NOT TO
BE TAKEN
OUT OF
THE
LIBRARY

UNIVER... ...TINGHAM
W... ...WN
FR... ...E LIBRARY

D0811126

NOTTINGHAM
UNIVERSITY LIBRARY

BRITAIN
1997

AN OFFICIAL HANDBOOK

Prepared by the Central Office of Information

© Crown Copyright 1996. Published in association with the Central Office of Information under licence from the Controller of Her Majesty's Stationery Office

Applications for reproduction should be made in writing to:
The Controller of Her Majesty's Stationery Office, St Clements House, 2–16 Colegate, Norwich NR3 1BQ

ISBN 0 11 702045 1

London: The Stationery Office

Published by The Stationery Office and available from:

The Publications Centre
(mail, telephone and fax orders only)
PO Box 276, London SW8 5DT
General enquiries 0171 873 0011
Telephone orders 0171 873 9090
Fax orders 0171 873 8200

The Stationery Office Bookshops
49 High Holborn, London WC1V 6HB
(counter service and fax orders only)
Fax 0171 831 1326
68–69 Bull Street, Birmingham B4 6AD
0121 236 9696 Fax 0121 236 9699
33 Wine Street, Bristol BS1 2BQ
01179 264306 Fax 01179 294515
9–21 Princess Street, Manchester M60 8AS
0161 834 7201 Fax 0161 833 0634
16 Arthur Street, Belfast BT1 4GD
0123 223 8451 Fax 0123 223 5401
The Stationery Office Oriel Bookshop,
The Friary, Cardiff CF1 4AA
01222 395548 Fax 01222 384347
71 Lothian Road, Edinburgh EH3 9AZ
(counter service only)

Customers in Scotland may mail, telephone
or fax their orders to:
Scottish Publication Sales,
South Gyle Crescent, Edinburgh EH12 9EB
0131 479 3141 Fax 0131 479 3142

Accredited Agents
(see Yellow Pages)

and through good booksellers

Contents

		Page
Foreword		vi
Visiting Wealth on the Nation, by Richard, 7th Earl of Bradford		vii
Britain and its People		1
1	Introduction	3
2	England	7
3	Northern Ireland	11
4	Scotland	18
5	Wales	24
6	The Social Framework	29
Government and Administration		45
7	Government	47
8	Justice and the Law	83
External Affairs		115
9	Overseas Relations	117
10	Defence	142
Economic Affairs		151
11	Economy	153
12	Overseas Trade	173
13	Employment	185
14	Industry and Government	203
15	Finance and Other Service Industries	219
16	Manufacturing and Construction Industries	242
17	Energy and Natural Resources	259
18	Agriculture, the Fishing Industry and Forestry	281
19	Transport and Communications	302
20	Science and Technology	325
The Environment		345
21	Sustainable Development	347
22	Environmental Protection	354
23	Local Development	375
24	Housing	385
Social and Cultural Affairs		395
25	Health and Social Services	397
26	Social Security	430
27	Education	442
28	Religion	466
29	The Arts	475
30	The Media	496
31	Sport and Active Recreation	519

Appendix 1: Government Departments and Agencies   540
Appendix 2: Recent Legislation   548
Appendix 3: Principal Abbreviations   550
Appendix 4: Calendar of Events 1997   551
Index   553

List of Illustrations

Diagrams

Availability of Certain Durable Goods   37
Changes in Average Household Food Consumption 1985–95   38
The Royal Family Tree   48
Recorded Crime in England and Wales 1945–1995   85
Government Receipts and Expenditure 1996–97   164
Geographical Distribution of Trade 1995   175
Full- and Part-time Employment in Great Britain   186
Type of Saving by Households   221
Technologies Supported under Recent NFFO   275
Land Use in Britain   282
Agricultural Land Use 1995   283
Public Expenditure under the CAP   290
Deaths on Britain's Roads 1926–1995   306
The European Ecolabel   352
Emissions of Sulphur Dioxide   361
Emissions of Carbon Dioxide   362
Broadleaved Tree Planting, 1980–81 to 1994–95   367
Tenure in Great Britain   386
House Prices 1983–1994   387
Type of Accommodation Occupied   388
Health Service Expenditure in England   403
Social Security Expenditure: Great Britain 1995–96   432

Maps

Physical Features
Population Density
Main Railway Passenger Routes   }   *endpapers*
Motorways and Major Trunk Roads
Major Conservation and Recreation Areas
Agricultural Land Use   }   between pp. 320 and 321
The European Union   119
The Commonwealth   122
The Assisted Areas   215
Oil   263
Gas   266
Electricity   270
Minerals   276

Photographs

The Royal Family
Theme Parks
Monuments
} between pp. 64 and 65

British Armed Forces in Bosnia
Construction
The Queen's Awards for Export
} between pp. 128 and 129

The Meteorological Office
Advances in Medicine
Satellites
} between pp. 192 and 193

The Environment

Reducing Pollution
The Individual and the Environment
Campaigns and Conferences
Industry
Conservation of Wildlife and the Countryside
The Built Environment
} between pp. 256 and 257

Transport
The Royal Mail
} between pp. 320 and 321

Costumes and Fabrics
Charities
Contemporary Music
} between pp. 384 and 385

Broadcasting
One Hundred Years of Cinema
Galleries and Exhibitions
} between pp. 480 and 481

Acknowledgments for photographs (photographs listed top to bottom, left to right); **Cover:** RSPB/C.H. Gomersall (front), R. Key/English Nature (back), P. Wakely/English Nature (spine); **Royal Family:** COI Pictures; **Theme Parks:** LEGOLAND Windsor Park, Ulster American Folk Park, Wales Tourist Board Photo Library, S.T.B./Still Moving Picture Co.; **Monuments:** Ray Martin, COI Pictures; **British Armed Forces in Bosnia:** COI Pictures; **Construction:** COI Pictures (except Birmingham waterfront); **Queens Awards:** COI Pictures (English Hop Products); **The Meteorological Office:** COI Pictures; **Advances in Medicine:** Glaxo-Wellcome, Zeneca, Zeneca, COI Pictures, COI Pictures; **Satellites:** ESA, Matra-Marconi Space; *The Environment* - **Reducing Pollution:** Institute of Arable Crops Research, COI Pictures; **The Individual and the Environment:** Jess Esposito (recycling initiative), COI Pictures; **Campaigns and Conferences:** COI Pictures, Greenpeace/Morgan; **Industry:** COI Pictures; **Conservation of Wildlife and the Countryside:** P. Wakely/English Nature (limestone pavement, saxifrage, Exmoor), COI Pictures (snow leopards, salmon eggs), Dyfed Wildlife Trust; **The Built Environment:** Historic Scotland, Carol McCorkell; **Transport:** J.D. Cable (train), Philippe Maille (taxi); **The Royal Mail:** COI Pictures; **Costumes and Fabrics:** COI Pictures; **Charities:** Barnado's, ACTIONAID, Age Resource/Age Concern, COI Pictures; **Contemporary Music:** Tom Sheehan/London Features International, Gerry Lane/London Features International; **Broadcasting:** BBC, COI Pictures; **One Hundred Years of Cinema:** BFI Stills, Posters and Designs (Saturday morning cinema and Empire, Leicester Square), Miramax International, COI Pictures, North of England Newspapers; **Galleries and Exhibitions:** COI Pictures, The Natural History Museum, London.

Foreword

Britain 1997 is the 48th in the series of annual Handbooks prepared by the Central Office of Information (COI). Drawing on a wide range of official and other authoritative sources, it provides a factual and up-to-date overview of government policy and other recent developments in Britain.

Handbook is widely recognised as an established work of reference, not only in Britain itself, but also overseas, where it is an important element of the information service provided by British diplomatic posts. It is sold by The Stationery Office and its agents throughout the world.

Features

As always, the text has been fully updated and revised. There are also more pages than ever before, with the usual charts, tables and graphs.

This year's *Handbook* has an environmental flavour to it. Britain's response to the challenge of 'sustainable development' is set out in Chapter 21, and there is an extended photographic section on Britain and the Environment. The Earl of Bradford has provided a lively introduction on tourism and the environment which forthrightly expresses his own viewpoint. This does not necessarily always coincide with the official government view!

Because of the environmental theme, we have switched to 'greener' paper. The text paper is 100% recycled and produced under entirely chlorine-free conditions. The paper for the photographic sections is 50% recycled and partly chlorine-free.

Coverage

Every effort is made to ensure that the information given in *Handbook* is accurate at the time of going to press. The text is generally based on information available up to September 1996.

As far as possible, *Handbook* presents information that applies to Britain as a whole. However, care should be taken when using *Handbook* to note whether the information given refers to:

- Britain, formally the United Kingdom of Great Britain and Northern Ireland;

- Great Britain, which comprises England, Wales and Scotland;

- England and Wales, which are grouped together for many administrative and other purposes; or, in some instances,

- England alone.

Acknowledgments

Britain 1997 has been compiled with the full co-operation of around 250 organisations, including other government departments and agencies. The editor would like to thank all the people from these organisations who have taken so much time and care to ensure that *Handbook's* high standards of accuracy have been maintained. Their contributions and comments have been extremely valuable.

Readers' Comments

We welcome readers' comments and suggestions on *Handbook*. These should be sent to:

The Editor
Britain: An Official Handbook
Publishing Services
Central Office of Information
Hercules Road
London SE1 7DU.

Richard, 7th Earl of Bradford, is a landowner, restaurateur and writer. He has a degree in agriculture from Trinity College, Cambridge and manages his family estate in Shropshire. His ancestral seat, Weston Park, is now owned by a charitable trust; it is a successful enterprise that hosts special events and offers accommodation and banqueting facilities for groups, as well as being open to the public. Lord Bradford is also President of the Wrekin Tourism Association, an active member of the House of Lords, and the owner of Porters English Restaurant in Covent Garden, London. What follows is his personal view.

Lord and Lady Bradford with their children at Weston Park.

Visiting Wealth on the Nation

Tourism and the Environment in Britain

What is mainly flat, mostly green and contributes around £22.7 billion to the Exchequer every year? Answer: Tourist Britain. The major draws are heritage, history, business, shopping and the countryside—though not necessarily in that order. Yet heritage and landscape can be literally 'loved to death'—threatened by the very multitudes that come to appreciate them.

So how can the conflicting demands of tourism and the environment be reconciled? This introduction sets out some of the problems and suggests some of the solutions, not forgetting that our country's economic future is at stake, for tourism is Britain's second largest, and fastest growing, industry.

In fact by the start of the next millennium, tourism *will* be the world's largest industry. Britain—given its relatively small size and lack of consistent weather—has performed reasonably well, but by comparison with Europe and the rest of the world, our figures have been gently slipping for some time. This is borne out by the figures in the Government's own recent document *Tourism: Competing with the Best*. For instance, our share of world tourism declined from 6 per cent in 1985 to only 4.7 per cent ten years later, and we are third from last in the league table of tourism growth in Europe between 1980 and 1992.

Our balance of payments performance has been even more dramatic—and extremely disappointing. A decent surplus of £500 million in 1985 became a huge deficit of £4.5 billion in 1994. Just consider what financial freedom the Chancellor would enjoy if he had that missing £5 billion each year to help him solve the balance of payments problem.

A Sound Investment

The fact is that spending money on tourism promotion is not like other forms of government expenditure. It is an investment that demonstrably pays off.

Tourism promotion puts people into work. The numbers presently employed in tourism and tourism-related industries are estimated at 1.475 million. Professor Stephen Wanhill, Professor of Tourism Studies at Cardiff University, has demonstrated that one new job can be created by an increased spend on tourism of just £28,500. That missing £5 billion could have created 175,000 jobs in Britain.

Wigan Pier—Reviving the Ruins

In 1981 unemployment in Wigan was 14 per cent and domestic tourism in the doldrums. The derelict industrial buildings at Wigan Pier—among them cotton mills and warehouses—stood as a symbol of urban decay.

However, as far back as 1975 the owners of the buildings had drawn up a plan for a commercial and leisure use for them. But it was not until the early 1980s that Wigan Council took up the idea. They had visited Bradford and seen how successfully the council there had marketed the area as a destination for short-break holidays (see p. xii).

Bringing in a marketing and tourism consultant, Wigan Council launched its project in 1982. Wigan Pier was opened by Her Majesty the Queen in 1986.

The unique complex of canalside buildings offers a host of attractions, among them a heritage centre, waterbuses and narrowboats, and exhibition facilities. Wigan Pier has won numerous awards, among them a Council of Europe Award for Environmental Conservation. It has created over 300 jobs, and the careful planning has paid handsome dividends: every year since its opening, Wigan Pier has attracted visitors far in excess of its annual target.

Tourism promotion generates revenue. The World Travel and Tourism Council's assessment is that the British travel and tourism industry will have contributed £22.7 billion in taxes in 1995.

Most of all, it yields a direct financial return to the Exchequer. An influential study by McKinsey, a respected firm of international consultants, has estimated that every extra pound spent on tourism promotion by the Government produces over four pounds in additional tax revenue—a staggering pay-off, quickly generated.

Instead, the total grant has been restrained in recent years. It was exactly the same in real terms in 1995 as it was in 1979, which disguises the fact that, since many of the British Tourist Authority's costs are in foreign currencies, there has actually been a reduction in its resources created by the fall in the value of the pound.

In addition, further cost burdens have been imposed on the tourism industry. In particular, VAT has been raised from 8 per cent in 1979 to 17.5 per cent now, and a new airport tax has been created. The yield for the first full year of operation is around £300 million. Surely it would make sense to put some of that money to good use by investing it in tourism promotion, instead of merely allowing our competitive disadvantage to grow.

It has been suggested that the industry should pay for its own promotion. However, of the 224,000 businesses in the tourism industry, 180,000 are owner-operated. Therefore, only the largest companies would be able to afford this, and the smaller ones would risk going out of business, to the detriment of employment.

If this suggestion were taken up, we would also be the only major tourist destination in the world not to fund tourism promotion centrally. Other countries are recognising the need to invest in promotion. Australia—where incidentally the Minister for Tourism holds Cabinet rank—is currently spending A$100 million (over £50 million) on worldwide television advertising, including A$30 million in Asia alone, the fastest growing market. Our total grant to the BTA and all the statutory bodies was only £92 million in 1995–96.

Therefore, just for fun, imagine what might happen if the Chancellor in his budget were to raise spending on tourism promotion to £5 billion. Think what room to manoeuvre the resulting revenue would offer.

Unfortunately, the consequent side effect would be that the country's infrastructure would totally collapse under the burden of increased tourist numbers. The Tower of London would be worn away into sand and Yorkshire Water would probably have to cease supplies completely!

Maintaining the Fabric

But, joking apart, even with the present volume of incoming visitors, there are very real problems as a consequence of increasing numbers, and it is obvious in certain areas of Britain that some constraints are required. Tourism must become environmentally sustainable and sensitive to the problems that it can create, both for the locality and for the people who try to live normally in it.

Examples of unsustainable tourism are now legion: the traffic nightmare in London—sometimes approaching gridlock outside the most popular attractions at the busiest times—caused mainly by the huge seasonal influx of coaches full of day trippers; the erosion of the paths in some parts of the Lake District or the Peak District National Park; and the strain placed on the infrastructure of many historic towns—Canterbury, Oxford, and York, for instance—by an uncontrolled invasion of tourists, causing inconvenience and annoyance to native and visitor alike.

Yet the majority of tourists visit Britain for a slice of authentic history and tradition, and it is impossible to re-create that in any way, when what they want is the genuine article.

Many major attractions like the Tower of London or St Paul's Cathedral have finite maximum numbers that they can accommodate at any given time, firstly to control damage but secondly to ensure that all the sightseers enjoy a happy rather than an overcrowded experience. It is interesting to note that, whereas there used to be plenty of free attractions in London, most have now started charging: the Natural History Museum in 1987, the Science Museum in 1988, and the Victoria and Albert Museum in 1996. The National Gallery is still free, as are the British Museum and the Tate Gallery, but these have donation boxes for voluntary contributions towards the upkeep of the buildings. In 1991 St Paul's Cathedral started charging again (Queen Victoria had ordered them to stop in 1851, in honour of the Great Exhibition!), to clear its debts and fund a planned programme of restoration.

A major problem with ever-greater numbers coming to London is trying to differentiate between those bringing positive economic benefits and those that merely 'clog up the streets'.

This is a necessary (though perhaps, in some respects, regrettable) step, if we are to encourage an increase in visitors that fall into the higher-spending category. Coaches full of day-trippers from across the Channel, arriving with their packed lunches and itinerary of free attractions, could actually end up costing the country more than they bring in. Perhaps those arriving via the ferry terminals and Eurotunnel should, like airline passengers, be obliged to pay some sort of tax, so that the country would at least be assured of a contribution towards the infrastructure costs generated by the 'cheaper' traveller.

It is also important, in these circumstances, not to continue expanding the numbers of visitors to London, but to ensure that they are more evenly distributed throughout the country. However, if we are going to restrict access effectively but fairly, at the same time we also need to foster an increase in the amount spent by tourists. Many attractions recognise that we need to raise the financial take from visitors in environmentally sensitive locations or simply where the existing facilities are under strain. Limiting numbers while increasing the amount they spend both maintains funds for upkeep and reduces the rate of deterioration.

Cambridge City Council, for example, has persuaded local accommodation providers to offer a considerable discount to people who are staying for more than just one night. This encourages them, instead of coming merely as day-trippers or overnight and contributing little to the area, to provide a more significant financial yield.

At the same time we must continue to concentrate on one immensely important and fast-growing sector of the market: the business or incentive traveller. There are two main reasons why we should target them: not only are they less seasonal—most valuable for spreading the load—but also the amount they spend tends to be higher—often considerably so.

Now that we have added to our range of facilities available for the business traveller—for example, with the National Exhibition Centre and the International Convention Centre, both in Birmingham, which seems to be achieving something of a lead in this field—we are better placed, but we should certainly not be complacent; we still lag far behind many of our leading competitors.

Branching Out

While it is critical to boost the business travel market, we should try to persuade the ordinary traveller to consider seeing more of Britain and, in particular, to get out of London, which, sadly, as far as many people are concerned, *is* Britain.

It should be obvious and is certainly vital that we look at boosting numbers by attracting more people to parts of the country that have room to entertain and indulge them.

Immediately we come up against a logistical problem, as all the major gateways into Britain are in the South East, and where you start your trip has an enormous influence on where you go. Heathrow and Gatwick are the dominant airports, while the ferry terminals at Dover and Folkestone occupy a similar standing. What's more, we now have the effect of Eurotunnel to contend with as well.

There is a constant call to increase the size of the two main airports, with many fundamental reasons being cited: the major airlines do not have enough space, there is demand from customers, the present facilities are becoming overcrowded, we need to retain their standing as major airports and as transport 'hubs' for the rest of Europe, we must avoid the danger of losing out to Amsterdam or Brussels, and so on.

The USA is in a much more fortunate position: throughout the Eastern seaboard there are many different, widely spread airline hubs—Atlanta, Charlotte, Orlando, JFK, Newark, Baltimore, Dallas, Philadelphia, Miami, Washington, Boston—which provide a wider choice and ensure that their tourist industry relies far less on New York than ours does on London.

Unfortunately, until we expand the perfectly viable alternatives, like Birmingham, Manchester, Prestwick, Cardiff, and Belfast, to a critical mass that will enable them to provide a range of services comparable to those of Heathrow or Gatwick, there will continue to be a bias towards London and the South East, and the strain on resources and infrastructure will grow.

Green for Go

In encouraging people to travel further afield, we must not lose sight of the problems that travel—be it hiking intrepidly up and down Scottish mountains or driving round to your local stately home of a Sunday afternoon—can cause: overcrowding, air pollution, and degradation of landscape, buildings and roads. Many local councils have adopted strategies to control the level of traffic in their area: park-and-ride schemes, to confine cars to a manageable area; downgrading roads so that they no longer appear on local tourist maps; placing special ticket machines in car parks so that users can, if they wish, make an additional contribution to the upkeep of the woodland served by the car park; and last but not least, integrating their traffic management schemes into partnerships with local public transport companies so as to offer a service that will tempt motorists out of their cars.

The National Trust is even conducting an 18-month experiment by running a property without a car park: Prior Park, near Bath. The Trust is funding a Sunday bus service from the city centre to Prior Park itself, as there was no existing Sunday service. Furthermore, members of the Trust have voted overwhelmingly to reduce the percentage of visitors arriving at Trust properties by car from 90 per cent to 60 per cent by the year 2020.

National Trust—Promoting Public Transport

The National Trust (NT) is a registered charity founded in 1895 'to preserve places of historic interest or natural beauty' for the public. It owns 240,000 hectares (600,000 acres) of countryside and 885 km (550 miles) of coastline, and protects over 200 historic houses, 160 gardens and 25 industrial sites.

In 1995 around 11 million visits were made to NT properties, and many more to woods, coastal areas and other open spaces. No one is more conscious than the NT of the threat to the built and the natural environment from people and pollution. It therefore promotes travel to its properties and sites by public transport. For each one listed in its handbook, the NT gives details on how to reach it by public transport. It also produces *Green Transport News*, a bulletin highlighting new transport links to NT properties and the reduced entry fees available to those who can present a bus or train ticket.

One example is Aberdulais Falls, in Wales. Those travelling by bus from Neath, three miles away, are entitled to discounted entry to see this spectacular waterfall and the hydro-electric scheme developed to harness the waters of the Dulais river—an all-round environmentally-friendly outing.

Off the Beaten Track

Despite the concentration on the South East as the point of access to Britain, there are countless examples of extraordinary regional success. Many people have been impressed by the achievements of Yorkshire, as it has found and developed many new points of interest: by exploiting its authors, its television series, particularly *Last of the Summer Wine* — and who would have thought that Bradford or Leeds would find so much to engross and allure the tourist?

(Incidentally, before any possible accusations of parochial self-interest are levelled at me, I am not choosing Bradford as an excellent example of tourism because of any family connection. My title, 'Earl of Bradford', is taken from the Hundred of South Bradford in Shropshire, where we still live.)

When Bradford decided to enter the holiday market in 1980, it was widely treated as something of a joke. What could a Northern industrial town, with declining traditional local industries, possibly have to offer the visitor?

Yet Bradford was actually blessed with a number of natural attractions: Haworth, home of the Brontë sisters; Saltaire model mill village and other fascinating Victorian industrial buildings; and particularly its proximity to the spectacularly scenic Yorkshire Dales.

The city council's Economic Development Unit initially targeted the travel trade by launching two themed 'short-stay' holidays, which generated—partly because the whole premise seemed so unlikely!—considerable publicity and sold very well. Bradford had made its mark.

One gratifying result of this success was that Bradford was chosen as the location for the new National Museum of Photography, Film and Television in 1983, while nearby Leeds has recently enticed the new Armoury to its city centre. The area now has over 50 attractions of international and local interest—there are even signs in Japanese to local landmarks around Haworth!

Today, the Bradford area draws more than six million visitors a year, worth somewhere around £120 million to the local economy, all of which has been achieved in a comparatively short time by an imaginative approach.

Capitalising on the Countryside

Similarly, as President of the Wrekin Tourism Association for the last fifteen years I have seen firsthand the enormous impact that success in attracting more tourists can have on a region—mainly achieved through innovative promotion and unselfish co-operation, aided by a progressive attitude from local government. Tourist expenditure in the area has leapt from around £3 million in 1980 to £54 million in 1995, and consequently employment has expanded from 180 to 2,400, and accommodation stock from 400 bed spaces to 3,000. This has happened because the number of incoming tourists has multiplied almost tenfold over the period, to a figure of 2,400,000.

Such success has, of course, been greatly assisted by the designation of Ironbridge Gorge as a world heritage site, but a whole raft of new attractions has risen up because of the popular demand that has now been generated.

With this growth many other businesses have been created, such as restaurants, leisure centres, an ice rink, and a bowling alley. So a strong case can be made for the theory that the development of facilities ostensibly to service the tourist industry has actually greatly

Peatlands Park—A Unique Habitat

Very little now remains of Europe's oldest natural living landscape—Ireland's bogland. In Northern Ireland only 9 per cent of lowland bog remains intact; in the uplands and hills the figure is about 14 per cent.

Overgrazing, drainage to reclaim the land for agriculture, and new peat extraction technology have all taken their toll. Yet these ancient peatlands have a vital ecological function to perform: they absorb carbon dioxide (CO_2) from the air and act as a filter to purify rainwater. Destruction of the bogland would release CO_2 into the atmosphere, contributing to global warming.

Peatlands are also an important habitat for birds. A large proportion of Ireland's curlews live there, as do rare birds of prey such as hen harriers and merlin.

Peatlands Park covers 700 acres of preserved bogland in County Armagh, Northern Ireland. It not only protects a threatened ecosystem, but raises concern for a landscape that was once taken for granted. Each year 100,000 people visit Peatlands Park, in school parties, family groups and as individuals, demonstrating that conservation of a rare environment can itself be exploited as a tourist attraction, raising funds to continue the valuable work—and raising consciousness.

enhanced the quality of life for residents of the Wrekin and indeed the whole of Shropshire.

It is interesting to note that while the number of hotel bedrooms in the Wrekin has expanded substantially, there has equally been an enormous increase in the quantity of bed-and-breakfast establishments. These enable people to stay cheaply, provide important competition in keeping hotel prices down and give a great boost to the rural economy.

Bed-and-breakfast establishments were once the mainstay of seaside accommodation, providing the British with their traditional form of holiday. The experience in general—and the landlady, in particular—was the butt of many jokes. Now offering bed-and-breakfast accommodation has become an important source of income for many people who live in the countryside, while providing a less costly and more informal way of exploring Britain. Many farmers appreciate that it can be as important a 'cash crop' as wheat or barley, though it places further demands on them, their spouses and family members.

It is estimated that over 18,000 farmers are currently running bed-and-breakfast accommodation, which brings in an average income of £6,700 per establishment. The total earnings from these enterprises are over £120 million per year, which in turn leads to invaluable sales revenue for many local tradesmen who supply the farms, from the newsagent to the milkman (unless, of course, the farm in question happens to be a dairy farm!).

Conservation through Reoccupation

It is always a great sadness to note the number of historic properties in Britain that have fallen into such a state of disrepair that they have had to be demolished. The inter-war period and the twenty years after the war were particularly bad in this respect. Even my own family had to blow up Tong Castle and pull down Leaton Knolls Hall in the 1950s: one was derelict and the other riddled with dry rot and every other known form of pest.

Fortunately this trend has been virtually halted. Larger houses are being converted— most of them sympathetically, as they are likely to be listed buildings—into individual dwelling units by enlightened architects such as Kit Martin.

Meanwhile, many smaller buildings or structures of historic interest, architectural merit or amenity value have been in a more critical position. As the properties were often unsuitable for full-time occupation and would have cost a small fortune to restore, the only option for owners was to raze or mothball.

Thus it was with great foresight that John and Christian Smith founded the Landmark Trust in 1965 to rescue such places. As well as the benefits of upkeep, the occupation of these properties by short-stay visitors offers valuable protection against vandalism.

The National Trust have followed a similar route with some of their less grand properties, and now let out a total of 120.

The Landmark Trust— Generating Funds for Conservation

One unusual form of accommodation for holiday-makers is supplied by the Landmark Trust. This registered charity specialises in rescuing small but historically interesting buildings (everything from barns to manor houses to Martello towers), many of them in remote locations. It restores them, furnishes them in the appropriate style, and then rents them out as self-catering holiday accommodation to people who want something out of the ordinary. The income the Trust receives from these lettings provides for the restoration and upkeep of the properties.

One of the Trust's most popular buildings is the Pineapple, an eccentric confection in stone dating from the 18th century, which is situated near Stirling, in Scotland.

Thanks to these two organisations, the traveller has a unique opportunity to enjoy Britain from a different viewpoint, while at the same time contributing to valuable conservation work.

Meeting the Millenium

We must attempt to ensure that we are not left out of the boon to our economy generated by tourism, by ensuring continued and increased investment in international promotion of the right kind.

We must look at developing more gateways into Britain and make sure that previously unexploited areas examine the benefits that they could derive from well-planned tourism, as we need to encourage people to spread themselves more thinly throughout Britain, rather than huddling together in the South East. We must always take care that tourism is to the advantage of the local environment and the local population, as well as to the Treasury.

We can change our approach, and in doing so, we can draw on the advice and best practice, both of the organisations mentioned here and of others, such as SustainAbility and the Campaign for Environmentally Responsible Tourism.

We cannot afford to create a situation in which the patient ends up on the critical list because our efforts at tourism promotion have achieved such a resounding success—purely in terms of numbers, without the accompanying, and most necessary, increase in spending—that our finite resource of 'real history' suffers irreversible damage at the hands (or feet) of the trampling hordes.

Further Reading

The Impact of Tourism on Rural Settlements. Rural Research Report 21. ISBN 1 869964 46 2. Rural Development Commission, 1996.

Sustainable Development: The UK Strategy. CM 2426. ISBN 0 10 124262 X. HMSO, 1994. £22.

Tourism. Planning Policy Guidance 21. ISBN 0 11 072726 2. HMSO, 1992. £3.90.

Tourism: Competing with the Best. Department of National Heritage. 1995.

Tourism 2000: A Strategy for Wales. ISBN 01 85013 058 2. Wales Tourist Board, 1994. £15.

. . . and for a more light-hearted view:
Stately Secrets: Behind-the-scenes Stories from the Stately Homes of Britain. Richard, Earl of Bradford. ISBN 0 86051 035 6. Robson Books, 1996. £7.99.

Contact Points

British Tourist Authority, English Tourist Board, Thames Tower, Black's Road, London W6 9EL. Tel: 0181 846 9000

The Landmark Trust, Shottesbrooke, Maidenhead, Berkshire, SL6 3SW. Tel: 01628 825925

The National Trust, 36 Queen Anne's Gate, London SW1H 9AS. Tel: 0171 222 9251

Northern Ireland Tourist Board, St Anne's Court, Belfast BT1 1NB. Tel: 01232 520700

Scottish Tourist Board, 23 Ravelston Terrace, Edinburgh EH4 3EU. Tel: 0131 317 7200

Wales Tourist Board/Bwrdd Croeso Cymru, Brunel House, 2 Fitzalan Road, Cardiff CF2 1UY. Tel: 01222 499909

Britain and its People

1 Introduction

Britain comprises Great Britain (England, Wales and Scotland) and Northern Ireland, and is one of the 15 member states of the European Union (EU). Its full name is the United Kingdom of Great Britain and Northern Ireland.

Physical Features

Britain constitutes the greater part of the British Isles. The largest of the islands is Great Britain. The next largest comprises Northern Ireland and the Irish Republic. Western Scotland is fringed by the large island chain known as the Hebrides, and to the north east of the Scottish mainland are the Orkney and Shetland Islands. All these, along with the Isle of Wight, Anglesey and the Isles of Scilly, have administrative ties with the mainland, but the Isle of Man in the Irish Sea and the Channel Islands between Great Britain and France are largely self-governing, and are not part of the United Kingdom.

With an area of about 242,000 sq km (93,000 sq miles), Britain is just under 1,000 km (about 600 miles) from the south coast to the extreme north of Scotland and just under 500 km (around 300 miles) across at the widest point.

The climate is generally mild and temperate. Prevailing winds are south-westerly and the weather from day to day is mainly influenced by depressions moving eastwards across the Atlantic. The weather is subject to frequent changes. In general, there are few extremes of temperature; it rarely rises above 32°C (90°F) or falls below −10°C (14°F).

Average annual rainfall is more than 1,600 mm (over 60 inches) in the mountainous areas of the west and north but less than 800 mm (30 inches) over central and eastern parts. Rain is fairly well distributed throughout the year, but, on average, March to June are the driest months and September to January the wettest.

During May, June and July (the months of longest daylight) the mean daily duration of sunshine varies from five hours in northern Scotland to eight hours in the Isle of Wight; during the months of shortest daylight (November, December and January) sunshine is at a minimum, with an average of an hour a day in northern Scotland and two hours a day on the south coast of England.

Geographical Facts

- Highest mountain: Ben Nevis, in the highlands of Scotland, at 1,343 m (4,406 ft)

- Longest river: the Severn, 354 km (220 miles) long, which rises in central Wales and flows through Shrewsbury, Worcester and Gloucester in England to the Bristol Channel

- Largest lake: Lough Neagh, Northern Ireland, at 396 sq km (153 sq miles)

- Highest waterfall: Eas a'Chual Aluinn, from Glas Bheinn, in the highlands of Scotland, with a drop of 200 m (660 ft)

- Deepest cave: Ogof Ffynnon Ddu, Wales, at 308 m (1,010 ft) deep

- Most northerly point on the British mainland: Dunnet Head, north-east Scotland

- Most southerly point on the British mainland: Lizard Point, Cornwall

Historical Outline

The name 'Britain' derives from Greek and Latin names probably stemming from a Celtic original. Although in the prehistoric timescale the Celts were relatively late arrivals in the

British Isles, only with them does Britain emerge into recorded history. The term 'Celtic' is often used rather generally to distinguish the early inhabitants of the British Isles from the later Anglo–Saxon invaders.

After two expeditions by Julius Caesar in 55 and 54 BC, contact between Britain and the Roman world grew, culminating in the Roman invasion of AD 43. Roman rule was gradually extended from south-east England to include Wales and, for a time, the lowlands of Scotland. The final Roman withdrawal in 409 followed a period of increasing disorder during which the island began to be raided by Angles, Saxons and Jutes from northern Europe. It is from the Angles that the name 'England' derives. The raids turned into settlement and a number of small English kingdoms were established. The Britons maintained an independent existence in the areas now known as Wales and Cornwall. Among these kingdoms more powerful ones emerged, claiming overlordship over the whole country, first in the north (Northumbria), then in the midlands (Mercia) and finally in the south (Wessex). However, further raids and settlement by the Vikings from Scandinavia occurred, although in the 10th century the Wessex dynasty defeated the invading Danes and established a wide-ranging authority in England. In 1066 England was invaded by the Normans (see p. 7), who then settled along with others from France.

Dates of some of the main events in Britain's history are given on p. 5. The early histories of England, Wales, Scotland and Northern Ireland are included in Chapters 2 to 5, which also deal with the main aspects of their social, economic and political life. Additional material is included on the political situation in Northern Ireland. Table 1.1 gives a selection of some of the main statistics for each of the four lands.

Wildlife

Britain is home to a great variety of wildlife, with an estimated 30,000 animal species, as well as marine and microscopic life; about 2,800 species of 'higher' plants; and many thousands of mosses, fungi and algae. The Government seeks to conserve species and habitats, and many of its strategies are

Table 1.1: General Statistics

	England	Wales	Scotland	Northern Ireland	United Kingdom
Population (1995) ('000)	48,708	2,913	5,132	1,642	58,395
Area (sq km)[a]	130,423	20,766	77,080	13,483	241,752
Population density (persons per sq km)	373	140	66	122	242
Gross domestic product (£ per head, 1994)	9,925	8,173	9,734	8,025	9,768
Employees in employment ('000, June 1996)	18,625	988	1,927	574	22,114
Percentage of employees (June 1996) in:					
services	76.6	70.6	73.9	73.7	76.1
manufacturing	17.6	22.9	16.4	17.8	17.7
construction	3.6	3.2	6.0	4.0	3.8
mining, energy and water supply	0.9	1.1	1.9	1.2	1.0
agriculture, forestry and fishing	1.3	2.1	1.8	3.3	1.5
Unemployment rate (per cent, seasonally adjusted, August 1996)	7.4	8.1	8.0	11.3	7.5

Sources: *Regional Trends, Annual Abstract of Statistics*, Office for National Statistics
[a]Figures for area are not on a strictly comparable basis; those for England and Wales include inland water, while those for Scotland and Northern Ireland are for the land area only.

Significant Dates

55 and 54 BC: Julius Caesar's expeditions to Britain

AD 43: Roman conquest begins under Claudius

122–38: Hadrian's Wall built

c409: Roman army withdraws from Britain

450s onwards: foundation of the Anglo-Saxon kingdoms

597: arrival of St Augustine to preach Christianity to the Anglo-Saxons

664: Synod of Whitby opts for Roman Catholic rather than Celtic church

789–95: first Viking raids

832–60: Scots and Picts merge under Kenneth Macalpin to form what is to become the kingdom of Scotia

860s: Danes overrun East Anglia, Northumbria and eastern Mercia

871–99: reign of Alfred the Great in Wessex

1066: William the Conqueror defeats Harold Godwinson at Hastings and takes the throne

1215: King John signs Magna Carta to protect feudal rights against royal abuse

1301: Edward of Caernarvon (later Edward II) created Prince of Wales

1314: battle of Bannockburn ensures survival of separate Scottish kingdom

1337: Hundred Years War between England and France begins

1348–49: Black Death (bubonic plague) wipes out a third of England's population

1381: Peasants' Revolt in England

1455–87: Wars of the Roses between Yorkists and Lancastrians

1477: first book to be printed in England, by William Caxton

1534–40: English Reformation; Henry VIII breaks with the Papacy

1536–42: Acts of Union integrate England and Wales administratively and legally and give Wales representation in Parliament

1547–53: Protestantism becomes official religion in England under Edward VI

1553–58: Catholic reaction under Mary I

1558: loss of Calais, last English possession in France

1558–1603: reign of Elizabeth I; moderate Protestantism established

1588: defeat of Spanish Armada

c1590–c1613: plays of Shakespeare written

1603: union of the two crowns under James VI of Scotland

1642–51: Civil Wars between King and Parliament

1649: execution of Charles I

1653–58: Oliver Cromwell rules as Lord Protector

1660: monarchy restored under Charles II

1688: Glorious Revolution; accession of William and Mary

1707: Act of Union unites England and Scotland

c1760s–c1830s: Industrial Revolution

1761: opening of the Bridgewater Canal ushers in Canal Age

1775–83: American War of Independence leads to loss of the Thirteen Colonies

1793–1815: Revolutionary and Napoleonic Wars

1801: Act of Union unites Great Britain and Ireland

1825: opening of the Stockton and Darlington Railway, the world's first passenger railway

1829: Catholic emancipation

1832: First Reform Act extends the franchise

1914–18: First World War

1921: Anglo–Irish Treaty establishes the Irish Free State; Northern Ireland remains part of the United Kingdom

1939–45: Second World War

1952: accession of Elizabeth II

1973: Britain enters European Community (now the European Union)

published in the 1994 document *Biodiversity: The UK Action Plan* (see p. 370).

> Although the Song Thrush (pictured on the front cover) is a widespread species, its numbers have more than halved in Britain over the last 25 years. Causes include environmetal factors such as changes in farming methods, which have affected its food supply and nesting sites, severe winter weather and dry soil conditions.
>
> Research is now being undertaken into appropriate remedial measures, including the promotion of sensitive farming options, with the aim of halting the decline in numbers of the Song Thrush by the year 2000.

Channel Islands and Isle of Man

Although the Channel Islands and the Isle of Man are not part of the United Kingdom, they have a special relationship with it. The Channel Islands were part of the Duchy of Normandy in the 10th and 11th centuries and remained subject to the English Crown after the final loss of Normandy to the French in the 15th century. The Isle of Man was under the nominal sovereignty of Norway until 1266, and eventually came under the direct administration of the British Crown in 1765. Today the territories have their own legislative assemblies and systems of law; the Isle of Man also has its own system of taxation. The British Government is responsible for their international relations and external defence.

Further Reading

Statlas UK: A Statistical Atlas of the United Kingdom. HMSO, 1995.

2 England

Early History	7	Transport	10
Government	7	Cultural and Social Affairs	10
The Economy	9	The Environment	10

England is predominantly a lowland country, although there are upland regions in the north (the Pennine Chain, the Cumbrian mountains and the Yorkshire moorlands) and in the south west, in Cornwall, Devon and Somerset. The greatest concentrations of population (see Table 2.1) are in London and the South East, the West Yorkshire and north-west industrial cities, the Midlands conurbation around Birmingham, the north-east conurbations on the rivers Tyne and Tees, and along the Channel coast. England's population is expected to rise from 48.5 million in 1993 to 51.9 million in 2016.

Early History

The name 'England' is derived from the Angles, one of the Germanic tribes which established monarchies in lowland Britain in the 5th century. The Anglo-Saxon kingdoms were initially fairly small and numerous, but gradually larger entities emerged. Eventually Wessex came to dominate, following its leading role in resisting the Danish invasions of the 9th century. Athelstan (924–39) used the title of 'King of all Britain', and from 954 there was only a single Kingdom of England. The present Royal Family is descended from the old royal house of Wessex.

In 1066 the last successful invasion of England took place. Duke William of Normandy defeated the English at the Battle of Hastings, and Normans and others from France came to settle. French became the language of the nobility for the next three centuries, and the legal and social structures were influenced by those prevailing across the Channel.

Almost all the English Crown's possessions in France were lost during the late Middle Ages. The union of England and Scotland in took place in 1707, leaving England as the most populous part of the British nation state.

Government

England has no government minister or department exclusively responsible for its central administration, in contrast to Wales, Scotland and Northern Ireland. Instead, there are a number of government departments, whose responsibilities in some cases also cover aspects of affairs in Wales and Scotland (see Appendices). A network of Government Offices for the Regions is responsible for the implementation of several government programmes (see p. 375) in the English regions.

There are currently 524 English parliamentary constituencies represented in the House of Commons. Changes approved following a 1995 boundary review (see p. 54) will increase this to 529 after the next general election. In August 1996 England had 310

Table 2.1: Population and Population Density Mid-1995*

	Population	People per sq km		Population	People per sq km
North	**3,099,800**	**201**	Greater London	6,967,500	4,415
Cleveland	560,100	939	Hampshire	1,605,700	425
Cumbria	490,200	72	Hertfordshire	1,005,400	613
Durham	607,800	250	Isle of Wight	124,600	328
Northumberland	307,700	61	Kent	1,564,300	414
Tyne and Wear	1,134,000	2,099	Oxfordshire	590,200	226
Yorkshire and Humberside	**5,025,000**	**326**	Surrey	1,041,200	621
Humberside	889,500	254	West Sussex	722,100	363
North Yorkshire	726,100	87	**South West**	**4,798,400**	**201**
South Yorkshire	1,305,400	837	Avon	978,700	734
West Yorkshire	2,104,000	1,034	Cornwall and Isles of Scilly	479,600	135
East Midlands	**4,102,200**	**263**	Devon	1,053,400	157
Derbyshire	954,100	363	Dorset	673,000	254
Leicestershire	916,900	359	Gloucestershire	549,500	207
Lincolnshire	605,600	102	Somerset	477,900	138
Northamptonshire	594,800	251	Wiltshire	586,300	169
Nottinghamshire	1,030,900	477	**West Midlands**	**5,294,900**	**407**
East Anglia	**2,104,900**	**167**	Hereford and Worcester	699,900	178
Cambridgeshire	686,900	202	Shropshire	416,500	119
Norfolk	768,800	143	Staffordshire	1,054,400	388
Suffolk	649,500	171	Warwickshire	496,300	251
South East	**17,870,200**	**656**	West Midlands (Metropolitan County)	2,627,800	2,924
Bedfordshire	543,100	440	**North West**	**6,412,000**	**873**
Berkshire	769,200	661	Cheshire	975,600	419
Buckinghamshire	658,400	351	Greater Manchester	2,578,000	2,005
East Sussex	726,500	405	Lancashire	1,424,000	464
Essex	1,569,900	427	Merseyside	1,434,400	2,189
			England	**48,707,500**	**373**

Source: Office of Population Censuses and Surveys
*This table does not reflect subsequent changes in local government structure (see pp. 75–6).

Table 2.2: Percentage Change in Population, Employment and Housing Stock

	Population 1981–94	Employment[a] 1981–95	Housing stock 1981–94
North	−0.6	0.4	7.8
Yorkshire and Humberside	2.2	3.5	9.0
East Midlands	6.5	7.6	14.0
East Anglia	11.1	26.4	19.4
South East	5.0	3.5	13.9
South West	9.5	17.8	17.5
West Midlands	2.1	1.1	9.8
North West	−0.7	−3.6	6.9
England	**4.0**	**4.6**	**12.2**

Source: *Regional Trends*
[a]Employees in employment plus self-employed.

Conservative Members of Parliament, 197 Labour, 15 Liberal Democrat and one independent, as well as the Speaker of the House of Commons.[1] Conservative support tends to be strongest in suburban and rural areas, and the Conservatives have a large majority of parliamentary seats in the southern half of England and in East Anglia. The Labour Party derives its main support from urban areas. Liberal Democrat support in England is particularly strong in the South West, where the party holds eight of its 15 English seats.

Local government is mainly administered through a two-tier system of counties subdivided into districts. However, there are a number of single-tier authorities, with more being introduced as part of the reform of the structure of local government in England (see pp. 75–6).

The English legal system comprises on the one hand a historic body of conventions known as 'common law' and 'equity', and, on the other, parliamentary and European Community (EC) legislation. In the formulation of common law since the Norman Conquest, great reliance has been placed on precedent. Equity law—law outside the scope of the common law or statute law—derives from the practice of petitioning the Lord Chancellor in cases not covered by common law.

The Church of England, which was separated from the Roman Catholic Church at the time of the Reformation in the early 16th century, is the Established Church (that is, the official religion of England); the Sovereign must always be a member of the Church and appoints its two archbishops and 42 other diocesan bishops (see p. 468).

The Economy

Considerable changes in the economy of England have occurred during the 20th century. In the second half of the century, jobs in service industries have grown and now account for three-quarters of employees in employment, with expansion having been particularly noticeable in financial and business services. Services account for three-quarters of gross domestic product (GDP) in London and the South East, and over a quarter of employees in Greater London work in financial services. London is one of the world's leading centres of banking, insurance and other financial services.

Manufacturing, although declining as a proportion of the employment base, remains important in a number of areas. In terms of GDP, it is most significant in the East Midlands (where manufacturing accounted for 29 per cent of the region's GDP in 1994), the North and the West Midlands. East Anglia has been the fastest-growing English region in terms of population since the 1960s. It is expected that it will continue to be the fastest growing region in the early years of the 21st century. Once largely agricultural, high-

---

[1] The Speaker of the House of Commons, who presides over the debates there (see p. 54), traditionally does not vote along party lines and so is not counted towards the strength of the party for which he or she was originally elected.

technology industry has in recent years developed in the region.

In agriculture, dairying is most common in the west of England; sheep and cattle are reared in the hilly and moorland areas of the North and South West. Arable farming, pig and poultry farming and horticulture are concentrated in the east and south.

Tourism and leisure now form one of England's biggest industries, worth £11,650 million in 1994 and contributing 5 per cent of GDP. About 1.5 million people work in tourism and leisure.

Transport

The motorway network comprises four long-distance routes linking London and the cities of the Midlands, the North and North West, and the South West; the London orbital route (M25); and over 30 shorter motorways. In all, there are about 3,200 km (2,000 miles) of motorway in England, plus about 14,400 km (9,000 miles) of other trunk roads.

The railway system has largely been privatised. Many of the passenger services have been franchised to the private sector and Railtrack, the infrastructure company, was floated on the Stock Exchange in May 1996.

Cultural and Social Affairs

London has a wealth of cultural centres, including four major art galleries and many renowned museums, together with theatres, ballet and opera houses and concert halls. Other major cities and towns also have a broad range of cultural interests. Many theatres outside London are used for touring by the national theatre, dance and opera companies. There is also a thriving popular culture in Britain, including numerous kinds of pop music, theatre styles such as pantomime and musicals, and performances by comedians. Safari, wildlife and theme parks all offer family activities and entertainment. Arts projects are benefiting from the proceeds of the National Lottery (see p. 42).

Further Reading

Regional Trends, annual report. HMSO.

Table 2.3: Attendances at English Tourist Attractions, 1995

		millions
Blackpool Pleasure Beach	F	7.3*
British Museum	F	5.7
National Gallery	F	4.5
Palace Pier, Brighton	F	3.8*
Alton Towers	P	2.7
Madame Tussaud's	P	2.7
Tower of London	P	2.5
Funland and Laserbowl, Trocadero, London	F	2.5*
Westminster Abbey	F	2.2
St Paul's Cathedral	P	2.2*
Canterbury Cathedral	P	1.9
Tate Gallery	F	1.8

Source: British Tourist Authority
F   Free admission
P   Paid-for admission
*   Estimated visitor numbers

Numerous regions and towns have associations with great English writers, artists and musicians, such as Stratford-upon-Avon (William Shakespeare), the Lake District (William Wordsworth), Stoke-on-Trent (Arnold Bennett), Haworth (the Brontë sisters), Dorset (Thomas Hardy), Essex and Suffolk (John Constable), Salford (L.S. Lowry), Worcestershire (Edward Elgar) and Aldeburgh (Benjamin Britten).

The Environment

Despite the relatively high population density and degree of urbanisation, there are still many unspoilt rural and coastal areas. There are seven National Parks, six forest parks, 36 designated 'areas of outstanding natural beauty', 22 environmentally sensitive areas, almost 200 country parks approved by the Countryside Commission, 800 km (500 miles) of designated heritage coastline, and about 2,000 historic buildings and some 3,600 gardens open to the public.

3 Northern Ireland

History	11	Security Policy	15
Government	12	The Economy	15
Human Rights	14	Cultural and Social Affairs	16

About half of the 1.6 million people in Northern Ireland are settled in the eastern coastal region, the centre of which is the capital, Belfast. Most industry is situated in this part of the province. Northern Ireland is at its nearest point only 21 km (13 miles) from Scotland. It has a 488-km (303-mile) border with the Irish Republic.

According to the 1991 Census, 50.6 per cent of the people regarded themselves as Protestants and 38.4 per cent as Roman Catholics. Most of the Protestants are descendants of Scots or English settlers who crossed to north-eastern Ireland; they are British by culture and tradition and committed to remaining part of the United Kingdom. The Roman Catholic population is mainly Irish by culture and history, and the majority of them favour a united Ireland.

History

During the tenth century Ireland was dominated by the Vikings. In 1169 Henry II of England launched an invasion of Ireland. He had been granted its overlordship by the English Pope Adrian IV, who was anxious to bring the Irish church into full obedience to Rome. Although a large part of the country came under the control of Anglo-Norman magnates, little direct authority was exercised from England during the Middle Ages.

The Tudor monarchs showed a much greater tendency to intervene in Ireland. During the reign of Elizabeth I, a series of campaigns was waged against Irish insurgents.

The main focus of resistance was the northern province of Ulster. After the collapse of this resistance in 1607 and the flight of its leaders, Ulster was settled by immigrants from Scotland and England.

The English civil wars (1642–51) led to further risings in Ireland, which were crushed by Oliver Cromwell. More fighting took place after the overthrow of the Roman Catholic James II in 1688. During the Battle of the Boyne in Ireland in 1690 the forces of James II, who was trying to regain the throne, starting in Ireland, were defeated by those of the Protestant William of Orange (William III).

Throughout most of the 18th century there was uneasy peace. In 1782 the Irish Parliament (dating from medieval times) was given legislative independence; the only constitutional tie with Great Britain was the crown. The Parliament, however, represented only the privileged Anglo-Irish minority, and Roman Catholics were excluded from it. In 1798 an abortive rebellion took place, led by Wolfe Tone's United Irishmen movement. Three years later Ireland was unified with Great Britain; under the 1801 Act of Union the Irish Parliament was abolished and Irish members sat in both houses of the Westminster Parliament in London.

The Irish question was one of the major issues of British politics during the 19th century and after. In 1886 the Liberal Government introduced a Home Rule Bill designed to give a new Irish Parliament devolved authority over most internal matters while reserving control over foreign and defence policy to Britain. This led to a split in the Liberal Party and the failure of the Bill. In 1893 a second Home Rule Bill was approved by the House of Commons but rejected by the House of Lords.

The issue returned to the political agenda in 1910 because Asquith's Liberal administration was dependent on support from the pro-Home Rule Irish Parliamentary Party. The controversy intensified as unionists and nationalists in Ireland formed private armies. In 1914 Home Rule was approved in the Government of Ireland Act. Implementation, however, was delayed by the outbreak of the First World War.

A nationalist rising in Dublin in 1916 was suppressed and its leaders executed. Two years later the nationalist Sinn Fein party won a large majority of the Irish seats in elections to the Westminster Parliament. Its members refused to attend the House of Commons and, instead, formed the Dail Eireann in Dublin. A nationalist guerrilla force called the Irish Republican Army began operations against the British administration in 1919.

The 1920 Government of Ireland Act provided for the establishment of two Home Rule parliaments, one in Dublin and the other in Belfast. The Act was implemented in 1921 in Northern Ireland, when six of the nine counties of the province of Ulster received their own Parliament and remained represented in, and subject to, the supreme authority of, the British Parliament.

In the South the guerillas continued to fight for independence. A truce was agreed in June 1921, followed by negotiations between the British Government and Sinn Fein. These were concluded in December 1921 with the signature of the Anglo-Irish Treaty establishing the Irish Free State, which became a republic in 1949.

From its creation in 1921, Northern Ireland's Parliament had a consistent unionist majority from which government ministers were drawn. The nationalist minority resented this persistent domination and their effective exclusion from political office and influence. Although an active and articulate civil rights movement emerged during the 1960s, reforms made in response were unable to forestall the development of serious sectarian rioting. This led to the introduction in 1969 of British Army support for the police. These sectarian divisions were subsequently exploited by terrorists from both sides, most notably by the Provisional Irish Republican Army (IRA), which claimed to be protecting the Roman Catholic minority.

Because of increased terrorism and inter-communal violence, the British Government took over responsibility for law and order in 1972. The Northern Ireland unionist Government resigned in protest at this decision and direct rule from London began.

Government

Under the system of direct rule, the United Kingdom Parliament approves all laws, and Northern Ireland's government departments are controlled by the Secretary of State—a Cabinet minister—and his ministerial team.

Seventeen members are elected to the House of Commons. In the most recent general election in April 1992 the Ulster Unionists won 9 seats, the Democratic Unionists 3, the Ulster Popular Unionists 1 and the nationalist Social Democratic and Labour Party (SDLP) 4. The Alliance Party, offering an alternative to Unionists and Nationalists, did not obtain a seat. Sinn Fein also fought the election but lost its only seat to the SDLP. The number of Commons seats in Northern Ireland will increase to 18 after the next general election (see p. 54).

Northern Ireland elects three members of the European Parliament.

Efforts to Achieve Devolved Government

Throughout the period of direct rule, successive British Governments have favoured a devolved administration widely acceptable to both unionist and nationalist political traditions. In 1974 a unionist–nationalist coalition Executive was formed but shortly collapsed as a result of a protest strike by those unionists opposed to power sharing. In 1982 an Assembly was elected by proportional representation but was dissolved four years later because no agreement could be reached between the parties on a devolved administration.

Following another government initiative, the four main constitutional parties (Ulster Unionists, Democratic Unionists, Alliance Party, and Social and Democratic Labour Party) held a series of talks with the Government and, where appropriate, the Irish Government, in 1991 and 1992 to see whether they could reach an agreement taking into account the three sets of relationships relevant to the Northern Ireland problem—within Northern Ireland itself; within the island of Ireland; and between the British and Irish Governments. The talks ended in November 1992 without agreement.

Since then, the British Government has been engaged in a series of bilateral talks with the Northern Ireland parties in order to explore the basis on which they might come together for further dialogue. This work led to the launch of the negotiations which started in June 1996. The aim of all these discussions was to produce a settlement attracting widespread agreement among the two political traditions in the North.

Relations with the Irish Republic

The British and Irish Governments have worked closely together in order to bring peace to Northern Ireland. The 1985 Anglo–Irish Agreement created an Intergovernmental Conference, in which both governments discuss issues such as improved cross border co-operation and security. The Irish Government can put forward views and proposals on matters related to Northern Ireland provided that these are not the responsibility of a devolved administration in Belfast.

The Downing Street Declaration

Signed in December 1993 by the two governments, the Downing Street Declaration is a statement of fundamental principles which made clear that the consent of a majority of people in Northern Ireland would be required before any constitutional change could come about. On this basis the British Government reiterated that it had no selfish strategic or economic interest in Northern Ireland and that, were a majority in Northern Ireland to wish it, the Government would introduce legislation to bring about a united Ireland. The Irish Government accepted that it would be wrong to attempt to impose a united Ireland without the freely given consent of the majority of people in Northern Ireland.

In August 1994 the IRA announced a complete cessation of its military operations. This was followed in October by a similar cessation by the loyalist paramilitary organisations. In December 1994 British officials, under the authority and political direction of ministers, started separate exploratory dialogues with Sinn Fein and with the Progressive Unionist and Ulster Democratic parties, the loyalist paramilitaries' political representatives, in order to explore the basis on which they could be admitted to the talks process and examine the practical consequences of an end to violence. In 1995 British ministers joined these dialogues, stressing the need for the decommissioning of illegally held weapons before these parties could take part in all-party negotiations.

Joint Framework Document

In February 1995 the British and Irish Governments published their 'Frameworks for the Future' document, which contains two sets of proposals. The first describes a shared understanding, prepared at the request of the Northern Ireland parties, between the two governments on new political arrangements between Northern Ireland and the Irish Republic and between the two governments based on agreement and co-operation to the mutual benefit of all. The other sets out the British Government's own understanding of potentially acceptable elements for new institutions in Northern Ireland which would improve local accountability as part of a comprehensive settlement. It draws closely on the work done in the 1992 round table discussions between the Government and the Northern Ireland parties and takes account of subsequent discussions with them.

The aim of 'Frameworks for the Future' is to serve as an aid to discussion and negotiation between the parties. It is not a blueprint and no solution will be imposed. In the view of the two governments, it contains the elements of what an overall settlement might look like. They believe it deals with the range of issues which the participants in the negotiations are likely to wish to consider.

Further Developments

In November 1995 the British and Irish Governments launched a Twin Track Initiative, which addressed the issues of decommissioning illegal arms through the establishment of an independent International Body and preparatory discussions with the parties on ground rules for political negotiations.

Chaired by former US senator George Mitchell, the International Body published its report in January 1996. It concluded that the paramilitary organisations would not decommisssion any arms before all-party talks and set out six principles of democracy and non-violence to which it said all parties should adhere. In addition, it set out guidelines on ways of decommissioning and proposed several confidence-building measures, including, if it were broadly acceptable, an elective process appropriately mandated and within the talks structure. All of these proposals were endorsed by the British Government.

The IRA announced the end of its ceasefire on 9 February 1996 and explosions for which the IRA claimed responsibility subsequently took place in London and Manchester. On 28 February, the British and Irish Prime Ministers set a date for all-party negotiations to begin—10 June 1996—following intensive multilateral consultations and an elective process. The two governments also agreed that there could be no question of ministerial meetings with Sinn Fein or of Sinn Fein

taking part in the negotiations until there was an unequivocal restoration of the IRA ceasefire.

Following the multilateral consultations with the Northern Ireland parties in March, the British Government published on 16 April draft elections legislation which became law on 29 April 1996. Under this an election took place on 30 May which produced 110 representatives, 5 from each of the 18 parliamentary constituencies and 2 from each of the 10 most successful parties across the Province. The representatives took their seats in a deliberative forum whose purpose is to discuss issues relevant to promoting dialogue and understanding within Northern Ireland. The Secretary of State invited the parties represented in the Forum to select negotiating teams to participate in negotiations launched by the British and Irish Prime Ministers on 10 June. In line with the policy set out in the February 1996 communiqué, nominations were not invited from Sinn Fein.

The two governments invited members of the independent International Body which examined the decommissioning issue to chair those aspects of the talks requiring independent chairmanship. The Secretary of State will chair those proceedings concerning internal institutions in Northern Ireland.

Human Rights

Economic and social deprivation persists on both sides of the Northern Ireland community. However, on all major social and economic indicators, Roman Catholics generally experience higher levels of disadvantage than Protestants, leading to feelings of discrimination and alienation which in turn influence attitudes to political and security issues. Government guidelines aim to promote fair treatment by ensuring that policies and programmes do not discriminate unjustifiably against, for example, people of different religious beliefs or political opinion, women, disabled people, ethnic minorities and people of different sexual orientation. The Government also provides grant aid to local government programmes designed to encourage mutual understanding and appreciation of cultural diversity; support is also given to the Cultural Traditions Programme, which attempts to show that different cultures do not have to lead to division. The aim of these initiatives is to encourage a more pluralistic and tolerant society with equal esteem for unionist and nationalist traditions. The Standing Advisory Commission on Human Rights advises the Secretary of State on the effectiveness of anti-discrimination laws and measures.

Direct or indirect discrimination in employment on grounds of religious belief or political opinion is unlawful. All public authorities and all those private employers with more than ten employees are required to register with the Fair Employment Commission. There is also compulsory monitoring of the religious composition of workforces, continual review of recruitment, training and promotion procedures and affirmative action if fair employment is not provided. Criminal penalties and economic sanctions exist for defaulting employers. The Fair Employment Tribunal deals with individual complaints about discrimination.

An independent Chief Electoral Officer maintains the accuracy of the electoral register, while electoral boundaries for parliamentary constituencies are determined by impartial statutory procedures conducted by the Boundary Commission for Northern Ireland. The Northern Ireland Ombudsman and Commissioner for Complaints deal with complaints by the public against government departments and local authorities. An independent commission supervises police investigations into the more serious complaints against police officers and, at its discretion, the investigation of other matters (see p. 91).

Security Policy

In order to protect the public, legislation gives the authorities exceptional powers to deal with and prevent terrorist activities. These include special powers of arrest for those suspected of certain serious terrorist offences, non-jury courts to try terrorist offences (see p. 96) and the banning of terrorist organisations. The legislation is subject to annual independent review and to annual approval by Parliament.

The Government hopes that, once a lasting peace is established, there will be no need for these exceptional powers and is keeping the requirement for such powers under continuing review.

An independent Commissioner observes and reports on the conditions under which terrorist suspects are detained by the security forces in police offices known as holding centres. The Commissioner submits an annual report to the Secretary of State which is published.

Statutory codes of practice apply to the detention, treatment, questioning and identification of suspects. A breach of any of the codes' provisions by a police officer is a disciplinary offence.

The Economy

Trends in output and employment tend to reflect those in Britain. However, seasonally adjusted unemployment (11.1 per cent in May 1996) is higher because a relatively high birth rate has led to a greater natural rate of population increase than in any other region in Britain.

Some 74 per cent of employees work in service industries and 18 per cent in manufacturing. The largest industrial employer is Short Brothers, owned by the Canadian company Bombardier, with some 5,100 employees engaged on the manufacture of aircraft and their components, guided missiles and related products and services. The shipbuilder Harland and Wolff employs 1,750 people.

In 1994–95 the value of exports increased by 21 per cent to £2,600 million. Exports account for 33 per cent of product sales. The Irish Republic is the most important market outside Britain, taking 8 per cent of exports in 1994–95.

Agriculture accounts for 5 per cent of gross domestic product or 8 per cent if ancillary industries are included. Some 10 per cent of the workforce is employed in agriculture, forestry, fishing and ancillary industries.

Tourism which is promoted by the Northern Ireland Tourist Board throughout the world, sustains about 12,500 jobs. A record 1.5 million people visited Northern Ireland in

1995 and it is hoped to attract 1.8 million in 1997.

Overseas and other companies are important investors, Northern Ireland attracting 9 per cent of all new investment jobs in Britain in 1995–96 even though it accounted for only 3 per cent of the British population. Around 200 externally owned companies employ almost 46,000 people, nearly half the manufacturing labour force. Many overseas companies use the region as a base for operations in the ever-increasing European market.

The United States is the most important single source of international investment for Britain and in particular for Northern Ireland. Almost 50 per cent of all inward investment to Britain originates in the US, while in Northern Ireland US companies represent a substantial proportion of the Province's manufacturing output.

The Industrial Development Board (IDB) encourages industrial development and new international investment. In 1995–96, 6,600 new jobs were created by new and established companies. In the same year the IDB successfully negotiated 35 new investments or expansions by externally owned companies; these are expected to result in 4,869 new jobs.

The Local Enterprise Development Unit assists the establishment and growth of small businesses as well as 45 local enterprise agencies run by people with business skills and expertise. The Training and Employment Agency is responsible for training the workforce. The Industrial Research and Technology Unit manages programmes aimed at increasing the quality and level of innovation and research.

Considerable public expenditure has been devoted to improving conditions in urban and rural areas. Since 1974 there has been a 92 per cent reduction in housing unfitness levels in Belfast.

The recently completed cross-harbour road and rail bridges have transformed Belfast's infrastructure at a cost of £89 million. The telecommunications firm BT has started work on its new £30 million riverside Laganside headquarters. Other important Laganside developments include Belfast City Council's new concert hall and conference centre, which is due to open in January 1997, and a 182-bedroom

Hilton International hotel, a £24 million project on which construction work began in 1996. More than 250 economic, social and environmental projects in the city's disadvantaged areas have been supported in a bid to improve education, training for adults, and job finding services for unemployed people.

In Londonderry major private and public sector developments recently completed or under way include a major city retail centre and multi-storey car park which provides employment for 1,200 people; a £6 million retail and car parking development elsewhere in the city; and an investment of £11 million in two new government office blocks providing accommodation for over 400 civil servants.

Northern Ireland has parity with England, Scotland and Wales on taxation and services. The British Government makes a contribution of over £3,000 million a year to maintain social services at the level of those in Great Britain, to meet the cost of security measures and to compensate for the natural disadvantages of geography and lack of resources.

In 1986 the British and Irish Governments established the International Fund for Ireland. Some three-quarters is spent in Northern Ireland, the rest going to border areas in the Republic. Programmes cover business enterprise, tourism, community relations, urban development, agriculture and rural development. Donors include the United States, the European Union, Canada and New Zealand.

Cultural and Social Affairs

Northern Ireland's cultural heritage is preserved and portrayed by the Ulster Museum in Belfast, the Ulster Folk and Transport Museum in County Down and the Ulster-American Folk Park in Omagh, which specialises in the history of Irish emigration to America. The Government recently announced the merger of these three museums. There are also several local museums and heritage centres which are mainly funded by local district councils.

Local arts festivals are an important feature of the arts calendar, the highlight being the Belfast festival, based at Queen's University. The Ulster Orchestra has a notable reputation. Government support for the arts is channelled through the Arts Council of Northern Ireland, which gives financial help and advice to opera and drama companies, orchestras and festivals, arts centres, galleries, theatres, writers and artistic groups.

Local district councils provide leisure facilities, including leisure centres and swimming pools. The Government finances the Sports Council for Northern Ireland, which promotes sport and physical recreation.

Health and personal social services correspond fairly closely to those in the rest of Britain.

Although publicly-financed schools must be open to children from all religions, in practice Roman Catholic and Protestant children are mainly educated in separate schools. There are 28 integrated schools for both Protestant and Roman Catholic children out of a total of 1,237 publicly-financed schools and this process is being encouraged by the Government (see p. 445.

Most housing is owner occupied. The Housing Executive (see p. 389) allocates public housing to those in greatest need.

Further Reading

A History of Ulster. Bardon, Jonathon. Blackstaff Press, 1992.

Northern Ireland (2nd edition). Aspects of Britain series, HMSO 1995.

Northern Ireland Expenditure Plans and Priorities. The Government's Expenditure Plans 1996–97 to 1998–99. HMSO, 1996.

Omnibus. A thrice-yearly magazine published by the Northern Ireland Information Service.

4 Scotland

Early History	18	The Environment	22
Government	19	Housing and Urban	
The Economy	20	Regeneration	22
Agriculture, Forestry and		Health	22
Fishing	21	Education	22
Energy and Water Resources	21	Cultural and Social Affairs	22
Transport	21		

Three-quarters of the population of Scotland and most of the industrial towns are in the central lowlands. The chief cities are Edinburgh (the capital), Glasgow, Aberdeen and Dundee. Just over half of Scotland consists of the sparsely populated highlands and islands in the north.

Scotland contains large areas of unspoilt and wild landscape, and the majority of Britain's highest mountains—nearly 300 peaks over 913 m (3,000 ft). The Grampians in the central highlands contain Ben Nevis (1,343 m, 4,406 ft), the highest peak in Britain.

Early History

At the time of the Roman invasion of Britain, what is now Scotland was mainly inhabited by the Picts. Despite a long campaign, Roman rule was never permanently extended to most of Scotland. In the sixth century, the Scots from Ireland settled in what is now Argyll, giving their name to the present-day Scotland. Lothian was populated by the Angles, while Britons moved north to Strathclyde. In the ninth century parts of Scotland were subject to raids by the Vikings; a united Scottish kingdom was established at this time.

The powerful English monarchy threatened Scottish independence in the Middle Ages, particularly under Edward I, and war between the two kingdoms was frequent. There were also, however, strong links with England; several Scottish kings held land and titles in

England and there was intermarriage between the Scottish and English royal families. Cultural influences on Scotland were also strong. Despite reverses such as the defeat of William Wallace's uprising in 1298, Robert the Bruce's victory over Edward II of England at Bannockburn in 1314 ensured the survival of a separate kingdom of Scotland.

The two crowns were eventually united when Elizabeth I of England was succeeded in 1603 by James VI of Scotland (James I of England), who was her nearest heir. Even so, England and Scotland remained separate political entities during the 17th century, apart from an enforced period of unification under Oliver Cromwell in the 1650s. The religions of the two kingdoms had also developed in different directions, with England retaining an Episcopalian church (governed by bishops)

Table 4.1: Population and Population Density

Council area	Population at 30 June 1995	Population density (people per sq km)
Aberdeen City	219,120	1,179
Aberdeenshire	226,530	36
Angus	111,770	51
Argyll and Bute	91,310	13
Clackmannanshire	48,820	312
Dumfries and Galloway	147,900	23
Dundee City	151,010	2,318
East Ayrshire	123,110	98
East Dunbartonshire	111,130	647
East Lothian	87,630	129
East Renfrewshire	88,150	510
Edinburgh, City of	447,550	1,706
Falkirk	142,800	477
Fife	351,600	266
Glasgow, City of	618,430	3,533
Highland	208,300	8
Inverclyde	88,690	548
Midlothian	79,880	224
Moray	87,150	39
North Ayrshire	139,520	158
North Lanarkshire	326,740	690
Orkney Islands	19,870	20
Perth and Kinross	132,820	25
Renfrewshire	178,340	682
Scottish Borders	106,200	22
Shetland Islands	23,090	16
South Ayrshire	114,570	95
South Lanarkshire	307,420	174
Stirling	82,280	37
West Dunbartonshire	96,290	594
West Lothian	149,540	352
Western Isles	29,040	9
Scotland	5,136,600	66

Source: General Register Office for Scotland.

and Scotland embracing a Presbyterian system (see p. 469). In 1707 both countries, realising the benefits of closer political and economic union, agreed on a single parliament for Great Britain. Scotland retained its own system of law and church settlement.

Government

Special arrangements are made for the conduct of Scottish affairs within the British system of government and separate Acts of Parliament are passed for Scotland where appropriate. There are 72 Scottish seats in the House of Commons. In August 1996 there were 49 Labour Members of Parliament, 10 Conservative, 9 Liberal Democrat and 4 Scottish Nationalist.

Scottish administration is the responsibility of the Secretary of State for Scotland, a member of the Cabinet, working through The Scottish Office, which has its headquarters in Edinburgh and an office in London.

Review of Scottish Government

In 1993 the Government issued a White Paper, *Scotland in the Union: A Partnership for Good*, following a wide-ranging examination of Scotland's place in Britain and the role of Parliament in Scottish affairs. This has led to a number of changes to improve the parliamentary arrangements for handling Scottish business. For example, the range of business handled by the Scottish Grand Committee (which consists of all 72 Scottish MPs) has been widened and the Committee now meets in Scotland as well as at Westminster. Other changes include improved scrutiny of Scottish legislation through two standing committees, which examine in detail Bills which are exclusively Scottish; and greater accountability of Scottish Office ministers through parliamentary question time (see p. 61).

Local Government Reform

A major change in the structure of local government took effect in April 1996. Under the Local Government etc. (Scotland) Act 1994, a single-tier structure of 29 councils replaced the 62 regional and district councils. The three islands councils—Orkney, Shetland and the Western Isles—were largely unaffected. Edinburgh, Glasgow, Dundee and Aberdeen now all have their own council.

Legal System

The principles and procedures of the Scottish legal system differ in many respects from those of England and Wales. These differences stem, in part, from the adoption of elements from other European legal systems, based on Roman law, during the 16th century. For example, a Scottish jury can give a verdict of 'not proven' as an alternative to 'not guilty', when the accused is acquitted.

Scotland has its own prosecution, prison and police services.

The Economy

Scotland has experienced the same pressure on its traditional industries as Wales and the north of England. However, since 1989 economic growth in Scotland has on average been greater than in Britain as a whole and it was less affected by the recession in the early 1990s than were other areas.

Industry

As traditional industries such as coal, steel and shipbuilding have declined, there has been growth in high-technology industries, such as chemicals, electronic engineering, information technology and lighter forms of mechanical and instrument engineering. Scotland has one of the biggest concentrations of the electronics industry in Western Europe, with around 200 plants employing some 46,000 workers. The industry accounts for around 20 per cent of manufacturing output in Scotland and is responsible for a significant proportion of Europe's output of personal computers, computer workstations and automated cash dispensers (see p. 249).

Some traditional industries, such as high-quality tweeds and other textiles, and food and drink products, remain important. There are 92 whisky distilleries in operation, mostly in the north-east. Whisky exports, valued at £2,300 million in 1995, represent about 15 per cent of Scotland's manufacturing exports.

Industrial Development

Government support for enterprise and training is channelled through Scottish Enterprise and Highlands and Islands Enterprise, which both have general functions in economic development, training and environmental improvement in the Scottish lowlands and the Highlands and Islands respectively. They contract with 22 Local Enterprise Companies (led by the private sector), which arrange the provision of training and business support.

Government measures have helped to attract firms to Scotland, and investment by overseas companies has made a significant contribution to the growth of modern technologically based industries. In 1995–96

Locate in Scotland and The Scottish Office Education and Industry Department helped to attract 84 inward investment projects to Scotland, involving planned investment of nearly £1,000 million. The projects are expected to create or safeguard over 12,500 jobs.

Services

A marked expansion has occurred in services, which now employ over 70 per cent of the workforce. Financial and business services are of growing importance, and in June 1995, 279,000 people were employed in the sector. There are four Scottish-based clearing banks and they have limited rights to issue their own banknotes.

> The Scottish financial sector ranks third in Europe in terms of the volume of equity funds under management and eleventh in the world. In a range of services, the sector has been a pioneer, for example, in the use of cash dispensers and electronic home banking. Scotland is a base for a large number of financial institutions, including insurance companies, unit trusts and investment trusts. Between 1989 and 1994 the total market value of funds under management by Scottish fund managers—including life assurance offices, specialist fund managers, banks and stockbrokers—rose by over 97 per cent to £136,000 million.

Tourism and leisure also make a significant contribution to the economy, directly providing over 180,000 jobs. In 1994 expenditure by tourists was valued at £2,005 million; there were 10.25 million tourist trips, including those originating in Scotland. A strategic plan for the development of the tourism industry, launched by the Government in 1994, is aiming to spread tourism throughout Scotland and increase tourism in off-peak periods.

Agriculture, Forestry and Fishing

About 76 per cent of the land area of Scotland is devoted to agriculture. Most of this is rough grazing for cattle and sheep. Scotland's cattle industry has a worldwide reputation, both for the quality of meat and for pedigree breeds. Arable farms are highly productive, and the principal crop is barley, which is used in the making of whisky.

Scotland accounts for over half of Britain's forest area and for just under half of timber production. Forestry is continuing to expand and many new woodlands are being created, including native pine forests.

Fishing remains important, particularly in the north-east and the islands. Scotland accounts for nearly three-quarters by weight and over 60 per cent by value of the fish landed in Britain by British vessels.

Energy and Water Resources

Offshore oil and gas production have made a significant contribution to the economy. Recent trends have been the exploitation of smaller resources and an increase in production.

Nuclear and hydro-electric generation supply a higher proportion of energy than in any other part of Britain. In 1995–96 the output from Scottish Nuclear's two nuclear power stations was equivalent to around 55 per cent of electricity sales in Scotland. British Energy—the holding company of Scottish Nuclear and Nuclear Electric—is one of the three largest electricity generators in Great Britain and was privatised in July 1996 (see p. 273); its head office is in Edinburgh.

With abundant rainfall, there is an extensive supply of water from upland sources. As a result of the changes in local government, three new public water authorities were set up in April 1996 to take over responsibility for water and sewerage services from the regional and islands councils.

Transport

Communications, both domestic and international, have improved in many parts of Scotland. Electrification of the Edinburgh to London railway was completed in 1991.

The road construction programme includes completion of the Central Scotland motorway network and of the upgrading to motorway standard of the A74 from Carlisle to Glasgow. A new bridge linking the Scottish mainland to the island of Skye was opened in October 1995 and is one of the world's longest span balanced cantilever bridges.

The Environment

Scotland's countryside contains a rich variety of wildlife, with some species not found elsewhere in Britain. There are 70 National Nature Reserves and 1,398 Sites of Special Scientific Interest. Four regional parks and 40 national scenic areas have been designated, covering 13 per cent of the land surface. Four of the 11 forest parks in Great Britain are in Scotland, and a fifth spans the border between Scotland and England.

Over 100 wildlife sites of European importance have been proposed for designation as Special Areas of Conservation under the European Community (EC) Habitats Directive. Under the EC's Wild Birds Directive, more than 50 sites have been designated as Special Protection Areas because of their importance to rare and migratory birds.

Housing and Urban Regeneration

The tenure pattern is somewhat different from that in the rest of Britain. Home ownership is increasing but, at 57 per cent, is still lower than in other areas of Britain. Some 33 per cent of housing is rented from the public sector, compared with 20 per cent for Britain as a whole. Projects to tackle the problems in inner city areas and some peripheral housing estates include a series of partnerships between The Scottish Office and other groups, such as local communities and the private sector (see pp. 380–1).

Health

There has been a general improvement in the health of people in Scotland, but for certain diseases, such as lung cancer and heart disease, the health record is not as good as elsewhere in Britain. In 1992 the Government issued a policy statement with a range of initiatives to improve health in Scotland and meet the targets for the year 2000 which had been announced in 1991. Progress is being made towards meeting some of these targets, with, for example, falls in mortality from coronary heart disease.

Education

The concept of universal education was accepted in Scotland as early as the 16th century. The Scottish education system has a number of distinctive features, for example, in examinations (see p. 452). Four of the 13 universities—St Andrews, Glasgow, Aberdeen and Edinburgh—were established in the 15th century. Record numbers of students are now entering higher education.

The Education (Scotland) Act 1996 contains provisions to strengthen the quality of pre-school education and to set up a new Scottish Qualifications Authority (which is intended to improve the educational pathways between schools, colleges and preparation for employment). The Act also aims to improve the operation of school boards and to extend parental choice on school places.

Cultural and Social Affairs

Gaelic, a language of ancient Celtic origin, is spoken by some 70,000 people, many of whom live in the islands of the Hebrides. The Government is encouraging people to learn more about the Gaelic language and culture. Government support for Gaelic covers three main areas: education, Gaelic organisations and television broadcasting.

> **Many Scots have achieved eminence in arts and sciences. A major programme of events during 1996, the bicentenary of the death of the poet Robert Burns, has commemorated his life and work. The programme took place both in Scotland and across the world.**

The annual Edinburgh International Festival is one of the world's leading cultural events. Held in August and September, it brings about £70 million into the Scottish economy each year. Edinburgh and the Mayfest international arts festival in Glasgow are the two largest arts festivals in Britain. Scotland possesses a number of major collections of the fine and applied arts. For example, Glasgow houses the Burrell Collection and the new Gallery of Modern Art, which was opened in 1996. A new Museum of Scotland is being built in Edinburgh to house the National Museums' Scottish collection. Each spring Edinburgh hosts the International Science Festival, the world's biggest science festival in a single city.

The predominant Church of Scotland is a Protestant church which is Presbyterian in form; it is governed by a hierarchy of church courts, each of which includes lay people.

The sport of golf originated in Scotland, and there are over 400 golf courses, including St Andrews, Gleneagles, Turnberry, Muirfield, Troon and Prestwick, which are internationally renowned. A wide range of outdoor activities, such as mountaineering, hill walking and fishing, are also pursued. Winter sports are becoming increasingly popular in the Cairngorm Mountains, Glencoe and a number of other areas.

Further Reading

Scotland. Aspects of Britain series, HMSO, 1993.

Scotland in the Union: A Partnership for Good. Cm 2225. HMSO, 1993.

Serving Scotland's Needs: The Government's Expenditure Plans 1996–97 to 1998–99. Departments of the Secretary of State for Scotland and the Forestry Commission. Cm 3214. HMSO, 1996.

5 Wales

Early History	24	Agriculture and Forestry	27
Language	24	Transport	27
Government	25	The Environment	27
The Economy	25	Cultural and Social Affairs	28

Two-thirds of the population of Wales live in the southern valleys and the lower-lying coastal areas. The chief urban centres are Cardiff (with a population of 306,500), Swansea and Newport in the south and Wrexham in the north. However, much of Wales is hilly or mountainous, with about a quarter of the land being 300 metres (980 ft) or more above sea level. The highest mountains are in Snowdonia and the tallest peak is Snowdon (1,085 m, 3,560 ft).

Wales is a principality; Prince Charles, the heir to the throne, was invested by the Queen with the title of Prince of Wales at Caernarfon Castle in 1969, when he was 20. The Welsh name of the country is Cymru.

Early History

After the collapse of Roman rule in Britain (see p. 4), Wales remained a Celtic stronghold, although often during Norman times within the English sphere of influence. For much of its early history, it was divided into a number of separate principalities, and unity was achieved only sporadically. In 1267 Llywelyn ap Gruffudd, who had achieved control over a large portion of Wales, was recognised as Prince of Wales by the English. However, following his death in battle in 1282, Edward I completed a successful campaign to bring Wales under English rule. The series of great castles that he had built in north Wales remain among Britain's finest historic monuments (see p. 373). Edward I's eldest son—later Edward II—was born at Caernarfon in 1284 and was given the title Prince of Wales, which continues to be borne by the eldest son of the reigning monarch.

Continued strong Welsh national feeling culminated in the unsuccessful rising led by Owain Glyndŵr at the beginning of the 15th century. The Tudor dynasty, which ruled England from 1485 to 1603, was of Welsh ancestry. The Acts of Union of 1536 and 1542 united England and Wales administratively, politically and legally.

Language

At the time of the 1991 census Welsh speakers made up 19 per cent of the population. In much of the rural north and west, Welsh remains the first language of most of the population. There is some evidence that the decline in the number of Welsh speakers is being halted, with greater numbers of children and young people able to speak Welsh, and a revival in the largely anglicised areas of south-east and north-east Wales.

The Government has reaffirmed its commitment to enhancing Welsh culture and developing greater use of the Welsh language. Bilingual education in schools is encouraged (see p. 28), and Welsh is now more widely used for official purposes and in broadcasting. There are also many more bilingual publications and most road signs are bilingual. Expenditure of £6.2 million directly in support of the language is planned in 1996–97.

The Welsh Language Act 1993 establishes the principle that, in the context of public business and the administration of justice in Wales, Welsh and English should be treated on an equal basis. The Act also put the Welsh Language Board (formerly an advisory body) on a statutory basis.

> **The Welsh Language Board aims to promote and facilitate the use of the Welsh language. In autumn 1996 the Board published its strategy for the future of the Welsh language. Three main priorities were identified:**
>
> - **increasing the number of Welsh speakers;**
> - **providing more opportunities to use the language; and**
> - **strengthening Welsh as a community language.**
>
> **The Board will seek to achieve these aims in partnership with the main interested parties in Wales.**

Government

The country elects 38 Members of Parliament (MPs) to the House of Commons. For the last 60 years the industrial communities have tended to support the Labour Party in elections, ensuring a Labour majority of seats. In September 1996 Wales had 27 Labour MPs, 6 Conservative, 4 Plaid Cymru (Welsh Nationalist) and 1 Liberal Democrat. Special arrangements exist for the discussion of Welsh affairs in the parliamentary Welsh Grand Committee, whose function is to consider matters relating exclusively to Wales; Bills are referred to it for consideration as to whether they should be given a second reading (see p. 61).

The Secretary of State for Wales, who is a member of the Cabinet, has wide-ranging responsibilities relating to the economy, education, welfare services and the provision of amenities. The headquarters of the administration is the Welsh Office in Cardiff; it also has an office in London. The legal system is identical to that in England.

Under the Local Government (Wales) Act 1994, local government has been reorganised. The former two-tier structure of eight county councils and 37 district councils has been abolished and succeeded by 22 unitary authorities. The authorities took up their new responsibilities in April 1996.

The Economy

Recent decades have seen fundamental changes in the basis of the Welsh economy. The dependence on refined fuels and coalmining has declined considerably, although steelmaking remains important. Wales accounts for over a third of Britain's steel output. The most notable features have been expansion in service industries and the development of a more diverse range of manufacturing industries, including many at the forefront of technology. Some 915 new plants have been created since 1980, providing around 62,000 new jobs.

In the service sector the most marked growth has been in financial and business services, and leisure services. Annual earnings from tourism are estimated at about £1,500 million and the industry employs directly or indirectly about 100,000 people. The Wales Tourist Board seeks to develop tourism in ways which will yield the optimum economic benefit for the people of Wales.

Table 5.1: Population Mid-1994

Council area	Population	Population density (people per sq km)
Blaenau Gwent	73,300	675
Bridgend	130,900	531
Caerphilly	171,000	616
Cardiff	306,500	2,206
Carmarthenshire	169,000	71
Ceredigion	69,700	39
Conwy	110,700	98
Denbighshire	91,300	108
Flintshire	145,300	334
Gwynedd	116,900	46
Isle of Anglesey	68,400	96
Merthyr Tydfil	59,500	535
Monmouthshire	84,200	99
Neath Port Talbot	140,100	318
Newport	137,400	725
Pembrokeshire	114,100	72
Powys	121,800	23
Rhondda, Cynon, Taff	239,000	562
Swansea	230,900	612
Torfaen	90,600	717
Vale of Glamorgan	118,900	355
Wrexham	123,500	247
Wales	**2,913,000**	**140**

Source: Welsh Office.

Wales is now an important centre for consumer electronics, information technology, automotive components, chemicals and materials, and food and drink. Around 35,000 people are employed in the manufacture of optical and electrical equipment, and the sector's output has risen by 44 per cent since 1990. Wales is responsible for around 10 per cent of world production of optical fibres. Over 20,000 people are employed in the automotive components sector, whose annual sales are about £1,700 million.

Although south Wales remains the principal industrial area, new industries and firms have been introduced in north-east Wales and light industry attracted to the towns in the rural areas of mid- and north Wales.

Inward Investment

Wales has been particularly successful in attracting investment from overseas companies and from elsewhere in Britain. Through its International Division, the Welsh Development Agency (WDA) seeks to attract investment into Wales and co-ordinates the approach for responding to the needs of investors. Since 1983 it has recorded over 1,500 projects, which promise capital investment of £8,000 million, the creation of over 87,000 new jobs and safeguarding over 54,000 existing jobs. Overseas-owned manufacturing companies employ more than 73,000 people. Among the projects in 1995–96 was a £300 million scheme announced by Ford to expand its engine plant at Bridgend. LG of

Korea has recently announced a £1,700 million project which will create 6,100 new jobs in two factories—one producing semiconductors and the other wide-screen television sets and components. This is the largest single inward investment project ever into Europe.

Economic Development

The economic programmes of the Welsh Office are complemented by the work of the WDA and the Development Board for Rural Wales, which have wide powers to promote economic, industrial and environmental change. In 1996–97 these bodies plan to undertake programmes involving expenditure of £130 million and £20 million respectively. One of the main areas of activity is providing accommodation for business, increasingly in partnership with the private sector. The WDA is also undertaking the largest land reclamation programme in Europe.

The south Wales valleys are one of the main areas to have been affected by the decline in traditional industries. A second five-year Programme for the Valleys was launched in 1993, with the objective of improving the economic, social and environmental conditions in the area. Under the new programme, the emphasis has moved away from centralised initiatives towards stronger partnerships between the Welsh Office, development agencies, local councils and the private and voluntary sectors. The Government has set a target of matching public sector investment in the area with private sector investment of £1,000 million by the year 2000. This is in line with its intention to maximise private sector investment in support of urban and rural regeneration. This private finance initiative is being extended during 1996 to the rest of Wales.

A development corporation has been set up to stimulate the regeneration of the Cardiff Bay area. A new barrage is being built across the harbour mouth and should be completed in 1998. It is expected that about 25,000 new jobs will be created in the Cardiff Bay area, 6,000 new homes built, 1 million sq m of business space created and over £1,175 million of private sector investment attracted. A key infrastructure project is the construction of a landscaped avenue linking the inner harbour with the city centre and incorporating a light rail link. A development contract is expected to be awarded early in 1997, with the intention of establishing the link in time for the Rugby World Cup in 1999 (see p. 28).

In March 1996 the Secretary of State for Wales issued a White Paper designed to encourage sustainable economic growth and community development in rural Wales (see p. 379).

Agriculture and Forestry

Agriculture occupies about 81 per cent of the land area. The main activities are sheep and cattle rearing in the hill regions and dairy farming in the lowlands. About 12 per cent of Wales is covered by woodland.

Transport

Completion of the M4 motorway in the south and of the conversion to dual carriageway of the A55 trunk road across the mainland in the north, both in 1994, have helped the Welsh economy. Great importance is attached to further improvements to these routes. Motorway links to England and the rest of Europe were considerably improved with the opening in June 1996 of the second motorway crossing of the Severn. The bridge, which cost £300 million, was built and is operated by a private sector company, Severn River Crossing plc. New publicly funded motorway links to the bridge have also been provided.

Passenger traffic at Cardiff International Airport has increased from 638,000 in 1990–91 to nearly 1.1 million in 1994–95.

The Environment

Wales has a rich and diverse natural heritage, and the environment in rural Wales is an important natural asset. About one-quarter of Wales is designated as a National Park or Area of Outstanding Natural Beauty (see p. 368). As well as three National Parks—Snowdonia, the Brecon Beacons and the Pembrokeshire Coast—and five Areas of Outstanding Natural Beauty, there are two national trails, 31 country parks and large stretches of heritage coast. There are 56 National Nature Reserves and over 900 Sites of Special Scientific Interest.

In February 1996 the tanker *Sea Empress* ran aground off Milford Haven (Pembrokeshire), resulting in one of Britain's largest oil spills. However, a major clean-up operation was immediately undertaken to minimise the damage, an operation which was scheduled to continue for some time. A thorough investigation into the cause of the incident is being conducted, and a committee has been established to assess the environmental impact.

Cultural and Social Affairs

Welsh literature is one of the oldest in Europe. The Welsh people have strong musical traditions and Wales is well known for its choral singing, while the Welsh National Opera has an international reputation. Special festivals, known as eisteddfodau, encourage Welsh literature and music. The largest is the annual Royal National Eisteddfod, consisting of competitions in music, singing, prose and poetry entirely in Welsh. Artists from all over the world come to the town of Llangollen for the annual International Musical Eisteddfod. New galleries and a permanent Evolution of Wales exhibition were opened at the National Museum of Wales in Cardiff in 1993. A third building at the National Library of Wales, costing some £11 million, was opened by the Queen in May 1996.

There is no established church, the Anglican church in Wales having been disestablished in 1920 following decades of pressure from adherents of the Methodist and Baptist churches. Methodism in particular spread rapidly in Wales in the 18th century, assuming the nature of a popular movement among Welsh speakers and finding strong support later in industrial communities.

An active local press includes a number of Welsh language publications. The fourth television channel, Sianel Pedwar Cymru (S4C), broadcasts most of its programmes in Welsh during peak viewing hours and is required to see that a significant proportion of programmes are in Welsh.

Although the National Curriculum (see p. 451) applies in both England and Wales, there are a number of distinct features to education in Wales. The content of several subjects is different in order to reflect the distinctive history, geography and cultural development of Wales. Welsh is also taught—as a first or second language—to most pupils between the ages of 5 and 16. In addition, subjects are taught in Welsh in about 500 schools, in both the primary and secondary sectors. Most of these are in the traditionally Welsh-speaking, largely rural areas, but there are also some in the anglicised, mainly industrial areas. There are 14 higher education institutions, of which eight form the collegiate University of Wales (founded in 1893), and 26 further education colleges.

Among many sporting activities, there is particular interest in rugby union football, which has come to be regarded as the Welsh national game. A new national rugby stadium is to be built in Cardiff and will cost some £114 million, of which £46 million will be provided by the Millennium Commission (see p. 43). It is due to open early in 1999 and will host the final of the 1999 Rugby World Cup.

Further Reading

The Government's Expenditure Plans 1996–97 to 1998–99. A Report by the Welsh Office and the Office of Her Majesty's Chief Inspector of Schools in Wales. Cm 3215. HMSO, 1996.

Statistical Focus on Wales. Welsh Office, 1996.

Wales. Aspects of Britain series, HMSO, 1993.

A Working Countryside for Wales. Cm 3180. HMSO, 1996.

6   The Social Framework

Population	29	The Economic and Social	
Language	33	Pattern	36
Ethnic and National			
Minorities	34		

Among the main social changes during the second half of the 20th century are longer life expectancy and a lower birth rate, reflected in a growing proportion of elderly people; a higher divorce rate; wider educational opportunities; technological progress and a higher standard of living.

POPULATION

According to mid-1994 estimates, Britain's population is 58.4 million, the 17th largest in the world. Statistics are derived from the census (taken every ten years), with allowance made for subsequent births and deaths (obtained from compulsory registration), and migration.

The population has been growing slowly since the early 1980s, thanks to increased longevity. On mid-1994-based projections, the population in Britain is forecast to rise to 59.4 million in 2001 and 60.5 million in 2011. However, the population is likely to start falling again from about 2025, owing to low birth rates (see below) and the post-war 'baby boom' generation dying out.

Birth Rates

In 1995 there were 732,000 live births in Britain, compared with 751,000 in 1994. The total period fertility rate (an indication of average family size) remains below 2.1, the level leading to the long-term replacement of the population, although it is projected that it will increase from 1.75 in 1995 to 1.8 for women born in or after 1980.

Contributory factors to the relatively low birth rate in recent years (12.6 live births per 1,000 population in 1995) include:

- the trends towards later marriage and towards postponing having children, which have led to an increase in the average age of women giving birth—28.5 years in England and Wales in 1995, compared with 26.8 in 1981;

- a preference for smaller families than in the past, which has led to a significant decline in the proportion of families with four or more children;[1] and

- more widespread and effective contraception, making it easier to plan families, and the greater prevalence of voluntary sterilisation for both men and women.

---

[1]In 1994–95, 20 per cent of households in Great Britain consisted of a married couple with one or two dependent children, compared with 5 per cent of households consisting of a married couple with three or more dependent children.

There were 178,300 legal abortions in Great Britain in 1994, down 6.5 per cent on 1991.

Mortality

At birth the expectation of life for a man is about 73 years and for a woman 79 years, compared with 49 years for men and 52 years for women in 1901.

There were 626,000 deaths in 1995, a death rate of 11.0 per 1,000 population. There has been a decline in mortality at most ages, particularly among children. The infant mortality rate (deaths of infants under one year old per 1,000 live births) was 6.2 in 1995; neonatal mortality (deaths of infants under four weeks old per 1,000 live births) was 4.2; and maternal mortality is about 0.07 per 1,000 total births. The decline in the mortality rate reflects better nutrition, rising standards of living, the advance of medical science, the increased availability of medical facilities, improved health measures, better working conditions, education in personal hygiene and the smaller size of families.

Deaths caused by circulatory diseases (including heart attacks and strokes) now account for nearly half of all deaths, and mortality from heart disease in Great Britain remains high compared with that of other developed countries. The next largest cause of death is cancer, which is responsible for nearly one-quarter of deaths.

Cigarette smoking is the greatest preventable cause of illness and death in Britain. However, there has been a significant decline in the prevalence of smoking, with 28 per cent of adult males and 26 per cent of adult females smoking cigarettes in 1994, compared with 52 and 41 per cent respectively in 1972.

Between 1990 and 1992 the Government set out strategies for continuing the overall improvement in health, emphasising disease prevention and health promotion (see p. 399). A number of government priorities, aimed at supporting the overall goals of improving the country's health and providing high-quality care for those who need it, have been listed. The Government is also pursuing a comprehensive strategy against drug misuse in Britain. Initiatives are aimed at reducing both the supply of, and demand for, drugs. From 1991 onwards, annual surveys have been carried out in England to monitor trends in health.

Marriage and Divorce

Britain has one of the highest marriage and divorce rates in the European Union. In 1993 there were 332,600 marriages in Britain, of which 38.7 per cent were remarriages of one or both parties. Some 25.1 per cent of marriages were remarriages where one or both parties had been divorced. Of the male population aged 16 or over in Great Britain in 1994, 61 per cent were married, 24 per cent single, 7 per cent cohabiting, 4 per cent widowed, 4 per cent divorced and 1 per cent separated. Among women, 54 per cent were married, 18 per cent single, 13 per cent widowed, 6 per cent cohabiting, 6 per cent divorced and 2 per cent separated. The average age for first marriages in England and Wales is now about 28.2 for men and 26.2 for women.

In 1995 there were 13.1 divorces for every 1,000 married couples in England and Wales. The rates for Scotland and Northern Ireland are lower than that for England and Wales. In 1995 167,748 divorces were granted in Britain. The average age of people at the time of divorce in England and Wales is now about 39.6 for men and 37.0 for women.

> Under the Family Law, couples seeking to divorce will have to go through a period of at least one year for reflection and consideration. This would allow time for conciliation, if that is possible, and so, it is hoped, keep a larger number of marriages intact of those that are capable of being saved.

Another feature, common to many other Western European countries, has been an increase in cohabitation, and 21 per cent of non-married men aged 16–59 in Great Britain were cohabiting in 1994. Between 1979 and 1994 the proportion of non-married women aged 18–49 who were cohabiting rose from 11 to 23 per cent. Cohabitation is particularly high (28 per cent) among divorced women, but recently the largest increase has been for single women.

Age and Sex Structure

The most significant changes in the age structure of the population have been the growing numbers of elderly people and the decline in the proportion of young people. The proportion of young people aged under 15 fell from 24.1 per cent of the population in 1971 to 9.4 per cent in 1995. During the period 1971–94 the proportion of elderly people (those aged 65 and over) increased from 13.2 to 15.7 per cent, while 18.2 per cent of the population were over the normal retirement ages (65 for men and 60 for women) in 1994, compared with 16.3 per cent in 1971.

There is a ratio of about 104 females to every 100 males in the population as a whole. There are about 3 per cent more male than female births every year. However, because of the higher mortality of men at all ages, there is a turning-point, at about 50 years of age, beyond which the number of women exceeds the number of men.

Distribution of Population

The population density is about 242 inhabitants per sq km, which is well above the EU average of about 153 per sq km. Of the four lands, England is the most densely populated, with 375 people per sq km. Scotland is the least densely populated, with 67 people per sq km. Wales and Northern Ireland have 140 and 122 people per sq km respectively.

Since the 19th century there has been a trend, especially in London, for people to move away from congested urban centres into the suburbs. Between the 1981 and 1991 censuses, all metropolitan counties (with the exception of West Yorkshire) experienced small decreases in population, the largest being in Merseyside (5 per cent). There has also been a geographical redistribution of the population, away from Scotland and the northern regions of England. The regions with the highest rates of increase in population between 1981 and 1991 were East Anglia (10

per cent) and the South West (8 per cent). Retirement migration is also a feature of population movement, the main recipient areas being the south coast of England and East Anglia.

Migration

From 1989 to 1994 some 1.1 million people left Britain (excluding the Channel Islands and the Isle of Man) to live abroad. About 1.2 million came from overseas to live in Britain, so that net immigration increased the population by about 94,000. These figures exclude migration to and from the Irish Republic, and are also likely to exclude people admitted as visitors who were subsequently granted an extension of stay for a year or more.

In 1994 the total inflow of people intending to stay in Britain for one year or more was 253,000, some 18 per cent more than in 1993. The outflow of people leaving to live abroad, at 191,000, was 13 per cent lower than in 1993.

Of the 191,000 departing residents in 1994:

- 29 per cent left for EU countries;
- 22 per cent for Australia, Canada, New Zealand or South Africa;
- 15 per cent for other Commonwealth countries;
- 13 per cent for the United States;
- 6 per cent for the Middle East; and
- 15 per cent for other countries.

Of the 253,000 new residents in 1994:

- 31 per cent came from EU countries;
- 16 per cent came from Australia, Canada, New Zealand or South Africa;
- 21 per cent from other Commonwealth countries;
- 12 per cent from the United States;
- 4 per cent from the Middle East; and
- 16 per cent from other countries.

Nationality

Under the British Nationality Act 1981 there are three main forms of citizenship:

- British citizenship for people closely connected with Britain;

- British Dependent Territories citizenship for people connected with the dependent territories (see p. 123); and

- British Overseas citizenship for those citizens of the United Kingdom and Colonies who did not acquire either of the other citizenships when the 1981 Act came into force.

British citizenship is acquired automatically at birth by a child born in Britain if his or her mother or father is a British citizen or is settled in Britain. A child adopted in Britain by a British citizen is also a British citizen. A child born abroad to a British citizen born, adopted, naturalised or registered in Britain is generally a British citizen by descent. The Act safeguards the citizenship of a child born abroad to a British citizen in Crown service, certain related services, or in service under a European Union institution.

British citizenship may also be acquired:

- by registration for certain children, including those born in Britain who do not automatically acquire such citizenship at birth, or who have been born abroad to a parent who is a citizen by descent;

- by registration for British Dependent Territories citizens, British Overseas citizens, British subjects under the Act, British Nationals (Overseas) and British protected persons after five years' residence in Britain, except for people from Gibraltar, who may be registered without residence;

- by registration for stateless people and those who have previously renounced British nationality; and

- by naturalisation for all other adults aged 18 or over.

Naturalisation is at the Home Secretary's discretion. Requirements include five years' residence, or three years if the applicant's spouse is a British citizen. Those who are not married to a British citizen are also required to have a sufficient knowledge of English, Welsh or Scottish Gaelic; they must also intend to have their main home in Britain or be employed by the Crown, by an international organisation of which Britain is a member, or by a company or association established in Britain.

Special arrangements covering the status of British Dependent Territories citizens connected with Hong Kong when the territory returns to the People's Republic of China in 1997 are made by the Hong Kong (British Nationality) Order 1986. Under this, such citizens are entitled, before 1997, to acquire a status known as British National (Overseas) and to hold a passport in that status. In addition, the British Nationality (Hong Kong) Act 1990 made provision for the registration as British citizens before 30 June 1997 of up to 50,000 people who are able to meet certain criteria and who are recommended by the Governor, together with their spouses and children who are still minors. By May 1996 almost all of these places had been filled.

In 1995, 40,500 people were granted British citizenship, in addition to about 26,000 people registered that year under the British Nationality (Hong Kong) Act 1990.

Immigration

Immigration into Britain is largely governed by the Immigration Act 1971 and the Immigration

Table 6.1: Acceptances for Settlement 1985–1995

	1985	1995
Pakistan	6,680	6,310
India	5,500	4,860
United States	4,170	3,960
Bangladesh	5,330	3,280
Nigeria	500	3,260
Australia	3,750	2,020
Japan	1,010	1,870
Ghana	660	1,820
Jamaica	350	1,400
New Zealand	2,280	1,390
Sri Lanka	930	1,370
Hong Kong	950	1,310
South Africa	790	1,300
Turkey	480	1,170
People's Republic of China	140	1,130
Iran	2,210	1,120
Philippines	750	1,090

Source: Home Office

Rules made under it. The Rules set out the requirements to be met by those who are subject to immigration control and seek entry to or leave to remain in Britain. New Immigration Rules came into effect in 1994. British citizens and those Commonwealth citizens who had the right of abode before January 1983 maintain the right of abode and are not subject to immigration control.

Under the Immigration Rules nationals of certain specified countries or territorial entities must obtain a visa before they can enter Britain. Other nationals subject to immigration control require entry clearance when coming to work or settle in Britain. Visas and other entry clearances are normally obtained from the nearest or other specified British diplomatic post in a person's home country.

Nationals of the European Economic Area (EEA)—EU member states plus Norway, Iceland and Liechtenstein—are not subject to substantive immigration control. They may work in Britain without restriction. Provided that they are working or able to support themselves financially, EEA nationals have a right to reside in Britain.

Britain has traditionally granted asylum to those fleeing persecution and respects its obligations under the United Nations Convention and Protocol relating to the Status of Refugees. These provide that refugees lawfully resident should enjoy treatment as least as favourable as that accorded to other foreign nationals. However, in recent years there has been a significant change in both the numbers and the motivation of those seeking asylum in Britain, with many asylum seekers motivated by economic rather than political factors. Between 1984 and 1995 the number of asylum seekers rose from 4,000 to 55,000 (including dependants); of these only 6 per cent were accepted as being genuine refugees. In common with other European countries, Britain has reviewed its procedures in order to curb abuse of the system while safeguarding the interests of genuine refugees. However, the upward trend of asylum applications has risen sharply during the last two years and further measures to discourage abuse have now been enacted by Parliament. The Asylum and Immigration Act 1996 gives the Government, among other things, the power to designate

selected countries of origin as not giving rise to serious risk of persecution. It makes appeals against return to EU, and certain other, safe third countries exercisable only after removal from Britain.

In 1995 9.6 million foreign and Commonwealth nationals (excluding EEA nationals) were admitted to Britain. About 55,000 people were accepted for settlement.

LANGUAGE

English is the main language spoken in Britain, and is also one of the most widely used in the world.[2] Recent estimates suggest that 310 million people speak it as their first language, with a similar number speaking it as a second language. It is an official language in a large number of overseas countries, and is widely used internationally as the main language for purposes such as air traffic control and academic gatherings.

Modern English derives primarily from one of the dialects of Anglo-Saxon. However, it has been very greatly influenced by other languages, particularly, following the Norman conquest, by French. French was the language of the nobility and the law courts for many years after 1066. The re-emergence of English as the universal language of England was signified by such events as the Statute of Pleadings in 1362, which laid down that English was to be used in court. The 14th century also saw the first major English literature since Anglo-Saxon days, with the writing of works such as *Piers Plowman* by William Langland and *The Canterbury Tales* by Geoffrey Chaucer. However, there remained great regional variations in the language, and spellings were not always standardised.

Following the introduction of the printing press to England by William Caxton in the late 15th century, there was a considerable flowering of English literature in the 16th and early 17th centuries. Writers such as William Shakespeare, Edmund Spenser and Christopher Marlowe produced work that is still famous today. Cranmer's prayerbook and the Authorised ('King James') Version of the

---

[2]For the Welsh language see p. 24; for Gaelic see p. 22.

Bible, which have had a profound effect on literature down to modern times, also date from this period. About this time, too, translations of Latin, Italian and other European works into English vastly expanded the English language. The work of early lexicographers, of whom the most famous was Samuel Johnson (1709–84), led to greater standardisation in matters such as spelling.

ETHNIC AND NATIONAL MINORITIES

For centuries people from overseas have settled in Britain, either to escape political or religious persecution or in search of better economic opportunities.

The Irish have long formed a large section of the population. Jewish refugees who came to Britain towards the end of the 19th century and in the 1930s were followed by other European refugees after 1945. Substantial immigration from the Caribbean and the South Asian sub-continent dates principally from the 1950s and 1960s, while many people of Asian descent moved to this country from eastern Africa. In recent years, the number of people coming from the South Asian sub-continent has remained roughly stable, but there has been a rise in immigration from some African countries, such as Ghana, Nigeria and South Africa (see Table 6.1).

The 1991 census included for the first time a question on ethnic grouping. This found that 94.5 per cent of the population belonged to the 'White' group, while just over 3 million people

(5.5 per cent) described themselves as belonging to another ethnic group (see Table 6.2).

Overall, just under half of the ethnic minority population were born in Britain. A higher proportion is under 16 than for the White group (33 per cent and 19 per cent respectively), but a much lower proportion is over pensionable age (3 per cent and about 17 per cent respectively).

Members of ethnic minority groups were heavily concentrated in industrial and urban areas, and over half lived in the South East, especially in London. The highest proportion was in the London borough of Brent: nearly 45 per cent of the population. Ethnic minority groups also accounted for over a third of the population in the London boroughs of Newham, Tower Hamlets and Hackney. Outside London the main concentrations were in Leicester, Slough, Luton, Bradford, the West Midlands and the Pennine conurbation. Regional concentrations varied among the ethnic groups. About three-fifths (60 per cent) of people from black ethnic groups lived in London, compared with about two-fifths (41 per cent) of Indians and just under one fifth (18 per cent) of Pakistanis, who were concentrated in other metropolitan areas such as the West Midlands and West Yorkshire.

According to the Labour Force Survey, economic activity rates for men of working age in Great Britain tend to be similar to those for the White groups. In summer 1995 they were 81.3 per cent for the Black group, 82.6 per cent for the Indian group, 70.5 per cent for the

Table 6.2: Population by Ethnic Group, 1991, Great Britain

	Number of people *(000s)*	Per cent
White	51,874	94.5
Other groups	3,015	5.5
of whom:		
Black	891	1.6
Indian	840	1.5
Pakistani	477	0.9
Bangladeshi	163	0.3
Chinese	157	0.3
Other	488	0.9

Source: Office for National Statistics

Pakistani/Bangladeshi population and 86.6 per cent for the white group. The variations are greater for women: 67.8 per cent of those from the Black ethnic group were economically active, compared with 65 per cent in the Indian group, 72.8 per cent in the White group and only 25.4 per cent in the Pakistani/Bangladeshi group.

Alleviating Racial Disadvantage

Although many members of the black and Asian communities are concentrated in the inner cities, where there are problems of deprivation and social stress, progress has been made over the last 20 years in tackling racial disadvantage in Britain.

Many individuals have achieved distinction in their careers and in public life, and the proportion of ethnic minority members occupying professional and managerial positions is increasing. There are at present six ethnic minority Members of Parliament, and the number of ethnic minority councillors in local government is growing. There has also been an expansion of commercial enterprise, and numerous self-help projects in ethnic minority communities have been established. Black competitors have represented Britain in a range of sporting activities (such as athletics, cricket and football), and ethnic minority talents in the arts and in entertainment have increasingly been recognised.

The principal means of combating disadvantage is through the economic, environmental, educational and health programmes of central government and local authorities. There are also special allocations, mainly through Home Office and Department of the Environment grants, which channel extra resources into projects of specific benefit to ethnic minorities. These include, for example, the provision of specialist teachers for children needing English language tuition. Cultural and recreational schemes and the health and personal social services also take account of the particular needs of ethnic minorities.

The Government is promoting equal opportunities for ethnic minorities through training programmes, including greater provision for unemployed people who need training in English as a second language.

Race Relations Legislation

The Race Relations Act 1976, which applies to England, Scotland and Wales, strengthened previous legislation passed in the 1960s. It makes discrimination unlawful on grounds of colour, race, nationality or ethnic or national origin in the provision of goods, facilities and services, in employment, in housing, in education and in advertising. The 1976 Act also gave complainants direct access to civil courts and, for employment complaints, to industrial tribunals. It is a criminal offence to incite racial hatred under the provisions of the Public Order Act 1986.

Legislation against racial discrimination in employment and in the provision of goods and services is to be introduced for Northern Ireland in late 1996.

Commission for Racial Equality

The Commission for Racial Equality was established by the 1976 Act. It has power to investigate unlawful discriminatory practices and to issue non-discrimination notices requiring such practices to cease. It has an important educational role and has issued codes of practice in employment, education, health care, maternity services and housing. It also provides advice to the general public about the Race Relations Act and may help individuals with their complaints about racial discrimination. In 1995 the Commission registered 1,682 applications for assistance and successfully handled 155 litigation cases. It can also undertake or fund research.

The Commission supports the work of 88 racial equality councils. These are autonomous voluntary bodies set up in most areas with a significant ethnic minority population to promote equality of opportunity and good relations at the local level. The Commission helps pay the salaries of officers employed by the racial equality councils, most of whom also receive funds from their local authorities. It also gives grants to ethnic minority self-help groups and to other projects run by or for the benefit of the minority communities.

THE ECONOMIC AND SOCIAL PATTERN

Marked improvements in the standard of living have taken place during the 20th century. According to a United Nations report on human development published in 1994, Britain ranked tenth out of 173 countries on a human development index that combines life expectancy, education levels and basic purchasing power.

Britain has also performed well economically. Growth between 1980 and 1990 was higher than in all other major EU countries except Spain. Following the recession of the early 1990s, Britain was one of the first countries to experience recovery. Gross domestic product in Britain grew by 2.5 per cent in 1995. Inflation has recently been around 3 per cent a year, with the underlying level of inflation the lowest for almost 50 years.

Income and Wealth

Wages and salaries remain the main source of household income for most people, although the proportion they contribute of household income (64 per cent in 1994–95, compared with 68 per cent in 1971) has been declining. Sources which have become more important include private pensions and annuities (6.4 per cent, up from 2.2 per cent in 1965) as the number of people who have made such provision has grown. Disposable income in 1995 was 32 per cent higher than in 1985 after allowing for inflation.

The proportion of household income that is paid in income tax and National Insurance contributions by a two-children family with a father on average earnings was 21.7 per cent in 1994–95. This figure has not changed significantly in recent years. The top 20 per cent of households by income received 44 per cent of income in 1994–95. Wealth is less evenly distributed, with the richest 10 per cent of the population having 48 per cent of marketable wealth in 1993. The inclusion of 'non-marketable' wealth, such as rights in occupational and state pension schemes, reduces this share substantially, to 33 per cent. Since the mid-1970s there has been little change in the distribution of marketable wealth.

A large proportion of personal wealth—28 per cent in 1994 —is in dwellings, down quite sharply from the level of immediately preceding years as house prices have fallen. The proportion of net wealth held in shares declined up to 1984, but has since increased. The Government's privatisation programme has contributed to the growth in share ownership. In 1993 about 10 million people— 22 per cent of the adult population in Great Britain—owned shares, compared with 7 per cent in 1979.

Eating and Drinking Habits

The general level of nutrition remains high. There has been a significant shift in eating patterns over the last decade, reflecting greater emphasis on health, frozen and convenience foods. Changes in household consumption of selected foods between 1985 and 1995 are shown in the diagram on p.38. Consumption of several items, such as packet sugar, eggs, fresh potatoes and fresh green vegetables, has declined substantially. Other changes include:

- a long-term decline in consumption of beef, lamb and pork—this has been partly offset by a continuing increase in poultry consumption, which has been at or close to record levels in recent years;

- an increase in purchases of semi-skimmed milk, with skimmed milk now constituting more than half of the total household consumption of liquid milk;

- a decline in the total consumption of cooking and spreading fats, with large falls in butter and lard usage being partly offset by rapid rises in the consumption of vegetable and salad oils and reduced-fat spreads;

- an increase in the consumption of rice and pasta, which may be partly responsible for the decline in the consumption of fresh potatoes;

- a trend away from consumption of some fresh green vegetables such as cabbages, peas and beans towards leafy salads and cauliflowers;

- a large increase in purchases of fruit juice; and

Availability of Certain Durable Goods

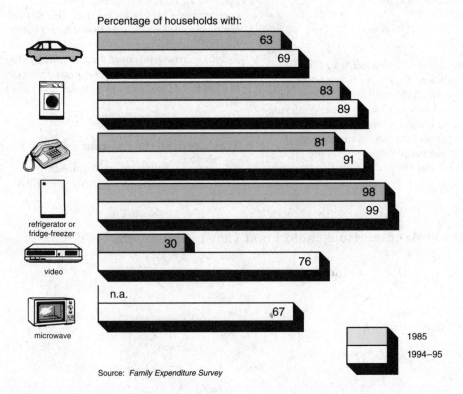

Percentage of households with:

	1985	1994–95
car	63	69
washing machine	83	89
telephone	81	91
refrigerator or fridge-freezer	98	99
video	30	76
microwave	n.a.	67

Source: *Family Expenditure Survey*

- a switch in fish consumption away from fresh white fish towards fat fish, canned fish and shellfish.

Average mineral and nutrient intakes are generally above the daily amounts recommended by the Department of Health. There has been a steady fall in the proportion of energy derived from fat. There is some evidence that health considerations influence food consumption, for example, the move away from whole milk and in the growth in low fat spread consumption. The Government encourages the widest availability of wholesome food, while giving high priority to consumer safety.

There has been an increase in the number of meals eaten away from home, for example, in restaurants or at work, and a growth in the consumption of food from 'take-away' and 'fast food' shops.

There has been little change in alcohol consumption in recent years. Beer is the most popular drink among male drinkers, whose overall consumption is significantly higher than that of women. Lager is now estimated to account for over half of all beer sales. The largest consumers of alcohol are those aged 18 to 24, with consumption generally declining with age. Consumption of table wine has grown, although there has been little change in the consumption of higher strength wines such as sherry and port.

A high proportion of beer is drunk in public houses ('pubs'), traditional social centres for many people, and in clubs. The Licensing Act 1988 relaxed restrictions on the opening hours of public houses, but this has not resulted in a significant increase in alcohol consumption. There are signs that they are becoming more popular with families: more meals are being served and the consumption of non-alcoholic drinks is increasing. Under the Deregulation and Contracting Out Act 1994, pubs can now apply for a children's certificate. This allows children under 14 into designated areas if accompanied by an adult.

Households

The average size of households in Great Britain has fallen from over four people in 1911 to three in 1961 and 2.4 in 1994. The fall reflects a greater number of people living on their own (12 per cent of adults in 1994) or in one-parent families, the increasing number of old people (more of whom are living alone) and the preference for smaller families.

A large proportion of households—67 per cent—own their own homes. Owner-occupation is higher for married couples than for single, divorced or widowed household heads. The number of owner-occupied dwellings rose from over 4 million in 1951 to 16 million at the end of 1995. Four-fifths of British households live in houses rather than flats.

Transport and the Environment

An important influence on the planning of housing and services has been the growth of

Changes in Average Household Food Consumption 1985–1995

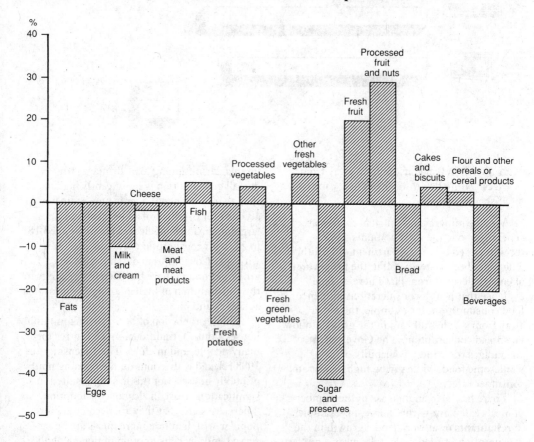

Note: Average household food consumption may be affected by changes in such factors as household composition and income as well as changes in eating habits.

Source: *National Food Survey*, MAFF

car ownership; in 1994–95, 69 per cent of households had the use of at least one car or van, including 24 per cent with the use of two or more. Greater access to motorised transport and the construction of a network of modern trunk roads and motorways have resulted in a considerable increase in personal mobility and changed leisure patterns. Most detached or semi-detached houses in new suburban estates have garages. Many out-of-town shopping centres, often including large supermarkets and do-it-yourself stores, have been built with the motorist in mind.

Cars, taxis and motor cycles accounted for 87 per cent of all passenger transport in Great Britain in 1994, compared with 57 per cent in 1961. To relieve road congestion, the Government regards carefully targeted improvements to the road system as essential. The Government is also seeking to use the planning system (see p. 381) to reduce people's need to travel without inhibiting their freedom to do so. A key part of this, especially in urban areas, will involve the promotion of public transport and cycling (see pp. 306–7). To help meet the British target for reducing carbon dioxide emissions (see p. 359), it is increasing fuel duty by 5 per cent a year in real terms.

Women

The economic and domestic lives of women have been transformed in the 20th century. These changes are due partly to women obtaining many political and legal rights previously open only to men. The growth of part-time and flexible working patterns has allowed more women to combine raising a family with paid employment. Women now make up nearly 46 per cent of the workforce in employment, with about 800,000 running their own businesses.

Responsibility for co-ordinating government policy on women's issues lies with a Cabinet Sub-committee for Women's Issues. The Women's National Commission, an official advisory committee, puts forward the views of women to the Government and other public bodies. About 50 of the main national women's organisations are represented on the Commission.

Britain participated fully in the United Nations Fourth World Conference on Women, held in Beijing in September 1995. The Conference adopted a 'Global Platform for Action' on a broad range of issues, such as the family, childbearing, inheritance rights, and women in power. The Government has announced plans to implement the Platform in Britain.

'Fair Play for Women' was introduced in England in 1994 as a joint initiative between the Government and the Equal Opportunities Commission (see below) and was based on a scheme in operation in Wales. During 1996 the initiative was extended to Scotland and Northern Ireland. It aims to help women realise their full capabilities, both in the community and at work.

The Government supports 'Opportunity 2000', an employer-led initiative to increase the participation of women in the workforce. Membership stands at over 300 employers, with organisations employing about a quarter of the workforce being committed to the campaign. Many member organisations are reinforcing their equal opportunities policies and practices, such as by offering job share arrangements and flexible working hours. Within the civil service, the proportion of posts at the top three grades filled by women rose from 5 per cent in 1984 to 11 per cent at the end of 1995. In 1991 the Government launched an initiative to increase the proportion of public appointments held by women. The proportion has subsequently risen from 23 to 30 per cent. In June 1996 there were 63 women MPs, compared with 19 in 1979.

In 1993 the Government introduced the Out of School Childcare Initiative to offer parents with children of school age the chance to participate more fully in the labour market. Around 52,000 childcare places in Great Britain have been created. A report published in January 1996 found that this had had a positive effect on the labour market, with significant benefits in particular for lone parents. Funding is being provided to create an additional 18,000 places. In Northern Ireland a similar initiative was launched in February 1996, to establish 3,000 childcare places.

Equal Opportunities

The Sex Discrimination Acts 1975 and 1986 make discrimination between men and women unlawful, with certain limited exceptions, in employment, education, training and the provision of housing, goods, facilities and services. Discriminatory job recruitment advertisements are unlawful. Complaints of discrimination concerning employment are dealt with by industrial tribunals; other complaints are taken before county courts in England and Wales or the Sheriff Court in Scotland. Under the Equal Pay Act 1970, as amended in 1984, women in Great Britain are entitled to equal pay with men when doing work that is the same or broadly similar, or work which is rated as equivalent or work which is of equal value. Parallel legislation on sex discrimination and equal pay is in operation in Northern Ireland.

The Equal Opportunities Commission (EOC), an independent statutory body, has the duties of working towards the elimination of sex discrimination and promoting equality of opportunity. The EOC may advise people of their rights under the Acts and may give assistance to help individuals conduct a case. It is empowered to carry out formal investigations and issue notices requiring discriminatory practices to stop. The EOC runs an 'Equality Exchange', with 500 members, which enables employers to exchange information on good practice.

The Voluntary Sector

There is a long tradition in Britain of voluntary service to the community. There are hundreds of thousands of voluntary organisations, ranging from national bodies to small local groups. One area of rapid expansion in the last 20 years or so has been 'self-help' groups. Examples include bodies which provide playgroups for pre-school children, or help their members to cope with a particular disability.

Voluntary organisations may be staffed by professional workers, but most rely on the efforts of volunteers at some level. It has been estimated that up to half of all adults take part in some form of organised voluntary work in the course of a year. Many volunteers are involved in work which improves the quality of life in their local communities or, more widely, give their time to help organise events or groups in areas as diverse as social welfare, education, sport, heritage and the arts. A very large number of volunteers are involved in activities to protect or improve the environment, working, for example, for the National Trust, which has over 2 million members (see p. 373). The Government greatly values the voluntary sector's contribution to society and, as a result, is keen to encourage productive partnerships between the statutory and voluntary sectors. For example, voluntary organisations are important providers of government-supported employment and training services for unemployed people.

'Make a Difference' Initiative

The Voluntary and Community Division within the Department of National Heritage[3] co-ordinates government policy towards the voluntary sector throughout Britain. It also aims to support a healthy and cost-effective voluntary sector and to promote volunteering throughout the community. Its 'Make a Difference' initiative, launched in 1994, brings together the business, voluntary and public sectors to promote volunteering. As one aspect of the initiative, a nationwide telephone helpline was set up in 1995. This aims to provide callers throughout Britain with information on how to get involved with local voluntary initiatives.

A national strategy on volunteering was published in 1995 (see 'Further Reading'). The Government's response includes:

- a pledge that by the end of 1997 there will be volunteering opportunities for all 15- to 25-year-olds who wish to volunteer;

---

[3]In May 1996 responsibility for the voluntary sector was transferred from the Home Office to the Department of National Heritage.

- completing and strengthening the network of volunteer bureaux to provide a focus for volunteering in every locality; and

- in partnership with the brewing company Whitbread, funding a nationwide Make a Difference Award to recognise outstanding contributions by voluntary organisations.

Funding

Voluntary organisations receive income from several sources, including:

- contributions from individuals, businesses and trusts;

- central and local government grants;

- earnings from commercial activities and investments; and

- fees from central and local government for those services which are provided on a contractual basis.

In 1994–95 direct grants to voluntary organisations from government amounted to £595 million.

Tax changes in recent budgets have helped the voluntary sector secure more funds from industry and individuals. The Gift Aid scheme provides tax relief on single cash donations of

at least £250. By March 1996 charities had received donations of more than £1,336 million under the scheme and had claimed tax repayments of £443 million on them. Under the Payroll Giving scheme, employees can also make tax-free donations to charity from their earnings. The scheme provides tax relief on donations of up to £1,200 a year.

Charities

In England and Wales over 181,000 charities are registered with the Charity Commission. Their combined annual turnover is around £11,500 million. The Commission also gives advice to trustees of charities on their administration. Organisations may qualify for charitable status if they are established for exclusively charitable purposes such as the relief of poverty, the advancement of education or religion, or the promotion of certain other purposes of public benefit. These may include good community relations, the prevention of racial discrimination, the protection of health and the promotion of equal opportunity. The Charity Commission also has a statutory responsibility to ensure that charities make effective use of their resources.

The Charities Acts 1992 and 1993 strengthened the Commissioners' power to

Table 6.3: Income of the Top Fund-raising Charities 1994–95

Charity	Total income	£ million Voluntary income[a]
National Trust	144.4	75.9
Save the Children Fund	91.9	41.3
Oxfam	86.7	53.7
British Red Cross Society	84.7	38.7
Barnardo's	84.5	33.9
Salvation Army	72.3	38.8
Royal National Lifeboat Institution	64.6	58.2
Cancer Research Campaign	59.1	55.9
Imperial Cancer Research Fund	53.6	45.6
Royal National Institute for the Blind	52.8	26.0
National Society for the Prevention of Cruelty to Children	43.1	35.3
Help the Aged	38.7	34.8
Cancer Relief Macmillan Fund	37.6	32.2

Source: Charities Aid Foundation
[a]Includes donations, legacies, covenants and Gift Aid and charity shop income.

investigate and supervise charities. For example, new measures to protect charities and donors from bogus fund-raisers came into force in 1995, while measures aimed at increasing the accountability of charities came into force in March 1996.

> The National Lottery Charities Board distributes the portion of the proceeds of the National Lottery allocated to charities. By August 1996 the Board had made over 4,700 grants totalling almost £320 million. Recipients ranged from large organisations such as Age Concern and Barnardo's to smaller local organisations such as the Ystrad Rhondda Boys Club and the Omagh and District Talking Newspaper.

The Charities Aid Foundation, an independent body, is one of the main organisations that aid the flow of funds to charity from individuals, companies and grant-making trusts.

Umbrella Organisations

The National Council for Voluntary Organisations is one of the main co-ordinating bodies in England, providing close links between voluntary organisations, government departments, local authorities, the European Commission and the private sector; around 650 national voluntary organisations are members. It also protects the interests and independence of voluntary agencies, and provides them with advice, information and other services. Councils in Scotland, Wales and Northern Ireland perform similar functions. The National Association of Councils for Voluntary Service is another umbrella organisation providing resources, with over 230 local councils for voluntary service throughout England. Their role is to encourage the development of local voluntary action, mainly in urban areas.

Leisure Trends

About 14 per cent of total household expenditure went on leisure goods and services in 1993. The most common leisure activities are home-based, or social, such as visiting relatives or friends. Television viewing is by far the most popular leisure pastime, and nearly all households have a television set, almost all of these having a colour set. Average viewing time is nearly 27 hours a week. Around 76 per cent of households now have at least one video recorder, compared with 30 per cent in 1985.

Listening to radio has been increasing, and averages over 10 hours a week. Purchases of compact discs have risen very rapidly, and since 1992 have exceeded the sales of audio cassettes. The proportion of households with a compact disc player has grown considerably, from 15 per cent in 1989 to 46 per cent in 1994–95.

Other popular pursuits include: reading, do-it-yourself home improvements, gardening and going out for a meal, for a drink or to the cinema. About half of households have a pet, the most common being dogs and cats, with roughly 7 million of each in Britain.

National Lottery

Launched in November 1994, the National Lottery has made a major impact in Britain and has grown to become the biggest lottery in the world. About 90 per cent of adults have participated and around 30 million regularly buy tickets. Lottery ticket sales amounted to nearly £5,000 million in 1995. There is a draw each week, with an average weekly jackpot fund of £10 million, while there are also 'instant' scratchcards. About £68 million is spent on the weekly draw, although this has exceeded £100 million when the jackpot has not been won and has been carried forward to the next week. Weekly sales of scratchcards are around £20 million.

Britain's National Lottery is the only one in Europe to involve private enterprise in its operation. Camelot Group plc, a private sector company, was awarded the contract to run the Lottery. The Lottery is regulated by the Director General of the National Lottery, who heads the Office of the National Lottery ('Oflot').

The Lottery has already raised large

Table 6.4: Awards to Good Causes March 1995-February 1996

	Number of awards	Amount awarded (£ million)
Arts Council of England	466	280.9
Scottish Arts Council	142	23.0
Arts Council of Wales	159	10.3
Arts Council of Northern Ireland	75	5.4
Total arts awards	**842**	**319.5**
Sports Council	911	152.1
Scottish Sports Council	166	18.5
Sports Council for Wales	111	9.8
Sports Council for Northern Ireland	100	6.6
Total sports awards	**1,288**	**186.9**
National Heritage Memorial Fund	221	117.0
Millennium Commission	310	443.4
National Lottery Charities Board	2,460	159.1
Total awards	**5,121**	**1,226.0**

Source: *The First Year Report on the Distribution of National Lottery Proceeds March 1995–February 1996.*
Note: Differences between totals and the sums of their component parts are due to rounding.

sums—£2,000 million by June 1996—for good causes, which receive 28 per cent of net proceeds. This is one of the highest proportions allocated to good causes by any national lottery. The remainder is divided between prizes (50 per cent), tax (12 per cent), retailers' commission (5 per cent) and operating costs and profit (5 per cent).

In the first year of lottery awards, over 5,000 projects benefited from awards totalling over £1,200 million. The awards are distributed between five good causes: sport, charities, the arts, heritage and projects to mark the millennium. Each receives one-fifth of the money generated for good causes. The amount distributed by each awarding body in 1995–96 is shown in Table 6.4.

A very wide range of projects are receiving funding through lottery awards. Some are large schemes, notably some of those supported by the Millennium Commission, such as £50 million for a new environmental Earth Centre at Conisbrough (South Yorkshire), £40 million for the redevelopment of Portsmouth Harbour and £22 million for a new botanic garden at Middleton. However, about 77 per cent of awards are for less than

£100,000. Awards made in the first year include, for example:

● 55 awards, worth £73 million, to museums;

● 33 awards, valued at £23 million, for environmental projects;

● 62 awards, worth £3.5 million, to amateur dramatics societies; and

● 47 awards, valued at £2.7 million, to churches.

In all, 247 awards went to youth projects and 107 to projects to help people with disabilities, while nearly 2,500 awards were made to charities working with disadvantaged people.

In April 1996 the Government announced changes to the rules on the distribution of lottery funds. As well as investment in buildings and equipment, lottery funds can now be spent on projects to develop people's talents and potential. New areas include:

● 'talent funds' to provide individual support to talented athletes and sports people, and to develop the creative abilities of individual performers and young artists;

● greater access to the arts, such as through supporting touring companies and subsidised ticket schemes for schools and community groups; and

● the restoration and renovation of run-down buildings of historical significance by local building preservation trusts.

Holidays

In 1995, 61 per cent of the adult population took at least one long holiday of four or more nights away from home. The number of long holidays taken by British residents was 59 million, of which 33 million were taken in Britain. The most frequented free attraction was Blackpool Pleasure Beach (Lancashire),

with an estimated 7.3 million visitors in 1995. The most popular holiday destinations are the West Country, Scotland, the south of England and Wales.

In 1995 the most popular destinations for overseas holidays by British residents were:

● Spain (27 per cent);

● France (10 per cent);

● Greece (8 per cent); and

● the United States (7 per cent).

In all, British residents took 26 million long holidays overseas in 1995, of which 58 per cent involved 'package' arrangements. About 73 per cent of all holidays abroad are taken in Europe, although more people are taking holidays further afield, for example to the United States. The proportion of adults taking two or more holidays a year was 27 per cent in 1995.

Further Reading

Ethnic Minorities. Aspects of Britain series, HMSO, 1991.

Immigration and Nationality. Aspects of Britain series, HMSO, 1992.

Make a Difference: An Outline Volunteering Strategy for the UK. Home Office, 1995.

Population. Aspects of Britain series, HMSO, 1995.

Women. Aspects of Britain series, HMSO, 1996.

Annual Reports
Family Spending. HMSO.

Living in Britain: Results from the 1994 General Household Survey. HMSO.

Social Trends. HMSO.

Women and Men in Britain. Equal Opportunities Commission.

Government and Administration

7   Government

The Monarchy	47	Improving Public Services	69
Parliament	51	The Civil Service	71
Her Majesty's Government	64	Local Government	75
The Privy Council	67	Pressure Groups	80
Government Departments	67		

The system of parliamentary government in Britain is not based on a written constitution, but is the result of gradual evolution over many centuries. The Monarchy is the oldest institution of government, dating back to at least the ninth century. Parliament is one of the oldest representative assemblies in the world. Among the most significant recent developments in government have been the steps taken to improve management. New management structures—such as the creation of executive agencies—have been developed; competition with the private sector has been introduced or extended; and arrangements for pay are changing. A Civil Service code has been introduced and measures to increase the openness of central government have been implemented. The aim of all these changes is to safeguard and improve the standards of the public services.

The British constitution, unlike that of most other countries, is not set out in any single document. Instead it is made up of statute law, common law and conventions. (Conventions are rules and practices which are not legally enforceable but which are regarded as indispensable to the working of government.)

The constitution can be altered by Act of Parliament, or by general agreement, and is thus adaptable to changing political conditions.

The organs of government overlap but can be clearly distinguished. *Parliament* is the legislature and the supreme authority. The *executive* consists of:

- the Government—the Cabinet and other Ministers responsible for national policies;

- government departments and agencies, responsible for national administration;

- local authorities, responsible for many local services; and

- public corporations, responsible for operating particular nationalised industries or other bodies, subject to ministerial control.

The *judiciary* (see Chapter 8) determines common law and interprets statutes.

The Monarchy

The Monarchy is the oldest institution of government. Queen Elizabeth II is herself directly descended from King Egbert, who

The Royal Family from the Reign of Queen Victoria to August 1996

QUEEN VICTORIA 1819–1901
m. Prince Albert of Saxe-Coburg and Gotha (Prince Consort)

KING EDWARD VII 1841–1910
m. Princess Alexandra of Denmark
(QUEEN ALEXANDRA 1844–1925)

2 brothers and 3 sisters

KING GEORGE V 1865–1936
m. Princess Mary of Teck (QUEEN MARY 1867–1953)

Duke of Windsor 1894–1972
KING EDWARD VIII
(abdicated 1936)
m. Wallis Simpson

KING GEORGE VI 1895–1952
m. Lady Elizabeth Bowes-Lyon
(QUEEN ELIZABETH the Queen Mother)

Mary, Princess Royal 1897–1965
m. Earl of Harewood
2 sons

Henry, Duke of Gloucester 1900–1974
m. Lady Alice Montagu Douglas Scott

George, Duke of Kent 1902–1942
m. Princess Marina of Greece

Prince John 1905–1919

Princess Alice 1843–1878
m. Grand Duke Louis of Hesse
3 brothers and 4 sisters

Princess Victoria 1863–1950
m. Marquess of Milford Haven
2 brothers and 4 sisters

Princess Alice 1885–1969
m. Prince Andrew of Greece
2 brothers and 1 sister

Philip, Duke of Edinburgh b. 1921
m. Princess Elizabeth (QUEEN ELIZABETH II)
4 sisters

QUEEN ELIZABETH II b. 1926
m. Philip, Duke of Edinburgh

Princess Margaret b. 1930
m. Antony, Earl of Snowdon (divorced 1978)

David, Viscount Linley b. 1961
m. Serena Stanhope

Lady Sarah Armstrong-Jones b. 1964
m. Daniel Chatto

Samuel Chatto b. 1996

Charles, Prince of Wales b. 1948
m. Lady Diana Spencer (divorced 1996)

Prince William of Wales b. 1982

Prince Henry of Wales b. 1984

Anne, Princess Royal b. 1950
m. (1) Captain Mark Phillips (divorced 1992)
(2) Commander Timothy Laurence

Peter Phillips b. 1977

Zara Phillips b. 1981

Andrew, Duke of York b. 1960
m. Sarah Ferguson (divorced 1996)

Princess Beatrice of York b. 1988

Princess Eugenie of York b. 1990

Prince Edward b. 1964

Edward, Duke of Kent b. 1935
m. Katherine Worsley

George, Earl of St Andrews b. 1962
m. Sylvana Tomaselli

Edward, Baron Downpatrick b. 1988

Lady Marina Windsor b. 1992

Lady Amelia Windsor b. 1995

Lady Helen Windsor b. 1964
m. Timothy Taylor

Columbus b. 1994

Lord Nicholas Windsor b. 1970

Princess Alexandra b. 1936
m. Hon. Angus Ogilvy

James Ogilvy b. 1964
m. Julia Rawlinson

Flora b. 1994

Marina b. 1966
m. Paul Mowatt

Zenouska b. 1990

Christian b. 1993

Prince Michael b. 1942
m. Baroness Marie-Christine von Reibnitz

Lord Frederick Windsor b. 1979

Lady Gabriella Windsor b. 1981

Richard, Duke of Gloucester b. 1944
m. Birgitte van Deurs

Alexander, Earl of Ulster b. 1974

Lady Davina Windsor b. 1977

Lady Rose Windsor b. 1980

Prince William 1941–1972

Order of Succession to the Throne

The Prince of Wales
Prince William of Wales
Prince Henry of Wales
The Duke of York
Princess Beatrice of York
Princess Eugenie of York
The Prince Edward
The Princess Royal
Peter Phillips
Zara Phillips
The Princess Margaret, Countess of Snowdon
Viscount Linley
Lady Sarah Chatto
Samuel Chatto
The Duke of Gloucester
Earl of Ulster
Lady Davina Windsor
Lady Rose Windsor
The Duke of Kent
Baron Downpatrick
Lady Marina Windsor
Lady Amelia Windsor
Lord Nicholas Windsor
Lady Helen Taylor
Columbus Taylor
Lord Frederick Windsor
Lady Gabriella Windsor

Dates relating to Queen Elizabeth II

Marriage:	20 Nov. 1947
Accession to throne:	6 Feb. 1952
Coronation:	2 June 1953
Birthday:	21 April
Official birthday celebration:	During June

united England under his rule in 829. The only interruption in the history of the Monarchy was the republic, which lasted from 1649 to 1660.

Today the Queen is not only Head of State, but also an important symbol of national unity. The Queen's title in Britain is: 'Elizabeth the Second, by the Grace of God of the United Kingdom of Great Britain and Northern Ireland and of Her other Realms and Territories Queen, Head of the Commonwealth, Defender of the Faith'.

In the Channel Islands and the Isle of Man the Queen is represented by a Lieutenant-Governor.

The Commonwealth

Although the seat of the Monarchy is in Britain, the Queen is also head of state of a number of Commonwealth states.[1] In each such state the Queen is represented by a Governor-General, appointed by her on the advice of the ministers of the country concerned and completely independent of the British Government. In each case the form of the royal title varies. Other Commonwealth states are republics or have their own monarchies.

In British dependent territories (see p. 123) the Queen is usually represented by governors, who are responsible to the British Government for the administration of the countries concerned.

Succession

The title to the Crown is derived partly from statute and partly from common law rules of descent. Despite interruptions in the direct line of succession, the hereditary principle upon which it was founded has always been preserved.

Sons of the Sovereign have precedence over daughters in succeeding to the throne. When a

[1]The other Commonwealth states of which the Queen is head of state are: Antigua and Barbuda, Australia, Bahamas, Barbados, Belize, Canada, Grenada, Jamaica, New Zealand, Papua New Guinea, St Christopher and Nevis, Saint Lucia, St Vincent and the Grenadines, Solomon Islands and Tuvalu.

daughter succeeds, she becomes Queen Regnant, and has the same powers as a king. The consort of a king takes her husband's rank and style, becoming Queen. The constitution does not give any special rank or privileges to the husband of a Queen Regnant.

Under the Act of Settlement of 1700, which formed part of the Revolution Settlement following the events of 1688 (see p. 5), only Protestant descendants of Princess Sophia, the Electress of Hanover (a granddaughter of James I of England and VI of Scotland) are eligible to succeed. The order of succession can be altered only by common consent of the countries of the Commonwealth of which the Queen is Sovereign.

Accession

The Sovereign succeeds to the throne as soon as his or her predecessor dies: there is no interregnum. He or she is at once proclaimed at an Accession Council, to which all members of the Privy Council (see p. 67) are summoned. The Lords Spiritual and Temporal (see p. 53), the Lord Mayor and Aldermen and other leading citizens of the City of London are also invited.

Coronation

The Sovereign's coronation follows the accession after a convenient interval. The ceremony takes place at Westminster Abbey in London, in the presence of representatives of the Houses of Parliament and of all the great public organisations in Britain. The Prime Ministers and leading members of the other Commonwealth nations and representatives of other countries also attend.

The Monarch's Role in Government

The Queen personifies the State. In law, she is head of the executive, an integral part of the legislature, head of the judiciary, the commander-in-chief of all the armed forces of the Crown and the 'supreme governor' of the established Church of England. As a result of a long process of evolution, during which the Monarchy's absolute power has been progressively reduced, the Queen acts on the advice of her Ministers. Britain is governed by Her Majesty's Government in the name of the Queen.

Within this framework, and in spite of a trend during the past hundred years towards giving powers directly to Ministers, the Queen still takes part in some important acts of government. These include summoning, proroguing (discontinuing until the next session without dissolution) and dissolving Parliament; and giving Royal Assent to Bills passed by Parliament. The Queen also formally appoints many important office holders, including government Ministers, judges, officers in the armed forces, governors, diplomats, bishops and some other senior clergy of the Church of England. She is also involved in pardoning people convicted of crimes; and in conferring peerages, knighthoods and other honours.[2] An important function is appointing the Prime Minister (see p. 64). In international affairs the Queen, as Head of State, has the power to declare war and make peace, to recognise foreign states and governments, to conclude treaties and to annex or cede territory.

With rare exceptions (such as appointing the Prime Minister), acts involving the use of 'royal prerogative' powers are now performed by government Ministers, who are responsible to Parliament and can be questioned about particular policies. Parliamentary authority is not required for the exercise of these prerogative powers, although Parliament may restrict or abolish such rights.

The Queen continues to play a role in the working of government. She holds Privy Council meetings, gives audiences to her Ministers and officials in Britain and overseas, receives accounts of Cabinet decisions, reads dispatches and signs state papers. She must be consulted on every aspect of national life, and must show complete impartiality.

Provision has been made to appoint a regent to perform these royal functions should the Queen be totally incapacitated. The regent would be the Queen's eldest son, the Prince of Wales, then those, in order of succession to the throne, aged 18 or over. In the event of her partial incapacity or absence abroad, the Queen may delegate certain royal functions to the Counsellors of State (the Duke of Edinburgh, the four adults next in line of succession, and the Queen Mother). However, Counsellors of State may not, for instance, dissolve Parliament (except on the Queen's instructions), nor create peers.

Ceremonial and Royal Visits

Ceremonial has always been associated with the British monarchy, and many traditional ceremonies continue to take place. Royal marriages and funerals are marked by public ceremony, and the Sovereign's birthday is officially celebrated in June by Trooping the Colour on Horse Guards Parade. State banquets take place when a foreign monarch or head of State visits Britain; investitures are held at Buckingham Palace and the Palace of Holyroodhouse in Scotland to bestow honours; and royal processions add significance to such occasions as the State opening of Parliament.

Each year the Queen and other members of the Royal Family visit many parts of Britain. They are also closely involved in the work of many charities. For example, the Prince of Wales is actively involved in The Prince's Trust, set up to encourage small firms and self-employment in inner cities, while the Princess Royal is President of the Save the Children Fund. The Queen pays state visits to foreign governments, accompanied by the Duke of Edinburgh. She also tours the other countries of the Commonwealth. Other members of the Royal Family pay official visits overseas, occasionally representing the Queen.

Royal Income and Expenditure

Until 1760 the Sovereign had to provide for payment of all government expenses, including

---

[2] Although most honours are conferred by the Queen on the advice of the Prime Minister, a few are granted by her personally—the Order of the Garter, the Order of the Thistle, the Order of Merit and the Royal Victorian Order.

the salaries of officials and the expenses of the royal palaces and households. These were met from hereditary revenues, mainly income from Crown lands, and income from some other sources granted to the Monarch by Parliament. The income from these sources eventually proved inadequate and in 1760 George III turned over to the Government most of the hereditary revenue. In return he received an annual grant (Civil List), from which he continued to pay royal expenditure of a personal character, the salaries of government officials, the costs of royal palaces, and certain pensions. The latter charges were removed from the Civil List in 1830.

Present Arrangements

Today the expenditure incurred by the Queen in carrying out her public duties is financed from the Civil List and from government departments, which meet the cost of, for example, the Royal Yacht and the aircraft of No 32 (The Royal) Squadron. All such expenditure is approved by Parliament. In 1991 Civil List payments were fixed at £7.9 million a year for ten years. About three-quarters of the Queen's Civil List provision is required to meet the cost of staff. They deal with, among other things, state papers and correspondence, and the organisation of state occasions, visits and other public engagements undertaken by the Queen in Britain and overseas. The Queen's private expenditure as Sovereign is met from the Privy Purse, which is financed mainly from the revenue of the Duchy of Lancaster;[3] her expenditure as a private individual is met from her own personal resources.

Under the Civil List Acts, other members of the Royal Family also receive annual parliamentary allowances to enable them to carry out their public duties. The Prince of Wales, however, receives no such allowance, since as Duke of Cornwall he is entitled to the income of the estate of the Duchy of Cornwall.

[3]The Duchy of Lancaster is an inheritance which, since 1399, has always been enjoyed by the reigning sovereign. It is kept quite apart from his or her other possessions and is separately administered by the Chancellor of the Duchy of Lancaster.

Each year the Queen refunds the Government for all parliamentary allowances paid to members of the royal family except the Queen Mother and the Duke of Edinburgh.

Since 1993 the Queen has voluntarily paid income tax on all personal income and on that part of the Privy Purse income which is used for private purposes. The Queen also pays tax on any realised capital gains on her private investments and on the private proportion of assets in the Privy Purse. Inheritance tax will not, however, apply to transfers from one sovereign to his or her successor, although any personal bequests other than to the successor will be subject to inheritance tax. In line with these changes the Prince of Wales pays income tax on the income from the Duchy of Cornwall so far as it is used for private purposes.

Parliament

Origins of Parliament

The medieval kings were expected to meet all royal expenses, private and public, out of their own revenue. If extra resources were needed for an emergency, such as a war, the Sovereign would seek to persuade his barons, in the Great Council—a gathering of leading men which met several times a year—to grant aid. During the 13th century several English kings found the private revenues and baronial aids insufficient to meet the expenses of government. They therefore summoned not only the great feudal magnates but also representatives of counties, cities and towns, primarily to get their assent to extraordinary taxation. In this way the Great Council came to include those who were summoned by name (those who, broadly speaking, were to form the House of Lords) and those who were representatives of communities—the commons. The two parts, together with the Sovereign, became known as 'Parliament' (the term originally meant a meeting for parley or discussion).

Over the course of time the commons began to realise the strength of their position. By the middle of the 14th century the formula had appeared which in substance was the same as that used nowadays in voting supplies to the Crown—that is, money to the government—

namely, 'by the Commons with the advice of the Lords Spiritual and Temporal'. In 1407 Henry IV pledged that henceforth all money grants should be approved by the House of Commons before being considered by the Lords.

A similar advance was made in the legislative field. Originally the King's legislation needed only the assent of his councillors. Starting with the right of individual commoners to present petitions, the Commons gained the right to submit collective petitions. During the 15th century they gained the right to participate in giving their requests—their 'Bills'—the form of law.

The subsequent development of the power of the House of Commons was built upon these foundations. The constitutional developments of the 17th century led to Parliament securing its position as the supreme legislative authority.

The Powers of Parliament

The three elements which make up Parliament—the Queen, the House of Lords and the elected House of Commons—are constituted on different principles. They meet together only on occasions of symbolic significance such as the State opening of Parliament, when the Commons are summoned by the Queen to the House of Lords. The agreement of all three elements is normally required for legislation, but that of the Queen is given as a matter of course.

Parliament can legislate for Britain as a whole, or for any part of the country. It can also legislate for the Channel Islands and the Isle of Man, which are Crown dependencies and not part of Britain. They have local legislatures which make laws on island affairs (see p. 6).

As there are no legal restraints imposed by a written constitution, Parliament may legislate as it pleases, subject to Britain's obligations as a member of the European Union. It can make or change any law, and overturn established conventions or turn them into law. It can even prolong its own life beyond the normal period without consulting the electorate.

In practice, however, Parliament does not assert its supremacy in this way. Its members bear in mind the common law and normally act in accordance with precedent. The House of Commons is directly responsible to the electorate, and in this century the House of Lords has recognised the supremacy of the elected chamber. The system of party government helps to ensure that Parliament legislates with its responsibility to the electorate in mind.

The European Union

As a member of the European Union, Britain recognises the various types of Community legislation and wider policies. It sends 87 elected members to the European Parliament (see p. 120).

The Functions of Parliament

The main functions of Parliament are:

- to pass laws;
- to provide, by voting for taxation, the means of carrying on the work of government;
- to scrutinise government policy and administration, including proposals for expenditure; and
- to debate the major issues of the day.

In carrying out these functions Parliament helps to bring the relevant facts and issues before the electorate. By custom, Parliament is also informed before important international treaties and agreements are ratified. The making of treaties is, however, a royal prerogative exercised on the advice of the Government and is not subject to parliamentary approval.

The Meeting of Parliament

A Parliament has a maximum duration of five years, but in practice general elections are usually held before the end of this term. The maximum life has been prolonged by legislation in rare circumstances such as the two world wars. Parliament is dissolved and writs for a general election are ordered by the Queen on the advice of the Prime Minister.

The life of a Parliament is divided into

sessions. Each usually lasts for one year—normally beginning and ending in October or November. There are 'adjournments' at night, at weekends, at Christmas, Easter and the late Spring Bank Holiday, and during a long summer break usually starting in late July. The average number of 'sitting' days in a session is about 159 in the House of Commons and about 140 in the House of Lords. At the start of each session the Queen's speech to Parliament outlines the Government's policies and proposed legislative programme. Each session is ended by prorogation. Parliament then 'stands prorogued' for about a week until the new session opens. Prorogation brings to an end nearly all parliamentary business: in particular, public Bills which have not been passed by the end of the session are lost.

The House of Lords

The House of Lords consists of the Lords Spiritual and the Lords Temporal. The Lords Spiritual are the Archbishops of Canterbury and York, the Bishops of London, Durham and Winchester, and the 21 next most senior diocesan bishops of the Church of England. The Lords Temporal consist of:

- all hereditary peers of England, Scotland, Great Britain and the United Kingdom (but not peers of Ireland);
- life peers created to assist the House in its judicial duties (Lords of Appeal or 'law lords');[4] and
- all other life peers.

Hereditary peerages carry a right to sit in the House provided holders establish their claim and are aged 21 years or over. However, anyone succeeding to a peerage may, within 12 months of succession, disclaim that peerage for his or her lifetime. Disclaimants lose their right to sit in the House but gain the right to vote and stand as candidates at parliamentary elections. When a disclaimant dies, the peerage passes on down the family in the usual way.

Peerages, both hereditary and life, are created by the Sovereign on the advice of the Prime Minister. They are usually granted in recognition of service in politics or other walks of life or because one of the political parties wishes to have the recipient in the House of Lords. The House also provides a place in Parliament for people who offer useful advice, but do not wish to be involved in party politics.

Peers who attend the House (the average daily attendance is about 360) receive no salary for their parliamentary work, but can claim for expenses incurred in attending the House (for which there are maximum daily rates) and certain travelling expenses.

In April 1996 there were 1,197 members of the House of Lords, including the two archbishops and 24 bishops. The Lords Temporal consisted of 755 hereditary peers who had succeeded to their titles, 12 hereditary peers who had had their titles conferred on them (including the Prince of Wales), and 404 life peers, of whom 24 were 'law lords'. There were 82 women peers.

Potential membership is about 1,200, but this number is reduced by about 70 by a scheme which allows peers who do not wish to attend to apply for leave of absence for the duration of a Parliament. In addition some hereditary peers do not establish their claim to succeed and so do not receive a writ of summons entitling them to sit in the House; there were 83 such peers in April 1996.

Officers of the House of Lords

The House is presided over by the Lord Chancellor, who takes his or her place on the woolsack[5] as ex-officio Speaker of the House. In his absence his place is taken by a deputy. The first of the deputy speakers is the Chairman of Committees, who is appointed at the beginning of each session and normally chairs Committees of the Whole House and some domestic committees.

The Clerk of the Parliaments is responsible

---

[4]The House of Lords is the final court of appeal for civil cases in Britain and for criminal cases in England, Wales and Northern Ireland.

[5]The woolsack is a seat in the form of a large cushion stuffed with wool from several Commonwealth countries; it is a tradition dating from the medieval period, when wool was the chief source of the country's wealth.

for the records of proceedings of the House of Lords and for the text of Acts of Parliament. He or she is the accounting officer for the cost of the House, and is in charge of the administrative staff of the House, known as the Parliament Office. The Gentleman Usher of the Black Rod, usually known as 'Black Rod', is responsible for security, accommodation and services in the House of Lords' part of the Palace of Westminster.

The House of Commons

The House of Commons is elected by universal adult suffrage (see below) and consists of 651 Members of Parliament—MPs. **(See below for future changes.)** In mid-1996 there were 63 women, three Asian and three black MPs. Of the 651 seats, 524 are for England, 38 for Wales, 72 for Scotland, and 17 for Northern Ireland.

General elections are held after a Parliament has been dissolved and a new one summoned by the Queen. When an MP dies or resigns,[6] or is given a peerage, a by-election takes place. Members are paid an annual salary (from 1 July 1996 to 31 March 1997) of £43,000 and an office costs allowance (from April 1996) of up to £46,364. Other allowances include travel allowances, a supplement for London members and, for provincial members, subsistence allowances and allowances for second homes. (For Ministers' salaries see p. 65.)

Officers of the House of Commons

The chief officer of the House of Commons is the Speaker, elected by MPs to preside over the House. Other officers include the Chairman of Ways and Means and two deputy chairmen, who act as Deputy Speakers. They are elected by the House on the nomination of the Government but are drawn from the Opposition as well as the government party. They, like the Speaker, neither speak nor vote

other than in their official capacity. Responsibility for the administration of the House rests with the House of Commons Commission, a statutory body chaired by the Speaker.

Permanent officers (who are not MPs) include the Clerk of the House of Commons, who is the principal adviser to the Speaker on its privileges and procedures. The Clerk's departmental responsibilities relate to the conduct of the business of the House and its committees. The Clerk is also accounting officer for the House. The Serjeant at Arms, who waits upon the Speaker, carries out certain orders of the House. He is also the official housekeeper of the Commons' part of the building, and is responsible for security. Other officers serve the House in the Library, the Department of the Official Report (*Hansard*), the Finance and Administration Department and the Refreshment Department.

Parliamentary Electoral System

For electoral purposes Britain is divided into constituencies, each of which returns one member to the House of Commons. To ensure that constituency electorates are kept roughly equal, four permanent Parliamentary Boundary Commissions, one each for England, Wales, Scotland and Northern Ireland, keep constituencies under review. They recommend any adjustment of seats that may seem necessary in the light of population movements or other changes. Reviews are conducted every 8 to 12 years. Elections are by secret ballot.

Planned Changes

The Commissions' last general reviews were approved by Parliament in 1995. As a result of their recommendations, the number of parliamentary constituencies—and thus the number of MPs—will increase from 651 to 659: England will get an extra five seats (from 524 to 529); Wales two (from 38 to 40) and Northern Ireland one (from 17 to 18). The number of seats in Scotland remains unchanged. The new boundaries will come

---

[6]An MP who wishes to resign from the House can do so only by applying for an office under the Crown as Crown Steward or Bailiff of the Chiltern Hundreds, or Steward of the Manor of Northstead.

into effect after the dissolution of Parliament[7] at the next general election.

Voters

British citizens, together with citizens of other Commonwealth countries and citizens of the Irish Republic resident in Britain, may vote provided they are:

- aged 18 or over;
- included in the annual register of electors for the constituency; and
- not subject to any disqualification.

People not entitled to vote include members of the House of Lords, foreign nationals, some patients detained under mental health legislation, sentenced prisoners and people convicted within the previous five years of corrupt or illegal election practices. Members of the armed forces, Crown servants and staff of the British Council employed overseas (together with their wives or husbands if accompanying them) may be registered for an address in the constituency where they would live but for their service. British citizens living abroad may apply to register as electors for a period of 20 years after they have left Britain.

Voting Procedures

Each elector may cast one vote, normally in person at a polling station. Electors whose circumstances on polling day are such that they cannot reasonably be expected to vote in person at their local polling station—for example, electors away on holiday—may apply for an absent vote at a particular election. Electors who are physically incapacitated or unable to vote in person because of the nature of their work or because they have moved to a new area may apply for an indefinite absent vote. People entitled to an absent vote may vote by post or by proxy, although postal ballot papers cannot be sent to addresses outside Britain.

Voting is not compulsory; 76.9 per cent of a total electorate of 43.3 million people voted in

the general election in April 1992. The simple majority system of voting is used. Candidates are elected if they have more votes than any of the other candidates (although not necessarily an absolute majority over all other candidates).

Candidates

British citizens and citizens of other Commonwealth countries, together with citizens of the Irish Republic, resident in Britain, may stand for election as MPs provided they are aged 21 or over and are not disqualified. Those disqualified include undischarged bankrupts; people sentenced to more than one year's imprisonment; clergy of the Church of England, Church of Scotland, Church of Ireland and Roman Catholic Church; peers; and holders of certain offices listed in the House of Commons Disqualification Act 1975.

A candidate's nomination for election must be proposed and seconded by two electors registered as voters in the constituency and signed by eight other electors. Candidates do not have to be backed by a political party. A candidate must also deposit £500, which is returned if he or she receives 5 per cent or more of the votes cast.

The maximum sum a candidate may spend on a general election campaign is £4,642 plus 3.9 pence for each elector in a borough constituency, or 5.2 pence for each elector in a county constituency. Higher limits have been set for by-elections in order to reflect the fact that they are often regarded as tests of national opinion in the period between general elections. The maximum sum is £18,572 plus 15.8 pence for each elector in borough seats, and 20.8 pence for each elector in county seats. A candidate may post an election communication to each elector in the constituency, free of charge. All election expenses, apart from the candidate's personal expenses, are subject to the statutory limit.

The Political Party System

The party system, which has existed in one form or another since the 18th century, is an essential element in the working of the

---

[7]That is, the Parliament elected on 9 April 1992.

constitution. The present system depends upon the existence of organised political parties, each of which presents its policies to the electorate for approval. The parties are not registered nor formally recognised in law, but in practice most candidates in elections, and almost all winning candidates, belong to one of the main parties.

For the last 150 years a predominantly two–party system has existed. Since 1945 either the Conservative Party, whose origins go back to the 18th century, or the Labour Party, which emerged in the last decade of the 19th century, has held power. A new party—the Liberal Democrats—was formed in 1988 when the Liberal Party, which traced its origins to the 18th century, merged with the Social Democratic Party, formed in 1981. Other parties include two nationalist parties, Plaid Cymru (founded in Wales in 1925) and the Scottish National Party (founded in 1934). In Northern Ireland there are a number of parties. They include the Ulster Unionist Party, formed in the early part of this century; the Democratic Unionist Party, founded in 1971 by a group which broke away from the Ulster Unionists; and the Social Democratic and Labour Party, founded in 1970.

Since 1945 eight general elections have been won by the Conservative Party and six by the Labour Party; the great majority of members of the House of Commons have belonged to one of these two parties. Table 7.1 shows the results of the general election of April 1992.

The party which wins most seats (although not necessarily the most votes) at a general election, or which has the support of a majority of members in the House of Commons, usually forms the Government. By tradition, the leader of the majority party is asked by the Sovereign to form a government. About 100 of its members in the House of Commons and the House of Lords receive ministerial appointments (including appointment to the Cabinet—see p. 65) on the advice of the Prime Minister. The largest minority party becomes the official Opposition, with its own leader and 'shadow cabinet'.

The Party System in Parliament

Leaders of the Government and Opposition sit on the front benches of the Commons with their supporters (the backbenchers) sitting behind them.

Similar arrangements for the parties also apply to the House of Lords; however, a significant number of Lords do not wish to be associated with any political party, and sit on the 'cross-benches'.

The effectiveness of the party system in Parliament rests largely on the relationship between the Government and the opposition parties. Depending on the relative strengths of the parties in the House of Commons, the Opposition may seek to overthrow the Government by defeating it in a vote on a 'matter of confidence'. In general, however, its aims are to contribute to the formulation of

Table 7.1: Results of the April 1992 General Election

Party	Members elected	Number of votes cast
Conservative	336	14,094,116
Labour	271	11,557,134
Liberal Democrats	20	5,998,446
Plaid Cymru (Welsh Nationalist)	4	
Scottish National	3	
Ulster Unionist (Northern Ireland)	9	
Ulster Democratic Unionist (Northern Ireland)	3	1,960,703
Ulster Popular Unionist (Northern Ireland)	1	
Social Democratic and Labour (Northern Ireland)	4	
Total	**651**	**33,610,399**

*a*These figures include votes for other parties whose candidates were unsuccessful policy and legislation by constructive criticism; to oppose government proposals it considers objectionable; to seek amendments to Government Bills; and to put forward its own policies in order to improve its chances of winning the next general election.

The detailed arrangements of government business are settled, under the direction of the Prime Minister and the Leaders of the two Houses, by the Government Chief Whips of each House in consultation with the Opposition Chief Whips. The Chief Whips together constitute the 'usual channels' often referred to when the question of finding time for a particular item of business is discussed. The Leaders of the two Houses are responsible for enabling the Houses to debate matters about which they are concerned.

Outside Parliament, party control is exercised by the national and local organisations. Inside, it is exercised by the Chief Whips and their assistants, who are chosen within the party. Their duties include keeping members informed of forthcoming parliamentary business, maintaining the party's voting strength by ensuring members attend important debates, and passing on to the party leadership the opinions of backbench members. Party discipline tends to be less strong in the Lords than in the Commons, since Lords have less hope of high office and no need of party support in elections.

The formal title of the Government Chief Whip in the Commons is Parliamentary Secretary to the Treasury. Of the other Government Whips, three are officers of the Royal Household (one of these is Deputy Chief Whip), five hold titular posts as Lords Commissioners of the Treasury and five are Assistant Whips. The Opposition Chief Whips in both Houses and two of the Opposition Assistant Whips in the Commons receive salaries. The Government Whips in the Lords hold offices in the Royal Household; they also act as government spokesmen.

Financial Assistance to Parties

Annual assistance from public funds helps opposition parties carry out parliamentary work at Westminster. It is limited to parties which had at least two members elected at the previous general election or one member elected and a minimum of 150,000 votes cast. The amount for the period 1 April 1996 to 31 March 1997 is £3,743.33 for every seat won at the 1992 general election, plus £7.48 for every 200 votes.

Parliamentary Procedure

Parliamentary procedure is based on custom and precedent, partly codified by each House in its Standing Orders. The system of debate is similar in both Houses. Every subject starts off as a proposal or 'motion' by a member. After debate, in which each member may speak only once, the motion may be withdrawn: if it is not, the Speaker or Chairman 'puts the question' whether to agree with the motion or not. The question may be decided without voting, or by a simple majority vote. The main difference of procedure between the two Houses is that the Speaker or Chairman in the Lords has no powers of order; instead such matters are decided by the general feeling of the House.

In the Commons the Speaker has full authority to enforce the rules of the House and must guard against the abuse of procedure and protect minority rights. The Speaker has discretion on whether to allow a motion to end discussion so that a matter may be put to the vote, and has powers to put a stop to irrelevance and repetition in debate, and to save time in other ways. In cases of grave disorder the Speaker can adjourn or suspend the sitting. The Speaker may order members who have broken the rules of behaviour of the House to leave the Chamber or can initiate their suspension for a period of days.

The Speaker supervises voting in the Commons and announces the final result. In a tied vote the Speaker gives a casting vote, without expressing an opinion on the merits of the question. Voting procedure in the House of Lords is broadly similar, although the Lord Chancellor does not have a casting vote.

Financial Interests

The Commons has a public register of MPs' financial (and some non-financial) interests. Members with a financial interest must declare it when speaking in the House or in Committee and must indicate it when giving notice of a question or motion. In other proceedings of the House or in dealings with other Members, Ministers or civil servants, MPs must also disclose any relevant financial interest. In November 1995 the House agreed that Members cannot advocate matters in the House which are related to the source of any financial interest that they enjoy.

In November 1995 the House of Lords passed a Resolution to establish a Register of Lords' Interests, on lines similar to that for MPs. The first Register was published in February 1996 and is open to public inspection.

Parliamentary Commissioner for Standards

Following recommendations of the Committee on Standards in Public Life (the Nolan Committee—see p. 71), the new post of Parliamentary Commissioner for Standards was created in November 1995. The Commissioner can advise MPs on matters of standards and conduct a preliminary investigation into complaints about alleged breaches of the rules. The Commissioner reports to the House of Commons Select Committee on Standards and Privileges.

Public Access to Parliamentary Proceedings

Proceedings of both Houses are normally public. The minutes and speeches (transcribed verbatim in *Hansard*, the official report) are published daily.

The records of the Lords from 1497 and of the Commons from 1547, together with the parliamentary and political papers of a number of former members of both Houses, are available to the public through the House of Lords Record Office.

The proceedings of both Houses of Parliament may be broadcast on television and radio, either live or, more usually, in recorded or edited form. Complete coverage is available on cable television.

The Law-making Process

Statute law consists of Acts of Parliament and delegated legislation made by Ministers under powers given to them by Act (see p. 60). While the law undergoes constant refinement in the courts (see p. 83), changes to statute law are made by Parliament.

Draft laws take the form of parliamentary Bills. Proposals for legislation affecting the powers of particular bodies (such as local authorities) or the rights of individuals (such as certain proposals relating to railways, roads and harbours) are known as Private Bills, and are subject to a special form of parliamentary procedure. Bills which change the general law and which constitute the more significant part of the parliamentary legislative process are Public Bills.

Public Bills can be introduced into either House, by a government Minister or by an ordinary ('private' or 'backbench') member. Most public Bills that become Acts of Parliament are introduced by a government Minister and are known as 'Government Bills'. Bills introduced by other members of Parliament are known as 'Private Members' Bills'.

The main Bills which constitute the Government's legislative programme are announced in the Queen's Speech at the State opening of Parliament, which usually takes place in November, and the Bills themselves are introduced into one or other of the Houses over the succeeding weeks.

Before a Government Bill is drafted, there may be consultation with professional bodies, voluntary organisations and other agencies interested in the subject, and interest and pressure groups which seek to promote specific causes. Proposals for legislative changes are sometimes set out in government 'White Papers', which may be debated in Parliament before a Bill is introduced. From time to time consultation papers, sometimes called 'Green Papers', set out government proposals which are still taking shape and seek comments from the public.

Passage of Public Bills

Public Bills must normally be passed by both Houses. Bills relating mainly to financial matters are almost invariably introduced in the Commons. Under the provisions of the Parliament Acts 1911 and 1949, the powers of the Lords in relation to 'money Bills' are very restricted. The Parliament Acts also provide for a Bill to be passed by the Commons without consent of the Lords in certain (very rare) circumstances.

The process of passing a Public Bill is similar in each House. On presentation the Bill is considered, without debate, to have been read for a first time and is printed (although a substantial number of Private Members' Bills are never printed). After an interval, which may be between one day and several weeks, a Government Bill will receive its second reading debate, during which the general principles of the Bill are discussed. If it obtains a second reading in the Commons, a Bill will normally be committed to a standing committee (see p. 60) for detailed examination and amendment. In the Lords, the committee stage usually takes place on the floor of the House, and this procedure may also be followed in the Commons if that House so decides (usually in cases where there is a need to pass the Bill quickly or where it raises matters of constitutional importance.) The Commons may also decide to divide the committee stage of a Bill between a standing committee and a committee of the whole House (which is commonly the case with the annual Finance Bill).

The committee stage is followed by the report stage ('consideration') on the floor of the House, during which further amendments may be made. In the Commons, this is usually followed immediately by the third reading debate, where the Bill is reviewed in its final form. In the Lords, a Bill may be further amended at third reading.

After passing its third reading in one House, a Bill is sent to the other House, where it passes through all its stages once more and where it is, more often than not, further amended. Amendments made by the second House must be agreed by the first, or a compromise reached, before a Bill can go for Royal Assent.

In the Commons the House may vote to limit the time available for consideration of a Bill. This is done by passing a 'timetable' motion proposed by the Government, commonly referred to as a 'guillotine'.

There are special procedures for Public Bills which consolidate existing legislation or which enact private legislation relating to Scotland.

Royal Assent

When a Bill has passed through all its parliamentary stages, it is sent to the Queen for Royal Assent, after which it is part of the law of the land and known as an Act of Parliament. The Royal Assent has not been refused since 1707. (A list of the main Public Bills receiving Royal Assent since autumn 1995 is given on p. 548.)

Limitations on the Power of the Lords

Most Government Bills introduced and passed in the Lords pass through the Commons without difficulty, but a Lords Bill which was unacceptable to the Commons would not become law. The Lords, on the other hand, do not generally prevent Bills insisted upon by the Commons from becoming law, though they will often amend them and return them for further consideration by the Commons.

By convention, the Lords pass Bills authorising taxation or national expenditure without amendment. Under the Parliament Acts 1911 and 1949, a Bill that deals only with taxation or expenditure must become law within one month of being sent to the Lords, whether or not they agree to it, unless the Commons directs otherwise. If no agreement is reached between the two Houses on a non-financial Commons Bill the Lords can delay the Bill for a period which, in practice, amounts to at least 13 months. Following this the Bill may be submitted to the Queen for Royal Assent, provided it has been passed a second time by the Commons. The Parliament Acts make one important exception: any Bill to lengthen the life of a Parliament requires the full assent of both Houses in the normal way.

The limits to the power of the Lords, contained in the Parliament Acts, are based on the belief that nowadays the main legislative function of the non-elected House is to act as a chamber of revision, complementing but not rivalling the elected House.

Private Members' Bills

Early in each session backbench members of the Commons ballot (draw lots) for the opportunity to introduce a Bill on one of the Fridays during the session on which such Bills have precedence over government business. The first 20 Members whose names are drawn win this privilege, but it does not guarantee that their Bills will pass into law. Members may also present a Bill on any day without debate, and on most Tuesdays and Wednesdays on which the Commons is sitting there is also an opportunity to seek leave to present a Bill under the 'ten minute rule'. This provides an opportunity for a brief speech by the Member proposing the Bill (and by one who opposes it).

Few of these Bills make further progress or receive any debate, but in most sessions a few do become law. Recent examples include the Marriage Act 1994, the Building Societies (Joint Account Holders) Act 1995 and the Wild Mammals (Protection) Act 1996. Private Members' Bills do not often call for the expenditure of public money; but if they do they cannot proceed to committee stage unless the Government decides to provide the necessary money. Peers may introduce Private Members' Bills in the House of Lords at any time. A Private Member's Bill passed by either House will not proceed in the other House unless taken up by a member of that House.

Private and Hybrid Bills

Private Bills are promoted by people or organisations outside Parliament (often local authorities) to give them special legal powers. They go through a similar procedure to Public Bills, but most of the work is done in committee, where procedures follow a semi-judicial pattern. Hybrid Bills are Public Bills which may affect private rights. As with Private Bills, the passage of Hybrid Bills through Parliament is governed by special procedures which allow those affected to put their case.

Delegated Legislation

In order to reduce unnecessary pressure on parliamentary time, primary legislation often gives Ministers or other authorities the power to regulate administrative details by means of secondary or 'delegated' legislation. To minimise any risk that delegating powers to the executive might undermine the authority of Parliament, such powers are normally delegated only to authorities directly accountable to Parliament. Moreover, Acts of Parliament which delegate such powers usually provide for some measure of direct parliamentary control over proposed delegated legislation, by giving Parliament the opportunity to affirm or annul it. Certain Acts also require that organisations affected must be consulted before rules and orders can be made.

A joint committee of both Houses reports on the technical propriety of these 'statutory instruments'. (One specific type of statutory instrument—known as a deregulation order—is subject to a different committee procedure in each House.) In order to save time on the floor of the House, the Commons uses standing committees to debate the merits of instruments; actual decisions are taken by the House as a whole. The House of Lords has appointed a delegated powers scrutiny committee which examines the appropriateness of the powers to make secondary legislation in Bills.

Parliamentary Committees

Committees of the Whole House

Either House may pass a resolution setting itself up as a Committee of the Whole House to consider Bills in detail after their second reading. This permits unrestricted discussion: the general rule that an MP or Lord may speak only once on each motion does not apply in committee.

Standing Committees

House of Commons standing committees debate and consider Public Bills at the committee stage. The committee considers the Bill clause by clause, and may amend it before reporting it back to the House. Ordinary standing committees do not have names but are referred to simply as Standing Committee A, B, C, and so on; a new set of members is appointed to them to consider each Bill. Each committee has between 16 and 50 members, with a party balance reflecting as far as possible that in the House as a whole. The standing committees include two Scottish standing committees, and the Scottish, Welsh and Northern Ireland Grand Committees.

The Scottish Grand Committee comprises all 72 Scottish members (and may be convened anywhere in Scotland as well as at Westminster). It may consider the principles of Scottish Bills referred to it at second and at third reading stages wherever it makes sense to do so. It also debates Scottish public expenditure estimates and any other matters concerning Scotland. Its business also includes questions tabled for oral answer, ministerial statements and other debates, including those on statutory instruments referred to it.

The Welsh Grand Committee, with all 38 Welsh members and up to five others, considers Bills referred to it at second reading stage, questions tabled for oral answer, ministerial statements, and other matters. The Northern Ireland Grand Committee debates matters relating specifically to Northern Ireland. It includes all 17 Northern Ireland members and up to 25 others.

There are also standing committees to debate proposed European legislation, and to scrutinise statutory instruments made by the Government.

In the Lords, various sorts of committees on Bills may be used instead of, or as well as, a Committee of the Whole House. Such committees include Public Bill Committees, Special Public Bill Committees, Committees off the Floor of the House and Scottish Public Bill Committees.

Select Committees

Select committees are appointed for a particular task, generally one of enquiry, investigation and scrutiny. They report their conclusions and recommendations to the House as a whole; in many cases their recommendations invite a response from the Government, which is also reported to the House. A select committee may be appointed for a Parliament, or for a session, or for as long as it takes to complete its task. To help Parliament with the control of the executive by

examining aspects of public policy, expenditure and administration, 17 committees, established by the House of Commons, examine the work of the main government departments and their associated public bodies. The Foreign Affairs Select Committee, for example, 'shadows' the work of the Foreign & Commonwealth Office. The committees are constituted on a basis which is in approximate proportion to party strength in the House.

Other regular Commons select committees include those on Public Accounts, Standards and Privileges, European Legislation, and the Parliamentary Commissioner for Administration (the 'Parliamentary Ombudsman'—see p. 63). Since 1995 there has also been a Deregulation Committee, which examines proposals and draft orders to be made under the Deregulation and Contracting Out Act 1994 (see Chapter 14). 'Domestic' select committees also cover the internal workings of Parliament.

In their examination of government policies, expenditure and administration, committees may question Ministers, civil servants and interested bodies and individuals. Through hearings and published reports, they bring before Parliament and the public an extensive body of fact and informed opinion on many issues, and build up considerable expertise in their subjects of inquiry.

In the House of Lords, besides the Appeal and Appellate Committees in which the bulk of the House's judicial work is transacted, there are two major select committees, on the European Community and on Science and Technology. Ad hoc committees may also be set up to consider particular issues (or, sometimes, a particular Bill), and 'domestic' committees—as in the Commons—cover the internal workings of the House.

Joint Committees

Joint committees, with a membership drawn from both Houses, are appointed in each session to deal with Consolidation Bills[8] and

[8]A Consolidation Bill brings together several existing Acts into one, with the aim of simplifying the statutes.

delegated legislation (see p. 60). The two Houses may also agree to set up joint select committees on other subjects.

Unofficial Party Committees

In addition to the official committees of the two Houses there are several unofficial party organisations or committees. The Conservative and Unionist Members' Committee (the 1922 Committee) consists of the backbench membership of the party in the House of Commons. When the Conservative Party is in office, Ministers attend its meetings by invitation and not by right. When the party is in opposition, the whole membership of the party may attend meetings. The then leader appoints a consultative committee, which acts as the party's 'shadow cabinet'.

The Parliamentary Labour Party comprises all members of the party in both Houses. When the Labour Party is in office, a parliamentary committee, half of whose members are elected and half of whom are government representatives, acts as a channel of communication between the Government and its backbenchers in both Houses. When the party is in opposition, the Parliamentary Labour Party is organised under the direction of an elected parliamentary committee, which acts as the 'shadow cabinet'.

Other Forms of Parliamentary Control

In addition to the system of scrutiny by select committees, both Houses offer a number of opportunities for the examination of government policy by both the Opposition and the Government's own backbenchers. In the House of Commons, the opportunities include:

1. Question Time, when for 55 minutes on Monday, Tuesday, Wednesday and Thursday, Ministers answer MPs' questions. The Prime Minister's Question Time is every Tuesday and Thursday when the House is sitting. Parliamentary questions are one means of seeking information about the Government's intentions. They are also a way of raising grievances brought to MPs' notice by constituents. MPs may also put questions to Ministers for written answer; the questions and answers are published in *Hansard*. There are some 50,000 questions every year.

2. Adjournment debates, when MPs use motions for the adjournment of the House to raise constituency cases or matters of public concern. There is a half-hour adjournment period at the end of the business of the day, while immediately before the adjournment for each recess three hours are spent discussing issues raised by private members. In addition, an MP wishing to discuss a 'specific and important matter that should have urgent consideration' may, at the end of Question Time, seek leave to move the adjournment of the House. On the very few occasions when leave is obtained, the matter is debated for three hours in what is known as an emergency debate, usually on the following day.

3. Early day motions (EDMs) provide a further opportunity for backbench MPs to express their views on particular issues. A number of EDMs are tabled each sitting day; they are very rarely debated but can be useful in gauging the degree of support for the topic by the number of signatures of other MPs which the motion attracts.

4. The 20 Opposition days each session, when the Opposition can choose subjects for debate. Of these days, 17 are at the disposal of the Leader of the Opposition and three at the disposal of the second largest opposition party.

5. Debates on three days in each session on details of proposed government expenditure, chosen by the Liaison Committee.

Procedural opportunities for criticism of the Government also arise during the debate on the Queen's speech at the beginning of each session; during debates on motions of censure for which the Government provides time; and during debates on the Government's legislative and other proposals.

House of Lords

Similar opportunities for criticism and examination of government policy are provided in the House of Lords at daily Question Time, during debates and by means of questions for written answer.

Control of Finances

The main responsibilities of Parliament, and more particularly of the House of Commons, in overseeing the revenue of the State and public expenditure, are to authorise the raising of taxes and duties, and the various objects of expenditure and the sum to be spent on each. It also has to satisfy itself that the sums granted are spent only for the purposes which Parliament intended. No payment out of the central government's public funds can be made and no taxation or loans authorised, except by Act of Parliament. However, limited interim payments can be made from the Contingencies Fund.

The Finance Act is the most important of the annual statutes, and authorises the raising of revenue. The legislation is based on the Chancellor of the Exchequer's Budget statement. This includes a review of the public finances of the previous year, and proposals for future expenditure (see p. 164). Scrutiny of public expenditure is carried out by House of Commons select committees (see p. 61).

European Union Affairs

To keep the two Houses informed of EU developments, and to enable them to scrutinise and debate Union policies and proposals, there is a select committee in each House (see p. 61), and two Commons standing committees debate specific European legislative proposals. Ministers also make regular statements about EU business.

The Commons' Ability to Force the Government to Resign

The final control is the ability of the House of Commons to force the Government to resign by passing a resolution of 'no confidence'. The Government must also resign if the House rejects a proposal which the Government considers so vital to its policy that it has declared it a 'matter of confidence' or if the House refuses to vote the money required for the public service.

Parliamentary Commissioner for Administration

The Parliamentary Ombudsman—officially known as the Parliamentary Commissioner for Administration—investigates complaints from members of the public (referred through MPs) alleging that they have suffered injustice arising from maladministration. The Ombudsman is independent of government and reports to a Select Committee of the House of Commons. The Ombudsman's jurisdiction covers central government departments and agencies and a large number of non-departmental public bodies. He or she cannot investigate complaints about government policy, the content of legislation or relations with other countries.

In making his investigations, the Commissioner has access to all departmental papers, and has powers to summon those from whom he wishes to take evidence. When an investigation is completed, he sends a report with his findings to the MP who referred the complaint (with a copy report for the complainant). In reports of justified cases, the Ombudsman normally recommends that the department provides redress (which can include a financial remedy for the complainant in appropriate cases). There is no appeal against the Ombudsman's decision. He submits an annual report to Parliament, and also publishes selected cases three times a year.

In 1995 the Ombudsman received 1,706 new complaints. He completed 245 investigations; of these he found 236 wholly or partly justified and 9 unjustified.

The Parliamentary Ombudsman also monitors the Code of Practice on Access to Official Information (see p. 71).

Parliamentary Privilege

Each House of Parliament has certain rights and immunities to protect it from obstruction in carrying out its duties. The rights apply collectively to each House and to its staff and individually to each member.

For the Commons the Speaker formally claims from the Queen 'their ancient and undoubted rights and privileges' at the beginning of each Parliament. These include freedom of speech; first call on the attendance of its members, who are therefore free from arrest in civil actions and exempt from serving on juries, or being compelled to attend court as witnesses; and the right of access to the Crown, which is a collective privilege of the House. Further privileges include the rights of the House to control its own proceedings (so that it is able, for instance, to exclude 'strangers'[9] if it wishes); to decide upon legal disqualifications for membership and to declare a seat vacant on such grounds; and to punish for breach of its privileges and for contempt. Parliament has the right to punish anybody, inside or outside the House, who commits a breach of privilege—that is, offends against the rights of the House.

The privileges of the House of Lords are broadly similar to those of the House of Commons.

Her Majesty's Government

Her Majesty's Government is the body of Ministers responsible for the conduct of national affairs. The Prime Minister is appointed by the Queen, and all other Ministers are appointed by the Queen on the recommendation of the Prime Minister. Most Ministers are members of the Commons, although the Government is also fully represented by Ministers in the Lords. The Lord Chancellor is always a member of the House of Lords.

The composition of governments can vary both in the number of Ministers and in the titles of some offices. New ministerial offices may be created, others may be abolished, and functions may be transferred from one Minister to another.

---

[9] All those who are not members or officials of either House.

Prime Minister

The Prime Minister is also, by tradition, First Lord of the Treasury and Minister for the Civil Service. The Prime Minister's unique position of authority derives from majority support in the House of Commons and from the power to appoint and dismiss Ministers. By modern convention, the Prime Minister always sits in the House of Commons.

The Prime Minister presides over the Cabinet (see p. 65), is responsible for the allocation of functions among Ministers and informs the Queen at regular meetings of the general business of the Government.

The Prime Minister's other responsibilities include recommending a number of appointments to the Queen. These include:

- Church of England archbishops, bishops and deans and some 200 other clergy in Crown 'livings';
- senior judges, such as the Lord Chief Justice;
- Privy Counsellors; and
- Lord-Lieutenants.

They also include certain civil appointments, such as Lord High Commissioner to the General Assembly of the Church of Scotland, Poet Laureate, Constable of the Tower, and some university posts; and appointments to various public boards and institutions, such as the BBC (British Broadcasting Corporation), as well as various royal and statutory commissions. Recommendations are likewise made for the award of many civil honours and distinctions and of Civil List pensions (to people who have achieved eminence in science or the arts and are in financial need). The Prime Minister also selects the trustees of certain national museums and institutions.

The Prime Minister's Office at 10 Downing Street (the official residence in London) has a staff of civil servants who assist the Prime Minister. The Prime Minister may also appoint special advisers to the Office to assist in the formation of policies.

Departmental Ministers

Ministers in charge of government departments are usually in the Cabinet; they

THE ROYAL FAMILY

The Queen and South African President Nelson Mandela drive along the Mall on the first day of his four-day state visit to Britain in July 1996.

On the 50th anniversary of UNICEF, the United Nations children's fund, the Duchess of Kent, as a patron, paid an eight-day visit to India to see the organisation's work.

The Prince of Wales examines the destruction at Sarajevo's National Library during a two-day trip to the former Yugoslavia.

THEME PARKS

Legoland, opened in March 1996, includes model European cities re-created in great detail using nearly 20 million Lego bricks, as well as interactive rides, shows, building workshops and power models.

The Ulster American Folk Park at Castletown, Northern Ireland, is an outdoor museum designed to tell the story of the many emigrants who left for America in the 18th and 19th centuries.

The Pirate Ship at Oakwood Park, Pembrokeshire, Wales. Other attractions include Megafobia, Europe's biggest wooden roller coaster, the waterfall ride, assault courses and the bobsleigh ride.

Deep Sea World is the national aquarium of Scotland, and features the world's largest underwater tunnel (pictured here), which holds 4,500 fish from 40 species native to British coastal waters and Europe's largest Sandtiger Shark collection.

MONUMENTS

The Glenfinnan Monument in the Scottish Highlands marks the place where the Jacobite Rising of 1745 began. Each year Highland games are held on the site in memory of those who died fighting for Bonnie Prince Charlie.

London's Big Ben clock tower is one of the city's best known landmarks. Here its face is cleaned for the first time in 11 years. Each of the 4 dials is 7 metres in diameter, and the work took a week to complete.

are known as 'Secretary of State' or 'Minister', or may have a special title, as in the case of the Chancellor of the Exchequer.

Non-departmental Ministers

The holders of various traditional offices, namely the Lord President of the Council, the Chancellor of the Duchy of Lancaster, the Lord Privy Seal, the Paymaster General and, from time to time, Ministers without Portfolio, may have few or no departmental duties. They are thus available to perform any duties the Prime Minister may wish to give them. In the present administration, for example, the Lord President of the Council is Leader of the House of Commons and the Chancellor of the Duchy of Lancaster is Minister for the Public Service.

Lord Chancellor and Law Officers

The Lord Chancellor holds a special position, as both a Minister with departmental functions and the head of the judiciary (see p. 111). The four Law Officers of the Crown are: for England and Wales, the Attorney General and the Solicitor General; and for Scotland, the Lord Advocate and the Solicitor General for Scotland.

Ministers of State and Junior Ministers

Ministers of State usually work with Ministers in charge of departments. They normally have specific responsibilities, and are sometimes given titles which reflect these functions. More than one may work in a department. A Minister of State may be given a seat in the Cabinet and be paid accordingly.

Junior Ministers (generally Parliamentary Under-Secretaries of State or, where the senior Minister is not a Secretary of State, simply Parliamentary Secretaries) share in parliamentary and departmental duties. They may also be given responsibility, directly under the departmental Minister, for specific aspects of the department's work.

Ministerial Salaries

A fundamental review of MPs' and Ministers' parliamentary pay and allowances was set up in February 1996. The Review Body (see Further Reading) reported in July and Parliament voted to accept its recommendations. As a result, until the next Parliament the salaries of ministers in the House of Commons range from £66,623 a year for junior Ministers to £86,991 for Cabinet Ministers. In the House of Lords salaries range from £43,632 for junior Ministers to £58,876 for Cabinet Ministers. The Prime Minister receives £101,557 and the Lord Chancellor £133,406.

Ministers in the Commons, including the Prime Minister, receive a full parliamentary salary of £43,000 a year (which is included in the above figures) in recognition of their constituency responsibilities and can claim the other allowances which are paid to all MPs.

The Leader of the Opposition in the Commons is entitled to a salary of £83,332 (including the full parliamentary salary);[10] two Opposition whips in the Commons and the Opposition Leader and Chief Whip in the Lords also receive salaries.

The Cabinet

The Cabinet is composed of about 20 Ministers (the number can vary) chosen by the Prime Minister and may include departmental and non-departmental Ministers.

The functions of the Cabinet are to initiate and decide on policy, the supreme control of government and the co-ordination of government departments. The exercise of these functions is vitally affected by the fact that the Cabinet is a group of party representatives, depending upon majority support in the House of Commons.

Cabinet Meetings

The Cabinet meets in private and its proceedings are confidential. Its members are bound by their oath as Privy Counsellors not to disclose information about its proceedings, although after 30 years Cabinet papers may be made available for inspection in the Public Record Office at Kew, Surrey.

---

[10]Since 1995 the Leader of the Opposition has declined the pay increases awarded; he draws instead a salary of £67,456.

Normally the Cabinet meets for a few hours each week during parliamentary sittings, and less often when Parliament is not sitting. To keep its workload within manageable limits, a great deal of work is carried on through the committee system. This involves referring issues either to a standing Cabinet committee or to an *ad hoc* committee of the Ministers directly concerned. The committee then considers the matter in detail and either disposes of it or reports upon it to the Cabinet with recommendations for action.

There are standing committees dealing with defence and overseas policy, economic and domestic policy, and legislation. The membership and terms of reference of all ministerial Cabinet committees are published by the Cabinet Office. Where appropriate, the Secretary of the Cabinet and other senior officials of the Cabinet Office attend meetings of the Cabinet and its committees.

Diaries published by several former Ministers have given the public insight into Cabinet procedures in recent times.

The Cabinet Office

The Cabinet Office is headed by the Secretary of the Cabinet (a civil servant who is also Head of the Home Civil Service) under the direction of the Prime Minister. It comprises the Cabinet Secretariat and the Office of Public Service (OPS).

The Cabinet Secretariat serves Ministers collectively in the conduct of Cabinet business, and in the co-ordination of policy at the highest level.

The Chancellor of the Duchy of Lancaster is in charge of the OPS and is a member of the Cabinet. The OPS is responsible for:

- raising the standard of public services across the public sector through the Citizen's Charter (see p. 69);
- promoting the Government's policies on competitiveness and deregulation;
- promoting openness in government; and
- improving the effectiveness and efficiency of central government, through, among other things, the establishment of executive agencies and the market testing programme (see p. 73).

The Historical and Records Section is responsible for Official Histories and managing Cabinet Office records.

Ministerial Responsibility

'Ministerial responsibility' refers both to the collective responsibility for government policy and actions which Ministers share, and to Ministers' individual responsibility for their departments' work.

The doctrine of collective responsibility means that the Cabinet acts unanimously even when Cabinet Ministers do not all agree on a subject. The policy of departmental Ministers must be consistent with the policy of the Government as a whole. Once the Government's policy on a matter has been decided, each Minister is expected to support it or resign. On rare occasions, Ministers have been allowed free votes in Parliament on government policies involving important issues of principle. In February 1994, for example, free votes were allowed on lowering the age of consent to homosexual sex from 21 to 18.

The individual responsibility of Ministers for the work of their departments means that they are answerable to Parliament for all their departments' activities. They bear the consequences of any failure in administration, any injustice to an individual or any aspect of policy which may be criticised in Parliament, whether personally responsible or not. Since most Ministers are members of the House of Commons, they must answer questions and defend themselves against criticism in person. Departmental Ministers in the House of Lords are represented in the Commons by someone qualified to speak on their behalf, usually a junior Minister.

Departmental Ministers normally decide all matters within their responsibility. However, on important political matters they usually consult their colleagues collectively, either through the Cabinet or through a Cabinet committee. A decision by a departmental Minister binds the Government as a whole.

On assuming office Ministers must resign directorships in private and public companies, and must ensure that there is no conflict between their public duties and private interests.

The Privy Council

The Privy Council was formerly the chief source of executive power in the State; its origins can be traced back to the King's Court, which assisted the Norman monarchs in running the government. As the system of Cabinet government developed in the 18th century, however, much of the role of the Privy Council was assumed by the Cabinet, although the Council retained certain executive functions. Some government departments originated as committees of the Privy Council.

Nowadays the main function of the Privy Council is to advise the Queen on the approval of Orders in Council, including those made under prerogative powers, such as Orders approving the grant of royal charters of incorporation and those made under statutory powers. Responsibility for each Order, however, rests with the Minister answerable for the policy concerned, regardless of whether he or she is present at the meeting where approval is given.

The Privy Council also advises the Sovereign on the issue of royal proclamations, such as those summoning or dissolving Parliament. The Council's own statutory responsibilities, which are independent of the powers of the Sovereign in Council, include supervising the registration authorities of the medical and allied professions.

Membership of the Council, with the style of 'Right Honourable', is retained for life, except for very occasional removals. It is accorded by the Sovereign on the recommendation of the Prime Minister (or occasionally, Prime Ministers of Commonwealth countries) to people eminent in public life—mainly politicians and judges—in Britain and the independent monarchies of the Commonwealth. Cabinet Ministers must be Privy Counsellors and, if not already members, are admitted to membership before taking their oath of office at a meeting of the Council. There are about 450 Privy Counsellors. A full Council is summoned only on the accession of a new Sovereign or when the Sovereign announces his or her intention to marry.

Committees of the Privy Council

There are a number of Privy Council committees. These include prerogative committees, such as those dealing with legislation from the Channel Islands and the Isle of Man, and with applications for charters of incorporation. Committees may also be provided for by statute, such as those for the universities of Oxford and Cambridge and the Scottish universities. Membership of such committees is confined to members of the current administration. The only exceptions are the members of the Judicial Committee and the members of any committee for which specific provision authorises a wider membership.

Administrative work is carried out in the Privy Council Office under the Lord President of the Council, a Cabinet Minister.

The Judicial Committee of the Privy Council is primarily the final court of appeal for British dependent territories and those independent Commonwealth countries which have retained this avenue of appeal after independence. The Committee also hears appeals from the Channel Islands and the Isle of Man, and from the disciplinary and health committees of the medical and allied professions. It has a limited jurisdiction to hear certain ecclesiastical appeals. In 1995 the Judicial Committee heard 69 appeals and 69 petitions for special leave to appeal.

The members of the Judicial Committee include the Lord Chancellor, the Lords of Appeal in Ordinary, other Privy Counsellors who hold or have held high judicial office and certain judges from the Commonwealth.

Government Departments

Government departments and their agencies, staffed by politically impartial civil servants, are the main instruments for implementing government policy when Parliament has passed the necessary legislation, and for advising Ministers. They often work alongside local authorities, statutory boards, and government-sponsored organisations operating under various degrees of government control.

A change of government does not necessarily affect the number or general functions of government departments, although major changes in policy may be accompanied by organisational changes.

The work of some departments (for instance, the Ministry of Defence) covers Britain as a whole. Other departments, such as the Department of Social Security, cover England, Wales and Scotland, but not Northern Ireland. Others, such as the Department of the Environment, are mainly concerned with affairs in England.

The ten Government Offices for the Regions are responsible for administering the main regional programmes of the Departments of Environment, Trade and Industry, Education and Employment, and Transport, as well as programmes from the Home Office; they also administer the Single Regeneration Budget (see p. 375).

Some departments which have direct contact with the public throughout the country (for example, the Department of Social Security) also have local offices.

Departments are usually headed by Ministers. In some departments the head is a permanent official, and Ministers with other duties are responsible for them to Parliament. For instance, Ministers in the Treasury are responsible for HM Customs and Excise, the Inland Revenue, the National Investment and Loans Office and a number of other departments, as well as executive agencies such as the Royal Mint. Departments generally receive their funds directly out of money provided by Parliament and are staffed by members of the Civil Service.

The functions of the main government departments and agencies are set out on pp. 540–7.

Non-departmental Public Bodies

Non-departmental public bodies (NDPBs) have a role in the process of national government but are not government departments nor parts of a department. There are three kinds: executive bodies, advisory bodies and tribunals. Tribunals are a specialised group of bodies whose functions are essentially judicial (see p. 111).

The function of NDPBs is regularly reviewed in a continuous programme. Once they are no longer needed in their existing form, the bodies are abolished, merged or privatised. The number of NDPBs decreased from 2,167 in 1979 to 1,227 in 1995, a reduction of 43 per cent. During the same period the number of staff they employed decreased from 217,000 to 109,200—a reduction of 50 per cent. See p. 71 for government plans to increase the public accountability of NDPBs.

Executive Bodies

Executive bodies normally employ their own staff and have their own budget. They are public organisations whose duties include executive, administrative, regulatory or commercial functions. They normally operate within broad policy guidelines set by departmental Ministers but are in varying degrees independent of government in carrying out their day-to-day responsibilities. Examples include the Commission for Racial Equality, the Police Complaints Authority, and the Public Health Laboratory Service.

Advisory Bodies

Many government departments are assisted by advisory councils or committees which carry out research and collect information, mainly to give Ministers access to informed opinion before they come to a decision involving a legislative or executive act. In some cases a Minister must consult a standing committee, but advisory bodies are usually appointed at the discretion of the Minister. Examples include the British Overseas Trade Board and the Farm Animal Welfare Council.

The membership of advisory councils and committees varies according to the nature of the work involved, but normally includes representatives of the relevant interests and professions.

In addition to standing advisory bodies, there are committees set up by government to examine specific matters and make recommendations. For example, the Committee on Standards in Public Life (the Nolan Committee—see p. 71) was set up in 1994, reporting directly to the Prime Minister.

For certain important inquiries, Royal Commissions, whose members are chosen for their wide experience, may be appointed. Royal Commissions examine evidence from government departments, interested organisations and individuals, and submit recommendations; some prepare regular reports. Examples include the standing Royal Commission on Environmental Pollution, set up in 1970, and the Royal Commission on Criminal Justice, which issued its report in 1993. Inquiries may also be undertaken by departmental committees.

Government Information Services

Each of the main government departments has its own information division, public relations branch or news department. These are normally staffed by professional information officers responsible for communicating their department's activities to the news media and the public (sometimes using publicity services provided by the Central Office of Information—see p. 545). They also advise their departments on the public's reaction.

The Lobby

As press adviser to the Prime Minister, the Prime Minister's Press Secretary and other staff in the Prime Minister's Press Office have direct contact with the parliamentary press through regular meetings with the Lobby correspondents. The Lobby correspondents are a group of political correspondents with the special privilege of access to the Lobby of the House of Commons, where they can talk privately to government Ministers and other members of the House. The Prime Minister's Press Office is the accepted channel through which information about parliamentary business is passed to the media.

Administration of Scottish, Welsh and Northern Ireland Affairs

Scotland

Scotland has its own system of law and wide administrative autonomy. The Secretary of State for Scotland, a Cabinet Minister, has responsibility in Scotland (with some exceptions) for a wide range of policy matters (see p. 546).

The distinctive conditions and needs of Scotland and its people are also reflected in separate Scottish legislation on many domestic matters. Special provisions applying to Scotland alone are also inserted in Acts which otherwise apply to Britain generally.

British government departments with significant Scottish responsibilities have offices in Scotland and work closely with The Scottish Office.

Wales

Since 1964 there has been a separate Secretary of State for Wales, who is a member of the Cabinet and is responsible for many aspects of Welsh affairs. (For further details see p. 547.)

Northern Ireland

Since the British Government's assumption of direct responsibility for Northern Ireland in 1972 (see p. 12), the Secretary of State for Northern Ireland, with a seat in the Cabinet, has been in charge of the Northern Ireland Office. He is assisted by two Ministers of State and two Parliamentary Under-Secretaries of State. The Secretary of State has overall responsibility for the government of Northern Ireland. He is directly responsible for political and constitutional matters, security policy and broad economic questions and other major policy issues, while responsibility for the Departments of Agriculture, Economic Development, Education, Environment, Finance and Personnel, and Health and Social Services is shared among the other Ministers.

Improving Public Services

The Citizen's Charter

The Citizen's Charter was launched by the Prime Minister in 1991 as a ten-year programme to raise the standard of public services and make them more responsive to the needs and wishes of their users. It is closely linked to other reforms, including the Next

Steps programme, efficiency measures and the Government's contracting out and market testing programmes (see p. 73).

The Charter applies to all public services, at both national and local levels, and to the privatised utilities. Most major public services have now published separate charters (by mid-1996 over 40 had been issued). In many cases separate charters have been published for services in Northern Ireland, Scotland and Wales. (Details of many of the charters can be found in the relevant chapters.)

The Principles of Public Service

The Charter sets out a number of key principles which users of public services are entitled to expect.

They include requirements for published standards of services and results achieved; comprehensive information on services; consultation with users of services; courteous and helpful service from public servants; effective redress if things go wrong, including well publicised and easy to use complaints procedures; and independent inspectorates and auditing.

Implementing the Charter

A Cabinet Minister, the Chancellor of the Duchy of Lancaster, is responsible for the Charter programme. The Chancellor of the Duchy is supported by the Citizen's Charter Unit within the OPS (see p. 66). The Prime Minister also receives advice on the Charter from an Advisory Panel drawn from business, consumer affairs and education. The Panel works with the Citizen's Charter Unit and officials in all the departments to implement and develop the Citizen's Charter programme. The Prime Minister holds regular seminars with Advisory Panel members and Cabinet Ministers to report on progress and plan further action.

Executive agencies (see p. 73) are expected to comply fully with the principles of the Citizen's Charter, and the pay of agency chief executives is normally directly related to their agency's performance. Performance-related pay is being introduced throughout the public service.

Projects to ensure that public service managers understand the benefits of the Charter programme and that users are aware of the standards of service they can expect to receive include:

Charter Mark Awards The Charter Mark Scheme was introduced in 1992 to reward excellence in delivering public services. Applicants have to demonstrate that they have achieved measurable improvements in the quality of services over the previous two years, and that their customers are satisfied with their services. Winners are judged by the Prime Minister's Citizen's Charter Advisory Panel.

In 1995 a record number of 740 applications were received and 224 awards were made. Winners came from all parts of the public sector throughout Britain. They included: St James's University Hospital Liver Unit (Leeds), Employment Service (Inverness), Merthyr Tydfil Libraries, the UK Passport Agency (London) and Northern Ireland Housing Executive (Lisburn).

Charter Quality Networks The Charter Unit has helped to set up a number of networks of groups of managers of public services to meet locally to exchange ideas on customer service and quality issues and share best practice. There are 24 Quality Networks around Britain, with over 1,000 members. The networks aim to help break down boundaries between public service organisations and encourage problem-sharing and solving.

Charter Quality Seminars and Workshops The Charter Unit runs and arranges a number of seminars and workshops to allow local public services managers and consumer groups to share experiences in delivering a high-quality service to their customers. Seminars have been held for local authorities; secondary, further and higher education; those involved in community care; services to road users; services in rural areas; and effective complaints handling.

Open Government

In line with Citizen's Charter principles of increased openness and accountability of public administration, the Government introduced the Code of Practice on Access to Official Information in 1994. Under the Code, government departments and bodies within the jurisdiction of the Parliamentary Ombudsman (see p. 63) are required to:

- publish facts and analysis with major policy decisions;
- open up internal guidelines about departments' dealings with the public;
- give reasons for administrative decisions to those affected;
- provide information about public services, including their cost, targets, performance, complaints and redress; and
- provide information in response to specific requests on policies, actions and decisions.

As examples of information which departments and public bodies volunteered to the public in 1995, the Ministry of Agriculture, Fisheries and Food made 124 internal guidance documents available through the Helpline Desk in its main library; and reports by the Social Services Inspectorate of inspections of voluntary children's homes were made public for the first time.

The Code allows independent review when applicants feel that the Code has not been properly applied. Complainants may be referred to the Parliamentary Ombudsman through an MP. Reports are made to Parliament by the Ombudsman if information has been improperly withheld. A similar Code of Practice on Openness in the National Health Service came into force in June 1995.

The Government is also to propose legislation to provide rights of access to health and safety information and personal records. These rights would add to a number of existing rights of access in specific areas such as environmental information.

Committee on Standards in Public Life

The Committee on Standards in Public Life (the Nolan Committee), set up in 1994, issued its first report in May 1995. It recommended, among other things, an independent element in the scrutiny of the conduct of MPs, in the acceptance of appointments by Ministers when they leave office, and of how Ministers make appointments to public bodies. The Government accepted the broad thrust of its recommendations. As a result:

- The first independent Commissioner for Public Appointments was appointed in November 1995. The Commissioner provides advice and guidance to departments and monitors, regulates and audits their procedures for making appointments to executive non-departmental public bodies and NHS bodies, ensuring that appointments are governed by the overriding principle of appointment on merit. The Commissioner published a code of practice in April 1996, and will publish an annual report containing the results of the monitoring of all departments' appointments procedures.

- In March 1996 the Government published the proposed text of the revised rules on the acceptance of appointments outside government by former civil servants; this brings special advisers within the system and enables the Prime Minister's Advisory Committee on Business Appointments to announce the reasons for its decisions and to advise a civil servant or Minister that the acceptance of a particular appointment is inappropriate.

- In March 1996 the Government also published a consultation paper which proposes action to improve the accountability of public bodies. *Spending Public Money: Governance and Audit Issues* includes a clear set of principles for the audit of public money, including how well it is spent. It also provides a framework for accountability.

The Civil Service

The Civil Service is concerned with the conduct of the whole range of government activities as they affect the community. These range from policy formulation to carrying out the day-to-day duties of public administration.

Civil servants are servants of the Crown. For all practical purposes the Crown in this context means, and is represented by, the Government of the day. In most circumstances the executive powers of the Crown are exercised by, and on the advice of, Her Majesty's Ministers, who are in turn answerable to Parliament. The Civil Service as such has no constitutional personality or responsibility separate from that of the Government of the day. The duty of the individual civil servant is first and foremost to the Minister of the Crown who is in charge of the Department in which he or she is serving. A change of Minister, for whatever reason, does not involve a change of staff. Ministers sometimes appoint special advisers from outside the Civil Service. The advisers are normally paid from public funds, but their appointments come to an end when the Government's term of office finishes, or when the Minister concerned leaves the Government or moves to another appointment.

A new Civil Service code came into force in January 1996, following publication in 1994 of *The Civil Service: Continuity and Change*, a White Paper on the role and future of the Civil Service. The Code provides a statement of the constitutional framework within which all civil servants work and the values they are expected to uphold. The Code includes an independent line of appeal to the Civil Service Commissioners (see p. 74) on alleged breaches of the Code.

The number of civil servants fell from 732,000 in April 1979 to 499,900 in January 1996, its lowest since 1939. This reflects the Government's policy of controlling the cost of the Civil Service and of improving its efficiency.

About half of all civil servants are engaged in the provision of public services. These include paying sickness benefits and pensions, collecting taxes and contributions, running employment services, staffing prisons, and providing services to industry and agriculture. A quarter are employed in the Ministry of Defence. The rest are divided between central administrative and policy duties; support services; and largely financially self-supporting services, for instance, those provided by National Savings and the Royal Mint. Four-fifths of civil servants work outside London.

The total also includes members of the Senior Civil Service—around 3,000 of the most senior managers and policy advisers. They are responsible for serving the collective interest of government with a focus and loyalty wider than their own departments and agencies.

Equality of Opportunity

The Government is committed to achieving equality of opportunity for all its staff. In support of this commitment, the Civil Service, which recruits and promotes on the basis of merit, is actively pursuing policies to develop career opportunities for women, ethnic minorities and people with disabilities. In April 1995:

- women represented 51.3 per cent of all non-industrial civil servants, and since 1987 the proportion of women in the top three grades of the service has more than doubled to almost 9 per cent;

- representation of ethnic minority staff among non-industrial civil servants had increased from 4.2 per cent in 1989 to 5.4 per cent, compared with 4.9 per cent, for the overall ethnic minority representation in the working population; and

- 2.8 per cent of disabled people were employed in the non-industrial home Civil Service, of whom 1.6 per cent were registered disabled, which is just above the proportion of registered disabled people in the workforce as a whole and twice the proportion employed in the private sector.

Progress is monitored and reported on regularly by the Cabinet Office (OPS).

Management Reforms

Civil Service reforms are being implemented to ensure improved management performance, in particular through the increased accountability of individual managers, based on clear objectives and responsibilities. These reforms include performance-related pay schemes and other incentives.

Executive Agencies: Next Steps Programme

The Next Steps Programme, launched in 1988, aims to deliver government services more efficiently and effectively within available resources for the benefit of taxpayers, customers and staff. This has involved setting up, as far as is practicable, separate units or agencies to perform the executive functions of government. Agencies remain part of the Civil Service but under the terms of individual framework documents they enjoy greater delegation of financial, pay and personnel matters. Agencies are headed by chief executives who are accountable to Ministers but who are personally responsible for day-to-day operations.

No agency can be established until the 'prior options' of abolition, privatisation and contracting out have been considered and ruled out. These 'prior options' are reconsidered when agencies are reviewed, normally after five years of operation.

At the end of 1995, 109 agencies were in existence, together with 23 Executive Units of Customs and Excise and 27 Executive Offices of the Inland Revenue. At that time over 366,000 civil servants—67 per cent of the total—worked in organisations run on Next Steps lines. At the same time a further 57 agency candidates—employing nearly 58,000 staff—had been identified as suitable for agency status.

In 1994–95, agencies met 83 per cent of their key performance targets—a small improvement on the previous year.

Efficiency Measures

In 1992 the Government increased its drive to secure the best value for money in the provision of public services through expanding competition and encouraging private sector involvement. Up to 1992, £20–25 million

worth of activities had been opened up to external competition. By March 1995 over £2,600 million of activities, covering 69,000 posts, had been reviewed; and in 1995–96 alone over £1,000 million of activities were reviewed.

Central Management and Structure

Responsibility for central co-ordination and management of the Civil Service is divided between the Cabinet Office (OPS) and the Treasury.

The OPS, which is under the control of the Prime Minister, as Minister for the Civil Service, oversees organisation, senior civil service pay, pensions and allowances, recruitment, retirement and redundancy policy, personnel management and statistics, and the overall efficiency of the Service.

The function of official Head of the Home Civil Service is combined with that of Secretary of the Cabinet.

At the senior levels, where management forms a major part of most jobs, there are common grades throughout the Civil Service. These unified grades 1 to 7 are known as the Open Structure and cover grades from Permanent Secretary level to Principal level. Within these grades each post is filled by the person considered to be best qualified, regardless of the occupational group to which he or she previously belonged.

Below this the structure of the non-industrial Civil Service is based on a system of occupational groups. These groups assist the recruitment and matching of skills to posts and offer career paths in which specialist skills can be developed. Departments and agencies are being encouraged to develop their own pay and grading arrangements. They are expected to produce value-for-money benefits which are greater than those available through centrally controlled negotiation. Since April 1996 all departments and agencies have been responsible for implementing their own systems of pay and grading of staff below senior levels.

The Diplomatic Service

The Diplomatic Service, a separate service of some 6,000 people, provides the staff for the

Foreign & Commonwealth Office (see p. 117) and for British diplomatic missions abroad.

The Diplomatic Service has its own grade structure, linked to that of the Home Civil Service. Terms and conditions of service are comparable, but take into account the special demands of the Service, particularly the requirement to serve abroad. Home civil servants, members of the armed forces and individuals from the private sector may also serve in the Foreign & Commonwealth Office and at overseas posts on loan or attachment.

Civil Service Recruitment

Recruitment is based on the principle of selection on merit by fair and open competition. Independent Civil Service Commissioners are responsible for approving the selection of people for appointment to the Senior Civil Service. Recruitment of all other staff is the responsibility of departments and executive agencies. Departments and agencies can choose whether to undertake this recruitment work themselves, to employ a private sector recruitment agency or to use the Government's Recruitment and Assessment Services Agency to recruit on their behalf.

People from outside the Civil Service may be recruited directly to all levels, particularly to posts requiring skills and experience more readily found in the private sector. The exchange of staff between the Civil Service and industry is also encouraged.

Since May 1995 departments and agencies have been required to publish information about their recruitment systems.

Training

Government departments and agencies provide training and development to meet their business needs, to improve performance, and to help staff respond effectively to changing demands. Most training and development takes place within departments and agencies. In addition, the Civil Service College provides management and professional training, mainly for those who occupy, or hope to occupy, relatively senior positions. Considerable use is made of other providers in the private and public sectors.

Civil servants aged under 18 may continue their general education by attending courses, usually for one day a week ('day release' schemes). All staff may be entitled to financial support to continue their education, mainly in their own time. There are also opportunities for civil servants to undertake research and study in areas of interest to them and to their department or agency.

Promotion

Departments are responsible for promotion up to and including Grade 4. In some cases centrally arranged postings are supplemented or replaced by schemes of job advertising. For about 150 of the most senior posts in the Civil Service, appointments and transfers are approved by the Prime Minister, who is advised by the Head of the Home Civil Service.

Political and Private Activities

Civil servants are required to perform loyally the duties assigned to them by the Government of the day, whatever its political persuasion. It is essential that Ministers and the public should have confidence that the personal views of civil servants do not influence the performance of their official duties, given the role of the Civil Service in serving successive governments formed by different parties. The aim of the rules which govern political activities by civil servants is to allow them, subject to these fundamental principles, the greatest possible freedom to participate in public affairs consistent with their rights and duties as citizens. The rules are therefore concerned with activities liable to give public expression to political views rather than with privately held beliefs and opinions.

The Civil Service is divided into three groups for the purposes of deciding the extent to which individuals may take part in political activities:

● those in the 'politically free' group, consisting of industrial staff and non-office grades, are free to engage in any political activity outside official time, including adoption as a prospective candidate for the British or the European

Parliament (although they would have to resign from the Service before giving their consent to nomination).

- those in the 'politically restricted' group, which comprises staff in Grade 7 and above as well as Administration Trainees and Higher Executive Officers (D), may not take part in national political activities but may apply for permission to take part in local political activities; and

- the 'intermediate' group, which comprises all other civil servants, may apply for permission to take part in national or local political activity, apart from candidature for the British or the European Parliament.

Where required, permission is granted to the maximum extent consistent with the Civil Service's reputation for political impartiality and the avoidance of any conflict with official duties. A code of discretion requires moderation and the avoidance of embarrassment to Ministers.

Generally, there are no restrictions on the private activities of civil servants, provided that these do not bring discredit on the Civil Service, and that there is no possibility of conflict with official duties. For instance, a civil servant must comply with any departmental instruction on the need to seek authority before taking part in any outside activity which involves official experience.

Security

Each department is responsible for its own internal security. As a general rule the privately-held political views of civil servants are not a matter of official concern. However, no one who is, or has been involved in, or associated with, activities threatening national security may be employed on work which is vital to the security of the State. Certain posts are not open to people who fall into this category, or to anyone whose reliability may be in doubt for any other reason.

The Security Commission may investigate breaches of security in the public service and advise on changes in security procedure if asked to do so by the Prime Minister after consultation with the Leader of the Opposition.

Local Government

Although the origins of local government in England can be traced back to Saxon times, the first comprehensive system of local councils was established in the late 19th century. Major reforms to the structure of local government are now being implemented.

Local Government Reform

A major reform of local government took place in 1974 in England and Wales and in 1975 in Scotland. This created two main tiers of local authority throughout England and Wales: counties and the smaller districts. Local government in London had been reorganised along the same lines in 1965. In Scotland functions were allocated to regions and districts on the mainland; single-tier authorities were introduced for the three Islands areas. In Northern Ireland changes were made in 1973 which replaced the two-tier county council and urban/rural council system with a single-tier district council system.

The Local Government Act 1985 abolished the Greater London Council and the six metropolitan county councils in England. Most of their functions were transferred to the London boroughs and metropolitan district councils respectively in 1986 (see below).

Local Government Commission

The Local Government Commission was established in 1992 to review the structure, boundaries and electoral arrangements of local government in England and to undertake periodic electoral reviews. So far most of its work has been to review the structure of local government in non-metropolitan England. The reviews considered whether the two-tier structure should be replaced by single-tier ('unitary') authorities in each area; for the most part the Commission recommended the retention of two-tier government, but suggested unitary authorities for some areas, especially the larger cities. The first changes, on the Isle of Wight, were implemented in April 1995. In April 1996 13 more unitary councils were established, and others will be set up in April 1997 or later years.

The Commission is now concentrating on reviews of local authority electoral arrangements, although it may also look at the boundaries of metropolitan areas where there is sufficient demand.

Scotland and Wales

In Scotland 29 new unitary councils replaced the previous system of nine regional and 53 district councils in April 1996 under the Local Government etc. (Scotland) Act 1994. The three Islands councils have remained in being. In Wales, under the Local Government (Wales) Act 1994, 22 unitary authorities replaced the previous eight county councils and 37 district councils, again in April 1996. The first elections for the new councils took place in 1995, with the new authorities acting in 'shadow' form until April 1996 to make preparations for their assumption of power.

Local Authorities' Powers

Local authorities derive their power from legislation. Although local authorities are responsible for administering certain services, Ministers have powers in some areas to secure a degree of uniformity in standards to safeguard public health or to protect the rights of individual citizens.

Relations with Central Government

The main link between local authorities and central government in England is the Department of the Environment. However, other departments such as the Department for Education and Employment and the Home Office are also concerned with various local government functions. In the rest of Britain the local authorities deal with the Scottish or Welsh Offices or the Department of the Environment for Northern Ireland, as appropriate.

Principal Types of Local Authority

Before the recent reforms, England outside Greater London was divided into counties,

sub-divided into districts. All the districts and the non-metropolitan counties had locally elected councils with separate functions. County councils provided large-scale services such as education and social services, while district councils were responsible for the more local ones (see p. 78). These arrangements are broadly continuing in areas where two-tier local government will remain. The new unitary authorities, where they are being created, bring all of these local authority functions together.

Greater London is divided into 32 boroughs and the City of London, each of which has a council responsible for local government in its area. In the six metropolitan counties there are 36 district councils; there are no county councils. A number of services, however, require a statutory authority over areas wider than the individual boroughs and districts. These are:

- waste disposal (in certain areas);
- the fire services, including civil defence; and
- (outside London) public transport.

These are run by joint authorities composed of elected councillors nominated by the borough or district councils. Local councils also provide many of the members of the police authorities (see p. 89).

In addition to the two-tier local authority system in England, over 8,000 parish councils or meetings provide and manage local facilities such as allotments and village halls, and act as agents for other district council functions. They also provide a forum for discussion of local issues. In Wales about 730 community councils have similar functions, and provision is made for local community councils in Scotland.

The boundaries and electoral arrangements of local authorities in England are kept under review by the Local Government Commission (see p. 75), and in Wales and Scotland by the Local Government Boundary Commissions.

In Northern Ireland 26 district councils are responsible for local environmental and certain other services. Statutory bodies, such as the Northern Ireland Housing Executive and area boards, are responsible to central government departments for administering other major services.

Election of Councils

Local councils consist of elected councillors. Councillors are paid a basic allowance but may also be entitled to additional allowances and expenses for attending meetings or taking on special responsibilities. Parish and community councillors cannot claim allowances for duties undertaken within their own council areas. In Scotland community councillors are not eligible for any form of allowance.

In England and Wales each council elects its presiding officer annually. Some districts have the ceremonial title of borough, or city, both granted by royal authority. In boroughs and cities the presiding officer is normally known as the Mayor. In the City of London and certain other large cities, he or she is known as the Lord Mayor. In Wales the presiding officer of the new authorities is called chairman in the case of counties and mayor in the case of county boroughs.In Scotland the presiding officer of the district council of each of the four cities—Aberdeen, Dundee, Edinburgh and Glasgow—is called the Lord Provost. In other councils he or she is known as a convenor or provost. District councils in Northern Ireland are presided over by a chairman. There are, however, a number of boroughs and cities where the presiding officer is the Mayor and in Belfast he or she is known as the Lord Mayor.

Most councillors are elected for four years. All county councils in England, London borough councils, and about two-thirds of non-metropolitan district councils are elected in their entirety every four years. In the remaining districts (including all metropolitan districts) one-third of the councillors are elected in each of the three years when county council elections are not held. Where new unitary authorities are being set up in England, Parliamentary Orders make the necessary provisions regarding elections. In Scotland local elections will now be held every three years, with the next elections due in 1999. Each election covers the whole council. In Wales elections for the full councils will continue to be held every fourth year, again with the next due in 1999.

Voters

Anyone may vote at a local government election in Britain provided he or she is:

- aged 18 years or over;
- a citizen of Britain or of another Commonwealth country, or of the Irish Republic, or (from 1996) a citizen of the European Union;
- not legally disqualified; and
- on the electoral register.

To qualify for registration a person must be resident in the council area on the qualifying date. In Northern Ireland there are slightly different requirements.

Candidates

Most candidates at local government elections stand as representatives of a national political party, although some stand as independents. Candidates must be British citizens, other Commonwealth citizens or citizens of the European Union, and aged 21 or over. In addition, they must also either:

- be registered as local electors in the area of the relevant local authority; or
- have occupied (as owner or tenant) land or premises in that area during the whole of the preceding 12 months; or
- have had their main place of work in the area throughout this 12-month period.

No one may be elected to a council of which he or she is an employee, and there are some other disqualifications. All candidates for district council elections in Northern Ireland are required to make a declaration against terrorism.

Electoral Divisions and Procedure

Counties in England are divided into electoral divisions, each returning one councillor. Districts in England and Northern Ireland are divided into wards, returning one councillor or more. In Scotland the electoral areas in the new councils are called wards and in Wales they are called electoral divisions; each returns one or more councillors. Parishes (in England) and communities (in Wales) may be divided into wards. Wards return at least one councillor.

The procedure for local government voting in Great Britain is broadly similar to that for parliamentary elections. In Northern Ireland local government elections are held by proportional representation, and electoral wards are grouped into district electoral areas.

Council Functions and Services

At present in England county councils are responsible for strategic planning, transport planning, highways, traffic regulation, education,[11] consumer protection, refuse disposal, the fire service, libraries and the personal social services. District councils are responsible for services such as environmental health, housing, decisions on most local planning applications, and refuse collection. Both tiers of local authority have powers to provide facilities such as museums, art galleries and parks; arrangements depend on local agreement. Where unitary authorities are created in non-metropolitan areas, they are generally responsible for both county and district level functions.

In the metropolitan counties the district councils are responsible for all services apart from the police, the fire service and public transport and, in some areas, waste disposal (see p. 76). In Greater London the boroughs and the Corporation of the City of London have similar functions, but London's metropolitan police force is responsible to the Home Secretary. Responsibility for public transport lies with London Transport (see p. 308).

Wales and Scotland now have unitary local authorities, responsible for a range of local government services. In Wales fire services are provided by three combined fire authorities. In Northern Ireland local environmental and

certain other services, such as leisure and the arts, are administered by the district councils. Responsibility for planning, roads, water supply and sewerage services is exercised in each district through a divisional office of the Department of the Environment for Northern Ireland. Area boards, responsible to central departments, administer education, public libraries and the health and personal social services locally. The Northern Ireland Housing Executive, responsible to the Department of the Environment for Northern Ireland, administers housing.

Changes in Local Government

There have been numerous changes in recent years in the way that local authorities approach their responsibilities. Many of these can be encapsulated under the term 'the enabling authority'. It is used to describe the general shift away from local authorities providing services directly and towards them arranging for services to be provided, or carrying out functions in partnership with other bodies. For example, councils often have nomination rights to housing association properties (see p. 389), so that they are acting not as provider but as 'gatekeeper'. Likewise, under the community care reforms, councils with social services responsibilities draw up care plans for those who need them (see p. 421), but the care is often provided by the private or voluntary sectors funded by the council, rather than directly by the local authority itself.

The Government introduced legislation in the 1980s to encourage local authorities to obtain better value for money in the services they provide. As a result, many services traditionally provided by the council's own staff, such as refuse collection and leisure management, must now be put out to competition with private firms. The process is known as compulsory competitive tendering (CCT). In-house teams may also bid for the work. The Government estimates that CCT has resulted in a cost saving of 7 per cent since its introduction. It has now been extended to local authorities' provision of a range of professional functions, such as legal and personnel services. The metropolitan districts and London boroughs already have some of

---

[11]Schools may, however, 'opt out' of local education authority control by obtaining grant-maintained status—see p. 444.

these new arrangements in place and these will be extended to the remaining authorities over the next few years.

Internal Organisation of Local Authorities

Local authorities have considerable freedom to make arrangements for carrying out their duties. Some decisions are made by the full council; many other matters are delegated to committees composed of members of the council. A council may delegate most functions to a committee or officer, although certain powers are legally reserved to the council as a whole. Parish and community councils in England and Wales are often able to do their work in full session, although they appoint committees from time to time as necessary.

In England and Wales committees generally have to reflect the political composition of the council (although the legislation governing this specifically excludes parish or community councils). In practice, this is often also the case in Scotland, although it is not enforced by legislation. People who are not members of the council may be co-opted onto decision-making committees and can speak and take part in debates; they cannot normally vote. Legislation also prevents senior officers and others in politically sensitive posts from being members of another local authority or undertaking public political activity. Some of these provisions have not been introduced in Northern Ireland.

The Government is looking at ways of improving the internal management of local authorities.

Public Access

The public (including the press) are admitted to council, committee and sub-committee meetings, and have access to agendas, reports and minutes of meetings and certain background papers. Local authorities may exclude the public from meetings and withhold these papers only in limited circumstances.

Employees

About 1.4 million people[12] are employed by local authorities in England. These include administrative, professional and technical staff, teachers, firefighters, and manual workers, but exclude those in law and order services. Education is the largest service, employing almost 45 per cent of all local government workers. Councils are individually responsible, within certain national legislative requirements, for deciding the structure of their workforces.

Senior staff appointments are usually made by the elected councillors. More junior appointments are made by heads of departments. Pay and conditions of service are usually a matter for each council, although there are scales recommended by national negotiating machinery between authorities and trade unions, and most authorities follow these.

Local Authority Finance

Local government expenditure accounts for about 25 per cent of public spending. The Government has sought to influence local government spending as part of a general policy of controlling the growth of public expenditure. Since 1984 the Government has had powers to limit or 'cap' local authority budgets (local authority taxation in Scotland) by setting a maximum amount for local authorities which have, in its view, set budgets which are excessive.

In 1995–96 expenditure by local authorities in Britain was about £74,800 million. Current expenditure amounted to £64,000 million; capital expenditure, net of capital receipts, was £6,700 million; and debt interest £4,100 million. Local government capital expenditure is financed primarily by borrowing within limits set by central government and from capital receipts from the disposal of land and buildings.

Local authorities in Great Britain raise revenue through the council tax, which meets about 20 per cent of their revenue expenditure. Their revenue spending is, however, financed

---

[12]Whole-time equivalents.

primarily by grants from central government and by the redistribution of revenue from the national non-domestic rate, a property tax levied on businesses and other non-domestic properties.

District councils in Northern Ireland continue to raise revenue through the levying of a domestic rate and business rates.

Financial Safeguards

Local councils' annual accounts must be audited by independent auditors appointed by the Audit Commission in England and Wales, or in Scotland by the Accounts Commission for Scotland. In Northern Ireland this role is exercised by the chief local government auditor, who is appointed by the Department of the Environment for Northern Ireland.

Local Government Complaints System

Local authorities are encouraged to resolve complaints through internal mechanisms, and members of the public will often ask their own councillor for assistance in this. Local authorities must also appoint a monitoring officer, whose duties include ensuring that the local authority acts lawfully in the conduct of its business.

Allegations of local government maladministration leading to injustice may be investigated by statutory independent Commissioners for Local Administration, often known as 'local government ombudsmen'. There are three of these in England, and one each in Wales and Scotland. A report is issued on each complaint fully investigated and, if injustice caused by maladministration is found, the local ombudsman normally proposes a remedy. The council must consider the report and reply to it.

An independent review of the local government ombudsman service in England began in 1995.

In Northern Ireland a Commissioner for Complaints deals with complaints alleging injustices suffered as a result of maladministration by district councils and certain other public bodies.

Pressure Groups

Pressure groups are informal organisations which aim to influence Parliament and Government in the way decisions are made and carried out, to the benefit of their members and the causes they support. There is a huge range of groups, covering politics, business, employment, consumer affairs, ethnic minorities, aid to developing countries, foreign relations, education, culture, defence, religion, sport, transport, social welfare, animal welfare and the environment. Some have over a million members, others only a few dozen. Some exert pressure on a number of different issues; others are concerned with a single issue. Some have come to play a recognised role in the way Britain is governed; others seek influence through radical protest.

While political parties seek to win political power, pressure groups aim to influence those who are in power, rather than to exercise the responsibility of government and to legislate.

Pressure Groups and Policy

Pressure groups operating at a national level have a number of methods for influencing the way Britain is governed. Action by them may highlight a particular problem, which is then acknowledged by the Government. Groups whose scale of membership indicates that they are broadly representative in their field may then be consulted by a government department, or take part in Whitehall working groups or advisory councils. If the Government considers that legislation is necessary, then proposals are drafted, which are circulated to interested groups for their comments. Legislation is then put before Parliament, and at various times during the passage of a Bill—especially at the committee stage—pressure groups have opportunities to influence its content. If the Act includes delegated legislation (see p. 60), pressure groups may be consulted and have the opportunity to provide information and express their views.

Pressure Groups and Government

The principle of consultation to gain the consent and co-operation of as wide a range of organisations as possible, and ensure the smooth working of laws and regulations, plays an important part in the relationship between government departments and interested groups.

In some instances a department is under legal obligation to consult interested groups. The Government has a duty to consult organised interests, providing the pressure groups involved have a broad enough membership for them to represent a majority view, and provided that they observe confidentiality about their discussions with the department. Members of pressure groups have direct expertise, and an awareness of what is practicable, and can give advice and information to civil servants engaged in preparing policy or legislation. In return, the pressure groups have the opportunity to express their opinions directly to the Government. The contacts between civil servants and pressure group representatives may be relatively informal—by letter or telephone—or more formal, through involvement in working parties or by giving evidence to committees of inquiry.

Administration by Pressure Groups

As well as providing information and opinions, pressure groups can also be involved in administering government policy. The Government also makes grants to pressure groups which, as well as speaking on behalf of their members or for an issue, also provide a service. Relate: National Marriage Guidance has received grants for the advice centres it runs, and government departments make grants to a number of pressure groups for research relating to public policy.

Pressure Groups and Parliament

Lobbying—the practice of approaching MPs or Lords, persuading them to act on behalf of a cause, and enabling them to do so by providing advice and information—is a form of pressure group activity which has substantially increased in recent years.

A common pressure group tactic is to ask members of the public to write to their MP about an issue—for example, the Sunday trading laws, or the plight of political prisoners in particular countries—in order to raise awareness and persuade the MP to support the cause.

Raising Issues in Parliament

Other ways through which pressure groups may exert influence include:

- suggesting to MPs or Lords subjects for Private Members' Bills (see p. 59); many pressure groups have ready-drafted legislation waiting to be sponsored;
- approaching MPs or Lords to ask parliamentary questions as a means of gaining information from the Government and of drawing public attention to an issue;
- suggesting to MPs subjects for Early Day Motions (see p. 62); and
- orchestrating public petitions as a form of protest against government policy, or to call for action. If the petition is to be presented in Parliament, it must be worded according to Commons or Lords rules, and be presented by an MP or Lord in his or her own House.

Parliamentary Lobbyists

Many pressure groups employ full-time parliamentary workers or liaison officers, whose job is to develop contacts with MPs and Lords sympathetic to their cause, and to brief them when issues affecting the group are raised in Parliament.

There are also public relations and political consultancy firms specialising in lobbying Parliament and Government. Such firms are employed by pressure groups—as well as by British and overseas companies and organisations—to monitor parliamentary business, and to promote their clients' interests where they are affected by legislation and debate.

Further Reading

The British System of Government (3rd edn). Aspects of Britain series, The Stationery Office, 1996.

The Citizen's Charter - Five Years On. Cm 3370. HMSO, 1996.

The Civil Service. Aspects of Britain series, HMSO, 1995.

The Civil Service: Continuity and Change. Cm 2627, HMSO, 1994.

The Civil Service: Taking Forward Continuity and Change. Cm 2748, HMSO 1995.

The First Report of the Committee on Standards in Public Life (Nolan Report). Cm 2850, HMSO, 1995.

Government and the Individual: The Citizen's Means of Redress. Aspects of Britain series, HMSO, 1996.

The Government's Response to the First Report from the Committee on Standards in Public Life. Cm 2931, HMSO, 1995.

Honours and Titles (2nd edn.). Aspects of Britain series, HMSO, 1996.

Local Government. Aspects of Britain series. HMSO, 1996.

The Monarchy. Aspects of Britain series. HMSO, 1991.

Open Government. Cm 2290. HMSO, 1993.

Organisation of Political Parties (2nd edn). Aspects of Britain series, HMSO, 1994.

Parliament (3rd edn). Aspects of Britain series, The Stationery Office, 1996.

Parliamentary Elections (2nd edn). Aspects of Britain series, HMSO, 1995.

Pressure Groups. Aspects of Britain series, HMSO, 1994.

Review of Parliamentary Pay and Allowances. Review Body on Senior Salaries: Report 38. (Cm 3330–1) HMSO, 1996.

8   Justice and the Law

Criminal Justice	84	Civil Courts	108
The Police Service	88	Administration of the Law	111
Criminal Courts	94	Government Responsibilities	111
Treatment of Offenders	101	Judges and Lawyers	112
Civil Justice	108	Legal Aid	112

Major reforms of criminal procedure have been introduced under the Criminal Procedure and Investigations Act 1996. The Act creates a statutory scheme for the disclosure of material by the prosecution and defence in criminal cases in England, Wales and Northern Ireland and introduces a number of measures to improve the effectiveness of pre-trial procedures. Other developments during the last year include the setting up of the national Crime Prevention Agency; proposals for tougher sentencing for repeat offenders and an end to automatic early release and parole from prison; and a review of rules and procedures of the civil courts in England and Wales.

England and Wales, Scotland, and Northern Ireland all have their own legal systems, with considerable differences in law, organisation and practice. All three have separate prosecution, prison and police services. Crime prevention policy and non-custodial treatment for offenders are similar throughout Britain. There are different civil court and civil law systems in England and Wales and in Scotland; Northern Ireland's system is in many ways similar to the English and Welsh model.

Common Law and Statute Law

One of the main sources of law in England and Wales and in Northern Ireland is common law, which has evolved over centuries from judges' decisions. It forms the basis of the law except when superseded by legislation. In Scotland, too, the doctrine of legal precedent has been more strictly applied since the end of the 18th century.

Much of the law, particularly that relating to criminal justice, is statute law passed by Parliament. If a court reaches a decision which is contrary to the intentions of Parliament, then Parliament must either accept the decision or pass amending legislation. Some Acts create new law, while others are passed to draw together existing law on a given topic. Parliament can repeal a statute and replace it with another.

European Community Law

European Community law, which applies to Britain by virtue of its membership of the European Union, derives from the European Community treaties and the legislation adopted under them. EC legislation has been adopted in most of the fields covered by the

Community treaties, including economic and social matters, agriculture and the environment. Where EC law is applicable, it takes precedence over domestic law. It is normally applied by the domestic courts, but the most authoritative rulings are given by the European Court of Justice in Luxembourg (see p. 120).

Certain changes to United Kingdom law have been made to bring it into line with rulings of the European Court of Human Rights (see p. 135).

Branches of the Law

There are two main branches of the law—criminal and civil. Criminal law is concerned with acts punishable by the State. Civil law covers:

- dealings or disputes between individuals about their rights, duties and obligations; and

- dealings or disputes between individuals and companies, and between one company and another.

Criminal Justice

Crime Statistics

Differences in the legal systems, police recording practices and statistical classifications make it impracticable to analyse in detail trends in crime for Britain as a whole. However, as elsewhere in the industrialised world, there has been a substantial rise in crime in Britain since the 1950s. Annual official statistics cover crime recorded by the police and can be affected by changes in the amount of crime that goes unreported.

Recorded crime in England and Wales (see Table 8.1) has been falling since 1993; in 1995 it was down by 491,500 offences on 1992 levels—the largest ever continuous fall in the number of annually recorded crimes. On only two other occasions this century have there been continuous annual falls: 1912–15 and 1951–54.

The Scottish police recorded 502,802 crimes in 1995 (the fourth successive year in which a decrease has occurred); of these, 195,188 were cleared up. In Northern Ireland, of the 68,808 recorded crimes in 1995, 24,838 were cleared up.

Crime tends to be concentrated in large cities and urban areas, although rural crime has increased in recent years. About 93 per cent of offences recorded by the police in England and Wales are directed against property but only 6 per cent involve violence. Rising affluence has provided more opportunities for casual property crime; for example, car crime accounts for about 26 per cent of all recorded crimes (and is currently the focus for much of the Government's crime prevention activity). The demand for, and supply of, illegal drugs has also been an increasing factor in the incidence of crime in recent years.

Table 8.1: Notifiable Crimes Recorded by the Police in England and Wales 1995

Offence Group	Recorded crimes	Crimes cleared up	Per cent
Violence against the person	212,588	163,485	77
Sexual offences	30,274	22,873	76
Burglary	1,239,484	259,719	21
Robbery	68,074	15,395	23
Theft and handling stolen goods	2,452,109	566,762	23
Fraud and forgery	133,016	65,935	50
Criminal damage[a]	699,694	134,246	19
Other	50,705	48,460	96
Total	**4,885,944**	**1,276,875**	**26**

Source: Home Office
[a]Excludes criminal damage of £20 or under.

Recorded Crime in England and Wales 1945–1995

Number of recorded crimes
(excluding criminal damage £20 and under)

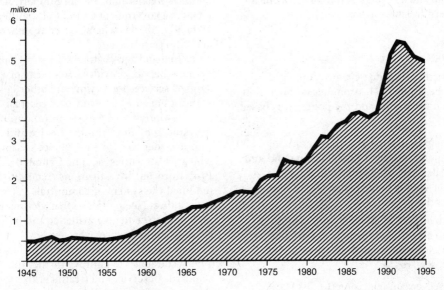

Source: *Protecting the Public* White Paper, Cm 3190

Regular crime surveys are undertaken in England and Wales and in Scotland. These indicate that many crimes go unrecorded by the police, mainly because not all victims report what has happened to them. The surveys confirm that most crimes are against property, in the form of theft and vandalism.

Most crime is committed by young males, is opportunist and is not planned by hardened professional criminals, although these do exist. There are about eight times as many male offenders as female.

Crime Prevention

In November 1995 the Government announced the creation of the Crime Prevention Agency. The aims of the Agency are to initiate and develop ideas to help prevent crime and reduce the fear of crime by following up new research, identifying good practice, and ensuring that guidance and advice are available.

Home Office support to police crime prevention work is provided by the Crime Prevention Centre, which is part of the Agency and which offers training and advice and promotes best practice. About 800 specialist crime prevention officers are employed in police forces across England and Wales, and crime prevention activities are being increasingly integrated into operational policing.

About 1,300 local crime prevention panels (including over 1,000 school-based youth panels) assist the police in preventing crime through publicity, marking goods and equipment, and fund-raising to buy security devices.

The work of the Crime Prevention Agency is overseen by the Crime Prevention Agency Board, which brings together the key bodies involved in promoting crime prevention: the Home Office, the Association of Chief Police Officers, Crime Concern (an independent organisation which encourages local initiatives and business participation in crime prevention), local authorities, police authorities and business.

There is a Crime Prevention Council in Scotland and a Crime Prevention Panel in Northern Ireland.

Initiatives

The Partners Against Crime campaign, which began in 1994, promotes co-operation between the public and the police. It is based on:

- Neighbourhood Watch schemes, of which there are 143,000 in England and Wales, covering some 6 million households (and also 3,600 schemes in Scotland); and
- Street Watch, in which local people, in agreement with the police, work out specific routes and regularly walk the chosen area.

Closed-circuit television (CCTV) surveillance systems have proved very effective in preventing and detecting crime, and in deterring criminals, in high streets, shopping centres, schools, industrial estates and other areas. The Government has encouraged the setting up of CCTV schemes across the country, and in October 1995 announced plans for financing a further 10,000 CCTV cameras over three years.

The Safer Cities Programme tackles crime and the fear of crime through joint crime prevention action by local government, private businesses, the police and voluntary agencies in England and Wales. The programme has supported nearly 4,500 schemes, with government funding of over £26 million. There is a parallel Safer Cities programme in Scotland, and similar projects are being funded by the Government in Northern Ireland.

Helping the Victim

The Government has emphasised the importance of victims' interests within the criminal justice system.

There are some 365 victim support schemes—with over 12,000 volunteer visitors throughout England and Wales—providing practical help and emotional support to victims of crime. The schemes are co-ordinated by a national organisation, Victim Support, which receives a government grant (£11.7 million in 1996–97). Similar schemes operate in Scotland and Northern Ireland.

In England and Wales the Crown Court Witness Service provides a full range of support services for victims and other witnesses in all 77 Crown Court centres.

A new offence of witness intimidation was introduced by the Criminal Justice and Public Order Act 1994 to protect victims who are also witnesses. The Criminal Procedure and Investigations Act 1996 modified the system of committal proceedings (see p. 95), so that victims will no longer have to give evidence and be cross-examined twice over.

A new Victim's Charter, published in June 1996, is designed to improve further the standards of service and treatment that victims receive from criminal justice agencies. It sets out 27 standards of service that victims can expect, and explains which agency is responsible for providing the service and how victims can complain if they do not get the level of service promised.

A scheme giving victims the opportunity formally to explain the effect of what happened to them, so that it may be taken into account by the criminal justice agencies before they decide how to deal with an alleged offender, is being introduced on a pilot basis in six police areas from autumn 1996.

Blameless victims of violent crime in England, Wales and Scotland, including foreign nationals, may be eligible for compensation from public funds; in 1995–96 £183 million was paid out under the Criminal Injuries Compensation Scheme. In Northern Ireland there are separate statutory arrangements for compensation for criminal injuries, and for malicious damage to property, including any resulting loss of profits.

Tackling Drug Misuse

The Government's comprehensive strategy for tackling drug misuse involves:

- international co-operation against production and trafficking (see p. 136);

- law enforcement by police and customs, and maintenance of tight domestic controls and effective deterrents (see below); and

- preventive education, publicity, and community action, and the treatment and rehabilitation of offenders (see pp. 411–3).

Recent Developments

The White Paper *Tackling Drugs Together*, published in May 1995, contained a new drugs strategy for England for 1995–98. This maintains the emphasis on law enforcement and reducing supply but recognises a need for stronger action on reducing demand for illegal drugs. The strategy seeks to involve the voluntary and private sectors, local authorities, schools, parents, health professionals and criminal justice agencies in a comprehensive programme to reduce supply, demand and misuse of illegal drugs. It aims to take action by vigorous law enforcement, accessible treatment and a new emphasis on education and prevention to:

- increase the safety of communities from drug-related crime;

- reduce the acceptability and availability of drugs to young people; and

- reduce the health risks and other damage related to drug misuse.

The Government recognises that these aims are best achieved through a co-ordinated multi-agency approach at both national and local level. One hundred and five Drug Action Teams have been set up across England to implement the strategy locally. The teams consist of senior representatives from the key statutory agencies: the police, probation and prison services, and health and local authorities. They have drawn up action plans for the next two years which focus on local priorities and specific local objectives.

In Scotland the report of the Ministerial Drugs Task Force, *Drugs in Scotland: Meeting the Challenge*, setting out a comprehensive strategy for action, was published in 1994. Its recommendations are being implemented, and, as in England, Drug Action Teams are

developing plans for their areas. A Northern Ireland policy statement was issued in 1995 and discussions have taken place on establishing a local co-ordination network. In Wales a strategy was published in May 1996.

In 1995–96 the European Drug Liaison Officer network of the National Criminal Intelligence Service (NCIS—see p. 89) contributed to the seizure of drugs with a street value of more than £243 million, an increase of 12.5 per cent over the previous year.

Strengthening the Law

In addition to wide-ranging legislation such as the Criminal Justice and Public Order Act 1994 and the Criminal Procedure (Scotland) Act 1995, giving the police and the courts greater powers to catch, convict and punish criminals, other important measures to strengthen the criminal justice system have been taken in recent years.

Courts in England and Wales have powers to order the confiscation of profits made by drug traffickers and other criminals. (Similar provisions are in place in Scotland and Northern Ireland.) These were first introduced in 1986, in relation to the proceeds of drug trafficking, and have since been considerably strengthened. The Proceeds of Crime Act 1995 brought the law on criminal proceeds into line with that on drug trafficking. In particular, the Act provided new powers for the courts to confiscate the proceeds of persistent offending. Such offenders can now be required to account for the lawful origin of all their property. If they cannot do so, the property is liable to confiscation. The legislation also closed the loophole which enabled some criminals to avoid payment by serving a term of imprisonment in default. The amount owing under a confiscation order is now liable to confiscation even when the offender has served a default term for failing to pay the order.

New powers to clamp down on money launderers[1] came into force in 1994, with

---

[1] Money laundering is the process by which illegally obtained money or other property—from drugs or arms trafficking, terrorist activities or other serious crimes—is given the appearance of having originated from a legitimate source.

heavy penalties for those who launder money gained from any sort of serious crime.

There are strict legislative controls on firearms. The police license the possession of firearms and have powers to regulate their safekeeping and movement. The private ownership of certain highly dangerous types of weapon, such as machine guns, high-powered self-loading rifles and burst-fire weapons, is banned.

It is illegal to manufacture, sell or import certain weapons such as knuckledusters or to carry a knife in a public place without good reason. Penalties for offences relating to the carrying of knives are being raised.

Measures to Combat Terrorism

Most of the powers which the police use to combat terrorism and the offences with which terrorists might be charged are contained in the general criminal law. However, the Prevention of Terrorism (Temporary Provisions) Act 1989 in Great Britain, and legislation relating specifically to Northern Ireland (see below), do confer some exceptional powers, and create additional offences, in order to combat terrorism.

The special counter-terrorist legislation gives the Secretary of State the power:

- to proscribe any organisation which appears to be concerned with terrorism in Northern Ireland; and
- to exclude from all or part of Britain people who are believed to be, or to have been, involved in terrorism connected with the affairs of Northern Ireland.

The police also have wider powers of arrest and greater powers of detention under the Prevention of Terrorism Act than under the general criminal law when dealing with suspected terrorists. They can arrest and detain someone for up to 48 hours (and for a further five days if a Secretary of State approves) on reasonable suspicion of involvement in terrorism. They also have powers to conduct security checks at ports, and special investigative powers for offences relating to the financing of terrorism.

Under the Criminal Justice and Public Order Act 1994, the police have powers to stop and search for articles which may be used for terrorist purposes, and a new offence of possession of such articles has been created.

Extended police powers to stop and search pedestrians, to search non-residential premises and unaccompanied goods at ports, to impose cordons, and to restrict parking and remove vehicles were introduced under the Prevention of Terrorism (Additional Powers) Act 1996.

Northern Ireland

Powers similar to those now provided in England and Wales under the Prevention of Terrorism (Additional Powers) Act 1996 have existed for a number of years in Northern Ireland under successive Northern Ireland (Emergency Provisions) Acts, which have a fixed lifespan. The provisions of the last such Act, which lapsed in August 1996, were largely renewed in successor legislation, namely the Northern Ireland (Emergency Provisions) Act 1996.

Despite the ceasefires declared by the paramilitary groupings in Northern Ireland in 1994, the Government did not think it would be prudent to remove emergency legislation from the statute book while illegal weaponry and explosives were still at large. The Provisional Irish Republican Army (PIRA) ended its ceasefire and returned to violence in mainland Britain in February 1996 (see p. 14).

THE POLICE SERVICE

The Home Secretary and the Scottish and Northern Ireland Secretaries, together with police authorities and chief constables, are responsible for the provision of an effective and efficient police service in Britain.

Organisation

There are 52 police forces in Britain, mainly organised on a local basis: 43 in England and Wales, eight in Scotland and one—the Royal

Ulster Constabulary (RUC)—in Northern Ireland. The Metropolitan Police Service and the City of London force are responsible for policing London. The police service is financed by central and local government.

At the end of 1995 police strength in England and Wales was about 127,000, of which the Metropolitan Police numbered 27,300. The establishment of the Royal Ulster Constabulary (RUC) was around 8,500. Police strength in Scotland was about 14,500. With the exception of the RUC, each force has volunteer special constables who perform police duties in their spare time, without pay, acting in support of regular officers. The Government is aiming to recruit a further 10,000 special constables by the end of 1996, so increasing the overall number by 50 per cent. In Northern Ireland there is a 5,000-strong reserve force.

Police forces are maintained in England and Wales by local police authorities, which appoint the chief constables and provide buildings and equipment. The Home Secretary is responsible for London's Metropolitan Police Service. In Scotland the new unitary councils act as police authorities. In Northern Ireland the Police Authority for Northern Ireland is appointed by the Secretary of State.

Provincial forces are headed by chief constables, who are responsible for the direction and control of their police forces and for the appointment, promotion and discipline of all ranks below assistant chief constable. On matters of efficiency they are generally answerable to their police authorities, to whom they must submit an annual report (with a copy to the Secretary of State). In the Metropolitan Police area the commissioner of police and his or her deputies are appointed on the recommendation of the Home Secretary.

Police forces are inspected by independent inspectors of constabulary, whose reports to central government are published.

Police officers are not allowed to join a trade union or to go on strike. All ranks, however, have their own staff associations.

Recent Reforms

In England and Wales the Police and Magistrates' Courts Act 1994 has changed the relationship between central government, police authorities and chief constables—improving the management of the police, reducing cumbersome central controls, and devolving more power and decision-making to the local level.

Under this legislation, new free-standing police authorities were set up in 1995 in each of the 41 police areas outside London. They were given greater responsibility for securing effective police performance and were made more accountable to the public. Appointments to police authorities now include independent members as well as local councillors and magistrates. The standard size of a police authority is set at 17 members: nine locally elected councillors, three magistrates and five independent members. The Home Secretary can increase the size of a police authority beyond 17 if local circumstances make it desirable. A 12-member Metropolitan Police Committee assists the Home Secretary, who acts as police authority for the Metropolitan Police. Police authorities, in consultation with the chief constables and local community, set local policing objectives, while the Government sets priority objectives for the police as a whole.

In Northern Ireland the Secretary of State has issued a White Paper proposing reforms to improve accountability and efficiency in the police service. Some of the proposals mirror changes made in England and Wales.

Police authorities in Scotland continue to be composed of elected councillors.

Co-ordination of Police Operations

Certain police services are provided centrally either by the Government or through co-operation between forces. In England and Wales these include criminal intelligence, telecommunications, and research and development. In Scotland the main common services are centralised police training, the Scottish Crime Squad and the Scottish Criminal Record Office.

The National Criminal Intelligence Service, with a headquarters in London and five regional offices, co-ordinates and provides information to the police and HM Customs about major criminals and organised crime, including drug trafficking. The Service also liaises with the International Criminal Police Organisation (INTERPOL), which promotes international co-operation between police forces.

Britain has taken the lead in developing, with other European Union countries, a European police organisation (EUROPOL) designed to provide Union-wide intelligence about serious crime (see p. 136).

All British police forces have fraud squads responsible for investigating financial and commercial fraud.

Six regional crime squads in England and Wales deal with serious crime which goes beyond individual force, regional or national boundaries.

The Government is taking steps to increase the capability of Britain's law enforcement agencies to gather and use intelligence when fighting organised crime. Legislation passed in 1996 enables the Security Service to support the law enforcement agencies in the prevention and detection of serious crime (extending its functions beyond the protection of national security and the safeguarding of Britain's economic well-being against threats from abroad). The Government also intends to:

- develop the National Criminal Intelligence Service's leading role in collecting and sharing intelligence to assist investigations, including a pivotal role in international co-operation;

- set up a unified Crime Squad for England and Wales to conduct investigations of organised criminals and support police forces in cases of serious crime; and

- establish a new statutory system for the authorisation of intrusive police surveillance operations by Chief Police Officers.

Information Technology

The Police National Computer provides all police forces in Britain with rapid 24-hour-a-day access to essential information. Phoenix—the Criminal Justice Record Service—went live on the Police National Computer in 1995, and gives the police direct on-screen access to national records of arrests, cautions, bail decisions and convictions. This will gradually replace the manual record-keeping service currently maintained on microfiche by the National Identification Service (NIS). Phoenix will eventually provide information direct to other agencies such as the courts, the Prison Service and the Crown Prosecution Service.

Scottish criminal records are held on computer at the Scottish Criminal Record Office, which has an automatic national fingerprint record system; the initial implementation of a similar national system in England and Wales (NAFIS) is planned for 1997–98.

The National Strategy for Police Information Systems, launched in 1994, aims to increase police effectiveness in England and Wales by developing common information technology applications, and a common technical infrastructure to deliver them. A new Police Information Technology Organisation (PITO) was officially launched in July 1996. It is responsible for specifying and procuring the delivery of national information technology systems (such as the Police National Computer) for the police service, and for promoting the National Strategy for Police Information Systems at force level. PITO will also be responsible for communications services, including the Police National Network (which provides telecommunications services to forces throughout Britain) and the next generation of police radio systems.

Firearms

Police officers in Great Britain do not normally carry firearms. About five per cent of officers are allowed to be issued with firearms, on the authority of a senior officer, where there is a special need. Most forces operate armed response vehicles which can be deployed quickly to contain firearms incidents. In Northern Ireland police officers are issued with firearms for their personal protection.

Forensic Science Service

The Forensic Science Service (FSS) provides scientific support in the investigation of crime.

Its customers include the police, the Crown Prosecution Service, coroners and defence solicitors.

In April 1996 the FSS merged with the Metropolitan Police Forensic Science Laboratory to form a single agency serving all police forces in England and Wales through six regional laboratories. The FSS holds and operates the national DNA database (see p. 93).

In Scotland forensic science services are provided by forces' own laboratories. Northern Ireland has its own forensic science laboratory.

Police Discipline

A police officer may be prosecuted if suspected of a criminal offence. Officers are also subject to a disciplinary code designed to deal with abuse of police powers and maintain public confidence in police impartiality. If found guilty of breaching the code, an officer can be dismissed from the force.

Revised disciplinary procedures for the police, similar to those in operation elsewhere in the public service, are being introduced. These provide for a more flexible system with greater line management involvement, the introduction of procedures for dealing with unsatisfactory performance and changes in the appeals procedures, which no longer involve the Secretary of State.

Members of the public have the right to make complaints against police officers if they feel that they have been treated unfairly or improperly. In England and Wales such complaints are investigated by the independent Police Complaints Authority. In Scotland complaints against police officers involving allegations of criminal conduct are referred to the procurator fiscal for investigation. The Scottish Inspectorate of Constabulary considers representations from complainants dissatisfied with the way the police have handled their complaints.

In Northern Ireland the Independent Commission for Police Complaints is required to supervise the investigation of complaints regarding death or serious injury and has the power to supervise that of any other complaint. In certain circumstances, the Secretary of State may direct the Commission to supervise the investigation of matters that are not the subject of a formal complaint. The Northern Ireland system is currently under review.

Community Relations

Police/community liaison consultative groups operate in every police authority; they consist of representatives from the police, local councillors and community groups.

Particular efforts are made to develop relations with young people through greater contact with schools. School governing bodies and head teachers have to describe in their annual reports the steps taken to strengthen their schools' links with the community, including the police.

Central guidance recommends that all police officers should receive thorough training in community and race relations issues. Home Office and police service initiatives are designed to tackle racially motivated crime and to ensure that the issue is treated as a police priority. Forces' responses to racial incidents are monitored by the Inspectorate of Constabulary. Discriminatory behaviour by police officers, either to other officers or to members of the public, is an offence under the Police Discipline Code.

All police forces recognise the need to recruit women and members of the ethnic minorities in order to ensure that the police represent the community.

Police Powers in England and Wales

The powers of a police officer to stop and search, arrest and place a person under detention are contained in the Police and Criminal Evidence Act 1984. The legislation and its accompanying codes of practice set out police powers and procedures in the investigation of crime, and safeguards for members of the public. An officer is liable to disciplinary proceedings if he or she fails to comply with any provision of the codes, and evidence obtained in breach of the codes may be ruled inadmissible in court. The codes must be readily available in all police stations for consultation by police officers, detained people and members of the public. (For information on police powers relating to the prevention of terrorism, see p. 88).

Stop and Search

A police officer has the power to stop and search people and vehicles if there are reasonable grounds for suspecting that he or she will find stolen goods, offensive weapons or implements that could be used for theft, burglary and other offences. The officer must make a record of the grounds for the search and of anything found. The person stopped is entitled to a copy of the search record. Under the Criminal Justice and Public Order Act 1994 a senior police officer (superintendent or above) who reasonably believes that serious incidents of violence may take place can authorise uniformed officers to stop and search people and vehicles for offensive weapons or dangerous implements. The authorisation must specify the timescale and area in which the powers are to be exercised.

Arrest

The police have various powers to arrest people suspected of having committed an offence. They may arrest on a warrant issued by a court, but can arrest without warrant for arrestable offences and serious arrestable offences.

An arrestable offence is an offence for which the sentence is fixed by law or for which the term of imprisonment is five years or more. Serious arrestable offences, such as murder, rape and manslaughter, fall within this category, but the seriousness of the offence allows the police greater opportunity to detain and interview suspects (see below). There is also a general power of arrest for all other offences if:

- it is impracticable or inappropriate to proceed by way of summons to appear in court; or
- a police officer has reasonable grounds for believing that arrest is necessary to prevent the person concerned from causing injury to any other person or damage to property.

Detention, Treatment and Questioning

If a person is suspected of involvement in an offence, he or she must be cautioned before the police ask any questions about the offence. The caution informs suspects that they do not have to say anything, but anything that they do say may be given in evidence in court. The caution also tells suspects that it may be harmful to their defence if they fail to mention something during questioning which they later rely on in court. A caution will also be given in similar terms when a suspect is charged. The caution reflects the requirements of the Criminal Justice and Public Order Act 1994, which allows a court to draw inferences from a defendant's failure to mention facts when questioned or charged.

Questions relating to an offence may not normally be put to people after they have been charged with that offence or informed that they may be prosecuted for it.

The length of time a suspect is held in police custody before charge is strictly regulated. For arrestable offences this may not exceed 24 hours. A person suspected of committing a serious arrestable offence can be detained for up to 96 hours without charge but beyond 36 hours only if a warrant is obtained from a magistrates' court. Reviews must be made of a person's detention at regular intervals—six hours after initial detention and thereafter every nine hours as a maximum—to check whether the criteria for detention are still satisfied. If they are not, the person must be released.

The tape recording of interviews with suspected offenders at police stations must be used when the police are investigating indictable offences and in certain other cases. The police are not precluded from taping interviews for other types of offences. The taping of interviews is regulated by a code of practice approved by Parliament, and suspects are entitled to a copy of the tape if they are charged or informed that they will be prosecuted.

A person who thinks that the grounds for detention are unlawful may apply to the High Court for a writ of *habeas corpus* against the person who detained him or her, requiring that person to appear before the court to justify the detention. *Habeas corpus* proceedings take precedence over others.

Recognising that the use of DNA analysis has become a powerful tool in the investigation of crime, the Government has extended police powers to take body samples from suspects. The police may take non-intimate samples without consent from anyone who is detained or convicted for a recordable offence, and use the samples to search against existing records of convicted offenders or unsolved crimes. A national DNA database, the first of its kind in the world, was introduced in 1995.

Charging

Once there is sufficient evidence, the police have to decide whether a detained person should be charged with an offence. They may issue a formal caution (see p. 102), which will be recorded and may be taken into account if the person reoffends.

If charged, a person may be kept in custody if there is a risk that he or she might fail to appear in court or might interfere with the administration of justice. When no such considerations apply, the person must be released on or without bail. When someone is detained after charge, they must be brought before a magistrates' court as soon as practicable. This is usually no later than the next working day.

Police Powers in Scotland

The police in Scotland can arrest a person without a warrant if he or she is seen committing a crime or is reasonably suspected of an offence against laws controlling the use of drugs. In other cases the police may seek a warrant to arrest a person suspected of a crime by applying to a Justice of the Peace (see p. 95).

As in England and Wales, Scottish police have powers to enter a building without a warrant from a court if they are in close pursuit of a person who has committed or attempted to commit a serious crime. A court can grant the police a search warrant giving them the power to search premises for stated items in connection with a crime. The police have statutory powers to search anyone if they have reasonable grounds to suspect him or her of carrying an offensive weapon.

There are powers to detain for questioning anyone the police suspect of committing an offence punishable by imprisonment. The suspect may not be detained for more than six hours. After this period the person must be either formally arrested and charged or

released. If held in a police station, the suspect has a right to have a solicitor and one other person informed about his or her whereabouts.

Once a person has been charged with a criminal offence, only voluntary statements will normally be allowed in evidence at the trial. The court will reject statements unless satisfied that they have been fairly obtained. Tape recording of interviews with suspects is common practice. Anyone arrested must be brought before a court on the first working day after arrest. In less serious cases, the police may release a person who gives a written undertaking to attend court at a later date.

Where the charges involve serious crime, the accused is brought before the sheriff in private, either to be committed for a period not exceeding eight days to allow further enquiries to be made or to be committed for trial.

The Criminal Procedure (Scotland) Act 1995 extends the range of samples which the police may take without warrant for DNA analysis.

Police Powers in Northern Ireland

The law in Northern Ireland relating to the powers of the police in the investigation of crime and to evidence in criminal proceedings is very similar to that in force in England and Wales.

Under emergency legislation designed to combat terrorism (see p. 88), people detained on suspicion of terrorist offences are kept at special holding centres, and may be held for up to 48 hours. Further extensions of up to five days require the consent of the Secretary of State.

Awaiting Trial

England and Wales

Most accused people are not remanded in custody to await trial except where strictly necessary. In England and Wales the court decides whether a defendant should be released on bail. Unconditional bail may be withheld only if the court believes that the accused would abscond, commit an offence, interfere with witnesses or otherwise obstruct the course of justice.

A court may also impose conditions before

granting bail. If bail is refused, the defendant may apply to a High Court judge or to the Crown Court for bail. In certain circumstances the prosecution may appeal to a Crown Court judge against the granting of bail by magistrates. An application can also be made to the Crown Court for conditions imposed by a magistrates' court to be altered. In some cases a court may grant bail to a defendant on condition that he or she lives in an approved bail or probation/bail hostel.

The Criminal Justice and Public Order Act 1994 gives the police powers of immediate arrest for breach of police bail and removes the presumption in favour of bail for people alleged to have offended while on bail. It also removes the right to bail for someone charged with murder, manslaughter or rape if previously convicted of the same offence.

Scotland

When arrested, an accused person in Scotland may be released by the police to await summons, on an undertaking to appear at court at a specified time, or be held in custody to appear at court on the next working day. Following that appearance, the accused may be remanded in custody until trial or released by the court on bail. If released on bail, the accused must undertake to appear at trial when required, not to commit an offence while on bail, and not to interfere with witnesses or obstruct the course of justice. The court may also impose additional conditions on the accused as appropriate (for example, to keep away from certain people or locations).

There is a right of appeal to the High Court by an accused person against the refusal of bail, or by the prosecutor against the granting of bail, or by either against the conditions imposed.

The Criminal Procedure (Scotland) Act 1995 gives the courts increased powers to sentence a person who commits an offence while on bail. A prison sentence may be increased by up to six months; a fine by up to £1,000. Bail will not be granted where an accused person is charged with murder, attempted murder, culpable homicide, rape or attempted rape and has a previous conviction for such a crime (in the case of culpable homicide involving a prison sentence).

Northern Ireland

In Northern Ireland bail may be granted by a resident magistrate except in cases dealt with under emergency provisions, where the decision is made by a judge of the High Court.

CRIMINAL COURTS

Prosecution

England and Wales

Once the police have instituted criminal proceedings against a person, the independent Crown Prosecution Service (CPS) takes control of the case, reviews the evidence and decides whether the case should be continued.

The CPS is headed by the Director of Public Prosecutions, who is accountable to Parliament through the Attorney General. It is divided into 13 geographical areas, each headed by a Chief Crown Prosecutor, and below these there are 99 branches. A 14th area (Central Casework) operates from London and York. Each branch has a number of teams, responsible for casework from particular police divisions and feeding into particular courts. Central Casework deals with some especially sensitive cases, including terrorist offences and breaches of the Official Secrets Act.

A prosecution will proceed only if the prosecutor is satisfied that there is, on the evidence, a realistic prospect of conviction, and if so, that it is in the public interest for the prosecution to proceed.

Scotland

The Lord Advocate is responsible for prosecutions in the High Court of Justiciary, sheriff courts and district courts. Private prosecutions are extremely rare. The High Court of Justiciary will only grant the right to prosecute to a private person in very exceptional cases. The Lord Advocate is advised by the Crown Agent, who is head of the Procurator Fiscal Service and is assisted in the Crown Office by a staff of legally qualified civil servants.

Prosecutions in the High Court of Justiciary are prepared by procurators fiscal and Crown Office officials. They are conducted by the Lord Advocate, the Solicitor General for

Scotland (the Lord Advocate's ministerial deputy) and advocate deputes, collectively known as Crown Counsel.

Crimes tried before the sheriff and district courts are prepared and prosecuted by procurators fiscal. The police and other law enforcement agencies investigate crimes and offences and report to the fiscal, who decides whether to prosecute, subject to the directions of Crown Counsel.

When dealing with minor crime, the fiscal can use alternatives to prosecution, such as formal warnings or diversion to social work. The Criminal Procedure (Scotland) Act 1995 extends the range of minor offences to which fiscal fines may apply.

Northern Ireland

The Director of Public Prosecutions for Northern Ireland, appointed by the Attorney General, prosecutes all offences tried on indictment and may do so in other (summary) cases. Most summary offences are prosecuted by the police.

Prosecutions for Fraud

The Serious Fraud Office prosecutes the most serious and complex cases of fraud in England, Wales and Northern Ireland. Investigations are conducted by teams of lawyers, accountants, police officers and other specialists. In Scotland the Crown Office Fraud Unit, which is part of the public prosecution service, directs the investigation and preparation for prosecution of serious and complex fraud cases.

Courts

England and Wales

Very serious offences such as murder, manslaughter, rape and robbery can only be tried on indictment in the Crown Court, where all contested trials are presided over by a judge sitting with a jury. Summary offences—the less serious offences and the vast majority of criminal cases—are tried by unpaid lay magistrates (see below) or, in a few areas, by a single paid stipendiary magistrate; both sit without a jury.

Offences in a third category—such as theft, the less serious cases of burglary and some assaults—are known as 'either-way' offences. They can be tried either by magistrates or by jury in the Crown Court. If magistrates are content to deal with the case, the accused has the right to choose trial by magistrates or trial by jury in the Crown Court.

All those charged with offences triable in the Crown Court must first appear before a magistrates' court, which decides whether to commit them to the Court for trial. Modifications to the existing committal procedures are due to be implemented in 1997. Under the modified system a magistrates' court will consider only documentary evidence and exhibits tendered by the prosecution, together with representations by both parties, when determining whether there is a case to answer. No witnesses are called to give evidence or be cross-examined. Existing procedures for transferring cases of serious or complex fraud or cases involving child evidence are not affected by the legislation.

The Government has been concerned that too many cases that could properly be tried in magistrates' courts go instead to the Crown Court. This causes delay in hearing cases, increased stress on victims and witnesses, and unnecessary additional expense for the criminal justice agencies. Under the Criminal Procedure and Investigations Act 1996 a defendant will be invited to indicate his or her plea before the magistrates decide whether they should hear the case or whether it should be heard in the Crown Court.

A magistrates' court, which is open to the public and the media, usually consists of three lay magistrates—known as Justices of the Peace—who are advised by a legally qualified clerk or a qualified assistant. There are about 30,000 lay magistrates serving some 400 courts. The few full-time, legally qualified stipendiary magistrates may sit alone and usually preside in courts where the workload is heavy.

Most cases involving people under 18 are heard in youth courts. These are specialist magistrates' courts which either sit apart from other courts or are held at a different time. Restrictions are placed on access by ordinary members of the public. Media reports must not identify a young person concerned in the proceedings, whether as defendant, victim or witness.

Where a young person under 18 is charged jointly with someone aged 18 or over, the case may be heard in an ordinary magistrates' court or the Crown Court. If the young person is found guilty, the court may transfer the case to a youth court for sentence.

An independent inspectorate monitors the administration of magistrates' courts in order to improve performance and spread good practice. It does not comment on the judicial decisions of magistrates or their clerks in particular cases.

The Crown Court sits at about 90 venues and is presided over by High Court judges, full-time circuit judges and part-time recorders. The kind of judge chosen to preside over a case depends on its complexity and seriousness. Crown Court organisation is based on six regional areas called circuits.

Charter for Court Users

A Courts Charter, setting out the standards of service in the High Court, Crown Court and county courts in England and Wales, came into operation in 1993. A new Charter for Court Users was launched in 1995, which increased the number of standards from 65 to 79 and tightened some of the existing ones. The new standards cover areas such as witness and juror care, and correspondence and complaints handling. The Charter does not cover the judiciary. Magistrates' courts are also developing their own charters, based on similar principles to the Courts Charter for the higher courts.

Scotland

The High Court of Justiciary tries the most serious crimes and has exclusive jurisdiction in cases involving murder, treason and rape. The sheriff court is concerned with relatively less serious offences and the district court with minor offences.

Criminal cases in Scotland are heard under solemn or summary procedure. In solemn procedure, an accused person's trial takes place before a judge sitting with a jury of 15 people. As in England and Wales, details of the alleged offence are set out in a document called an indictment. In summary procedure the judge sits without a jury.

All cases in the High Court and the more serious ones in sheriff courts are tried by a judge and jury. Summary procedure is used in the less serious cases in the sheriff courts, and in all cases in the district courts. District court judges are lay Justices of the Peace. In Glasgow there are also stipendiary magistrates, who are full-time lawyers with the same powers as a sheriff in summary procedure.

Children under 16 who have committed an offence are normally dealt with by children's hearings (see p. 26).

The levels of service which citizens are entitled to expect from the main criminal justice agencies are set out in the Justice Charter for Scotland.

Northern Ireland

Cases involving minor summary offences are heard by magistrates' courts presided over by a full-time, legally qualified resident magistrate. Young offenders under 17 are dealt with by a juvenile court consisting of the resident magistrate and two specially qualified lay members, at least one of whom must be a woman.

The Crown Court deals with criminal trials on indictment. It is served by High Court and county court judges. Contested cases are heard by a judge and jury, although people charged with terrorist-type offences are tried by a judge sitting alone because of the possibility of jurors being intimidated by terrorist organisations.

In non-jury Crown Court trials the onus remains on the prosecution to prove guilt beyond reasonable doubt and defendants have the right to be represented by a lawyer of their choice. The judge must set out in a written statement the reasons for convicting and there is an automatic right of appeal against conviction and sentence on points of fact as well as of law.

Trial

Criminal trials in Britain have two parties: the prosecution and the defence. The law presumes the innocence of an accused person until guilt has been proved by the prosecution. An accused person has the right to employ a legal adviser and may be granted legal aid from public funds (see p. 113). If remanded in custody, he or she may be visited by a legal adviser to ensure a properly prepared defence.

Pre-Trial Preparation

The Criminal Procedure and Investigations Act 1996 (mainly applicable in England and Wales but also to some extent in Northern Ireland) provides for reform of the law on prosecution and defence disclosure of evidence, and other measures to improve pre-trial procedures. At present the prosecution in Crown Court cases must disclose to the defence any material that may possibly be relevant to an issue in the case, unless the material is sensitive and a court rules that it may be withheld. In contrast, the accused generally need not disclose anything about his or her defence before the trial. Under the new legislation clear limits will be placed on what the police and prosecution disclose to the defence, and sensitive material will be protected more effectively. The defence will also be required to disclose before the trial the general nature of its case, and the matters on which it takes issue with the prosecution, with its reasons. Defence disclosure will be mandatory in the Crown Court, but voluntary in the magistrates' court. This part of the Act applies to Northern Ireland.

The legislation will also:

- create a statutory scheme for pre-trial hearings in the Crown Court in England and Wales, with the aim of ensuring that potentially difficult cases come to court as thoroughly prepared and as well presented as they can be; and
- give judges a new power to make a binding ruling on the admissibility of evidence or other point of law in any case before the start of a trial.

Other measures to improve pre-trial preparation in the Crown Court in England and Wales include a new scheme of plea and directions hearings. These short hearings provide an opportunity for judges to ensure that cases are properly prepared and that cases which are likely to be uncontested are dealt with quickly.

In Scotland, the prosecution in solemn cases must give the defence advance notice of the witnesses it intends to call and of the documents and other items on which it will rely. In summary cases this is usually done as a matter of practice, although there is no obligation on the Crown to do so. The Criminal Procedure (Scotland) Act 1995 strengthens the procedures for judicial examination of the accused person before trial, introducing an enhanced system of intermediate diets (sittings of the sheriff and district courts in advance of the trial) to establish the state of readiness of both the defence and the prosecution. Mandatory intermediate diets in summary cases have been in force in most Scottish courts since April 1996.

Trial Procedure

Criminal trials normally take place in open court and rules of evidence, which are concerned with the proof of facts, are rigorously applied. If evidence is improperly admitted, or excluded, a conviction can be quashed on appeal. In Scotland hearsay evidence may be admitted in particular circumstances.

During the trial the defendant has the right to hear and cross-examine prosecution witnesses. He or she can call his or her own witnesses who, if they will not attend voluntarily, may be legally compelled to do so. The defendant can also address the court in person or through a lawyer, the defence having the right to the last speech before the judge sums up.

The defendant cannot be questioned without consenting to be sworn as a witness in his or her own defence, although a court in England and Wales may draw inferences from a refusal to give evidence (see p. 92). Similar provision exists in Northern Ireland. When a defendant does testify, he or she may be cross-examined about character or other conduct only in exceptional circumstances. Generally the prosecution may not introduce such evidence.

In Scotland, the Criminal Procedure (Scotland) Act 1995 removes the prohibition on the prosecutor to comment on an accused person's failure to give evidence. Cross-examination about the character or other conduct of the accused may be made in certain circumstances.

Child Witnesses

Legislation in 1988 abolished the presumption in England and Wales that children were incompetent as witnesses. It also introduced the system which allows children to give their evidence at court by means of a closed–circuit television link. Building on that, the Criminal Justice Act 1991 extended the closed–circuit television provisions, forbade the cross-examination of a child directly by the accused, and provided for a video–recorded interview with a child victim or witness to be admissible in court as his or her main evidence. The Criminal Justice and Public Order Act 1994 further clarifies the law on child evidence in England and Wales, by requiring judges to admit the evidence of a child unless he or she is incapable of giving intelligible testimony. It is for the jury to decide what weight should be placed on a child's evidence. The provisions in the 1991 and 1994 Acts were replicated for Northern Ireland in legislation passed in 1995.

In Scotland live television links installed in a number of criminal courts enable children to give their evidence without entering the courtroom. A child's evidence may also be given from behind a screen in the courtroom. There is also provision for a child to give video–recorded evidence before or during the trial. The child who has given evidence in this manner is not subject to cross-examination on that evidence in court.

Fraud Proceedings

In complex fraud cases the judge may order a preparatory Crown Court hearing to be held. This takes place in open court but is subject to restrictions on press reporting. This provides an opportunity for the judge to determine questions on admissibility of evidence and any other questions of law relating to the case. The judge also has the power to order the prosecution and the defence to provide each other with certain statements and to prepare the case in such a way that it is easier to understand. Appeals may be made to the Court of Appeal regarding certain decisions of the judge in the preparatory hearings.

The Jury

In jury trials the judge decides questions of law, sums up the evidence for the jury, and discharges or sentences the accused. The jury is responsible for deciding questions of fact. In England, Wales and Northern Ireland the verdict may be 'guilty' or 'not guilty', the latter resulting in acquittal. If the jury cannot reach a unanimous decision the judge may allow a majority verdict provided that, in the normal jury of 12 people, there are no more than two dissenters.

In Scotland the jury's verdict may be 'guilty', 'not guilty' or 'not proven'; the accused is acquitted if either of the last two verdicts is given. The jury consists of 15 people and a verdict of 'guilty' can be reached only if at least eight members are in favour. As a general rule no one may be convicted without corroborated evidence from at least two sources.

If the jury acquits the defendant, the prosecution has no right of appeal and the defendant cannot be tried again for the same offence (although the provisions of the Criminal Procedure and Investigations Act 1996 will enable a retrial in England, Wales or Northern Ireland of a case which resulted in an acquittal if the acquittal had been tainted by a conviction for interference with, or intimidation of, jurors or witnesses).

A jury is independent of the judiciary. Any attempt to interfere with a jury is a criminal offence. Potential jurors are put on a panel before the start of the trial. In England and Wales the prosecution and the defence may challenge individual jurors on the panel, giving reasons for doing so. In Northern Ireland each defendant has the right to challenge up to 12 potential jurors without giving a reason. In Scotland, new legislation provides for improved procedures for the selection of juries, including the abolition of peremptory challenge.

People between the ages of 18 and 70 (65 in Scotland) whose names appear on the electoral register are, with certain exceptions, liable for jury service and their names are chosen at random. Ineligible people include judges and people who have within the previous ten years been members of the legal profession or the police, prison or probation services. People convicted of certain offences within the previous ten years cannot serve on a jury. Anyone who has received a prison sentence of five years or more is disqualified for life. People on bail are also ineligible to sit on juries.

Sentencing

If a person is convicted, the magistrate or judge (or their Scottish equivalent) decides on the most appropriate sentence, taking into account the facts of the offence, the circumstances of the offender, any previous convictions or sentences and any statutory limits on sentencing. The defence lawyer may make a speech in mitigation.

Courts in England and Wales must obtain a 'pre-sentence' report from the probation service on offenders under the age of 18 in cases involving an offence triable either way before passing a custodial or more complex community sentence. In most other circumstances, such reports are discretionary.

The Criminal Justice and Public Order Act 1994 provides for sentence discounts for those pleading guilty at an early stage in the court process in England and Wales.

Protecting the Public, a White Paper issued in April 1996, contains new sentencing proposals under which:

- offenders sentenced to custody would serve the full term ordered by the court, abolishing automatic early release and parole (see p. 104);
- automatic life sentences would be imposed on offenders convicted for a second time of a serious sexual or violent offence; and
- mandatory minimum prison sentences would be imposed on drug dealers and burglars for repeat offences.

In Scottish cases a court must obtain a social enquiry report before imposing a custodial sentence if the accused is under 21 or has not previously served a custodial sentence. A report is also required before making a probation or community service order (see p. 102), or in cases involving people subject to supervision.

The Criminal Procedure (Scotland) Act 1995 makes provision for the High Court to issue guidelines on sentencing to the lower courts, encouraging consistency in sentencing in similar cases. The legislation also enables courts to take into account, when deciding the appropriate sentence, the fact that an accused person pleaded guilty, and the timing and circumstances in which the plea was made.

Appeals

England and Wales

A person convicted by a magistrates' court may appeal to the Crown Court against the sentence if he or she has pleaded guilty. An appeal may be made against both conviction and sentence, or sentence alone, if a 'not guilty' plea has been made. The High Court hears appeals on points of law and procedure—by either prosecution or defence—in cases originally dealt with by magistrates. If convicted by the Crown Court, a defendant may seek leave to appeal to the Court of Appeal (Criminal Division) against both the conviction and the sentence imposed. The House of Lords is the final appeal court, but will only consider cases that involve a point of law of general public importance and where leave to appeal is granted.

The Attorney General (see p. 111) may seek a ruling of the Court of Appeal on a point of law which has been material in a case where a person is tried on indictment. The Court has power to refer the point to the House of Lords if necessary. The ruling will constitute a binding precedent, but an acquittal in the original case is not affected.

The Attorney General can apply for leave to refer to the Court of Appeal a sentence which, in his or her view, appears unduly lenient. This power covers offences triable on indictment and certain offences triable either way (where sentence has been passed in the Crown Court). Such triable 'either-way' offences are indecent assault, making threats to kill, and cruelty to, or neglect of, a child. The Attorney General's power also covers certain types of serious or complex fraud. The Court of Appeal may, if it decides to quash the original sentence, impose in its place any sentence which the original sentencing court had the power to impose.

The Criminal Appeal Act 1995 provides for the creation of a Criminal Cases Review Commission to operate in England, Wales and Northern Ireland. This body, independent of both Government and the courts, will examine possible miscarriages of justice in cases tried on indictment or summarily and decide whether to refer them to the courts on the grounds of sentence and conviction. It will direct and supervise investigations undertaken on its behalf and approve the appointment of investigating officers. Referral of a case will require some new argument or evidence not previously raised at the trial or on appeal.

The final decision on any case referred rests with the respective Courts of Appeal in England and Wales and Northern Ireland (if the case was tried originally on indictment) or with the Crown Court following a referral in a summary case. The power of the Home Secretary (and the Secretary of State in Northern Ireland) to investigate and refer possible miscarriages of justice to the Court of Appeal is being relinquished.

The legislation also clarifies the grounds for allowing and dismissing an appeal: the Court of Appeal will allow any appeal where it considers the conviction unsafe and will dismiss it in any other case.

Scotland

All appeal cases are dealt with by the High Court of Justiciary. In both solemn and summary procedure, a convicted person may appeal against conviction, or sentence, or both. The Court may authorise a retrial if it sets aside a conviction. There is no further appeal to the House of Lords. In summary proceedings the prosecutor may appeal on a point of law against acquittal or sentence. The Lord Advocate may seek the opinion of the High Court on a point of law in a case where a person tried on indictment is acquitted. The

acquittal in the original case is not affected. The Crown has a right of appeal against lenient sentences in both solemn and summary procedure.

The Criminal Procedure (Scotland) Act 1995 introduces a requirement for leave to appeal. This involves a single judge assessing whether there are arguable grounds for an appeal. The legislation also reduces the number of High Court judges required to consider appeals against sentence only from three to two.

A person convicted on indictment may petition the Secretary of State to refer the case to the High Court on the ground that a miscarriage of justice has occurred. If the case is referred, then it will be dealt with as though it were a normal appeal.

Northern Ireland

In Northern Ireland, appeals from magistrates' courts against conviction or sentence are heard by the county court. An appeal on a point of law alone can be heard by the Northern Ireland Court of Appeal, which also hears appeals from the Crown Court against conviction and/or sentence. Procedures for a further appeal to the House of Lords are similar to those in England and Wales.

A person convicted of a terrorist offence in a non-jury court has an automatic right of appeal against conviction and/or sentence.

The new Criminal Cases Review Commission (see above) will operate in Northern Ireland as well as in England and Wales.

Coroners' Courts

In England and Wales the coroner must hold an inquest if the deceased died a violent or unnatural death, a sudden death where the cause is unknown, or in prison or in other specified circumstances. In Northern Ireland in such circumstances the coroner investigates the matter to decide whether an inquest is necessary. The coroner's court establishes how, when and where the deceased died. A coroner may sit alone or, in certain circumstances, with a jury.

In Scotland the local procurator fiscal

inquires privately into all sudden and suspicious deaths and may report the findings to the Crown Office. When appropriate a fatal accident inquiry may be held before the sheriff; this is mandatory in cases of death resulting from industrial accidents and of deaths in custody.

TREATMENT OF OFFENDERS

The Government believes that prison is the right response to the most serious, dangerous and persistent offenders. It also considers that there should be effective and demanding punishment within the community to deal with offenders for whom a prison sentence is not appropriate. Fines continue to represent an appropriate penalty for other less serious offences.

Legislation sets the maximum penalties for offences, the sentence being a matter for the courts subject to these maximums (but see p. 99 for Government proposals on mandatory sentences for persistent offenders). The Court of Appeal issues guidance on sentencing to the lower courts when points of principle have arisen on individual appeal cases.

In Scotland, where many offences are not created by statute, the penalty for offences at common law ranges from absolute discharge to life imprisonment.

Non-custodial Treatment

Non-custodial sentences include:

- fines;
- compensation orders;
- probation orders;
- supervision orders;
- community service orders;
- a combination order, which includes elements of probation and community service; and
- a supervised attendance order (Scotland only).

Fines

About 80 per cent of offenders are punished with a fine. There is no limit to the fine which the Crown Court (and High Court of Justiciary and the sheriff court in Scotland under solemn procedure) may impose on indictment. The maximum fine that can be imposed by a magistrates' court in England and Wales (and a sheriff court in Scotland under summary procedure) is £5,000. When fixing the amount of a fine, courts are required to reflect the seriousness of the offence and to take into account the financial circumstances of the offender.

Probation

The locally organised probation service in England and Wales supervises offenders in the community under direct court orders and after release from custody. It also provides offenders in custody with help and advice.

A court probation order requires the offender to maintain regular contact with the probation officer, who is expected to supervise the offender and to confront him or her with the consequences of his or her offence. Special conditions attached to the order may require the offender to attend a day centre for up to 60 days. Probation is intended as a punishment, although the time spent by offenders under supervision in the community offers an opportunity for constructive work to reduce the likelihood of reoffending.

A probation order can last from six months to three years; if the offender fails to comply with any of the requirements of the order, he or she can be brought before the court again. A probation order can be combined with a community service order.

In England and Wales the probation service also administers supervision orders, and the community service scheme, and supervises those released from prison on parole.

The statutory Probation Inspectorate monitors the work of the voluntary and private sectors with the probation service, in addition to its inspection and advisory duties.

In Scotland local authority social work departments supervise offenders on probation and community service, and offenders who are subject to supervision when released from custody.

In Northern Ireland the service is administered by the government-funded

Probation Board, whose membership is representative of the community.

Community Service

In England and Wales offenders aged 16 or over convicted of imprisonable offences may, with their consent, be given community service orders. The court may order between 40 and 240 hours' unpaid service to be completed within 12 months. Examples of work done include decorating the houses of elderly or disabled people and building adventure playgrounds. In Scotland the minimum number of hours for which a community service order can be made has been increased from 40 to 80 and the maximum, in higher courts, from 240 to 300.

In England and Wales the court may make an order combining community service and probation. In Scotland a probation order may include a condition of unpaid work.

Curfew Order

The Criminal Justice and Public Order Act 1994 provides for the use of curfew orders with electronic monitoring in selected areas in England and Wales. Courts in the trial areas can require offenders to remain at home for periods of between two and 12 hours a day. The order can be combined with probation or community service. A decision on whether to extend the order to courts throughout England and Wales will be taken in the light of extended trials.

Supervised Attendance Order

In Scotland supervised attendance order schemes have been piloted in a number of areas. They provide an alternative to imprisonment for fine default, and incorporate aspects of work and training. Their use is being extended to form an alternative in the first instance to fines for young offenders.

Compensation

The courts may order an offender to pay compensation for personal injury, loss or damage resulting from an offence. In England and Wales courts must give reasons for not awarding compensation to a victim. Compensation takes precedence over fines.

Other Measures

A court in England and Wales may discharge a person either absolutely or conditionally if it believes that it is not necessary to inflict punishment. If conditionally discharged, the offender remains liable to punishment for the offence if convicted of another offence within a period specified by the court (not more than three years).

Courts may also require an offender to keep the peace and/or be of good behaviour. If this requirement is not complied with, the offender is liable to forfeit a sum of money. Similar powers are available to courts in Northern Ireland.

Courts have the power to defer sentence, so as to enable the court, in subsequent dealings with the offender, to have regard to his or her conduct or any changes in circumstances.

The police have discretion whether to charge an offender or formally to caution him or her. Cautioning is a form of warning and no court action is taken. New guidelines designed to stop the use of cautions for serious offences and to cut the number of repeated cautions were published by the Government in 1994. Cautioning is not available in Scotland.

Custody

England and Wales

A custodial sentence is the most severe penalty available to the courts. It is imposed where the offence is so serious that only such a sentence would be appropriate, or where there is a need to protect the public from a sexual or violent offender. A court must explain to the offender why it is passing a custodial sentence. The length of the sentence must reflect the seriousness of the offence.

A magistrates' court cannot impose a term of more than six months' imprisonment for an individual offence tried summarily. It can impose consecutive sentences for 'either-way' offences, subject to an overall maximum of 12 months' imprisonment. If an offence carries a higher maximum penalty, the court may commit the offender for sentence at the Crown Court. The Crown Court may impose a custodial sentence for any term up to life, depending on the seriousness of the offence and the maximum penalty available.

If a court decides that an offence is sufficiently serious to justify an immediate custodial sentence of not more than two years, the sentence may be suspended for a period of at least one year and not more than two years if exceptional circumstances justify the suspension. If the offender commits another imprisonable offence during the period of suspension, the court may order the suspended sentence to be served in addition to any punishment imposed for the second offence. When passing a suspended sentence, the court must consider whether it would also be appropriate to impose a fine or make a compensation order. The court may also order the offender to be supervised by a probation officer if the suspended sentence is for more than six months.

There is a mandatory sentence of life imprisonment for murder throughout Britain. Life imprisonment is the maximum penalty for a number of serious offences such as robbery, rape, arson and manslaughter.

Northern Ireland

In Northern Ireland the position is generally the same as for England and Wales. A magistrates' court, however, cannot commit an offender for sentencing at the Crown Court if it has tried the case.

Scotland

In Scottish trials on indictment the High Court of Justiciary may impose a sentence of imprisonment for any term up to life, and the sheriff court any term up to three years. The sheriff court may send any person to the High Court for sentence if the court considers its powers are insufficient. In summary cases the sheriff or stipendiary magistrate may normally impose up to three months' imprisonment or six months' for some repeated offences. The district court can impose a maximum term of imprisonment of 60 days.

Prisons

The Prison Service in England and Wales, the Scottish Prison Service and the Northern Ireland Prison Service are all executive agencies (see p. 73). Government ministers remain accountable for policy but the Chief Executives are responsible for the delivery of services.

Prisoners are housed in accommodation ranging from open prisons to high security establishments. In England, Wales and Scotland sentenced prisoners are classified into different risk-level groups for security purposes. Women prisoners are held in separate prisons or in separate accommodation in mixed prisons. There are no open prisons in Northern Ireland, where the majority of offenders are serving sentences for terrorist offences. People awaiting trial in custody have certain rights and privileges not granted to convicted prisoners. Where possible, they are separated from prisoners who have been convicted and sentenced.

There are 134 prison establishments in England and Wales and 22 in Scotland. Thirty eight establishments in England and Wales hold young offenders (22 of which are dedicated to young offenders only) and five cater for them in Scotland. Northern Ireland has four prisons and one young offenders' centre. Four of these establishments have been built since 1972.

Although many prisons were built in the 19th century, a major refurbishment and prison-building programme in England and Wales over recent years has led to improvements in prison conditions. All prisoners in England and Wales now have access to sanitation 24 hours a day, as do an increasing proportion (currently two-thirds) in Scotland.

The average prison population in 1995 was 51,000 in England and Wales, 5,626 in Scotland and 1,762 in Northern Ireland.

Private Sector Involvement

Under the Criminal Justice Act 1991, the Home Secretary has the power to contract out the management of prisons in England and Wales to the private sector, as well as escort and guarding functions. All escort services will be provided by the private sector by 1997, leaving police and prison officers free to concentrate on their own core duties.

Four prisons (which remain part of the Prison Service) are now managed by private contractors: The Wolds in Humberside, which opened in 1992; Blakenhurst prison in Worcestershire, which opened in 1993; and Doncaster prison and Buckley Hall prison in Rochdale, which opened in 1994. The first three prisons to be designed, constructed, managed and financed under the Private Finance Initiative (PFI—see p. 162) are expected to be in full operation in 1998–99 in Merseyside, Nottinghamshire and South Wales.

The Prison Service is also continuing to contract out services both nationally and locally, including education services in prison and catering.

In Scotland education services in prisons are contracted out, and a new prison near Kilmarnock is to be built and managed under the PFI.

Early Release of Prisoners

The remission and parole systems in England and Wales were reformed by the Criminal Justice Act 1991, with revised arrangements for the early release of prisoners and for their supervision and liabilities after release. The Parole Board continues to advise the Home Secretary on the early release or recall of long-term prisoners.

At present prisoners sentenced to less than four years are released once they have served half of their sentence. Long-term prisoners (those sentenced to four years or more) become eligible to be considered for early release once they have served half of their sentence; if not found suitable for parole they are released automatically at the two-thirds point. The Parole Board has the final decision on the early release of prisoners sentenced to four years or more, but less than seven years, after 1 October 1992 (when the 1991 Act came into effect). In other cases the Board makes a recommendation to the Home Secretary about a prisoner's suitability for parole. All prisoners sentenced to a year or

more are released on licence to be supervised until the three-quarters point of the sentence. If ordered by the sentencing court, sex offenders may be supervised to the end of the sentence. If convicted of another offence punishable with imprisonment and committed before the end of the original sentence, a released prisoner may be required by the court to serve all or part of the original sentence outstanding at the time the fresh offence was committed.

In Scotland similar arrangements apply except that the Parole Board has the power to release prisoners from halfway through their sentence if they are serving between four and ten years. Those serving ten years or more may only be released with the consent of the Secretary of State. All prisoners sentenced to four years or more are supervised from release until the end of their sentence.

In Northern Ireland prisoners serving a sentence of more than five days are eligible for remission of half their sentence. Remission for those convicted of terrorist offences and serving sentences of five years or more is one-third. However, under legislation in force since November 1995, prisoners have been eligible for release at the halfway point in their sentence but remain under licence (until the two-thirds point) and may be subject to recall during that period. If convicted of another terrorist offence before the expiry of the original sentence the prisoner must complete that sentence before serving any term for the second offence.

In *Protecting the Public* (see p. 99), the Government proposed major changes to the arrangements for the early release of prisoners in England and Wales. Offenders sentenced to custody would serve the full term ordered by the court, and automatic early release and parole would be abolished. Instead, offenders who co-operated with the prison regime and behaved well would be able to earn up to 20 per cent off their sentence. On release, offenders sentenced to 12 months or more would be supervised by the probation service for a period equivalent to 15 per cent of their original prison sentence.

Similar changes have been proposed in Scotland.

Life Sentence Prisoners

People serving life sentences for the murder of police or prison officers, terrorist murders, murder by firearms in the course of robbery and the sexual or sadistic murder of children are normally detained for at least 20 years.

The release on licence of prisoners serving mandatory life sentences for murder may only be authorised by the Home Secretary on the recommendation of the Parole Board and after consultation with the judiciary. A similar policy applies in Scotland.

The Home Secretary is required to release prisoners serving life sentences for offences other than murder after an initial period set by the trial judge if so directed by the Parole Board. The Board has to be satisfied that the protection of the public does not require their further confinement. These provisions conform with the requirements of the European Convention on Human Rights. Similar procedures apply in Scotland.

On release, life sentence prisoners remain on licence for the rest of their lives and are subject to recall if their behaviour suggests that they might again be a danger to the public.

In Northern Ireland the Secretary of State reviews life sentence cases on the recommendation of an internal review body.

Repatriation

Sentenced prisoners who are nationals of countries which have ratified the Council of Europe Convention on the Transfer of Sentenced Persons, or similar international arrangements, may apply to be returned to their own country to serve the rest of their sentence there.

Independent Oversight of the Prison System

Every prison establishment and young offender institution in England and Wales has a board of visitors (a visiting committee in Scotland). They are volunteers drawn from the local community and appointed by the Secretary of State. Board members, who are independent of the prison and the Prison Service, visit the prison frequently, hear any complaints by prisoners and report as necessary to the Secretary of State.

Independent Prisons Inspectorates report to the respective Secretaries of State on the treatment of prisoners and prison conditions. Each establishment is visited about every three years. The Inspectorates submit annual reports to Parliament.

In England and Wales prisoners who fail to get satisfaction from the Prison Service's internal request and complaints system may complain to the Prisons Ombudsman. The Ombudsman is independent of the Prison Service and investigates complaints from individual prisoners concerning decisions relating to them which have been taken by Prison Service staff, or other people working in prisons.

In Scotland, prisoners who exhaust the internal grievance procedure may make application to the Scottish Prisons Complaints Commission, which is independent of the Scottish Prison Service.

Prison Industries

Prison industries aim to give inmates work experience which will assist them when released and to secure a return which will reduce the cost of the prison system. The main industries are clothing and textile manufacture, engineering, woodwork, laundering, farming and horticulture. A few prisoners are employed outside prison, some in community service projects.

Prison Education

Full-time education of 15 hours a week is compulsory for young offenders below school leaving age. For older offenders it is voluntary. Many prisoners study for public examinations, including those of the Open University. Competitive tendering for the provision of education services in prisons in England, Wales and Scotland has taken place and contracts have been awarded, many to further and higher education establishments. There are also some facilities available for prisoners to gain vocational qualifications.

Physical education is voluntary for adult offenders but compulsory for young offenders. Practically all prisons have physical education facilities, some of which are purpose-built.

Opportunities are given for inmates to obtain sporting proficiency awards. Inmates also compete against teams in the local community.

Health Care

The Health Care Service for Prisoners in England and Wales is responsible for the physical and mental health of all those in custody. A Health Advisory Committee provides independent medical advice to government ministers, the Prison Service Chief Executive and the Director of Health Care.

A greater emphasis is being placed on 'buying in' health care services either from the National Health Service (NHS—see p. 397) or from the independent sector.

The Prison Service is committed to transferring mentally disordered offenders to the care and treatment of the NHS and social services where possible. The most dangerous offenders in this category are confined in the special hospitals of Ashworth, Rampton and Broadmoor.

In Scotland general medical services are provided mainly by visiting general practitioners (GPs). Psychiatric and psychological services are bought in from local health boards responsible for the NHS.

Privileges and Discipline

Prisoners may write and receive letters and be visited by relatives and friends, and those in all establishments in England, Wales and Scotland may make telephone calls. Privileges include a personal radio; books, periodicals and newspapers; watching television; and the opportunity to buy goods from the prison shop with money earned in prison. Depending on the facilities available, prisoners may be granted the further privileges of dining and recreation with other inmates.

To maintain discipline, control and order the Prison Service in England and Wales is:

- developing incentive-based regimes, so that prisoners must earn privileges through responsible behaviour and will lose them for misbehaviour;
- providing special units with facilities for dealing with violent or disruptive prisoners; and

- implementing a comprehensive strategy on drug misuse, including mandatory drug testing.

Offences against prison discipline are dealt with by prison governors who act as adjudicators.

Religion

Anglican, Church of Scotland, Roman Catholic and Methodist chaplains provide opportunities for worship and spiritual counselling, supported by visiting ministers of other denominations and faiths as required.

Preparation for Release

The Prison Services in England and Wales and in Scotland have a duty to prepare prisoners for release. Planning for safe release starts at the beginning of an offender's sentence and ties in with all the training, education and work experience provided. It is designed to help prisoners reintegrate into society and cope with life without reoffending. Risk assessment and confronting offending behaviour are essential elements of this process. Sentence planning is being extended progressively to all prisoners serving substantial sentences, in conjunction with extended arrangements for aftercare.

Prisoners may be released on temporary licence for short periods but, under a new system introduced in England and Wales in April 1995, they are subject to a rigorous risk assessment and are released only for precisely defined and specific activities which cannot be provided in Prison Service establishments. Similar arrangements are in place in Scotland.

The Pre-Release Employment Scheme in England and Wales and the Training for Freedom Scheme in Scotland enable selected long-term prisoners to spend some time before release in certain hostels attached to prisons in order to help them readapt to society. Hostellers work in paid employment in the community and return to the hostel each evening. Periods of temporary release on resettlement licence enable hostellers to renew ties with their families.

In Northern Ireland prisoners serving fixed sentences may have short periods of pre-release home leave. Prisoners who have served 11 years or more are also eligible for leave at Christmas and a seven-day allowance to be taken during the year. Life sentence prisoners are given a nine-month pre-release programme which includes employment outside the prison.

Aftercare

Professional support is given to offenders after release. All young offenders and all adult offenders in England and Wales sentenced to 12 months' imprisonment and over are supervised on release by the probation service—or, in the case of certain young offenders, by local authority social services departments. In Scotland this support is provided by local authority social work services, although not all adult offenders are subject to supervision on release. Offenders sentenced to less than 12 months are not subject to statutory supervision on release, but probation service supervision is available on a voluntary basis if the offender requests it.

Young Offenders

England and Wales

Criminal proceedings cannot be brought against children below the age of 10. Offenders between the ages of 10 and 18 fall within the jurisdiction of youth courts. Sixteen- and 17-year-olds may be given the same probation, curfew and community service orders as older offenders; also available to the court are the same supervision orders or attendance centre orders as are given to younger offenders.

Under a supervision order—which may remain in force for not more than three years—a child (10–13 years old) or young person (14–17 years old) normally lives at home under the supervision of a social worker or a probation officer. The order may require the offender to live in local authority accommodation and/or participate in specified activities at specified times.

Anyone under 21 years of age found guilty of an offence for which an adult may be imprisoned can be ordered to go to an attendance centre, as can an offender who

refuses to comply with another order (for example, default in paying a fine or breach of a probation order). The maximum number of hours of attendance is 36 (or 24 if the offender is aged under 16) spread over a period; the minimum is 12 hours. The order aims to encourage offenders to make more constructive use of their leisure time.

Crown Court powers to order long periods of detention for young offenders who commit serious crimes are extended under the provisions of the Criminal Justice and Public Order Act 1994 to include 10- to 13-year-olds. The courts may detain 10- to 13-year-olds convicted of an offence for which an adult can be jailed for 14 years or more (including rape, arson, domestic burglary and robbery). Previously they could be given long terms of detention only if they had been convicted of murder or manslaughter. Courts may also detain any 10- to 15-year-old convicted of indecent assault on a woman, where previously only 16- and 17-year-olds could be detained for this offence. Any offender aged 14 or over who is convicted of causing death by dangerous or drunken driving may also be detained. Detention may be in a local authority secure residential unit, a centre managed by the Youth Treatment Service or a young offender institution.

The basic custodial sentence for those aged 15 to 21 is detention in a young offender institution. Alternatives include fines and compensation, attendance centre orders and community service orders.

The Criminal Justice and Public Order Act 1994 extends the powers given to the courts in the area of parental responsibility. Under the legislation courts can order parents to ensure their children comply with community sentences. In every case in which an offender aged between 10 and 15 years receives a community sentence, the court is under a duty to consider such an order. Courts have a power, as opposed to a duty, in the case of 16- and 17-year-olds. Courts will also be empowered to impose a secure training order on persistent offenders aged between 12 and 14. The order means a period of detention in a secure training centre followed by a period of supervision; it will be available for young offenders who have committed three or more imprisonable offences and who have failed to respond to punishment in the community. (The order will be implemented once the new secure training centres are available.) A further provision doubles the maximum sentence for 15- to 17-year-olds in a young offender institution from one to two years.

In September 1995 the Government announced plans for a tough, disciplined and demanding new regime for young offenders, involving an intensive daily schedule of training, education, work and other physical activity, and designed to break the cycle of reoffending. The initiative is being introduced on a pilot basis in two young offender institutions from mid-1996.

Scotland

Criminal proceedings may be brought against any child aged eight years or over, but the instructions of the Lord Advocate are necessary before anyone under 16 years of age is prosecuted.

Most children under 16 who have committed an offence or are considered to be in need of care and protection may be brought before a children's panel. The panel, consisting of three lay people, determines in an informal setting whether compulsory measures of care are required and, if so, the form they should take. An official known as the reporter decides whether a child should come before a hearing. If the grounds for referral are not accepted by the child or parent, the case goes to the sheriff for proof. If he or she finds the grounds established, the sheriff remits the case to the reporter to arrange a hearing. The sheriff also decides appeals against a hearing's decision.

Young people aged between 16 and 21 serve custodial sentences in a young offender institution. Remission of part of the sentence for good behaviour, release on parole and supervision on release are available.

Northern Ireland

Those aged between 10 and 16 who are charged with a criminal offence are normally brought before a juvenile court. If found guilty of an offence punishable in the case of an adult by imprisonment, the court may order the offender to be placed in care, under supervision or on probation. The offender may also be required to attend a day attendance centre, be sent to a training school or committed to residence in a remand home. Non-custodial options are the same as in England and Wales.

Offenders aged between 16 and 24 who receive custodial sentences of less than four years detention serve them in a young offenders' centre.

Civil Justice

The Civil Law

The civil law of England, Wales and Northern Ireland covers business related to the family, property, contracts, and torts (non-contractual wrongful acts suffered by one person at the hands of another). It also includes constitutional, administrative, industrial, maritime and ecclesiastical law. Scottish civil law has its own, broadly similar, branches.

CIVIL COURTS

England and Wales

Civil cases are heard in county courts and the High Court. Magistrates' courts have a concurrent jurisdiction with county courts and the High Court in cases relating to children.

The jurisdiction of the 250 county courts covers:

- actions founded upon contract and tort;
- trust and mortgage cases;
- actions for the recovery of land;
- cases involving disputes between landlords and tenants;
- complaints about race and sex discrimination;
- admiralty cases (maritime questions and offences) and patent cases; and
- divorce cases and other family matters.

Specialised work is concentrated in certain designated courts. In some types of case, for example admiralty cases, a county court is restricted to an upper financial limit.

For small claims (up to the value of £3,000), there are special arbitration facilities and simplified procedures. Special care centres and family hearing centres deal with contested family matters involving children.

The High Court, which is divided into three divisions, deals with the more complicated civil cases. Its jurisdiction covers mainly civil and some criminal cases; it also deals with appeals from tribunals (see p. 111) and from magistrates' courts in both civil and criminal matters. The three divisions are:

- the Family Division, which is concerned with family law, including adoption and divorce;
- the Chancery Division, which deals with corporate and personal insolvency; disputes in the running of companies, between landlords and tenants and in intellectual property matters; and the interpretation of trusts and contested wills; and
- the Queen's Bench Division, which has a wide and varied jurisdiction, including contract and tort cases. It also deals with applications for judicial review. Maritime law and commercial law are the responsibility of the Division's admiralty and commercial courts.

In the event of overlapping jurisdiction between the High Court and the county courts, cases of exceptional importance, complexity or financial substance are reserved or transferred for trial in the High Court.

Appeals

Appeals in family cases which have been heard by magistrates' courts go to the Family Division of the High Court. Appeals from the High Court and county courts are heard in the Court of Appeal (Civil Division), and may go on to the House of Lords (the final national court of appeal in civil and criminal cases).

The Law Lords deal with cases submitted to the House of Lords. They are professional judges who have been given life peerages (see p. 53). A group of five judges usually deals with cases. The Lord Chancellor is President of the House in its judicial capacity.

Scotland

The civil courts in Scotland are the Court of Session and the sheriff court, which have the same jurisdiction over most civil litigation. However, cases with a value of less than £1,500 are dealt with only by the sheriff court. Appeals from the sheriff court may be made to the sheriff principal or directly to the Court of Session.

The Court of Session sits in Edinburgh, and in general has jurisdiction to deal with all kinds of action. It is divided into the Outer House (a court of first instance) and the Inner House (mainly an appeal court). Appeals to the Inner House may be made from the Outer House and from the sheriff court. From the Inner House an appeal may go to the House of Lords.

The Scottish Land Court deals exclusively with matters concerning agriculture. Its chairman has the status and tenure of a judge of the Court of Session and its other members are lay specialists.

Northern Ireland

Civil cases up to a limited and specified monetary value are dealt with in county courts. The magistrates' court in Northern Ireland also deals with certain limited classes of civil case. The superior civil law court is the High Court of Justice, from which an appeal may be made to the Court of Appeal. The House of Lords is the final civil appeal court. Appeals from county courts are dealt with by the High Court or the Court of Appeal.

Civil Proceedings

England and Wales

Civil proceedings are started by the aggrieved person. Actions in the High Court are usually begun by a writ served on the defendant by the plaintiff, stating the nature of the claim. Before the case is tried, documents (pleadings) setting out the scope of the dispute are filed with the court; the pleadings are also served on the parties to the case. County court proceedings are initiated by a summons, usually served on the defendant by the court. Child care cases are initiated by an application in the magistrates' courts.

The High Court and the county courts can order pre-trial exchange of witness statements, and may impose penalties in costs on parties who unreasonably refuse to admit facts or to disclose documents before trial.

Civil proceedings, as a private matter, can usually be abandoned or ended by settlement between the parties at any time. Actions brought to court are usually tried without a jury, except in defamation, false imprisonment or malicious prosecution cases or where fraud is alleged, when either party may apply for trial by jury. The jury decides questions of fact and determines the damages to be paid to the injured party; majority verdicts may be accepted. The Court of Appeal can increase or reduce damages awarded by a jury if it considers them inadequate or excessive.

A decree of divorce must be pronounced in open court, but a procedure for most undefended cases dispenses with the need to give evidence in court and permits written evidence to be considered by the county court district judge.

In civil cases heard by a magistrates' court, the court issues a summons to the defendant setting out details of the complaint and the date on which it will be heard. Parties and witnesses give their evidence at the court hearing. Family proceedings are normally heard by not more than three lay justices, including both men and women. Members of the public are not allowed to be present. The court may make orders concerning residence, contact and supervision of children, and in some cases maintenance payments for spouses and children.

Most judgments are for sums of money and may be enforced, in cases of non-payment, by seizure of the debtor's goods or by a court order requiring an employer to make periodic payments to the court by deduction from the debtor's earnings. Other court remedies may include an injunction restraining someone from performing an unlawful act. Refusal to obey a court order may result in a fine or imprisonment for contempt of court.

Normally the court orders the costs of an action to be paid by the party losing it, but, in the case of family law maintenance proceedings, a magistrates' court can order either party to pay the whole or part of the other's costs.

Reform Proposals

The final report of a two-year inquiry into access to civil justice in England and Wales (the Woolf Report—see Further Reading) was published in July 1996. The report proposes a new system of case management where the courts would take greater responsibility for the progress of litigation. Its recommendations include, among other things, detailed proposals for:

- a new fast track procedure, with fixed legal costs, for all personal injury cases up to £10,000 and other cases between £3,000 and £10,000;

- the use of pre-action protocols to encourage a more co-operative approach to the resolution of disputes and promote fair settlements, avoiding litigation wherever possible; and

- increased access to justice in several special areas of litigation, including medical negligence, housing, multi-party actions and judicial review.

The report is accompanied by a draft of new Civil Proceedings Rules, which would harmonise and simplify procedures for all High Court and county court cases and replace the two separate rule books for the Supreme Court and the county courts.

Scotland

Proceedings in the Court of Session or ordinary actions in the sheriff court are initiated by serving the defender with a summons or, in sheriff court cases, an initial writ. A defender who intends to contest the action must inform the court; if he or she fails to do so, the court normally grants a decree in absence in favour of the pursuer. Where a case is contested, both parties must prepare written pleadings. Time is allowed for either party to adjust their pleadings in the light of what the other has said. At the end of this period a hearing will normally be arranged.

In cases involving sums between £750 and £1,500 in the sheriff court, a statement of claim is incorporated in the initial writ. The procedure is designed to enable most actions to be settled without the parties having to appear in court. Normally they, or their representatives, need appear only when an action is defended.

Tribunals

Tribunals exercise judicial functions separate from the courts and are intended to be more accessible, less formal and less expensive. They are normally set up under statutory powers, which also govern their constitution, functions and procedure. Tribunals often consist of lay people, but they are generally chaired by a legally qualified person.

Some tribunals settle disputes between private citizens. Industrial tribunals, for example, have a major role in employment disputes. Others, such as those concerned with social security, resolve claims by private citizens against public authorities. A further group, including tax tribunals, decide disputed claims by public authorities against private citizens. Tribunals usually consist of an uneven number of people so that a majority decision can be reached.

In the case of some tribunals a two-tier system operates, with an initial right of appeal to a lower tribunal and a further right of appeal, usually on a point of law, to a higher one, and in some cases to the Court of Appeal. Appeals from single-tier tribunals can usually be made only on a point of law to the High Court in England and Wales, to the Court of Session in Scotland, and to the Court of Appeal in Northern Ireland.

The independent Council on Tribunals exercises general supervision over many tribunals. A Scottish Committee of the Council exercises the same function in Scotland.

Administration of the Law

GOVERNMENT RESPONSIBILITIES

England and Wales

The Lord Chancellor is the head of the judiciary and a senior Cabinet Minister. His administrative responsibility for the Supreme Court (comprising the Court of Appeal, High Court and Crown Court) and the county courts in England and Wales is exercised through the Court Service. He also has ministerial responsibility for the locally administered magistrates' courts. He advises the Crown on the appointment of most members of the higher judiciary, and he appoints most magistrates. He is also responsible for promoting general reforms of the civil law and for the legal aid schemes.

The Home Secretary has overall responsibility for criminal law, the police service, the prison system, the probation and after-care service, and for advising the Queen on the exercise of the royal prerogative of mercy.

The Attorney General and the Solicitor General are the Government's principal legal advisers and represent the Crown in appropriate domestic and international cases. They are elected members of the House of Commons and hold ministerial posts. The Attorney General is also Attorney General for Northern Ireland. As well as exercising various civil law functions, the Attorney General has final responsibility for enforcing the criminal law. The Solicitor General is the Attorney's deputy. As head of the Crown Prosecution Service, the Director of Public Prosecutions is subject to superintendence by the Attorney General, as are the Director of the Serious Fraud Office and the Director of Public Prosecutions for Northern Ireland.

Scotland

The Secretary of State for Scotland is responsible for Scottish criminal law, crime prevention, the police, the penal system and legal aid. He or she is advised on parole matters by the Parole Board for Scotland, and is also responsible for substantive civil law.

The Secretary of State recommends the appointment of all judges other than the most senior ones, appoints the staff of the High Court of Justiciary and the Court of Session, and is responsible for the administration and staffing of the sheriff courts.

The Lord Advocate and the Solicitor General for Scotland, both government ministers, are the chief legal advisers to the Government on Scottish questions and the principal representatives of the Crown for the purposes of prosecutions and other litigation in Scotland. The Lord Advocate has ministerial responsibility for the law of evidence (civil and criminal) and for jurisdiction and procedures of the civil courts in Scotland.

Northern Ireland

Court administration is the responsibility of the Lord Chancellor, while the Northern Ireland Office, under the Secretary of State, deals with policy and legislation concerning criminal law, the police and the penal system. The Lord Chancellor has general responsibility for legal aid, advice and assistance.

JUDGES AND LAWYERS

Judges are not subject to ministerial direction or control. They are normally appointed from practising barristers (advocates in Scotland), or solicitors (see below). Lay magistrates in England and Wales and Scottish district court justices are trained in order to give them sufficient knowledge of the law, including the rules of evidence, and of the nature and purpose of sentencing.

In Northern Ireland members of a lay panel who serve in juvenile courts undertake training courses; resident magistrates are drawn from practising solicitors or barristers.

The Legal Profession

The legal profession is divided into two branches: barristers (advocates in Scotland) and solicitors. Barristers and advocates advise on legal problems submitted through solicitors or other recognised professional bodies and present cases in all courts. Solicitors undertake legal business for individual and corporate clients; they can also, after appropriate training and accreditation, present cases in all courts.

Although people are free to conduct their own cases, most people prefer to be legally represented, especially in more serious cases.

The Legal Services Ombudsman for England and Wales conducts investigations into the way professional bodies handle complaints against barristers, solicitors and licensed conveyancers. There is a separate Ombudsman for Scotland.

LEGAL AID

A person who needs legal advice, assistance or representation may be able to get help with legal costs from the legal aid scheme. People who qualify for help may have all their legal costs paid for, or may be asked to contribute towards them, depending on their means.

Legal Advice and Assistance

Legal advice is available under the Legal Advice and Assistance ('Green Form') Scheme in England and Wales. People whose income and capital are within certain limits are entitled to free advice from a solicitor on most legal matters. The scheme provides for up to three hours' work for matrimonial cases where a petition is drafted and two hours for other work. Similar schemes operate in Northern Ireland and Scotland.

Legal Aid in Civil Proceedings

Civil legal aid may be available for most civil proceedings to those who satisfy the financial eligibility conditions. Applicants for legal aid must also show that they have reasonable grounds for taking, defending or being a party to proceedings. Legal aid may be refused if it is considered unreasonable that an applicant should receive it in the particular circumstances. In England and Wales payments to lawyers are made through the Legal Aid Fund, administered by the Legal Aid Board. Scotland has a separate Legal Aid Fund, administered by the Scottish Legal Aid Board. In Northern Ireland legal aid is administered by the Law Society for Northern Ireland.

In certain limited circumstances the successful unassisted opponent of a legally aided party may recover his or her costs from the Legal Aid Board. Where the assisted person recovers or preserves money or property in the proceedings, the Legal Aid Fund will usually have a first charge on that money or property to recover money spent on the assisted person's behalf.

Legal Aid in Criminal Proceedings

In criminal proceedings in England, Wales and Northern Ireland legal aid may be granted by the court if it appears to be in the interests of justice and if a defendant is considered to require financial assistance.

The Legal Aid Board in England and Wales makes arrangements for duty solicitors to assist unrepresented defendants in the magistrates' courts. Solicitors are available, on a 24-hour basis, to give advice and assistance to those being questioned by the police. The services of a solicitor at a police station and of the duty solicitor at court are not means-tested and are free.

Where legal aid is granted for criminal cases in Northern Ireland it is free. There is a voluntary duty solicitor scheme at the main magistrates' court in Belfast.

Scotland

A duty solicitor is available to represent people in custody on their first appearance in the sheriff courts and the district courts without enquiry into the person's means. In other cases, a person seeking legal aid in summary criminal proceedings must apply to the Scottish Legal Aid Board, which must be satisfied that the costs of the case cannot be met by the applicant without undue hardship, and that it is in the interests of justice that legal aid is awarded.

In solemn proceedings the court decides on the availability of legal aid and must be satisfied that the accused cannot meet the costs of the defence without undue financial hardship. Where legal aid is granted to the accused in criminal proceedings, he or she is not required to pay any contribution towards expenses.

Proposed Changes to Legal Aid in England and Wales

In a White Paper published in July 1996, the Government proposed far-reaching changes to the legal aid system in order to make it more cost-effective and to concentrate available resources on the most deserving cases. The main changes would:

- regulate the allocation of financial resources through predetermined budgets reflecting local demand within national priorities;
- introduce contracts between providers of legal services and the Legal Aid Board for specified services of defined quality at an agreed price (this is being implemented with immediate effect);
- introduce a stricter merits test for assessing whether civil cases should be given legal aid; and
- increase potential liability of assisted people to contribute to their own and, in civil cases, their opponents' costs.

Free Representation Units

The Bar Council, the barristers' professional body, supports a Free Representation Unit for clients at a variety of tribunals for which legal aid is not available. Most of the representation by the London unit is carried out by Bar students supported and advised by full-time case workers. Elsewhere, barristers do such work through regional units. A special Bar unit, based in London, was formed in early 1996 through which more senior barristers provide representation in cases which might otherwise not be heard.

Law Centres

In some urban areas law centres provide free legal advice and representation. They may employ a salaried lawyer and many have community workers. Much of their time is devoted to housing, employment, social security and immigration problems. Although there is a restriction on cases they will accept, most law centres will give preliminary advice.

Advice at minimal or no cost may be available in Citizens Advice Bureaux, consumer and housing advice centres and in specialist advice centres run by voluntary organisations.

Further Reading

Access to Justice—Final Report, the Rt Hon the Lord Woolf. HMSO, 1996.

Britain's Legal Systems (2nd edition). Aspects of Britain series, HMSO, 1996.

Criminal Justice (2nd edition). Aspects of Britain series, HMSO, 1995.

Departmental Report of The Lord Chancellor's and Law Officers' Departments: The Government's Expenditure Plans 1996–97 to 1998–99. HMSO, 1996.

Drugs in Scotland: Meeting the Challenge. The Scottish Office, 1994.

Home Office Annual Report 1996: The Government's Expenditure Plans 1996–97 to 1998–99. HMSO, 1996.

Protecting the Public. The Government's Strategy on Crime in England and Wales. Cm 3190. HMSO, 1996.

Report of the Royal Commission on Criminal Justice. HMSO, 1993.

Striking the Balance: the Future of Legal Aid in England and Wales. Cm 3305. HMSO, 1996.

Tackling Drugs Together. A Strategy for England 1995–1998. HMSO, 1995.

External Affairs

9　Overseas Relations

Administration of Foreign Policy	117
International Organisations	118
Britain's Dependent Territories	123
European Union Policy	125
International Peace and Security	129
Central and Eastern Europe and Central Asia	130
Other Regions	131
Arms Control	133
Human Rights	134
International Crime	136
Development Co-operation	136
Cultural Relations	140

The aims of British foreign policy are to promote and protect the security and prosperity of the peoples of Britain and its Dependent Territories and to contribute to a safer and fairer international order. To these ends, Britain is a member of some 80 international organisations, including the United Nations (UN), the Commonwealth, the North Atlantic Treaty Organisation (NATO) and the European Union (EU). It plays an active part in maintaining international peace and security and has been fully involved in efforts to bring about a negotiated settlement in former Yugoslavia. The British aid programme is centred on the needs of the poorest countries.

ADMINISTRATION OF FOREIGN POLICY

Foreign & Commonwealth Office

The Foreign & Commonwealth Office (FCO) is in charge of overall foreign policy and is headed by the Foreign and Commonwealth Secretary, who is assisted by five ministers without Cabinet rank. One of these is the Minister for Overseas Development, who is responsible for the Overseas Development Administration (ODA). The FCO's Permanent Under-Secretary of State is a civil servant who heads the Diplomatic Service and provides advice to the Foreign and Commonwealth Secretary on all aspects of foreign policy.

Of about 6,000 staff of the FCO's Diplomatic Wing appointed in Britain, nearly 2,500 serve overseas, of whom 167 are seconded from other government departments and other public and private organisations. British diplomatic missions also employ about 7,440 locally engaged staff.

Some 26 per cent of frontline staff overseas deal with political and economic work, while 35 per cent are engaged on commercial and inward investment work, 14 per cent on entry clearance to Britain, 7 per cent on consular work, 5 per cent on aid administration, 5 per cent on information and 8 per cent on other activities, such as culture, science and technology.

The FCO administers pre-entry control overseas for people wishing to enter Britain. Applications for entry clearance are dealt with by the visa section or consulate of a British mission.

Britain is committed to maintaining a worldwide diplomatic presence and has diplomatic or consular relations with 188 countries. There are also missions at nine international organisations or conferences.

The FCO's only executive agency, Wilton Park International Conference Centre (at Wiston House in West Sussex), contributes to the solution of international problems by organising conferences in Britain, attended by politicians, business people, academics and other professionals from all over the world.

Other Departments

Other government departments are also concerned with overseas relations and foreign policy. The Ministry of Defence maintains military liaison with Britain's NATO and other allies, in addition to controlling and administering the armed forces (see p. 149). The Department of Trade and Industry (DTI) has an important influence on international trade policy and commercial relations with other countries, including EU member states. The FCO and DTI have a joint export promotion organisation—Overseas Trade Services (see p. 181). The Treasury is involved in British international economic policy and is responsible for Britain's relations with the World Bank and other international financial institutions.

When other departments are involved, the FCO decides policy in consultation with them. The department with the main interest usually takes the lead, particularly in EU matters and international economic policy. The FCO co-ordinates British EU policy through the Cabinet Office European Secretariat.

The British Council is responsible for British cultural relations with other countries (see p. 140).

INTERNATIONAL ORGANISATIONS

United Nations

Britain is a founder member of the United Nations and one of the five permanent members of the Security Council, along with China, France, Russia and the United States. In 1996 it was the fifth largest contributor to the UN regular budget. It is also one of the leading contributors to UN peacekeeping operations (see p. 129). Britain is fully committed to the purposes and principles of the UN Charter, including the maintenance of international peace and security, the development of friendly relations among nations, the achievement of international co-operation on economic, social, cultural and humanitarian issues and the protection of human rights and fundamental freedoms.

European Union

Britain is a member of the European Union, which comprises the European Community (EC) and intergovernmental co-operation on foreign and security policy, and on justice and home affairs. The EU is an association of 15 democratic nations; its members are Austria, Belgium, Britain, Denmark, Finland, France, Germany, Greece, the Irish Republic, Italy, Luxembourg, the Netherlands, Portugal, Spain and Sweden.

As one of the five most populous countries, Britain provides two of the 20 members of the European Commission, which puts forward legislative proposals, executes the decisions taken by the Council of the European Union and ensures that European Community rules are correctly observed. Britain is represented at every meeting of the Council, which is the main decision-making body. Each Council consists of government ministers from the 15 member states, representing national interests in the subjects under discussion—for example, trade, agriculture or transport. When a member state has the Presidency of the Union (for a period of six months), its ministers are responsible for chairing meetings of the Council. The Committee of Permanent Representatives, consisting of member states' ambassadors to the European Union, prepares the work of the Council. European

The European Union

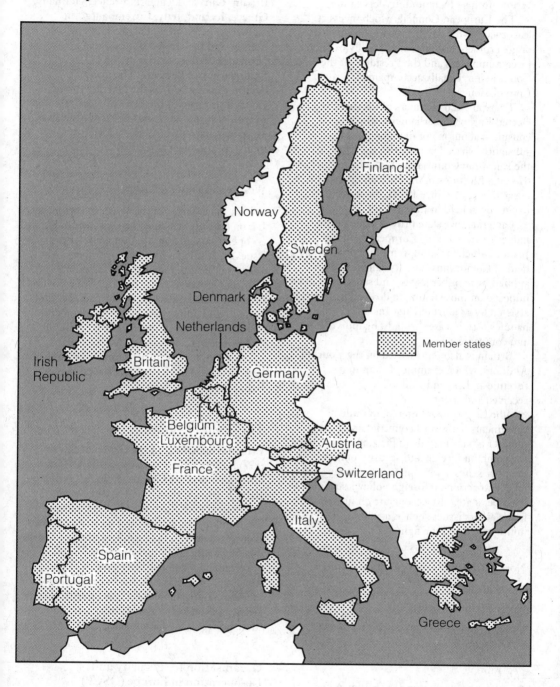

Community policies are implemented by various forms of Community legislation.

The European Council, which meets at least twice a year, comprises the heads of state or government accompanied usually by their foreign ministers and the President of the Commission, usually accompanied by a Commissioner.

There are 626 members of the directly elected European Parliament, which is consulted about major decisions and has substantial shared power with the Council over the European Community budget. Britain has 87 seats. Elections to the Parliament take place every five years (since 1979), the most recent having been held in June 1994.

Each member state provides one of the judges to serve on the European Court of Justice, which is the supreme authority in the field of Community law. Its rulings must be applied by member states, and sanctions can be imposed on those failing to do so. The Court is assisted by a Court of First Instance, which handles certain cases brought by individuals and companies.

Britain is also represented on the Court of Auditors, which examines Community revenue and expenditure to see that it is legally received and spent.

The Community enters into trade agreements with third countries and has a number of substantial aid programmes. Under the common foreign and security policy, member states agree common positions and take joint action on foreign policy issues. Member states also co-operate on justice and home affairs issues such as asylum, immigration and the fight against crime.

North Atlantic Treaty Organisation

Membership of NATO is central to British defence policy (see p. 143). NATO is based on the principle of collective security and its core functions are to:

- provide a foundation for security in Europe;

- deter aggression and defend member states against it; and

- provide a forum for Allied transatlantic consultation.

Each of the 16 member states (Belgium, Britain, Canada, Denmark, France, Germany, Greece, Iceland, Italy, Luxembourg, the Netherlands, Norway, Portugal, Spain, Turkey and the United States) has a permanent representative at NATO headquarters in Brussels. The main decision-taking body is the North Atlantic Council. It meets at least twice a year at foreign minister level, and weekly at the level of permanent representatives. Defence ministers also meet at least twice a year.

Western European Union

Britain is a member of the Western European Union (WEU), which is the main forum for co-operation and consultation on defence issues for NATO's European members. The WEU's other full members are Belgium, France, Germany, Greece, Italy, Luxembourg, the Netherlands, Portugal and Spain. Iceland, Norway and Turkey are associate members; Austria, Denmark, Finland, the Irish Republic and Sweden are observers. 'Associate partnership' (a new form of membership) has been extended to 10 Central European and Baltic states.

The Group of Seven

Britain is a member of the Group of Seven (G7) leading industrialised countries. The other members are Canada, France, Germany, Italy, Japan and the United States. As an informal organisation, the G7 has no legal force and no secretariat. Its Presidency rotates each year between the members, the key meeting being an annual summit of heads of government. Originally formed in 1975 to discuss economic issues, the G7 agenda now includes political issues such as international crime and terrorism. Russia has participated in these political discussions since 1994.

Organisation for Security and Co-operation in Europe (OSCE)

Britain is a signatory to the 1975 Helsinki Final Act, which established a framework for co-operation between OSCE states on

European security (see p. 135), respect for human rights and economic matters. It was agreed that the Helsinki commitments should be reviewed at regular follow-up conferences.

The 1990 Charter of Paris committed the signatories to democracy, human rights and market economies. The OSCE has a Secretariat in Vienna, where Britain has a permanent delegation. Day-to-day business is conducted in the Permanent Council. A Prague office organises the twice-yearly meetings of senior officials.

The OSCE has 54 members, including every country in Europe, the states of the former Soviet Union, and the United States and Canada. The Federal Republic of Yugoslavia was suspended in 1992. All states participate on an equal basis, and decisions are taken by consensus.

The main areas of OSCE work are:

- early warning of potential conflict through preventive diplomacy missions and the work of the OSCE High Commissioner on National Minorities;

- providing advice on human rights, democracy and law through the OSCE Office for Democratic Institutions and Human Rights in Warsaw (see p. 135); and

- promoting security through arms control and military confidence building.

Council of Europe

Britain is a founding member of the Council of Europe, which is open to any European democracy accepting the rule of law and the protection of fundamental human rights and freedoms. The 39 member states co-operate on culture, education, sport, health, anti-crime policy, measures against drug trafficking, youth affairs and the improvement of the environment. The Council adopted its European Convention on Human Rights in 1950 (see p. 135).

The Commonwealth

There are 53 members of the Commonwealth, including Britain. It is a voluntary association of states, nearly all of which were British territories but are now independent. The members are Antigua and Barbuda, Australia, Bahamas, Bangladesh, Barbados, Belize, Botswana, Britain, Brunei Darussalam, Cameroon, Canada, Cyprus, Dominica, The Gambia, Ghana, Grenada, Guyana, India, Jamaica, Kenya, Kiribati, Lesotho, Malawi, Malaysia, Maldives, Malta, Mauritius, Mozambique (the most recent country to join, in November 1995), Namibia, Nauru, New Zealand, Nigeria, Pakistan, Papua New Guinea, St Kitts and Nevis, St Lucia, St Vincent and the Grenadines, Seychelles, Sierra Leone, Singapore, Solomon Islands, South Africa, Sri Lanka, Swaziland, Tanzania, Tonga, Trinidad and Tobago, Tuvalu, Uganda, Vanuatu, Western Samoa, Zambia and Zimbabwe. Nauru and Tuvalu are special members, entitled to take part in all Commonwealth meetings and activities, with the exception of the biennial Commonwealth heads of government meetings. South Africa rejoined in 1994 after an absence of 33 years.

Consultation between member states takes place through:

- meetings of heads of government;

- specialised conferences of other ministers and officials;

- diplomatic representatives known as high commissioners; and

- non-governmental organisations.

The Queen is recognised as head of the Commonwealth and is head of state in Britain and 15 other member countries. In 1997 Britain will host the Heads of Government Meeting for the first time in 20 years.

The Commonwealth Secretariat in London promotes consultation, disseminates information, and organises heads of government meetings, ministerial meetings and other conferences. It administers co-operative programmes agreed at these meetings, including the Commonwealth Fund for Technical Co-operation, which provides consultancy services and training awards to Commonwealth developing countries.

The Commonwealth Institute is the centre of Commonwealth education and culture in Britain.

The Commonwealth

Membership of the Commonwealth enables Britain to play a responsible part alongside other nations in aiding the democratisation and progress of the developing world. About 56 per cent of British bilateral aid to developing countries went to Commonwealth countries in 1994–95.

Other International Bodies

Britain belongs to many other international bodies, and was a founder member of the International Monetary Fund (IMF) and the World Bank. The IMF regulates the international financial system and provides a source of credit for member countries facing balance-of-payments difficulties. The World Bank provides loans to finance economic and social projects in developing countries.

In addition, Britain, along with 24 other industrialised countries, belongs to the Organisation for Economic Co-operation and Development (OECD), which promotes economic growth, support for less developed countries and worldwide trade expansion.

Other organisations to which Britain belongs or extends support include the regional development banks in Africa, the Caribbean, Latin America and Asia.

BRITAIN'S DEPENDENT TERRITORIES

Britain's Dependent Territories have a combined population of over 6 million, the vast majority of whom live in Hong Kong. Most territories have considerable self-government, with their own legislatures. Governors appointed by the Queen are responsible for external affairs, internal security (including the police) and the public service. Certain responsibilities are delegated to locally elected ministers but the ultimate responsibility for all government affairs rests with the Foreign and Commonwealth Secretary. The British Indian Ocean Territory, the British Antarctic Territory, and South Georgia and the South Sandwich Islands have commissioners, not governors; a commissioner is not responsible for external affairs. Britain seeks to provide the territories with security and political stability, ensure

efficient and honest government, and help them achieve economic and social development on a par with neighbouring countries.

The territories are: Anguilla; Bermuda (where, in a referendum in August 1995, voters rejected decisively the principle of independence from Britain); British Antarctic Territory; British Indian Ocean Territory; British Virgin Islands; Cayman Islands; Falkland Islands; Gibraltar; Hong Kong; Montserrat; Pitcairn, Ducie, Henderson and Oeno; St Helena and St Helena Dependencies (Ascension and Tristan da Cunha); South Georgia and the South Sandwich Islands; and Turks and Caicos Islands.

British policy is to help the inhabitants of the Dependent Territories to take independence if they want it and where it is practicable, and to do so in accordance with treaty obligations. The reasonable needs of the Dependent Territories are a first call on the British aid programme.

Hong Kong

Under the Second Convention of Peking, signed in 1898, China granted Britain a 99-year lease for 92 per cent of Hong Kong's present-day territory, known as the New Territories. Since this lease runs out on 30 June 1997, Britain is committed under international law to return the New Territories to China. The remaining, densely populated, eight per cent of Hong Kong's territory— Hong Kong Island and Kowloon Peninsula—was ceded to Britain in perpetuity earlier in the nineteenth century. Because this area would be unviable on its own, Britain decided, under the terms of the 1984 Sino-British Joint Declaration, to return the entire territory of Hong Kong to China with effect from 1 July 1997, in return for guarantees about Hong Kong's future way of life.

Thereafter Hong Kong will become a Special Administrative Region (SAR) of China. Apart from the fields of foreign affairs and defence, the Hong Kong SAR will enjoy a high degree of autonomy, with its own government and legislature composed of Hong Kong people. In addition, Hong Kong's capitalist system, freedoms, currency and financial markets will remain intact.

Britain is pledged to co-operate with China in bringing about a smooth transition in 1997. The main forum for decisions between Britain and China on the implementation of the Joint Declaration is the Sino-British Joint Liaison Group (JLG) which will be working hard in the last months before the handover to ensure that all outstanding transitional issues are resolved.

One area of disagreement between Britain and China concerns the legislature. The Chinese Government has said that it will replace in July 1997 the Legislative Council elected in 1995. Britain does not accept the need for the replacement of a body for which Hong Kong people voted in record numbers. The electoral arrangements in 1995 were consistent with both the Joint Declaration and the Basic Law, China's mini-constitution for Hong Kong. The British Government, therefore, continues to see no justification for the so-called 'Provisional Legislature' which will be installed in July 1997.

Britain will have a strong commitment to Hong Kong well beyond 1997. The JLG continues until January 2000 and many of the guarantees in the Joint Declaration last until 2047. There will still be three million British passport-holders in Hong Kong. Britain's commercial interests will remain substantial since Hong Kong is its second greatest export market in Asia.

The Falkland Islands

The Falkland Islands are the subject of a territorial claim by Argentina but the inhabitants wish to remain under British sovereignty. The British Government does not accept the Argentine claim and is committed to defending the Islanders' right to live under a government of their own choice. This right of self-determination is set out in the 1985 Falkland Islands Constitution.

In 1982 Argentina invaded and occupied the Islands, but its forces were expelled by British troops following Argentina's failure to abide by United Nations resolutions requesting its forces to withdraw. Britain and Argentina, while sticking to their respective positions on sovereignty, maintain diplomatic relations and continue to discuss their common interests in the South Atlantic region, such as fisheries conservation and the exploitation of oil reserves. An agreement on oil exploration co-operation was signed in September 1995, enabling the Falkland Islands to launch an oil licensing round.

Gibraltar

Gibraltar was ceded to Britain in 1713 by the Treaty of Utrecht. It is the subject of a territorial claim by Spain. Under the Treaty, Spain has the right of first refusal should Britain ever decide to relinquish sovereignty.

Britain is committed to honouring the wishes of the people of Gibraltar on their future. This is set out in the 1969 Gibraltar Constitution.

Over the years, Spain has used various means to pursue its national objectives regarding Gibraltar, in particular pressure at the border, where the periodic imposition of strict controls has caused severe delays and substantial damage to Gibraltar's economy.

Gibraltar is part of the European Union within the United Kingdom member state, although it is outside the common customs system and does not participate in the Common Agricultural or Fisheries policies or the value added tax regime.

Gibraltar has recently introduced strict anti-money laundering legislation (see also p. 136) and has taken action to deter drug smuggling from Morocco to Spain and tobacco smuggling to Spain.

Caribbean Dependent Territories

The Dependent Territories Regional Secretariat in Barbados administers aspects of British government policy towards the Caribbean territories (Anguilla, the British Virgin Islands, the Cayman Islands, Montserrat, and the Turks and Caicos Islands). Jointly agreed country policy plans for each territory receiving British aid have been introduced or are under discussion.

In London an FCO minister chairs the Ministerial Group for the Caribbean Dependent Territories, drawn from a number of government departments and agencies and benefiting from wider expertise than the FCO or the ODA alone can offer. It meets two or three times a year. Policy initiatives by the group are supported by the Good Government Fund which, among other objectives, pays for British personnel on loan to local governments to help them fight drug trafficking and other criminal activity. Assistance is also given to local disaster response teams. In addition, the Group monitors a programme of action designed to improve regulation of the offshore finance sector and anti-money laundering measures.

EUROPEAN UNION POLICY

Britain regards the EU as a means of safeguarding political stability in Europe and generating economic prosperity. British trade with Europe has risen by almost twice the rate of that with the rest of the world. EU membership has also been a key factor in attracting inward investment into Britain. Moreover, the creation of the internal European market has helped remove barriers to trade between member states and thereby increase consumer choice and prosperity.

The Government wants Britain to be an active participant in the EU but is opposed to a gradual centralisation of powers in Brussels and the development of a federal Europe. Instead, it favours an EU which respects cultural and political diversity and which concentrates only on action that needs to be taken at European level. It believes that the great bulk of decisions should continue to be taken by national governments. It is opposed to harmonisation for its own sake or to any further European integration not driven by the prospect of practical benefit to member states.

Britain welcomed the accession of Austria, Finland and Sweden in 1995 and favours enlargement of the EU as a means of consolidating democracy in eastern and central Europe and healing the divisions originally created by the Cold War. It therefore supports the eventual membership of Bulgaria, the Czech Republic, Estonia, Hungary, Latvia, Lithuania, Poland, Romania, Slovakia and Slovenia, all of which have applied to join and have agreements with the EU designed to lead towards membership. The EU is also committed to starting accession negotiations with Cyprus and Malta six months after the current intergovernmental conference (IGC—see p. 126) ends.

Background

The Union had its origins in the post-Second World War resolve by Western European nations, particularly France and Germany, to prevent wars breaking out again between themselves. The 1957 Rome Treaty, which established the European Community, defined its aims as the harmonious development of economic activities, a continuous and balanced economic expansion and an accelerated rise in the standard of living. These objectives were to be achieved by the creation of a common internal market, including the elimination of customs duties between member states, free movement of goods, people, services and capital, and the elimination of distortions in competition within this market. These objectives were reaffirmed by the 1986 Single European Act, which agreed measures to complete the internal market.

Maastricht Treaty

The 1992 Maastricht Treaty amended the Rome Treaty and made other new commitments, including moves towards economic and monetary union. It established the EU, which comprises the European Community and intergovernmental arrangements regarding a common foreign and security policy (see p. 118) and increased co-operation on interior/justice policy issues (see p. 83). The Maastricht Treaty also codified the principle of subsidiarity under which action should be taken at European level only if its objectives cannot be achieved by member states acting alone and can be better achieved by the Community. Under an agreement reached in 1992, a subsidiarity test is applied to all European Commission proposals for action.

In addition, the Treaty introduced the concept of European Union citizenship as a supplement to national citizenship.

Following ratification by Britain and the other member states, the Treaty came into force in November 1993.

Intergovernmental Conference

Following on from the Maastricht Treaty, an intergovernmental conference (IGC) was convened by EU heads of government at Turin in March 1996 to consider further treaty amendments.

> The British Government wants the IGC to focus on making the EU more relevant and acceptable to the people of Europe by improving practical co-operation, which produces the real benefits of the EU, decentralising powers and strengthening the principle of subsidiarity. It is, therefore, opposed to the extension of European Community powers and to more majority voting in the Council. The IGC must also prepare the institutions of the EU for enlargement.

Any amendments to the treaties can only be agreed by unanimity and cannot enter into force until they have been ratified by each individual member state according to its own constitutional procedures; in Britain's case this is passage through Parliament of an Act amending the 1972 European Communities Act.

Economic and Monetary Union

The Maastricht Treaty provides for progress towards economic and monetary union (EMU) in three stages: the first—completion of the single market—ended at the end of 1993. The second stage, which began on 1 January 1994, includes the establishment of a European Monetary Institute with a largely advisory and consultative role. Although the Institute is preparing for stage 3, monetary policy remains a national responsibility. Member states co-ordinate economic policies in the context of agreed non-binding policy guidelines. The British Government is participating in stage 2.

The third stage is a single currency for EU member states. Under the Treaty this is envisaged by 1 January 1999, although member states will have to satisfy certain criteria on inflation rates, government deficit levels, currency fluctuation margins and interest rates. A special protocol, negotiated by the British Government, recognises that Britain is not obliged or committed to move to this final stage of EMU.

The Community Budget

The Community's revenue consists of:

- levies on agricultural imports;
- customs duties;
- the proceeds of a notional rate of value added tax of up to 1.4 per cent on a standard 'basket' of goods and services; and
- contributions from member states based on gross national product (GNP).

Britain has an annual rebate worth some £2,000 million because of the fact that, without it, the British net contribution would be far greater than that justified by its share of Community GNP.

An agreement on future finance was reached at the European Council summit in Edinburgh in 1992. Under the agreement, the overall revenue ceiling was maintained at 1.2 per cent of Community GNP until 1995. It is then rising in steps, reaching 1.27 per cent in 1999. Agricultural spending will be less than half the budget by the end of the century, compared with 80 per cent in 1973 and 60 per cent at present. It was also agreed that more resources would be allocated to the poorer regions of the Union.

Single Market

The single market, providing for the free movement of people, goods, services and capital, is largely complete in legislative terms. It covers, among other benefits, the removal of customs barriers, the liberalisation of capital movements, the opening of public procurement markets and the mutual recognition of professional qualifications. The single market is designed to reduce business costs, stimulate efficiency, increase consumer choice and encourage the creation of jobs and wealth. The British Government is supporting continuing work on extending the single market to important areas such as telecommunications and energy.

Under the European Economic Area (EEA) Agreement, which entered into force on 1 January 1994, most of the EU single market measures have been extended to Iceland, Norway and Liechtenstein.

Transport

The concept of a common transport policy was laid down in the Treaty of Rome, and Britain fully supports the extension of competition and deregulation in transport. Liberalisation measures relating to civil aviation, shipping, and road haulage and passenger services are described in Chapter 19.

Trans-European Networks

The EU is working towards the completion of trans-European networks in the fields of transport, energy and telecommunications. The aim is to improve the interconnection and interoperability of national networks. Of the 14 priority transport projects which have been endorsed by the European Council, Britain has an interest in four. One of these is the planned construction of a new rail link between London and the Channel Tunnel (see p. 311). Ten priority energy projects have been endorsed, but none with a British interest. Britain has an interest in three non-priority projects, including the Bacton–Zeebrugge gas link.

Trade

Britain is the world's fifth largest trading nation. EEA member states comprise the world's largest trading bloc, accounting for about 40 per cent of all trade. The British Government fully supports an open world trading system, on which EU member states depend for future economic growth and jobs.

Under the Rome Treaty, the European Commission speaks on behalf of Britain and the other member states in international trade negotiations, such as the recently concluded GATT Uruguay Round, which led to the creation of the World Trade Organisation (WTO). The Commission negotiates on a mandate agreed by the Council. For further information on trade, see Chapter 12.

The Environment

European Union member states are at the forefront of many international measures on environmental issues, such as air quality standards and the depletion of the ozone layer. For further information, see Chapter 22.

Agriculture and Fisheries

The Common Agricultural Policy (CAP) is designed to secure food supplies and to stabilise markets. It has also, however, created overproduction and unwanted food surpluses, placing a burden on the Community's budget.

The Common Fisheries Policy is concerned with the conservation and management of fishery resources.

The operation of these policies, and Britain's advocacy of CAP reform, are described in Chapter 18.

Regional and Infrastructure Development

There are a number of Structural Funds designed to:

- promote economic development in underdeveloped regions;
- regenerate regions affected by industrial decline;
- combat long-term unemployment and facilitate the entry of young people into the labour market;
- help workers adapt to industrial changes and to advances in production systems;
- speed up the adjustment of production, processing and marketing structures in agriculture; and
- promote development in rural areas.

Infrastructure projects and industrial investments are financed by the European Regional Development Fund. The European Social Fund supports training and employment measures for the unemployed and young people. The Guidance Section of the European Agricultural Guidance and Guarantee Fund supports agricultural restructuring and some rural development measures. The Financial Instrument of Fisheries Guidance supports the modernisation of the fishing industry.

A Cohesion Fund, set up under the Maastricht Treaty, is designed to reduce disparities between levels of development in the poorer and richer member states.

Other initiatives aim to assist the development of new economic activities in regions affected by the restructuring of traditional industries, such as steel, coal and shipbuilding.

The European Investment Bank, a non-profit-making institution, lends at competitive interest rates to public and private capital investment projects. Lending is directed towards:

- less-favoured regions;
- transport infrastructure;
- protection of the environment;
- improving industrial competitiveness; and
- supporting loans to small and medium-sized enterprises.

Employment and Social Affairs

In Britain's view, Community social policy should be primarily concerned with helping member states to create jobs and maintain a well-educated and trained workforce. The Government supports:

- freedom of movement for workers, mutual recognition of professional and vocational qualifications, equal opportunities at work and measures which genuinely safeguard health and safety at work; and
- practical measures to increase jobs and cut unemployment which do not place more costs on employers.

At Maastricht the Government opposed the extension of Community social policy and qualified majority voting into new areas of social affairs on the grounds that this would damage competitiveness and destroy jobs. It also stressed that the main responsibility for such policies should remain with individual member states. It therefore negotiated the Social Protocol to the Maastricht Treaty, which allows other member states to agree social legislation in these areas which is not applicable in Britain. The British Government is committed to maintaining this arrangement during the current discussions in the intergovernmental conference (see p. 126).

Research and Development

Research collaboration among member states is promoted primarily through a series of framework programmes defining priorities and setting out the overall level of funding. The British Government actively encourages British companies and organisations to participate in collaborative research and development (R & D) with European partners (see p. 342).

The Fourth Framework Programme, adopted in April 1994, focuses on generic and precompetitive research which is of use to a number of industries. It covers information and communications technologies, industrial technologies, the environment, life sciences and technology, energy, transport and socio-economic research. The programme also provides for international co-operation, dissemination of research, and training and mobility of researchers.

Common Foreign and Security Policy

The common foreign and security policy (CFSP), established by the Maastricht Treaty, is intergovernmental, decisions being taken by unanimity. This co-ordination of foreign policy among EU member states has progressed, with less emphasis being placed on declaratory statements. Successful common policies have been agreed on issues such as the delivery of humanitarian aid to Bosnia and the administration of the Bosnian town of Mostar, assistance to the Middle East peace process (including the organisation of Palestinian elections), election monitoring in Russia and South Africa and the promotion of nuclear non-proliferation.

One of the main weaknesses of the CFSP so far has been the practical implementation of policy initiatives. During the current IGC, the Government is pressing for a strengthening of the CFSP Secretariat charged with implementing policy and for more co-ordination between member states. In particular, Britain wants more planning and analysis in the CFSP Secretariat and is prepared to consider the idea of appointing a single figure, answerable to member

BRITISH ARMED FORCES IN BOSNIA

There are an estimated 6 million unexploded mines in the former Yugoslavia; over the past few years Britain's Royal Engineers have been carrying out mine-awareness training for thousands of inhabitants, concentrating on those people returning to areas of high risk.

Camouflaged Gurkha soldiers take part in a training exercise in preparation for peacekeeping duties in Bosnia. One hundred infantry soldiers of the Royal Gurkha Rifles, from Nepal, have joined 13,000 British troops as part of NATO's Implementation Force.

CONSTRUCTION

The new road bridge linking England and Wales across the River Severn opened in June 1996, completing Europe's biggest bridge-building project.

Birmingham's regenerated city centre canalside has helped attract huge investment to the area, and won the 1995 international award for Excellence on the Waterfront.

This canal near Leeds, part of the Aire and Calder Navigation, is the first canal to be built in Britain for 90 years. It is used by freight barges and leisure boats, and has a new lock, two lock-keeper's cottages, a weir, a marina, three bridges and a nature reserve.

The largest Hindu temple to be built outside India is at the Swaminarayan Hindu Mission in north London. Opened in 1995, it was funded mainly by donations from Britain's Gujarati community.

THE QUEEN'S AWARDS FOR EXPORT

English Hop Products, Kent, exports to many countries, including Russia, the United States, India and Japan. Hops are used to flavour beer and other malt products.

Burberrys, the internationally renowned clothing manufacturer based in London, has won its sixth Export Award. As well as its famous raincoats, such as the one pictured here, it exports a range of other clothing, knitwear, sportswear and accessories to 46 countries.

Dairy Produce Packers, Co. Londonderry, Northern Ireland, is a major supplier of dairy products to international customers in the catering and fast food businesses.

states' foreign ministers, to represent EU foreign policy to the outside world.

The Treaty differentiates between security and defence policy, confirming that defence issues are a matter for the Western European Union (see p. 120). There is, however, a commitment to 'the eventual framing of a common defence policy, which might in time lead to a common defence'.

INTERNATIONAL PEACE AND SECURITY

Britain maintains that states should not use, or threaten, force against other sovereign states and that they should resolve their disputes by peaceful means. The United Nations is the principal body responsible for the maintenance of international peace and security.

Britain considers that prevention of conflict is better than cure. It is, therefore, particularly active in looking for ways of strengthening the capacity of the UN and other international organisations to predict and prevent conflicts before they arise.

Britain and UN Peacekeeping

Britain supports UN efforts to increase the effectiveness of its peacekeeping capacity and has pressed for the strengthening of the UN's Department of Peacekeeping Operations. Ten British officers are currently serving in the Department and are performing operational, financial and other specialist functions.

In 1994 Britain launched an initiative calling for action on conflict in Africa, progressing from early warning and preventive diplomacy through to humanitarian and peacekeeping operations on the ground. It has also taken the lead in the UN's efforts to reform the funding, administration and logistics of peacekeeping operations. Together with the United States, Canada and other member states, Britain has made practical proposals for improving support for UN missions and modernising the UN's procurement policies.

Britain pays an assessed share of the costs of UN peacekeeping (nearly 6.6 per cent of the total), contributing about £137 million in 1995. In April 1996 over 12,500 British personnel were engaged in operations in support of UN Security Council resolutions, with a further 425 under direct UN command.

British Contributions to UN Operations

Bosnia

Britain is continuing to work for peace and stability in former Yugoslavia. Since the outbreak of inter-ethnic hostilities in mid-1991 the European Union and the UN have sought to bring about a negotiated and lasting settlement for the area as a whole.

In December 1995 the Dayton Peace Agreement for Bosnia was signed in the United States, and Britain is playing a central role in its implementation. Over 10,000 British personnel are participating in the NATO-led Implementation Force, which comprises about 60,000 troops from all NATO nations and 16 other countries, including Russia and a number of other Partnership for Peace (see p. 143) members. The main task of the force is to assist in implementing the agreement's territorial and other provisions. These include monitoring compliance, establishing secure conditions for elections and assisting humanitarian organisations.

Africa

In 1994 Britain deployed a battalion to serve for three months with the UN mission in Rwanda, where it repaired over 800 UN vehicles, rebuilt bridges and restored utilities. Another battalion was sent in 1995 to help establish infrastructure for the UN peacekeeping mission in Angola.

Cyprus

Britain continues to provide the largest contingent (about 400 strong) to the UN Force in Cyprus, which was established in 1964 to help prevent the recurrence of fighting on the island between Greek and Turkish Cypriots. Since the serious hostilities of 1974, when Turkish forces occupied the northern part of the island, the Force has been responsible for maintaining the ceasefire and control of a buffer zone between the two communities.

Iraq/Kuwait

In 1991 a Security Council resolution established a demilitarised zone extending 10 km into Iraq and 5 km into Kuwait to deter violations of the boundary and to observe hostile or potentially hostile actions. Britain, with the other permanent members of the Security Council, contributes 15 observers to the 1,000-strong UN Iraq/Kuwait observer mission (UNIKOM). Royal Air Force aircraft are continuing reconnaissance missions over Iraq to monitor Iraqi military activity and police the 'no fly' zones from which Iraqi aircraft are excluded (see p. 147).

Georgia

Ten British officers are deployed as military observers in Georgia as part of a 127-strong UN observer mission. The mission was established by the Security Council in August 1993 to observe and monitor the ceasefire established following violent conflict between the Georgian armed forces and Abkhaz separatists.

CENTRAL AND EASTERN EUROPE AND CENTRAL ASIA

Since the disintegration of the Warsaw Pact and the formation of democratically elected governments in Eastern and Central Europe and Central Asia, the European security situation has been transformed.

In 1990 NATO Allies and former Warsaw Pact states signed a joint declaration in Paris saying that:

- they were no longer adversaries and would build new partnerships;
- they would maintain only enough military forces to prevent war and provide for effective defence; and
- they would form the North Atlantic Co-operation Council to foster co-operation and understanding.

In 1994 a NATO summit meeting invited the non-NATO states in Eastern and Central Europe and Central Asia to join a Partnership for Peace initiative in order to:

- develop a practical working relationship; and
- enlist the Partners' assistance in peacekeeping operations and guide their armed forces towards compatibility with those of NATO countries.

The Partnership for Peace, which now includes 26 countries, also monitors matters such as the Partners' respect for international treaties, civilian control of the military and openness in defence budgeting.

Economic Help

Britain and other Western countries are taking action to help deal with the vast economic problems following the fall of Communism, and to promote the development of market economies. The IMF and World Bank, with Britain's active support, provide advice and finance to nearly all countries in the region, while the European Bank for Reconstruction and Development channels Western investment. The European Community's PHARE scheme is assisting Central European countries in the process of reform and the development of infrastructure. Eastern Europe and Central Asia receive help through a parallel programme (TACIS), which concentrates on financial services, transport, energy (including nuclear safety) and humanitarian needs. Britain's Export Credit Guarantee Department provides insurance cover for exporters to a number of countries.

Know How Fund

The Know How Fund is Britain's programme of bilateral technical assistance to the countries of Central and Eastern Europe and Central Asia. It aims to support their transition to pluralist democracy and a market economy by providing British skills and by encouraging British investment in the region.

In Central and Eastern Europe, and especially Russia, the Fund's main priorities are developing financial services, including banking, insurance, audit and privatisation; management training; small and medium-sized enterprise development; public administration; and employment services. Agriculture, energy and health care management are also priorities in some countries.

The Know How Fund also finances activities promoting good government and civil society, such as parliamentary exchanges, police training, development of legal services, and media development and training.

The Fund spent over £86.5 million in 1995–96 and over £300 million since its inception in 1989.

Europe (Association) Agreements

The European Union has strengthened relations with Bulgaria, the Czech Republic, Estonia, Hungary, Latvia, Lithuania, Poland, Romania, Slovakia and Slovenia by signing Europe (Association) Agreements with these countries. The agreements envisage accession to the European Union when these countries are able to assume the obligations of membership.

The EU has signed partnership and co-operation agreements with Russia, Ukraine, Moldova, Kazakhstan, Kyrgyzstan, Belarus, Georgia, Armenia, Azerbaijan and Uzbekistan. A Trade and Co-operation Agreement is in force with Albania.

The purpose of all these agreements is to reduce trade barriers, develop wide-ranging co-operation and increase political dialogue at all levels.

OTHER REGIONS

The Middle East

Middle East Peace Process

Britain warmly welcomed the breakthrough in the Middle East peace process in 1993, when Israel and the Palestine Liberation Organisation (PLO) agreed to mutual recognition and signed a Declaration of Principles on interim self-government for the Palestinians in Israeli-held territories occupied in 1967. The first stage of the Declaration was implemented in May 1994, when the Palestinians adopted self-government in the Gaza Strip and the Jericho area. In October 1994 a peace treaty between Israel and Jordan was formally signed. Britain continues to encourage peace negotiations between Israel, Syria and Lebanon.

A further major advance was achieved in September 1995, when Israel and the PLO reached an interim agreement providing for a phased Israeli troop withdrawal from occupied Palestinian areas of the West Bank and for elections to a new Palestinian Council with legislative and executive powers. The British Government applauded the agreement, recognising the difficult compromises made on both sides. Britain took part in the EU-co-ordinated international observation of the Palestinian elections in January 1996.

Along with its European Union partners, Britain continues to support peace moves, politically and economically, and is committing £87 million over three years in aid to the Palestinians and the peace process through bilateral and multilateral channels. Many programmes are already under way and are designed to support Palestinian administration, police training, the Palestinian Monetary Authority, legal structures and the judiciary, water management and health care.

In June 1996, following a general election in Israel the previous month which led to a change of government, Britain and its EU partners reiterated their support for the peace process, and appealed to all parties in the region to avoid and prevent actions which might prejudice further negotiations. In response to conflict between Palestinians and Israeli forces in the West Bank and Jerusalem in September 1996, the British Government appealed to Israeli and Palestinian leaders to step back from confrontation and return to the path of trust and reconciliation.

The Gulf Conflict

As a permanent member of the UN Security Council, Britain strongly condemned Iraq's invasion of Kuwait in August 1990 and supported all the Council's resolutions designed to force Iraqi withdrawal and restore international legality. Because of Iraq's failure to withdraw, its forces were expelled in February 1991 by an international coalition led by the United States, Britain, France and Saudi Arabia, acting under a UN mandate.

UN Security Council Resolution 687,

adopted in April 1991, formalised the ceasefire in the Gulf War and stipulated conditions for Iraqi acceptance, including measures to prevent the development of weapons of mass destruction, recognition of the border with Kuwait and the payment of compensation to those who suffered as a result of the invasion of Kuwait. The resolution, fully supported by Britain, imposed sanctions on Iraq which remain in force until the Security Council is satisfied that Iraq is fully in compliance with it.

As part of the agreement ending hostilities, the Security Council authorised the creation of a Special Commission (UNSCOM) to supervise the elimination of Iraq's weapons of mass destruction. Britain has provided considerable support to UNSCOM and the International Atomic Energy Authority in the form of personnel, equipment and information since the first inspection in 1991.

The Security Council approved a separate resolution (688) in response to continued oppression by the Iraqi regime of the civilian population in northern Iraq and the marshes of southern Iraq. British military aircraft help to police the 'no fly' zones which operate over both areas to monitor Iraqi actions and to deter air attacks.

Iraqi troop movements threatening Kuwait in September/October 1994 were countered by swift military reinforcements by Britain and its coalition partners. In September 1996 Britain supported United States air raids on Iraqi military installations following an advance by Iraqi troops into the Kurdish areas of northern Iraq.

Sub-Saharan Africa

For many years, Britain has been concerned with the affairs of sub-Saharan Africa, where positive developments have included the abolition of apartheid and the establishment of a non-racial democracy in South Africa and free elections in Kenya, Malawi, Uganda and Zambia.

Since the election of President Mandela's government in 1994, South Africa's relations with Britain have broadened into new areas, ranging from development assistance to military advice, and sporting links to scientific co-operation. There has also been a steady flow of ministerial visits to and from South Africa, the most notable being that of the British Prime Minister in 1994.

The British Government is supporting the South African Government in its efforts to tackle the economic distortions and inequalities inherited from the apartheid era.

> In addition to a £100 million aid package over the three years from 1994 to 1996 and an additional £60 million announced during President Mandela's state visit to Britain in July 1996, Britain is supporting South Africa's development through trade and investment and through official export credit guarantees.

Britain is the second highest exporter to South Africa and its largest foreign investor, with a market value of between £8,000 million and £10,000 million. Nine of the top twenty foreign employers in South Africa are British. South Africa also has a significant investment in Britain. In addition there is a British investment promotion scheme designed to encourage more small and medium-sized businesses to invest in South Africa.

The importance of British–South African relations was symbolised by the historic state visits of the Queen in 1995 and of President Mandela in 1996, the latter being accompanied by a high-level ministerial team and a large trade delegation.

Asia–Pacific Region

The dynamic growth of the East Asian economies has made the Asia–Pacific region increasingly important in world affairs. There is also an encouraging trend towards political liberalisation. Britain has a long association with the region and is giving it an even higher priority in its foreign policy. Close relations are maintained with Japan, China, the ASEAN countries (Brunei, Indonesia, Malaysia, the Philippines, Singapore, Thailand and Vietnam), Australia and New Zealand. Britain has defence links with some countries in the region.

In South Asia the Indo-British Partnership initiative, established in 1993, is continuing to promote commercial and investment links between Britain and India.

Britain has stepped up political dialogue with countries in the region, developing British commercial activity through more trade and investment, and the setting up of business councils, joint commissions or industrial co-operation agreements. In addition Britain is working even more closely with governments there on international problem-solving. It is also taking advantage of growing opportunities for English language teaching, co-operation in science and technology, and educational exchanges.

Britain has welcomed the Asia–Europe Meeting (ASEM) process which held its first meeting in Bangkok in March 1996. Intended to balance existing transatlantic and transpacific relationships, ASEM will foster closer economic and political ties between European Union countries, the seven ASEAN nations, China, Japan and Korea. The second meeting will take place in Britain in 1998.

North and Latin America

Britain has long-established political, trade and cultural links with the United States. As founding members of NATO, both countries are deeply involved in Western defence arrangements (see p. 143) and, as permanent members of the UN Security Council, work closely together on major international issues. Strong links are also maintained with Canada, with whom Britain shares membership of the Commonwealth, NATO and other key international organisations.

Important British connections with Latin America date from the participation of British volunteers in the wars of independence in the early 19th century. Britain has welcomed the fact that democratically elected governments are now the norm in the region; this, together with the trend towards freer market economies, presents many opportunities for Britain to strengthen its relations with Latin American governments. In 1995 the British Government launched a Latin American trade campaign—Link into Latin America—to promote trade and investment. There has been considerable British investment in Latin America as a result of the free market economic policies and economic growth of the last few years.

ARMS CONTROL

Britain plays a major role in international efforts to control weapons of mass destruction, conventional weapons and related exports.

Weapons of Mass Destruction

Nuclear Weapons

The main instrument for controlling nuclear weapons is the 1968 Nuclear Non-Proliferation Treaty (NPT). Britain took an active part in negotiating the treaty and more recently in securing its indefinite extension in 1995. It is now working to ensure a successful follow-up to the other decisions taken during the 1995 negotiations.

As part of this effort Britain played an important role in negotiations on the recently agreed Nuclear Test Ban Treaty which it signed in September 1996. Britain has made it clear that it will respond to the challenge of multilateral talks on the global reduction of nuclear arms in a world in which those of the United States and Russian forces are counted in hundreds rather than thousands. Meanwhile, Britain has already made substantial reductions in its nuclear forces.

Biological Weapons

Britain played a large part in promoting the 1972 Biological Weapons Convention, which provides for a world-wide ban on such weapons. Unfortunately, it has no verification mechanism so Britain is taking part in international efforts to develop one. Britain will chair a review conference at the end of 1996 attended by parties to the convention.

Chemical Weapons

The 1993 Chemical Weapons Convention provides for a worldwide ban on chemical weapons. Britain made a particular contribution to the negotiations on the convention's extensive verification provisions. British efforts are now concentrated on ensuring that the Organisation of the Prohibition of Chemical Weapons, established under the convention, can implement the verification provisions effectively once the convention enters into force.

Conventional Weapons

In Europe

Britain and its NATO allies have contributed to a number of conventional arms control measures designed to contribute to European security. These include:

- the Conventional Armed Forces in Europe Treaty (the CFE Treaty), committing all NATO members and all members of the former Warsaw Pact to limit five major classes of offensive conventional weapons; and

- the Open Skies Treaty, which, when it comes into force, will allow regular flights by aircraft over the entire territories of the same states to monitor their military capabilities and activities.

A wide range of confidence- and security-building measures have been developed under the auspices of the Organisation for Security and Co-operation in Europe. Britain continues to play a full part in implementing and developing these measures. It will participate fully in a new process aimed at adapting the CFE Treaty in order to take account of changes in the European security situation. It will also press for the entry into force of the Open Skies Treaty, and will continue to contribute to arms control efforts relevant to maintaining peace in former Yugoslavia.

Around the World

In 1991 Britain pressed successfully for the establishment of a United Nations Register of Conventional Arms, aimed at making it easier to monitor any excessive arms build-up by any country in the world. During 1995–96 Britain helped secure changes to the 1981 United Nations Weaponry Convention which substantially strengthen its provisions on anti-personnel landmines and add new ones on blinding laser weapons.

Britain continues its strong support for the UN Register and is pressing for international agreement on a total ban on anti-personnel mines.

Export Controls

In addition to efforts to control weapons of mass destruction and conventional arms, it is also necessary to control the export of directly related items and of so-called dual-use items. Dual-use items may have a quite legitimate civilian use but could also have a weapons-related one. Britain participates actively in all the major export control arrangements related to these types of weapons and missiles.

HUMAN RIGHTS

The protection of human rights is an important part of British foreign policy. Universal respect for human rights is an obligation under the UN Charter, reinforced by human rights law in the form of UN and regional human rights treaties. Britain played a key role at the 1993 UN World Conference on Human Rights in Vienna, which reaffirmed that human rights are a legitimate concern of the international community. The expressions of concern about human rights do not, therefore, constitute interference in the internal affairs of another state.

The Universal Declaration of Human Rights was adopted by the UN General Assembly in 1948. Since this is not a legally binding document, the General Assembly adopted two international covenants in 1966, placing legal obligations on those states ratifying or acceding to them. The covenants came into force in 1976, Britain ratifying both in the same year. One covenant deals with economic, social and cultural rights and the other with civil and political rights. States which are parties to the covenants undertake to submit periodic reports detailing compliance with their terms. Each covenant has a UN treaty monitoring committee which examines these reports. Britain recognises the competence of these committees to receive and consider state-to-state complaints.

Other international conventions to which Britain is a party include those on:

- the elimination of racial discrimination;
- the elimination of all forms of discrimination against women;
- the rights of the child;
- torture and other cruel, inhuman or degrading treatment or punishment;
- the prevention of genocide;
- the abolition of slavery; and
- the status of refugees.

The Council of Europe

Britain is bound by the Council of Europe's Convention for the Protection of Human Rights and Fundamental Freedoms, which covers:

- the right to life, liberty and a fair trial;
- the right to marry and have a family;
- freedom of thought, conscience and religion;
- freedom of expression, including freedom of the press;
- freedom of peaceful assembly and association;
- the right to have a sentence reviewed by a higher tribunal; and
- the prohibition of torture and inhuman or degrading treatment.

Complaints about violations of the Convention are made to the European Commission of Human Rights in Strasbourg. Although one state may lodge a complaint against another, most complaints are brought against states by individuals or groups. The Commission decides whether cases are admissible and, if so, examines the matter with the parties with a view to achieving a settlement. If this fails, the Commission or the state concerned can refer the case to the European Court of Human Rights, which rules on whether the Convention has been breached. Britain has signed and ratified the 11th Protocol to the Convention, which concerns the replacement of the existing Commission and Court with a full-time Court.

Organisation for Security and Co-operation in Europe

The OSCE's human rights body, the Office for Democratic Institutions and Human Rights in Warsaw, is responsible for furthering human rights, democracy and the rule of law. It provides a forum for meetings and expert seminars to discuss the implementation of commitments in the area of human rights. The Office shares and exchanges information on the building of democratic institutions and the holding of elections in participating states. It also co-ordinates the monitoring of elections and provides expertise and training on constitutional and legal matters.

Westminster Foundation for Democracy

The Westminster Foundation for Democracy, an independent non-departmental public body established in 1992, provides assistance in building and strengthening pluralist democratic institutions overseas. It receives an annual grant from the Foreign & Commonwealth Office (£2.5 million in 1995–96) and raises funds through donations from other organisations.

The three main political parties (see p. 56) are each represented on the Foundation's Board of Governors and are appointed by the Foreign and Commonwealth Secretary after consultations with the parties. There is also a representative from one of the smaller political parties and non-party figures drawn from business, trade unions, the academic world, the media and other non-government sectors.

The Foundation is fully independent in its decision-taking, the British Government having no right of veto over the projects which the Board chooses to support. The FCO provides a non-voting member of the Board to act as a channel of communications and provide factual advice when required.

The Foundation supports projects which promote the development of:

- electoral systems, administration and monitoring;
- parliaments or other representative institutions;
- political parties;
- independent media;

- trade unions; and
- human rights groups.

Efforts are being concentrated on three priority areas—Central and Eastern Europe, Russia and Central Asia, and Anglophone Africa. The Foundation also gives sympathetic consideration to worthwhile projects in other parts of the world.

INTERNATIONAL CRIME

The British Government attaches great importance to action against international terrorism and to international co-operation against drug traffickers and organised crime. Britain and the other members of the European Union have agreed not to export arms or other military equipment to countries clearly implicated in supporting terrorist activity, and to take steps to prevent such material being diverted for terrorist purposes.

It is EU policy that no concessions should be made to terrorists or their sponsors, and that there should be solidarity among member states in the prevention of terrorism.

Britain participates actively in international forums on co-operation against the illegal drugs trade, maintains a substantial programme of overseas assistance in this field and stations drug liaison officers in a number of countries in order to liaise with the host authorities in the fight against drug trafficking. Britain is one of the main contributors to the UN International Drug Control Programme, providing £4.26 million in 1995–96. In December 1995, a British–French initiative to combat drug trafficking in the Caribbean secured support from the EU, and has since been extended to Latin America.

EU member states are setting up a central European Police Office (EUROPOL) to provide a Union-wide centre for the exchange and analysis of intelligence about serious international crime. As a step in this process, the EUROPOL Drugs Unit has already been established. EU member states also belong to the International Criminal Police Organisation (INTERPOL). British liaison with INTERPOL is provided by the National Criminal Intelligence Service (see p. 89).

Co-operation between the governments of EU member states on justice and home affairs takes place under the provisions of the Maastricht Treaty (see p. 125). A number of conventions have been agreed under these arrangements, including those on EUROPOL, extradition and the protection of the European Community's financial interests.

Britain plays a leading role in supporting international and regional initiatives to counter money laundering.

DEVELOPMENT CO-OPERATION

The objective of Britain's official overseas aid effort is to improve the quality of life of people in poorer countries by contributing to sustainable development and reducing poverty and suffering. To achieve this, the aid programme is aiming:

- to encourage sound development policies, efficient markets and good government;
- to help people achieve better education and health and to widen opportunities, particularly for women;
- to enhance productive capacity and to conserve the environment; and
- to promote international policies for sustainable development and to increase the effectiveness of multilateral development institutions.

Britain's aid programme (the sixth largest in the world), which is delivered through the Foreign & Commonwealth Office's Overseas Development Administration (ODA), amounted to £2,314 million in 1994–95. Of this, 87 per cent went to developing countries and 10 per cent to countries in transition in Central and Eastern Europe and the former Soviet Union. (The remaining three per cent comprises mainly administrative costs.) About 48 per cent was given directly to individual countries and the remainder channelled through international bodies, such as the European Union, the United Nations and the World Bank group of institutions. In addition, over £276 million was invested in developing countries by the Commonwealth Development Corporation in 1995 (see p. 137). Some of the aid budget goes to programmes administered by the British Council (see p. 140) and by over 110 non-governmental organisations (such as Oxfam and Save the Children Fund).

Economic Reform

Britain works closely with developing countries and countries in Eastern Europe and Central Asia to promote sound economic management and create efficient market economies. Britain's aid programme helps British experts to assist countries design and implement changes to their economies, for example, tax reform, privatisation, civil service reform and management of the financial sector. Aid is also used to support imports of essential goods and pay for important public services in countries such as Tanzania, Uganda, Ghana and Zambia, which are reforming their economies. In Eastern Europe and Central Asia know-how from Britain has been very important in helping countries privatise old state assets and support the growth of new small businesses.

The Private Sector

The Commonwealth Development Corporation (CDC) is the Government's main instrument within the aid programme for encouraging private-sector investment in developing countries. It provides loans, equity funds and management services for financially viable investments in agriculture, fisheries, minerals, industry, transport, communications and housing. At the end of 1995 it had investments and commitments worth nearly £1,490 million in 369 enterprises in 50 countries.

The ODA itself supports private sector development by providing British expertise and financial support through schemes such as:

- business management training in Zimbabwe;
- setting up an enterprise centre to give advice and help for small firms in Namibia;
- privatising farms in Russia; and
- supporting new stock markets in Eastern Europe.

Good Government

Assistance for good government is a major priority for the British aid programme. In 1994–95 there were 180 new projects—up by 30 per cent on the previous year—and expenditure totalled about £164 million. The aim is to help promote democracy, human rights and the rule of law and assist governments to become more accountable and competent. British assistance includes:

- support for civil service and local government reform;
- electoral assistance;
- reform of the police and judiciary;
- projects to control corruption; and
- advice on the promotion and protection of human rights.

Reducing Poverty

About three-quarters of British bilateral aid to developing countries goes to the poorest ones. In India, Pakistan and Bangladesh projects include rural development, urban slum upgrading and the provision of health, family planning and education services for poor people. Some of the ODA's projects to help the poor are carried out in conjunction with non-governmental organisations. In Nepal, for example, WaterAid has built a gravity-fed water system, piping water from springs in the hills to tapstands in the village so that all the houses now have latrines and access to water.

Britain is at the forefront of efforts to relieve the heavy burden of debt on many developing countries. The ODA has written off over £1,200 million of British aid loans to 31 of the poorest countries. Britain has also initiated a number of schemes for debt relief, including the present rescheduling arrangements agreed by western creditor governments (the Paris Club) in 1995. These terms allow for up to two-thirds relief on the eligible debt of the poorest, most indebted countries that have a good record of economic reform. Nineteen countries have benefited so far from these higher rates of debt relief.

Britain is also working with the international financial institutions, such as the World Bank and the International Monetary

Fund, to examine further measures to tackle the problem of multilateral debt for the poorest, most indebted countries.

Education

ODA education policy is in line with the principles agreed at the 1990 World Conference on 'Education for All', to which other major international institutions subscribe. ODA projects focus on primary and tertiary education and concentrate on key areas such as:

- curriculum development;
- teacher education;
- examination reform;
- the development of learning materials, including books;
- the planning, financing and administration of education; and
- the provision of school buildings and equipment.

In 1994–95 some 9,500 students and trainees from developing countries, mainly postgraduates, received ODA support to study and train in Britain under technical co-operation training arrangements and three scholarship schemes—the Commonwealth Scholarship and Fellowship Plan, the British Chevening Scholarships (see p. 463) and the ODA Shared Scholarships Scheme. Part of Britain's grant aid to South Africa is a £2 million project that will provide bursaries and loans to 1,200 university and technical students from disadvantaged communities studying science, engineering, commerce and medicine.

Health

Britain's objective in health and population policy is to help countries obtain the best possible use of limited resources by improving the relevance, effectiveness and coverage of health services, in particular by increasing access to essential health care for women and children. Over 10 per cent of the aid programme is spent on health and population activities.

Through its *Children by Choice, Not Chance*

policy, Britain seeks to ensure that more women and men can receive good quality family planning and reproductive health care, allowing them to choose the size of their families and the spacing and timing of the birth of their children. The policy also enables women to go through pregnancy and childbirth more safely. Over £180 million has been committed for new population and reproductive health projects since the International Conference on Population and Development in Cairo in 1994.

The British aid programme also aims to reduce suffering from communicable diseases, especially tuberculosis, malaria and HIV/AIDS. In 1995 Britain was the largest bilateral donor to the World Health Organisation's anti-tuberculosis programme. Britain has also strongly supported the establishment of the new joint UN programme on HIV/AIDS.

Britain funds a strong programme of technology development and research—about £8 million annually—in four priority areas:

- health care management and health sector reform;
- reproductive health;
- communicable diseases; and
- health care in unstable living environments.

Promoting Opportunities for Women

In the last few years Britain has made considerable progress in supporting the advancement of women in the aid programme. In 1994–95 over 16 per cent of bilateral aid was targeted at improving women's as well as men's needs, compared with 12 per cent the previous year. Making women and men more equal will improve the quality of life for people in poorer countries.

At the Fourth World Conference on Women in Peking in 1995 the governments of 189 countries committed themselves to the long term goal of gender equality. The Conference adopted an action plan to promote a more equal partnership between women and men in the home, in communities and at all levels of political and economic life. The ODA is already addressing many of these concerns through its bilateral aid programme and in the support it gives to multilateral and non-governmental organisations.

Projects designed to help women and girls gain greater access to education, health and incomes will continue to play a key role in the British aid programme. The ODA is also committed to giving more support to:

- help institutions in partner governments to train staff and develop systems to address gender issues in policies and programmes, such as economic reform and public expenditure;

- improve data collection and statistical analysis to measure and value women's, as well as men's, work;

- revise legal frameworks to promote gender equality;

- promote women's participation in government and politics; and

- assist non-governmental organisations concerned with the promotion of gender equality.

The Environment

Protection and sustainable management of the environment are key aims of the British aid programme. In 1994–95 the ODA committed over £285 million bilaterally in support for over 260 projects aimed at protecting the environment, promoting cleaner technologies or supporting sustainable agriculture. Activities ranged from preparing integrated coastal zone management plans in South Africa, Eritrea and Ghana, to funding country studies on climate change and desertification.

In addition to helping countries address national environmental problems, Britain takes action on global environmental concerns shared by all countries.

The Global Environment Facility (GEF) is a trust fund of over $2,000 million which helps developing countries and countries with economies in transition to meet the incremental costs of protecting the world's environment in four main areas:

- climate change;

- biodiversity;

- pollution of international waters; and

- protection of the ozone layer (for countries in transition only).

Britain has committed £130 million to the GEF and is the Fund's fifth largest donor.

Climate Change

Britain signed the Convention on Climate Change at the 1992 Earth Summit and ratified it in the following year. The aim of the Convention is to stabilise atmospheric concentrations of greenhouse gases at a level which will prevent dangerous climate change. It commits all parties to prepare national programmes identifying the sources of such gases and steps to limit emissions. Britain believes that the best way of assisting developing countries to reduce greenhouse gas emission is through energy efficiency programmes. In 1994–95 Britain committed £48 million for development projects that promote energy efficiency.

Ozone Depletion

The Montreal Protocol's Multilateral Fund helps developing countries to meet some of the extra costs of phasing out ozone-depleting substances. Britain has so far committed $40 million to the Fund, which will be replenished in 1997.

Biodiversity

The Rio Biodiversity Convention, which Britain signed in June 1992 and ratified a year later, requires countries to take action to halt the loss of animal and plant species and preserve genetic resources, and to produce plans for conserving them.

Britain is helping countries to fulfil their obligations under the Convention through its contributions to the GEF, the British bilateral aid programme, and the Darwin Initiative for the Survival of Species, which was launched at the Earth Summit in 1992. Since 1994 Britain has committed £48 million to projects promoting biodiversity.

Forestry

The ODA has about 200 forestry projects under way or under preparation in 41 countries, at a total cost of over £180 million. The aim is to help developing countries utilise their forests sustainably and to reduce the rate of deforestation. When sustainably managed, forests can be an invaluable resource for communities in developing countries and represent a major habitat for biological diversity. Forests are also important for the world's climate, since trees absorb carbon dioxide, a gas which contributes to global warming.

Natural Resources

The ODA spends some £100 million a year on helping developing countries to promote sustainable and efficient management of their renewable resources in areas such as small-scale agriculture, animal production, fisheries, forestry and wildlife. This involves working directly with communities as well as helping governments to formulate and implement appropriate policies.

Examples of ODA natural resources programmes include:

- helping Botswana develop better rangelands and wildlife management systems;
- working through the non-governmental organisation CARE to help farmers in Bangladesh farm fish in their rice fields;
- supporting community-based forestry management in Nepal; and
- developing sustainable land-use systems in the buffer zones around national parks and protected areas in Bolivia.

In addition to programmes in individual developing countries, Britain spends around £20 million a year on technology development and research in agriculture, forestry, livestock and fisheries.

Britain is also a founder member of, and contributor to, the Consultative Group on International Agricultural Research, which is dedicated to improving food security through sustainable agriculture. Research through the Group helps to increase the supply of staple foods, preserve plant genetic resources and strengthen scientific capacity in developing countries.

The ODA's scientific executive agency, the Natural Resources Institute, was privatised in

1996 and continues to be a multi-disciplinary centre of expertise on which the ODA can draw. In 1995 the Agency's work for the ODA included:

- research into replacing a chemical pesticide causing ozone depletion with a more environmentally-friendly technique for fumigating crops;
- management and conservation of forestry and fisheries; and
- the provision of advice on the storage, handling and marketing of food and cash crops after harvest.

Emergency Relief

The ODA's Disaster Unit co-ordinates the British Government's provision of humanitarian aid, which takes the form of financial grants, practical items such as tents, blankets and medical supplies, or staff with needed skills. The unit works closely with the International Red Cross and Red Crescent, the European Union and voluntary agencies. Through its Disaster Relief Initiative, the unit also mounts its own response to emergencies overseas; for example, road convoys and engineering projects in former Yugoslavia, and water tankerage for Rwanda refugees.

The ODA also funds over £3 million each year for disaster mitigation projects, such as a volcanic hazards mapping project in Chile and a disaster management programme in Bangladesh run by OXFAM.

In 1994–95 Britain spent nearly £334 million on emergencies; £209 million was provided bilaterally, of which £85 million was channelled through non-governmental organisations

CULTURAL RELATIONS

The British Council is Britain's principal agency for cultural relations overseas, with 228 offices in 109 countries (compared with 108 offices in 79 countries in 1979). Its purpose is to promote a wider knowledge of Britain and the English language and to encourage cultural, scientific, technological and educational co-operation between Britain and other countries. The Council:

- helps people to study, train or make professional contacts in Britain;

- enables British specialists to teach, advise or establish joint projects abroad;
- teaches English and promotes its use;
- provides library and information services;
- promotes scientific and technical training, research collaboration and exchanges; and
- makes British arts and literature more widely known.

The Council runs 185 libraries, resource centres and information centres (including 40 in Central and Eastern Europe), and 95 English language teaching centres. In 1994–95 ten million loans of books and other materials were made to 500,000 library members. The Council funds over 9,000 scientific visits and more than 1,300 research links. Additionally, it administers over 400,000 British professional and academic examinations each year. The Council is financed partly by a grant from the Foreign & Commonwealth Office. The training and education programmes organised by the Council as part of the British aid programme are another important source of income. One third of its income comes from other earnings.

Educational Exchanges

The British Council recruits teachers for work overseas, organises short overseas visits by British experts, encourages cultural exchange visits, and organises academic interchange between British universities and colleges and those in other countries. It arranges over 50,000 visits to and from Britain each year.

The ODA helps fund certain Council programmes, such as:

- recruitment of staff for overseas universities;
- secondment of staff from British higher education establishments; and
- organisation of short-term teaching and advisory visits.

The Central Bureau for Educational Visits and Exchanges, which is part of the British Council, promotes partnerships and exchanges between schools, teachers, students and pupils throughout Europe. Opportunities for young people include school and class links and English language summer camps. For the post-16 age group, there are work placements and English language assistants' posts as well as other exchange programmes.

The Arts

The British Council initiates or supports more than 2,000 arts and literature events each year. These activities include tours by British theatre companies, orchestras, choirs, opera and dance companies, and jazz, rock and folk groups, as well as visits by individual actors, musicians and artists. The Council also arranges for directors, designers, choreographers and conductors to work in other countries. In addition, it organises and supports literature, fine arts and other cultural exhibitions, and British participation in book fairs and international film festivals.

Further Reading

Britain and Development Aid. Aspects of Britain series, HMSO, 1995.

British Council Annual Report.

British Overseas Aid Annual Review 1995. Overseas Development Administration, 1996.

Departmental Report 1996: The Government's Expenditure Plans 1996–97 to 1998–99. Foreign & Commonwealth Office, including Overseas Development Administration. Cm 3203. HMSO, 1996.

European Union. Aspects of Britain series, HMSO, 1994.

Statement on the Defence Estimates 1996. HMSO, 1996.

10 Defence

Introduction	142	Nuclear Forces	147
North Atlantic Treaty Organisation	143	Defence Equipment Programmes	147
United Kingdom Defence Policy	144	The Armed Forces	148
		Administration	149

Britain's defence policy supports its wider security policy, which is to maintain the country's freedom and territorial integrity, and that of its Dependent Territories, as well as its ability to pursue its legitimate interests at home and abroad. As a member of NATO (North Atlantic Treaty Organisation), Britain makes a significant contribution to maintaining stability throughout Europe and has been providing a major part of the NATO peace implementation force in Bosnia.

INTRODUCTION

With the reduction in the potential strategic threats facing Britain as a result of the end of the Cold War, progress has been made in security-building and co-operation with states in central and eastern Europe. However, the end of East–West confrontation has been followed by problems of instability, nationalism and extremism within parts of Europe and beyond. These developments are the major factors shaping defence policy today. Britain and its NATO allies have responded to these changes by adapting their policies and the structure of their armed forces to meet the defence requirements of the future.

NATO remains the foundation of Britain's defence and security policies. In addition, Britain works to increase security through its membership of the Western European Union (WEU), the European Union (EU—see p. 118), the Organisation for Security and Co-operation in Europe (OSCE—see p. 120) and the United Nations (UN—see p. 118). These organisations have been involved in negotiating an end to conflicts, in peacekeeping deployments and in humanitarian missions.

Britain and the other WEU member states are developing the WEU as the body which will provide political authority and direction for European operations in the future. At the January 1994 NATO Summit it was decided that NATO assets could be made available for European/WEU operations. In co-operation with NATO, Britain and the rest of the WEU are supporting the implementation of conflict prevention and crisis management measures.

The current fundamental restructuring of Britain's armed forces recognises the need for flexibility in the face of future uncertainty. The armed forces are, therefore, equipped to take part in combined operations, ranging from small-scale peacekeeping or humanitarian missions to large-scale high-intensity conflict.

A permanent Joint Headquarters, at Northwood in London, and a Joint Rapid Deployment Force became operational in 1996. They will strengthen Britain's ability to project military forces worldwide in support of its interests and will enable the three armed Services to work together more effectively.

The highest priority continues to be placed on maximising the cost-effectiveness and military capabilities of the armed forces. Published in 1993, the Defence Costs Study—*Front Line First* (see p. 149)— examined all areas of administration and support to the front line to ensure that the money spent contributes to fighting capability.

NORTH ATLANTIC TREATY ORGANISATION

NATO has provided Britain's main means of defence against a major external threat for over 45 years. It is the only security organisation with the military means to back up its security guarantees and has consequently undertaken action on behalf of the UN in former Yugoslavia. NATO unites the interests of Europe and North America in the pursuit of peace, stability and well-being in the whole of Europe. Most of Britain's forces are committed to NATO.

Adaptation of NATO

As part of its continuing post-Cold War evolution NATO launched a number of important initiatives at the 1994 Summit, including the creation of the Combined Joint Task Force concept, the Partnership for Peace, the enlargement of NATO, and the development of a stronger European defence identity. NATO also agreed to intensify and expand its efforts against the proliferation of weapons of mass destruction (see p. 133).

Combined Joint Task Force

The Combined Joint Task Force concept will enable NATO to carry out a wide range of crisis management missions, such as support for peacekeeping operations under the auspices of the UN and the OSCE. It also gives NATO the flexibility within the Alliance's command structures to involve other non–NATO countries in its operations.

Partnership for Peace

The Partnership for Peace seeks to deepen co-operative political and military ties between NATO and the central and eastern European countries. It also promotes better co-operation between military forces engaged in multinational operations such as peacekeeping and humanitarian relief. By April 1996, 27 states had signed the Partnership for Peace, including Russia, almost all the central and eastern European states, Sweden, Finland, Austria, Malta and most of the central Asian and Trans-Caucasian states of the former Soviet Union.

In addition to its work within NATO on Partnership for Peace, Britain has signed formal Memoranda of Understanding on bilateral defence contacts with 16 central and eastern European countries. The Memoranda are designed to promote stability in the region, encourage openness in all military affairs and develop closer co-operation between the states concerned and Western security institutions. Britain's contacts include exchanges between Ministers and senior military and civilian staff, the provision of places on British military training courses, English language training and assistance with the development of expertise in defence management.

NATO Enlargement

NATO is committed to opening Alliance membership to other European countries. Following a study into the principles guiding enlargement and their implications, NATO agreed to intensify discussions with interested members of the Partnership for Peace and to work towards strengthening ties between NATO and all Partner countries. These discussions will lead in due course to individual countries being invited to apply for NATO membership.

European Defence Identity

The Alliance is also taking steps to develop, within an adapted NATO, a stronger European defence identity that would permit the creation of effective forces capable of operating under the control of the WEU in line with the objectives agreed at the 1994 Summit.

NATO Force and Command Structures

The size, availability and deployment of NATO forces reflect the Alliance's defensive nature. NATO strategy involves:

- deployment in Europe of smaller and highly mobile flexible forces;
- a reduced reliance on nuclear weapons;
- a higher proportion of forces kept at lower levels of readiness;
- increased importance of mobile reserves and augmentation forces; and
- the continuing need for force modernisation.

Forces available to NATO fall into three categories: immediate and rapid reaction, main defence and augmentation forces.

Under the present structure, major NATO commands exist for Allied Command Europe and Allied Command Atlantic. Among the sub-commands covering Britain is Allied Forces North West Europe, which incorporates the land mass of Britain and Norway, the United Kingdom air defence region and the North Sea; it is commanded from headquarters at RAF High Wycombe, in Buckinghamshire. NATO members have agreed that the command structure should be renovated to reflect the new circumstances and challenges facing the Alliance; changes, once agreed, will be made over the next few years.

UNITED KINGDOM DEFENCE POLICY

The aim of Britain's defence strategy is:

- to deter any threats to, and, if necessary, defend the freedom and territorial integrity of, Britain and its Dependent Territories; this includes providing

support as necessary for the civil authority in countering terrorism;

- to contribute to the promotion of Britain's wider security interests, including the protection of freedom, democratic institutions and free trade; and
- to promote peace and help maximise Britain's international prestige and influence.

Within this aim is a range of tasks which define the military activities to be undertaken by the Ministry of Defence and the armed forces in order to give effect to defence and security policy.

Britain and its Dependencies

The armed forces continue to have day-to-day responsibility for safeguarding Britain's territory, airspace and territorial waters. They also provide for the security and reinforcement, as necessary, of the Dependent Territories and, when required, support for the civil authorities in Britain and the Dependent Territories.

Maritime Defence

The Royal Navy ensures the integrity of British territorial waters and the protection of British rights and interests in the surrounding seas. The maintenance of a 24-hour, year-round presence in British waters provides considerable reassurance to merchant ships and other mariners. The Royal Air Force (RAF) also contributes to maritime requirements, for instance through the Nimrod MR2 force, which provides air surveillance of surface vessels and submarines.

Land Defence

Regular Army units committed to activities in defence of Britain and its Dependent Territories include 24 Infantry battalions and seven Home Service battalions. Tasks include contributing to the security of national and NATO nuclear forces, military support to the machinery of government in war, military aid to the civil power throughout Britain and its

Dependent Territories, maintaining the security of the Dependent Territories and State ceremonial and public duties.

Air Defence

Air defence of Britain and the surrounding seas is maintained by a system of layered defences. Continuous radar cover is provided by the Improved United Kingdom Air Defence Ground Environment (IUKADGE), supplemented by the NATO Airborne Early Warning Force, to which the RAF contributes six E-3D aircraft. The RAF also provides six squadrons of all-weather Tornado F3 air defence aircraft, supported by tanker aircraft and, in wartime, an additional F3 squadron and armed Hawk trainer aircraft. Royal Navy air defence destroyers can be also linked to the IUKADGE, providing radar and electronic warfare coverage and surface-to-air missiles. Ground-launched Rapier missiles defend the main RAF bases. Naval aircraft also contribute to British air defence.

Overseas Garrisons

Britain maintains garrisons in Hong Kong, Gibraltar, the Sovereign Base Areas of Cyprus and the Falkland Islands. The Hong Kong garrison is being reduced in stages until 1997, when the territory will revert to Chinese sovereignty (see p. 123). Gibraltar provides headquarters and communications facilities for NATO in the western Mediterranean, and Cyprus acts as a base for operations in the Middle East and North Africa.

Northern Ireland

The armed forces provide support to the Royal Ulster Constabulary (RUC) in maintaining law and order and countering terrorism. There are currently 18 major units in the infantry role assigned to Northern Ireland, including six Home Service battalions of the Royal Irish Regiment. The number of those major units deployed to the province at any one time is dependent on the prevailing security situation. The Royal Navy patrols territorial waters around Northern Ireland and its inland waterways in order, among other things, to deter and intercept the movement of terrorist weapons. The Royal Marines provide troops to meet Navy and Army commitments, while RAF helicopters provide support to ground forces.

Other Tasks

Other tasks include the provision of:

- military assistance to civil ministries, including assistance to maintain the essentials of life in the community and carrying out work of national importance;
- military aid to the civil community, including during emergencies;
- military search and rescue;
- military intelligence and surveillance; and
- physical protection and security.

Britain and its Allies

The foundation of Britain's defence is provided through its membership of NATO.

Maritime Forces

Most Royal Navy ships are committed to NATO. Permanent contributions are made to NATO's standing naval forces in the Atlantic, the English Channel and the Mediterranean. The main components of the Fleet are:

- three aircraft carriers operating Sea Harrier aircraft and Sea King anti-submarine helicopters;
- 35 destroyers and frigates;
- 12 nuclear-powered attack submarines; and
- amphibious forces, including two assault ships and a helicopter carrier which is currently under construction.

For information on Britain's independent nuclear deterrent see p. 147.

Land Forces

The multinational Allied Command Europe Rapid Reaction Corps (ARRC) is the key land component of NATO's rapid reaction forces. Britain is the lead nation of the Corps, which became fully operational in April 1995.

Britain is fully committed to the continuing effectiveness of the ARRC. It is commanded by a British general and some 55,000 British regular troops are assigned to it. This includes Britain's contribution, as the ARRC's lead nation, of some 60 per cent of the headquarters staff and Corps level combat support and combat service support units. Britain also provides two of the ten divisions available to the Corps—an armoured division of three armoured brigades stationed in Germany, and a mechanised division of two mechanised brigades and an airborne brigade based in Britain. An air-mobile brigade, assigned to one of the ARRC's two multinational divisions, is also located in Britain. A British contingent is present in Bosnia as part of an international peacekeeping force from NATO and non-NATO countries (see p. 129).

Air Forces

The RAF makes a major contribution to NATO's Immediate and Rapid Reaction Forces. Around 100 fixed-wing aircraft and 40 helicopters are allocated to support these Reaction Forces. Tornado F3 and Rapier surface-to-air missiles form part of the Supreme Allied Commander Europe's Immediate Reaction Force, while Harrier, Tornado GR1 and GR1a provide offensive support and tactical reconnaissance to the Rapid Reaction Force. Chinook and Puma helicopters provide troop airlift facilities for the ARRC (see above) or other deployed land forces. Tornado F3 and Tornado GR1b aircraft support NATO's maritime reaction forces.

Modified RAF Tornado GR1 aircraft (designated GR1b), equipped with the Sea Eagle missile, have the task of maritime attack. The Tornado GR1b force has been in service since March 1994. The RAF will continue to provide Nimrod maritime patrol aircraft and search and rescue helicopters.

Since 1991 the number of RAF squadrons in Germany has been reduced to four Tornado GR1 strike/attack squadrons, two Harrier offensive support squadrons and a Puma/

Chinook support helicopter squadron at RAF Bruggen and RAF Laarbruch. It is intended that RAF Laarbruch will close in 1999 and, subject to consultation, RAF Bruggen will close in 2002; the aircraft squadrons and the support helicopters currently based there will be withdrawn to existing bases in Britain. Meanwhile these aircraft and personnel, alongside the continuing and significant Army presence in Germany, are a visible sign of Britain's commitment to the defence of Europe.

Other Forces

Britain contributes to NATO's maritime augmentation forces. These are held at the lowest state of readiness and in peacetime comprise ships mainly in routine refit or maintenance. It also contributes special forces to support reaction and main defence force deployments for surveillance, reconnaissance, offensive action and military assistance operations. The United Kingdom Amphibious Force, together with its Dutch counterpart, is assigned to the Supreme Allied Commander Atlantic for the reinforcement of Norway and could be deployed by the Supreme Allied Commander Europe, for example, with the ARRC. The Force is also a candidate for a range of WEU operations. RAF fighter and transport aircraft will also be available for WEU operations.

Wider Security Interests

Military tasks to promote Britain's wider security interests may be undertaken unilaterally or multilaterally with support from NATO or directly for UN or OSCE operations.

United Nations Operations

Britain remains a major contributor to UN operations. Contingents are currently deployed in Cyprus, where Britain is the largest UN contributor, and Iraq/Kuwait.

Other Operational Deployments

Royal Navy ships of the Armilla Patrol continue to provide reassurance and assistance to entitled merchant shipping in the Gulf area and regularly participate in maritime exercises with navies of Gulf states and Gulf war coalition allies. The Patrol also conducts interception and boarding operations to ensure that ships do not breach UN sanctions against Iraq (see p. 130).

The number of operations against trafficking in illicit drugs has increased in recent years, especially in the Caribbean, where the West Indies Guardship and other Royal Navy ships work closely with the authorities of the United States, the Dependent Territories and the Regional Security System to combat drug trafficking. Although primary responsibility for this work rests with other government departments, the armed forces assist where this can be done without detriment to the performance of other military tasks.

British Garrisons

A British garrison is maintained in Brunei, South-East Asia, at the request of the Brunei Government. A British military presence is maintained in Belize, Central America, in the form of a jungle training support unit. The withdrawal of the full British garrison was completed in 1994.

Military Assistance

During 1995–96, some 4,270 students from 117 countries attended military training courses in Britain. On 1 January 1996, 353 British Service personnel (61 Royal Navy and Royal Marines, 226 Army and 66 Royal Air Force) were on loan in 22 countries. Their duties include assisting, advising and training the armed forces of the country or territory to which they are loaned.

NUCLEAR FORCES

Britain's operationally independent nuclear deterrent forces continue to provide the ultimate guarantee of national security. All of these forces are also allocated to NATO and make an important contribution to the Alliance's strategy of war prevention.

British nuclear forces currently comprise two Vanguard class ballistic missile submarines, carrying Trident missiles procured from the United States and equipped with British nuclear warheads, together with free-fall nuclear bombs carried by RAF Tornado aircraft. A third Vanguard class submarine will enter service in 1998 and a fourth around the turn of the century. Four submarines will ensure that Britain can maintain continuous deterrent patrols throughout the 25-year life of the Trident force.

Adjusting to improving strategic circumstances, Britain is deploying far fewer warheads on each submarine than the Trident system's theoretical maximum. The assignment of Trident to both the strategic and sub-strategic nuclear roles is also allowing reductions in the size of Britain's nuclear deterrent forces. All nuclear free-fall bombs will be taken out of service by the end of 1998, and Trident will then provide Britain's single nuclear system.

DEFENCE EQUIPMENT PROGRAMMES

Modern equipment is essential if one of the key aims of Britain's force restructuring programme is to be achieved, namely that of increasing the flexibility and mobility of the armed forces. The outcome of the Defence Costs Study (see p. 149) has enabled the British Government to preserve the front line (and its essential operational support) and to make a number of important improvements in the armed forces.

Current and planned front-line improvements for the Royal Navy equipment programme include:

- the introduction of the rest of the Trident submarines;
- an invitation to tender for the design and building of a second batch of Trafalgar class submarines to enter service at the beginning of the next century;
- a substantially modernised destroyer and frigate fleet, including the introduction of a new air defence frigate developed collaboratively with France and Italy;

- a follow-on batch of 7 Sandown class single role minehunters;

- introduction of a new helicopter carrier, planned to enter service in 1998, to enhance Britain's amphibious forces;

- 18 new Sea Harrier F/A2 aircraft and the upgrading of the existing Harriers to F/A2 standard; and

- the building of replacements for the assault ships *Fearless* and *Intrepid*.

The Army front line is being enhanced by:

- the introduction of an all-Challenger 2 tank fleet;

- Westland Apache attack helicopters to replace the Lynx in the anti-armour role;

- improved Rapier and new Starstreak missiles to improve air defence;

- a new medium-range anti-tank missile; and

- a new generation of combat radios.

Improvements for the RAF include:

- the Eurofighter 2000 from the beginning of the next century;

- upgrading of the Jaguar, Tornado GR1 (to GR4), and Tornado F3 aircraft;

- refurbishment of the Nimrod maritime patrol aircraft;

- orders for new air-launched anti-armour and stand-off missiles; and

- orders for further EH101 and Chinook support helicopters and the introduction of Hercules C130J aircraft from 1997.

THE ARMED FORCES

Personnel

It is predicted that by April 1997 the strength of the armed forces will be around 111,000 in the Army, about 57,000 in the RAF and about 46,000 in the Royal Navy. In April 1996 regular reserves totalled 263,800 and volunteer reserves and auxiliary forces almost 62,000. Civilian staff numbers are planned to fall from 127,700 (in April 1996) to 115,800 (102,600 British-based and 13,200 locally engaged) by 2002.

Commissioned Ranks

Commissions, either by promotion from the ranks or by direct entry based on educational and other qualifications, are granted for short, medium and long terms. All three Services have schemes for school, university and college sponsorships.

Commissioned ranks receive initial training at the Britannia Royal Naval College, Dartmouth; the Royal Military Academy, Sandhurst; or the Royal Air Force College, Cranwell. This is followed by specialist training, which may include degree courses at service establishments or universities.

Higher training for officers is currently provided by the Royal Naval College and Joint Services Defence College, Greenwich; the Army Staff College, Camberley; and the Royal Air Force Staff College, Bracknell. The Defence Costs Study (see p. 149) concluded that courses should be subsumed into a tri-Service course which will reinforce the joint approach to the tactical and operational levels of conflict. As such, the Joint Services Command and Staff College will be established in 1997 at Camberley. The Higher Command and Staff Course, conducted at Camberley, will remain as a focus for the study of the operational level of command, but will be expanded from 24 to 30 officers for each course to increase the joint service aspect.

Non-commissioned Ranks

Engagements for non-commissioned ranks in the Army and the RAF range from six months to 22 years; they can be for a maximum of 37 years in the Royal Navy (22 years in the Royal Marines). There is a wide choice of engagement length and terms of service. Subject to a minimum period of service, entrants may leave at any time, giving 18 months' notice (12 months for certain engagements). Discharge may also be granted on compassionate or medical grounds.

Throughout their Service careers, non-commissioned personnel receive basic training supplemented by specialist training. Study for educational qualifications is encouraged and Service trade and technical training lead to nationally recognised qualifications.

Reserve Forces

Reserve forces are a central component of Britain's armed forces. They include members who become reservists following a period of regular service (regular reserve); others are volunteers who train in their spare time. Volunteer reserve forces include the Royal Naval Reserve, the Royal Marines Reserve, the Territorial Army, the Royal Auxiliary Air Force and the Royal Air Force Volunteer Reserve. Reserves are available to support regular forces, either as units or as individuals, in time of tension or war. In particular, reserves can provide skills and units not available or required in peacetime. Reserves are also a valuable link between the Services and the civil community. New legislation (the Reserve Forces Act 1996) allows more flexible use of the Reserves, especially the Volunteer Reserves, in roles such as peacekeeping, humanitarian and disaster relief operations.

ADMINISTRATION

The Defence Budget

The estimated defence budget for 1996–97 is £21,425 million, with expenditure plans for 1997–98 and 1998–99 of £21,923 million and £22,624 million respectively. The Government anticipates a reduction of 14.5 per cent in real terms between 1992–93 and 1997–98. By 1998–99 defence spending will reduce to 2.7 per cent of gross domestic product; the current average for NATO countries is 2.3 per cent.

Defence Management

The Ministry of Defence has a dual role as a Department of State and the highest military headquarters of the armed forces. A unified Central Staff made up of military officers and civilians is responsible for defence policy, resource allocation and equipment requirements, direction of operations at the highest level, and management policy for the armed forces and the Ministry of Defence.

Department support services are provided to the Head Office, Commands and budget-holders by, among others, the Procurement Executive, the Defence Intelligence Service, the Defence Estates Organisation, and the Defence Export Services Organisation.

Each Service's Chief of Staff is responsible, through the Chief of the Defence Staff and the Secretary of State for Defence, for the fighting effectiveness, efficiency and morale of his Service. They and the other senior officers and officials at the head of each of the Department's main functions form a single body responsible for all the activities of the Ministry of Defence and the armed forces. This corporate board is chaired by the permanent civilian head of the Department, the Permanent Under-Secretary.

Since 1991, military and civilian managers have been given ever greater authority and responsibility for fulfilling their objectives through the most efficient use of the resources allocated to them. This is aimed at achieving greater value for money and clearer direction and accountability. The Defence Costs Study examined all aspects of the Ministry of Defence other than the front line itself. Its aim was to identify cost savings that could be made in the support area without reducing front-line effectiveness, and the study teams examined over 30 functional areas. As a result, in 1994 proposals were announced for savings of £750 million in 1996–97, rising to more than £1,000 million a year by the end of the decade, together with a number of improvements in the equipment programme.

Wherever possible the Study sought to identify and implement changes designed to achieve greater working efficiency rather than financial savings. Major emphasis was placed on a clearer definition of the role of the Head Office, further delegation of responsibility to Commands and budget-holders outside London and the rationalisation of many Commands, and training and support activities on a joint-Service basis.

Defence Procurement

About 40 per cent of the defence budget is spent on military equipment, including the procurement of spares and associated costs. The aim is to procure equipment, works and services from the suppliers offering the best value for money, taking all relevant factors into account. When assessing options, particular consideration is given not just to the initial procurement cost of a project, but also to the costs that could be necessary to support it through its Service life. Competition is fundamental to obtaining value for money and takes place wherever possible. In general, competitions are open to prime and sub-contractors from overseas. Britain also seeks to promote market liberalisation for defence equipment worldwide.

International Procurement Collaboration

International collaborative projects are becoming increasingly important as equipment development and production costs increase and defence budgets are reduced. Britain favours such co-operation wherever it makes economic and military sense by providing value for money and improving standardisation. It therefore plays an active role in NATO's Conference of National Armaments Directors, which promotes equipment collaboration between NATO members. Britain is also a member of the WEU's Western European Armaments Group, which is the main European forum for consultations about armaments.

Current collaborative programmes include:

- development of the Eurofighter 2000 (with Germany, Italy and Spain);

- anti-tank guided weapons (with Belgium, France, Germany and the Netherlands);

- a new air defence frigate (with France and Italy);

- the Multiple Launch Rocket System (with the United States, Germany, France and Italy);

- the EH101 helicopter (with Italy);

- anti-air missiles (with France and Italy); and

- a multi-role armoured vehicle (with France and Germany).

Further Reading

Britain, NATO and European Security. Aspects of Britain series. HMSO, 1994.

The Government's Expenditure Plans 1996–97 to 1998–99. Departmental Report by the Ministry of Defence. HMSO, 1996.

Statement on the Defence Estimates 1996. HMSO, 1996.

Front Line First: The Defence Costs Study. HMSO, 1994.

NATO at a Glance. NATO, 1996.

Economic
Affairs

11 Economy

Economic Background   153
Economic Strategy   157
National Income and
  Expenditure   159
Public Finance Strategy   161
Main Programmes and Priorities 161
Control of Public Expenditure 163
Main Sources of Revenue   165
Public Sector Financial
  Operations   171

The British economy emerged from recession in 1992 and is continuing to grow, with inflation remaining at historically low levels. Output is currently more than 7 per cent above the previous peak reached in 1990. Growth has taken place across a broad front, with major contributions coming from exports and consumer spending. The current economic climate is also characterised by falling unemployment and low interest rates. The economy is based primarily on private enterprise, with the private sector accounting for 82 per cent of output and 79 per cent of employment. Government economic policies are designed to help businesses and individuals generate sustainable economic growth and rising prosperity by creating a stable economic environment with permanently low inflation and sound public finances, and by allowing markets to operate efficiently.

ECONOMIC BACKGROUND

Output

From 1981 to 1990 the British economy experienced nine years of sustained growth at an annual average rate of over 3 per cent. In the early 1990s, Britain, in common with other major industrial countries, experienced recession, with output falling by over 3 per cent between mid-1990 and mid-1992. Economic recovery began in the second half of 1992 and output has increased each year since then. Values for some of the main economic indicators in selected years since 1985 are shown in Table 11.1.

Following a rise in gross domestic product (GDP) of 4 per cent in 1994, economic growth slowed to 2.5 per cent in 1995 as the Government tightened monetary policy to ward off emerging inflationary pressures. In the second quarter of 1996 GDP was 2.2 per cent higher than a year earlier. GDP growth is expected to be stronger in the second half of 1996 and through 1997.

Recent decades have generally seen the fastest growth in the services sector (finance, tourism, shipping and aviation, and so on), which now accounts for around two-thirds of GDP, compared with about one-half in 1950. Manufacturing contributes less than one-quarter of GDP, compared with over a third in 1950.

Output of the services industries reached a record level in 1995, up 2.9 per cent on the

153

Table 11.1: Economic Indicators

	1985	1990	1995
Gross domestic product[a]	468,071	551,118	584,340
Exports[a]	109,163	133,165	166,773
Imports[a]	105,957	148,285	169,092
Consumers' expenditure[a]	276,742	347,527	364,045
Gross domestic fixed capital formation[a]	81,575	107,577	99,302
Percentage increase in Retail Prices Index	6.7	9.5	3.4
Workforce in employment (000s)	24,712	27,198	25,751
Percentage of workforce unemployed	10.9	5.8	8.2

Sources: *United Kingdom National Accounts 1996 Edition; Economic Trends; Labour Market Trends*
[a]£ million at 1990 market prices.

previous year. In the second quarter of 1996 services output was 3.2 per cent higher than a year earlier.

Manufacturing output was adversely affected by oil price rises and bouts of stagnation in the world economy in the 1970s and early 1980s. A period of growth then occurred until 1990, when manufacturing output again fell significantly during the recession. Manufacturing growth resumed slowly in 1992, and in 1995 there was a 2.2 per cent increase in manufacturing output.

Oil and gas output reached a peak in the mid-1980s and then declined. Since 1991 it has recovered, with exceptionally high increases in 1993 and 1994, when output grew by 14 and 24 per cent respectively. It was up by 5.7 per cent in 1995, and in the three months to August 1996 was 8.3 per cent higher than a year earlier.

Table 11.2 shows output and employment in 1994 and 1995, and Table 11.3 compares GDP by industry in 1985 and 1995.

Productivity

Between 1980 and 1994 output per head increased by an average of 2.1 per cent a year in the economy as a whole and by 4.6 per cent a year in manufacturing. Output per head in the whole economy rose by 1.8 per cent in 1995, although the rise in manufacturing was lower, at 1.1 per cent.

Investment and Profitability

During the 1980s fixed capital investment increased by about 4 per cent a year on average. It declined during the recession of the

Table 11.2: Output and Employment (Indices: 1990 = 100)

	Output		Employment[a]	
	Index 1994	Index 1995	Index 1994	Index 1995
Agriculture, hunting, forestry and fishing	98.0	98.6	100.0	98.7
Production industries	103.2	105.9	80.6	81.2
of which: Electricity, gas and water	113.1	116.7 }	65.1	59.3
Mining and quarrying	132.4	139.3		
Manufacturing	99.3	101.5	82.0	83.1
Construction	90.5	89.6	76.3	73.7
Services	105.3	108.4	99.7	101.4
GDP	**103.7**	**106.2**		
Employees in employment			94.2	95.4

Sources: *United Kingdom National Accounts 1996 Edition; Labour Market Trends*
[a]Employment figures relate to Great Britain and cover employees in employment at June on a seasonally adjusted basis.

Table 11.3: Gross Domestic Product by Industry[a]

	1985		1995	
	£ million	per cent	£ million	per cent
Agriculture, hunting, forestry and fishing	6,110	2.0	11,896	2.0
Electricity, gas and water supply	8,204	2.7	15,787	2.6
Mining and quarrying, including oil and gas extraction	23,096	7.5	14,575	2.4
Manufacturing	75,761	24.6	131,658	21.8
Construction	18,424	6.0	31,815	5.3
Wholesale and retail trade, repairs, hotels and restaurants	40,734	13.2	84,706	14.0
Transport, storage and communications	24,246	7.9	50,835	8.4
Financial and business activities, real estate and renting	61,870	20.1	158,224	26.2
Public administration, defence and social security	21,516	7.0	39,510	6.5
Education, health and social work	28,323	9.2	72,972	12.1
Other services	11,705	3.8	23,255	3.8
Total	319,989	103.9	635,233	105.1
Adjustment for financial services	−12,087	−3.9	−30,794	−5.1
Statistical discrepancy	—	—	−180	—
GDP at factor cost	**307,902**	**100.0**	**604,259**	**100.0**

Source: *United Kingdom National Accounts 1996 Edition*
[a]Before provision for depreciation but after deducting stock appreciation.
Note: Differences between totals and the sums of their component parts are due to rounding.

early 1990s, but has recovered since 1992, although it fell very slightly in 1995; in the second quarter of 1996 investment grew by 3.2 per cent, compared with a year earlier.

Between 1980 and 1995 the private sector's share of fixed capital investment increased from 70 to 83 per cent, due in part to privatisation (see p. 207). In the same period, there was a rise in the share of investment undertaken by the services sector and a fall in that carried out by manufacturing. Table 11.4 shows investment by business sector.

A recent survey disclosed that Britain had 16 of the 25 most profitable quoted companies in Europe. The rate of return on capital employed in non-oil industrial and commercial companies in Britain increased in the late 1980s to the highest levels for 20 years. It then declined, but since 1992 there has been a recovery. Non-oil corporate earnings grew strongly in 1995, when net profitability of industrial and commercial companies reached 9 per cent.

Inward Investment

Britain is recognised as a prime location for inward direct investment and over 8,000 overseas companies are currently operating in Britain, including more than 4,200 from the United States, over 1,000 from Germany and 210 from Japan. Attractions include Britain's membership of the European Union (EU) and proximity to other European markets, its open trading system and 'enterprise culture', stable labour relations and comparatively low personal and corporate taxation. Overseas-owned firms are offered the same incentives as British-owned ones.

Table 11.4: Gross Domestic Fixed Capital Formation (Investment) by Sector 1995

	£ million at market prices	£ million at 1990 prices	Index at 1990 prices (1990 = 100)
Agriculture, hunting, forestry and fishing	933	856	62.6
Mining and quarrying, including oil and gas extraction	4,463	4,509	95.9
Electricity, gas and water	4,802	4,434	93.5
Manufacturing	15,237	12,638	88.8
Construction	770	661	68.5
Services	53,861	52,543	94.0
Dwellings	21,837	19,947	93.0
Transfer costs	3,482	3,714	87.3
Whole economy	**105,385**	**99,302**	**92.3**

Source: *United Kingdom National Accounts 1996 Edition*

In recent years Britain has received the greatest share of inward investment into the European Union, including about 40 per cent of Japanese and of US investment. It is second only to the United States as a destination for international direct investment.

Inflation

During most of the 1950s and the 1960s the inflation rate in Britain rarely rose above 5 per cent. However, in 1971 it reached double figures, climbing to 27 per cent in 1975. Contributory factors included oil price rises in 1973 and increases in the money supply and public spending. Inflation fell in the early 1980s and stayed low for a number of years, before picking up towards the end of the decade and reaching a peak of 10.9 per cent during 1990.

Since then inflation has declined substantially. For the Retail Prices Index (RPI—which records the price of goods and services purchased by households in Britain), the annual rate was 2.1 per cent in August 1996. The RPI excluding mortgage interest payments ('underlying' inflation) was 2.8 per cent in August 1996. Underlying inflation has now been below 4 per cent for four years, the longest period for almost 50 years.

Labour Market

Following an increase of over 3 million between 1983 and 1990, the workforce in employment fell by around 2 million in the early 1990s. With economic recovery, employment levels have stabilised at an earlier stage than in previous cycles and are now rising.

Unemployment increased during the early 1990s, reaching nearly 3 million on a seasonally adjusted basis in 1992, 10.6 per cent of the workforce. Since then it has fallen by over 870,000. In August 1996 it was 2.1 million—7.5 per cent of the workforce—the lowest level for more than five years (see p. 188).

The number of working days lost through industrial disputes in 1994 and 1995 was the lowest since records began over 100 years ago.

Overseas Trade

Britain has an open economy in which international trade plays a vital part. The share of GDP accounted for by exports of goods and services was 28 per cent in 1995. Investment income on overseas assets now accounts for around 30 per cent of all Britain's overseas earnings.

Membership of the European Union has had a major impact on Britain's pattern of trade. Between 1972—the year before Britain became a member—and 1995 the share of its exports of goods going to other EU members rose from 40 per cent to almost 60 per cent. Imports have followed a similar trend, rising from 45 per cent to 57 per cent. Germany, Britain's most important trading partner, accounts for 13 per cent of Britain's exports and nearly 16 per cent of its imports.

Since 1983 Britain has had a deficit on its trade in goods. In 1995 it stood at £11,600 million, about £800 million higher than in 1994. Nevertheless, exports have recently performed strongly as a result of improved competitiveness and a sharp recovery in world trade.

Substantial earnings from trade in services and from overseas investments kept the balance of payments current account in surplus between 1980 and 1985, but it has been in deficit since then. The deficit rose slightly from £2,419 million in 1994 to £2,892 million in 1995, although these figures were the lowest levels for nearly a decade. In 1995 exports of services amounted to 23 per cent of exports of goods and services combined.

Energy

With the exploitation of oil and natural gas from the Continental Shelf, particularly under the North Sea, Britain is self-sufficient in energy in net terms and expects to remain so for some years. In 1995 it was the world's ninth largest oil producer. The extraction of oil and gas accounted for 2.1 per cent of GDP in 1995, while crude oil and petroleum products made up about 6 per cent of exports of goods.

The benefits to the balance of payments began to appear in the second half of the 1970s, and in 1980 Britain had its first surplus on oil trade. Exports, mainly to other EU countries, are equivalent to 75 per cent of domestic oil and gas production. They are partly offset in balance-of-payments terms by imports of other grades of crude oil from the Middle East and elsewhere.

ECONOMIC STRATEGY

The Government's strategy is directed at providing the stability needed by business and individuals to plan ahead and generate lasting economic expansion and prosperity. It seeks to do this by creating a stable macroeconomic environment and by means of structural policies to improve the long-term performance of the economy.

The Government's economic policy is outlined in the medium-term financial strategy, which is published each year at the time of the Budget. Within this strategy, the role of monetary policy is to secure permanently low inflation, while fiscal policy is designed to maintain sound public finances.

Macroeconomic policy is focused on creating a stable economic environment. Microeconomic policies seek to improve the working of markets and encourage enterprise, efficiency and flexibility through measures such as privatisation, developing new partnerships with the private sector, deregulation, promoting competition, trade liberalisation, labour market reform, better training, and tax reforms.

Monetary Policy

Since 1992 the Government has set an explicit target of keeping underlying inflation within a range of 1 to 4 per cent, bringing it down to the lower half of this range—2.5 per cent or less—by the end of the present Parliament, and a target of 2.5 per cent or less subsequently.

Short-term interest rates remain the key instrument of monetary policy. Monetary policy takes time to influence inflation: hence, interest rate decisions are based on an assessment of the prospects for underlying inflation in one to two years' time. That assessment is based on a wide range of information, including monetary and other financial indicators, activity indicators and measures of costs.

Since 1994 a record has been published of the monthly monetary meeting between the Chancellor of the Exchequer and the Governor of the Bank of England. This, together with the Bank's Quarterly Inflation Report—which is prepared independently of the Treasury—and full explanations whenever interest rates are changed, is designed to make Britain's monetary policy framework as open as possible.

Fiscal Policy

The Government aims to bring the Public Sector Borrowing Requirement (PSBR) back towards balance over the medium term, and in particular to ensure that the Government borrows no more than is required to finance net capital spending. It is committed to reducing the share of public expenditure in national income to below 40 per cent of GDP, and at the same time constantly improving value for money and providing extra resources for priority services (see pp. 161–2).

Within the overall policy of moving towards a balanced budget, the Government aims to reduce taxes when possible so as to leave businesses and individuals with more of their own money. The basic rate of income tax has been cut from 33 to 24 per cent, and a lower rate of 20 per cent now applies on the first £3,900 of taxable income (see pp. 166–7).

Supply-side Policies

The Government is trying to improve the supply response, and thus the efficiency, of the economy through microeconomic policies. Action has been taken to expose as much of the economy to market forces as possible. Direct controls—for example, on pay, prices, foreign exchange, dividend payments and commercial credit—have been abolished and competition in domestic markets strengthened.

A substantial number of activities have been transferred from the public to the private sector through privatisation and contracting out. In addition, the Government is seeking greater efficiency and value for money in the public sector through market testing and competitive tendering, efficiency reviews and scrutinies, and better financial management. The Government's Private Finance Initiative aims to provide high quality capital assets and services to the public using private-sector financing and know-how (see pp. 162–3).

Measures have been implemented to reduce regulatory burdens on business and administrative obstacles facing small firms and self-employed people (see p. 208). Where there is evidence of market failure, and government intervention can be cost-effective and is likely to cause minimal distortion, efforts have been made to increase the flow of investment funds to small firms, help facilitate innovation in industry and attract industry to the inner cities. Steps have been taken to encourage saving and share ownership; TESSAs (Tax Exempt Special Savings Accounts) and Personal Equity Plans are recent examples (see Chapter 15).

The Government has sought to increase work incentives by reducing personal income tax rates whenever possible, raising tax thresholds and reforming the benefits system. It has also, through the tax system, encouraged the extension of share ownership among employees. A scheme of income tax relief has been introduced to encourage the spread of profit-related pay. The Government has expanded training opportunities and put in place a new training framework, with a greater role for employers, so that training better reflects labour market needs.

Since 1994 the Government has issued an annual White Paper with measures designed to improve business competitiveness. The first contained over 60 new measures, many relating to improving education and training and the performance of small businesses (see p. 206). The most recent, published in June 1996, included new analysis on skills and competitiveness in firms, with over 130 examples of excellence for firms to follow. It contained further measures on education and training, and measures to attract more inward investment, create new jobs and raise living standards.

Economic Management

HM Treasury has prime responsibility for the formulation and conduct of economic policy, which it carries out in conjunction with the Bank of England (the central bank—see pp. 222–3) and other government departments —Trade and Industry, Education and Employment, the Environment, Transport, and the Ministry of Agriculture, Fisheries and Food. While the Chancellor of the Exchequer makes the decisions about whether to change interest rates, the Governor of the Bank of England is responsible for deciding the precise timing of any interest rate change.

Several other bodies deal with specific aspects of economic policy and the regulation of certain sectors of the economy. These include the Office of Fair Trading and the Monopolies and Mergers Commission (see pp. 208–9), with responsibilities for protecting consumers and ensuring markets work effectively and fairly.

The Government makes known its economic policies and keeps in touch with developments throughout the economy by means of informal and continuous links with representatives from the industrial, financial and commercial sectors as well as other interested parties. This includes the Panel of Independent Forecasters, which reports to the Chancellor twice a year on the current position of, and future prospects for, the economy. Final responsibility for the broad lines of economic policy rests with the Cabinet.

NATIONAL INCOME AND EXPENDITURE

The value of all goods and services produced in the economy is measured by GDP. This may be expressed either in terms of market prices (the prices people pay for the goods and services they buy) or at factor cost (the cost of the goods and services before adding taxes and subtracting subsidies). It can also be expressed in current prices or in constant prices (that is, removing the effects of inflation to measure the volume of growth in the economy). In 1995 GDP at current factor cost totalled £604,259 million. Between 1985 and 1995 the index of GDP at constant factor cost increased by 25 per cent.

Table 11.5 gives figures for GDP, at both current market prices and current factor cost. It also shows the components of two other main aggregates, gross national product and national income.

Table 11.6 shows the categories of total final expenditure in 1995. Consumers' expenditure accounted for over 49 per cent of total final expenditure, and exports of goods and services for 22 per cent.

Personal Incomes and Expenditure

Personal disposable income consists of personal incomes after deductions—mainly taxation and social security contributions. This rose from £243,413 million in 1985 to £502,433 million at current prices in 1995. Personal disposable income in 1995 was 3 per cent higher in real terms than in 1994. Consumers' expenditure, though, rose by only 2 per cent in real terms and there was a rise in the savings ratio (see p. 160).

Consumers' expenditure amounted to 89 per cent of post-tax personal income in 1995.

Table 11.5: Gross Domestic Product, Gross National Product and National Income

	£ million 1985	£ million 1995
Total final expenditure	456,332	903,557
less imports of goods and services	−98,988	−203,086
Statistical adjustment	—	419
GDP at market prices	357,344	700,890
plus net property income from abroad	2,296	9,572
Gross national product at market prices	359,640	710,462
GDP at factor cost	307,902	604,259
plus net property income from abroad	2,296	9,572
Gross national product at factor cost	310,198	613,831
less capital consumption	−41,883	−72,884
National income (net national product at factor cost)	268,315	540,643

Source: *United Kingdom National Accounts 1996 Edition*
Note: Differences between totals and the sums of their component parts are due to rounding.

Table 11.6: Total Final Expenditure in 1995 at Market Prices

	£ million	per cent
Consumers' expenditure	447,247	49.5
General government final consumption	149,474	16.5
Gross domestic fixed capital formation	105,385	11.7
Value of physical increase in stocks and work in progress	3,851	0.4
Total domestic expenditure	705,957	78.1
Exports of goods and services	197,600	21.9
Total final expenditure	903,557	100.0

Source: *United Kingdom National Accounts 1996 Edition*
Note: Differences between totals and the sums of their component parts are due to rounding.

Table 11.7 shows the changing pattern of consumers' expenditure from 1985 to 1995. Declining proportions are being spent on food and alcoholic drink, tobacco, clothing and footwear, and fuel and power. Over the longer term, as incomes rise, people tend to spend increasing proportions on services. Spending on leisure pursuits and tourism, health and financial services have all shown significant growth in recent years. Housing, food, alcoholic drink, tobacco, clothing and footwear, and fuel and power together accounted for 45 per cent of the total in 1995.

The ratio of saving to personal disposable income declined substantially during the 1980s. However, in 1992 it increased to 11.9 per cent, falling to 10.1 per cent in 1994, but rising again to 11 per cent in 1995.

Sources of Income

The proportion of total personal pre-tax income accounted for by income from employment was 60 per cent in 1995; average gross weekly earnings in April 1996 in Great Britain were £392 for full-time male workers and £283 for full-time female workers. The three other main sources of personal income were self-employment (11 per cent), rent, dividends and interest (14 per cent), and social

Table 11.7: Consumers' Expenditure in 1985 and 1995 at Market Prices

	1985	1995	
	per cent	per cent	£ million
Food (household expenditure)	14.1	10.9	48,850
Alcoholic drink	7.2	5.9	26,355
Tobacco	3.2	2.6	11,655
Clothing and footwear	6.9	5.8	25,801
Housing	15.0	16.2	72,589
Fuel and power	4.9	3.4	15,117
Household goods and services	6.5	6.2	27,806
Transport and communications	17.5	17.4	77,803
Recreation, entertainment and education	9.3	10.5	46,918
Other goods and services	14.6	19.3	86,193
Other items[a]	0.9	1.8	8,160
Total	100.0	100.0	447,247

Source: *United Kingdom National Accounts 1996 Edition*
[a]Household expenditure overseas plus final expenditure by private non-profit-making bodies, minus expenditure by foreign tourists in Britain.
Note: Differences between totals and the sums of their component parts are due to rounding.

Table 11.8: Public Expenditure Plans

	1995–96 Estimated outturn	1996–97	1997–98
		Forecast	
Control Total	255.6	260.2	268.2
Cyclical social security	14.5	14.3	14.6
Central government debt interest	20.1	22.2	25.0
Accounting adjustments[a]	9.4	10.0	9.3
General government expenditure (X)[b]	299.6	306.8	317.1
Privatisation proceeds	–2.4	–4.5	–2.0
Lottery-financed spending and interest and dividend receipts	5.6	5.8	6.5
General government expenditure	302.7	308.1	321.6

£ thousand million

Source: *Summer Economic Forecast 1996.*
[a]A number of adjustments are needed to relate the Control Total to the broader concept of general government expenditure.
[b]The measure in which the Government's objective for public expenditure is now expressed.
Note: Differences between totals and the sums of their component parts are due to rounding.

security benefits and other current grants from government (15 per cent).

PUBLIC FINANCE STRATEGY

General government expenditure (GGE) is the total public expenditure by central and local government, including central government support for nationalised industries and other public corporations. In terms of the Government's measure GGE (X) (see p. 163), it is expected to be around £306,800 million in 1996–97 (see Table 11.8). The Government's policy is to reduce public spending to below 40 per cent of national income. Public expenditure as a proportion of GDP is expected to fall from 43 per cent in 1992–93 to 40.5 per cent in 1997–98 and below 40 per cent shortly afterwards.

The Public Sector Borrowing Requirement rose rapidly during the early 1990s, largely reflecting the impact of the recession, but since then it has fallen and in 1995–96 amounted to £32,200 million, 5 per cent of GDP. The Government's tax and spending policies are designed to ensure that the PSBR returns towards balance over the medium term. The PSBR is forecast to fall to £26,900 million in 1996–97 (see Table 11.9) and to be close to zero by the end of the 1990s.

MAIN PROGRAMMES AND PRIORITIES

The diagram on p. 164 shows the main categories of expenditure, together with the main sources of revenue. The government departments with the largest spending programmes are:

- the Department of Social Security (with planned expenditure of £76,800 million in 1996–97, excluding 'cyclical' social security);

- the Department of the Environment (£39,500 million, of which £31,300 million is on local government);

- the Department of Health (£33,800 million); and

- the Ministry of Defence (£21,400 million).

Planned spending is being concentrated on priority areas, with higher expenditure on schools, health and the police. These increases are being funded from savings elsewhere, for example, in housing, defence, roads and employment measures.

A greater contribution is being made by the private sector in the provision of public services through the Private Finance Initiative and challenge funding (see below). In addition, the costs of government are being strictly controlled, with the running costs of government departments planned to fall by 12 per cent in real terms by 1998–99. Under reforms to government (see Chapter 7), departmental expenditure is being contained in a variety of ways, including cutting bureaucracy, waste and management overheads; rationalising functions and activities; and contracting out services.

Tackling the growth in social security expenditure (which has been running at higher levels than planned) is the Government's most important priority in controlling public expenditure. A new campaign against social security fraud is planned (see p. 431), and tax evasion in other areas, such as vehicle excise duty, is also being tackled.

Local authorities spend about £75,000 million a year, around a quarter of public expenditure. The main categories of expenditure are education, law and order, personal social services, housing and other environmental services, and roads and transport.

Private Finance Initiative

The Private Finance Initiative (PFI), launched in 1992, aims to bring the private sector more directly into the provision of public services. It enables the Government to obtain the benefits of private sector capital and management experience. Under the PFI, the public sector acts as a purchaser rather than a provider of services. The aim is to obtain better value for money for the taxpayer while also providing new business opportunities for the private sector. Partnership between the public and private sectors is a key feature of the PFI. The public sector specifies the services and the level of performance, and the private sector competes for the opportunity to deliver the service. By combining responsibility for design, construction, finance and operation, lasting partnerships can be developed.

By the end of 1998–99 contracts involving capital investment of about £14,000 million are expected to have been awarded under the PFI. The largest single PFI project is the £3,000 million Channel Tunnel Rail Link (see p. 312).

Other transport projects include a number of 'design, build, finance and operate' road projects, the largest of which is the £200 million M1–A1 link road near Leeds; a £400 million contract for new trains on London Underground's Northern Line; the Croydon Tramlink; and the extension of the Docklands Light Railway to Lewisham (see p. 312). PFI projects in other sectors include:

● several redevelopment and improvement projects in the National Health Service (see p. 404);

Table 11.9: Projected Public Expenditure, Receipts and Borrowing Requirement

	£ thousand million		
	1995–96	1996–97	1997–98
General government expenditure	302.7	308.1	321.6
of which: Control Total	*255.6*	*260.2*	*268.2*
General government receipts	268.9	280.4	298.2
of which: income tax	*68.1*	*68.9*	*72.9*
corporation tax	*23.6*	*25.7*	*27.3*
VAT	*43.1*	*46.7*	*49.8*
excise duties	*28.4*	*31.1*	*33.7*
social security contributions	*44.5*	*46.6*	*48.8*
Public sector borrowing requirement (PSBR)	32.2	26.9	23.1
PSBR as percentage of GDP	5	4	3

Source: *Summer Economic Forecast 1996.*

- new prisons in Bridgend in south Wales and Fazakerley (Merseyside) (see p. 104); and over 100 information technology projects;
- with a capital value of about £2,000 million, which are in progress or being considered.

The Government has set up the Private Finance Panel (comprising high-level representatives from the public and private sectors) to provide independent assistance and advice with projects. The Panel has identified over 1,000 potential projects, worth a total of some £25,000 million, for consideration by the Government.

Challenge Funding

Partnerships between the public and private sectors on capital projects are also being encouraged by 'challenge funding', under which funding for public sector projects is allocated on a competitive basis. So far this approach has been used mainly in urban regeneration. For example, successful bids for projects supported by the Single Regeneration Budget (see pp. 375–6) have involved a wide range of schemes from the public, private and voluntary sectors. Challenge funding schemes are being investigated in other areas, such as schools refurbishment and tackling benefit fraud.

CONTROL OF PUBLIC EXPENDITURE

The Government's objective of reducing public expenditure is expressed in terms of GGE (X), which excludes from general government expenditure privatisation proceeds, spending financed out of the proceeds of the National Lottery (see pp. 42–3), and interest and dividend receipts. GGE (X) is a key measure and is used in the medium-term financial strategy (see p. 157), where public spending is set in the context of broader economic policy.

The Government seeks to achieve its public expenditure objective by planning and controlling a narrower target: the Control Total, which covers about 85 per cent of government expenditure. The Control Total includes:

- expenditure for which central government is itself responsible;
- the support it provides or approves for local authority expenditure;
- local authority self-financed expenditure;
- the external financing requirements of public corporations, including nationalised industries; and
- a reserve to cover unanticipated expenditure.

It excludes accounting adjustments and the two main items of expenditure most affected by the economic cycle–debt interest and cyclical social security. Annual ceilings are set for the growth of the Control Total, in line with the Government's medium-term objectives.

Planning Cycle and the Unified Budget

The present planning system took effect with the introduction of the unified Budget arrangements in November 1993, under which the Government presents taxation and spending proposals to Parliament at the same time. The Budget now covers both the Government's taxation plans for the coming financial year and its spending plans for the next three years. The proposals are announced to the House of Commons by the Chancellor of the Exchequer in the Budget statement and are published in the *Financial Statement and Budget Report*. This report also contains a review of recent developments in the economy, together with an economic forecast, and sets out the fiscal and monetary framework within which economic policy operates. This is the medium-term financial strategy.

The Budget statement is followed by the presentation to Parliament of a set of Budget resolutions in which the tax proposals are embodied. These resolutions are the foundation of the Finance Bill, published in January. The Provisional Collection of Taxes Act 1968 allows the tax authorities to collect taxes provisionally, at the levels provided by the Budget proposals, pending enactment of the Finance Bill.

Government Receipts and Expenditure 1996–97

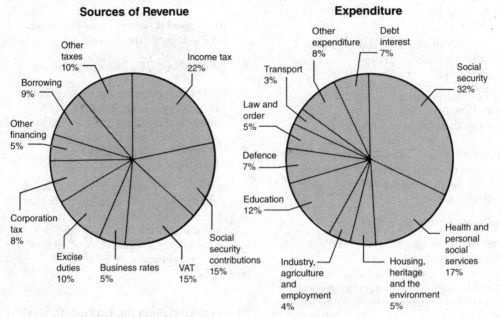

Sources of Revenue

Other taxes 10%
Income tax 22%
Borrowing 9%
Other financing 5%
Corporation tax 8%
Excise duties 10%
Business rates 5%
VAT 15%
Social security contributions 15%

Expenditure

Other expenditure 8%
Debt interest 7%
Transport 3%
Social security 32%
Law and order 5%
Defence 7%
Education 12%
Health and personal social services 17%
Industry, agriculture and employment 4%
Housing, heritage and the environment 5%

Note: As a result of rounding and omission of minor items, percentages do not add up to 100.

Source: HM Treasury

Public Expenditure Survey

Departmental spending decisions are based on allocating available resources within agreed ceilings for aggregate spending; resources are devoted to priority areas, with an emphasis on obtaining maximum value for money. The process of deciding the individual departmental allocations within the overall target takes place each autumn in the Public Expenditure Survey. The outcome is announced in the Budget.

Estimates

Individual reports for government departments setting out expenditure plans are published between February and April. These Estimates, which each government department submits to the Treasury, give details of the cash requirements for the coming financial year. After Treasury approval, these Supply Estimates are presented to Parliament. Parliamentary authorisation is required for the major part of the new spending plans for the year ahead announced in the Budget.

Parliament approves them as part of the annual Appropriation Act. Supplementary Estimates may also be presented to Parliament during the course of the year to reflect any necessary changes to the original main Estimate.

If any Supply Estimate is overspent, the Committee of Public Accounts (see p. 165) may investigate before Parliament is asked to approve any Excess Vote to balance the account. In each parliamentary session, up to three 'Estimates days' are available for debates on the Supply Estimates, following scrutiny by select committees of the House of Commons.

Cash Limits

The Government sets cash limits on just over 60 per cent of Supply expenditure—expenditure financed out of money voted by Parliament in the Supply Estimates. The imposition of cash limits indicates that the Government intends to avoid extra provision for programmes even in the event of unexpected increases in costs. They cover the major part of grants to local authorities, which are financed out of Supply expenditure. Cash limits also apply to some expenditure not voted in the Estimates. Running cost limits are imposed on the administrative costs of central government, which are identified separately in the Estimates.

Those Estimates not subject to cash limits mainly finance demand-led services like income support from the Department of Social Security. In such cases, once policy and rates of payment are determined, expenditure depends on factors beyond the direct control of government—such as the number of eligible recipients.

Changes in Government Accounting Procedures

Government proposals to change accounting and budgeting procedures by government departments were set out in a White Paper in 1995. Cash-based government accounts will be replaced by more commercial 'resource accounting' and budgeting methods, a process already adopted in executive agencies and the National Health Service. The new methods are designed to strengthen cash management, bring improved efficiency and focus more on departmental objectives and outputs in terms of resources used rather than the money available for spending. Departments will have their own balance sheets showing assets and liabilities. Resource accounting is expected to be introduced for most departments in April 1997 and the remainder in April 1998. The first resource-based Public Expenditure Survey is expected to be produced in 2000. In February 1996 the Financial Reporting Advisory Board was set up to provide independent advice to the Government on the new accounting principles.

Central Government Funds

The Government's sterling expenditure is largely met out of the Consolidated Fund, an account at the Bank of England into which tax receipts and other revenues are paid. Any excess of expenditure over receipts is met by the National Loans Fund, which is another official sterling account at the Bank of England and is the repository for funds borrowed by the Government. The National Insurance Fund, into which contributions are paid by employers and employed people, is used mainly to pay for social security benefits.

Examination and Audit of Public Expenditure

Examination of public expenditure is carried out by select committees of the House of Commons. These study in detail the activities of particular government departments and cross-examine ministers and officials.

The Committee of Public Accounts considers the accounts of government departments, executive agencies and other public sector bodies, and reports by the Comptroller and Auditor General (see below) on departments and their use of resources. It submits reports to Parliament. The Government's formal replies to the reports are presented to Parliament in the form of Treasury minutes, and the reports and minutes are usually debated annually in the Commons.

Audit of the Government's spending is exercised through the functions of the Comptroller and Auditor General, the head of the National Audit Office, who has two distinct functions:

- as Comptroller General, responsibility for ensuring that all revenue and other public money payable to the Consolidated Fund and the National Loans Fund is duly paid and that all payments from these funds are authorised by statute; and

- as Auditor General, responsibility for certifying the accounts of all government departments and executive agencies and those of a wide range of other public sector bodies; scrutinising the economy, efficiency and effectiveness of their operations; examining revenue accounts and inventories; and reporting the results of these examinations to Parliament.

MAIN SOURCES OF REVENUE

The main sources of revenue are:

- taxes on income (together with profits), which include personal income tax, corporation tax and petroleum revenue tax;
- taxes on expenditure, which include VAT (value added tax) and customs and excise duties; and

- National Insurance contributions, which give entitlement to a range of benefits.

Among the other sources are inheritance tax, capital gains tax, and the council tax and business rates.

Taxation Policy

The overall level of taxation—around 36 per cent of GDP—is below the average for member states of the Organisation for Economic Co-operation and Development. The Government's programme of tax reform has sought to maintain a climate in which business can thrive and individual initiative is rewarded. Its aims include:

- keeping the overall tax burden as low as possible through firm control over public expenditure;
- reducing marginal tax rates of income and profits to sharpen incentives to work and create wealth;
- maintaining a broad tax base, which helps to keep tax rates low and avoids distorting commercial decisions; and
- shifting the balance of taxation from taxes on income to taxes on expenditure.

Steps have also been taken to close tax loopholes. The Government is committed to simplifying the administration of the tax system, both for individuals and for companies. For example, tax law is to be rewritten so that it is easier to understand.

Tax Measures in the 1995 Budget

The November 1995 Budget aimed to cut tax in a way designed to improve incentives and boost enterprise. Taxes for 1996–97 were reduced by over £3,000 million. Measures included:

- cutting the basic rate of income tax from 25 per cent in 1995–96 to 24 per cent in 1996–97;
- widening the lower rate band (20 per cent) by £700 (see Table 11.10);
- increasing personal allowances by £100 more than 'indexation' (allowing for the effects for inflation);
- reducing taxes on savings income, such as bank and building society deposits, for

basic rate taxpayers, from 25 to 20 per cent; and

- introducing measures to help protect family savings, with a large increase in the starting point for inheritance tax (see p. 169) and a doubling to £16,000 in the level of assets below which people are eligible for help for care in residential and nursing homes.

Measures to boost enterprise included cutting the small companies' rate of corporation tax (see p. 168) from 25 to 24 per cent, a series of changes to stimulate employee share ownership, and extra help for businesses facing higher non-domestic rates bills. The Budget's measures for taxes on spending included raising in real terms road fuel duties by 5 per cent and tobacco duties by 3 per cent, thereby continuing the policy announced in the November 1993 Budget to curb vehicle emissions and encourage people to stop smoking. The tax on road fuel gases—compressed gas and liquid petroleum gas—was reduced, as these fuels produce significantly lower levels of emissions of major pollutants.

A new landfill tax, first announced in the 1994 Budget, was introduced in October 1996. It is intended to promote a more sustainable approach to waste management by encouraging business and consumers to produce less waste and dispose of less waste in landfill sites, and to provide an additional incentive for recycling. The tax is levied at £2 a tonne on inactive waste (such as bricks) which does not decay or contaminate land and £7 a tonne on other waste. To avoid imposing additional costs on business, cuts in employers' National Insurance contributions will be made in April 1997.

Collection of Taxes and Duties

The Inland Revenue assesses and collects taxes on income, profits and capital, and stamp duty. HM Customs and Excise collects the most important taxes on expenditure (VAT and most duties). Vehicle excise duty is the responsibility of the Department of Transport. National Insurance contributions are the responsibility of the Department of Social Security, although they are mainly collected by the Inland Revenue. The council tax and business rates are collected by local authorities.

In March 1996, as part of a series of measures designed to help small firms, the Government announced that the tax and National Insurance contributions systems for new businesses would be streamlined, for example, by adopting a single form of registration for new self-employed business people for VAT, PAYE income tax (see below) and National Insurance contributions.

Taxes on Income

Income Tax

Taxes on individual incomes are generally progressive in that larger incomes bear a greater amount of tax. Income tax is imposed for the year of assessment beginning on 6 April. The tax rates and bands for 1995–96 and 1996–97 are shown in Table 11.10 and apply to total income, including earned and investment income. Of nearly 26 million income taxpayers, around 6.3 million are expected to pay only lower rate tax in 1996–97, about 17.3 million will be basic rate taxpayers and 2 million will be in the higher rate tax band.

A number of allowances and reliefs reduce an individual's income tax liability, and the main allowances are shown in Table 11.10. All taxpayers, irrespective of sex or marital status, are entitled to a personal allowance against income from all sources. Married women pay their own tax on the basis of their own income. In addition, there is a married couple's allowance, which may be allocated to either partner or they may receive half each. Wives can elect to receive half the allowance as of right. Tax relief for some allowances, including the married couple's allowance, was restricted to 20 per cent from April 1994, and this was reduced to 15 per cent in April 1995.

Among the most important reliefs is that for mortgage interest payments on borrowing for house purchase up to the statutory limit of £30,000. Relief, which has been limited to 15 per cent since April 1995, is usually given 'at source', that is, repayments which the borrower makes to

Table 11.10: Tax Bands and Allowances £

	1995–96	1996–97
Income tax allowances:		
Personal allowance	3,525	3,765
Married couple's allowance, additional personal allowance and widow's bereavement allowance[a]	1,720	1,790
Allowances for those aged 65–74:		
personal allowance	4,630	4,910
married couple's allowance[a]	2,995	3,115
Allowances for those aged 75 and over:		
personal allowance	4,800	5,090
married couple's allowance[a]	3,035	3,155
Income limit for age-related allowances	14,600	15,200
Blind person's allowance	1,200	1,250
Bands of taxable income:		
Lower rate of 20 per cent	0–3,200	0–3,900
Basic rate[b]	3,201–24,300	3,901–25,500
Higher rate of 40 per cent	over 24,300	over 25,500

Source: HM Treasury.

[a]Tax relief for these allowances is restricted to 15 per cent. The additional personal allowance may be claimed by a taxpayer who is single, separated, divorced or widowed and who has a child at home.
[b]Basic rate is 25 per cent for 1995–96 and 24 per cent for 1996–97.

the lender are reduced to take account of tax relief and the tax refund is passed directly by the tax authorities to the lender rather than to the individual borrower. Employees' contributions to their pension schemes also qualify for tax relief within limits laid down by Parliament.

In general, income tax is charged on all income which originates in Britain—although some forms of income are exempt, such as certain social security benefits—and on all income arising abroad of people resident in Britain. Britain has entered into agreements with many countries to provide relief from double taxation; where such agreements are not in force unilateral relief is often allowed. British residents working abroad for the whole year may benefit from 100 per cent tax relief.

Most wage and salary earners pay their income tax under a Pay-As-You-Earn (PAYE) system whereby tax is deducted and accounted for to the Inland Revenue by the employer, in a way which enables most employees to pay the correct amount of tax during the year.

A new self assessment system for collecting personal taxation is being introduced. It will apply to everyone who fills in a tax return (about 9 million people). Taxpayers will be able to calculate their own liability to tax, although they can choose to have the calculations done by the Inland Revenue. A uniform set of dates will apply for the payment of income tax and capital gains tax. The 'preceding year' basis of income tax for the self-employed will be replaced by a simpler 'current year' basis; people who have become self-employed since April 1994 are already being taxed on the latter basis.

A new legal requirement to keep records of income and capital gains from all sources was introduced in April 1996. The first 'new style' tax returns will be sent out to taxpayers in April 1997.

Corporation Tax

The rates of company tax in Britain are lower than in most other industrialised countries.

Companies pay corporation tax on their income and capital gains after deduction of certain allowances and reliefs. A company which distributes profits to its shareholders is required to pay advance corporation tax (ACT) on these distributions to the Inland Revenue. This ACT can be set against the company's liability to corporation tax, subject to a limit. Shareholders resident in Britain receiving dividends from British-resident companies are entitled to a tax credit, which is equivalent to the ACT paid. This satisfies some or all of their liability to income tax on dividend income.

The main rate of corporation tax is 33 per cent, with a reduced rate of 24 per cent for small companies (those with profits below £300,000 in a year). Relief is allowed for companies with profits between £300,000 and £1.5 million, so that the company's overall rate is between the main rate and the small companies' rate. Relief for capital expenditure on plant and machinery, on scientific research and on industrial and agricultural buildings is available in the form of capital allowances, which are deducted from profits.

Petroleum Revenue Tax

Petroleum revenue tax (PRT), deductible in computing profits for corporation tax, is charged on profits from the production—as opposed, for example, to the refining—of oil and gas in Britain and on its Continental Shelf under licence from the Department of Trade and Industry. Each licensee of an oilfield or gasfield is charged at a rate of 50 per cent on the profits from that field after deduction of certain allowances and reliefs. New fields given consent for development on or after 16 March 1993 and gas from certain fields sold under contracts negotiated before 1975 are not liable to PRT.

Taxes on Capital

The Government's aim is to reduce taxes on capital—inheritance tax and capital gains tax—and to abolish them eventually.

Inheritance Tax

Inheritance tax is essentially charged on estates at the time of death and on gifts made within seven years of death; most other lifetime transfers are not taxed. There are several important exemptions. Generally, transfers between spouses are exempt, and gifts and bequests to British charities, major political parties and heritage bodies are also normally exempt. In general, business assets are now exempt from inheritance tax, so that most family businesses can be passed on without a tax charge.

Tax is charged at a single rate of 40 per cent above a threshold. This threshold was raised from £154,000 to £200,000 in April 1996. Only about 2 per cent of estates will now be liable for an inheritance tax bill.

Capital Gains Tax

Capital gains tax (CGT) is payable by individuals and trusts on gains realised from the disposal of assets. CGT is payable on the amount by which total chargeable gains for a year exceed the exempt amount (£6,300 for individuals and £3,150 for trusts in 1996–97). For individuals, CGT is calculated at income tax rates, as if the amount were additional taxable income, while there are special rates for trusts. Only gains arising since March 1982 are subject to tax. Indexation relief is given to take account of the effects of inflation, and this can reduce a gain but no longer create or enhance a capital loss—capital losses may be set against capital gains during the same year or a subsequent year. Gains on some types of asset are exempt from CGT. These include the principal private residence, government securities, certain corporate bonds, and gains on shares and corporate bonds owned under Personal Equity Plans (see p. 230).

For companies capital gains are charged to corporation tax, although there is no annual exempt amount.

Taxes on Expenditure

Value Added Tax

VAT is a broadly based expenditure tax, with a standard rate of 17.5 per cent and a reduced rate of 8 per cent on domestic fuel and power. It is collected at each stage in the production and distribution of goods and services by taxable persons. The final tax is payable by the consumer. When a taxable person purchases taxable goods or services, the supplier charges VAT—the taxable person's input tax. When the taxable person supplies goods or services, the customers are then in turn charged VAT, which is the taxable person's output tax. The difference between the output tax and the input tax is paid to, or repaid by, Customs and Excise.

The annual level of turnover above which traders must register for VAT is £47,000. Certain goods and services are relieved from VAT, either by being charged at a zero rate or by being exempt.

- Under zero rating, a taxable person does not charge tax to a customer but reclaims any input tax paid to suppliers. Among the main categories where zero-rating applies are goods exported to other countries, and goods shipped as stores on ships and aircraft; most food; water and sewerage for non-business use; domestic and international passenger transport; books, newspapers and periodicals; construction of new residential buildings; young children's clothing and footwear; drugs and medicines supplied on prescription; specified aids for handicapped people; and certain supplies by or to charities.

- For exempt goods or services, a taxable person does not charge any output tax but is not entitled to reclaim the input tax. The main categories where exemption applies are many supplies of land and buildings; insurance; postal services; betting; gaming (with certain important exceptions); lotteries; finance; much education and training; and health and welfare.

The Government has announced a number of changes designed to simplify VAT. These include implementing the EC's Second VAT Simplification Directive.

Customs Duties

Customs duties are chargeable on goods from outside the EU in accordance with its Common Customs Tariff. Goods can move freely across internal EU frontiers without making customs entries at importation or stopping for routine fiscal checks. For commercial consignments, excise duty and VAT are charged in the member state of destination, at the rate in force in that state.

Excise Duties

Hydrocarbon oils used as road fuel bear higher rates of duty than those used for other purposes, although the rate of duty on unleaded petrol is lower than that on leaded. Kerosene, most lubricating oils and other oils used for certain industrial processes are free of duty. There are duties on spirits, beer, wine, made-wine (wine with added constituents, such as fruit juice), cider and perry, charged according to alcoholic strength and volume. Spirits used for scientific, medical, research and industrial processes are generally free of duty. Cigarette duty is charged partly as a cash amount per cigarette and partly as a percentage of retail price. Duty on other tobacco products is based on weight.

Duties are charged on off-course betting, pool betting, gaming in casinos, bingo and amusement machines. Rates vary with the particular form of gambling. Duty is charged either as a percentage of gross or net stakes or, in the case of amusement machines, as a fixed amount per machine according to the cost of playing and the prize level. Some of these duties were reduced in the 1995 Budget in response to growing competition from the National Lottery (see pp. 42–3). On the Lottery there is a 12 per cent duty on gross stakes, but no tax on winnings.

Vehicle excise duty (VED) on a privately-owned motor car, light van or taxi with fewer than nine seats is £140 a year. The duty on goods vehicles is levied on the basis of gross weight and, if over 12 tonnes, according to the number of axles; it is designed to ensure that such vehicles at least cover their share of the full costs of road use through the tax paid (VED and fuel duty). Duty on taxis and buses varies according to seating capacity, and duty on motor cycles according to engine capacity. Privately owned vehicles over 25 years old—cars, taxis, motor cycles and non-commercial vehicles—are now exempt from VED following the 1995 Budget.

Other taxes include a 2.5 per cent tax on most premiums for general insurance, and a duty on air passengers of £5 for flights to internal destinations and those in the European Economic Area and £10 elsewhere.

Stamp Duty

Certain kinds of transfer are subject to stamp duty. These include purchases of houses, at 1 per cent of the total price if this exceeds £60,000. Transfers of shares attract duty at 0.5 per cent of the cost, while certain instruments, such as declarations of trust, have small fixed duties of 50p or £1. Transfers by gift and transfers to charities are exempt.

Taxpayer's Charter

The Taxpayer's Charter sets out the standard of service that people can expect from the Inland Revenue and HM Customs and Excise. Both departments should be fair, helpful, courteous, efficient and accountable, and keep taxpayers' financial affairs private.

Other Revenue

National Insurance Contributions

There are five classes of National Insurance contribution:

- Class 1—paid by employees and their employers;
- Class 1A—paid by employers on the cash equivalent of the benefit of cars and fuel provided to their employees for private use;
- Class 2—paid by the self-employed;
- Class 3—paid voluntarily for pension purposes; and
- Class 4—paid by self-employed people on their taxable profits between £6,860 and £23,660 a year (in addition to their Class 2 contribution).

Details of the rates of contribution are given in Chapter 26, Social Security, on pp. 431–2.

Local Authority Revenue

Local authorities in Great Britain have four main sources of revenue income: grants from central government; council tax; non-domestic rates; and sales, fees and charges. About 80 per cent of expenditure (excluding sales, fees and charges) is financed by government grants and redistributed business rates.

Non-domestic rates are a tax on the occupiers of non-domestic property. The rateable value of property is assessed by reference to annual rents and reviewed every five years; the most recent revaluation in Great Britain took place in April 1995. As this resulted in some very large local and sectoral changes in rateable values, a transitional scheme was introduced to phase in increases and reductions in rates bills. The non-domestic rate is set nationally by central government and collected by local authorities. It is paid into a national pool and redistributed to local authorities in proportion to their population. In Northern Ireland, rates are not payable on industrial premises or on commercial premises in enterprise zones. Certain other properties in Northern Ireland, such as freight transport and recreational premises, are partially derated.

Domestic property in Great Britain is generally subject to the council tax, which replaced the community charge in 1993. Each dwelling is allocated to one of eight valuation bands, based on its capital value in April 1991. Capital values are based on the amount each dwelling might have sold for on the open market, subject to certain assumptions, if it had been sold on 1 April 1991. Discounts are available for dwellings with fewer than two resident adults. A council tax payer on a low income may receive council tax benefit of up to 100 per cent of the tax bill (see p. 439).

In Northern Ireland, rates—local domestic property taxes based on the value of the property—are collected by local authorities.

PUBLIC SECTOR FINANCIAL OPERATIONS

Debt Management

The Government funds its borrowing requirement by selling debt to the private sector. Public sector borrowing, or debt repayment, each year represents an addition to,

or subtraction from, the net debt of the public sector. This debt is the consolidated debt of the public sector less its holdings of financial assets. Net public sector debt held outside the public sector amounted to £323,000 million at the end of March 1996, representing 44.5 per cent of GDP in 1995–96. This is expected to rise to 46.5 per cent of GDP by the end of March 1998, but thereafter to fall steadily as the PSBR is brought towards balance.

The funding requirement for 1996–97 is forecast to be about £42,700 million, of which National Savings products (see p. 227) are assumed to contribute about £3,000 million, with gilt-edged stock contributing the balance.

Gilt-edged Stock

The major debt instrument is known as gilt-edged stock ('gilts') as there is no risk of default. Gilts are marketable and widely traded. Pension funds and life insurance companies have the largest holdings. The Government publishes an annual debt management report which sets out the framework for issuing gilts in the coming year. Gilts are sold by the Bank of England on the Government's behalf. Issues are primarily by auction (broadly monthly), supplemented by *ad hoc* 'tap' sales. Gilts include 'conventionals', which pay fixed rates of interest and redemption sums; index-linked stocks, on which principal and interest are linked to inflation through the movement in the Retail Prices Index; and floating-rate gilts, with payments linked to short-term interest rates.

A series of changes has been implemented to increase the efficiency and liquidity of the gilts market, so enhancing the overall efficiency of Britain's financial system. Among these was a new open sale and repurchase ('repo') market in gilts, launched in January 1996.

Bills

Sterling Treasury bills are sold at a weekly tender; the majority have a maturity of three months. These are currently used to manage the money markets and meet the weekly cash needs of the Government, rather than to meet the Government's annual borrowing needs.

The Government also issues bills denominated and payable in European Currency Units (ECUs). The proceeds are added to the official foreign exchange reserves rather than being used to finance public expenditure.

Other Public Sector Borrowing

The bulk of public corporations' borrowing is funded by central government, although their temporary borrowing needs are met largely from the market, usually under Treasury guarantee. That part of local authority borrowing met by central government is supplied by authorisation of Parliament through the Public Works Loan Board from the National Loans Fund. The Board remains an independent body even though it is merged for administrative purposes with the former National Debt Office, forming the National Investment and Loans Office. Local authorities may also borrow directly from the market, both short-term and long-term, through a range of instruments.

Further Reading

Better Accounting for the Taxpayers' Money—The Government's Proposals: Resource Accounting and Budgeting in Government. Cm 2929. HMSO, 1995.

Debt Management Report, annual report, HM Treasury.

Financial Statement and Budget Report, annual report, HMSO.

The Government's Expenditure Plans 1996–97 to 1998–99: HM Treasury, Chancellor of the Exchequer's Smaller Departments. Cm 3217. HMSO, 1996.

Summer Economic Forecast, annual report, HMSO.

United Kingdom National Accounts, annual report, HMSO.

12 Overseas Trade

Trade in Goods	173	Controls on Trade	180
Other Transactions	178	Government Services	181
Commercial Policy	178	Balance of Payments	182

Overseas trade has been of vital importance to the British economy for hundreds of years. With only about 1 per cent of the world's population, Britain is the fifth largest trading nation, accounting for around 5 per cent of world trade. Some 100,000 companies based in Britain currently sell their products overseas. As a member of the European Union (EU), it is part of the world's largest established trading group, responsible for 40 per cent of world exports. Having a far higher degree of inward and outward investment than any other leading economy, relative to gross domestic product (GDP), Britain is taking advantage of increasing global free trade.

Britain exports more per head than the United States and Japan. Its overseas sales of goods and services are equivalent to about a quarter of GDP. Receipts from trade in services and investment income make up about one-half of Britain's total overseas earnings, and Britain consistently runs large surpluses on these accounts. Britain is the world's second biggest overseas investor and the leading destination for inward direct investment into the EU. British investors have more overseas direct investments than foreign firms have in Britain.

The British Government is a strong supporter of an open multilateral trading system and advocates further trade liberalisation. World trade is set to grow by 5 to 10 per cent a year in the next ten years, due in part to the successful conclusion of the Uruguay Round of negotiations under the General Agreement on Tariffs and Trade (GATT) in 1993. This led to the creation in 1995 of the World Trade Organisation (WTO), of which Britain is a founder member.

TRADE IN GOODS

In 1995 Britain's exports of goods were valued at about £152,300 million and imports at £164,000 million on a balance-of-payments basis (see Table 12.1). Between 1994 and 1995 the volume of exports of goods rose by 7 per cent and their value by 13 per cent. Over the same period, imports grew by 4 per cent by volume and 13 per cent in terms of value. Re-exporting plays a prominent role in trade: a recent survey found that nearly half of British importers export products.

Commodity Composition

Britain has traditionally been an exporter of manufactured goods and an importer of food and basic materials. In 1970 manufactures

Table 12.1: Overseas Trade 1993–95

	1993	1994	1995
Value (£ million)[a]			
EXPORTS			
Goods	121,398	134,666	152,346
Oil	7,962	8,494	8,687
Other goods	113,436	126,172	143,659
Services	38,599	41,399	45,254
Goods and services	**159,997**	**176,065**	**197,600**
IMPORTS			
Goods	134,858	145,497	163,974
Oil	5,520	4,591	4,457
Other goods	129,338	140,906	159,517
Services	33,083	36,652	39,112
Goods and services	**167,941**	**182,149**	**203,086**
Volume indices (1990 = 100)			
EXPORTS			
Goods			
All goods	107.4	118.5	127.1
Non-oil goods	106.3	116.7	126.2
Services	105.6	111.5	119.2
Goods and services	**107.0**	**116.8**	**125.2**
IMPORTS			
Goods			
All goods	104.8	109.2	113.8
Non-oil goods	104.7	110.1	115.4
Services	101.3	112.0	115.1
Goods and services	**104.1**	**109.7**	**114.0**
Price indices (1990 = 100)			
EXPORTS			
All goods	116.2	118.6	126.4
Non-oil goods	118.5	121.6	129.7
IMPORTS			
All goods	112.3	116.1	127.8
Non-oil goods	113.6	117.8	129.6
TERMS OF TRADE[b]			
All goods	103.5	102.2	98.9
Non-oil goods	104.3	103.2	100.1

Source: *United Kingdom Balance of Payments 1996 Edition*
[a]Balance-of-payments basis.
[b]Export price index as a percentage of import price index.

Table 12.2: Sector Analysis of Trade in Goods 1995[a]

£ million

	Exports	Imports	Balance
Food, beverages and tobacco	11,161	15,237	−4,076
Basic materials	2,932	6,441	−3,509
Oil	8,687	4,457	4,230
Other mineral fuels and lubricants	563	1,102	−539
Semi-manufactured goods	43,437	45,035	−1,598
Finished manufactured goods	83,783	90,180	−6,397
Commodities and transactions not classified according to kind	1,783	1,522	261
Total	**152,346**	**163,974**	**−11,628**

Source: *United Kingdom Balance of Payments 1996 Edition*   [a]Balance-of-payments basis

accounted for 85 per cent of its exports; this fell to around 67 per cent by the mid-1980s as North Sea oil exports increased their share. The proportion of manufactures in exports has since risen, to 84 per cent in 1995 (see Table 12.2). Britain has not, however, had a surplus on manufactures since 1982. Machinery and transport equipment account for about 43 per cent of exports and 41 per cent of imports (see Table 12.3). Aerospace,

chemicals and electronics have become increasingly significant export sectors, while textiles have declined in relative importance. Britain is Europe's biggest exporter of computers, television sets and microchips; many of the firms involved are large multinationals from the Far East and the United States.

Since the mid-1970s North Sea oil has made a substantial contribution to Britain's

Geographical Distribution of Trade 1995

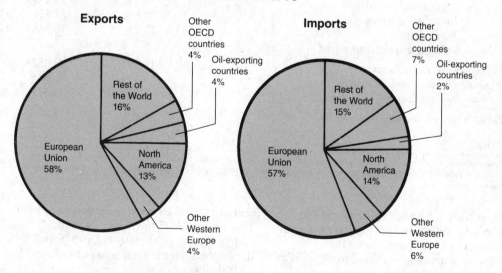

Note: Differences between totals and the sums of their component parts are due to rounding.

Source: *United Kingdom Balance of Payments 1996 Edition*

Table 12.3: Commodity Composition of Visible Trade 1995[a]

£ million

	Exports	Imports
Food and live animals	7,087	13,520
Beverages and tobacco	4,150	2,492
Crude materials	2,731	6,351
of which: Wood, lumber and cork	44	1,221
Pulp and waste paper	65	1,058
Textile fibres	640	682
Metal ores	766	1,498
Fuels	9,295	5,875
Petroleum and petroleum products	8,729	4,666
Coal, gas and electricity	567	1,211
Animal and vegetable oils and fats	223	601
Chemicals	21,147	17,837
of which: Organic chemicals	4,983	4,799
Inorganic chemicals	1,244	1,131
Plastics	3,307	4,669
Manufactures classified chiefly by material	22,569	28,205
of which: Wood and cork manufactures	190	1,068
Paper and paperboard manufactures	2,346	5,216
Textile manufactures	3,308	4,905
Iron and steel	4,380	3,667
Non-ferrous metals	2,877	3,847
Metal manufactures	3,103	3,313
Machinery and transport equipment	65,823	69,047
Mechanical machinery	18,631	15,438
Electrical machinery	30,896	32,321
Road vehicles	11,788	18,133
Other transport equipment	4,512	3,155
Miscellaneous manufactures	18,992	23,057
of which: Clothing and footwear	3,473	6,824
Scientific and photographic	5,985	5,545
Other commodities and transactions	1,756	1,359
Total	**153,761**	**168,335**

Source: *Monthly Digest of Statistics*[a] On an overseas-trade-statistics basis, seasonally adjusted. This differs from a balance-of-payments basis in that, for imports, it includes the cost of insurance and freight, and, for both exports and imports, includes returned goods.

overseas trade in terms of both exports and import substitution. In 1995 exports of fuels in volume terms were over six times their 1975 level, while imports were around three-fifths of the 1975 figure. The share of fuels in exports rose from 4 to 22 per cent by the mid-1980s, when the value of North Sea oil and gas production was at its peak, falling back to 6 per cent in 1995. The import share decreased from 19 per cent in 1975 to 13 per cent in the mid-1980s and to 3.5 per cent by 1995. In 1995 the surplus on trade in oil amounted to over £4,000 million.

Imported manufactures have taken a greater share of the domestic market in recent decades. The share of finished manufactures in total imports rose from 25 per cent in 1970 to 55 per cent in 1995, while the share of basic materials fell from 15 to 4 per cent between 1970 and 1995. The percentage of food, beverages and tobacco in total imports has been dropping since the 1950s, down to 9 per cent in 1995, as a result both of the extent to which food demand has been met from domestic agriculture and of the decline in the proportion of total expenditure on food.

Geographical Distribution

Britain's overseas trade is mainly with other developed countries. In 1970 these accounted for 70 per cent of exports and imports; by 1995 the shares were 80 and 83 per cent respectively. The proportion of Britain's trade with non-oil developing nations declined from about 24 per cent in 1970 to 13 per cent in the late 1980s and early 1990s, but has risen since 1992 to 16 per cent of trade in 1995.

In 1972, the year before Britain joined the European Community, 40 per cent of its trade in goods was with the other 14 countries which presently make up the European Union. The proportion rose to 57 per cent in 1995. Western Europe as a whole took 62 per cent of British exports in 1995.

In 1995 EU countries accounted for eight of Britain's top ten export markets and seven of the ten leading suppliers of goods to Britain (see Table 12.4). In 1990 Germany overtook the United States to become Britain's biggest overseas market for goods; Germany is also Britain's largest single supplier. In 1995 it took 13 per cent of Britain's exports and supplied nearly 16 per cent of its imports.

There have been a number of other changes in the pattern of Britain's overseas trade in recent years. Exports to Japan, which is presently Britain's tenth largest export market, rose by 26 per cent in 1995. Japan has steadily increased its share of Britain's imports and

Table 12.4: Britain's Main Markets and Suppliers 1995[a]

	Value (£ million)	Share (per cent)
Main markets		
Germany	20,154	13.1
United States	18,023	11.7
France	15,192	9.9
Netherlands	12,256	8.0
Belgium/Luxembourg	8,295	5.4
Italy	7,853	5.1
Irish Republic	7,724	5.0
Spain	6,064	3.9
Sweden	4,113	2.7
Japan	3,784	2.5
Main suppliers		
Germany	26,106	15.5
United States	20,280	12.0
France	16,256	9.7
Netherlands	11,371	6.8
Japan	9,630	5.7
Italy	8,189	4.9
Belgium/Luxembourg	7,975	4.7
Irish Republic	6,994	4.2
Switzerland	5,150	3.1
Sweden	4,497	2.7

Source: *Monthly Digest of Statistics*
[a]On an overseas-trade-statistics basis, seasonally adjusted.

now accounts for 6 per cent. In 1995 there was a significant increase in Britain's exports to most of the expanding markets in newly industrialising Asia, of around 12 per cent, including Hong Kong, Singapore, South Korea, Taiwan and Thailand, while exports to India grew by 28 per cent. Exports to South Africa also rose substantially in 1995, by 30 per cent.

OTHER TRANSACTIONS

Other transactions fall into three main groups:

- internationally tradeable services;
- investment income on external assets; and
- non-commercial transfers (chiefly between governments, between the British Government and EU organisations, and between private individuals).

Services range from banking, insurance and stockbroking, tourism, and shipping and aviation to specialist services such as engineering consultancy, computer programming and training. Financial services make a major contribution to overseas earnings: net overseas receipts from services rendered and investment income were £20,400 million in 1995, up from £18,800 million in 1994.

Earnings from trade in services as a whole rose by 9 per cent in 1995 to over £45,000 million (see Table 12.5). There was an overall surplus on services of £6,100 million, compared with £4,700 million in 1994.

Earnings on investment income rose by nearly 20 per cent to £93,100 million in 1995, while debits rose by a similar proportion to almost £83,600 million (see Table 12.6). The surplus on investment income was a record level of nearly £9,600 million. Within this there were surpluses on earnings from direct investment of £12,900 million and from portfolio investment of over £3,000 million, although these were partly offset by a deficit on bank borrowing and lending.

Transfers have almost always been in deficit, amounting to nearly £7,000 million in 1995—with a deficit on government transfers of £7,200 million and a surplus on private sector transfers of £200 million.

COMMERCIAL POLICY

Britain remains committed to the open multilateral trading system and to the further liberalisation of world trade. To this end it has taken a leading part in the activities of such organisations as the WTO, the International Monetary Fund (IMF) and the Organisation for Economic Co-operation and Development (OECD).

GATT/World Trade Organisation

The eighth and final GATT round—the Uruguay Round—was launched in 1986 and successfully concluded in 1993. It was the largest-ever international trade negotiation and is leading to a reduction in tariffs on goods and a liberalising of trade in services and agriculture.

Table 12.5: Britain's Trade in Services 1995

			£ million
	Credits	Debits	Balance
Private sector and public corporations	44,773	36,611	8,162
Sea transport	4,550	4,715	−165
Civil aviation	5,931	6,272	−341
Travel	11,906	15,609	−3,703
Financial services (net credits)	5,778	— }	12,371
Other business services	16,608	10,015 }	
General government	481	2,501	− 2,020
Total	45,254	39,112	6,142

Source: *United Kingdom Balance of Payments 1996 Edition*

Table 12.6: Investment Income and Transfers 1995

£ million

	Credits	Debits	Balance
Investment income	93,139	83,567	9,572
General government	1,641	4,360	−2,719
Private sector and public corporations	91,498	79,207	12,291
Transfers	6,135	13,113	−6,978
General government	3,697	10,877	−7,180
Private sector	2,438	2,236	202
Total	99,274	96,680	2,594

Source: *United Kingdom Balance of Payments 1996 Edition*

Creation of the WTO—which now has over 120 member states—has put the new arrangements on a permanent institutional footing. A GATT report has estimated that annual world income will be boosted by at least £330,000 million by 2005, as a result of the Uruguay agreement. The Government estimates that it will lead to a rise in Britain's GDP of 2 per cent after ten years.

The main features of the new agreement, which is gradually being brought into force, are as follows:

- There will be overall tariff reductions across all countries of about 40 per cent (tariff reductions by the EU will average over 33 per cent) and member states have undertaken not to raise tariffs again on 95 per cent of world trade.

- With the formation of the General Agreement on Trade in Services, services are being brought within the framework of GATT multilateral trade rules. Any remaining restrictions on trade in services are being made transparent and non-discriminatory.

- Agriculture is coming fully under the rules of multilateral trade for the first time; there will be a 36 per cent reduction in tariffs as well as substantial cuts in subsidies.

- Agreed multilateral rules govern trade-related intellectual property rights, providing protection for holders of trademarks, patents, copyrights and design rights.

- Trade in textiles, where restrictions on imports have been allowed under the Multi-Fibre Arrangement (MFA—see p. 180) to balance the interests of exporters and importers, is being reintegrated into the rules of the WTO over ten years.

Britain is now focusing on ensuring that unfinished Uruguay Round business is brought to a successful conclusion and that the multilateral trading system of the WTO works properly in practice. It is also seeking to make further progress, through the WTO, in reducing external barriers to trade. Increasingly, the focus for trade negotiations has shifted from the elimination of border barriers to examining the impact of domestic policies on trade. Policies on competition, investment, procurement, subsidies, standards, intellectual property rights, rules of origin, regulation and financial services are all being discussed. The first WTO ministerial conference will be held in Singapore in December 1996.

European Union

Austria, Finland and Sweden are the latest members of the European Union, joining in 1995. The single European market 'opened for business' in 1993, with the essential legislation in place for the free movement of goods, services, people and capital within the EU. The main changes were:

- the ending of routine customs clearance of commercial goods at national frontiers within the EU;

- the introduction of the right to trade

financial services throughout the EU on the basis of a single home authorisation 'passport' (see p. 222); and

- deregulation of airlines, with national flag carriers losing preferential treatment.

Member states are now concentrating on ensuring that the market operates efficiently and completing work in energy and telecommunications liberalisation. The DTI's Single Market Compliance Unit helps companies that encounter prohibited barriers to trade to overcome them.

Special Trading Arrangements

The EU has association and co-operation agreements with virtually all non-member countries with a Mediterranean coastline, plus Jordan; these give preferential access to EU markets. Non-preferential co-operation agreements have also been made with countries in South Asia and Latin America, as well as with the People's Republic of China, the Association of South East Asian Nations, the Andean Pact and the Central American states. Trade relations with the developing countries of Africa, the Caribbean and the Pacific are governed by the Lomé Convention, which gives these countries tariff-free access, subject to certain safeguards, to the EU for industrial and agricultural products.

Tariff preference is also given to developing countries under the Generalised System of Preferences. This applies to industrial products, including textiles and certain (mainly processed) agricultural products. The scheme focuses benefits on poorer producers and countries.

Europe (Association) Agreements are in place between the EU and Poland, Hungary, the Czech Republic, Slovakia, Bulgaria, Romania, Slovenia and the Baltic states. They are designed to facilitate closer political and economic ties and the eventual creation of a free trade area with a view to those countries becoming full members of the EU. A trade and economic co-operation agreement has also been made with Albania. Partnership and co-operation agreements have been concluded with ten states of the former USSR (see p. 131).

CONTROLS ON TRADE

With the completion of the single European market, all routine internal border controls and requirements were removed for trade in EU goods between the members of the EU. This has substantially cut travel times and costs; for example, freight journey times by road from Britain to Italy have been reduced by up to 24 hours.

Import Controls

Following the completion of the single European market, all national quantitative restrictions have been abolished. However, some EU-wide quotas have been imposed on a small range of non-textile and clothing products from the People's Republic of China, while EU imports of some steel products from Russia, the Ukraine and Kazakhstan are also restricted. Quantitative restrictions on textiles and clothing stem from the MFA, under which there is a series of bilateral agreements. Some quotas are also maintained against non-WTO countries. The MFA restrictions will be eliminated by 2005 as part of the WTO agreement.

Imports from certain countries remain subject to sanctions controls or embargo agreed by, for example, the United Nations. Imports of certain other goods from all countries are prohibited or restricted in order to protect human, animal or plant life and health. These include firearms and ammunition; nuclear materials; certain drugs; explosives; endangered wildlife and derived products; and certain agricultural, horticultural and food products.

Export Controls

The great majority of British exports are not subject to any government control. Controls on certain strategic goods are imposed for a variety of reasons, including foreign policy and non-proliferation concerns, the need to comply with international treaty commitments, the operation of sanctions and national security. The scope of export controls is limited to what is necessary to meet these concerns. Most controls apply on a worldwide basis, although certain sanctions and embargoes are applied against specific countries as a result of agreement by members of bodies such as the United Nations.

There are controls relating to the export of conventional military equipment and firearms as well as dual-use industrial goods that can be used for civil and military purposes. Most dual-use industrial goods are allowed to move within the EU without an export licence.

Controls on conventional weapons and equipment for their manufacture date back to an agreement by members of the Co-ordinating Committee for Multilateral Export Controls (COCOM). Although this body has been disbanded, ex-members are maintaining the controls in their present form. A new forum, the Wassenaar Arrangement, is expected to agree new lists shortly. Lists of controls on certain dual-use related goods are agreed by members of the Australia Group, the Nuclear Suppliers Group and the Missile Technology Control Regime; Britain is a member of all three. The aim of these groups is to help prevent the spread of chemical, biological and nuclear weapons and missile systems for their delivery.

GOVERNMENT SERVICES

The Government assists exporters by creating economic conditions favourable to the export trade and by providing practical help, advice and financial support. This includes a wide range of services and assistance to meet the requirements of exporters, especially small and medium-sized enterprises.

Export Promotion Services

Overseas Trade Services (OTS) comprises the leading government departments engaged in export promotion, including the Department of Trade and Industry (DTI), the Foreign & Commonwealth Office (FCO), the Industry Department of the Welsh Office, Scottish Trade International and the Industrial Development Board of Northern Ireland. There are over 2,000 staff worldwide, based at the DTI in London, in regional offices and Business Links (see p. 212) around Britain, and at 218 diplomatic posts overseas.

OTS gathers and disseminates export intelligence, helps in researching potential markets, and supports firms participating in trade fairs and missions. In 1995–96 around £225 million was spent on support for exporters.

In England the development of local Business Links is making OTS more accessible to potential users. The DTI is financing 70 'export development counsellors' in Business Links to give advice to exporters and outward investors at local business level.

OTS works closely with over 100 'export promoters' seconded from private industry, as well as with the British Overseas Trade Board (BOTB), the BOTB's Area Advisory Groups and with FCO posts abroad. The BOTB's aims are to:

- help guide the Government's export promotion efforts, including the provision of export services; and

- provide advice on policy issues affecting international trade and exports.

The BOTB's Area Advisory Groups, which are made up of business people with expert knowledge of trade with particular world markets, provide advice on the world's main trading areas. The Overseas Projects Board advises on major project business overseas, and the Small Firms Committee gives guidance on matters relating to small businesses. Some 200 businessmen and women are involved in the Board's work.

OTS pays special attention to the promotion of exports to its top priority areas in Western Europe, North America, and Japan and the fast-growing countries of the Asia–Pacific Rim. These three areas contain the world's largest and richest markets, and account for around four-fifths of Britain's exports. Emerging markets in other areas, such as Latin America, where some countries have been achieving rapid growth rates, are also being targeted.

The Government has set a target of introducing 30,000 firms to new export markets by the year 2000. It has also announced:

- an improved programme of trade fair and mission support;

- a programme of 'British Excellence' fairs in key markets;
- additional commercial staff abroad and 14 new overseas posts;
- 'export vouchers' for small and medium-sized enterprises to help them buy assistance at Business Links; and
- an 'Export Challenge' for trade associations, to encourage them to improve the international competitiveness of the sectors they represent.

British Invisibles

British Invisibles is an organisation which promotes the international activities of financial institutions and business services. Its role is to suggest and, where possible, implement measures for boosting such earnings in Britain and abroad. It also seeks to increase awareness of London as an international financial centre and of the role of the service sector in the British economy.

Export Insurance

ECGD (Export Credits Guarantee Department) is a government department responsible to the President of the Board of Trade. It helps British firms overcome many of the risks of selling and investing overseas. ECGD supports British exporters of capital goods and services sold on medium- and long-term credit by: '

- guaranteeing exporters and financing banks against the risk of non-payment by overseas buyers/borrowers;
- giving interest rate support to British banks, allowing overseas borrowers access to funds at fixed, often favourable, rates of interest; and
- providing reinsurance to British private-sector insurance companies covering exports sold on short-term credit.

In order to encourage investment in less developed countries, ECGD also insures investment earnings against the main political risks, such as war, expropriation and restrictions on repatriation of profits.

Particular attention is paid to ensuring that sufficient cover capacity is available for exports to ECGD's main markets, such as China, Saudi Arabia and Indonesia. The Asia–Pacific region is currently ECGD's largest source of new business.

ECGD's premium rates have been reduced by 25 per cent overall since 1992 and cover has been resumed for almost 30 markets worldwide.

BALANCE OF PAYMENTS

The balance-of-payments statistics record transactions between residents of Britain and non-residents. The transactions are classified into two groups: current account, and

Table 12.7: Britain's Balance of Payments 1991–95

£ million

	1991	1992	1993	1994	1995
Current account					
Trade in goods and services	−6,720	−8,154	−7,944	−6,084	−5,486
Investment income	150	3,124	2,197	8,691	9,572
Transfers balance	−1,383	−5,102	−5,007	−5,027	−6,978
Current balance	−7,954	−10,133	−10,756	−2,419	−2,892
Transactions in assets and liabilities					
British external assets	−18,683	−81,600	−155,611	−35,147	−124,045
British external liabilities	26,128	86,565	168,691	32,497	124,491
Balancing item	509	5,168	−2,324	5,069	2,446

Source: *United Kingdom Balance of Payments 1996 Edition*
Note: Differences between totals and the sums of their component parts are due to rounding.

transactions in Britain's external assets and liabilities, sometimes known as the capital account. The current account records trade in goods and services, including finance, tourism and transport; transactions in investment income; and transfers. Capital transactions include inward and outward investment, overseas transactions by banks in Britain, external borrowing and lending by residents in Britain and drawings on and accruals to the official reserves.

Britain has no exchange controls; residents are free to acquire foreign currency for any purpose, including direct and portfolio investment overseas. There are also no controls on the lending of sterling abroad and non-residents may acquire sterling for any purpose. Gold may be freely bought and sold. Exchange controls were abolished in 1979, and Britain meets in full its obligations on capital movements under an OECD code and under EC directives.

Britain's balance of payments current account deficit remains modest, at less than 1 per cent of GDP. It has been in deficit since 1986, although the deficits recorded in 1994 and 1995 were the lowest since 1986, at £2,400 million and £2,900 million respectively (see Table 12.7). Since 1983 Britain has had a deficit on trade in goods, and this amounted to £11,600 million in 1995. However, it has usually run large surpluses on trade in services

and investment income. In 1995 the surplus on services rose by £1,400 million and that on investment income by £900 million, but the deficit on transfers grew by nearly £2,000 million.

Inward and Outward Investment

The Government welcomes both outward and inward investment.[1] Outward investment helps to develop markets for British exports while providing earnings in the form of investment income. Inward investment is promoted by DTI's Invest in Britain Bureau (IBB—see p. 218) as a means of introducing new technology, products, management styles and attitudes; creating or safeguarding employment; and increasing exports or substituting imports. In recent years Japanese investment has helped transform the automotive industries in Britain.

The IBB was notified of 477 new inward investment projects from 29 countries in 1995–96. The projects are expected to create

[1] A distinction needs to be made between capital flows and capital holdings. Flows comprise transactions resulting in a change of ownership of financial assets and liabilities between British residents and non-residents, while holdings are measured by the total values of British external assets and liabilities at the end of the year. Income earned on external assets is dealt with in the section on other transactions.

Table 12.8: Summary of Transactions in External Assets[a] and Liabilities[b] 1993–95

£ million

	1993	1994	1995
Overseas direct investment in Britain	10,298	6,823	20,480
Overseas portfolio investment in Britain	45,466	32,609	16,859
British direct investment overseas	−17,026	−18,363	−25,546
British portfolio investment overseas	−84,828	17,968	−40,327
Borrowing from overseas	115,790	−7,435	85,436
Deposits and lending overseas	−52,450	−33,088	−57,735
Official reserves[a]	−698	−1,045	200
Other external liabilities of general government	−2,864	500	1,715
Other external assets of central government	−609	−619	−637
Total	**13,080**	**−2,650**	**446**

Source: *United Kingdom Balance of Payments 1996 Edition*
[a] Increase −/decrease +
[b] Increase +/decrease −
Note: Differences between totals and the sums of their component parts are due to rounding.

nearly 48,300 jobs. Inward investment is playing an increasingly important role in Britain's economy, with overseas firms providing 18 per cent of all manufacturing jobs, 24 per cent of net output, 32 per cent of manufacturing investment and about 40 per cent of manufacturing exports. At present Britain has over 40 per cent of US and Japanese investment in the EU. Inward investment has benefited a range of industries, including communications and the information sector, electronics, medical equipment, pharmaceuticals, financial services, food and drink, and the automotive industry.

At the end of 1995 the stock of inward direct investment (investment in branches, subsidiaries and associated companies which gives the investor an effective role in their management) was £150,400 million. The stock of direct investment overseas by British residents was £213,800 million at the end of 1995. The stock of overseas portfolio investment in Britain amounted to £309,000 million at the end of 1995, while the stock of British portfolio investment overseas was £482,000 million. An analysis of transactions in Britain's external assets and liabilities for 1993–95 is given in Table 12.8. Britain's identified external assets at the end of 1995 exceeded liabilities by nearly £50,000 million.

At the end of 1994, 81 per cent of outward direct investment was in developed countries, with 35 per cent in the EU and 32 per cent in the United States. Investment from developed countries accounted for 97 per cent of overseas direct investment in Britain: 41 per cent originated in the United States and 33 per cent in the EU.

Further Reading

Overseas Trade. Aspects of Britain series, HMSO, 1994.

United Kingdom Balance of Payments 1996 Edition. Office for National Statistics, HMSO.

Trade and Industry. The Government's Expenditure Plans 1996–1997 to 1998–1999. HMSO, 1996.

Department of Trade and Industry 1995. Annual Report. DTI, 1996.

13 Employment

Patterns of Employment	185	Terms and Conditions of	
Training, Education and		Employment	194
Enterprise	188	Industrial Relations	196
Recruitment and Job-finding	192	Health and Safety at Work	200

Britain has a higher proportion of the adult population in work—70 per cent—and a lower level of unemployment than any other major European Union (EU) country. Features of the changing labour market include the growing proportion of women in the workforce and increases in part-time employment, among both women and men, and in temporary employment. About three-quarters of employees now work in the service sector, compared with less than one-fifth in manufacturing. Industrial relations have been transformed, and the number of working days lost in 1994 and 1995 were the lowest annual totals recorded. Health and safety at work has improved, with fatalities from accidents at work at a record low level.

PATTERNS OF EMPLOYMENT

The total workforce in 1996 was almost 28 million. The workforce in employment in June 1996 totalled 25.8 million (see Table 13.1), of whom 22.1 million (nearly 11.2 million men and almost 11 million women) were classed as employees in employment. Employment is recovering from the fall during the recession of the early 1990s. Since December 1992 (the most recent employment trough) the workforce in employment has grown by over 480,000.

The long-term trend has been for a move away from full-time employment towards part-time employment (see graphs on p. 186), while the number of women in employment has grown considerably; women now make up 46 per cent of all in employment. Since 1986 part-time employment in Great Britain has risen by 26 per cent to 6.4 million in spring 1996: 5.2 million women and 1.2 million men.

About 45 per cent of women in employment were working part-time, compared with 8 per cent of men. Around 1.3 million people had two or more jobs. Nearly 1.6 million people were engaged in temporary jobs, of whom 51 per cent were on fixed-period contracts. Contracting out by firms of specialist and non-core functions has increased. 'Teleworking'—people working from home using information technology—is also becoming more widespread, for example, in journalism, consultancy and computer programming.

About 3.3 million people are self-employed in Britain, 19 per cent more than in 1986. The sectors with the highest concentrations of self-employed people are agriculture and construction. Around 18 per cent of men and 7 per cent of women in employment are self-employed.

Table 13.1: Workforce in Employment in Britain

Thousands, seasonally adjusted, June

	1986	1991	1994	1995	1996
Employees in employment	21,377	22,250	21,646	21,951	22,116
Self-employed	2,792	3,413	3,290	3,343	3,282
HM Forces	322	297	250	230	221
Work-related government-supported training programmes[a]	226	353	302	227	200
Workforce in employment	**24,716**	**26,313**	**25,488**	**25,751**	**25,819**

Source: Office for National Statistics
[a]Not seasonally adjusted.

Government Policy

Britain now has one of the least regulated labour markets among the major industrialised nations. This has arisen following action taken by the Government, with the aim of creating an economic climate in which business can flourish and create more jobs. These include:

- increasing the flexibility of the labour market, for example, by promoting decentralised and flexible pay arrangements;

- removing regulations which have restricted job creation; and

- encouraging better training, especially through employer-led Training and

Full- and Part-time Employment in Great Britain, Seasonally Adjusted

Full-time

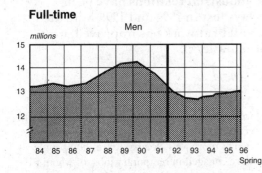

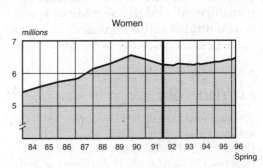

Part-time

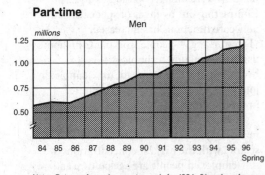

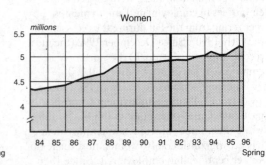

Note: Data are for spring quarters only for 1984–91 and are for every quarter for 1992 onwards. Data from spring 1992 contain unpaid family workers.

Source: *Labour Force Survey Quarterly Bulletin*

Enterprise Councils and, in Scotland, Local Enterprise Companies (see p. 188).

In the EU the Government emphasises the importance of improving competitiveness, creating jobs and tackling unemployment. In European Councils and other fora it consistently argues for attention to be paid to tackling unemployment rather than to the creation of legislation which it considers to be unnecessary and damaging, and which adds to the burdens of business and makes it more difficult to retain or create jobs. Britain has welcomed the conclusions of successive European Councils in recent years which have put the need to tackle unemployment at the top of the EU's employment agenda, and it has been active in sharing information about its policies, programmes and experiences with other member states.

Occupational Changes

There has been a gradual move away from manual occupations towards non-manual occupations, which are now held by nearly three-fifths of people in employment in Great Britain. Self-employment is highest in craft and related occupations (29 per cent of those in this sector in Great Britain in spring 1996), followed by managers and administrators (18 per cent).

Employment by Sector

As in other industrialised countries, there has been a marked shift in jobs from manufacturing to service industries (see Table 13.2). In the last 40 years the proportion of employees in employment engaged in service industries has more than doubled, to nearly 76 per cent. In June 1996 there were 16.4 million employees in the service sector in Great Britain, about 2.1 million more than in 1986 (see Table 13.3). Business activities, distribution, hotels and restaurants, education, medical services and social work experienced significant increases. Employment in the sector of public administration, defence and compulsory social security, however, has fallen.

Most other sectors—manufacturing, construction, agriculture, and mining, energy and water supply—have experienced lower levels of employment. By 1996 manufacturing accounted for 18 per cent of employees in employment, compared with 42 per cent in 1955. Traditional manufacturing industries, such as steel and shipbuilding, have recorded particularly large falls in employment. In August 1996 employment in the main manufacturing sectors in Great Britain included:

- 700,000 employees in non-metallic mineral products, metal and metal products;
- 491,000 in electrical and optical equipment;
- 436,000 in paper, pulp, printing, publishing and recording media;
- 422,000 in food products, beverages and tobacco; and

Table 13.2: Employees by Main Sector in Britain (at June)

	1991	1994	1995	1996
Thousands				
Service industries	16,187	16,293	16,577	16,783
Manufacturing industries	4,319	3,923	4,021	4,017
Mining, energy and water supply	381	264	239	209
Other industries	1,363	1,167	1,114	1,107
Per cent of employees				
Service industries	72.8	75.3	75.5	75.9
Manufacturing industries	19.4	18.1	18.3	18.2
Mining, energy and water supply	1.7	1.2	1.1	0.9
Other industries	6.1	5.4	5.1	5.0

Source: Office for National Statistics

Table 13.3: Employees in Employment in Services in Great Britain

Thousands: seasonally adjusted, June

	1986	1991	1994	1995	1996
Wholesale and retail trade, and repairs	3,287	3,532	3,583	3,630	3,668
Hotels and restaurants	988	1,188	1,145	1,206	1,230
Transport and storage	846	897	867	857	854
Postal services and telecommunications	435	455	420	420	433
Financial services	881	1,024	965	979	974
Real estate	157	186	250	260	270
Renting, research, computer and other business activities	1,777	2,167	2,205	2,340	2,483
Public administration, defence and compulsory social security	1,418	1,403	1,384	1,347	1,334
Education	1,617	1,791	1,772	1,781	1,764
Health activities	1,307	1,493	1,481	1,519	1,539
Social work activities	707	800	900	902	933
Other community, social and personal activities	841	865	913	917	877
All services	**14,261**	**15,802**	**15,885**	**16,157**	**16,360**

Source: Office for National Statistics

- 346,000 in clothing, textiles, leather and leather products.

Unemployment

Unemployment in Britain—as measured by the number of people claiming unemployment-related benefits and adjusted for seasonal variation—has fallen by over 870,000 since the end of 1992. This decline has occurred in all regions, and the number of long-term unemployed (who have been out of work for a year or more) has fallen by about 20 per cent. The level of unemployment is below the EU average and the rates of youth and female unemployment are below those in most other EU countries. In August 1996 claimant unemployment totalled 2.1 million, 7.5 per cent of the workforce. It ranged from 5.8 per cent in East Anglia to 11.3 per cent in Northern Ireland.

The Government has introduced a wide range of measures to help combat unemployment. In 1996–97 about 1.5 million places on employment and training schemes are being offered to help unemployed people.

TRAINING, EDUCATION AND ENTERPRISE

The Government's aim is to support economic growth and improve Britain's competitiveness by raising standards of educational achievement and skill. It encourages employers to invest in training through Investors in People (see p. 190) and the development of National Vocational Qualifications (NVQs—see pp. 458–9). In addition, individuals are encouraged to take responsibility for their own training and development. Key initiatives are Career Development Loans and tax relief. Britain is acknowledged as an innovative world leader in open and flexible learning, for example, through the Open University.

Training and Enterprise Councils

There are 81 Training and Enterprise Councils (TECs) in England and Wales. They are independent companies with employer-led boards. Seven TECs have merged with local chambers of commerce to form Chambers of Commerce, Training and Enterprise, while a number of other TECs are considering possible mergers.

The objective of TECs is to foster local economic development and stimulate employer investment in skills—in particular through the Investors in People standard—within their area. Their special focus is to strengthen the skills base and assist local enterprise programmes which are funded by the Government.

TECs manage the provision of training and enterprise programmes which are funded by the Government. For 1996–97, £1,200 million is being provided by the Department for Education and Employment to TECs in England to deliver its programmes. TECs also have access to funding from other government departments. For example, the Department of Trade and Industry funds TECs to deliver enterprise programmes (see Chapter 14) and TECs are lead partners in many of the projects funded through the Single Regeneration Budget (see p. 375).

In 1996–97 the Government set aside £55 million over a three-year period for a discretionary fund for TECs to use on local projects on training and enterprise. The fund operates under 'challenge' principles, and the prime basis for funding is the extent to which projects attract private finance.

TECs are accountable to the Government through their contracts. The Government Offices for the Regions are responsible for managing and overseeing the overall government contract with TECs.

Local Enterprise Companies

A separate network of 22 Local Enterprise Companies (LECs) exists in Scotland. These have wider-ranging responsibilities than the TECs, covering economic development and environmental improvement. LECs operate training programmes but, unlike TECs, have no responsibility for work-related further education. They run under the supervision of the two enterprise bodies: Scottish Enterprise and Highlands and Islands Enterprise (see p. 216).

Industry Training Organisations

Industry Training Organisations (ITOs) act as the focal point for training matters in their particular sector of industry, commerce or public service. Their role is to ensure that the skills needs of their sectors are being met and that occupational standards are being established and maintained for key occupations. There are over 120 independent ITOs, covering sectors employing about 85 per cent of the civilian workforce. The National Council of Industry Training Organisations, a voluntary body set up to represent the interests of ITOs, aims to improve their effectiveness, for example, by encouraging good practice.

By September 1997 a new network of National Training Organisations will replace ITOs, 'lead bodies' and occupational standards councils (OSCs). Lead bodies and OSCs have the prime function of representing occupational groups (a function also carried out by many ITOs) in developing occupational standards and NVQs and their Scottish equivalent.

National Targets for Education and Training

The National Targets for Education and Training were launched by the Confederation of British Industry in 1991 and are supported by the Government and many national and local organisations, including all TECs, LECs and ITOs, and other major education, training and employer bodies. The principal aim of the Targets is to improve Britain's international competitiveness by raising standards and attainment levels in education and training through ensuring that:

- all employers invest in employee development to achieve business success;
- everyone has access to education and training opportunities, leading to recognised qualifications which meet their needs and aspirations; and
- all education and training develops self-reliance, flexibility and breadth, through fostering competence in core skills.

The independent National Advisory Council for Education and Training Targets (NACETT) and the Advisory Scottish Council for Education and Training Targets monitor progress towards the Targets.

The Targets cover both young people and the workforce as a whole. Following a review by NACETT, new, more challenging Targets were set in 1995, relating to the year 2000. The 'Foundation Learning' Targets are that:

- by the age of 19, 85 per cent of young people should achieve five GCSEs at grade C or above, an intermediate GNVQ or NVQ level 2;[1]
- 75 per cent of young people should achieve level 2 competence in communication, numeracy and information technology by the age of 19, with 35 per cent reaching level 3 by the age of 21; and
- by 21, 60 per cent of young people should achieve two GCE A levels, an Advanced GNVQ or NVQ level 3.

The 'Lifetime Learning' Targets are that:

- 60 per cent of the workforce should be qualified to the standard of NVQ level 3, an Advanced GNVQ or two GCE A levels;
- 30 per cent of the workforce should have a vocational, professional, management or academic qualification at NVQ level 4 or above; and
- 70 per cent of organisations employing 200 or more people and 35 per cent of those employing 50 or more should be recognised as Investors in People.

Separate targets, set within the framework of the national targets, are in force in Scotland.

Training for Work

The Government's Training for Work programme is designed to help unemployed and disadvantaged adults to find jobs through training and work experience. The programme is open to those aged 18 to 63 who have been unemployed for six months or longer, although some groups with special needs can join earlier. Training is carried out by training providers under contract with the local TEC

or LEC. Each new trainee receives an individually adapted package of training and/or structured work activities. Planned expenditure in England in 1996–97 is £485 million, when about 197,000 people are expected to join the programme.

Investors in People

Investors in People is the main initiative in support of employers' investment in people. It is based on a rigorous national standard which helps companies to improve their performance by linking the training and development of all employees directly to the achievement of business objectives. TECs and LECs provide advice and information to help organisations to work towards the standard. Some 25,000 organisations, employing more than 5 million people, have made a commitment to work towards the Investors in People standard. By mid-1996 more than 4,000 organisations had achieved the standard. Reported benefits include increased productivity, higher profits, lower rates of sickness and absenteeism, and improved morale.

National Training Awards

The National Training Awards are an annual competition designed to promote good training practice by example, rewarding those who have carried out exceptionally effective training. In 1996, 93 awards (including 56 to employers and 23 to training providers) were presented to national winners, who were selected from about 250 regional winners.

Career Development Loans

Career development loans are available to help people to pay for vocational education or training in Great Britain. Loans of between £200 and £8,000 are provided through four major banks, and interest payments on the loans during training and for one month after training are funded by the Department for Education and Employment. The loans help to pay for courses lasting up to two years. More than 80,000 people have borrowed over £250 million through the programme since 1988 to pay for training. Over two-thirds of people go directly into employment following the training.

[1] For information on General National Vocational Qualifications (GNVQs) and examinations, see Chapter 27.

Small Firms Training Loans

Small Firms Training Loans were introduced in 1994. The programme helps firms with 50 or fewer employees to meet a range of training-related expenses, including training consultancy. Loans of between £500 and £125,000 are available through seven major banks and repayments can be deferred for up to 12 months.

Skills for Small Businesses

In 1995 Skills for Small Businesses was introduced. It is designed to help companies by training selected key workers—one per company—who then pass on their knowledge and expertise to other employees. Under the £63 million programme run by TECs, there is provision for training up to 24,000 key employees.

A Skills Challenge competition was held by the Department for Education and Employment and the Department of Trade and Industry in 1995–96. Groups of at least ten small companies were invited to bid for awards to develop innovative solutions to shared training needs. A total of 74 awards were made under the scheme, worth about £3.5 million.

Improving the Training Market

The Improving the Training Market programme covers a range of activities funded by the Department for Education and Employment aimed at improving the quality, impact and cost-effectiveness of vocational education and training. Priority is being given to encouraging investment by individuals in learning, supporting the implementation of new qualifications and developing frameworks for the new Modern Apprenticeships (see below).

Training for Young People

The Government is committed to ensuring that high-quality further education or training is available for all young people who can benefit from it. All those aged 16 or 17—and some aged 18 or above in special circumstances—who are not in full-time education, a job or a Modern Apprenticeship are guaranteed the offer of a suitable training opportunity.

The objectives of the two main youth programmes—Modern Apprenticeships and Youth Training—are to:

- provide participants with training leading to vocational qualifications at NVQ/SVQ levels 2 and 3 or above and with broad-based skills necessary to become flexible and self-reliant employees; and
- to meet the skill needs of the national and local economies.

The delivery of training is arranged through TECs and LECs.

Following a review of the qualifications framework for those aged 16 to 19 (see p. 457), the Government announced in July 1996 proposals for a major strengthening of training for young people from September 1997. They will include the introduction of National Traineeships for training to NVQ levels 1 and 2, and these will draw on the best features of current arrangements, including Modern Apprenticeships. They will offer a broad and flexible learning programme, including the key skills of communication, numeracy and information technology.

Modern Apprenticeships

'Modern Apprenticeships' became fully operational in 1995 following prototype schemes which had been run in 17 sectors. They are designed to build on the best features of existing apprenticeships and to increase significantly the number of young people trained to technician, supervisory and equivalent levels. Over 30,000 young people have begun Modern Apprenticeships, which are now in operation in over 50 industry sectors. A £3 million government advertising campaign was launched in 1996 to encourage more young people to take up Modern Apprenticeships.

Youth Credits

Youth Credits are intended to offer young people more individual choice and a greater sense of personal responsibility when buying training. Each credit has a financial value and can be presented to an employer or training provider in exchange for training. In England 16- and 17-year-old school- and college-leavers can obtain access to Youth Training or Modern Apprenticeships.

Skillseekers, the equivalent training credit scheme in Scotland, has been gradually extended following a pilot scheme in 1991, and by 1996 all young people leaving full-time education were eligible for the scheme.

Northern Ireland

The Training and Employment Agency, an executive agency within the Department of Economic Development, has primary responsibility for training and employment services. Its overall aim is to assist economic development and help people to find work through training and employment services delivered on the basis of equality of opportunity. Its budget in 1996–97 is £210 million.

The Agency has encouraged the formation of a sector training council in each of the main sectors to advise on employers' training needs and develop sectoral training strategies. In addition, the Agency supports company training through its Company Development Programme and encourages management development by providing training programmes and seminars for existing and future managers.

Northern Ireland has its own range of training and employment programmes for people seeking work. Its Jobskills programme is designed to raise skill levels and enhance the employment prospects of school-leavers and unemployed adults. The programme is incentive-based and focuses on the achievement of NVQs. In order to combat the high level of long-term unemployment in Northern Ireland, the Agency operates the Action for Community Employment Scheme and is running a two-year pilot Community Work Programme. The latter is being tested in three areas of the Province with high unemployment levels. Participants receive a weekly allowance in addition to their benefit and are given the opportunity to develop their skills, undertaking work of benefit to the community, to become better equipped to find permanent employment.

RECRUITMENT AND JOB-FINDING

There are a variety of ways in which people find jobs. These include replying to advertisements in the national, local or specialist press; direct approaches to employers; and through a Jobcentre or employment agency.

Government Employment Services

The Government provides a range of services to jobseekers through the Employment Service, an executive agency within the Department for Education and Employment. These include:

- a network of local offices, at which people can find details of job opportunities;
- advice and guidance so that people can find the best route back into employment, for example, by training; and
- a range of special programmes.

The Employment Service has about 1,100 Jobcentres and employs about 42,000 staff. In 1995–96 it placed over 1.9 million unemployed people into jobs and conducted over 3.25 million advisory interviews to help people find appropriate work or places on employment and training programmes.

The Jobseeker's Charter contains provisions governing the standard of service to users. These include provisions on the speed of service, and ensuring that vacancies on display boards at offices are both up to date and available, and that those entitled to benefit receive the correct payments promptly. A revised Charter will be issued after the introduction of the Jobseeker's Allowance (see below).

The Employment Service is an active participant in the European Employment Services Network (EURES), a partnership between the employment services in the member states of the EU. EURES facilitates the circulation of vacancies in member states through a computer network.

THE METEOROLOGICAL OFFICE

The Meteorological Office, based in Berkshire, provides a range of weather forecasting services for its customers, which include international shipping and cargo companies.

Weatherproof instruments such as these produced by Sewills, Liverpool, are used by the Meteorological Office because of their ability to withstand all extremes of weather.

ADVANCES IN MEDICINE

Banding and inspection of Retrovir capsules—used in the treatment of AIDS—at Glaxo Wellcome, Dartford, Kent. Glaxo Wellcome is the largest pharmaceutical company in the world.

Pharmaceutical production at Zeneca's plant in Macclesfield, Cheshire. The British pharmaceutical industry is the world's fourth-biggest exporter of medicines.

A cancer care centre in Miami, USA, owned by British company Zeneca.

This non-invasive device, developed by Moor Instruments, Axminster, Devon, uses a low-power laser beam to build up a colour-coded image of blood flow. It has applications in many areas, including research into breast cancer, rheumatology, neurology and vascular surgery.

A method of obtaining human and veterinary vaccines and immunotherapeutics from plants has been patented by Axis Genetics, based near Cambridge. It is expected to be available for commercial production in the near future.

SATELLITES

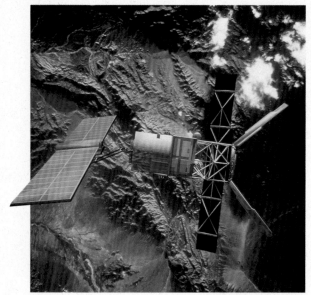

The European Space Agency's ERS (remote sensing) satellites, for which British companies supplied key instruments, are capable of operating 24 hours a day and of returning images of the earth through bad weather and in darkness.

The Skynet 4 British military communications satellite undergoing tests at Matra Marconi Space, Stevenage, Hertfordshire.

Advisory Services

Through the main Jobcentre services, unemployed people have access to vacancies, employment advice and training opportunities. Advisers provide unemployed people with information on employment and training opportunities available locally.

> A new Jobseeker's Allowance replaced unemployment benefit and income support for unemployed people in October 1996 (see p. 438). It is intended to improve the operation of the labour market by helping people in their search for work and to secure better value for money by targeting resources more closely on those needing financial support. To receive the allowance each unemployed person will have to complete a Jobseeker's Agreement, which will include the steps that the jobseeker has agreed to take in order to find work.
>
> The Employment Service is investing £70 million in a new computer system to support the operation of Jobseeker's Agreements and to help unemployed people to compete effectively for jobs and find employment as quickly as possible.

New Client Advisers interview newly unemployed people to check their eligibility for benefit. Together with the unemployed person, they agree a 'Back to Work Plan', which sets out specific courses of action to improve the prospects of finding a job. Thereafter unemployed people are required to attend a Restart advisory interview every six months. Restart interviews are intended to offer help and advice to unemployed people while they are on the unemployment register. Following the establishment of the Jobseeker's Allowance, a new in-depth interview will be introduced after 13 weeks of unemployment. The unemployed will then be expected to widen the range of jobs being considered if they have been unable to find work in their normal occupation.

The Employment Service has a wide variety of programmes. Those designed to help the long-term unemployed include:

- '1-2-1', a programme offering 239,000 places in 1996–97, which is designed to provide intensive help with looking for jobs for those who have been unemployed for over a year;

- Jobplan, which provides guidance and other support to enable those unemployed for a year to assess their skills, qualities and training needs, and to act as an introduction to future job and training options;

- Jobclubs, where participants are given training and advice in job-hunting skills and have access to facilities to help an intensive job search;

- Restart courses, designed to rebuild self-confidence and motivation, and including help with job-hunting skills;

- Work Trials, which encourage employers to take on people who have been unemployed for at least six months for a trial period of up to three weeks, during which they can assess their potential; and

- Project Work Pilots, a pilot scheme running for 15 months from April 1996 in two areas—in Hull, and Medway and Maidstone (Kent)—in which those aged 18–50 and unemployed for two years or more are offered an intensive period of help with finding a job; if this proves unsuccessful, they then have to take up a place on a programme combining work experience and job search.

Help for People with Disabilities

Most disabled people assisted by the Employment Service are helped through its mainstream services, and have priority access to most of the main programmes for unemployed people. Services for people with disabilities who need more specialist help to get or keep a job are available through Disability Employment Advisers based in Jobcentres. The advisers are members of local integrated specialist teams—Placing Assessment and Counselling Teams.

These services include:

- the Access to Work programme, which helps people with disabilities to overcome barriers to employment; and
- the Supported Employment Programme, which provides job opportunities to around 21,800 people with severe disabilities who can work but, because of their limited productivity, are unlikely to obtain and keep jobs in open employment without some support.

Employment Agencies

There are many private employment agencies, including several large firms with many branches. The total value of the market has been estimated at about £8,000 million a year.

The main trade body for the employment agency industry is the Federation of Recruitment and Employment Services, which regulates the activities of its members by means of a Code of Good Recruitment Practice and by specialist section codes of practice.

The law governing employment agencies is less restrictive than that of most other EU countries. Under the Deregulation and Contracting Out Act 1994 (see p. 208), the licensing of employment agencies was abolished in 1995. The Act contains powers to prohibit people from operating agencies if it is not appropriate that they should do so. Agencies have to comply with statutory standards of conduct. This includes a general prohibition on charging fees to jobseekers, although there are conditional exceptions for entertainment and modelling agencies.

TERMS AND CONDITIONS OF EMPLOYMENT

Employment Rights

Employment protection legislation provides a number of safeguards for employees. For example, most employees have a right to a written statement setting out details of the main conditions, including pay, hours of work and holidays. Many rights have long applied to part-time workers. In 1995 the Government introduced regulations under which part-time employees now qualify for all statutory employment rights on exactly the same basis as full-time employees.

Employees with the necessary period of continuous employment with their employer (two years) are entitled to lump-sum redundancy payments if their jobs cease to exist (for example, because of technological improvements or a fall in demand) and their employers cannot offer suitable alternative work. Where employers are insolvent, redundancy payments are met directly from the National Insurance fund.

Minimum periods of notice when employment is to be terminated are laid down for both employers and employees. Most employees who believe they have been unfairly dismissed have the right to complain to an industrial tribunal. If the complaint is upheld, the tribunal may make an order for re-employment or award compensation.

All pregnant employees, regardless of length of service, have the right to 14 weeks' statutory maternity leave with all their non-wage contractual benefits maintained, and protection against dismissal because of pregnancy.

New rights for disabled people in employment in Great Britain are contained in the Disability Discrimination Act 1995 (see p. 424). Virtually all the employment-related provisions will take effect in December 1996. Disabled people will have the right not to be discriminated against in the field of employment. Employers with 20 or more employees will have a duty not to discriminate against disabled employees or applicants. Among other things, this will mean that such employers may have to make a reasonable adjustment where their workplace or working arrangements put disabled people at a substantial disadvantage compared with non-disabled people. A Code of Practice gives guidance to employers on the new requirements.

Legislation forbids any employment of children under 13 years of age, and employment in any industrial undertaking of children who have not reached the statutory minimum school-leaving age, with some exceptions for family undertakings. The Government has announced proposals to update the law and to bring it into line with the European Community (EC) Directive on the Protection of Young People at Work. The main changes planned would involve a permitted list of occupations for those aged 13, and require children to have a period free from work during school holidays.

Equal Opportunities

The Race Relations Act 1976 makes it generally unlawful to discriminate on grounds of colour, race, nationality (including citizenship) or ethnic or national origin, in employment, training and related matters. The Department for Education and Employment's Race Relations Employment Advisory Service promotes those government policies aimed at combating racial discrimination in employment and at promoting fair treatment and equality of opportunity in employment. Advisers provide employers with advice and practical help in developing and implementing effective equal opportunity strategies.

The Sex Discrimination Act 1975, as amended, makes it generally unlawful in Great Britain to discriminate on grounds of sex or marital status when recruiting, training, promoting, dismissing or retiring staff. The Equal Pay Act 1970 makes it generally unlawful to discriminate between men and women in pay and other terms and conditions of employment. The Act was significantly extended in 1984 to meet EU requirements by providing for equal pay for work of equal value.

Practical advice to employers and others on the best arrangements for implementing equal opportunities policies in Great Britain is given in codes of practice from the Commission for Racial Equality and from the Equal Opportunities Commission (see p. 40). The Government is encouraging voluntary action by employers to increase the employment opportunities for women and supports the 'Opportunity 2000' campaign (see p. 39). The Government's Campaign for Older Workers encourages employers to recruit and retain workers on merit, irrespective of age.

Similar legislation to that in Great Britain on equal pay and sex discrimination applies in Northern Ireland; legislation on race relations is planned. Discrimination in employment on grounds of religious belief or political opinion is unlawful. The Fair Employment Commission (see p. 15) has the task of promoting equality of opportunity and investigating employment practices, with powers to issue legally enforceable directions.

Industrial Tribunals

Industrial tribunals in Great Britain have jurisdiction over complaints on a range of employment rights, including unfair dismissal, redundancy pay, equal pay, and sex and race discrimination. They received 108,800 applications in 1995–96 and the number of cases continues to grow steadily. In July 1996 the Government issued for consultation a draft Bill designed to implement the majority of the proposals contained in a 1994 Green Paper on resolving disputes on employment rights. The draft Bill includes provisions to promote the use of voluntary alternatives to tribunal hearings (such as independent, binding arbitration), to streamline and improve tribunal procedures, and to rename industrial tribunals as 'employment tribunals' to reflect their modern role.

Northern Ireland has its own separate tribunal system, which is being reviewed in conjunction with work by the Standing Advisory Commission on Human Rights on the functioning of the Province's fair employment legislation. Reform of tribunals in Northern Ireland will take into account the operation of the Fair Employment Tribunal, which operates alongside, and as an integral part of, the tribunals' administration.

Earnings

According to the official New Earnings Survey, the average weekly earnings, unaffected by absence and including overtime payments, in Great Britain in April 1996 of full-time employees on adult rates were £352. Earnings were higher for non-manual employees (£390) than for manual employees (£281). Managerial and professional groups are the highest paid. The sectors with the highest average weekly earnings were mining and quarrying (£475) and financial services (£453).

Overtime and other additional payments are particularly important for manual employees, for whom such additional payments represented over one-fifth of earnings. About 49 per cent of manual employees and 18 per cent of non-manual employees received overtime payments.

In the year to July 1996 the underlying average increase in earnings in Great Britain was about 3.75 per cent, compared with a rise of 2.2 per cent in the Retail Prices Index.

Fringe Benefits

A variety of fringe benefits are used by employers to provide additional rewards to their employees, including schemes to encourage employee financial participation in their companies, pension schemes, private medical insurance, subsidised meals, company cars and childcare schemes.

Many employees are covered by pension schemes provided by their employers. Such benefits are more usual among clerical and professional employees than among manual workers. Over 11 million people in Britain are members of occupational schemes.

Company cars are provided for employees in a wide variety of circumstances. It is estimated that around 1.7 million people have a company car and around half of these receive fuel for private motoring in their cars.

The Government has introduced tax reliefs to encourage employers to set up financial participation schemes, and give employees a direct financial stake in the business they work for. Profit-related pay (PRP) schemes link part of pay to changes in a business's profits. By the end of September 1995 over 10,500 PRP schemes were registered with the Inland Revenue, covering more than 2.6 million people. Employee share schemes allow employees to receive low-cost or free shares from their employer without paying income tax. Many companies have adopted such schemes. The 1995 Budget contained a series of measures to encourage companies to adopt employee participation schemes and to involve more of their workforce in them. Measures include more flexible arrangements for profit-sharing and savings-related schemes, and a new company share option plan enabling employees to exercise options over shares worth up to a maximum of £30,000 free of income tax.

Hours of Work

Most full-time employees have a basic working week of between 34 and 40 hours, and work a five-day week. When overtime is taken into account, average weekly hours worked in Great Britain in April 1996 were 41.7 for men and 37.6 for women. Both male and female full-time employees tend to work more hours than in other EU countries. Hours worked tend to be longest in agriculture, construction and transport and communications, and shortest in most service industries. More men than women work overtime, and those in manual occupations generally work more overtime than employees in non-manual jobs. Flexible working hours were worked by about 15 per cent of female and 10 per cent of male full-time employees in Britain in spring 1995.

In general, there are no limits on hours worked by adults except in a few occupations (such as for drivers of goods and public service vehicles).

Holidays with Pay

There are no general statutory entitlements to holidays, and holiday entitlements are determined by negotiation. Holiday entitlements (excluding public holidays) generally provide for at least four weeks' paid holiday a year for full-time workers. According to the Labour Force Survey in autumn 1995, holiday entitlements in Great Britain averaged 24 days for full-time employees and 13 days for part-time employees. Non-manual workers tend to have longer holidays than manual workers. Holiday entitlements may also be dependent upon length of service.

INDUSTRIAL RELATIONS

The structure of industrial relations in Britain has been established mainly on a voluntary basis. The system is based chiefly on the organisation of employees and employers into trade unions and employers' associations, and on freely conducted negotiations at all levels.

Trends in Bargaining and Pay

There has been a considerable reduction in the proportion of employees and workplaces where pay is determined by collective bargaining. Around 48 per cent of employees in employment in Great Britain work in firms where trade unions negotiate on pay and conditions of employment. Private sector employees are much less likely to be covered by collective bargaining than are public sector employees.

Where agreements in the private sector are industry-wide, they are often supplemented by local agreements in companies or factories (plant bargaining). Where there is no collective bargaining, pay is usually determined by management at local level. Most medium and large employers make some use of performance-related pay systems such as merit pay, profit-related pay (see p. 196) and individual payment by results. Private sector organisations are more likely than public sector bodies to use performance-related pay.

Performance-related pay has, though, become much more widespread in the public sector, as part of the Government's policy of improving the quality of public services. Another feature is the delegation of pay determination to a local level, such as to self-governing National Health Service Trusts and to grant-maintained schools. Since April 1996 all government departments and agencies have had responsibility for negotiating pay and conditions of staff below senior levels.

'New-style' agreements, often associated with overseas-owned companies, have become more widespread. Features normally include flexibility in working practices, recognition of a single union for all of a company's employees and 'single status', involving the elimination of the traditional distinction between managers, supervisors and other employees.

Employee Involvement

Employers use a variety of methods of informing and consulting their employees, not only through committees but also through direct communication between management and employees. These methods include employee bulletins and reports, quality circles, and attitude surveys.

Some of the largest British-based multinational companies, such as ICI and United Biscuits, have set up works councils covering consultation arrangements, in line with the EC's Directive on Works Councils. However, the Government has refused to accept the Directive and believes that companies should be free to develop employee involvement arrangements which are appropriate to their own circumstances and the needs of their employees.

Trade Unions

Trade unions have members in nearly all occupations. They are widely recognised by employers in the public sector and in large firms and establishments. As well as negotiating pay and other terms and conditions of employment with employers, they provide benefits and services such as educational facilities, financial services, legal advice and aid in work-related cases. In recent years many unions have extended considerably the range of services for members.

At the end of 1994 there were 8.3 million trade union members in Britain, 5 per cent fewer than a year earlier and the lowest number since 1945. The decline in membership reflects the moves away from manufacturing and public services, both of which have a relatively high level of membership, and the growth in part-time employment. About 58 per cent of union members were male and 42 per cent female. While male membership of trade unions fell by nearly 9 per cent in 1994, there was a slight increase in the number of female union members.

Unison, with about 1.4 million members, is the biggest union in Britain, accounting for 17 per cent of all union members. It was formed in 1993 from a merger of three unions: the Confederation of Health Service Employees, the National Union of Public Employees and the National and Local Government Officers' Association. Three other unions have over 500,000 members:

- the Transport and General Workers Union (with 897,000 members);
- GMB (740,000)—a general union with members in a range of public and private sector industries; and
- the Amalgamated Engineering and Electrical Union (726,000).

The number of unions has declined by around a third in the last 20 years, mainly as a result of mergers. At the end of 1995 there were 256 trade unions on the list maintained by the Certification Officer, who, among other duties, is responsible for certifying the independence of trade unions. To be eligible for entry on the list a trade union must show that it consists wholly or mainly of workers and that its principal purposes include the regulation of relations between workers and employers or between workers and employers' associations. A further 25 unions were known to the Certification Officer.

Trade union organisation varies widely, but there is usually a national executive council or committee. Many unions also have regional and district organisations, while local branches cover one or more workplaces. Elected workplace representatives are often called 'shop stewards'. Where two or more unions have members in the same workplace, shop stewards' committees may be formed to discuss matters of common concern.

Trades Union Congress

In Britain the national body of the trade union movement is the Trades Union Congress (TUC), founded in 1868. Its affiliated membership comprises 71 trade unions, which together represent some 6.75 million people, or about 80 per cent of all trade unionists in Britain.

The TUC's objectives are to promote the interests of its affiliated organisations and to improve the economic and social conditions of working people. It deals with all general questions which concern trade unions, both nationally and internationally, and provides a forum in which affiliated unions can collectively determine policy. There are six TUC regional councils for England and a Wales Trades Union Council. The annual Congress meets in September to discuss matters of concern to trade unionists. A General Council represents the TUC between annual meetings.

The TUC plays an active part in international trade union activity, through its affiliation to the International Confederation of Free Trade Unions and the European Trade Union Confederation. It also nominates the British workers' delegation to the annual International Labour Conference.

Scotland and Northern Ireland

Trade unions in Scotland also have their own national central body, the Scottish Trades Union Congress, which in many respects is similar in constitution and function to the TUC. Nearly all trade unions in Northern Ireland are represented by the Northern Ireland Committee of the Irish Congress of Trade Unions (ICTU). Most trade unionists in Northern Ireland are members of unions affiliated to the ICTU, while the majority also belong to unions based in Great Britain which are affiliated to the TUC. The Northern Ireland Committee of the ICTU enjoys a high degree of autonomy.

Legal Framework

The Government's reforms of industrial relations and trade union law have changed the balance of power between trade unions and employers, and between trade unions and their own members. For example, since 1980 employers have been able to decide whether or not to bargain with a trade union or continue to do so. Legislation for Great Britain is consolidated in the Trade Union and Labour Relations (Consolidation) Act 1992, as amended by the Trade Union Reform and Employment Rights Act 1993. There is broad parity of provision in respect of industrial relations and trade union law in Northern Ireland.

There were 415,000 working days lost in 235 stoppages of work as a result of industrial action in 1995 (see Table 13.4). The number of days lost in 1994 and 1995 were the lowest annual figures since records began in 1891.

Union Membership and Non-membership Rights

All individuals have the right under the law not to be dismissed or refused employment (or the services of an employment agency) because of membership or non-membership of a trade union. Individuals who believe that they have been dismissed or refused employment on such grounds may complain to an industrial tribunal. All employees who are union members also have the right not to have union membership subscriptions deducted from their pay unless they have authorised this, and authorisation has to be renewed every three years.

The Conduct of Union Affairs

The law requires a trade union to elect every member of its governing body, its general secretary and its president. Elections must be held at least every five years and be carried out by a secret postal ballot under independent scrutiny. Any union member who believes that the union has not complied with the statutory requirements may complain to the courts or to the Certification Officer.

A trade union may establish a political fund if it wishes to use its money for what the law defines as 'political objects'. If a union wishes to set up a political fund, its members must first agree in a secret ballot a resolution adopting those political objectives as an aim of the union. The union must also ballot its members every ten years to maintain the fund. Union members have a statutory right to opt out of contributing to a political fund.

The law also gives all union members a statutory means of redress if unjustifiably disciplined by their union, for example, for refusing to take part in industrial action or for crossing a picket line. Members also have the right to inspect their union's accounting records and obtain an annual statement from the union about its financial affairs.

Industrial Action

For most of the 20th century trade unions enjoyed wide immunity protecting them from legal proceedings for organising industrial action, so that the organisation of almost any industrial action was protected. Legislative reforms have restricted the scope of these immunities. To have the benefit of statutory immunity (that is, to be 'lawful'), the organisation of industrial action must now be wholly or mainly in contemplation or furtherance of a trade dispute between workers and their own employer, and must not:

- involve workers who have no dispute with their own employer (so-called 'secondary' action);

Table 13.4: Industrial Disputes 1985–1995

	Working days lost (thousands)	Working days lost per 1,000 employees[a]	Workers involved (thousands)	Number of stoppages
1985	6,402	299	791	903
1986	1,920	90	720	1,074
1987	3,546	164	887	1,016
1988	3,702	166	790	781
1989	4,128	182	727	701
1990	1,903	83	298	630
1991	761	34	176	369
1992	528	24	148	253
1993	649	30	385	211
1994	278	13	107	205
1995	415	19	174	235

Source: Office for National Statistics
[a]Based on the mid-year (June) estimates of employees in employment.

- involve unlawful forms of picketing;
- be to establish or maintain a union-only labour agreement (the 'closed shop'); or
- be in support of any employee dismissed while taking unofficial industrial action.

Before calling for industrial action, a trade union must first obtain the support of its members in a secret postal ballot and must notify employers of its intention to conduct such a ballot. The union must also provide employers, in writing, with at least seven days' notice of official industrial action following a ballot, and with details of the ballot result.

Any trade union member has the right to restrain the union from calling on him or her, and other members, to take action unless a properly conducted secret ballot has supported the action. Anyone deprived of goods or services because of unlawful organisation of industrial action has the right to obtain a court order to stop this happening.

Employers' Organisations

Many employers in Britain are members of employers' organisations, some of which are wholly concerned with labour matters, although others are also trade associations concerned with commercial matters in general. With the move away from national pay bargaining, many employers' associations have moved towards concentrating on areas such as supplying information for bargaining purposes and dealing with specialist issues. As with some of the larger trade unions, a number of employers' associations are increasingly concerned with legislation and other issues relating to Europe.

Employers' organisations are usually established on an industry basis rather than a product basis, for example, the Engineering Employers' Federation. A few are purely local in character or deal with a section of an industry or, for example, with small businesses; most are national and are concerned with the whole of an industry. In some of the main industries there are local or regional organisations combined into national federations. At the end of 1995, 114 listed and 115 unlisted employers' associations were known to the Certification Officer.

Most national organisations belong to the Confederation of British Industry (see p. 205), which represents directly or indirectly some 250,000 businesses.

Advisory, Conciliation and Arbitration Service

The Advisory, Conciliation and Arbitration Service (ACAS) is an independent statutory body which has a general duty of promoting the improvement of industrial relations. ACAS aims to operate through the voluntary co-operation of employers, employees and, where appropriate, their representatives. Its main functions are collective conciliation, provision of arbitration and mediation facilities, advisory mediation services for preventing disputes and improving industrial relations through the joint involvement of employers and employees, and the provision of a public enquiry service. ACAS also conciliates in disputes on individual employment rights.

In 1995 ACAS:

- received 1,321 requests for collective conciliation, of which nearly half related to pay or other terms and conditions of employment;
- received nearly 91,600 individual conciliation cases, 15 per cent more than in 1994;
- assisted with 539 joint working exercises; and
- dealt with almost 538,400 enquiries through its public enquiry points.

In Northern Ireland the Labour Relations Agency, an independent statutory body, provides services similar to those provided by ACAS in Great Britain.

HEALTH AND SAFETY AT WORK

Health and safety standards in Britain are among the best in the world. Recent statistics indicate a reduction in the rate of major and other reported injuries to employees. In 1994–95 the number of deaths for employees and the self-employed from accidents at work fell to 263, the lowest figure recorded. The decline reflects improvements in safety, together with a change in industrial structure away from old heavy industries which tend to have higher risks. About 18 million working days a year are lost as a result of work-related injuries and 13 million from work-related illnesses.

The principal legislation is the Health and Safety at Work etc. Act 1974. It imposes general duties on everyone concerned with work activities, including employers, the self-employed, employees, and manufacturers and suppliers of materials for use at work. Associated Acts and regulations deal with particular hazards and types of work. Employers with five or more staff must prepare a written statement of their health and safety policy and bring it to the attention of their staff.

The Control of Substances Hazardous to Health Regulations 1988 (which were revised in 1994) constitute one of the most important sets of regulations made under the 1974 Act. They replaced a range of outdated legislation by a comprehensive and systematic approach to the control of exposure to virtually all substances hazardous to health.

Health and Safety Commission

The Health and Safety Commission (HSC) has responsibility for developing policy on health and safety at work, including proposals for new or revised regulations and approved codes of practice. Recent work has concentrated on achieving a simpler and more effective system of health and safety regulation. This is expected to reduce the volume of health and safety legislation by 40 per cent, primarily through repealing outdated or unnecessary regulations.

The HSC has advisory committees covering subjects such as toxic substances, genetic modification and the safety of nuclear installations. There are also several industry advisory committees, each of which deals with a specific sector of industry.

Health and Safety Executive

The Health and Safety Executive (HSE) is the primary instrument for carrying out the

HSC's policies and has day-to-day responsibility for enforcing health and safety law, except where other bodies, such as local authorities, are responsible. Its field services and inspections are carried out by the Field Operations Division. This incorporates the Factory, Agricultural and Quarries inspectorates, together with the regional staff of the Employment Medical Advisory Service and the Field Consulting Groups, which provide technical support to the inspectorates.

In 1995 the HSE launched a major campaign to reduce the number of people—2.2 million a year—who suffer work-related ill health. The campaign is designed to raise awareness of health risks at work, and to persuade managers to ensure that working conditions do not cause illness among their employees.

The HSE's Directorate of Science and Technology provides technical advice on industrial health and safety matters. The Health and Safety Laboratory provides scientific and medical support and testing services, and carries out research.

In premises such as offices, shops, warehouses, restaurants and hotels, health and safety legislation is enforced by inspectors appointed by local authorities, working under guidance from the HSE. Some other official bodies work under agency agreement with the HSE.

Northern Ireland

The general requirements of the Northern Ireland health and safety legislation are broadly similar to those for Great Britain. They are enforced mainly by the Department of Economic Development and the Department of Agriculture through their health and safety inspectorates, although the district councils have an enforcement role similar to that of local authorities in Great Britain. There is a Health and Safety Agency, roughly corresponding to the HSC but without its policy-making powers, and an Employment Medical Advisory Service.

Further Reading

Employment. Aspects of Britain series, HMSO, 1994.

Labour Market Trends. Department for Education and Employment and Office for National Statistics. Monthly.

Labour Force Survey Quarterly Bulletin. Office for National Statistics.

14 Industry and Government

Structure and Organisation
of Industry   203

Government Policy   205

The private sector is responsible for over three-quarters of total economic activity. Since 1979 the Government has reduced the state-owned sector of industry by about two-thirds under its privatisation programme. It believes that economic decisions are best taken by those competing in the market place, and that its primary roles are to help keep inflation low, maintain sound public finances and create the right climate for markets to work better. Government schemes do, however, provide direct assistance or advice, mainly to small and medium-sized businesses without the resources of large companies.

STRUCTURE AND ORGANISATION OF INDUSTRY

In some sectors a small number of large companies and their subsidiaries are responsible for a substantial proportion of total production, for instance in the chemical, motor vehicle, aerospace and transport equipment industries. Private enterprises account for by far the greater part of activity in the agricultural, manufacturing, construction, distributive, financial and other service sectors. The private sector contributed 78 per cent of total domestic expenditure in 1995, general government 21 per cent and public corporations under 1 per cent.

About 250 British industrial companies each have an annual turnover of over £500 million. Eleven British firms are among the top 25 European companies in terms of capital employed and 16 in terms of profitability. Small businesses now contribute 40 per cent of Britain's business turnover, employing over 50 per cent of the private sector workforce. Industries with the fastest growth rates in recent years are in the services sector, particularly finance, property, and professional and business services.

Legal Framework

All British companies are registered with the Registrar of Companies in Cardiff, Edinburgh or Belfast. Companies with a place of business or branch in Britain, but which are incorporated overseas, are also required to register.

Legislation deals with capital structure, rights and duties of directors and members, and the preparation and filing of accounts (see p. 204). Most corporate businesses are 'limited liability' companies. The liability of members of a limited company is restricted to contributing an amount related to their shareholding (or to their guarantee where companies are limited by guarantee). In the case of unincorporated businesses, such as sole proprietorships or partnerships, individuals are personally liable for any business debts, except where a member of a partnership is a limited liability company or a limited member of a limited partnership.

Companies may be either public or private. A company must satisfy certain conditions before it can become a public limited company (plc). It must:

- be limited by shares or guarantee and have a share capital;
- state in its memorandum of association that it is to be a public limited company;
- meet specified minimum capital requirements; and
- have as the suffix to its name the words 'public limited company' or 'plc'.

All other British companies are private companies and are generally prohibited from offering their shares to the public.

Industrial Financing

Over half of companies' funds for investment and other purposes is generated internally. Banks are the chief external source of finance, but companies have increasingly turned to equity finance. The main forms of short-term finance in the private sector are bank overdrafts, trade credit and factoring (making cash available to a company in exchange for debts owing to it).

Types of medium- and long-term finance include bank loans, mortgaging of property and the issue of shares and other securities to the public through the London Stock Exchange. The leasing of equipment may also be regarded as a form of finance. Other sources of funding for industry include government, the European Union (EU) and specialist financial institutions, such as financing and leasing, factoring, and venture capital companies.

Venture Capital

Venture capital, or private equity capital, provides long-term unsecured capital for companies which are starting up or expanding as well as those undergoing management buy-outs and buy-ins. It is available principally from institutions, including independent funds and wholly-owned subsidiaries or divisions of financial institutions, such as banks. The

British Venture Capital Association has 108 full members, which represent every major source of venture capital in Britain.

> Nearly £14,100 million has been invested by venture capital companies in over 14,000 businesses since 1984, with £2,535 million having been invested in 1,163 businesses in 1995. In that year, 53 per cent of venture capital deals were in expansion stage companies. Some 73 per cent of the total amount was invested in management buy-outs and buy-ins.

'Business angels', or private investors, are an increasingly important source of smaller amounts of venture capital. The Government's Enterprise Investment Scheme (EIS) and Venture Capital Trusts (VCTs) seek to encourage private investment in smaller unquoted trading companies by offering individuals tax incentives. The EIS allows business angels to take a position on the board of the investee company, while VCTs are more suited to less active investors. VCTs are similar in structure to investment trusts: they invest in unquoted trading companies and are quoted on the Stock Exchange.

Taxation

Rates of corporate taxation have been progressively reduced in recent years (see p. 168). The main rate of corporation tax is 33 per cent, with a reduced rate of 24 per cent for small firms (those with annual profits of less than £300,000). For companies with profits of between £300,000 and £1.5 million, the overall corporation tax rate is between the main rate and the rate for small firms. Expenditure on business plant and machinery, industrial building, and scientific research qualifies for annual allowances against profit for tax purposes.

Company Law

Laws relating to companies are designed to meet the need for proper regulation of business, maintain open markets and to create safeguards for those wishing to invest in companies or do business with them. They take account of EC directives on company law, and on company and group accounts and their auditing. The Government's aim is to achieve these objectives while imposing as small a burden as possible on business. Hence, it has removed from certain types of small companies the statutory obligation to have their accounts audited, and has introduced a simple procedure for dissolving private companies that are no longer operational. Additionally, it is taking steps to encourage the use of summary financial statements and to simplify statutory accounting requirements.

The 1992 Cadbury Committee Report on the management of companies recommended that company boards should comply with a Code of Best Practice. This is underpinned by a Stock Exchange requirement for firms to state whether they are complying with the Code and give reasons for areas of non-compliance. Standards of disclosure have improved since 1992 and they indicate a high level of compliance with the Cadbury recommendations, especially among larger companies. Shareholders, including institutional shareholders, are encouraged by the Government to play a more active role in overseeing management.

Insider dealing in shares is a criminal offence and inspectors may be appointed to investigate possible insider dealing. A licensing procedure ensures the professional competence, integrity and independence of people acting as trustees of bankrupt individuals, or as liquidators, receivers or administrators of insolvent companies.

Industrial Associations

The Confederation of British Industry (CBI) is the largest employers' organisation in Britain, representing about 250,000 companies. Most national employers' organisations, trade associations, and some chambers of commerce are also members.

The CBI aims to ensure that the Government, national and international institutions and the public understand the needs, intentions and problems of business, so as to help create a climate of opinion in which business can operate efficiently and profitably. It campaigns to lessen the administrative and regulatory burdens on business, tackle handicaps on competition, and help improve the performance of companies. It offers members a forum, a lobby and a range of advisory services. The CBI also conducts surveys of activity in manufacturing, distribution, financial services, the regions, innovation, and pay and productivity. It has 12 regional offices and an office in Brussels. The CBI is the British member of the Union of Industrial and Employers' Confederations of Europe.

Chambers of commerce represent business views to the Government at national and local levels. They promote local economic development—for example, through regeneration projects, tourism, inward investment promotion and business services, including overseas trade missions, exhibitions and training conferences. Member firms are also supplied with information about overseas buyers and product sourcing. The Association of British Chambers of Commerce represents about 200,000 businesses in 196 chambers of commerce and trade.

The Institute of Directors (IOD) has 35,000 members in Britain, many of whom are from small businesses. It provides business advisory services on a range of matters affecting company directors, such as corporate management, insolvency and career counselling, and represents the interests of members to authorities in Britain and the EU.

Trade associations represent companies producing or selling a particular product or group of products. They exist to supply common services, regulate trading practices and represent their members to government departments.

GOVERNMENT POLICY

The Department of Trade and Industry (DTI) is the department mainly responsible for the Government's relations with industry and commerce. Specific areas of responsibility, which are dealt with in this chapter, include company law, small firms, competition policy and consumer affairs, intellectual property, and regional industrial development and inward investment. The Department of the Environment oversees provision of regional industrial aid through the Government Offices for the Regions. The Scottish, Welsh and Northern Ireland Offices are responsible for industrial policies in their areas. Export promotion and technology and innovation, which are also part of DTI's remit, are dealt with in Chapters 12 and 20 respectively. The DTI's duties regarding industrial relations are covered in Chapter 13.

The Department of Trade and Industry seeks to help British industry to compete successfully in domestic and overseas markets. It has specified its objectives as:

- identifying business needs through close contact with individual sectors;

- ensuring these needs are taken into account by Government and the EU;

- identifying influences on competitiveness at home and abroad;

- working for global trade liberalisation worldwide and helping businesses take advantage of market opportunities at home and abroad;

- widening choice and stimulating enterprise by promoting competition and privatisation;

- maintaining confidence in markets and protecting consumers through fair regulation;

- reducing unnecessary regulatory and administrative burdens on business;

- promoting innovation and best practice in quality, design and management;

- fostering the creation and development of small and medium-sized businesses;

- responding to the needs of different regions and areas with special difficulties; and

- taking account of environmental issues when developing government policies and stimulating an effective business response to environmental developments.

Competitiveness White Papers

A White Paper on Competitiveness, issued by the Government in 1994, contained a programme of measures to help British business compete effectively in world markets (see p. 158). These were introduced to improve education and training, help small firms to be more innovative and to increase exports, boost regional economies and attract more inward investment. A follow-up White Paper was published a year later, detailing progress since 1994 and setting out new policies and initiatives, in particular for smaller companies. Some of the more important measures are covered in this chapter and also in Chapter 13.

Third Competitiveness White Paper

In June 1996 the Government published a further White Paper in this series, *Competitiveness: Creating the Enterprise Centre of Europe*. This contains an analysis of British industry's competitiveness, focusing on education and training as well as the comparative performance of British companies in both manufacturing and services. It outlines a range of new measures to improve the education and training framework, help attract more inward investment, create new jobs and raise living standards. There are also new proposals for simplifying government support for business and providing better assistance for small businesses.

Review of Business Support

The Government is presently consulting business and other interested parties on proposals to reduce the number and complexity of its business support services; delegate more of the design and delivery of these services to local level—principally through Training and Enterprise Councils (TECs) and Business Links; adopt challenge funding for a proportion of locally delivered support so that only the best projects are financed; and extend challenge funding to most sectoral support.

Small Firms

A small firms' benchmarking service will be made available locally. Measures to encourage better payment practice towards small businesses will include a new payment performance league table for government departments; local government will be expected to operate a similar scheme. Payment performance league tables are also being considered for the private sector. Additionally, the tax and National Insurance Contributions (NICs) systems are to be further streamlined (see pp. 165–171).

Single European Market

The Government believes that the single European market (see p. 180) is beneficial to the economy of each member state, and that removal of trade barriers should lead to a reduction in business costs and greater competition and efficiency, aiding consumers and job and wealth creation.

Specific advantages of the single market include:

- wider consumer choice;
- removal of barriers to trade through mutual recognition of standards and harmonisation;
- liberalisation of public procurement;
- the right to trade financial services throughout the EU on the basis of a single authorisation 'passport' (see p. 222);
- mutual recognition of professional and vocational qualifications; and
- a reduction in export business bureaucracy.

Privatisation

The Government is of the view that the best way to improve the performance of public sector companies and nationalised industries is to expose them to market forces, through privatisation and the promotion of competition. Privatisation has also provided an opportunity to widen and deepen share ownership by encouraging both employees and the public to take a direct stake in industry. In major flotations, employees in privatised companies are normally given a preferential right to buy shares in the new privatised companies.

Since 1979 the Government has privatised 50 major businesses, with net proceeds to the end of 1995–96 of about £64,000 million; more

than 950,000 jobs have been transferred to the private sector. Recent privatisations include British Coal, the electricity industry in Northern Ireland, London's buses and the Government's residual shareholdings in BT (British Telecom), National Power and PowerGen. The modern advanced gas-cooled reactor nuclear power stations were privatised in July 1996 (p. 273). Passenger services of British Rail are being franchised to the private sector; Railtrack was privatised in May 1996 (p. 310). Privatisation is also being extended to non-core government activities (including a number of research laboratories—p. 330) and other public sector areas.

Benefits

The Government believes that the economy has benefited through higher returns on capital in the privatised industries, which now have to compete for funds in the open capital markets. It considers that the consumer has gained from downward pressure on prices and from rising standards of service.

The Government has established a system of independent regulation for the privatised utilities. In each of the privatised utility sectors—telecommunications, electricity, gas and so on—a regulatory body has been appointed with a wide range of powers and duties to promote competition and the interests of consumers. These usually include considering all complaints and representations about the company's services. Each privatised utility operates under a pricing policy set by the regulator, which often limits annual price increases to significantly less than the rate of inflation.

Nationalised Industries

The remaining major nationalised industries are the Post Office, London Transport, and the Civil Aviation Authority. Managing boards are appointed by ministers, who have power to give general directions but are not engaged in day-to-day management. Managing boards and staffs of nationalised industries are not civil servants.

The Government considers that nationalised industries should act as commercial enterprises and has set guidelines to which they are expected to conform. These involve:

- clear government objectives;
- regular corporate plans and performance reviews;
- agreed principles relating to investment appraisal and pricing;
- financial targets and performance aims;
- external financing limits; and
- systematic monitoring.

Deregulation

The Government's aim is to reduce or simplify administrative and legislative 'burdens' on business, particularly small businesses, where the burden of compliance is most demanding, given limited financial resources and staffing levels. A small firms 'litmus test' is helping to ensure that compliance costs for new regulations are not unduly high. Deregulation policies are designed to help businesses to contain costs, operate more efficiently and trade more competitively.

Under its Deregulation Initiative, the Government is reducing burdens on business by:

- achieving more efficient regulation, and cutting unnecessary controls and the cost of compliance with essential regulation;
- ensuring that the views of business, and potential costs of compliance, are taken into account in framing new regulations and in negotiating EU proposals;
- increasing official awareness of the needs of business through training and better consultation and communication; and
- improving the quality of service to business generally, whether provided by central or local government.

Existing regulations affecting companies are being reviewed by government departments with the help of business people. The Deregulation and Contracting Out Act enables the Government to amend or repeal primary legislation imposing unnecessary burdens on business.

Regulation of Markets

The aim of Government competition policy is to encourage and enhance the competitive process. When the competitive process is frustrated intervention may be justified. The purpose is not to protect particular firms that may be adversely affected by competition. The law provides several ways in which market situations can be examined and, if necessary, altered.

Responsibility for competition policy lies with the President of the Board of Trade. Competition law is administered by the Director General of Fair Trading, the Monopolies and Mergers Commission (MMC) and the Restrictive Practices Court. The main legislation comprises:

- the Fair Trading Act 1973 and the Competition Act 1980, which deal with mergers and monopolies, and anti-competitive practices respectively;
- the Restrictive Trade Practices Act 1976, which regulates agreements between people or companies that could limit their freedom to operate independently; and
- the Resale Prices Act 1976, covering attempts to impose minimum prices at which goods can be sold.

Government proposals to reform competition laws include plans to prohibit cartels and restrictive trade agreements, and to strengthen the powers of the Director General of Fair Trading to deal with abuse of market power.

Competition policy is also governed by European Community rules. These apply only where an agreement or practice has an effect on trade between member states. Enforcement of these rules is primarily the responsibility of the European Commission, which has powers to investigate and terminate alleged infringements and to impose fines. The Director General assists the European Commission in the application of European Community competition law.

Monopolies

A simple monopoly is defined as a situation where a business supplies or purchases 25 per cent or more of a particular product or service in Britain, or a defined part of it. A complex monopoly is a situation where a group of companies or people together have 25 per cent or more of the market and behave in a way that adversely affects competition.

The Director General may enquire into possible abuse of a monopoly position and take various measures to remedy the situation. If there is 'prima facie' evidence of such an abuse, the matter can be referred for further investigation by the independent Monopolies and Mergers Commission, whose members include businessmen and women, lawyers, economists and trade unionists.

If the MMC finds that a monopoly situation operates, or could be expected to operate, against the public interest, the President of the Board of Trade can either make an order to prevent further harm or ask the Director General to obtain undertakings from those involved to remedy the situation.

Mergers

A merger is defined as occurring when two or more enterprises come under common ownership or control. It qualifies for investigation by the MMC where a market share—in Britain or a substantial part of it—reaches 25 per cent or more, or is increased, and the total value of gross assets to be taken over exceeds £70 million.

Qualifying mergers are considered by the Director General of Fair Trading, who then advises the Secretary of State for Trade and Industry. There is a voluntary procedure for pre-notification of proposed mergers which offers prompt clearance of straightforward cases. The majority of mergers are not found to operate against the public interest and are allowed to take place. However, under the Fair Trading Act, the Secretary of State can refer a merger for further investigation by the MMC if such a merger could lead to a significant reduction in competition or raise other matters of public concern. Alternatively, the Director General of Fair Trading may be asked to obtain suitable undertakings from the companies involved to remedy the adverse effects identified. The Secretary of State may accept undertakings by the parties concerned

to dispose of assets or to behave in a certain way so that there is no need for a full investigation by the MMC.

If a merger or proposed merger is referred and the MMC finds that it could be expected to operate against the public interest, the Secretary of State can prohibit it or allow it subject to certain conditions being met. Where the merger has already taken place, action can be taken to reverse it. There are special provisions for newspaper and water company mergers.

Certain mergers with an EC dimension, assessed by reference to turnover, come under the exclusive jurisdiction of the European Commission. The Commission can ban mergers if it concludes that they create or strengthen a dominant position which would significantly impede effective competition within the EU or a substantial part of it; alternatively, it may negotiate undertakings to correct the adverse effect.

Anti-competitive Practices

The Director General of Fair Trading can investigate any course of conduct by a business which appears to be anti-competitive. If a practice is found to be anti-competitive, undertakings may be sought from the business responsible for the conduct. In the event of a suitable undertaking not being given, the matter may be referred to the MMC. In the case of an adverse finding by the MMC, the Secretary of State for Trade and Industry has powers to take remedial action. Companies are not covered by the legislation if they have a turnover of below £10 million, or have less than 25 per cent of a relevant market in Britain.

Restrictive Trade Practices

Most commercial agreements containing restrictions on matters such as prices and other conditions of sale and parties or areas to be dealt with have to be submitted to the Director General of Fair Trading for registration. Legal proceedings are normally initiated by the Director General against blatantly anti-competitive agreements which have not been notified.

Once an agreement has been registered, the Director General is under a general duty to refer it to the Restrictive Practices Court. The Court must declare the restrictions in the agreement contrary to the public interest unless the parties can satisfy it that the restrictions fall within set public interest criteria. Restrictions declared contrary to the public interest by the Court are void, and the Court has the power to order the parties not to implement them.

In practice, however, the great majority of agreements are never brought to court, because the restrictions they contain are not significant enough to warrant such action.

Resale Price Maintenance

It is in general unlawful for suppliers to stipulate to dealers a minimum resale price for their goods or to make it a condition of supply that their goods be sold at a specified price. It is also unlawful for suppliers to seek to impose minimum resale prices by withholding supplies of goods or by discriminating against price-cutting dealers in other ways.

There is, however, the possibility of exemption for particular classes of goods by the Restrictive Practices Court on public interest grounds. These exemptions remain in force until it can be shown by the Director General of Fair Trading, or third parties, to the Court's satisfaction that there has been a material change in circumstances from the time the exemptions were first granted. Two exemptions are currently in force: on books (Net Book Agreement) and in respect of certain pharmaceuticals. The Net Book Agreement is being reviewed by the Court, though its publisher members have withdrawn from the arrangement. The Office of Fair Trading is considering the decision to exempt pharmaceuticals.

Consumer Protection

Consumer protection is an integral element in the fair and efficient operation of markets. The Government believes that consumers' interests are best served by open and competitive markets offering the widest choice of goods and services. There are, however, laws to ensure that consumers are adequately protected.

Legislation covers the sale and supply of goods and services. The Sale of Goods Act 1979 (as amended in 1994) ensures that consumers are entitled to receive goods which fit their description and are of satisfactory quality. The Trade Descriptions Act 1968 prohibits misdescriptions of goods, services, accommodation and facilities. False or misleading indications about prices of goods are covered by the Consumer Protection Act 1987. This Act also requires information or instructions relating to goods to be marked on or to accompany the goods or to be included in advertisements. The marking and accuracy of quantities are regulated by weights and measures legislation. Another law provides for the control of medical products, and certain other substances and articles, through a system of licences and certificates. Under EC legislation, it is a criminal offence to supply unsafe consumer products. A range of public safety information for consumers is made available by the DTI.

The Director General of Fair Trading promotes good trading practices and acts against malpractice. Under the Fair Trading Act, the Director General can recommend legislative or other changes to stop practices adversely affecting consumers' economic interests; encourage trade associations to develop codes of practice promoting consumers' interests; and disseminate consumer information and guidance. The Director General can also take assurances as to future conduct from traders who persistently breach the law to the detriment of consumers. Other regulations empower the Director General to act against traders using unfair contract terms.

The Consumer Credit Act 1974 is intended to protect consumers in their dealings with credit businesses. Businesses connected with the consumer credit or hire industry or which supply ancillary credit services, for example, credit brokers, debt collectors, debt counsellors and credit reference agencies, require a consumer credit licence. The Director General is responsible for administering the licensing system, including revoking licences of those unfit to hold them.

Under other regulations, the Director General also has powers to take court action to prevent the publication of misleading advertisements and powers to prohibit unfit people from carrying out estate agency work.

The EU's consumer programme covers activities such as health and safety, protection of the consumer's economic interests, promotion of consumer education and strengthening the representation of consumers. The views of British consumer organisations on EU matters are represented by the Consumers in Europe group (UK). British consumer bodies also have a voice on the European consumer 'watchdog' body, the Bureau Européen des Unions de Consommateurs.

Consumer Advice and Information

Advice and information on consumer matters are given by Citizens Advice Bureaux, trading standards and consumer protection departments of local authorities (in Northern Ireland the Department of Economic Development), and, in some areas, by specialist consumer advice centres.

The independent, non-statutory National Consumer Council (and associated councils for Scotland and Wales), which receives government finance, presents the consumer's view to government, industry and others. The General Consumer Council for Northern Ireland has wide-ranging duties in consumer affairs in general.

Consumer bodies for privatised utilities investigate questions of concern to the consumer. Some trade associations in industry and commerce have established codes of practice. In addition, several private organisations work to further consumer interests. The largest is the Consumers' Association, funded by the subscriptions of its 1 million members.

Education and Training

A well-educated and well-trained workforce is essential for achieving economic prosperity, especially at a time of intense international competition and rapid technological advance. The Government aims to ensure that

education and training are broadly based and that people of all ages can acquire economically relevant knowledge and skills.

New initiatives on education and training outlined in the competitiveness White Papers include:

- improved careers information, education and guidance for young people;
- a strengthening of academic and vocational qualifications;
- new modern and accelerated apprenticeships;
- initiatives to help firms develop and implement training plans;
- making training loans available to smaller firms; and
- a competition open to small firms for the best co-ordinated training projects.

A package of proposed measures for Scotland was announced in 1995.

Training and Enterprise Councils and Local Enterprise Companies

The Government has set up a network of 81 business-led Training and Enterprise Councils in England and Wales. Scottish Enterprise and Highlands and Islands Enterprise (see p. 216) run 22 local enterprise companies (LECs) in Scotland.

TECs and LECs are independent companies managed by boards of directors, the majority of whom are drawn from private sector business. They provide training, vocational education and enterprise programmes on behalf of the Government and encourage employers to develop the potential of all their employees through, for instance, the attainment of the Investors in People standard (see p. 190). In addition, they offer advisory and training services to businesses, including schemes to enhance the expertise of managers. In Scotland LECs supply the full range of services offered by the Enterprise bodies—support and advice to businesses, environmental renewal, training programmes for young and long-term unemployed people and encouragement to businesses to invest in management and skills. TECs and LECs also have a key role in regeneration and economic development activities locally and in setting up Business Links and similar operations in Scotland and Wales.

Management Education and Development

The DTI, in conjunction with the Department for Education and Employment (DFEE), works with industry, higher education institutions and business schools to spread awareness about best management practices and to encourage continuous professional development. Performance standards for all levels of management have been devised.

The 'Managing in the 90s' programme aims to improve the competitiveness of business by promoting best management practice. It is concerned with making businesses aware of the need for change and providing them with guidance on how to identify the changes required. Delivered mainly through Business Links and sectoral organisations, the programme offers a range of material and activities which are constantly being developed in response to market needs. These include help with networking (a scheme which encourages businesses to share their costs or capacity) and benchmarking (another programme which assists firms to reach international standards through objective assessments of performances and comparisons with leading companies).

Management education is available at many universities and colleges of higher and further education. Regional management centres have been established in England and Wales by associations of these colleges, and there are several similar organisations in Scotland. Universities run full-time postgraduate programmes at business schools, such as those of London, Manchester, Durham, Warwick and Strathclyde universities.

The British Institute of Management encourages excellence in management. Other bodies are concerned with standards and training in specialised branches of management. The employer-led Management Charter Initiative (MCI) is the operating arm of the National Forum for Management Education and Development and the leading industrial body for management standards.

About 2,500 employers, representing a quarter of the total workforce, are members of the MCI, which has 82 local networks working with local employers.

Business Support Services

To encourage the development of small firms, the DTI has established a network of more than 200 Business Links in England. This programme is designed to bring together in a single point of access organisations supporting enterprise, such as local companies, Training and Enterprise Councils, chambers of commerce, local authorities and enterprise agencies. Business Links are local, commercial partnerships, in which larger firms can make contacts and expertise available to smaller firms. Some 600 personal business advisers offer small firms a full range of business consultancy and other services, calling on specialist counsellors for, for example, marketing, export development, design, and innovation and technology. In addition, since April 1996 regional staff from four government departments (Environment, Trade and Industry, Education and Employment, and Transport) seconded to Business Links are providing services to businesses. Business Links are also the access point for a regional supply network designed to help both purchasers find competitive suppliers and suppliers exploit new markets. Every company in England now has easy access to a Business Link. Further measures to help small firms, available through Business Links, were outlined in the 1995 competitiveness White Paper:

- an extra £100 million over four years to develop existing management initiatives and make available locally designed business development programmes;

- more advice on innovation and technology, including overseas development; and

- free export help to small firms through export vouchers to develop and implement their export strategies.

In Scotland Business Shops are run by local partnerships between Local Enterprise Companies, local authorities and business support organisations; trained advisers provide information and direct enquiries to the business support services of local partners. Similar arrangements have been set up in Wales through Business Connect, which has a network of business support centres. In Northern Ireland small firms are helped by the Local Enterprise Development Unit's network of regional offices, which provide co-ordinated advice and support.

Consultancy

Business Links are responsible for supplying a flexible consultancy and diagnostic service, which gives assessments of smaller firms' strengths and weaknesses and draws up plans for their future development. A similar service is available in Scotland through Business Shops in lowland Scotland and Business Information Source in the Highland and Islands area. Since 1995 small and medium-sized companies can also use a new consultancy brokerage service to assist them in selecting consultants.

Small Firms Schemes

The SPUR scheme offers grants of up to £170,000 to businesses with no more than 250 employees for the development of new, technologically advanced products and processes. Under a new SPUR–PLUS scheme, larger grants up to £450,000 are available for exceptional projects.

SMART is an annual competition providing grants to individuals and businesses with up to 50 employees to support them in innovative technological projects with commercial potential. Firms which have completed their SMART projects are eligible for enhanced SPUR grants to develop their product. In 1995 SMART grants were made to over 220 new projects. In addition, levels of funding for SPUR and SMART schemes in designated eligible areas are increased by contributions from the European Regional Development Fund (ERDF—p. 217).

Other government assistance to small businesses includes:

- the Small Firms Loan Guarantee Scheme, which helps businesses with viable proposals to obtain finance where conventional loans are unavailable as a result of a lack of financial security or previous performance; redesigned and extended in March 1996, the scheme gives banks and other financial institutions a government guarantee on a certain percentage of the loan in return for a premium payment; £275 million was guaranteed in 1995–96;

- an initiative to encourage informal investment for small firms from a wider range of sources;

- a programme to encourage small and medium-sized firms to make better use of new information technology;

- the Business Start-Up scheme, enabling unemployed people to claim an allowance while establishing a new business; and

- an initiative which allows small firms to develop key workers' training skills in-house.

Design, Quality and Standards

The effective use of design is fundamental in the creation of innovative products, processes and services. The British design consultancy industry has an annual estimated turnover of £1,000 million and employs around 18,000 people.

The DTI encourages firms to invest in design which can contribute to international competitiveness; it also supports the benefits of good design through the independent Design Council. The Council acts primarily as a provider of analysis and advice on design policy to government, business and education. Design services for industry are supplied through Business Links in England (and equivalent bodies in Scotland and Wales), with financial support from the DTI (see p. 212).

The Government urges business to consider quality at all stages of design, production, marketing and delivery to customers. Accreditation is a key method of improving quality and competitiveness. Through its support for consultancy projects, the Government helps small and medium-sized firms to learn about and apply quality management techniques based on a national standard—BS EN ISO 9000— meeting international requirements. In order to increase customer confidence, companies are encouraged to obtain assessment and certification to this standard. The competence and performance of organisations undertaking such certification are officially accredited by the United Kingdom Accreditation Service. Companies certified by accredited bodies are permitted to use the national 'crown and tick' accreditation mark.

The DTI is responsible for policy relating to the National Measurement System. This provides, through a number of DTI-funded agencies, many of the physical measurement standards and associated calibration facilities necessary so that measurements in Britain are made on a common basis and to the required accuracy. Several of these agencies have been privatised or contracted out.

British Standards Institution

The British Standards Institution (BSI) is Britain's national standards body and is the British member of the European and international standards organisations. It works with industry, consumers and government to produce standards relevant to the needs of the market and suitable for public purchasing and regulatory purposes.

Government support for the BSI is directed particularly towards European and international standards work. Harmonised standards contribute to the aim of removing technical barriers to trade in the EU. Hence, over 90 per cent of the BSI's work is concentrated on European or international standards. The Kitemark is the BSI's registered product certification trade mark.

Awards

The Queen's Awards for Export, Technological and Environmental Achievement recognise outstanding performance in their respective fields. Awarded annually, they are valid for five years and are granted by the Queen on the advice of the Prime Minister, assisted by an Advisory Committee consisting of senior representatives from business, trade unions and government departments. Any self-contained 'industrial unit' in Britain is eligible to apply, regardless of size, provided it meets the scheme's criteria.

Other awards include the Export Award for Smaller Businesses (for firms employing fewer than 200 people) and the MacRobert Award for engineering in Britain made by the Fellowship of Engineering for successful technological innovation.

Industrial and Intellectual Property

The Government supports innovation by protecting the rights of the originators of inventions, industrial designs and trade marks, together with copyright in literary, artistic and musical works. These matters are the responsibility of the DTI's Patent Office, which includes the Design Registry and the Trade Marks Registry. Patent protection is also available under the European Patent Convention and the Patent Co-operation Treaty. Benefits may be claimed in other countries by virtue of separate conventions on industrial property, literary and artistic work, and music and broadcasting. Recent measures giving greater protection to industrial and intellectual property owners include:

- the adoption of EC directives on copyright which harmonise rental and lending rights of performers, record producers and broadcasters, and legal protection of computer programs; and

- a new EC regulation on counterfeit and pirated goods.

Regional Industrial Development

Industrial policy is designed to encourage enterprise and economic growth in all areas of Britain. Where additional help is needed, it is focused on the Assisted Areas (Development Areas and Intermediate Areas), which cover around 35 per cent of Britain's working population. The promotion of inward investment is a key element in the Government's regional policy (see p. 217).

The main regional policy instruments are:

- Regional Selective Assistance, available in the Assisted Areas, for investment

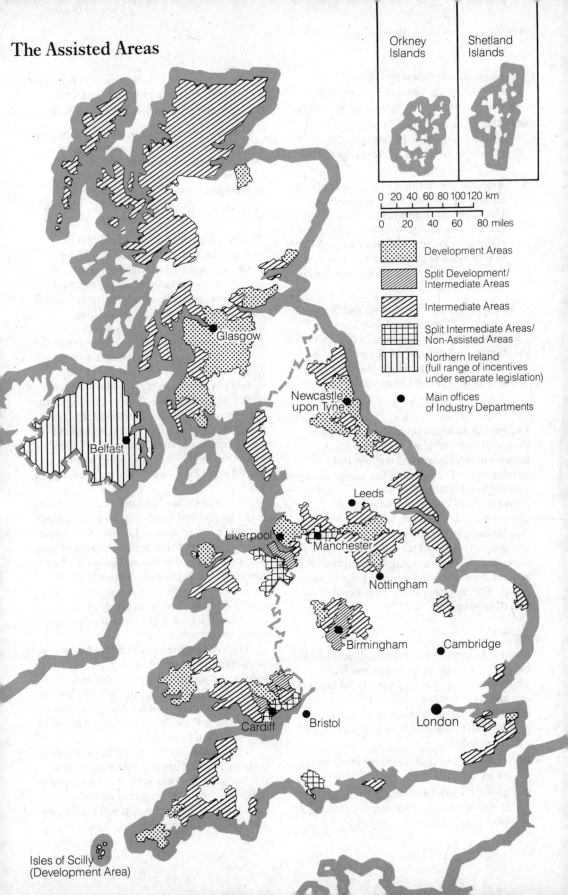

The Assisted Areas

Orkney Islands

Shetland Islands

0 20 40 60 80 100 120 km

0 20 40 60 80 miles

Development Areas

Split Development/ Intermediate Areas

Intermediate Areas

Split Intermediate Areas/ Non-Assisted Areas

Northern Ireland (full range of incentives under separate legislation)

● Main offices of Industry Departments

Glasgow

Belfast

Newcastle upon Tyne

Leeds

Liverpool

Manchester

Nottingham

Birmingham

Cambridge

Cardiff

Bristol

London

Isles of Scilly (Development Area)

projects undertaken by firms in manufacturing and some service sectors that will create or safeguard employment;

- Regional Investment Grants, for firms with no more than 25 employees in Development Areas or areas affected by colliery closures; and
- Regional Innovation Grants, for firms employing no more than 50 people in Development, Intermediate, Task Force and City Challenge areas or localities affected by colliery closures (see p. 269), as well as some other areas covered by EU schemes; they are also available in certain Scottish urban areas.

Regional Selective Assistance and Regional Investment and Innovation Grants are administered by the Government Offices for the Regions in England, the Scottish Office Industry Department and the Welsh Office Industry and Training Department.

England

English Partnerships promotes job creation, inward investment and environmental improvement through reclamation and development of vacant, derelict, under-used or contaminated land and buildings. The Rural Development Commission advises the Government on economic and social development in the countryside, promotes jobs and supports essential services. The Commission's resources are concentrated in areas of greatest need, known as priority areas (see p. 379), covering about 35 per cent of the area of England.

Scotland

Scottish Enterprise and Highlands and Islands Enterprise manage government and EU support to industry and commerce, in lowland and highland Scotland respectively, operating mainly through the network of LECs (see p. 211). The two bodies have a broad range of duties, including:

- attracting inward investment and encouraging exports;
- giving financial and management support to new businesses and assisting existing ones to expand;

- improving the environment by reclaiming derelict and contaminated land; and
- increasing job opportunities and skills.

A major initiative was launched by Scottish Enterprise in 1995 to increase the rate of business start-ups, with the objective of creating an additional 25,000 businesses in Scotland by 2000.

Wales

The Welsh Development Agency (WDA), with a budget of £120 million in 1996–97, promotes industrial efficiency and seeks to improve the environment. In conjunction with the private sector, it provides affordable, high-quality sites and premises for existing businesses and inward investors, spending £850 million on property development in the last 20 years. Since 1990, it has attracted over £240 million of private sector investments through Welsh Property Venture. It tries to attract investment into Wales and co-ordinates the approach for responding to the needs of investors. Over 1,500 projects—involving £8,500 million of capital investment, creating more than 90,000 jobs, and safeguarding 50,000 other jobs—have been generated since 1983.

The WDA's land reclamation programme is the largest and most sustained landscape improvement project in Europe. It has spent £314 million to bring 6,500 hectares of land into productive use; the reclamation of a further 1,250 hectares is currently in progress. Since 1991 the Agency has spent nearly £120 million on urban regeneration and attracted over £225 million of private sector investment.

The WDA's Business Services focuses on developing stronger regional clusters (such as supply and services chains), improving standards and efficiency, and helping Welsh companies to exploit new technology. Since 1991 Source Wales has helped firms to secure £21 million of business.

The Land Authority for Wales is a public body with a fundamental role in economic regeneration. It works with the private and public sectors, providing land for industrial and commercial projects that will create jobs and facilities (see p. 379).

The Development Board for Rural Wales promotes the economic and social well-being of rural mid-Wales. It is concentrating investment in market towns, especially those in the west, in order to help stimulate business confidence and prosperity. Priority is also being given to activities in smaller communities.

Northern Ireland

Industrial development policy in Northern Ireland is the responsibility of the Department of Economic Development and is delivered through various agencies:

- the Industrial Development Board, which deals with overseas companies considering Northern Ireland as an investment location, as well as the development of local companies with more than 50 employees;
- the Local Enterprise Development Unit, which promotes enterprise and the development of small businesses;
- the Industrial Research and Technology Unit, providing advice and assistance on research and development, innovation and technology transfer; and
- the Training and Employment Agency, which helps with in-company training and management development.

A variety of schemes are on offer to help companies with marketing, exporting, product development and design, improved productivity and quality, training, and research and development. A full range of assistance is made available to those companies able to demonstrate development potential and a prospect of long-term competitive growth. This assistance includes capital grants, loans and share capital investment.

European Union Regional Policy and Aid

The EU seeks to reduce disparities between the different regions of the Union. The principal responsibility for helping poorer areas remains with national authorities, but the EU complements schemes by awarding grants and loans from various sources, including the European Regional Development Fund (ERDF).

The European Investment Bank (see p. 128) offers loans for public and private capital investment schemes. Assisted projects typically include improvements to and building of infrastructure projects; construction of trans-European transport links (like the Channel Tunnel); support for business and tourism development; and capital investment in industry, such as factory construction.

EU Structural Funds, especially the ERDF, play an important role in regional development. Three areas—Northern Ireland, the Highlands and Islands, and Merseyside—are eligible for assistance; they are receiving around £2,000 million of EU funding over the period 1994–99. The ERDF also provides finance for areas of industrial decline and for rural development. Structural Funds are made available to areas suffering from a decline in the coal, steel, textile, fishing and defence industries.

Inward Investment

Inward investment is increasingly important to Britain's economy. It helps to develop and modernise the industrial base by introducing new products and processes, as well as bringing in management expertise. It provides new jobs and boosts output, exports and tax revenues.

Overseas companies are responsible for 18 per cent of British manufacturing employment, 32 per cent of capital investment, 24 per cent of output and 40 per cent of exports. A total of £20,500 million was invested in 1995, and, since 1979, inward investment has accounted for over 700,000 jobs.

Britain is the EU's major location for inward investment from North America and the Asia Pacific region, attracting about 40 per cent of investment from these areas. For the prospective inward investor Britain's strengths include its competitive costs, favourable regulatory regime, open markets, skilled and flexible workforce, and high quality communications.

A growing proportion of inward investment has been through expansion or reinvestment by existing investors. This is likely to continue as firms rationalise their European operations. The DTI's Invest in Britain Bureau (IBB) and its regional partners give high priority to 'caring for' existing foreign investors, to ensure that they are aware of the advantages of remaining and expanding in Britain.

Overall policy and co-ordination of overseas promotion of inward investment are the responsibility of the IBB, which represents Britain as a whole. It is supported in Britain by several territorial and regional bodies and overseas it operates through British Embassies, High Commissions and Consulates-general.

Similar advice and assistance to that provided in England by regional development organisations is available through:

● Locate in Scotland, operated jointly by the Scottish Office Industry Department and Scottish Enterprise;

● the Welsh Office Industry and Training Department and the Welsh Development Agency's International Division; and

● the Industrial Development Board in Northern Ireland.

Further Reading

Competitiveness: Helping Business to Win. Cm 2563, HMSO, 1994.

Competitiveness: Forging Ahead. Cm 2867, HMSO, 1995.

Competitiveness: Creating the Enterprise Centre of Europe. Cm 3300, HMSO, 1996.

Department of Trade and Industry 1996: The Government's Expenditure Plans 1996–97 to 1998–99. Cm 3205, HMSO 1996.

Government and Industry. Aspects of Britain series, HMSO, 1995.

15 Finance and Other Service Industries

Financial Services	219	Special Financing Institutions	230
Development of Financial		Financial Markets	231
Services	220	**Other Services**	**233**
Supervision	220	Distribution and Sales	233
Bank of England	222	Hotels, Holiday Centres,	
Banks and Building Societies	223	Public Houses and Catering	237
Insurance	228	Tourism, Travel and Leisure	238
Investment	229	Business Services	239

The service industries, which include finance, retailing, tourism and business services, contribute about 65 per cent of gross domestic product and 75 per cent of employment. Overseas earnings from services amounted to around 35 per cent of the value of exports of manufactures in 1995. The number of employees in services rose from over 13 million in 1983 to 16.8 million by June 1996, much of the rise being accounted for by growth in part-time (principally female) employment. London remains a world leader in the provision of financial and business services, employing 850,000 people. Financial services make a substantial contribution to Britain's balance of payments.

Average real disposable income per head increased by about three-quarters between 1971 and 1994 and this was reflected in a rise in consumer spending on financial, personal and leisure services. Demand for travel, hotel and restaurant services has risen in Britain as real incomes in Britain and other countries have increased.

Britain is a major financial centre, housing some of the world's leading banking, investment, insurance, futures and other financial services, commodities and shipping markets. Business services include advertising, market research, management consultancy, exhibition and conference facilities and computing.

By the year 2000, tourism is expected to be the world's biggest industry, and Britain is one of the world's leading tourist destinations. The industry is one of Britain's largest, employing about 7 per cent of the workforce. The wholesaling, retailing and repairs sector is also a major employer, employing 13 per cent of the workforce.

Financial Services

Historically the heart of the financial services industry in Britain has been located in the famous 'Square Mile' in the City of London, and this remains broadly the case. The markets for financial and related services have grown and diversified greatly during the last 25 years. The City is the largest financial centre in

Europe. Other financial centres are Edinburgh (the fourth largest in Europe), Manchester, Cardiff, Liverpool, Leeds and Glasgow.

An important feature of the City of London is the size of its international activities. It is noted for having:

- more overseas banks than any other financial centre;

- a banking sector that accounts for about a fifth of total international bank lending;

- the world's largest international insurance market;

- the biggest market in the world for trading overseas equities, accounting for 55 per cent of their global turnover;

- the world's largest foreign exchange market, handling 30 per cent of worldwide dealing in 1995;

- the world's second largest fund management centre, with over £490,000 million of institutional equity holdings;

- one of the world's biggest financial derivatives markets;

- the greatest concentration of international bond dealers;

- important markets for transactions in commodities; and

- a full range of ancillary and support services—legal, accountancy and management consultancy—which contribute to London's strength as a financial centre.

British financial institutions' net overseas earnings amounted to £20,400 million in 1995, 8.5 per cent higher than in 1994.

DEVELOPMENT OF FINANCIAL SERVICES

The growth in international movements of capital in the 1960s and 1970s mainly took the form of increased bank lending and foreign exchange trading. London became the international centre of this activity, particularly in the eurocurrency markets (see p. 232). During the 1980s, with increasing international competition in financial services and developments in technology, London's securities markets grew rapidly. Edinburgh also developed as a centre for fund management.

Another feature has been a significant deregulation of Britain's financial services. Major landmarks include:

- the abolition of exchange controls in 1979;

- the abolition in 1981 of the Reserve Asset Ratio requirement, under which banks had to hold 12.5 per cent of their deposits as liquid assets with the Bank of England;

- 'Big Bang' in 1986 (see p. 231);

- the Building Societies Act 1986 and subsequent proposals to further ease controls on building societies (see p. 226); and

- the Friendly Societies Act 1992 (see p. 226).

Traditional distinctions between financial institutions have been eroded, so that single firms supply a broader range of services, in both domestic and international markets. In the British market recent developments have included:

- new financial products, such as TESSAs and Personal Equity Plans (see p. 230);

- growth in the use of debit and credit cards;

- greater use in the delivery of services by telephone, as in insurance, home banking and mortgages;

- intense competition between financial institutions in providing services to personal customers; and

- changes in the structure of the banking and building society sectors, with several mergers or takeovers, while a number of large building societies are in the process of converting to banks.

In 1995 the Government set up the City Promotion Panel. This is developing better co-ordination of the international promotion of financial services and considering the sector's response to changing products and technology.

SUPERVISION

The Government is committed to improving market efficiency by providing a regulatory

Type of Saving by Households in Great Britain 1994–95

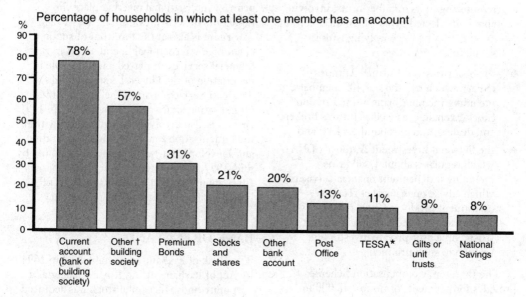

Percentage of households in which at least one member has an account

Source: *Family Resources Survey*

† Excluding current accounts and TESSAs.

* Tax Exempt Special Savings Accounts, which were introduced in 1991, allow tax-free investment with a bank or building society of up to £9,000 over five years. By June 1995 over 4.3 million TESSAs had been opened and more than £26,500 million invested.

regime in which free and fair competition can take place. It keeps the regulatory system under review to ensure that there is an appropriate balance between facilitating market developments and maintaining investor protection.

HM Treasury is the government department with responsibility for financial services. In particular, it is responsible for legislation covering the regulation of banks, building societies, friendly societies and investment businesses. It also oversees the Securities and Investments Board (SIB—see below).

The Department of Trade and Industry (DTI) is responsible for company law and insolvency matters, and for investigations and prosecutions under the Financial Services, Insolvency and Companies Acts. Investigations are carried out with the Serious Fraud Office (see p. 95). The DTI's duties include prudential supervision of insurance undertakings, supervision of European Community (EC) insurance directives, and general questions

affecting the insurance industry. It also has powers to investigate 'insider dealing' —securities trading carried out on the basis of privileged access to relevant information.

Regulation of Investment Businesses

Under the Financial Services Act 1986, investment businesses (those dealing in, arranging, managing or giving advice on investments or operating collective investment schemes) require authorisation and are subject to rules on the conduct of business. Most of the powers in the Act have been transferred to the SIB, which is responsible for recognising a number of 'front-line' regulators: self-regulating organisations (SROs) and recognised professional bodies (RPBs). Most investment businesses are authorised under the Act by virtue of membership of one of these. The SROs are:

● the Investment Management Regulatory Organisation (IMRO), which regulates about 1,100 fund management firms—

IMRO has announced a pilot project to test more targeted supervision and monitoring of its member firms, involving about 50 selected firms which meet certain criteria relating to complying with its standards;

- the Securities and Futures Authority (SFA), which has about 1,400 members, including member firms of the London Stock Exchange, as well as futures brokers and dealers, and eurobond dealers; and
- the Personal Investment Authority (PIA), which regulates about 4,000 firms, including independent financial advisers, which advise on or market retail investment products (such as life assurance, personal pensions and unit trusts) or act for private investors in relation to such products.

The Investors Compensation Scheme provides for payments of up to £48,000 to private investors if a firm regulated by an SRO or by SIB cannot meet its investment business liabilities. The funds for paying compensation come from other investment firms. Since its establishment in 1988 the scheme has helped customers of over 250 firms, and paid out £103 million to 9,100 investors.

International Agreements

The Treasury negotiates and implements EC directives relating to financial services and is responsible for arrangements with overseas regulators for exchanging information. Various EC directives deliver a 'passport' to banking, investment and insurance firms, allowing them to operate throughout the European Union (EU) on the basis of their home state authorisation. As part of this process, two EC directives entered into force in January 1996:

- the Investment Services Directive, which allows investment services firms to offer their services throughout the EU; and
- the Capital Adequacy Directive, which sets minimum capital requirements for the operations of banks and investment firms.

Britain plays a major role in encouraging international regulatory co-operation, particularly in the Bank for International

Settlements and the International Organisation of Securities Commissions (IOSCO—the primary international meeting place for regulators of securities).

Britain is also at the forefront of action to encourage international liberalisation in financial services. It played a leading role in negotiation of the General Agreement on Trade in Services, part of the World Trade Organisation series of agreements (see p. 179). Britain is also involved in negotiations within the Organisation for Economic Co-operation and Development, with the aim of reaching by mid-1997 a Multilateral Agreement on Investment that will set high standards of liberalisation and investment protection.

BANK OF ENGLAND

The Bank of England was established in 1694 by Act of Parliament and Royal Charter as a corporate body. Its capital stock was acquired by the Government in 1946. As Britain's central bank, the Bank of England's overriding objective is to maintain a stable and efficient monetary and financial framework for the effective operation of the economy. In pursuing this goal, it has three main purposes:

- maintaining the integrity and value of the currency;
- maintaining the stability of the financial system, both in Britain and internationally; and
- seeking to ensure the effectiveness of the financial services sector.

The Bank's primary objective is to support the Government in achieving permanently low inflation within the monetary policy framework (see p. 157). Unlike some other central banks, the Bank of England has no statutory independence. Decisions on interest rates are taken by the Chancellor of the Exchequer, and the Bank's role is to advise him and implement his decisions.

Once policy is decided, the Bank implements this through its operations, primarily in the money market. In general, the operation of the Government's accounts —including the weekly issue of Treasury bills—tends to create a daily shortage of funds in the banking system. The Bank acts to relieve this shortage either by buying bills from, or lending funds to, the discount houses (see p. 227). Daily 'open market operations' are supplemented by a fortnightly 'gilt repo' facility with banks, building societies and gilt-edged market makers.

The Bank is also responsible for providing advice on and implementing the Government's exchange rate policy. It acts as the Treasury's agent in managing the Government's reserves of gold and foreign exchange and its foreign currency borrowing, and it undertakes foreign exchange transactions on behalf of government departments and other central banks. As the Government's debt management agent, it sells gilt-edged stock through regular auctions supplemented by occasional 'tap' issues (see p. 171). The Bank also provides the principal stock registration service for the Government.

The Bank provides banking services to its customers, principally the Government, the banking system and other central banks. It plays a key role in payment and settlement systems. The Bank has sole right in England and Wales to issue banknotes, which are backed by government and other securities. The profit from the note issue is paid directly to the Government. Three Scottish and four Northern Ireland banks also issue notes, which have to be fully backed by Bank of England notes.

Supervision

The Bank has statutory responsibility for the supervision of the banking system in Britain within the framework of the Banking Act 1987 and legislation implementing EC directives. The aim is to protect bank depositors. The Act sets out a number of minimum standards which banks are required to meet on the integrity and competence of directors and management, the adequacy of capital and of cash flow, and the appropriateness of systems and controls to deal with the various risks that banks experience.

If a bank fails to meet the criteria, its activities may be restricted or it may even be closed. If a bank fails, there is a limited amount of protection available to small depositors financed by levies on the banking system. In exceptional circumstances, the Bank may

organise financial support for a bank in difficulty to prevent a loss of confidence spreading to the banking system as a whole.

The Bank also has formal responsibility for supervising firms in the wholesale markets for sterling, foreign exchange and bullion, and monitors links between the various financial markets.

Financial Developments

The Bank works to ensure that London maintains its position as a leading international financial centre by monitoring its development and identifying weaknesses and competitive threats. It is also concerned that the financial sector should provide efficient services to industry in Britain. The Bank sometimes facilitates collective initiatives where the interests of the financial institutions differ.

The Bank is playing a full part in the technical preparations for economic and monetary union within the EU (see p. 126).

BANKS AND BUILDING SOCIETIES

In addition to banks, other financial institutions offer banking services, notably the building societies and National Savings. Indeed, the distinction between banks and building societies in particular is becoming less clear, as both types of institution diversify their services.

A distinction can still be made, however, between 'retail' and 'wholesale' banking:

- Retail banking is primarily for personal customers and small businesses. Its main services are cash deposit and withdrawal facilities, and money transmission systems.
- Wholesale business involves taking large deposits at higher rates of interest, deploying funds in money-market instruments (see p. 232) and making large loans and investments. Nearly all banks in Britain engage in some wholesale activities and some, such as the merchant and overseas banks, centre their business on them. Many of the dealings are conducted on the inter-bank market—that is, between banks themselves.

In 1996 there were 375 institutions authorised under the Banking Act 1987, including clearing banks, investment banks, branches of overseas banks from outside the EU, discount houses, and banking subsidiaries of both banking and non-banking institutions from Britain and overseas. A further 103 branches of banks from other EU countries were entitled to take deposits in Britain. Of the total of 515 institutions permitted to take deposits in Britain, 300 were members of the British Bankers' Association, the main representative body for British banks.

Retail Banks

The major retail banks offer a full range of financial services to both individuals and companies. Services generally available include interest-bearing current accounts, deposit accounts, credit and debit cards, and various kinds of loan arrangements. A growing range of other facilities is offered by many banks, such as mortgages, insurance, investment advice, pensions products and share-dealing services. Around three-quarters of adults in Britain have a current account and over one-third a deposit account.

HSBC (including its subsidiary Midland) is the largest bank in Britain. Lloyds TSB Group became the second biggest following the merger in December 1995 of Lloyds and TSB. The other major banks in England and Wales are Barclays, National Westminster and Abbey National; and in Scotland, the Bank of Scotland and the Royal Bank of Scotland. Among the smaller retail banks are the Clydesdale Bank, the Co-operative Bank, the Yorkshire Bank and Alliance & Leicester Giro. Northern Ireland is served by branch networks of four major banking groups. During 1997 three of the largest building societies are due to join the banking sector following their flotations on the stock market (see p. 226).

The main retail banks operate through over 11,350 branches and sub-branches in Britain. At the end of 1995 Lloyds TSB had the largest number, with 2,858 branches, followed by National Westminster (2,215), Barclays (2,050), Midland (1,701), the Royal Bank of Scotland (687), Abbey National (678) and the Bank of Scotland (411).

With the growth of financial services and fewer restrictions on competition among financial institutions, the major banks have diversified their operations. Most now own finance houses, leasing and factoring companies, merchant banks, securities dealers, insurance companies and unit trust companies, and some have set up subsidiaries to provide venture capital for companies (see p. 230). Most retail banks maintain overseas subsidiaries and are active in eurocurrency markets (see p. 232).

The banks offer loan facilities to companies and have become important suppliers of finance for small firms. A loan guarantee scheme is supported by the banks, under which 70 per cent (85 per cent in certain cases) of the value of bank loans to small companies is guaranteed by the Government.

The total liabilities/assets of banks in Britain amounted to over £1,476,000 million at the end of 1995. Liabilities are made up of sterling deposits, foreign currency deposits, items in suspense or transmission, and capital and other funds. The banks' main liquid assets consist of money at call (mainly short-term loans to discount houses), their holdings of Treasury and other bills, short-dated British government securities and balances at the Bank of England.

Payment Systems

Apart from credit and debit card arrangements, the main payment systems are run by three separate companies operating under an umbrella organisation, the Association for Payment Clearing Services (APACS). One system covers bulk paper clearings—cheques and credit transfers. A second deals with high-value clearings for same-day settlement, namely the nationwide electronic transfer service Clearing House Automated Payment System (CHAPS). A third covers bulk electronic clearing for standing orders and direct debits. Membership of each company is open to any bank, building society or other financial institution meeting the criteria for appropriate supervision and volume of transactions; 22 banks and building societies are members of one or more clearing companies.

In May 1996 the Government issued proposals to allow electronic clearing of cheques. This is expected to lead to savings in costs for the banks of around £30 million.

Plastic Cards

The use of plastic cards has become very widespread, and around 92 million are in circulation. Among the main types are cheque guarantee cards, debit cards, credit cards, charge cards and cash cards. Cards frequently combine functions. One of the most popular uses is for obtaining cash from automated teller machines (ATMs). All the major retail banks and building societies participate in nationwide networks of ATMs, which give customers access to cash and other services for up to 24 hours a day. About 21,000 ATMs were in operation at the end of 1995.

> According to a report by the Credit Card Research Group, total spending using credit cards rose by 15 per cent in 1995 to £41,000 million, while expenditure using debit cards grew by 26 per cent to £28,000 million.

Cheque guarantee cards entitle holders to cheque-cashing facilities in participating institutions and guarantee retailers that transactions up to the specified guarantee limit—typically £50 or £100—will be honoured. Eurocheques supported by a eurocheque card are available from all major banks. They may be used to obtain cash or make payments in Britain, elsewhere in Europe and in a few other overseas countries. Cheques are made out in the currency of the country in which they are being used.

Credit cards are mainly issued by banks. Most cards are affiliated to one of the two major international credit card organisations, Visa and MasterCard. There are a growing number of 'affinity' cards, where the card is linked to an organisation such as a charity or trade union. Credit card users receive a statement each month and must pay off a minimum of the amount owed, interest then becoming chargeable on the remainder. A majority of users, though, choose to pay off the full amount owed each month. Charge cards, like credit cards, enable holders to make retail payments, but often have no credit limit or a very high limit. They are usually available only to those with relatively high incomes or assets; the credit balance must be settled in full each month. Some of the major retailers issue credit cards or charge cards for use within their own outlets.

More people are now paying for goods by debit cards issued by the major banks and building societies. Payments are deducted directly from the purchaser's current account. There are two debit card schemes in operation: Visa Delta and Switch.

Electronic Banking

Many banks and building societies offer home banking services, under which customers use a telephone to obtain account information, make transfers and pay bills. One of the largest operators is First Direct (a subsidiary of Midland), with over 600,000 customers. Some banks and building societies offer a home banking service for customers with a personal computer. Other innovations include banking services over the Internet and self-service kiosks containing ATMs and video links to banks' central facilities. The most recent development has been the launch of a new type of electronic card which is 'charged' with money from the card holder's bank account. The cards can be used to purchase goods or services at participating retailers through electronic tills, while some can carry foreign currency value for travelling overseas.

Building Societies

Building societies are mutual institutions, owned by their savers and borrowers, and are, with the banks, the main source of housing finance in Britain. They make long-term mortgage loans, mostly at variable rates of interest, against the security of property —usually private dwellings purchased for owner-occupation. Competition between lenders for business intensified in the first half of the 1990s when house prices fell and fewer people moved house. Remortgaging, whereby a borrower changes lender or switches to a different mortgage from the same lender, has become much more significant. In 1995 remortgaging accounted for around a quarter by value of total mortgage loans.

Around 60 per cent of adults have building society savings accounts. Societies are extending their services, for example by providing current account facilities such as cheque books and ATMs.

Structure

There are 77 authorised building societies, of which 76 are members of the Building Societies' Association. Building societies' assets totalled approximately £300,000 million at the end of 1995; they advanced about £34,000 million in new mortgages in 1995. The Council of Mortgage Lenders is a trade body established in 1989 for all mortgage lending institutions, including building societies, insurance companies, finance houses and banks. Its duties include representing member institutions in discussions with the Government on a broad range of issues.

> **The building society industry is undergoing a period of considerable change, which is particularly affecting the biggest societies. Three of the largest—the Halifax (which merged with the Leeds Permanent in August 1995), the Woolwich, and the Alliance & Leicester—have announced their intention to become retail banks, with the aim of facilitating expansion and offering a wider range of financial services. Subject to approval from their members and the Building Societies Commission (see below), all are expected to become banks during 1997. The banks will be public limited companies and will be responsible to shareholders rather than to members. Conversion to banks normally involves bonus payments to members, often·in the form of free shares in the new company.**

Another society, the Northern Rock, also plans to become a bank. Three others have been or are being acquired by banks:

- the Cheltenham & Gloucester was taken over by Lloyds in August 1995;
- the National & Provincial was acquired by Abbey National in August 1996; and

- the Bristol & West is to be acquired by the Bank of Ireland in 1997.

When all these changes have been implemented, the largest society will be the Nationwide.

Diversification

The Building Societies Act 1986 enabled societies to diversify into banking and other services and established the Building Societies Commission to carry out the prudential supervision of building societies.

Following a review of the 1986 Act, steps have been taken to extend the powers of building societies and remove or reduce certain statutory burdens. For example, societies are now able to raise up to 50 per cent (up from 40 per cent) of their funds on the wholesale market, to make unsecured loans to businesses, and, since July 1996, to wholly own insurance companies.

The Government is planning further relaxations. Consultation has taken place on a draft Building Societies Bill. Under the Bill, societies would be able to undertake a wider variety of services, subject to meeting certain criteria. However, lending for home ownership would remain the key business with:

- at least 75 per cent of a society's assets having to be loans secured on residential property (although for the first time this would include rented property); and
- a minimum of 50 per cent of funds in the form of shares from members.

Other provisions of the Bill include proposals to increase the accountability of societies to their members, for example, by requiring societies to get members' permission if they wished to move into a major new area of business.

Friendly Societies

Friendly societies have traditionally been unincorporated societies of individuals, offering their members a limited range of financial services, particularly provision for retirement and against loss of income through sickness or unemployment. The Friendly Societies Act 1992 enabled friendly societies to incorporate, take on new powers and offer a broader range of financial services through subsidiaries. It also established a Friendly Societies Commission to administer a system of regulation and to promote the financial stability of societies. Over 120 friendly societies are authorised to accept new business.

Merchant Banks

Merchant banks have traditionally been concerned primarily with accepting, or guaranteeing, commercial bills and with sponsoring capital issues on behalf of their customers. Today they undertake a diversified range of activities. After 'Big Bang' (see p. 231) some merchant banks acquired securities trading operations. Merchant banks have important roles in equity and debt markets and the provision of advice and financial services to industrial companies, especially where mergers, takeovers and other forms of corporate reorganisation are involved. Management of investment holdings, including trusts, pensions and other funds, is another important function. The sector is split between independent houses and those which are part of larger banking groups.

Overseas Banks

A total of 263 banks incorporated overseas have branches in Britain, including 28 from Japan and 23 from the United States; 80 institutions incorporated in Britain are subsidiaries of overseas companies. They offer a comprehensive banking service in many parts of the world and engage in financing trade not only between Britain and other countries but also between third-party countries.

British-based Overseas Banks

A small number of banks have their head offices in Britain, but operate mainly abroad, often specialising in particular regions. Standard Chartered, which is represented in Asia, Africa and the Middle East, is the major example of this type of bank. It has a network of over 600 offices in more than 40 countries.

Discount Houses

There are seven discount houses authorised under the Banking Act 1987. They act as financial intermediaries between the Bank of England and the rest of the banking sector, promoting an orderly flow of short-term funds. They guarantee to tender for the whole of the weekly offer of the Government's Treasury bills, which are instruments to raise funds over a period of up to three months. In return for acting as intermediaries, the discount houses have secured borrowing facilities at the Bank of England, acting as 'lender of last resort'. Assets of the discount houses consist mainly of Treasury and commercial bills, negotiable certificates of deposit and short-term loans. Their liabilities are for the most part short-term deposits.

National Savings

National Savings, a government executive agency, is a source of finance for government borrowing and aims to encourage saving by offering personal savers a range of investments. Certain National Savings products offer tax exempt returns. In September 1996 the total amount invested in National Savings was £61,657 million. Sales of National Savings products totalled £11,597 million in 1995–96. After allowing for repayments, the net contribution to government funding was £5,123 million. The largest single contribution, of £2,231 million, was from Pensioners Bonds, whose contribution more than doubled, reflecting decisions in the 1995 Budget to raise the maximum holding and cut the eligible age for the bonds from 65 to 60.

Another significant contribution from National Savings in 1995–96, of £1,485 million, came from Premium Bonds, where interest is in the form of prizes. Each month there are 350,000 prizes. Since their introduction in 1956, Premium Bonds have paid out over 57 million prizes, worth £3,518 million. The top prize in the monthly draw is now £1 million. Over 23 million people hold Premium Bonds.

Other important products include:

- Savings Certificates, which pay either a fixed rate of interest alone or a lower fixed rate of interest combined with index-linking (rising in line with the Retail Prices Index);

- Income and Capital Bonds;
- Children's Bonus Bonds, which are designed to accumulate capital sums for those under 21;
- Ordinary and Investment Accounts, where deposits and withdrawals can be made at post offices throughout Britain; and
- FIRST Option Bonds, which offer a guaranteed rate of interest that is fixed for one year.

INSURANCE

London is the world's leading centre for insurance and for placing international reinsurance. It handles an estimated 20 per cent of the general insurance business placed on the international market. EC directives to create a single European market in insurance came into force in 1994. As well as the British companies and Lloyd's (see below), a large number of overseas firms are represented, with which many British companies have formed close relationships. Authorised insurance companies are supervised by the Department of Trade and Industry under the Insurance Companies Act 1982.

Main Types of Insurance

There are two broad categories of insurance: long-term life insurance, where contracts may be for periods of many years; and general insurance, including accident and short-term health insurance, where contracts are for a year or less.

Long-term Insurance

As well as providing life cover, life insurance is a vehicle for saving and investment because premiums are invested in securities and other assets. About 65 per cent of households have life assurance cover. Total long-term insurance assets under management by companies in 1995 were £555,686 million on behalf of their worldwide operations. Long-term insurance is handled by around 200 companies.

General Insurance

General insurance business is undertaken by insurance companies and by underwriters at Lloyd's. It includes fire, accident, general liability, motor, marine, aviation and transport risks. Total worldwide premium income of members of the Association of British Insurers (ABI) in 1995 was £36,800 million, of which £21,200 million was earned in Britain.

Structure of the Industry

At the end of 1995, 826 companies were authorised to carry on one or more classes of insurance business in Britain. The industry employs about 207,000 people directly, plus a further 126,000 auxiliary staff. Around 450 companies belong to the ABI.

The industry includes both public limited companies and mutual institutions—companies owned by their policyholders. The five largest life insurance companies are Prudential, Standard Life (the largest mutual life insurance company in Europe), Norwich Union, Legal and General, and Scottish Widows. Like the banking and building society sectors, the industry is undergoing a period of structural change. Norwich Union has announced that it plans to become a public limited company instead of a mutual insurer. In 1996 Royal Insurance and Sun Alliance merged to create Royal and Sun Alliance. This is now Britain's largest general insurance company and the sixth largest life insurer.

Lloyd's

Lloyd's, the origins of which go back to the 17th century, is an incorporated society of private insurers in London. Although its activities were originally confined to marine insurance, it also engages in other classes of insurance business, such as aviation and motor insurance.

Lloyd's is not a company but a market for insurance administered by the Council of Lloyd's and Lloyd's Regulatory and Market Boards. Business is carried out for individual elected underwriting members, or 'names', trading with unlimited liability in competition with each other and with insurance companies. Since 1994 corporate members with limited liability have also traded in the market. Both are required to satisfy certain financial requirements and maintain set levels of deposits at Lloyd's.

Net premium income in 1995 was £5,700 million. For the 1996 year of account, there is total market capacity of £9,993 million provided by nearly 13,000 members grouped into 167 syndicates. Each syndicate is managed by an underwriting agent responsible for appointing a professional underwriter to accept insurance risks and settle claims on the syndicate members' behalf. With the exception of motor insurance business, insurance may only be placed through accredited Lloyd's brokers, who negotiate with Lloyd's syndicates on behalf of the insured. Reinsurance constitutes a large part of Lloyd's business.

Lloyd's has suffered severe losses, partly caused by a series of natural disasters and also as a result of claims arising from asbestosis and pollution. The Council is taking action to reconstruct the market. This includes a £3,200 million offer to names (which was accepted in August 1996) and proposals to deal with past debts and outstanding liquidation. Liabilities relating to the losses from 1992 and earlier years will be reinsured through a new company, Equitas.

Institute of London Underwriters

The Institute of London Underwriters, formed in 1884 as a trade association for marine underwriters, provides a market where member insurance companies transact marine, energy, commercial transport and aviation business. It issues combined policies in its own name on risks which are underwritten by member companies. The gross premium income processed by the Institute for its member companies in 1995 was £1,868 million. About half of the 58 member companies are branches or subsidiaries of overseas companies.

Insurance Brokers

Insurance brokers acting on behalf of the insured are a valuable part of the company market and play an essential role in the Lloyd's market. Smaller brokers mainly deal with the general public or specialise in a particular type of commercial insurance. Medium to large brokers almost exclusively handle commercial insurance, with the largest dealing with risks worldwide. Some brokers specialise in reinsurance business. The Insurance Brokers (Registration) Act 1977 makes provision for the voluntary registration and regulation of insurance brokers by the Insurance Brokers Registration Council. Only those registered with the Council can use the title 'insurance broker'. There are about 14,600 individuals registered with the Council, the majority of whom are employed by about 2,450 limited companies. Just over 2,000 individuals carry on business in their own right, trading as sole proprietor, or in partnership.

Other independent intermediaries may also arrange insurance, but are not allowed to use the title 'insurance broker'. There are about 7,000 independent intermediaries operating under the ABI's code of practice.

INVESTMENT

Britain has a great deal of expertise in fund management, which involves managing funds on the investor's behalf, or advising investors on how to invest their funds. The main types of investment fund include pension schemes, life assurance, unit trusts and investment trusts.

Pension Funds

Over 11 million people belong to occupational pension schemes and more than 5 million to personal pension schemes. Most occupational pension schemes pay benefits related to final salary, although a growing number are on a 'money purchase' basis where benefits depend on the size of the accrued funds. Benefits are normally funded in advance by employer and employee contributions, which are held and invested by trustees on behalf of beneficiaries. Pension funds are major investors in securities markets, holding around 30 per cent of securities listed on the London Stock Exchange. Total British pension fund net assets were worth about £500,000 million at the end of 1995.

Unit Trusts

Authorised unit trusts are open-ended collective funds which pool investors' money, and funds are divided into units of equal size. People with relatively small amounts to invest are able to benefit from diversified and expertly managed portfolios. The industry has grown rapidly during the last decade, and in 1996 there were over 1,660 authorised unit trusts. By June 1996 total funds under management were £126,000 million. Some are general funds, investing in a wide variety of British or international securities, while there are also many specialist trusts. Unit trust management groups are represented by the Association of Unit Trusts and Investment Funds and regulated by the PIA and IMRO. The trusts themselves are authorised by the SIB.

Open-ended Investment Companies

From early 1997 a new type of scheme—open-ended investment companies (OEICs)—will be available. OEICs will be similar to unit trusts, but an investor in an OEIC will buy shares rather than units in the company. The new schemes should enable British companies to compete on an equal footing with similar schemes operating elsewhere in the EU.

Investment Trusts

Investment trust companies, which also offer the opportunity to diversify risk on a relatively small lump-sum investment or through regular savings, are listed on the London Stock Exchange and their shares are traded in the usual way. They must invest mostly in securities, and the trusts themselves are exempt from tax on gains realised within the funds. Assets are purchased mainly out of shareholders' funds, although investment trusts are also allowed to borrow money for investment. There were 320 members of the Association of Investment Trust Companies in June 1996, with £56,000 million worth of assets under management. The three largest trusts are the venture capital company 3i Group, Foreign and Colonial, and Alliance.

Growth in Share Ownership

Privatisation (see p. 207) and employee share schemes (see p. 196) have both helped to increase share ownership, in line with the Government's policy of encouraging wider share ownership. About 10 million adults—22 per cent of the adult population in Great Britain—hold shares.

> The value of shares in Britain's listed companies in 1994 was £762,000 million, of which shares held by individuals accounted for £155,000 million (20 per cent). Financial institutions held £446,000 million (59 per cent), of which pension funds accounted for £212,000 million. Most of the remaining shares were in the hands of overseas investors.

Another major stimulus to raising share ownership by individuals has been the introduction of Personal Equity Plans (PEPs), which allow tax-free investment in shares, including investment trust companies and in unit trusts. In July 1995 PEPs were extended to cover certain corporate bonds (except those issued by financial services companies), preference shares and 'convertibles' (bonds or preference shares which can eventually be converted into a company's ordinary shares). Up to £6,000 in a single tax year may be invested in a general PEP and up to £3,000 in a single company PEP. Dividends and capital gains on assets held in a PEP are exempt from income tax and capital gains tax, and withdrawals from PEPs are normally tax free.

Since their introduction in 1987, more than £28,000 million had been invested in over 8 million PEPs by April 1996. In 1995–96, 1.5 million general PEPs and 220,000 single company PEPs were opened.

SPECIAL FINANCING INSTITUTIONS

Several specialised institutions offer finance and support to personal and corporate sector borrowers. Among public sector agencies are Scottish Enterprise, Highlands and Islands

Enterprise, the Welsh Development Agency, the Industrial Development Board for Northern Ireland (see pp. 216–217) and ECGD (see p. 182). The main private sector institutions are described below.

Finance and Leasing Companies

The Finance and Leasing Association represents the interests of firms offering motor finance, consumer credit, and business finance and leasing. Its 158 full and associate members undertook new business worth £32,000 million in 1994.

Factoring Companies

Factoring comprises a range of financial services allowing companies to obtain finance in exchange for outstanding invoices due to them. Factoring has developed as a major financial service since the early 1960s. Member companies of the Association of British Factors and Discounters handled business worth £30,400 million in 1995.

Venture Capital Companies

Venture capital companies offer medium- and long-term equity financing for new and developing businesses when such funds are not readily available from traditional sources, such as the London Stock Exchange or banks. The British Venture Capital Association has 108 full members, which make up over 99 per cent of the industry. A record amount—over £2,500 million—was invested by these venture capital firms in over 1,100 businesses in 1995.

To help encourage the availability of equity and long-term finance for smaller 'unlisted' businesses, the Finance Act 1995 provided for the establishment of venture capital trusts (VCTs, see p. 204). By May 1996 the first 12 VCTs had raised over £160 million.

FINANCIAL MARKETS

The City of London's financial markets include the London Stock Exchange, the foreign exchange market, the financial futures and options market, eurobond and eurocurrency markets, Lloyd's insurance market (see p. 228), and bullion and commodity markets. The securities markets are supervised jointly by the Treasury, the Bank of England, SIB and the London Stock Exchange, among others.

London Stock Exchange

The London Stock Exchange plays a vital role in maintaining London's position as a major financial centre. Its main administrative centre is in London and there are regional offices in Belfast, Birmingham, Glasgow, Leeds and Manchester. As a result of a set of legal reforms implemented in 1986 and known as 'Big Bang', the Exchange has changed radically over recent years. The most fundamental change has been the move away from the traditional market floor to screen-based trading.

The Exchange provides a trading platform for domestic equities with its automated price information system, SEAQ, which continuously updates share prices and can be viewed on a wide range of information systems. For trading in foreign equities, London's leading international equity market is supported by the Exchange's electronic price quotation system, SEAQ International.

About 2,600 British and overseas companies, with a combined market capitalisation of £3,370,000 million, are listed on the Exchange. In 1995 turnover of British and Irish equities reached £646,000 million, while turnover of foreign equities amounted to £791,000 million.

Changes now affecting the Stock Exchange are among the most significant since 'Big Bang'. Among these is a new 'order-driven' system now being planned. Under this, share transactions between buyers and sellers would be dealt with directly by computer, rather than being passed through market-making firms under the current 'quote-driven' system. The new system, with a public limit order book for the top 100 stocks, is expected to begin operating during 1997.

The London Stock Exchange's new public equity market, AIM, began operating in 1995, mainly for small, newly established or developing companies wishing to raise public finance and to have their shares more widely traded. By mid-1996 more than 150 companies had raised over £120 million on the market. Tradepoint, a computer-based, order-driven share dealing system in competition with the London Stock Exchange, also started operation in 1995.

> CREST, a new computerised settlement system for shares and other securities developed by a project team from the Bank of England, was inaugurated in July 1996. There will be a transitional period, expected to last until April 1997, during which CREST will gradually take on the settlement of all securities traded in Britain. Computerised settlement should increase efficiency and lower the cost by eliminating much of the paperflow currently involved. It should also assist in reducing settlement risk. CREST is owned and operated by CRESTCo, a private sector consortium representing a wide spread of City interests.

The gilt-edged market (see p. 171) allows the Government to raise money by issuing loan stock through the Bank of England. The London Stock Exchange offers a secondary or trading market where investors can buy or sell gilts. Turnover in the market totalled £1,576,000 million in 1995.

Money Markets

The London money markets comprise the interbank deposit markets plus a range of other instruments, usually short term in maturity. Banks are the major participants in these markets, and are supervised by the Bank of England.

Euromarkets

Markets operate for currencies lent or invested outside their domestic marketplace, particularly as a means of financing international trade and investment. Transactions can thus be carried out in eurodollars, eurodeutschemarks, euroyen and so on. London is at the heart of the euromarkets and houses most of the leading international banks and securities firms. Distinctions between markets have been breaking down and euromarkets form a major part of the wider international money and capital markets. Participants include multinational trading corporations, financial companies, governments, and international organisations like the World Bank and the European Investment Bank.

The euro-securities markets have grown considerably in recent years because the instruments traded on them— including eurobonds, euro-medium-term notes (EMTNs) and euro-commercial paper—are seen as flexible alternatives to bank loans. British building societies are prominent among EMTN issuers. There is a growing private-sector market in ECU-denominated deposits, securities and eurobonds.

Foreign Exchange Market

London is the world's biggest centre for foreign exchange trading, accounting for about 30 per cent of global net daily turnover in foreign exchange. Average daily turnover in London amounted to about £294,000 million in 1995, nearly 60 per cent higher than in 1992.

The foreign exchange market consists of telephone and electronic links between the participants, which include banks, other financial institutions and several foreign exchange broking firms acting as intermediaries. It provides those engaged in international trade and investment with foreign currencies for their transactions. The banks are in close contact with financial centres abroad and are able to quote buying and selling rates for both immediate ('spot') and forward transactions in a range of currencies and maturities. The forward market enables traders and dealers who, at a given date in the future, wish to receive or make a specific foreign currency payment, to contract in advance to sell or buy the foreign currency involved for sterling at a fixed exchange rate.

Derivatives

Financial derivatives are contracts to buy or sell, at a future date, financial instruments such as equities, bonds or money-market instruments. Their use has grown rapidly, especially among companies and investment institutions, and instruments have become more complex, as advances have been made in information technology. Derivatives offer a means of protection against changes in prices, exchange rates and interest rates. They include:

- futures—agreements to buy or sell financial instruments or physical commodities at a future date;
- options—the right to buy or sell financial instruments or physical commodities for a stated period at a predetermined price; and
- 'over-the-counter' products, including swaps—a foreign exchange swap can convert a money-market instrument in one currency into a money-market instrument in another.

Financial Futures and Options

Banks, other financial institutions, brokers and individual traders are members of the London International Financial Futures and Options Exchange (LIFFE). Futures contracts cover the purchase or sale of a fixed amount of a commodity or financial instrument at a given date in the future at a price agreed at the time of trade. There is also dealing in options on the equity of prominent British companies and in stock index options. LIFFE has the most internationally diverse range of financial futures and options products of any exchange in the world. Its turnover totalled nearly 133 million contracts in 1995, making it the world's third largest futures and options exchange. In 1995 LIFFE announced links with exchanges in Chicago and Tokyo, and also a merger with the London Commodity Exchange, which took place in September 1996. At the London Commodity Exchange, futures in grains and potatoes are traded, as are futures and options on 'soft' commodities (cocoa and coffee). White sugar, raw sugar and dry freight index futures contracts are also traded.

London Bullion Market

Around 60 banks and other financial trading companies participate in the London gold and silver markets, which, like the foreign exchange market, trade by telephone or other electronic means. Members of the London Bullion Market Association meet twice daily to establish a London fixing price for gold—a reference point for worldwide dealings. The silver fixing is held once a day. Although much interest centres upon the fixings, active dealing takes place throughout the day. London is the hub of the international bullion market.

Commodity, Shipping and Freight Markets

Britain is a major international centre for commodities trading and the home of many related international trade organisations. The London Metal Exchange is the primary base metals market in the world, trading both spot and forward contracts in aluminium, aluminium alloy, copper, lead, nickel, tin and zinc. The International Petroleum Exchange is Europe's only energy futures exchange. The Baltic Exchange, which finds ships for cargoes and cargoes for ships throughout the world, is the world's leading international shipping market.

Other Services

DISTRIBUTION AND SALES

The distribution of goods, including food and drink, to their point of sale by road, rail, air and sea is a major economic activity. The large retailers and wholesalers of food and drink and clothing operate, either directly or through contractors, extensive distribution networks.

Wholesaling

In 1994 there were 118,000 businesses, with a workforce of 800,000 and a turnover of £297,000 million (see Table 15.1), engaged in wholesaling and dealing in Great Britain.

In the food and drink trade almost all large retailers have their own buying and central distribution operations. Elsewhere in the trade,

Table 15.1: Wholesale Trade in Great Britain 1994

	Number of businesses	Turnover[a] (£ million)
Food and drink	15,754	52,539
Petroleum products	938	37,871
Clothing, furs, textiles and footwear	9,813	11,142
Coal and oil merchants	2,681	2,948
Builders' merchants	3,989	9,415
Agricultural supplies and livestock dealing	2,812	8,183
Industrial materials	5,527	26,827
Scrap and waste products	3,084	2,062
Industrial and agricultural machinery	8,663	25,806
Operational leasing	2,239	2,582
Other goods	62,271	117,520
Total wholesaling and dealing	**117,771**	**296,895**

Source: *Business Monitor SDA26. Wholesaling, 1996*
[a]Excludes value added tax.

voluntary 'symbol' groups (for example, Spar and VG) have been formed by wholesalers and small independent retailers. This has helped many smaller retail outlets, including traditional 'corner shops' and village stores, to stay in business, as it has given them the benefits of bulk buying and co-ordinated distribution.

London's wholesale markets play a significant part in the distribution of foodstuffs. New Covent Garden is the main market for fruit and vegetables, Smithfield for meat and Billingsgate for fish.

The Co-operative Wholesale Society (CWS) is the principal supplier of goods and services to the Co-operative Movement and was a founder member of the Co-operative Retail Trading Group. Formed in 1993 to act as a central marketing, buying and distribution partnership for retail co-operative societies, the Group now accounts for 65 per cent of Co-op food trade. The CWS is also the largest co-operative retailer in Europe, with 660 stores located in Scotland, Northern Ireland, the east and south Midlands, and south-east and northern England.

Retailing

In 1994 there were 197,000 retail businesses, with 290,000 outlets, employing 2.4 million people in Great Britain (see Table 15.2). These range from national supermarket chains to corner grocery shops and newsagents. During recent years the large multiple retailers have grown considerably, tending to reduce numbers of stores but increase outlet size and diversify product ranges. Some, like Marks & Spencer, J. Sainsbury and Tesco, have acquired retailers or made franchise arrangements abroad. Small independent businesses and retail co-operative societies have declined markedly. The number of grocery outlets, for instance, has fallen from 67,000 in the 1970s to the present-day total of 40,000. Sunday trading laws have been relaxed to allow retailers to open for limited periods on Sundays; smaller retailers are permitted to open for longer hours than the larger supermarkets and department stores in order to help their competitive position.

The biggest supermarket groups are Tesco, J. Sainsbury, Safeway and Asda, all of which are among the ten largest food retailers in Europe. These four have a market share of around 40 per cent of all food and drink sold. Other important retailers are Marks & Spencer, Somerfield and Kwik Save—the latter is the leading discount food retailer in Britain. Since the early 1990s several overseas discount food retailers, such as Aldi of Germany and Denmark's Netto, have entered the British market.

Table 15.2: Retail Trade in Great Britain 1994

	Number of businesses	Number of outlets	Number of people engaged ('000s)	Turnover[a] (£ million)
Non-specialised stores	21,146	36,910	917	69,014
Specialised stores	175,417	253,086	1,462	87,635
of which:				
Food, drinks or tobacco	45,971	59,814	270	13,103
Pharmaceuticals, cosmetics and toilet articles	7,275	12,529	88	5,860
Businesses having:				
1 outlet	173,113	173,113	708	35,328
2–9 outlets	22,212	51,575	270	15,401
10–99 outlets	1,096	18,840	301	20,412
100 or more outlets	141	46,466	1,100	85,508
of which:				
All businesses selling food, drinks or tobacco	66,575	92,600	1,020	70,906
Total retail trade	**196,563**	**289,996**	**2,379**	**156,649**

Source: *Business Monitor SDA25. Retailing, 1996*
[a]Includes value added tax.

Retail co-operative societies are voluntary organisations controlled by their members, membership being open to anyone paying a small deposit on a minimum share. Of the 5,000 retail co-operative outlets, over half sell food and groceries.

Alcoholic drinks are sold mainly in specialist 'off licences' and supermarkets, which have roughly equal sales. The principal off-licence chains are Cellar Five, Oddbins, Threshers and Victoria Wine.

The leading mixed retail businesses include Marks & Spencer, Boots, Woolworth (part of Kingfisher), Storehouse, W. H. Smith, Argos, Littlewoods, Savacentre (J. Sainsbury), John Menzies, Sears, Burton Group and House of Fraser.

Several chains of DIY (Do-It-Yourself) superstores cater for people wishing to carry out their own repairs and improvements on their homes and gardens; they stock a large range of tools, decorating and building materials, kitchen and bathroom fittings, garden products and so on. The three biggest are B&Q, Texas and Do It All, which together have around 650 outlets.

About 18 million people regularly buy all kinds of goods and services through mail order catalogues like Freemans, Great Universal Stores, Empire and Littlewoods. In 1994 sales by general mail order totalled £6,000 million. The largest selling items are clothing, footwear, furniture, household textiles and domestic electrical appliances.

Shopping Facilities

Britain has a wide range of complementary shopping facilities inside and outside town and city centres. Government policy is to encourage a balanced mixture of facilities that will satisfy the needs of all consumers, whether they have access to a car or not, and enable businesses of all sizes and types to prosper.

One of the most significant trends in retailing has been the spread of superstores, many of which have been built away from urban centres in recent years. The supermarket groups have around 1,000 superstores between them. While the 100 largest retailers account for about three-fifths of retail sales, there continues to be a demand for the products and services provided by small, specialised shops. Encouraged by the Government, the main multiple grocery companies are turning their attention back to town centres, redeveloping existing stores and building smaller outlets. Examples include Tesco's 'Metro' format and J. Sainsbury's 'Capital' stores.

Regional out-of-town shopping centres have been established on sites offering good access and parking facilities. One of the first was the Metro Centre at Gateshead, which is the largest of its kind in Europe. Other centres include Merry Hill at Dudley in the West Midlands, Meadowhall in Sheffield and the Lakeside Centre at Thurrock in Essex. About one-half of total food sales are accounted for by superstores away from town centres, compared with a fifth at the beginning of the 1980s. Retailers of non-food goods, such as DIY products, toys, furniture and electrical appliances, sportswear, and office and computer products, have also built outlets away from urban centres. There is a strong trend towards grouping retail warehouses into retail parks, often with food and other facilities.

All new retail development requires planning permission from the local government planning authority. These authorities must consult central government before granting permission for developments of 20,000 sq m (215,000 sq ft) or more. The Government's policy is to encourage the provision of a broad range of shopping facilities to the public. At the same time, it seeks to ensure that the effects of major new retail developments, especially those outside urban centres, do not undermine the viability of existing town centres. It is intensifying efforts to help revitalise shopping and other facilities in town centres where this is needed.

Other Trends

Many of the large multiple groups sell a much greater number of goods and services than previously. For example, large food retailers are increasing their range of foods. Increased emphasis is also being placed on selling own-label goods (which now account for up to one-half of goods on sale) and environmentally

friendly products, including organic produce. Most superstores and supermarkets offer fresh food, such as meat, fish, vegetables and, in many cases, bread baked on the premises, as well as packaged foods. In-store pharmacies and dry-cleaners are now a feature of many large supermarkets, which have in recent years also begun selling books, magazines, newspapers and pre-recorded video cassettes. The major supermarket chains have their own petrol stations at some of their bigger outlets (see p. 237).

'Stores within stores' are becoming more common; for example, sportswear and sports goods retailers are to be found in many of the big mixed retail stores, while Laura Ashley, the furnishings and fabrics retailer, has facilities in Homebase (a DIY chain owned by J. Sainsbury).

Several large retailers have issued their own credit cards for regular customers in an attempt to encourage sales, particularly of high-value goods. 'Loyalty' cards have also been introduced by some supermarket groups, offering regular customers cash discounts related to the size of their purchases. Marks & Spencer offers financial services.

Franchising

About 470 franchisors operate in Britain, with 26,000 outlets and yearly sales of nearly £6,000 million. Franchising is a business in which a company owning the rights to a particular form of trading licenses them to franchisees, usually by means of an initial payment with continuing royalties. The main areas are cleaning services, film processing, print shops, hairdressing and cosmetics, fitness centres, courier delivery, car rental, engine tuning and servicing, and fast food retailing. Familiar high street names include McDonalds, Body Shop (environmentally friendly cosmetics and other products) and Kall Kwik (fast printing).

Information Technology

Information technology is central to distribution and retailing. Computers monitor stock levels and record sales figures through electronic point-of-sale (EPOS) systems. EPOS systems read a bar-code printed on the retail product that holds price and product information and can be used to generate orders for stock replenishment as well as totalling up bills and providing a receipt for customers.

Techniques such as 'just-in-time' ordering, in which produce arrives at the store at the last possible moment before sale, have become widespread as a result. Most large retailers have set up electronic data interchange (EDI) systems; these enable their computers to communicate with those of their suppliers, and transmit orders and invoices electronically, so reducing errors and saving time.

EFTPOS (electronic funds transfer at point of sale) systems enable customers to pay for purchases using debit cards which automatically transfer funds from their bank account. Several major EFTPOS schemes are in operation and the number of terminals is growing rapidly.

'Superscan' technology—which involves customers using an electronic scanning device to work out their own bills, thus avoiding the need to queue at a check-out—is undergoing trials in a number of supermarkets. Electronic home shopping, using a television and telephone, and 'online' shopping, where personal computers are linked to databases, are also starting to be introduced.

Vehicle, Vehicle Parts and Petrol Retailing

In 1996 over 300,000 people were employed in Great Britain in retailing motor vehicles and parts, and in petrol stations. Many businesses selling new vehicles are franchised by the motor manufacturers. Drive-in fitting centres sell tyres, exhaust systems, batteries, clutches and other vehicle parts; the largest chains include Kwik-Fit and ATS.

Over one-third of petrol stations are owned by oil companies. The three companies with the largest number of outlets are Shell, Esso and BP. Unleaded petrol accounts for more than half of petrol sold. The majority of petrol stations are self-service.

The number of petrol stations has been reduced by about a half in the last decade or so as owners focus on larger sites that can accommodate the broad range of retail services, including food, that are now commonly available at petrol stations. About one-fifth of petrol sold in Britain comes from supermarket forecourts.

Rental Services

A broad range of rental services, many franchised, are on offer throughout Britain (see p. 236). These include hire of cars and other vehicles, televisions and video cassette recorders, household appliances such as washing machines and tumble dryers, tools and heavy decorating equipment (ladders, floor sanders and so on) and video films and computer games. Retailing of many types of service is dominated by chains, though independent operators are still to be found in most fields.

Auction Houses

Britain attracts buyers and sellers from around the world and has a long tradition of expertise and innovation in auctioneering. Its chief auction houses are active in the international auction markets for works of art, trading on their acknowledged expertise. The two largest houses, Sotheby's and Christie's, are established worldwide. The former handled sales valued at £1,050 million in 1995, while Christie's sales amounted to £931 million. Phillips and Bonhams are also prominent auctioneers.

HOTELS, HOLIDAY CENTRES, PUBLIC HOUSES AND CATERING

The hotel and catering trades, which include public houses (pubs) and licensed bars, employ 1.3 million people in Britain, including:

- 289,200 in hotels;
- 327,000 in pubs and bars;
- 295,500 in restaurants;
- 138,300 in clubs; and
- 115,700 in contract catering.

Around 165,000 self-employed people also work in these sectors.

There are 52,000 hotels in Great Britain. The largest hotel business is Forte Hotels Ltd, now owned by Granada Group plc, with 260 hotels in Britain and overseas. At the other end of the scale, numerous guest houses and hotels (many individually owned) have fewer than 20 rooms. Holiday centres, including holiday camps with full board, self-catering centres and caravan parks, are run by Butlins, Holiday Club, Center Parcs, Warner Holidays and Pontin's.

Britain's 100,000 restaurants offer cuisine from virtually every country in the world. Chinese, Indian, Italian and Greek restaurants are among the most popular. 'Fast food' restaurants, an area where franchising plays a significant role, are widespread. They specialise in selling hamburgers, chicken, pizza and a variety of other foods to be eaten on the premises or taken away. The most well-known chains include McDonalds (hamburgers), Burger King (hamburgers), KFC (chicken) and Pizza Hut. Traditional fish and chip shops are the other main providers of cooked take-away food. Sandwich bars are common in towns and cities, typically in areas with high concentrations of office workers.

About 77,100 pubs sell beer, wines, soft drinks and spirits to adults for consumption on the premises, and most also serve hot and cold food. Many pubs are owned by the large brewing companies, which either provide managers to run them or offer tenancy agreements; these pubs tend to sell just their own brands of beer, although some also offer 'guest' beers. Others, called 'free houses', are independently owned and managed and frequently serve a variety of beers. Wine bars are normally smaller than pubs and tend to specialise in wine and food; they more closely resemble bars in other parts of Europe.

Pubs and bars are permitted by law to open from 11.00 to 23.00 from Monday to Saturday (on Sunday they may open between 12.00 and 22.30). The introduction of liquor licences for 'café-style' premises allows children under 14 to accompany adults to selected places where alcoholic drinks are served.

TOURISM, TRAVEL AND LEISURE

In the region of 1.7 million people are employed in tourism and related activities; of these, 188,000 are self-employed. About 8 per cent of small businesses are engaged in tourism. The industry contributed £37,000 million to the economy in 1995—5 per cent of GDP. Britain is the world's fifth largest tourist destination in the world in terms of earnings from visitors. Although its share of world tourism earnings fell from 6 to 4.4 per cent in the ten years to 1994, this rose again to 5 per cent in 1995.

Britain's tourist attractions include theatres, museums, art galleries, and historic houses, as well as shopping, sports and business facilities. Domestic and foreign tourists play an ever more important role in supporting Britain's national heritage, creative arts and, to a lesser extent, sport.

The number of 'theme parks' has grown steadily in recent years and they now attract more than 15 million visitors a year. Alton Towers (Staffordshire), Chessington World of Adventures and Thorpe Park (both in Surrey) are three of the biggest; 2.7 million people visit Alton Towers annually, the largest number of visitors for any paid-for tourist attraction (see Table 2.3, p. 10). As well as spectacular 'white knuckle' rides and attractions and overhead cable cars and railways, some parks also feature displays of domesticated and wild animals.

Domestic tourism was worth around £12,800 million in 1995 (see p. 44). Of British residents opting to take their main holiday in Britain, around 40 per cent choose a traditional seaside destination, such as Blackpool (Lancashire), Bournemouth (Dorset), Great Yarmouth (Norfolk) and Torquay and other resorts in Devon and Cornwall. Short holiday breaks (one to three nights), valued at £2,500 million in 1995, make up an increasingly significant part of the market. Shopping accounts for about a fifth of all expenditure on day trips. Scotland has several skiing resorts.

The number of overseas visitors coming to Britain has more than doubled in the last 20 years. In 1995 a record 23.7 million—13 per cent more than in 1994—spent £11,885 million. An estimated 63 per cent were from Western Europe and 16 per cent from North America, with the United States supplying the largest number of any single country. Business travel accounts for £3,242 million, 27 per cent of all overseas tourism revenue.

Most British holiday-makers wishing to go overseas buy 'package holidays' from travel agencies, where the cost covers both transport and accommodation. The most popular package holiday destinations are Spain, France and Greece. Long-haul holidays to places like the United States, the Caribbean and Australia have become popular as air fares have come down. Winter skiing holidays to resorts in Austria, France, Italy and Switzerland and other countries inside and outside Europe continue to attract large numbers of Britons.

Britain has around 7,000 travel agencies, nearly all of which belong to the Association of British Travel Agents (ABTA). Although most are small businesses, a few large firms, such as Lunn Poly and Thomas Cook, have hundreds of branches. Some 620 tour operators are members of ABTA; about half are both retail agents and tour operators. ABTA operates financial protection schemes to safeguard its members' customers and maintains codes of conduct drawn up with the Office of Fair Trading, a government department. It also offers a free consumer affairs service to help resolve complaints against members and a low-cost independent arbitration scheme for members' customers.

Tourism Promotion

The Department of National Heritage is responsible for tourism in England, and the Scottish, Welsh, and Northern Ireland Offices have responsibility for tourism in their respective countries. The government-supported British Tourist Authority (BTA) promotes Britain overseas as a tourist destination through 42 offices worldwide and encourages the development of tourist facilities in Britain to meet the needs of overseas visitors. The tourist boards for England, Scotland, Wales and Northern Ireland, which also receive government finance, encourage the development and promotion of domestic tourism and work with the BTA to promote Britain overseas.

In 1995 the Government published plans to develop Britain's tourism industry by:

- raising standards of hotel and other accommodation;
- improving overseas marketing of Britain as a tourist destination;
- promoting London more effectively; and
- making holiday booking arrangements easier.

The BTA and the national tourist boards inform and advise the Government on issues of concern to the industry. They also help businesses and other organisations to plan by researching and publicising trends affecting the industry. The national tourist boards work closely with regional tourist boards, on which local government and business interests are represented. The national tourist boards offer financial assistance to the industry. There are over 800 local Tourist Information Centres in Britain.

Accommodation classification and quality grading schemes are operated by the national tourist boards, including the Crown scheme for hotels, guest houses, inns, bed and breakfast and farmhouse holiday accommodation. A new Lodge category has been introduced for purpose-built accommodation alongside motorways and major roads. Common standards are applied throughout Britain, and all participating establishments are inspected every year.

BUSINESS SERVICES

Exhibition and Conference Centres

Britain is one of the world's three leading countries for international conferences—the others being the United States and France.

London and Paris are the two most popular conference cities. A large number of other towns and cities in Britain have facilities for conferences and exhibitions. Total spending in 1994 on conferences, exhibitions and incentive travel amounted to £604 million.

Among the most modern purpose-built conference and exhibition centres are the International Conference Centre in Birmingham; the Queen Elizabeth II and Olympia Conference Centres, both in London; and Cardiff International Arena, a 5,000-seat multi-purpose facility. Others are located in Brighton (East Sussex), Harrogate (North Yorkshire), Bournemouth (Dorset), Birmingham, Manchester, Nottingham and Torquay (Devon). In Scotland both Glasgow and Aberdeen have exhibition and conference centres, and a new International Conference Centre was opened in Edinburgh in September 1995.

Other large exhibition facilities are situated in London at the Barbican, Earls Court, Alexandra Palace and Wembley Arena. An exhibition and conference facility is planned for London Docklands, to be completed in 1998 at an estimated cost of £100 million. The £29 million Belfast Waterfront Hall is due to be opened in 1997.

Many of the larger sites belong to a marketing group, Conventions Great Britain.

Advertising, Sponsorship and Public Relations

Britain is a major centre for creative advertising, and multinational corporations often use advertising created in Britain for marketing their products globally. British agencies have strong foreign links through overseas ownership and associate networks.

Spending on advertising in 1995 amounted to £10,959 million, a rise of 4.5 per cent in real terms on the previous year. The press accounted for 55 per cent of the total, television for 28 per cent, direct mail for 10 per cent, and posters, transport, commercial radio and cinema for the rest. The largest advertising expenditure is on food, household durables, cosmetics, office equipment, motor vehicles and financial services. Among the biggest spenders in 1996 are BT, Ford,

Dixons, McDonalds, Tesco, J. Sainsbury and the National Lottery (see p. 42). British television advertising receives many international awards.

Campaigns are planned by around 2,000 advertising agencies. In addition to their creative, production and media buying roles, some agencies offer integrated marketing services, such as consumer research and public relations. Leading agencies include Abbott Mead Vickers BBDO, J Walter Thompson, Leo Burnett, and Ogilvy and Mather Advertising.

Government advertising campaigns—crime prevention, health promotion, road safety and so on—are often organised by the Central Office of Information, an executive agency of the Government (see p. 545), which is able to secure large discounts because of its centralised buying power.

Many advertising agencies have sponsorship departments, which arrange for businesses to sponsor products and events, including artistic, sporting and charitable events. In return for financial or other support, the sponsoring company is associated with a worthy product or event, thereby raising its profile with consumers.

Britain's public relations industry has grown rapidly over the past ten years and is now the most developed in Europe. In 1994 it had an estimated turnover of £1,000 million.

Computing Services

The computing services industry comprises software houses; production of packaged software; consultancy; information technology 'outsourcing'; processing services; and the provision of complete computer systems. It also includes companies that provide information technology education and training; independent maintenance; support, contingency planning and recruitment; and contract staff.

The turnover of companies in the Computing Services & Software Association, which represents about 75 per cent of the industry in Britain, totalled £7,000 million in 1995. Important areas for software development include data and word processing, telecommunications, computer-aided design and manufacturing, defence and consumer electronics.

Management Consultancy

Management consultants provide advice and technical assistance to business and government clients. Typically, consultants identify and investigate problems and opportunities, recommend appropriate action and help to implement recommendations.

Many British-based consultancies operate internationally; the most recent trend has been for the largest firms to set up offices in Eastern Europe and the Pacific Rim. The 30 member firms of the Management Consultancies Association are among the largest in the industry and account for more than half of management consultancy work. They range from Andersen Consulting and CMG Management, with a strong technical bias, to Coopers & Lybrand and PA Consulting group, which specialise in market/industry sectors. In 1995 member firms earned over £1,000 million in Britain and nearly £200 million overseas.

Market Research

The market research profession in Britain has developed markedly in the past decade and now accounts for 9 per cent of worldwide market research spending. It has a wide range of domestic and overseas clients, including government bodies. The Association of Market Survey Organisations is the main trade organisation, with 33 member companies. In 1995 its members earned £380 million out of an estimated total market research industry turnover of over £600 million.

Further Reading

Financial Services. Aspects of Britain series, HMSO, 1995.

16 Manufacturing and Construction Industries

Introduction	242	Construction	256
Sectors of Manufacturing	242		

Britain became the world's first industrialised country in the mid-19th century. Wealth was based on manufacturing iron and steel, heavy machinery and cotton textiles, and on coal mining, shipbuilding and trade. Manufacturing still plays an important role and Britain excels in high-technology industries such as pharmaceuticals, electronics (including computers), aerospace and offshore equipment, where British companies are among the world's largest and most successful. The British construction industry has made its mark around the world and continues to be involved in some of the most prestigious international building projects.

Introduction

Manufacturing accounted for about a sixth of gross domestic product (GDP) in 1995 and for about the same proportion of employment. More than four-fifths of visible exports consisted of manufactured or semi-manufactured goods. Almost all manufacturing is carried out by private sector businesses. Around one-fifth of manufacturing jobs are provided by overseas companies.

Following the recession in the early 1990s, which led to a decline in manufacturing output, output rose by 4.2 per cent in 1994 and by 2.2 per cent in 1995 (see Table 16.2). Employment in manufacturing in 1995 was 4 million compared with 5 million in 1985. Total capital investment in manufacturing rose by nearly 13 per cent in 1995 to £15,237 million, comprising £12,824 million in plant and machinery, £1,610 million in new building work and £803 million in vehicles.

The construction industry contributed 5 per cent of GDP and about 1.8 million people worked in the industry in 1995, 7 per cent of the total number of employees and self-employed. Following a period of marked decline as recession affected the industry in the early 1990s, output has remained below the 1990 level. Total domestic fixed capital investment was £770 million in 1995.

Sectors of Manufacturing

Relative sizes of enterprises and the main sectors are shown in Tables 16.1 and 16.2. Table 16.3 indicates output and investment. A more detailed description of some of the main sectors is given below.

Mineral and Metal Products

British producers delivered 16 million tonnes of finished steel in 1995, of which just under 50 per cent was exported. Over the past ten years annual steel industry exports have

Table 16.1: Manufacturing—Size of Businesses by Turnover and Employment

Annual turnover (£'000)	Number of businesses 1995	Employment size	Number of businesses 1995
1–49	30,915	1–9	110,350
50–99	27,115	10–19	18,720
100–249	34,750	20–49	15,050
250–499	20,740	50–99	5,905
500–999	15,205	100–199	3,180
1,000–1,999	10,320	200–499	1,980
2,000–4,999	8,080	500–999	650
5,000–9,999	3,325	1,000+	475
10,000+	4,330		
Total	**154,780**	**Total**	**156,310**

Source: *Size, Analysis of United Kingdom Business. Business Monitor PA 1003*
*a*Includes secondary non-manufacturing activity.

increased by 50 per cent, to nearly 8 million tonnes, creating a favourable balance of trade in steel products (£2,700 million in 1995).

The major areas of steel production are in south Wales and northern England, with substantial further processing in the Midlands. Major restructuring in the steel industry took place during the 1980s and early 1990s. Productivity and efficiency have improved and the industry is now one of the lowest-cost producers in Europe.

British Steel is the fourth largest steel company in the world, employing 41,000 people and producing about three-quarters of Britain's crude steel in 1995. The company's output is based on flat steel products, plate, heavy sections and tubes. These are used principally in the construction, automotive,

Table 16.2: Indices of Manufacturing Output (1990 = 100)

1992 Standard Industrial Classification Category	Share of output 1990 (weight per 1,000)	1993	1994	1995
Food and beverages	29	100.3	101.8	104.1
Tobacco products	2	98.7	105.1	100.8
Textiles and leather products	14	89.4	90.5	89.7
Wood and wood products	4	89.3	95.5	91.2
Pulp, paper products, printing and publishing	26	99.0	101.5	102.6
Solid and nuclear fuels, oil refining	7	114.9	115.4	128.5
Chemicals and man-made fibres	24	107.6	112.3	117.5
Rubber and plastics products	10	99.8	109.6	114.5
Other non-metallic mineral products	9	88.9	92.7	92.1
Basic metals and metal products	27	84.8	86.7	87.4
Machinery and equipment	21	85.0	89.2	88.7
Electrical and optical equipment	27	101.2	112.0	119.2
Transport equipment	27	87.8	92.3	93.1
Other manufacturing	6	88.4	90.0	85.2
Total	**232**	**95.3**	**99.3**	**101.5**

Source: *United Kingdom National Accounts 1996 Edition*

Table 16.3: Output and Investment in Manufacturing

1992 Standard Industrial Classification Category	Gross output (£ million) 1995	Gross domestic fixed capital formation (£ million) 1995
Solid and nuclear fuels, oil refining	2,932	493
Chemicals and man-made fibres	15,149	
Other non-metallic mineral products	4,617	4,044
Basic metals and metal products	14,218	
Machinery and equipment	11,015	
Electrical and optical equipment	16,322	4,962
Transport equipment	12,321	
Food and beverages	17,364	
Tobacco products	1,279	
Textiles and leather products	7,097	
Wood and wood products	1,546	5,738
Pulp, paper products, printing and publishing	16,590	
Rubber and plastics products	7,045	
Other manufacturing	4,163	
Total	131,658	15,237

Source: *United Kingdom National Accounts 1996 Edition*

engineering, transport, metal goods, packaging and energy industries. British Steel owns UES Holdings, Europe's biggest producer of engineering steels—these are specialist grades used to make products such as forgings for the automotive and aerospace industries.

Other important steel producers in Britain include Caparo, Allied Steel and Wire, Co-Steel Sheerness, the Glynwed Group and the stainless steel producer Avesta Sheffield. Products manufactured by these companies include reinforcing bars for the construction industry, wire rod, hot rolled and cold finished bars and other special steels for the aerospace and offshore oil and gas industries.

Output of non-ferrous metals and their alloys includes primary and secondary (recycled) aluminium and copper, as well as aluminium and copper and copper alloy semi-manufactures. The production of metal relies mainly on imported ores and recycled material of both domestic and overseas origin. Copper and copper alloy semi-manufactures are used in a wide variety of electrical switchgear, wire and cable, tube and fittings for plumbing, and valves and components for the engineering and transport industries.

Britain is a major producer of specialised alloys for high-technology requirements in the aerospace, electronic, petrochemical, and nuclear and other fuel industries. Titanium and titanium alloys, which are light, strong and flexible, are used in aircraft manufacturing, power generation and North Sea oil production. Nickel alloys are utilised in aero-engines for high-temperature environments. In recent years considerable progress has been made in producing 'superplastic' alloys, which are more ductile and elastic than conventional alloys. Aluminium alloys, including aluminium lithium (developed by British Alcan Aluminium), are ideal for use in aircraft, being lighter, stronger and more rigid than normal aluminium. Aluminium alloys typically make up three-quarters of an airframe.

Ceramics

The ceramics industry manufactures clay products, such as domestic pottery, sanitaryware and tiles, and clay pipes for the building trade. Domestic tableware production includes fine china, earthenware and stoneware. Tableware is produced predominately in Stoke-on-Trent. Britain is the world's leading manufacturer and exporter of fine bone china; Waterford Wedgwood, Spode and Royal Doulton are among the more famous names.

Research is being conducted into ceramics for use in house building and diesel and jet engines. Important industrial ceramics invented in Britain include some forms of silicon carbide and sialons, which can withstand ultra-high temperatures.

Glass Products

Flat glass is manufactured through the float glass process, which was developed by Pilkington Brothers and licensed to glassmakers throughout the world. Pilkington has also produced an energy-saving window glass which reflects room heat without impairing visibility and an automotive glass that prevents car interiors overheating and being damaged by heat and sunlight. United Glass is a leading manufacturer of bottles and other glass containers. Glass-reinforced cement composites for the construction industry were invented in Britain in the early 1970s and are made under licence in over 40 countries.

China Clay

Britain is the world's second biggest exporter of china clay (kaolin), four-fifths of which is used in paper-making. In 1995, 2.2 million tonnes were sold overseas. The main company is ECC International Europe, part of the English China Clays Group.

Chemicals and Related Products

Pharmaceuticals and basic industrial chemicals are the two biggest sectors of the chemical industry, which is the third largest in Europe. Its products underpin almost all other industrial processes and products. The industry is at the forefront of modern technology, spending over 7 per cent of total sales on research and development (R & D). It provides direct employment for about 326,000 people. Over half of its output is exported, making it British manufacturing's greatest single export earner. Exports in 1995 were worth £21,300 million, while imports (mainly consisting of plastics and organic chemicals) were valued at £17,300 million.

Many major chemical companies in Britain are multinationals; several are subsidiaries of overseas companies and others are specialist manufacturers of pharmaceuticals, such as Glaxo Wellcome (see p. 246). Imperial Chemical Industries (ICI), the sixth largest chemical company in the world, manufactures industrial chemicals, paints, materials and explosives. Zeneca produces pharmaceuticals, agrochemicals and seeds, and specialty chemicals (see below). Teesside, which has been particularly successful in attracting investment from some of the largest domestic and overseas chemical firms, now rivals Rotterdam as Europe's largest petrochemicals zone.

Traditionally, Britain has been a major producer of basic industrial chemicals, such as basic organic and inorganic chemicals, plastics and fertilisers, which together comprise around two-fifths of output. The most rapid growth in recent years has been in pharmaceuticals.

Sales of basic organic chemicals amounted to £4,600 million and those of other basic industrial chemicals to £8,000 million in 1994. The most important bulk products are ethylene, propylene and benzene. Britain is the world's fourth biggest producer of specialised organic chemicals, with over 7.5 per cent of the world market.

Much inorganic chemical production consists of relatively simple bulk chemicals, such as sulphuric acid and metallic and non-metallic oxides, serving as basic materials for industry. Specialty chemicals include pharmaceutical ingredients, essential oils and flavourings, adhesives and sealants, and explosives, including those used for car safety airbags. Investment in environmentally safe products and processes, for example substitutes for chlorofluorocarbons (CFCs), is increasing.

A sizeable proportion of world R & D in agrochemicals is conducted in Britain. Notable British discoveries include diquat and paraquat herbicides, pyrethroid insecticides, systemic fungicides and aphicides, genetically engineered microbial pesticides and methods of encouraging natural parasites to eradicate common pests in horticulture.

Exports of soap and detergent preparations in 1995 were valued at £570 million. This sector is dominated by Lever Brothers (part of Unilever) and the US-owned Procter and Gamble.

Plastics

Around 230,000 people are employed by over 4,500 firms involved in the plastics industry. Of this, plastic processing—the conversion of plastics materials into finished or sub-assemblies of final products—accounts for 170,000 people and about 400 firms. Total turnover of the industry was £18,000 million in 1995; exports reached £3,500 million that year. Production includes packaging and building, electrical, automotive, houseware and clothing products. Britain's plastic processing industry continues to be a world leader in material specification and design with new processes allowing stronger plastics to replace other materials or spread into new applications.

Paints

Sales of paint, varnishes and painters' fillings were worth £2,700 million in 1994. ICI is the world's largest paint manufacturer. Among its specialised products are new ranges of synthetic resins and pigments, powder coatings, non-drip and quick-drying paints and paints needing only one top coat. Its best-known consumer product is the 'Dulux' paint range. Two of the more significant innovations have been solid emulsion paint and a temporary water-based finish which can be removed easily by chemical treatment, for vehicle bodies and road markings.

Pharmaceuticals

The British pharmaceutical industry is the world's third biggest exporter of medicines, accounting for around 11 per cent of the world market. About 300 pharmaceutical manufacturers and research organisations operate in Britain, including several multinational corporations. The British-owned group Glaxo Wellcome became the largest pharmaceutical company in the world when Glaxo took over Wellcome in 1995. Zeneca is the world's second biggest manufacturer of cancer therapies. There are also many medium-sized and smaller specialist companies. Total sales in 1995 were around £10,000 million, of which £4,900 million was accounted for by overseas sales. The main overseas markets are Western Europe and North America, with Japan an expanding market.

Some 75,000 people work in the industry, of whom more than a quarter are engaged in R & D. The industry, which is largely based in the South East and East Anglia, invested £2,000 million in R & D in 1995. This sum amounts to one-fifth of British industry's R & D and represents about a tenth of total world expenditure on pharmaceuticals R & D. Progress in devising vaccines has helped to reduce dramatically the impact of infectious diseases such as polio, whooping cough, mumps and measles.

British firms discovered and developed five of the world's 20 best-selling medicines, including Glaxo Wellcome's ulcer treatment Zantac, the best-selling medicine in the world, and Zeneca's beta-blocker Tenormin, for treating high blood pressure. Among Zeneca's newer products are Zestril (for combating high blood pressure), Zoladex (a prostate cancer therapy) and Diprivan (an anaesthetic).

Other major developments pioneered in Britain are semi-synthetic penicillins and cephalosporins, both powerful antibiotics, and new treatments for asthma, arthritis, migraine and coronary heart disease. The world's ninth largest pharmaceutical company, SmithKline Beecham, manufactures four of the world's top-selling antibiotics; it also developed Augmentin, used to treat a range of infections that have become resistant to antibiotics. Glaxo Wellcome's drug zidovudine (AZT) is one of the most widely used anti-viral agents for the treatment of HIV infection. Zofran, an anti-nausea drug for countering the unpleasant side-effects of cancer treatments also produced by Glaxo Wellcome, is one of the company's most successful new medicines.

British companies lead in the development of molecular graphics. These contribute to the rational design of new and improved medicines through a computer-aided technique for analysing the structures of complicated organic molecules.

A growing trend is the production of generic medicines. These are versions of branded medicines whose patents have expired. They are mostly unbranded and cheaper than the branded originals. About 50 per cent of doctors' prescriptions in Britain are for generic medicines.

Biotechnology

The Government estimates that world markets for biotechnology products could exceed £70,000 million by the year 2000. The British biotechnology industry is second only in pre-eminence to that of the United States. As well as Zeneca, Glaxo Wellcome and SmithKline Beecham, around 30 smaller independent firms, including British Biotech, Celltech, Xenova and Cantab, contribute to the sector.

Biotechnology has improved the specificity of pharmaceuticals through greater understanding of disease at the molecular level. It has enabled companies to manufacture products using genetic modification. British Biotech is developing a potentially important anti-cancer drug, Marimastat, which can be taken orally and is claimed to have few serious adverse side-effects. Among other major advances in the development of drugs are human insulin and interferons, genetically engineered vaccines, antibiotics produced by fermentation, and alternative bactericidal drugs based on Nisin, a food preservative made in Britain. Agricultural products include infection-resistant crops. Medical diagnostic devices are another strong sector and the industry produces the world's best-selling biosensor.

A second generation of vaccines based on recombinant DNA technology includes SmithKline Beecham's Engerix-B vaccine against hepatitis. Therapies based on correcting the function of defective genes are

under development. Diseases being targeted include those where a single defective gene needs correcting, such as in cystic fibrosis, and those where there are genetic and environmental components, like cardiovascular disease.

Specialist products of Britain's small and medium-sized biotechnology firms comprise, among other items, medical diagnostics and microbial pesticides. Celltech was the first company licensed by the United States Government for the large-scale production of monoclonal antibodies, proteins which can seek out a particular substance in the body. They are used to diagnose diseases, identify different blood types and can be employed in the treatment of a range of conditions, including cancer.

Fibres

The main types of synthetic fibre are still those first developed in the 1940s: regenerated cellulosic fibres such as viscose, and the major synthetic fibres like nylon polyamide, polyester and acrylics. Extensive research continues to produce a wide variety of innovative products; antistatic and flame-retardant fibres are examples. More specialist products include the aramids (with very high thermal stability and strength), elastanes (giving very high stretch and recovery) and melded fabrics (produced without the need for knitting or weaving).

Courtaulds, one of Britain's biggest chemical companies, was responsible for developing Tencel, a solvent-spun, biodegradable fibre. This is twice as strong as cotton while being soft enough to be used by designers of luxury garments.

Mechanical Engineering

The mechanical engineering sector has about 28,000 firms employing over 440,000 people. In 1995 exports totalled £14,600 million, with a trade surplus of £2,300 million. Output includes pressure vessels, heat exchangers and storage tanks for chemical and oil-refining plant, steam-raising boilers (including those for power stations), nuclear reactors, water and sewage treatment plant, and fabricated steelwork for bridges, buildings and industrial installations.

Machine-building is an area where British firms excel, especially in construction and earth-moving equipment, wheeled tractors, internal combustion engines, textile machinery, medical equipment, fork-lift trucks, pumps and compressors. Britain is one of the world's major producers of tractors, which make up around three-quarters of the country's total output of agricultural equipment. Sales of wheeled tractors in 1994 were valued at £860 million. Among leading tractor manufacturers are Massey Ferguson, JCB, Case and New Holland.

Widely-used technical innovations include computer-controlled tractors, a highly efficient pesticide sprayer and combined mower/conditioners that reduce the drying time for grass. Much new machinery is designed for use in a variety of conditions to meet the needs of overseas farmers.

Britain is a leading producer of machine tools. Almost all are purchased by the engineering, aerospace, automotive and metal goods industries. The machine tools sector was badly affected by the recent recession, but has now recovered strongly, with exports doing especially well. Turnover of machine tools was valued at £1,600 million in 1994, 15 per cent more than in 1993; exports account for a third of turnover. British manufacturers have made technological advances in probes, sensors, co-ordinate measuring devices, laser melting and the installation of flexible manufacturing systems. Computer numerical-controlled machines account for an increasing proportion of output. Of the top six machine tool companies in Britain, five are foreign-owned; the 600 Group is the biggest British company.

Most sales of textile machinery are to export markets. British innovations include computerised colour matching and weave simulation, friction spinning, high-speed computer-controlled knitting machines and electronic jacquard attachments for weaving looms.

Britain's mining and tunnelling equipment industry leads in the production of coal-cutting and road-heading (shearing) equipment, hydraulic roof supports, conveying equipment, flameproof transformers, switchgear, and subsurface transport equipment and control systems. JCB, Britain's biggest construction equipment manufacturer, is the world's leading manufacturer of backhoe loaders and telescopic handlers. Sales of construction equipment, such as excavators and backhoe loaders, rose in 1994 to £569 million.

The mechanical lifting and handling equipment industry produces cranes and transporters, lifting devices, escalators, conveyors, powered industrial trucks and air bridges, as well as electronically controlled and automatic handling systems. In 1994 sales in this sector were worth £2,300 million. Britain is also a major producer of industrial engines, pumps, valves and compressors, and of pneumatic and hydraulic equipment. Companies like Babcock manufacture steam generators and other heavy equipment for power plants. Despite an overall decline in the castings industry, some foundries have invested in new melting, moulding and quality control equipment.

Electrical, Electronic and Instrument Engineering

Making extensive use of the most advanced technologies, the electrical engineering industry manufactures a broad range of products: power plant, cable, transformers and switchgear, lighting, electrical installation products, and heating, ventilating and air conditioning equipment. GEC-Alsthom is one of only a handful of firms in the world which can supply the major components for a complete power station project.

The domestic electrical appliance sector is dominated by a few large firms. Britain has the fifth largest electronics industry in the world. Products include computers, communications equipment and a large range of components. Exports of computer hardware and software increased by 27 per cent in 1995; sales of telecommunications and sound equipment overseas were up 33 per cent.

The major electronic consumer goods produced are television sets and high-fidelity audio and video equipment. Several leading Japanese companies have established manufacturing bases in Britain. British manufacturers have a worldwide reputation for high-quality goods aimed at the upper end of the market.

> Scotland's 'Silicon Glen' employs 46,000 people in electronics. The electronics industry in Scotland currently produces 12 per cent of Europe's semiconductors, over 35 per cent of its personal computers, about 45 per cent of its computer workstations and over 50 per cent of its automated cash dispensers. Major Japanese, US and other overseas companies located in the area include IBM, NEC, Compaq and Digital, which are supplied by a strong indigenous electronic components sector.

Computers

This sector produces an extensive range of systems, central processors and peripheral equipment, from large computers for large-scale data-processing and scientific work to mini- and microcomputers for control and automation systems and for home, educational and office use. Between 1994 and 1995 turnover of electronic data processing equipment rose from £13,250 million to £14,900 million.

Britain's biggest computer manufacturer is the largely Japanese-owned ICL. Other companies, such as Psion, have concentrated on developing new products for specialised markets. These include hand-held, pocket-sized computers, increasingly used by company sales forces, and notebook and pen computers.

British firms make computer applications software, and are particularly strong in specialist markets such as artificial intelligence, computer-aided design, mathematical software, geographical information systems and data visualisation. The world's first modem (computer telephone link) for portable computers was designed in Britain. Psion is a pioneer of the 'palmtop' computer, which has the equivalent power of a desktop machine. All-Voice Computing is a market leader in devising software for voice-activated word processing.

British firms and research organisations, with government support, have been involved in the development and application of the family of 'three-five' semiconductor materials, such as gallium arsenide; these are used in a number of microwave devices and in the production of faster-working computers. Major advances are being made by British firms and academic institutions in the field of 'virtual reality', a three-dimensional computer simulation technique with a host of industrial and other applications. It is being used to design buildings and a range of products, including cars, pharmaceuticals and machine tools.

Communications Equipment

Britain's main communications products are switching and transmission equipment, telephones and terminals. As the telecommunications market has become fully liberalised (see p. 319), there has been a growing demand for equipment and services. GPT is Britain's foremost telecommunications manufacturer; its product range includes PBXs (private branch exchanges), transmission systems and videoconferencing equipment.

Innovative work is being stimulated by the expansion of cable television and the growth in value added network services. There has been rapid expansion in the market for cellular telephones since the second half of the 1980s.

Transmission equipment and cables for telecommunications and information networks include submarine and high-specification data-carrying cables. Supported by a technically advanced cable industry, BT has led in the development of optical fibre communications systems. It has paved the way for simpler and cheaper optical cables by laying the first non-repeatered cable over 100 km (62 miles) long, and by developing the first all-optical repeater.

More than half of the world's undersea communications cables have been made and laid by STC Submarine Systems, which, with its US and French partners, completed the laying of the first transatlantic optical fibre cable in 1988. Now part of Canada's Northern Telecom, STC is building the first fibre-optic cable linking Canada and Europe. The cable, which is being made in Britain and the United States, will carry up to 30,000 telephone calls simultaneously down each of two pairs of optical fibres.

Britain also has a world lead in the transmission of computerised data along telephone lines for reproduction on television screens.

Another sector of the industry manufactures radio communications equipment, radar, radio and sonar navigational aids for ships and aircraft, thermal imaging systems, alarms and signalling equipment, public broadcasting equipment and other capital goods. Radar was invented in Britain and British firms are still in the forefront of technological advances. Racal Avionics' X-band radar for aircraft ground movement control is in use at airports in several overseas countries. Solid-state secondary surveillance radar, manufactured by Cossor Electronics, is being supplied to 50 overseas civil aviation operators. Cable and Wireless's submarine cable-laying robot 'CIRRUS', which can work at depths of up to 1 km (3,280 ft), is controlled entirely by a computer on its mother ship.

Medical and Other Electronic Equipment

A range of electronic measurement and test equipment is made in Britain, as well as analytical instruments, process control equipment, and numerical control and indication equipment for use in machine tools. Companies such as GEC and Oxford Instruments produce electronic medical equipment, including ultrasound scanners, electromyography systems and patient monitoring systems for intensive and coronary care and other uses. Britain pioneered magnetic resonance imaging.

The indigenous electronics components industry is supplemented by subsidiaries of leading overseas companies. An area of rapid change in which Britain is particularly strong is the manufacture of advanced components, such as integrated circuits.

The instrument engineering industry makes measuring, photographic, cinematographic and reprographic equipment; watches, clocks and other timing devices; and medical and surgical instruments. Total turnover of this sector amounted to £9,000 million in 1995.

Overseas sales of scientific and photographic equipment were worth £6,000 million in 1995.

Motor Vehicles

Around 800,000 people are employed by vehicle and automotive components manufacturers. Car output is dominated by seven groups, accounting for 99 per cent of the total: Rover (a subsidiary of BMW), Ford (including Jaguar), Vauxhall, Peugeot-Talbot, Honda, Nissan and Toyota. The remainder is in the hands of smaller, specialist producers such as Rolls-Royce, whose cars are renowned for their quality and durability. Rover's production includes the highly successful Land Rover four-wheel drive vehicles and a full range of family cars. Investment continues on a large scale: nearly £4,000 million in the past five years by Ford; around £500 million a year by Rover with the backing of BMW; and since their arrival in the mid-1980s, Nissan, Toyota and Honda have invested more than £3,000 million.

A period of major change has accompanied the arrival of these three Japanese manufacturers. Their management approach, high productivity, quality, workforce commitment and co-operative partnerships have had a positive effect on established car and component manufacturers alike.

> Car production has recovered strongly following the recession: in 1995, 1.5 million cars were manufactured, the highest figure since 1974, due in large part to a strong export performance. A total of 745,000 passenger cars were exported in 1995, almost three and a half times as many as in 1988.

The motor components industry consists of up to 6,000 companies, including large conglomerates such as Lucas, GKN and T&N, and is ranked as one of Britain's major industries. Lucas is merging its business with that of Varity of the United States, becoming one of the top ten automotive components suppliers in the world.

Shipbuilding and Marine Engineering

Order books of British merchant shipbuilders for new building were estimated to be worth £200 million at the end of 1995; merchant ship repairers had a turnover of £300 million in 1995. The marine equipment industry is a major contributor to the shipbuilding industry, as equipment installed in a ship's hull accounts for about 50 per cent of its total cost. Some 800 firms offer a complete range of products, from diving equipment to sophisticated navigational systems, 75 per cent of which is exported.

More than two decades of oil and gas exploitation in the North Sea have generated a major offshore industry (see p. 267). Shipbuilders and fabricators build floating production units and semi-submersible units for drilling, production and emergency/maintenance support, drill ships, jack-up rigs, modules and offshore loading systems. UIE Scotland, Highlands Fabricators, John Brown and McDermott Scotland are among the larger manufacturers and designers. In 1996 Harland and Wolff of Belfast was awarded a £70 million contract by BP to build the hull for the world's largest newly constructed floating oil production vessel.

Several thousand firms supply other products needed by the offshore industry —such as diving equipment and helicopters— as well as services, including consultancy, design, project management and R & D. Their experience of North Sea projects has enabled them to establish themselves in oil and gas markets throughout the world.

Aerospace

Britain's aerospace industry is the third largest in the Western world, after the United States and France. Only nine firms employ 2,500 people or more, and two-thirds of the 540 core aerospace companies have fewer than 50 employees. Around 200 companies, employing over 130,000 people, belong to the Society of British Aerospace Companies. Total sales of the industry amounted to £12,000 million in 1994, with exports contributing £7,500 million. Aircraft and parts account for around two-fifths of overseas sales, with engines and parts, missiles and aerospace equipment (including satellite equipment) making up the rest.

Reductions in defence orders following the end of the Cold War, accompanied by fierce international competition in the defence products market, have forced the aerospace industry to contract and to improve its efficiency and competitiveness. An increase in the amount of collaborative development of civil and military aircraft and engines, as well as aviation equipment and satellites, is leading to significant savings on the costs of long-term programmes.

The industry's activities cover designing and constructing airframes, aero-engines, guided weapons, simulators and space satellites, flight controls including 'fly-by-wire' and 'fly-by-light' equipment (see p. 327), avionics and complex components, with their associated services. In order to improve fuel economy, engine and airframe manufacturers have been using lighter materials such as titanium and carbon-fibre composites (see p. 244), combined with advanced avionics and improved aerodynamic techniques.

Civil Aircraft

As one of the leading British exporters of manufactured goods, British Aerospace (BAe) produces both civil and military aircraft, as well as guided weapons and aircraft components.

BAe has a 20 per cent share of the European consortium Airbus Industrie. It designs and supplies the wings for the whole family of Airbus airliners, from the short- to medium-haul A320 series (the first civil airliner to use fly-by-wire controls—see p. 327) to the large long-range four-engined A340.

With Aerospatiale of France and Italy's Alenia, BAe has formed a new regional aircraft alliance which jointly markets turboprops and jet aircraft with between 29 and 115 seats; these include BAe's Avro RJ family of regional 'quiet jet' airliners and the 29-seat Jetstream 41 turboprop airliner.

The Canadian-owned Short Brothers of Belfast, with 9,000 employees, is engaged in the design and production of major civil aircraft sub-assemblies, advanced engine nacelles and components for aerospace manufacturers as well as in the provision of aviation support services. It is a leading supplier to Boeing and McDonnell Douglas among others. Shorts is a partner in manufacturing the 50-seat Canadair Regional Jet airliner; the Learjet 45, a small business jet aircraft; and the Bombardier Global Express long-range business jet.

Pilatus Britten-Norman manufactures the Islander light utility aircraft, which has had sales in over 100 countries. Slingsby Aviation produces several versions of the T67 Firefly two-seater training and acrobatic aircraft for customers around the world (see below).

Military Aircraft and Missiles

British Aerospace is one of the world's top defence companies, with more than four-fifths of its military production having been exported in 1995. Among its military aircraft is the Harrier, a unique vertical/short take-off and landing (V/STOL) military combat aircraft. BAe also produces the Hawk fast-jet trainer and, with McDonnell Douglas, the Goshawk T45 carrier jet trainer. It has a 33 per cent share in the development of the Eurofighter 2000, which had its maiden flight in 1994. This collaborative programme involves companies from Britain, Germany, Italy and Spain.

The Tornado combat aircraft is built by a company set up jointly by BAe, Alenia and Daimler-Benz Aerospace. A £5,000 million order for 48 Tornado bombers for Saudi Arabia was confirmed in 1993, making it one of Britain's biggest ever export deals. Together with Alenia, Daimler-Benz and Aerospatiale, BAe has formed a new company, a military subsidiary of Airbus Industrie, to manage the Future Large Aircraft military transport programme. The United States Air Force has chosen Slingsby Aviation's T67 Firefly training aircraft as its new basic trainer and 113 aircraft are being built. Slingsby also designs and makes composite components for the aviation and other industries.

BAe is a major supplier of tactical guided weapon systems for use on land, at sea and in the air. BAe is merging its missile business with that of France's Matra corporation to form Europe's largest guided weapons concern. Shorts Missile Systems Ltd (SMS) is a joint venture between Shorts and Thomson-CSF of France in the area of very short range air defence systems.

Helicopters

Westland Helicopters (part of the GKN group) manufactures the Sea King, Lynx and Apache military helicopters, and, in partnership with Agusta of Italy, the multi-role EH101 medium-lift helicopter. Over 1,000 Westland helicopters are in service in 19 countries. Orders currently being fulfilled include ones for the Royal Navy (for the EH101), Royal Air Force (EH101 and Sea King), and the British Army (Apache), and customers from Brazil (Lynx), Norway (Sea King) and Italy (EH101). Major Sea King upgrading programmes are being undertaken for Australia, Belgium and Norway.

Aero-engines

Rolls-Royce is one of the world's three prime manufacturers of aero-engines, with a turnover in 1995 of £2,400 million for its aerospace division. The Group's commercial aero-engine company makes engines for airliners and regional, executive and corporate jets. Over 50,000 Rolls-Royce engines are in service with more than 300 airlines in over 100 countries. More than 80 per cent of Boeing 757 operators have selected RB211-535 engines.

The company's latest large engine, the Trent, powers the new generation of wide-body twin-engined airliners, such as Boeing's 777 and the Airbus A330. The Trent 800 has run at over 100,000 lb thrust.

Rolls-Royce is a partner in the five-nation International Aero Engine consortium, which manufactures the low-emission V2500 aero-engine, now in service on the Airbus A320 and A321 as well as the McDonnell Douglas MD90. It is also in partnership with BMW, producing engines for large corporate jets and regional aircraft.

Rolls-Royce produces military engines for both aircraft and helicopters, and is a partner in the EJ200 engine project for the Eurofighter

2000. It also owns the Allison Engine Company of the United States, which is a world leader in helicopter and large turboprop engines.

The company also manufactures gas turbines for power generation, for oil and gas pumping and marine propulsion. Turnover of Rolls-Royce's industrial power group amounted to £1,200 million in 1995, of which 70 per cent came from overseas sales.

Aviation Equipment

Around one-third of the aerospace industry is devoted to designing and manufacturing aviation equipment. British firms have made significant technological advances. Manufacturers like Dowty, GEC-Marconi, Lucas, Smiths Industries, Racal, Normalair-Garrett and BAe provide equipment and systems for engines and aircraft propellers, navigation and landing systems, engine and flight controls, environmental controls and oxygen breathing and regulation systems, electrical generation, mechanical and hydraulic power systems, cabin furnishings, flight-deck controls and information displays. GEC-Marconi is the world's largest manufacturer of head-up displays (HUDs).

British firms have made important advances in developing ejection seats, firefighting equipment and flight simulators, as well as fly-by-wire and fly-by-light technology, where control surfaces on the wings and elsewhere are moved by means of automatic electronic signalling and fibre optics respectively, rather than by mechanical means. GEC-Marconi supplies the fly-by-wire system for the Boeing 777. Britain's aerospace companies provide radar and air traffic control equipment and ground power supplies to airports and airlines worldwide.

Space Equipment and Services

Over 400 companies employing almost 6,500 people are engaged in industrial space activities. The industry is strong in the development and manufacture of civil and military communications satellites and associated Earth stations and ground infrastructure equipment. In the field of Earth observation, it plays a leading role in manufacturing platforms, space radar and meteorological satellite hardware, and in the exploitation of space data imaging products. Through its participation in the Intelsat, Inmarsat, Eutelsat and Astra European space projects, Britain has become Europe's biggest user of space. The British Government is the fourth largest contributor to the European Space Agency (ESA).

The largest British space company is Matra Marconi Space UK, which, with its French partner, is one of the world's leading space companies. Its current major activities include manufacture of the Skynet 4 military communications satellites, payloads for the Koreasat and Inmarsat 3 communications spacecraft and the European Polar Platform and space radar systems. The company carried out instrumentation work on the SOHO scientific satellite launched in 1995 to study the Sun.

The National Remote Sensing Centre has a major role in developing the market for Earth observation data, an area in which other British firms—notably Logica, Vega, Science Systems and Cray—have major interests. SERCO is Europe's biggest supplier of technical services in space.

GEC-Marconi produces inertial guidance systems as well as electronics components; Pilkington dominates the world market in solar array cover glasses.

Food and Drink

Britain has a large food and drink manufacturing industry, which has accounted for a growing proportion of total domestic food supply in recent decades. In the last few years, it has increased productivity and undergone restructuring, partly in order to take advantage of the single European market. Approximately 450,000 people are employed in the industry.

Frozen foods and chilled convenience foods, such as ready-prepared meals, salads and pasta, together with yogurts, dairy desserts and 'instant snacks', have formed some of the fastest-growing sectors of the food market in recent years. Companies have introduced new low-fat and fat-free products such as spreads and ice creams to meet growing consumer demand. There has also been a rise in sales of products for vegetarians.

Around one-half of liquid milk in Britain is distributed through a doorstep delivery system employing about 28,500 people; the proportion is, however, declining. Household milk consumption per head—2.1 litres (3.6 pints) a week—is among the highest in the world. Consumption of skimmed and semi-skimmed milk continues to rise as people seek to reduce the fat content in their diet.

Milk for manufacturing purposes goes principally into butter, cheese, condensed milk, dried whole and skimmed milk powder, cream and other products like yogurt. The British dairy industry accounted for 60 per cent of butter supplies to the domestic market in 1995 and 72 per cent of cheese supplies. Butter exports in 1995 were worth £117 million. The other main exports are skimmed milk powder and whole milk powder, valued at £233 million in total, and cheese at £140 million.

About three-quarters of bread is produced in large bakeries. Household expenditure on bread amounts to about £2,000 million a year. A significant increase in the varieties available, greater awareness of the nutritional value of bread and the growth of the sandwich market have helped stabilise consumption in the last few years. Sales of ready-made sandwiches are now an estimated £6,000 million a year. Exports of biscuits were valued at £370 million in 1995 and those of chocolate and sugar confectionery at £350 million.

Of major significance among the alcoholic drinks produced in Britain is Scotch whisky, which is one of Britain's top export earners. There are about 100 distilleries in Scotland. Each of these produces either malt whisky or grain whisky. The raw material of the former is malt (that is, malted barley) and the latter other grain mixed with malt. Most Scotch whisky consumed is a blend of malt and grain whisky. Examples of well known brands of such blended Scotch whisky are as J & B, Johnnie Walker, Famous Grouse, Bell's and Teacher's. Some 13,000 people work in the industry and a further 45,000 are employed in supplying ingredients and materials used by the industry. Almost 90 per cent of Scotch whisky production is exported, to over 200 countries. The value of whisky exports was £2,300 million in 1995, Europe taking 42 per cent and the United States 13 per cent by volume.

In 1995 purchases of beer in Britain amounted to £14,000 million, about 3 per cent of consumers' expenditure. The brewing industry has four major national brewery groups—Scottish Courage, Bass, Whitbread and Carlsberg-Tetley—and about 480 regional and local brewers. British malt, which is made almost entirely from home-grown barley, is used by brewers throughout the world. Demand for traditional cask-conditioned ales ('real ale') remains buoyant, while lager now accounts for just over half of all beer sales. In recent years there has been a shift towards stronger bottled beers, a significant proportion of which are imported.

Cider is made primarily in south-west England, Gloucestershire, Herefordshire and Worcestershire.

Some 420 vineyards and 120 wineries in Britain (mainly in southern England) produce an average of 1.8 million litres of wine a year, most of which is white wine. Quality is improving rapidly through use of the latest wine-making technology.

The soft drinks industry, which had a turnover of £2,300 million in 1994, produces carbonated drinks, concentrates, fruit juices, and natural mineral and bottled waters. A highly competitive industry, it is the fastest growing sector of the grocery trade, introducing many innovative products.

Tobacco

The British tobacco industry manufactures nearly all cigarettes and tobacco goods sold in Britain. Almost all domestic output is provided by three major manufacturers (Imperial Tobacco, Gallaher and Carreras Rothmans). The industry specialises in the production of high-quality cigarettes made from flue-cured tobacco and achieves significant exports. Europe, the Middle East and Africa are important markets.

Textiles and Clothing

These products make a substantial contribution to the British economy in terms of employment, exports and turnover. Together with the footwear and leather industries, they employ around 420,000 people. For textiles, there is a high degree of regional concentration, particularly in North West England, West Yorkshire (mainly wool), the East Midlands (knitwear), Scotland and Northern Ireland. The clothing industry is scattered throughout Britain, with significant concentrations in Manchester, Leicester and London. The principal products are spun yarns, woven and knitted fabrics, apparel, industrial and household textiles, and carpets based chiefly on wool, cotton and synthetic fibres. Exports of textiles, clothing and footwear totalled more than £6,000 million in 1995.

The textile and clothing industry has around 14,000 firms, comprising a few large multi-process companies and two of the world's largest firms—Coats Viyella and Courtaulds Textiles—as well as a large number of small and medium-sized firms.

The international Multi-Fibre Arrangement (MFA—see p. 179) has allowed a measure of restraint on imports into the European Union from low-cost countries; however, the MFA is being phased out over ten years to the year 2005. Increased investment in new machinery and greater attention to design, training and marketing have helped the industry to raise its competitiveness. New technologies, largely designed to improve response times and give greater flexibility in production, are being used throughout the industry.

Britain's wool textile industry is one of the most important in the world. West Yorkshire is the main producing area, but Scotland is also famous as a specialist producer of high-quality yarns and tweeds. Raw wool is scoured and cleaned in Britain in preparation for woollen and worsted spinning and weaving (worsted is fine wool fabric often used for making suits). British mills also process rare fibres such as cashmere and angora. Sales of the wool textile industry amounted to £1,200 million in 1995.

Low-cost competition has cut progressively into British markets for cotton and allied products. Production includes yarn and fabrics of cotton, synthetic fibres and cotton-synthetic mixes, with large-scale dyeing and printing of cotton and synthetic fibre fabric. The linen industry is centred in Northern Ireland.

The high quality and variety of design make Britain one of the world's leading producers of woven carpets. Over half the value of carpet and rug output is made up of tufted carpets. Woven carpets, mainly Axminster, account for most of the remaining sales. There is a higher wool content in woven types, although in these, too, considerable use is being made of synthetic fibres.

Industrial textiles account for an increasing proportion of textile industry output, covering products such as conveyor belting and geotextiles used in civil engineering. Many of these are non-woven. Synthetic polypropylene yarn is used in the manufacture of carpet backing and ropes, and woven into fabrics for a wide range of applications in the packaging, upholstery, building and motor vehicle industries.

The clothing industry is more labour intensive than textiles, with about 7,700 companies. While a broad range of clothing is imported from Europe and Asia, British industry supplies about one-half of domestic demand. Exports have risen since the British fashion designer industry regained prominence during the 1980s, and traditional British tailoring enables branded clothing companies such as Burberry's to compete successfully overseas. The hosiery and knitwear industry comprises about 1,500 companies, mainly in the East Midlands and Scotland.

Paper, Printing and Publishing

There are 108 paper and board mills employing 20,500 people. Among the largest British groups are Shotton, St Regis and Bridgewater. Production has been concentrated in large-scale units to enable the industry to compete more effectively within the single European market. Between 1985 and 1995 output increased by two-thirds. Over half the industry is made up of forestry product companies from Scandinavia, North America, Australia and elsewhere. There has been a significant trend towards waste-based packaging grades. Usage of recycled waste paper is increasing and research is helping to extend it. In 1995 the total amount of waste paper used in British newspapers accounted for four-fifths of newsprint produced. Waste paper provides over half of the industry's fibre needs.

Employment in the paper products, printing and publishing industries is 450,000. Much printing and publishing employment and output is in firms based in south-east England. Mergers have led to the formation of large groups in newspaper, magazine and book publishing. More than £2,800 million worth of books were sold in Britain in 1994. The book-publishing industry is a major exporter, selling one-third of production in overseas markets. Security printers (of, for example, banknotes and postage stamps) are also important exporters, the major company being De La Rue.

Construction

Annual output of the construction industry is around £50,000 million. Most construction work is done by private firms, 98 per cent of which employ fewer than 25 people. While only 84 out of a total of nearly 195,000 firms employ more than 600 people directly, these companies undertake about 20 per cent of all construction in Britain. Some larger firms own quarries and factories for materials manufacture, and sophisticated plant. Some undertake responsibility for all stages of projects from initial design to final construction.

Efficiency and productivity in construction have benefited from greater off-site fabrication of standardised components and from computerised techniques such as computer-aided design, computerised stock ordering and job costing, electronic load safety measures for cranes, and distance measuring equipment.

Building Materials and Products

A vast range of products is used in the construction process, from structural steel, glass and bricks to tiles and bathroom fittings. These materials are estimated to make up around 40 per cent of the value of construction output. In 1995 sales of construction materials were worth about £20,000 million, with exports amounting to £3,500 million.

Most crushed rock, sand and gravel that is quarried by the aggregates industry is used in construction. The brick industry, one of Britain's oldest, is regarded as the world's most technically advanced. Portland cement, a 19th-century British innovation, is the most widely used chemical compound in the world.

Britain is also a world leader in the manufacture of glass used in windows, doors and cladding. Pilkington developed the float process for manufacturing distortion-free flat glass (see p. 245), which is licensed throughout the world. Substantially more energy-efficient, flat glass is used to allow more light into buildings and to provide insulation against heat loss in winter. The manufacture and supply of windows and doors is carried out by a large number of companies operating in one of three product sectors—timber, metal (aluminium and steel) and UPVC.

Project Procurement, Management and Financing

The most common basis of procurement for construction projects is a lump–sum contract with provision for variation. The largest projects are often carried out under the direction of construction managers or management contractors. Clients generally employ architects, project managers or civil engineers to advise on the feasibility of projects, draw up plans, and inspect and supervise the construction work.

Private and public sector projects are managed in a variety of ways. Most clients invite construction firms to bid for work by competitive tender, having used the design services of a consultant. The successful contractor will then undertake on-site work with a number of specialist sub-contractors. Alternative methods of contracting are becoming more common: for example, contracts might include subsequent provision of building maintenance or a comprehensive 'design-and-build' service, where a single

THE ENVIRONMENT

Reducing Pollution

The Institute of Arable Crops Research, Bristol, has found that using less intensive, more sustainable, systems of production can mean less reliance on agrochemicals. This reduces environmental risk, while maintaining profitable production.

The Coal Clough Wind Farm, near Burnley, Lancashire, has 24 turbines with a capacity of 9.6 megawatts, and serves about 7,500 homes. It saves 36,000 tons of carbon dioxide emissions and 165 tons of sulphur dioxide emissions each year.

The Individual and the Environment

Children at St. Edward's R.C. Primary School learn about recycling under Westminster City Council's Recycling Initiative.

As awareness of air pollution from motor vehicle traffic increases, use of the bicycle is again being encouraged. The aerobike, pictured here, has been designed to be fast and manoeuvrable, with air suspension to give a smoother ride.

The photovoltaic roof of this house in Oxford uses the sun's energy to generate enough electricity to heat the house, provide hot water and power the owner's electric car. There is even a surplus to sell to the National Grid.

The Henry Doubleday Research Organisation's organic allotment in Yalding, Kent, where the wisdom of gardeners from past centuries is combined with present-day scientific knowledge to produce organic vegetables, fruit and flowers.

Campaigns and Conferences

The closing ceremony of the first International Children's Conference on the Environment. Held in Eastbourne, East Sussex, the event was attended by 800 children from all over the world. Here Britain's Environment Secretary, John Gummer, helps to cut a special cake to mark the event.

Environmental pressure group Greenpeace patrols sensitive areas of the North Sea in its campaign for the regulation of industrial fishing.

Industry

Garden benches made from Durawood, a product made by British company Save Wood Products from polystyrene packaging waste. It reproduces the aesthetic and physical properties of wood and yet retains the benefits of plastic, needing no protective treatment.

The world's biggest flue gas desulphurisation plant—and Britain's single largest environmental project—at Drax Power Station, Yorkshire. The process removes more than 90 per cent of sulphur dioxide from the Drax chimney gases.

Conservation of Wildlife and the Countryside

Limestone pavements like Scar Close, North Yorkshire, are of geological and biological significance. The most important limestone pavements have been designated Sites of Special Scientific Interest (SSSIs), and additional measures are being taken to protect them under the EC Habitats Directive.

Measures are being taken under the Government's Biodiversity Action Plan to halt the decline of the yellow marsh saxifrage, threatened throughout much of Europe.

A Site of Special Scientific Interest within Exmoor National Park, Devon. Designation as an SSSI helps to protect this site.

Britain has a worldwide reputation for the conservation and breeding of endangered species, such as these snow leopard cubs. Born and reared at Marwell Zoological Park, Hampshire, their natural habitat is the mountains of central Asia.

Salmon eggs have been planted in specially cleaned areas of certain river beds by the former National Rivers Authority to help safeguard salmon stocks, which have fallen to very low levels in some areas of England.

Grey seals on Skomer Island Nature Reserve, off the coast of Pembrokeshire, Wales.

The Built Environment

Conservation work at Brodie Castle, Nairn, Scotland; the original structure dates back to the 15th and 16th centuries.

The Craft Village in Derry, Northern Ireland, contributes to the city's regeneration. Projects undertaken by Derry's Inner City Trust and the North West Centre for Learning and Development have helped to rebuild the city centre following years of political unrest.

company accepts responsibility for every stage of a project.

> Under the Government's Private Finance Initiative (see p. 162), private sector companies have become more heavily involved in constructing large-scale public infrastructure projects, including the new Ashford International Passenger Station and the Heathrow Express line presently under construction. The Channel Tunnel Rail Link (CTRL) and the Thameslink 2000 railway will also be built by a private sector concerns. The CTRL will be a 110-km (68-mile) high-speed railway costing about £3,000 million; the £650 million Thameslink 2000 scheme will extend services between north and south London through the City. The Government has also approved schemes for 80 'DBFO' ('Design, Build, Finance and Operate') road contracts.

The Government provides substantial work for the construction industry. Recently, several projects have been built and paid for by private consortia, which then charge the public for their use for a fixed period of time before transferring ownership back to the public sector; these are known as 'BOOT' ('Build, Own, Operate and Transfer') schemes. Two examples are the toll bridge over the River Thames at Dartford, Kent, and the second River Severn toll bridge, which opened in June 1996 (see p. 305).

Major Construction Projects in Britain

The most important recent construction project is the Channel Tunnel, the largest single civil engineering project ever undertaken in Europe (see p. 311). Completed in 1993, its estimated cost was £10,000 million. Building work was carried out by a consortium of ten French and British contractors working together as Transmanche Link (TML). The tunnel is nearly 50 km (31 miles) long and is 70 m (230 ft) below sea level at its deepest.

Associated projects included new international stations at Waterloo in London and Ashford, Kent, and an international terminal at Folkestone.

Other major building projects in hand or recently completed are the M25 motorway widening scheme, the M74 in Scotland, the A50/A564 in Derbyshire, the extensive development in London's Docklands, and the Sizewell B nuclear power station in Suffolk. Both Stansted and Manchester airports have been substantially redeveloped. There has also been large-scale redevelopment of sports stadiums, including Twickenham and Murrayfield (in Edinburgh) rugby grounds, and Manchester United and Arsenal football grounds. A new £16 million football stadium has been built to house Middlesbrough football club. Major redevelopment work is taking place at the Wimbledon lawn tennis complex.

Housing

During 1995 construction of 170,000 dwellings was started in Great Britain. Starts by private enterprise were 136,000, by housing associations 33,000 and in the public sector 1,100. Around 188,000 dwellings were completed: 148,000 by the private sector, 38,000 by housing associations and 2,000 by the public sector. The total value of new housing orders was over £5,600 million.

Building Regulations

The Department of the Environment's building regulations prescribe minimum standards of construction in England and Wales. Administered and enforced by local government, the regulations apply to new building, the installation or replacement of fittings, alterations and extensions to existing buildings, and certain changes of use of existing buildings. Similar controls apply in Scotland and Northern Ireland. An alternative to local authority building control involves private certification of compliance with building regulations. The British Standards Institution is providing much of Britain's contribution to the drafting of European standards, which are increasingly replacing national construction standards.

Research and Advisory Services

The Building Research Establishment, a government executive agency which is to be privatised in 1997, provides advice and research services to Government and industry on the design, construction and performance of buildings, together with the health and safety of people in and around buildings. Its areas of expertise include prevention and control of fires and protection of the environment. It actively supports the development of European codes and standards, and has strong links with a variety of international organisations. Major construction and materials firms, universities, colleges and research associations, as well as the British Board of Agrément, carry out research and provide advisory services. The Building Centre supplies exhibition and information services on materials, products, techniques and building services.

Overseas Contracting and Consultancy

British companies are engaged in many major projects throughout the world and have been in the forefront of management contracting and of 'design and construct' operations. They are increasingly engaged in developing privately financed projects. Contractors and consultants undertake the supervision and all or part of the construction of a project. Consultants are engaged in the planning, design and supervision of construction projects. British companies have a reputation for integrity and independence.

British contractors are currently active in over 100 countries, and have a permanent presence in 98 of them. In 1995 they secured new international business valued at £5,500 million, 45 per cent more than in 1994, with the main increases reported in Europe and Asia; about 35 per cent of all new contracts came from North America. Important international contracts won in 1995–96 included:

- various joint ventures connected with the new Hong Kong airport—landslide infrastructure, an air cargo complex and bridges;
- an office complex and shopping mall in Accra, Ghana;
- a joint venture in connection with the Oresund Crossing between Sweden and Denmark;
- a new headquarters building for the National Bank of Bahrain; and
- Phase 2 of the Ashgabat airport, Turkmenistan.

British engineering consultants are engaged in projects in 140 countries, having offices in most of those countries. In 1995 members of the Association of Consulting Engineers were engaged in new work overseas valued at £28,100 million. The capital value of projects under way at the end of 1995 was £82,000 million. British consulting engineers had estimated gross earnings in 1995 of £730 million from overseas commissions. The three largest categories of work covered roads, bridges and tunnels; thermal power stations; and water supply. The largest markets were the Far East, Africa, India and the Middle East. Major international projects include:

- airports in Israel and Hong Kong;
- land planning and development in the People's Republic of China;
- railways in Thailand and Malaysia;
- water works in Turkey; and
- harbours in Russia.

Further Reading

Aerospace Industry. Aspects of Britain series, HMSO, 1993.

Overseas Trade. Aspects of Britain series, HMSO, 1994.

Telecommunications. Aspects of Britain series, HMSO, 1994.

17 Energy and Natural Resources

Energy Resources	259	Coal	269
Energy Policy	260	Electricity	269
Energy Consumption	260	New and Renewable Sources	
Energy Efficiency	261	of Energy	274
Oil and Gas Exploration		Non-energy Minerals	275
and Production	262	Water	278
Gas Supply Industry	268		

In 1995 offshore oil and gas production reached record levels. Cumulative production of oil (1,835 million tonnes since 1975) is about one-fifth of maximum estimated recoverable reserves. Coal output from deep mines increased by 10 per cent. Parts of the nuclear electricity supply industry have been privatised.

Energy production directly employs about 200,000 people—5 per cent of industrial employees. The energy sector accounts for 5 per cent of gross domestic product (GDP), 8 per cent of total investment, 30 per cent of industrial investment, and 6 per cent of all expenditure by the production industries on research and development. It also includes three of Britain's 15 largest companies, both for profitability and for capital employed—Shell, BP and British Gas. Greater competition in energy markets has meant a continuing fall in real prices to virtually all consumers. The value of non-fuel minerals output exceeded £2,000 million in 1994. Water company investment of £400 million aims to ensure uninterrupted water supplies in 1996–97.

Energy Resources

Britain has the largest energy resources in the European Union (EU) and is a major world producer of oil and natural gas—known as primary sources. The other main primary sources are coal, nuclear power and some water power; secondary sources (derived from primary sources) are electricity, coke and smokeless fuels, and petroleum products.

In the early 1970s imports accounted for over 50 per cent of Britain's fuel consumption. In 1995, however, Britain was again a net exporter of fuels—40 million tonnes of oil equivalent—representing a surplus of £3,695 million, £514 million higher than in 1994.

Coal still supplies a significant proportion of the country's primary energy needs—23 per cent of total home consumption in 1995. Nuclear power provided about 27 per cent of electricity generated by the British electricity companies in 1995.

Ownership and Extraction

Gold, silver, oil, unworked coal and natural gas in Great Britain are owned by the Crown. Other minerals are mainly privately owned. Ownership of minerals normally belongs to the owner of the land surface, but not always in areas with a long history of mining. Mining and quarrying are usually carried out by privately owned companies.

In Northern Ireland the Crown owns gold and silver, while rights to exploit petroleum and other minerals (except 'common substances', such as sand and gravel, and crushed rock) are vested in the Department of Economic Development. On the United Kingdom Continental Shelf (UKCS; see map, p. 263) the right to work all minerals except coal is vested in the Crown. The Coal Authority owns almost all the unworked coal in Great Britain and has exclusive rights to work coal, or license others to do so, both on land and under the sea.

ENERGY POLICY

The Government's energy policy aims to ensure secure, diverse and sustainable supplies of energy in the forms that people and businesses want, and at competitive prices. Health, safety and environmental policies, as well as EU and other international commitments, have also to be borne in mind.

Key objectives are to:

- encourage competition among producers and choice for consumers, with a legal and regulatory framework to enable markets to work well;

- ensure service in a commercial environment, with customers paying the full cost of energy resources they consume;

- privatise state-owned industries where possible;

- take care that the energy sector does not have an adverse impact on the environment; and

- promote energy efficiency and renewable sources.

The independent regulators (see pp. 269 and 271) encourage the development of competition and protect the interests of consumers by administering price controls and enforcing standards of service in remaining areas of monopoly.

International Developments

Britain's membership of the EU and of the International Energy Agency (IEA: an autonomous part of the Organisation for Economic Co-operation and Development, with 23 member countries) enables it to collaborate on international energy matters. The EU's Energy Policy White Paper, published at the end of 1995, stresses competitiveness, security of supply, the environment, and particularly the need for market integration—beyond the completion of the internal market in electricity and gas.

Energy Report

The Government's third annual Energy Report, published (in two volumes) for the Department of Trade and Industry (DTI) in April–May 1996, is an essential source of information about Britain's energy industries. Volume 1 surveys the year's progress in all of them and describes, for example, further changes in the structure and ownership of the energy sector, and Britain's export potential in energy-related equipment. Volume 2 is a detailed survey of UKCS oil and gas resources in 1995, and includes outline reviews of each offshore and onshore oil and gas field.

The independent Energy Advisory Panel has assisted in the report's preparation.

ENERGY CONSUMPTION

During 1984–95, when Britain's GDP rose by about 30 per cent, final energy consumption on an 'energy supplied' basis increased by only 11 per cent. Since 1970, despite a 65 per cent rise in GDP, primary energy consumption has remained fairly constant, although, after temperature correction, it has risen for the last four years in succession. Energy consumption by final users in 1995 amounted to 150.9

Table 17.1: Inland Energy Consumption (in terms of primary sources)[a]

Million tonnes oil equivalent

	1985	1991	1992	1993	1994	1995
Oil	73.5	77.8	78.3	78.9	78.0	76.2
Coal	64.8	67.6	63.6	55.6	52.2	49.8
Natural Gas	51.8	54.1	55.0	62.6	64.8	70.0
Nuclear Energy	16.5	17.4	18.5	21.5	21.2	21.4
Hydro-electric power	0.4	0.4	0.5	0.4	0.5	0.5
Net imports of electricity	–	1.4	1.4	1.4	1.5	1.4
Total	**207.0**	**218.7**	**217.2**	**220.4**	**218.2**	**219.3**

Source: Department of Trade and Industry
[a]Adjustments in the figures for recent years are the result of methodological review.
Note: Differences between totals and the sums of their component parts are due to rounding.

million tonnes of oil equivalent[1] on an 'energy supplied' basis, of which transport consumed 34 per cent, industrial users 24 per cent, domestic users 28 per cent, and commerce, agriculture and public services 14 per cent. Warmer weather in 1995 helped bring final consumption as a whole down by 0.5 per cent from the 1994 figure.

ENERGY EFFICIENCY

In 1994 energy consumption in Britain's housing, offices and industrial buildings was worth about £17,500 million. The Environmental and Energy Management Directorate (EEMD) of the Department of the Environment estimates that 20 per cent—or £3,500 million—could be saved through investment in cost-effective energy efficiency measures. Such improvements offer a fast means of reducing carbon dioxide (CO_2) emissions. The EEMD encourages investment in these improvements through various programmes (see below). Its budget for 1996–97 has been increased to £131 million.

The Energy Efficiency Best Practice programme prepares and promotes authoritative information, guides and case studies on energy efficiency techniques and technologies in industry and buildings. The programme has an overall target of stimulating annual energy savings worth £800 million by the year 2000.

Combined Heat and Power

Combined Heat and Power (CHP) is the simultaneous generation of electricity and usable heat from the same plant. It harnesses the heat usually discarded during power generation. CHP can increase overall efficiency to as much as 70–90 per cent, compared with 30–50 per cent for conventional electricity generation. This also benefits the environment by reducing emissions of greenhouse gases. In summer 1996 total installed capacity of CHP in Britain was approximately 3,500 megawatts (MW)—about 5 per cent of Britain's generating capacity—on nearly 1,300 sites, with another 200 MW in construction or committed.[2]

Environmental and Energy Management Schemes

The Home Energy Efficiency Scheme is the Government's major domestic energy efficiency programme. It offers grants for loft insulation, tank and pipe lagging, draught-proofing, and energy advice to the neediest and most vulnerable households. Almost 2 million homes have been insulated since the scheme started in January 1991.

Since 1 April 1996 householders aged over 60 who qualify only on grounds of age (that is, they do not receive a qualifying benefit) have been asked to pay a contribution towards the cost of work carried out in their homes. This

[1]1 tonne of oil equivalent = 41.868 gigajoules.

[2]1 MW = 1,000 kilowatts (kW).

will help maintain the level of assistance given to low-income and disabled householders while saving some £31 million on the cost of the scheme. About 642,000 grants were paid in 1995–96.

The Small Company Environmental and Energy Management Assistance Scheme (SCEEMAS) meets up to 50 per cent of consultancy costs when small manufacturing businesses (less than 250 employees) set up an environmental management system, which has been validated by an external verifier, in support of the EU Eco-Management and Audit Scheme (see p. 252) in Britain.

The Energy Design Advice Scheme, funded by the DTI, makes low-energy building design expertise more accessible for all those working on the design of new and restored buildings.

> About 90 per cent of signatories to the EEMD's Making a Corporate Commitment campaign, which underlines good energy management on business premises, planned further investment in 1996. Over 1,900 organisations have joined the campaign.

Publicity campaigns (the latest being 'Wasting Energy Costs the Earth'), which include extensive media coverage, tell householders how they can combat global warming by improving the energy efficiency of their homes. Light-bulbs which carry EU ecolabels and produce a threefold (and more) reduction in total ecosystem mercury are one way of doing this.

Every new home in England and Wales now carries the Standard Assessment Procedure (SAP) for home energy rating, which demonstrates energy efficiency and impact on the environment.

The Energy Saving Trust is an independent organisation which aims to stimulate investment in energy efficiency and the development of appropriate goods and services. Its new £3 million campaign shows energy saving in a fashionable light. Government funding is £50 million in 1996–99.

OIL AND GAS EXPLORATION AND PRODUCTION

For centuries small quantities of oil have been produced in mainland Britain. The first onshore oil, in the 1820s, came from the Tar Tunnel at Ironbridge (Shropshire). Production, mostly from Lanarkshire shales, reached 3.25 million tonnes in 1913. The first onshore production well was at Hardstoft (Derbyshire) after the First World War. Some 250 onshore wells came into operation in 1939–40, though by the early 1960s they were producing only 150,000 tonnes a year—about 0.3 per cent of refinery output. Britain was almost wholly dependent for its oil supplies on imports. However, the first notable offshore discovery of oil in the UKCS (the Arbroath field) was made in 1969 and the first oil brought ashore, from the Argyll field, in 1975. In 1995, output of crude oil and natural gas liquids (NGLs) in Britain averaged 2.70 million barrels (about 357,000 tonnes) a day, making Britain the world's ninth largest producer.

Structure of the Industry

Exploration and production are carried out under licence by the private sector. The two leading British oil companies are British Petroleum (BP) and Shell Transport and Trading, which has a 40 per cent interest in the Royal Dutch/Shell Group of Companies. BP and Shell retain their position as the two largest industrial companies in Britain in terms of turnover.

The Government's main sources of revenue from oil and gas activities are Petroleum Revenue Tax, which was levied on all fields approved between 1975 and March 1993; Corporation Tax, which is charged on the profits of oil and gas companies in much the same way as any other industry and is the only tax on profits of fields approved after March 1993; and royalty, which applies only to fields approved before April 1982.

Economic and Industrial Aspects

In 1995 UKCS oil and gas production accounted for some 2 per cent of Britain's

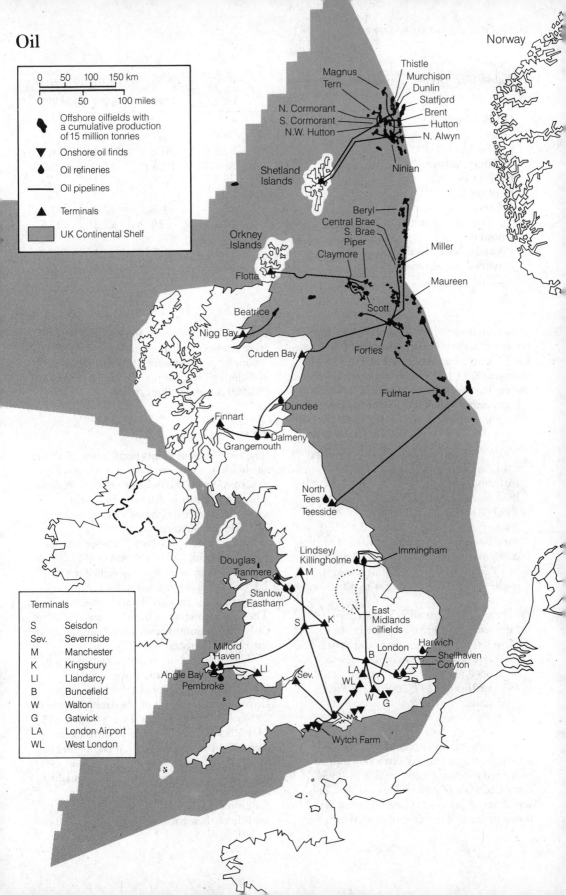

Oil

Norway

Scale:
0 50 100 150 km
0 50 100 miles

- Offshore oilfields with a cumulative production of 15 million tonnes
- ▼ Onshore oil finds
- ♦ Oil refineries
- Oil pipelines
- ▲ Terminals
- UK Continental Shelf

Terminals

S	Seisdon
Sev.	Severnside
M	Manchester
K	Kingsbury
Ll	Llandarcy
B	Buncefield
W	Walton
G	Gatwick
LA	London Airport
WL	West London

Magnus
Tern
Thistle
Murchison
Dunlin
Statfjord
N. Cormorant
S. Cormorant
N.W. Hutton
Brent
Hutton
N. Alwyn
Ninian

Shetland Islands

Beryl
Central Brae
S. Brae
Piper
Claymore
Miller
Maureen

Orkney Islands

Flotta

Beatrice
Nigg Bay
Cruden Bay

Scott
Forties
Fulmar

Finnart
Dundee
Dalmeny
Grangemouth

North Tees
Teesside

Douglas
Tranmere
Lindsey/Killingholme
Immingham
M

Stanlow
Eastham
East Midlands oilfields

S
K

Milford Haven
Harwich
London
Shellhaven
Coryton
Angle Bay
Pembroke
Ll
B
Sev.
LA
WL
W
G

Wytch Farm

Table 17.2: Oil Statistics					*Million tonnes*
	1985	**1992**	**1993**	**1994**	**1995**
Oil Production					
land	0.4	4.0	3.7	4.6	5.1
offshore	127.2	85.2	90.2	114.4	116.7
Refinery output	72.9	85.8	89.6	86.6	86.1
Deliveries	69.8	75.5	75.8	75	74
Exports					
Crude, NGL, feedstock	83	57.9	64.3	82.4	82.6
refined petroleum	14.8	20.3	23	22.2	21.6
Imports					
Crude, NGL, feedstock	35.6	57.7	61.7	53.1	48.7
refined petroleum	13.1	10.6	10.1	10.4	9.9

Source: Department of Trade and Industry

gross national product. Total revenues from the sale of oil and gas produced from the UKCS in 1995 are estimated at £10,550 million and £4,160 million respectively. Taxes and royalty receipts attributable to UKCS oil and gas came to about £2,350 million in 1995–96.

> Since 1965 the industry has generated trading profits of some £175,000 million, of which £64,000 million have been reinvested in the industry, £79,000 million paid to the Exchequer, and £33,000 million left for disposal by the companies. Total company income was £18,000 million in 1995, including £4,000 million, its highest ever, from the gas production sector.
>
> Proceeds from the sale of oil in 1995 were up 11 per cent on 1994; those from the sale of gas were up 8 per cent. Total value of oil and gas produced onshore is estimated at £490 million in 1995, compared with £385 million in 1994.

Gross capital investment from British sources in the oil and gas extraction industry recovered to some £4,200 million in 1995, compared with £3,500 million in 1994. This was about 18 per cent of British industrial investment and 4 per cent of gross domestic fixed capital formation. Some 29,000 people were employed offshore in September 1995, of whom 93 per cent were British nationals. In addition, oil and gas provide employment for 270,000 in support industries.

Licensing

The Government grants licences which allow the holders to explore for and produce oil and gas from specific offshore or onshore areas. In addition to awarding these licences, the Government must approve all proposed wells and field development plans.

Since 1964, 16 offshore licensing rounds have been held, and by the end of 1995, 5,848 wells had been or were being drilled in the UKCS: 1,878 exploration wells, 1,131 appraisal wells and 2,839 development wells. The record number of licences awarded in the early 1990s confirms companies' confidence in the British industry.

The 16th offshore round, which closed in March 1995, invited applications for 164 blocks in lightly explored areas around the British coast and West of Shetland. Awards for 26 blocks West of Shetland were made on 18 May 1995 and for 53 blocks in the remaining areas on 4 July, bringing the total number of blocks licensed in the round to 79. Some of these blocks are in environmentally sensitive areas; the licences are subject to strict conditions to ensure no adverse effects on wildlife or their habitats. A further 275 blocks have been offered for licence in the 17th offshore round, which closes in November 1996. These are in frontier areas, such as west of the Hebrides and the South West Approaches, and again will be subject to conditions designed to protect the environment.

Britain's largest onshore oilfield, at Wytch Farm (Dorset), produced 90 per cent of the total of just over 5 million tonnes of crude oils and NGLs originating onshore in 1995, up 8.5 per cent on 1994. In addition to minor production from various mining licensees, there are 19 other onshore fields in Lincolnshire, Nottinghamshire and Leicestershire. At the end of 1995, 149 landward licences were in force, covering an area of 20,078 sq km (7,752 sq miles). A further 22 licences were awarded in March 1996 under the seventh onshore licensing round, which closed in November 1995.

North Sea Fields

There were 143 offshore fields producing at the end of March 1996 (72 oil, 62 gas and 9 condensate). Nearly all of the fields discovered in the North Sea during 1965–75 have been developed and expansion of more recent finds is also in progress. A total of 26 new offshore development projects (16 of them for oil) were approved during 1995.

The fields with the largest cumulative production totals are Forties, Brent, Ninian and Piper. Remaining recoverable reserves of UKCS oil in the 'proven' plus 'probable' categories amount to 3,285 million tonnes, while the total remaining potential of the UKCS could be in the range of 3,640 to 8,630 million tonnes on current estimates.

Offshore Gas

Public supply of manufactured gas in Britain began in the early 19th century in central London. Gas used to be produced from coal, but during the 1960s growing imports of oil made possible town gas from oil-based feedstocks. After the first commercial natural gas discovery in the West Sole field in 1965 and the start of its exploitation in 1967,

supplies of offshore natural gas grew rapidly and by 1977 natural gas had replaced town gas in the public supply system in Great Britain.

Natural gas accounts for 70.6 per cent of total inland primary fuel consumption in Britain. In 1995 indigenous production of natural gas amounted to 75,404 million cubic metres. This included 4,881 million cubic metres of gas used for drilling, production and piping operations on North Sea platforms and at terminals. Total availability of UKCS gas amounted to 75,081 million cubic metres. Just under 1,000 million cubic metres of UKCS gas were exported and about 1,500 million cubic metres were imported from Norway.

> Up to the end of 1995 some £16,300 million had been spent on developing natural gas resources on the UKCS and 1,106,743 million cubic metres had been produced. Britain is the world's fifth largest gas producer—after Russia, the United States, Canada and the Netherlands.

Production from the three most prolific of the 67 offshore gasfields—Leman, Indefatigable (South) and the Hewett area—has accounted for over half the total gas produced so far in the UKCS. Associated gas,[3] delivered to land via the Far North Liquids and Associated Gas System (FLAGS) and from the Scottish Area Gas Evacuation System (SAGE), makes additional significant contributions. The south basin fields and the South Morecambe field in the Irish Sea produce more gas in winter. Gas from the twin North Sean and South Sean fields augments supplies to meet peak demand on very cold days in winter.

The partially depleted Rough field is used as a major gas store. Gas is drawn from the national transmission system in summer and injected into the Rough reservoir for rapid recovery during peak winter periods.

Remaining recoverable gas reserves in present discoveries are estimated at between

---

[3]Mainly methane, produced and used on oil production platforms.

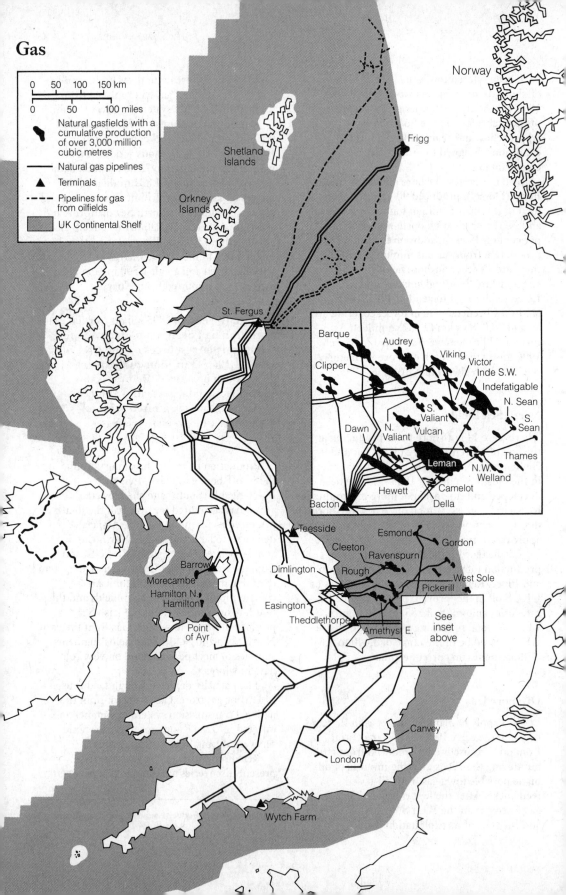

Gas

Natural gasfields with a cumulative production of over 3,000 million cubic metres

— Natural gas pipelines

▲ Terminals

- - - Pipelines for gas from oilfields

UK Continental Shelf

Scale: 0, 50, 100, 150 km; 0, 50, 100 miles

Norway

Frigg

Shetland Islands

Orkney Islands

St. Fergus

Inset:

Barque

Audrey

Viking

Victor

Inde S.W.

Clipper

Indefatigable

N. Sean

S. Sean

Dawn

N. Valiant

S. Valiant

Vulcan

Leman

Thames

N.W. Welland

Hewett

Camelot

Della

Bacton

Main map:

Teesside

Barrow

Morecambe

Hamilton N.

Hamilton

Point of Ayr

Dimlington

Cleeton

Rough

Ravenspurn

Esmond

Gordon

West Sole

Pickerill

Easington

Theddlethorpe

Amethyst E.

See inset above

Canvey

London

Wytch Farm

700,000 million and 1.92 million million cubic metres. If possible gas from existing discoveries and potential future discoveries are added, the remaining total reserves are estimated to be in the range of 1.233 million million to 3.7 million million cubic metres. Britain's offshore natural gas reserves are likely to meet most of home demand well into the next century.

Pipelines

Some 8,300 km (5,188 miles) of major submarine pipeline transports hydrocarbons from one field to another and to shore. Major crude oil onshore pipelines (from harbours, land terminals or offshore moorings to refineries) include those connecting Grangemouth to Finnart, Cruden Bay to Grangemouth, and Purbeck to Southampton. Onshore pipelines also carry refined products to major marketing areas; for example, a 423-km (263-mile) pipeline runs from Milford Haven to the Midlands and Manchester, while similar pipelines run from Fawley to Wolverhampton and from Lindsey to north London. Chemical pipelines include one from Mossmorran to Grangemouth and another (405 km; 252 miles) from Grangemouth to Stanlow.

Five pipeline terminals on the North Sea coast—Bacton (Norfolk), Theddlethorpe (Lincolnshire), Easington and Dimlington (Yorkshire) and St Fergus (Grampian), and one in Barrow in Furness (Cumbria)—supply a national and regional high- and low-pressure pipeline system some 267,300 km (167,060 miles) long, which transports natural gas around Great Britain. A pipeline taking natural gas from Scotland to Northern Ireland carried its first gas in autumn 1996. Other recently built onshore natural gas pipelines run by independent operators run from Horndon to Barking (Essex), and Point of Ayr to Connah's Quay (Clwyd).

The national and regional pipeline network is owned by TransCo, the transportation and storage business of the privatised British Gas. A network code between British Gas and its competitors allows open access to the national network of gas pipelines and storage systems.

Decommissioning

The Petroleum Act 1987 provides for the decommissioning of redundant offshore oil and gas installations and pipelines on the UKCS. Government consent is required and each application is examined on an individual basis. Although sea disposal is consistent with Britain's international obligations, abandonment of the Brent Spar storage and loading buoy was postponed in summer 1995 while Shell assessed alternative solutions. The Government has appointed an independent and international group of experts to examine the scientific evidence on deep-sea disposal, with special reference to the Brent Spar.

Offshore Safety

Offshore health and safety are the responsibility of the Health and Safety Executive (HSE; see p. 201). Government funding for the HSE's Offshore Safety Division reached £23 million in 1995–96.

Offshore Supplies

The Oil, Gas and Petrochemicals Supplies Office (OSO) of the DTI assists British companies in supplying goods and services to oil and gas projects, including petrochemicals, in a world market worth over £210,000 million. It helps, for example, to develop new technologies through R&D, and advises companies taking part in promotional events, such as ministerial visits, missions, exhibitions and conferences.

The IEA's latest forecasts attribute most of the recent rise in North Sea output to new medium-size fields coming on stream, a process made possible by the British industry's Cost Reduction in the New Era initiative, which has led to substantial falls in project costs.

Research

The DTI's oil and gas division funds an improved oil recovery programme and a reservoir programme. These provide technical support and expertise to ensure maximum recovery of hydrocarbons from British fields, for example, by achieving economic production of viscous crude oil.

The DTI also takes part in R&D clubs. These have undertaken work on horizontal and multilateral wells, gas condensate reservoir management, and fluid behaviour, at universities such as Heriot-Watt, Exeter, and Liverpool, and at Imperial College London.

Oil Consumption

Deliveries of petroleum products for inland consumption (excluding refinery consumption) in 1995 included just under 22 million tonnes of motor spirit, 13.4 million tonnes of DERV fuel, 7.7 million tonnes of aviation turbine fuel, 7.2 million tonnes of gas oil and 8 million tonnes of fuel oils.

Gas Consumption

Demand for gas has risen markedly since 1991. In 1993 consumption grew by 12 per cent, with a further 6 per cent each in 1994 and 1995. Sales of natural gas in Britain totalled 804 terawatt[4] hours (TWh) in 1995. About 35 per cent (282 TWh) of this is for industrial and commercial purposes (172 TWh and 110 TWh respectively); 326 TWh were sold to domestic users.

Industrial gas prices have fallen by 48 per cent in real terms since privatisation in 1986, and domestic prices by 24 per cent. Natural gas accounted for about a third of final consumption of energy in 1995.

Oil Refineries

In 1995 Britain's 14 refineries processed 92.7 million tonnes of crude and process oils (a fraction down on 1994). About 80 per cent of output (by weight) is in the form of lighter, higher-value products such as gasoline, DERV and jet kerosene. By comparison, the proportion of Western European refinery output accounted for by these higher-value products (including orimulsion) is about 70 per cent.

---

[4] 1 TW = 1,000 gigawatts. 1 GW = 1,000 MW.

Trade

In 1995, Britain's refinery sector exported 26.2 million tonnes of refined petroleum products and NGLs (separated at North Sea terminals), 30 per cent of its output (worth £1,133 million to the balance of payments). Virtually all exports went to Britain's partners in the EU and the IEA, the largest markets being France, the Irish Republic, Italy, the Netherlands and Germany, and, outside the EU, the United States.

GAS SUPPLY INDUSTRY

Structure of the Industry

The Government has progressively introduced competition in gas supply since 1986 and there is now an open supply market above the 2,500-therm threshold, with all companies using British Gas's pipeline network.

The Gas Act 1995 creates a new regulatory framework extending competition to residential consumers throughout Great Britain. This is to take place in three stages:

● From 1996 in south-west England, in an area covering 500,000 consumers;

● From 1997 in south-east England, enlarging the market to 2 million; and

● From 1998 throughout England and Scotland to 18 million consumers.

Three separate classes of licence will be issued to:

● *Public Gas Transporters* (PGTs), firms operating a pipeline system and contracting with gas shippers to transport gas;

● *Gas Shippers*, who arrange with a PGT for gas to be conveyed through its pipeline system; and

● *Gas Suppliers*, companies which sell gas to consumers and are also the consumers' point of contact.

The Network Code (see above) defines the rights and responsibilities of all users of the gas transportation system. The Gas Act 1995 required British Gas to separate its activities between the parent and a subsidiary company, British Gas Trading Ltd, because the same corporate entity is not permitted to hold both a PGT licence and a supplier's licence. British Gas has announced plans to take the company separation further and demerge, in 1997, into two separately listed companies: British Gas Energy and TransCo International.

Competition

Some ten suppliers (including British Gas) competed at the launch of the pilot project in south-west England at the end of April 1996. New suppliers have been offering price savings of 15 per cent and above over British Gas's tariffs. At the end of 1995 British Gas's share of the commercial and industrial markets in Britain was some 35 per cent.

An excess of supply over demand in 1995 (a 'gas bubble') has depressed the spot price of gas below levels previously considered possible. British Gas and other competitors are now contracted to buy gas at prices substantially above the present market level. British Gas has been discussing a possible renegotiation of contracts with producers.

In May 1996 the Office of Gas Supply (Ofgas) published its initial proposals for the TransCo price review, which would lead to a significant reduction in TransCo's prices and in consumers' bills. Ofgas announced its final plans in August.

COAL

The size of the British coal industry has reduced drastically since the 1960s. Yet coal mining in Britain can be traced back to Roman times. Taxes raised on its sale helped pay for rebuilding London, and St Paul's Cathedral, after the Great Fire of 1666. Coal played a crucial part in the industrial revolution of the 18th and 19th centuries. In its peak year, 1913, the industry produced 292 million tonnes of coal, exported 74 million tonnes and employed over a million workers. In 1947 (when 200 million tonnes were produced) the coal mines passed into public ownership, and the National Coal Board (now British Coal) was set up.[5] In

1955 there were 850 British Coal collieries in operation. Its mining activities were privatised at the end of 1994. At the end of 1995, 32 large deep mines were operating in the private sector, employing about 13,500 mineworkers.

Coal Authority

Set up under the Coal Industry Act 1994, the Coal Authority took over ownership of coal reserves from British Coal. It licenses coal-mining; holds, manages and disposes of interests in unworked coal and coal mines; provides information about mining plans and geological data; and deals with subsidence and damage claims in former mining areas.

Market for Coal

In 1995 inland consumption of coal was 77 million tonnes, of which about 78 per cent was by electricity generators, 11 per cent by coke ovens and 3.7 per cent by domestic users. Exports were 0.9 million tonnes, while imports amounted to 15.9 million tonnes.

Production

Total production from deep mines rose from 31.9 million tonnes in 1994 to 35.1 million tonnes in 1995, thus reversing the decline of deep-mine production.

At the end of 1995, 91 opencast sites were in operation. Total opencast output fell from 16.8 million tonnes in 1994 to 16.4 million in 1995.

Coal Research

The Government aims to secure a strong industrial base to commercialise clean coal technologies by encouraging collaboration between industry, universities and organisations overseas. It has allotted some £5.7 million to research in 1996–97.

ELECTRICITY

England and Wales

The main generating companies in England and Wales, National Power, PowerGen, and British Energy and Magnox Electric (see

---

[5]British Coal continues to have residual functions in 1996–97.

Electricity

Orkney Islands

Shetland Islands

0 20 40 60 80 100 120 km

0 20 40 60 80 miles

☐ Conventional power stations (220 MW and over) under construction

■ Conventional power stations (220 MW and over)

★ CCGT power stations (220 MW and over)

● Nuclear power stations

○ Under construction

◆ Power-producing reactors of the UKAEA or BNFL

★ Hydro-electric power stations (over 45 MW capacity)

▲ Pumped storage schemes

Dounreay ◆

Fasnakyle ★

▲ Foyers

Peterhead ■

Rannoch ★   Errochty ★
Cruachan ▲
Lochay ★   Clunie
Sloy ★

Kincardine
Longannet ■
Cockenzie ■   Torness ●
■ Inverkip
● Hunterston B

Chapelcross ◆

Coolkeeragh ■

Ballylumford ■
Kilroot ■

★ Galloway

Blyth A ■
Blyth B ■

Hartlepool ●

Calder Hall ◆
Roosecote ★   Teesside ★
Heysham II ●
Heysham I ●

Ferrybridge C ■   Drax ■
Deeside ★   Fiddler's   Eggborough ■   Brigg ■   Killingholme
Wylfa ●   Ferry   Keadby ■★   PowerGen ★
Dinorwig ▲   Cottam ■   Killingholme ★
Connah's   Ince ■   West Burton ■   ☐ Humber ★
Quay ★   Spondon   High Marnham ■
Ffestiniog ▲   Ratcliffe-on-Soar ■   Peterborough ★
Rheidol ★   Corby ★   ☐ King's Lynn ★
Rugeley B ■   Willington B ■   Sizewell
Drakelow   Little Barford ★   ●
C   Rye House ★   Sizewell
Ironbridge ■   ●
Barking   Bradwell ●
Pembroke ■   Didcot B ★   Kingsnorth
Aberthaw ■   ☐ Didcot A   Tilbury ■   Grain ■
● Oldbury   Littlebrook   Medway ★
☐ Seabank ★
Hinkley Point A ●   Hinkley Point B ●   Dungeness A ●
Dungeness B ●

below), sell electricity to suppliers through a market known as the pool. The National Grid (NGC) owns and operates the transmission system, transferring electricity in bulk across the national grid.

Distribution—the transfer of electricity from the national grid to consumers via local networks—is carried out by the 12 regional electricity companies (RECs). Supply is the purchase of electricity from generators and its sale to customers. Until 1998 RECs have a monopoly of all franchise sales (to consumers taking 100 kW or less) in their regions. These RECs are known as first-tier suppliers. Above 100 kW the market is already open to competition, and consumers may have contracts with a second-tier supplier, who could be one of the generators, an REC from a different region, or an independent supplier.

With the expiry in March 1995 of the Government's special shares in the English and Welsh RECs, take-overs within the electricity market became possible. Ownership of seven of the 12 RECs has now changed. After the disposal of 6,000 MW of their coal-fired plant by National Power and PowerGen, Eastern Group is also a significant generator, with some 8 per cent of the market. In April 1996, however, the Government disallowed National Power's bid for Southern Electric and PowerGen's for Midlands Electricity on the grounds that they would be detrimental to competition, given the current state of the electricity market.

Scotland

ScottishPower plc and Scottish Hydro–Electric plc generate, transmit, distribute and supply electricity. They are also contracted to buy all the output from Scottish Nuclear Ltd.

Associated Functions

The Electricity Association is the main trade association for the electricity industry. It carries out certain service and co-ordinating functions for its members, which include the transmission, supply and main generator companies in Britain. Regulation of the industry is primarily the responsibility of the Office of Electricity Regulation, headed by the Director General of Electricity Supply (DGES), whose duties include the promotion of competition and the protection of consumer interests.

Northern Ireland

Responsibility for transmission, distribution and supply of electricity lies with Northern Ireland Electricity (NIE) plc, privatised in 1993. Three private companies generate electricity from four power stations. The largest power station, Ballylumford, is being converted from oil to gas firing and accounts for almost half Northern Ireland's generating capacity (2,243 MW). Regulation of the industry is the responsibility of the Office of Electricity Regulation (NI), headed by the DGES (NI).

Consumption

In 1995 sales of electricity through the distribution system in Britain amounted to 290.76 TWh. Domestic users took 35 per cent of the total, industry 33 per cent, and commercial and other users the remainder.

Generation

Since 1989, 15 new companies have entered electricity generation in Britain, bringing the total number in this field to 27.

According to the NGC's Seven Year Statement, National Power's 28 fossil-fuelled power stations, together with its five hydro schemes, generate about 35 per cent of the electricity supplied to the transmission and distribution networks in England and Wales. PowerGen's 17 fossil-fuelled power stations and other, renewable, schemes together generate about 26 per cent. The nuclear stations in Great Britain generate almost 27 per cent. The NGC's pumped-storage business, now known as First Hydro, has been sold to Mission Energy, subsidiary of a US electricity producer.

In 1995–96, 44 per cent of electricity generated in Scotland was produced by Scottish Nuclear's two stations. In addition to nuclear generation, Scotland's electricity needs are met from hydro, coal, and gas—a total

Table 17.3: Generation by and Capacity of Power Stations owned by the Major Power Producers in Britain.

	Electricity generated (GWh)			Per cent 1995	Output capacity (MW)
	1985	1990	1995[a]		
Nuclear plant	56,354	61,308	85,298	27	12,374
Other conventional steam plant	216,255	230,376	169,866	55	38,242
Gas turbines and oil engines	1,084	432	190	–	1,890
Pumped storage plant	2,831	1,982	1,552	1	2,788
Natural flow hydro-electric plant	3,447	4,393	4,096	1	13,919
CCGTs	–	–	48,720	16	9,216
Renewables other than hydro	–	4	570	–	71
Total	279,972	289,495	310,292	100	65,900
Electricity supplied (net)[a]	258,242	277,978	292,211	–	–

Source: Department of Trade and Industry

[a]Electricity generated less electricity used at power stations (both electricity used on works and that used for pumping at pumped-storage stations).

Note: Differences between totals and the sums of their component parts are due to rounding.

output capacity of approximately 9,700 MW. Scottish Nuclear sells 74.9 per cent of its output to ScottishPower and the rest to Hydro-Electric.

Non-nuclear power stations owned by Britain's major power producers consumed 50 million tonnes of oil equivalent in 1995, of which coal accounted for 70 per cent, natural gas 23 per cent and oil 6 per cent.

Other power producers, and an increasing number of small 'autogenerators' (who produce power for their own use), have equal access with the major generators to the grid transmission and local distribution systems.

In 1995 installation and commissioning of flue gas desulphurisation (FGD) equipment, to control acid emissions, were completed at PowerGen's 2 GW Ratcliffe station (Leicestershire). Early in 1996 all six generating units at National Power's Drax station (North Yorkshire) operated with FGD. A ten-year programme to control emissions of oxides of nitrogen (NO_x) through the installation of low-NO_x burners at 12 major power stations in England and Wales is in progress. ScottishPower is fitting low-NO_x burners at Longannet and Cockenzie.

Combined Cycle Gas Turbines

In 1995, CCGTs accounted for about 16 per cent of the electricity generated by major

power producers, compared with 8 per cent in 1993. This increase has been balanced by a fall in coal- and oil-fired generation.

CCGTs tend to be quicker and cheaper to build and operate than conventional plant, and the fuel efficiency of CCGT technology continues to improve. They use natural gas, at present a cheaper fuel, and give out almost no sulphur dioxide and some 55 per cent less CO_2 than coal-fired plant. In England and Wales, 16 such stations (total declared net capacity 9.05 GW) are generating electricity. About 5 GW of CCGT capacity is under construction. (Between the winters of 1994–95 and 1995–96 National Power and PowerGen mothballed 2.3 GW of coal- and oil-fired capacity.)

Exports

The NGC and Electricité de France run a 2,000-MW cross-Channel cable link, providing for the transmission of electricity between the two countries. The link has generally been used to supply baseload electricity—power that needs to be generated and available round the clock—from France to England. Imports met about 5 per cent of Britain's electricity needs in 1995.

Some of Scotland's capacity is exported to England and Wales. Transmission lines linking the Scottish and English grid systems enable cross-border trading. This interconnector's capacity is now 1,600 MW and there are plans to increase it to 2,200 MW in 1997. The Government will decide about a 250-MW undersea-cable interconnector between Scotland and Northern Ireland when it has considered the reports of two public inquiries.

Nuclear Power

After the Government's Nuclear Review in 1995, the nuclear industry in Britain was substantially restructured in preparation for privatisation in July 1996. Nuclear Electric and Scottish Nuclear became wholly owned subsidiaries of British Energy. Nuclear Electric operates the five Advanced Gas-cooled Reactor stations (AGRs) in England and Britain's first pressurised water reactor (PWR) at Sizewell (Suffolk). They have an aggregate capacity of 7,200 MW and in 1995–96 an output of over 43 TWh—equivalent to about 15 per cent of current sales demand in England and Wales. Scottish Nuclear operates two AGR stations with an aggregate capacity of about 2,400 MW and output of 17.6 TWh in 1995–96—about 55 per cent of Scottish electricity sales. A third nuclear generator, Magnox Electric, will remain in the public sector and own the older Magnox stations. Six of these are operational and three others have closed and are being decommissioned.

Factors influencing privatisation were: reduced uncertainties about the costs of managing spent nuclear fuel, waste, and decommissioning plant; considerably improved AGR performance; and the start of operations at Sizewell B PWR in January 1995. The review also concluded that while nuclear power has diversity of supply and environmental advantages, there is no wider economic case for funding new nuclear stations. British Energy will be responsible for the liabilities associated with its assets. Station decommissioning costs will be met through a segregated fund, with a £230 million initial endowment from the companies and further annual payments set independently.

The Government concluded that premium payments to Nuclear Electric under the non-fossil fuel levy should end on privatisation, except to allow Magnox Electric to collect sums due to it but unpaid before privatisation. This enabled the levy rate to reduce from 10 per cent to 3.7 per cent. The levy will continue to cover British Nuclear Fuels (BNFL) and renewables. It does not apply in Scotland, where, under the Nuclear Energy Agreement (NEA), ScottishPower and Hydro-Electric have contracted to take all of the electricity generated by Scottish Nuclear Ltd until 2005. With privatisation the premium element of the NEA has ceased. Scottish Nuclear's income under the NEA now depends on the market rate in England and Wales.

British Nuclear Fuels

BNFL, owned by the Government, provides nuclear fuel cycle services both in Britain and overseas. In 1995–96 BNFL sheared and dissolved over 200 tonnes of spent fuel at its thermal oxide reprocessing plant (THORP) at Sellafield (Cumbria). THORP's first ten years are fully committed, with orders from Britain and overseas. Some 40 per cent of the second ten years' capacity has also been sold. The Sellafield Mixed Oxide Fuel plant, due to become operational in late 1997, will blend plutonium recovered from reprocessing with uranium, to make mixed oxide fuel for use in reactors. A subsidiary company, BNFL Inc, continues to win contracts for restoring redundant facilities and dealing with radioactive material from the United States defence programme.

AEA Technology

AEA Technology plc is an international business which provides science and engineering services to the worldwide nuclear industry and to other industrial sectors. In 1994–95 its turnover was £257 million. The Government privatised AEA Technology plc in 1996.

United Kingdom Atomic Energy Authority

UKAEA is responsible for the safe and cost-effective maintenance and decommissioning of its redundant nuclear facilities used for Britain's nuclear R&D programme. UKAEA owns sites from

Caithness to Dorset and is also responsible for Britain's fusion programme (see below).

Nuclear Research

The Government plans to spend £14.6 million in 1996–97 on fusion research. About half of this is Britain's contribution to the EU Joint European Torus nuclear project at Culham (Oxfordshire). EU member states have agreed in principle to extend it to the end of 1999.

The DTI also funds assessments of advanced reactor safety and of international safety standards, and the transfer of technology to help improve nuclear safety in the former Soviet Union, and in central and eastern Europe.

Nuclear Safety

In Britain responsibility for ensuring the safety of nuclear installations falls to nuclear operators and is assured through a rigorous system of regulatory control enforced by the nuclear industry's independent regulator, the HSE's Nuclear Installations Inspectorate (NII).

Through the licensing regime, the NII has extensive powers to ensure that operators apply high standards of safety in the design, construction, operation and eventual decommissioning of nuclear installations. This includes constant monitoring and assessment of plant and the power to require improvements and ultimately to close an installation if not satisfied with its safety.

Monitoring ensures that any potential safety problems are avoided or dealt with at an early stage. In order to take account of privatisation, the NII has now issued all nuclear sites in Britain with replacement site licences. The process of relicensing the sites involved NII's detailed scrutiny of the proposed new arrangements for managing safety at each site. It concluded that all licensees had adequate resources, experience and arrangements to ensure safety at nuclear sites.

Discharges of radioactive waste have to be kept within the limits and conditions set by authorisations granted under the Radioactive Substances Act 1993. Within maximum dose limits, operators of nuclear facilities have to keep discharges as low as reasonably achievable and failure to do so makes them liable to prosecution.

Britain is one of 62 signatories to the Nuclear Safety Convention agreed in Vienna in 1994. Each signatory will produce a national report on its performance against a range of nuclear safety obligations set out in the Convention.

Britain's main contribution to the international effort to improve safety in central and eastern Europe and in the former Soviet Union is channelled through EU assistance programmes. In addition, Britain has contributed £18.25 million to the Nuclear Safety Account managed by the European Bank for Reconstruction and Development, which is funding urgent improvements to higher-risk plants in Bulgaria, Lithuania and Russia. (A project for Chernobyl in Ukraine is currently being finalised.)

International attention focuses on implementing the G7/Ukraine Memorandum of Understanding, signed on 20 December 1995, on the closure of Chernobyl by 2000.

Emergency Plans

The precautions taken in the design and construction of nuclear installations in Britain, and the care taken in their operation and maintenance, reduce the chance of accidents which might affect the public to an extremely low level. However, all operators are required, as a condition of their site licences, to prepare emergency plans, including those for dealing with an accidental release of radioactivity. These are regularly tested in exercises witnessed by the NII.

International conventions exist for early notification of a nuclear accident which may have possible transboundary effects, and on the mutual provision of assistance in the event of a nuclear accident or radiological emergency.

NEW AND RENEWABLE SOURCES OF ENERGY

The Government encourages development of new and renewable energy sources wherever

Technologies supported under recent NFFO and renewables obligations in Britain[1]

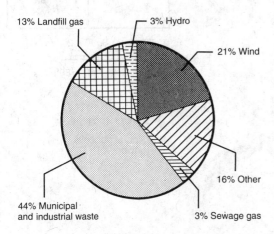

13% Landfill gas

3% Hydro

21% Wind

16% Other

3% Sewage gas

44% Municipal and industrial waste

[1] Contracted capacity (MW DNC) under all Orders.
Source: Department of Trade and Industry.

400–500 MW of contracted capacity) and SRO-2 (70–80 MW of contracted capacity), and a second Northern Ireland Order (45 MW of contracted capacity), are due to be made Orders in early 1997.

The NFFO has encouraged the best wind resource in Europe (66 MW operating capacity in Britain), with turbines (average capacity 300–400 kW) in small clusters, and in wind farms of up to 100 machines. Capacity provided by energy from waste exceeds 100 MW, while 119 MW of sewage gas and landfill gas plant is currently generating. In the energy crop sector, the development of agricultural waste and forestry waste is making progress, with 25 MW of plant in operation.

they have prospects of being economically attractive and environmentally acceptable. It is working towards 1,500 MW (3 per cent of Britain's current requirements) of new electricity generating capacity from renewable energy sources, for Britain as a whole, by 2000.

The non-fossil fuel obligation (NFFO) is used to provide a guaranteed market for the most promising forms of renewable generation. NFFO Orders place a legal obligation on the RECs to contract for specified amounts of electricity from specified non-fossil sources. The extra costs to the RECs of paying above the pool price are met from the fossil fuel levy paid by licensed electricity suppliers.

Three renewables Orders have been made for England and Wales and one each (in 1994) for Scotland and Northern Ireland. At the end of March 1996, 151 projects contracted in England and Wales under the first three Orders (NFFO-1-3) were operating, with a declared net capacity of 335 MW. The first Scottish Renewables Order (SRO) was for 76 MW capacity. Proposals for NFFO-4 (some

Some 21 MW of hydro capacity, a proved and commercial technology, operates under NFFO arrangements. However, there is little scope for further development of large-scale hydro in Britain. The greatest potential use for photovoltaics (PV) within Britain is for building-integrated systems, in which energy generated can supplement mains supplies. The Government has supported the installation of PV cladding at the University of Northumbria at Newcastle.

International collaboration is undertaken through multilateral and bilateral arrangements within the IEA and the EU. JOULE-THERMIE is an EU programme which aims to reduce harmful emissions through the introduction of renewables into Europe's energy systems, and the improved conversion and use of energy. Its budget is 1,000 million ECU (£750 million) over four years. Many British companies receive funding from this source.

Non-energy Minerals

Output of non-energy minerals in 1994 totalled 353 million tonnes, valued at £2,010 million. Construction raw materials, in particular aggregates, form the bulk, but their

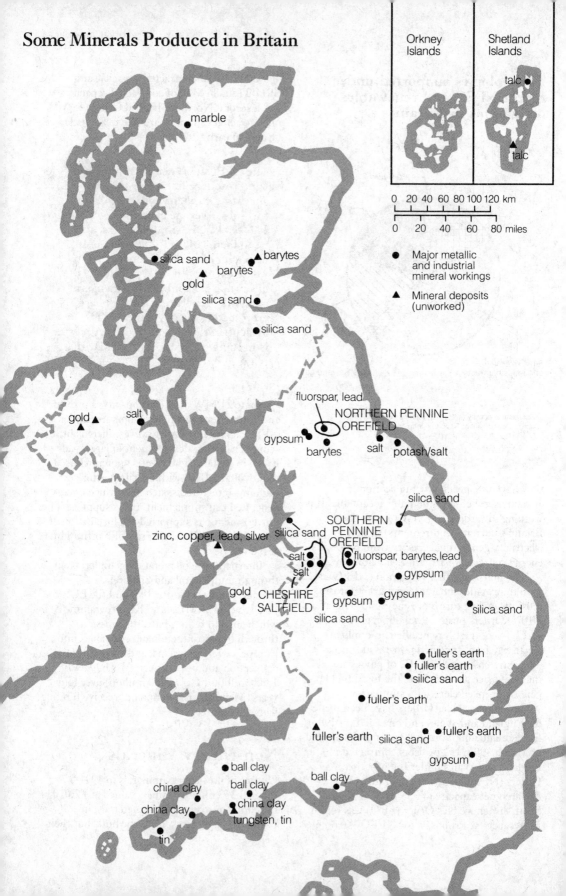

Some Minerals Produced in Britain

Orkney Islands

Shetland Islands

talc

talc

0 20 40 60 80 100 120 km

0 20 40 60 80 miles

● Major metallic and industrial mineral workings

▲ Mineral deposits (unworked)

marble

● silica sand

▲ barytes

▲ gold

barytes

● silica sand

● silica sand

● gold ▲

● salt

fluorspar, lead

NORTHERN PENNINE OREFIELD

gypsum ●

barytes

salt ●

● potash/salt

silica sand ●

SOUTHERN PENNINE OREFIELD

zinc, copper, lead, silver ▲

silica sand

● salt

● fluorspar, barytes, lead

● gypsum

● salt

gold ●

CHESHIRE SALTFIELD

gypsum ● ● gypsum

silica sand

● silica sand

● fuller's earth

● fuller's earth

● silica sand

● fuller's earth

▲ fuller's earth

silica sand ●

● fuller's earth

● gypsum

● ball clay

ball clay

ball clay ●

china clay

china clay ●

china clay

▲ tungsten, tin

tin

production declined in 1995. The total number of employees in the extractive industry was some 30,000 in 1994.

Exploration and Development

The Environment Act 1995 provides for a review of mineral sites with planning permissions in England and Wales granted between 1948 and 1982. No minerals development may be carried out on a dormant site (as distinct from an active site) until a new scheme of conditions has been approved by the local minerals planning authority. Development of minerals planning policy is supported across the whole of Britain by research carried out under the Department of the Environment's Geological and Minerals planning research programme.

In June 1996 revised Minerals Planning Guidance for England was issued which will help industry to bring forward development proposals which satisfy the environmental concerns of site operation and restoration, and accord with the principles of sustainable development. English Guidance for the provision of aggregates is looking for less

reliance on traditional land-won sources, with a doubling of recycled and secondary material by the year 2006. Where environmentally acceptable, coastal superquarries may make an increased contribution to English aggregate supplies. Scottish Office Guidance sets limits of no more than four superquarries in Scotland over the period to 2009.

The British Geological Survey's long-term minerals reconnaissance programme for the DTI described six new areas with mineral potential in Britain in 1995.

In Wales some 2,000 tonnes of gold ore a year come from the Gwynfynydd mine, and the nearby Clogau mine has been reopened. Production at the underground gold mine at Cononish, near Tyndrum (Perthshire), is expected to start in 1997. Published plans for the open pit mine at Cavanacaw in Northern Ireland suggest an annual production of 12,000 oz (373 kg) of gold and 15,000 oz (466 kg) of silver.

Production

In terms of value, production of limestone and dolomite was estimated at £596 million in

Table 17.4: Production of Some of the Main Non-energy Minerals

million tonnes

	1985	1989	1995
Sand and gravel	107.7	138.4	104.0
Silica sand	4.2	4.4	4.2
Igneous rock	38.6	54.5	50.0
Limestone and dolomite	95.6	132.7	113.0
Chalk[a]	12.0	13.9	10.0
Sandstone	13.2	19.6	17.0
Gypsum	3.1	4.0	2.0
Salt, including salt in brine	7.1	6.8	7.1
Common clay and shale	18.9[a]	19.4	14.0[a]
China clay	2.9	3.1	2.7[b]
Ball clay	0.6	0.8	0.9
Fireclay[a]	0.8	1.1	0.7
Iron ore	0.3	0.0	0.0
Potash	0.6	0.8	1.0
Fluorspar	0.2	0.1	0.1
Fuller's earth	0.2	0.2	0.1

Source: *British Geological Survey, United Kingdom Minerals Yearbook*
[a]Great Britain only.
[b]Moisture-free basis.

1994, sand and gravel £489 million, clays £298 million (with china clay valued at £220 million), igneous rock £248 million, sandstone £91 million, potash £83 million, salt £62 million, chalk £44 million, silica sands £40 million, gypsum and anhydrite £18 million, fluorspar £7 million and tin £6 million. In 1994 the production of metals in non-ferrous ores totalled 3,900 tonnes, mainly lead, and tin from Cornwall. In 1995 South Crofty, the one remaining Cornish tin mine and one of the very few sources of tin in the EU, produced 1,971 tonnes of tin-in-concentrate, a 2 per cent increase on 1994 and equivalent to about 20 per cent of Britain's demand.

Water

About 75 per cent of Britain's water supplies are obtained from surface sources such as mountain lakes, reservoirs and river intakes; and about 25 per cent from groundwater. In spring 1995 reservoirs were more than 95 per cent full after one of the wettest winters on record. By contrast summer 1995 and winter 1995–96 were exceptionally dry, and some reservoirs in north and south-west England were less than half full in spring 1996. Scotland has a relative abundance of unpolluted water from upland sources, and Northern Ireland also has abundant supplies for domestic use and for industry.

About 99 per cent of the population in Great Britain and 97 per cent in Northern Ireland are served by the public water supply system. Water put into this system (including industrial and other uses) in England and Wales amounted to 17,087 megalitres (Ml) a day in 1994–95, of which average domestic daily consumption per household was estimated at 380 litres. An average of 2,263 Ml a day was supplied in Scotland in 1994–95. In Northern Ireland the figure was 686 Ml a day.

Some 53,648 Ml a day were abstracted in England and Wales in 1994, of which public water supplies accounted for 16,735 Ml a day. The electricity generating companies and other industry took 27,732 Ml a day; fish farming, cress growing and amenity ponds 3,983 Ml a day; and agriculture 119 Ml a day, with spray irrigation accounting for a further 285 Ml a day.

England and Wales

The Secretaries of State for the Environment and for Wales are responsible for the statutory structure under which the Director General of Water Services and the Environment Agency are the principal regulators of the water industry in England and Wales. The Director General is responsible for the economic regulations of the water industry. The Environment Agency is responsible for the regulation of the water environment. The Drinking Water Inspectorate regulates drinking water quality. The Minister of Agriculture, Fisheries and Food and the Secretary of State for Wales are responsible for policy relating to land drainage, flood protection, sea defence, and the protection and development of inland and coastal fisheries.

Water Companies

The ten water service companies have statutory responsibilities for water supply, its quality and sufficiency, and for sewerage and sewage treatment. The supply-only companies, of which there were 29 in the private sector in 1989, now, after various mergers, number 19. They supply water to nearly a quarter of the population.

The companies determine their own methods of charging—usually on the basis of the former rateable value of the property to which water is supplied. In the Government's view, metering is the fairest way of paying for water. In general, companies require new properties and those substantially converted to have metered supplies. Most commercial and industrial concerns are now metered.

A system of economic regulation and guaranteed standards of service is overseen by Ofwat, the Office of Water Services. The Director General has a duty to ensure that water companies are able to finance the carrying-out of their statutory obligations; to promote economy and efficiency within the water industry and, where appropriate, competition (see below); to protect the interests of customers; and to ensure that there is no undue preference or discrimination in the fixing of charges. The Director General also sets limits to the rate at which water companies can increase their prices.

Over 99 per cent of the population is connected to mains drinking water supplies. These supplies are of high quality and all are safe to drink. In 1994 (the latest year for which data have been collated) over 99 per cent of the nearly 3.5 million tests carried out showed compliance with the relevant drinking water quality standards. In Britain some of these standards are stricter than those in the EC drinking water directive, and have been set to provide additional protection for public health. The remaining standards are in line with what the directive requires.

Environment Agency

The statutory duties and powers of the Environment Agency (see p. 355), which took over the functions of the National Rivers Authority (NRA) on 1 April 1996, include regulation of the water environment—for example, management of water resources and pollution control; flood defence, fisheries, recreation, and conservation; and some navigation duties and operations in England and Wales. Its responsibilities extend to all rivers, lakes, reservoirs, estuaries, coastal waters and water stored naturally underground. Its consent is needed for the abstraction of water and the discharge of effluent.

During 1994–95 the NRA (with an estimated expenditure of £438.7 million) investigated 35,000 pollution incidents, successfully prosecuted 316 polluters (with fines totalling nearly £1 million) and inspected and monitored 19,000 abstraction licences and 14,000 discharge consents.

Ensuring Supplies

Since 1990–91, the water companies have invested over £17,000 million in improving their operations, efficiency and service. In 1995–96 they announced planned investment of over £400 million to ensure supplies in the event of further drought during 1996–97. Ofwat has set the water companies a one-year deadline to bring down leakage levels or face the prospect of mandatory targets.

Husbanding of precious resources and difficulties in meeting peak demand have emphasised the need for a proper framework for water management—balancing customers' expectations, the cost of providing the service, and protecting the environment. In a period of changing patterns of, and demand for, water use, the Government points to the need for water companies to:

- understand better the present and likely future demands for water;

- introduce selective metering and appropriate tariff structures to influence demand, particularly for inessential uses of water; and

- promote the efficient use of water by customers, as required in a new statutory duty.

Competition

In April 1996 a government consultation document outlined proposals for competition in the water supply industry. These include:

- introduction of 'common carriage' arrangements, whereby suppliers compete for customers through the shared use of water mains;

- extending the scope for 'inset appointments' to allow a new water or waste water undertaker to supply an area within an existing undertaker's area; and

- removing the restrictions on cross border supply to enable a water undertaker to provide water for non-domestic purposes to customers within another undertaker's area.

Scotland

In Scotland, since April 1996, responsibility for public water supply, sewerage and sewage disposal rests with three public water authorities, North, West and East of Scotland Water Authorities. The Scottish Water and Sewerage Customers Council, a body set up in 1995 to protect and represent all customers of the new water authorities, is financed by an annual levy on the authorities.

The Secretary of State for Scotland and the water authorities are responsible for promoting conservation and effective use of water resources and provision of adequate water supplies. He has a duty to promote the cleanliness of rivers and other inland waters, and the tidal waters of Scotland. Also from April 1996, the Scottish Environment Protection Agency took over statutory responsibility for water pollution control from the Scottish river purification authorities.

Charging for water supply accords with type of consumer: domestic consumers pay water charges based on their council tax band or metered charges; non-domestic consumers pay non-domestic water rates, or metered charges. For sewerage services, domestic consumers pay a sewerage charge based on their council tax band, and non-domestic consumers pay non-domestic sewerage rates and, where appropriate, trade effluent charges. Charges and rates are decided by each water authority with the agreement and approval of the Customers Council.

Northern Ireland

The Department of the Environment for Northern Ireland is responsible for public water supply and sewerage throughout Northern Ireland. It is also responsible for the conservation and cleanliness of water resources and, with the Department of Agriculture, may prepare a water management programme with respect to water resources in any area. A domestic water charge is contained in the regional rate, while agriculture, commerce and industry pay metered charges.

Research

Several organisations and centres of expertise provide water research services to government, the Environment Agency, water undertakers and the Scottish Environment Protection Agency.

Research carried out by institutes of the Natural Environment Research Council (see p. 333) embraces river modelling, water quality, climate change, effects on resources and the impact of pollution on freshwater.

Among its various roles the Institute of Hydrology studies the statistics of floods and droughts.

Further Reading

Digest of Environmental Statistics. No 18, 1996. Department of the Environment. HMSO.

Digest of United Kingdom Energy Statistics 1996. Department of Trade and Industry. HMSO.

Energy and Natural Resources. Aspects of Britain series. HMSO, 1992.

The Energy Report 1: Change and Opportunity (1996). Department of Trade and Industry. HMSO.

The Energy Report 2: Oil and Gas Resources of the United Kingdom (1996). Department of Trade and Industry. HMSO.

United Kingdom Minerals Yearbook 1995. British Geological Survey. HMSO.

18 Agriculture, the Fishing Industry and Forestry

Agriculture	281	Role of the Government	289
Production	283	Control of Diseases and Pests	295
Food Safety	288	The Fishing Industry	296
Exports	288	Research	299
Marketing	289	Forestry	300

Total income from farming in Britain is estimated to have risen 22 per cent in real terms between 1994 and 1995. The Government has continued to expand the role of incentive schemes which can be used to secure environmentally beneficial management of agricultural land. In particular, there will be a major expansion of the Countryside Stewardship scheme. Britain has sustained pressure to apply improved animal welfare standards throughout Europe. In response to concerns over BSE (a fatal disease in cattle that may be transmissible to humans), Britain is taking a number of measures with the aim of resuming exports of British beef and beef products.

In response to the need to conserve fish stocks, £26 million was spent on the decommissioning of fishing boats between 1993 and 1995. Scotland has maintained its place as the largest producer of farmed salmon in the EU.

Agriculture

In 1995 British agriculture employed 2.1 per cent of the total workforce. Food, feed and beverages again accounted for about 10 per cent of Britain's imports by value. The agricultural contribution to gross domestic product (GDP) was £9,000 million in 1995, 1.5 per cent of the total. Britain is a major agricultural exporter—of livestock, food products, agrochemicals and agricultural machinery.

In October 1995 the Government published a White Paper, *Rural England: a Nation Committed to a Living Countryside*, jointly produced by the Ministry of Agriculture, Fisheries and Food (MAFF) and the Department of the Environment. The White Paper comprehensively reviews rural policies and covers economic, social and environmental issues affecting today's countryside. It sets out objectives for the countryside and actions to support them.

The White Paper also makes clear its overall objective for agriculture: an efficient, prosperous and outward-looking industry able to operate in increasingly open world markets, providing high-quality raw materials at competitive prices for the domestic food industry and paying due regard to public health and the environment. The key to this, the Government believes, lies with progressive reductions in production-related support and the eventual abolition of supply controls, within the competing framework of a common European Union (EU) agricultural policy avoiding national subsidies.

The White Paper announced the transfer of the Countryside Stewardship scheme from the Countryside Commission to MAFF. It also highlighted government progress with innovative projects for improving the economy of the most disadvantaged rural areas under Objective 5b of the European Structures Initiative.

The Government published a progress report in October 1996, on how *Rural England* commitments have developed over the year.

In *Rural Scotland: People, Prosperity and Partnership*, published in December 1995, the Government also recognises that agricultural and other traditional land uses still have great importance in rural communities. While changes in support arrangements are essential, that support should be better targeted to meet the needs of such communities.

MAFF has published 21 customer service standards in accordance with the principles of the Citizen's Charter (see pp. 69–70). MAFF's regional administrative structure consists of nine Regional Service Centres (RSCs), at Bristol, Cambridge, Carlisle, Crewe, Exeter, Northallerton, Nottingham, Reading and Worcester. Their work relates to payments under domestic and EU schemes, licensing and various other services provided to farmers and growers. Within available resources, the Centres aim to administer the schemes efficiently, providing the best possible service consistent with the need to prevent fraud and to avoid EU-imposed penalties. An independent survey in 1995 showed that nearly 90 per cent of customers rated RSC service as good or better.

The ten MAFF Inspectorates (such as the Fatstock Inspectorate, the Sea Fisheries Inspectorate, or the Plant Health and Seeds Inspectorate) enforce quality and health standards in animals, fish, and crops. Six MAFF executive agencies conduct regular customer satisfaction surveys. The Scottish Office Agriculture, Environment and Fisheries Department (SOAEFD) sets out its standards of service and performance targets in charter standard statements called *Serving Scottish Farmers* and *Serving Crofting*.

Land Use

In 1995, as in 1994, there were 11.3 hectares (27.9 million acres) under crops and grass. A further 5.8 million hectares (14.3 million acres) were used for rough grazing, most of it in hilly areas. Soils vary from the thin poor ones of highland Britain to the rich fertile soils of low-lying areas, such as the fenlands of eastern England. The climate is generally temperate, though rainfall distribution over Britain is uneven. The South East receives only about 600 mm (24 inches) a year, compared with over 1,500 mm (59 inches) in parts of west Scotland, Cumbria and Wales.

Land Use in Britain

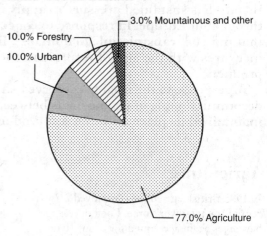

3.0% Mountainous and other
10.0% Forestry
10.0% Urban
77.0% Agriculture

Farming

In 1995 there were some 234,900 farm holdings in Britain (excluding minor holdings too small to be surveyed on a regular basis), with an average area of 72.4 hectares (178.9 acres)—again excluding minor holdings. About two-thirds of all agricultural land is

Agricultural Land Use 1995

TOTAL AREA ON
AGRICULTURAL HOLDINGS

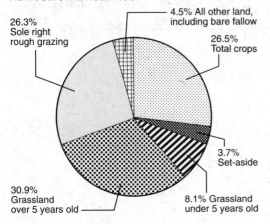

26.3%
Sole right
rough grazing

4.5% All other land,
including bare fallow

26.5%
Total crops

3.7%
Set-aside

30.9%
Grassland
over 5 years old

8.1% Grassland
under 5 years old

CROPS

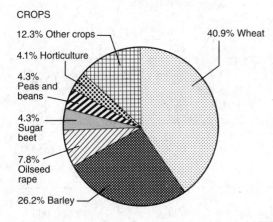

12.3% Other crops

4.1% Horticulture

4.3%
Peas and
beans

4.3%
Sugar
beet

7.8%
Oilseed
rape

26.2% Barley

40.9% Wheat

owner-occupied. Some 44 per cent of holdings are smaller than 8 European size units (ESU).[1] Labour productivity increased by 25.9 per cent during 1985–95. Total income from farming (that of farmers, partners, directors and their spouses, and family workers—see Table 18.1) was estimated at £5,044 million in 1995, 25.6 per cent more (at current prices) than in 1994. In real terms this measure of

---

[1]ESUs measure the financial potential of the holding in terms of the margins which might be expected from stock and crops. 8 ESU is judged the minimum for full-time holdings.

income is about 49 per cent higher than in the mid-1980s. Conditions contributing to this increase include:

- favourable weather;

- high world prices for some basic commodities, including cereals; and

- the increasing value of EU payments to farmers in respect of, for example, setting land aside.

At the end of 1994 the industry's gross capital stock, valued at 1990 prices, amounted to nearly £34,000 million, of which buildings and works made up just under two-thirds. The level of capital stock is now estimated to be some 1.3 per cent below the 1984–86 average.

PRODUCTION

Home production of the principal foods is shown in Table 18.2 as a percentage by weight of total supplies. Total new supply is home production plus imports less exports. It may be augmented (or reduced) by a decrease (or increase) in stocks. The result is described as 'total domestic uses'.

Livestock

Over half of full-time farms are devoted mainly to dairy farming or to beef cattle and sheep. The majority of sheep and cattle are reared in the hill and moorland areas of Scotland, Wales, Northern Ireland and northern and south-western England. British livestock breeders have developed many of the cattle, sheep and pig breeds with worldwide reputations, for example, the Hereford and Aberdeen Angus beef breeds, the Jersey, Guernsey and Ayrshire dairy breeds, Large White pigs and a number of sheep breeds. Britain is an exporter of semen and embryos from high-quality donor animals, but has been forced to stop sales abroad because of the EU ban on beef products (see below). Livestock totals are given in Table 18.3.

Cattle and Sheep

Cattle and sheep constitute about 42 per cent of the value of Britain's gross agricultural

Table 18.1: Labour Force in Agriculture

	'000 persons 1984–86 average	'000 persons 1995
Workers		
Regular whole time		
hired: male	109	70
female	10	10
family: male	31	20
female	5	3
Total	155	103
Regular part-time		
hired: male	19	19
female	22	18
family: male	13	13
female	7	7
Total	61	56
Seasonal or casual		
male	58	57
female	39	27
salaried managers[a]	8	8
Total workers	321	251
Farmers, partners and directors		
whole-time	200	170
part-time	92	112
Total farmers, partners and directors	292	282
Total farmers, partners, directors and workers	614	533
Spouses of farmers, partners and directors (engaged in farm work)	76	75
Total labour force (including farmers and their spouses)[b]	690	608

Source: *Agriculture in the United Kingdom 1995*
[a]This figure relates to Great Britain only.
[b]Figures exclude schoolchildren and most trainees.
Note: Differences between totals and the sums of their component parts are due to rounding.

output. Dairy production is the largest part of the sector, followed by cattle and calves, and then fat sheep and lambs. Most dairy cattle in Britain are bred by artificial insemination. In 1995 the average size of dairy herds was 67 (excluding minor holdings), while the average yield of milk for each dairy cow was 5,366 litres (1,180 gallons). Average household consumption of liquid (including low-fat) milk per head in 1995 was 1,881 millilitres (3.31 pints) a week.

More than half of home-fed beef production originates from the national dairy herd, in which the Holstein Friesian breed is predominant. The remainder is derived from suckler herds producing high-quality beef calves, mostly in the hills and uplands. The traditional British beef breeds (see above) and, increasingly, imported breeds such as Charolais, Limousin, Simmental and Belgian Blue, are used for beef production. In 1995 the size of

Table 18.2: British Production as a Percentage of Total New Supplies

Food Product	1984–86 average	1995 (provisional)
Beef and veal	98	107
Eggs	97	97
Milk for human consumption (as liquid)	100	100
Cheese	67	73
Butter	64	62
Sugar (as refined)	54	67
Wheat	110	119
Potatoes	92	88

Source: MAFF

the beef-breeding herd continued to expand—by 2 per cent. The dairy herd decreased by 4 per cent.

In spring 1996 the announcement of a possible link between Bovine Spongiform Encephalopathy (BSE) and Creutzfeldt-Jakob disease in humans caused considerable damage to the beef market in Britain and resulted in an EU worldwide ban on British beef and beef products. Among government measures to protect public and animal health, restore confidence and maintain the stability of the beef supply chain were:

- a ban on the sale of meat from cattle over 30 months old (subsequently amended to allow meat from herds with a very low risk of BSE to be sold up to the age of 42 months;

- a ban on the removal of any meat from the head except for the tongue;

- the recall of all meat and bone feed from farms, manufacturers and merchants;

- the prohibition of the sale and use of meat and bone meal in all animal feed and as fertiliser on agricultural land;

- aid schemes for the slaughtering and rendering sectors; and

- voluntary schemes for the disposal of unsaleable beef stocks.

Britain has a tradition of sheep production, with more than 60 native breeds and many

Table 18.3: Livestock and Livestock Products

	1984–86 average	1993	1994	1995 (provisional)
Cattle and calves ('000 head)	12,908	11,729	11,834	11,733
Sheep and lambs ('000 head)	35,830	43,901	43,295	42,771
Pigs ('000 head)	7,832	7,754	7,797	7,534
Poultry ('000 head)[a]	116,616	132,300	130,027	130,939
Milk (million litres)	15,549	14,096	14,302	13,950
Hen eggs (million dozen)	853	791	792	792
Beef and veal ('000 tonnes)	1,113	884	945	1,004
Mutton and lamb ('000 tonnes)	304	391	391	401
Pork ('000 tonnes)	733	821	851	808
Bacon and ham ('000 tonnes)	206	181	188	196
Poultry meat ('000 tonnes)	882	1,075	1,147	1,222

Source: MAFF

[a] Includes ducks, geese and turkeys. Figures for turkeys are for England and Wales only.

cross-bred varieties. Sheepmeat production is the main source of income for sheep farmers, and wool provides additional return.

Grass (including silage) covers most British agricultural land and supplies 60–80 per cent of the feed for cattle and sheep. Grass production has been enhanced by the increased use of fertilisers, methods of grazing control, and improved herbage conservation for winter feed. Certain sheep and cattle feed extensively on rough grazings, producing young animals for fattening elsewhere.

The Integrated Administration and Control System (IACS), an EU-wide anti-fraud measure, requires farmers to submit an annual application giving field-by-field details of their farmed land. This serves as a basis for administrative and on-farm checks on their entitlement to aid under area-based Common Agricultural Policy (CAP) schemes. Essential features of the IACS are systems for uniquely identifying farmers' fields and animals. Details of farmers' IACS applications and the results of checks are stored in a computerised database.

Pigs

Pig production occurs in most areas but is particularly important in East Anglia and Yorkshire. There is an increasing concentration into larger breeding units—about 20 per cent of holdings with breeding sows account for 80 per cent of the national breeding herd, which comprises some 750,000 sows. Britain is broadly self-sufficient in pork and exports to such destinations as Germany, Italy, France, Japan and Korea. However, bacon is imported from Denmark, the Netherlands and the Irish Republic. Pig breeding companies in Britain supply about 8 per cent of the genetically improved pigs and sows bought by the world's pig farmers.

Poultry

Britain's more efficient poultry industry owes much to high husbandry standards and the use of improved genetic stock. The increase in demand is partly satisfied by imports. Poultry production in 1995 was 1.22 million tonnes—a small increase on 1994. Broiler production, at 948,000 tonnes, was 54,000 tonnes above the level for 1994. Broilers from the 9 per cent of holdings with over 100,000 table birds account for well over a half of the total flock. Hen eggs went up from 885 million dozen in 1994 to 887 million dozen in 1995. Britain remains almost self-sufficient in poultry meat and eggs (see Table 18.2).

Animal Welfare

Public interest in farm animal welfare in Britain is traditionally high. During 1995, MAFF ministers answered 209 parliamentary questions on the subject and 23,000 letters—20 per cent of the Ministry's correspondence. The Government expects high welfare standards on farms, during transport and at abattoirs. It receives advice from the Farm Animal Welfare Council and from government animal welfare research programmes.

In 1995 public awareness and concern focused on the welfare of animals in transit. The Government applies tight welfare controls to alternative export routes set up after the decision of the major ferry companies in 1994 to stop carrying live food animals from Britain. In June 1995 the EU adopted new rules, to be implemented by 31 December 1996, on animal welfare in transit. These set:

- maximum journey times;
- feeding and watering intervals; and
- new enforcement measures, including a system of licensing for transporters of livestock.

Britain has also been pressing for the welfare standards for rearing calves across Europe to be brought up to the level which applies here. Pressure from Britain resulted in new EU proposals (January 1996) for a ban on veal crates and for calves to be housed in groups.

Crops

The farms devoted primarily to arable crops are found mainly in eastern and central-southern England and eastern

Scotland. The main crops are shown in Table 18.4. In Britain in 1995 the area planted to cereals totalled 3.2 million hectares (7.9 million acres), an increase of 4.5 per cent on 1994, largely as a result of a further reduction in the set-aside rate (see p. 290). High cereals market prices coupled with the arable area payments contributed to a 20 per cent increase (£484 million) in the value of output. Production of wheat, barley and oats was up on 1994, reflecting the near ideal growing conditions in many regions.

Large-scale potato and vegetable cultivation can be found on the fertile soils throughout Britain, often with irrigation. Principal areas are the peat and silt fens of Cambridgeshire, Lincolnshire and Norfolk; the sandy loams of Norfolk, Suffolk, West Midlands, Nottinghamshire, South Yorkshire and Lincolnshire; the peat soils of South Lancashire; and the alluvial silts of parts of the Thames and Humber valleys. Early potatoes are produced in Shropshire, Pembrokeshire, Cornwall, Devon, Essex, Kent and Cheshire. Production of high-grade seed potatoes is confined to Scotland, Northern Ireland and the Welsh borders.

Sugar from home-grown sugar beet provides 67 per cent of home needs, most of the remainder being refined from raw cane sugar imported under the Lomé Convention (see p. 180).

Horticulture

In 1995 the land utilised for horticulture (excluding potatoes and peas for harvesting dry) was about 187,000 hectares (462,000 acres).

Table 18.4: Main Crops

	1984–86 average	1993	1994	1995 (provisional)
Wheat				
Area ('000 hectares)	1,946	1,759	1,811	1,859
Production ('000 tonnes)	13,639	12,890	13,314	14,310
Yield (tonnes per hectare)	7.01	7.33	7.35	7.70
Barley				
Area ('000 hectares)	1,954	1,164	1,106	1,192
Production ('000 tonnes)	10,273	6,038	5,945	6,833
Yield (tonnes per hectare)	5.26	5.19	5.37	5.73
Oats				
Area ('000 hectares)	112	92	109	112
Production ('000 tonnes)	544	479	597	617
Yield (tonnes per hectare)	4.87	5.21	5.48	5.52
Potatoes				
Area ('000 hectares)	139	170	164	171
Production ('000 tonnes)	6,882	7,065	6,531	6,396
Yield (tonnes per hectare)	36.41	41.56	39.82	37.40
Oilseed rape				
Area ('000 hectares)	288	418	496	439
Production ('000 tonnes)	922	1,100	1,254	1,235
Yield (tonnes per hectare)	3.21	2.63	2.53	2.81
Sugar beet				
Area ('000 hectares)	203	197	195	196
Production ('000 tonnes)	8,284	9,666	8,720	8,600
Yield (tonnes per hectare)	41.51	49.06	35.25	43.88

Sources: *Agriculture in the United Kingdom 1995* and *Agricultural Census, June 1995*

Vegetables grown in the open accounted for 69 per cent of this, orchards for 15 per cent, soft fruit for 6 per cent and ornamentals (including hardy nursery stock, bulbs and flowers grown in the open) for 7 per cent. More than one vegetable crop is, in some cases, taken from the same area of land in a year, so that the estimated area actually cropped for horticulture in 1995 was 233,000 hectares (577,000 acres).

Mushrooms, carrots and lettuces are the single most valuable horticultural crops, with farm gate values of £166 million, £120 million and £108 million respectively in 1995.

Apple output was valued at £80 million; those of strawberries and raspberries at £58 million and £33 million respectively.

Field vegetables account for 55 per cent of the value of horticultural output and are widely grown throughout the country. Some are raised in blocks of compressed peat or loose-filled cells, a technique which reduces root damage and allows plants to establish themselves more reliably and evenly.

Glasshouses are used for growing tomatoes, cucumbers, sweet peppers, lettuces, flowers, pot plants and nursery stock. Widespread use is made of automatic control of heating and ventilation, and semi-automatic control of watering. Low-cost plastic tunnels extend the season for certain crops previously grown in the open.

Alternative Crops

The Government supports R&D into crops for renewable raw materials for industrial and energy uses. MAFF funding alone is £1.47 million in 1996–97.

FOOD SAFETY

EU food law harmonisation covers food safety, fair trading and informative labelling. The Government's system for identifying food safety risks involves food surveys, investigations and research, the results of which are published. Food law enforcement falls mainly to local authorities.

The Government relies on expert independent advisory committees, such as the Advisory Committee on the Microbiological

Safety of Food and the Food Advisory Committee, which provide systematic assessments of risk.

Following the concern about BSE in 1996 (see p. 285) the Government further reinforced measures to prevent potentially infected material from entering the food chain.

EXPORTS

Provisional data for 1995 suggest that the value of exports related to agriculture (food, feed and drink), at some £9,896 million, was about 9 per cent greater than in 1994. The main markets are France (£1,600 million), the Irish Republic (£1,000 million) and Spain (£700 million). Exports to the EU are worth £6,400 million. Other key markets are the United States (£600 million) and Japan (£200 million).

Cereals and cereal dried products are the largest category of British food exports, worth £1,322 million in 1995. Exports include specialities such as fresh salmon, biscuits, jams and conserves, soft drinks and tea, as well as beef and lamb carcasses, and cheese.

Worldwide sales of Scotch whisky increased by 6 per cent in 1995. Over 90 per cent of whisky production is exported. Exports to the EU alone were worth £880 million; to the Americas £663 million, to Japan £121 million, and worldwide £2,319 million. Certain markets grew markedly: for example, Brazil by 43 per cent and Korea by 24 per cent.

The Scotch whisky industry employs some 13,000 people directly. Because of strong local linkages a total of 61,000 jobs in Scotland are dependent on the industry.

The export trade in beef and beef products, which reached 291,000 tonnes in 1995 (worth about £616 million), compared with about 250,000 tonnes in 1994, was hit by the BSE crisis.

Export promotion for food and drink is headed by Food From Britain, an organisation funded by MAFF (£5.3 million in 1995–96) and industry. For agricultural products and machinery, and food processing equipment, MAFF co-ordinates export promotion and organises trade fairs and ministerial visits to other countries. Its presence at overseas trade fairs during 1995 attracted close on 2,000 serious enquiries for British agricultural products.

One of the world's largest agricultural events, the annual Royal Agricultural Show, held at Stoneleigh in Warwickshire, enables visitors to see the latest techniques and improvements in British agriculture. Some 200,000 visitors attended in 1996, of whom 20,000 were from overseas. Other major agricultural displays include the Royal Smithfield Show, held every other year in London, which exhibits agricultural machinery, livestock and carcasses; the Royal Highland Show (June); the Royal Welsh Show (July); and the Royal Ulster Agricultural Show.

The horticulture industry set up a Horticultural Export Bureau in 1996, to link producers, exporters and overseas buyers by means of a database; provide market intelligence; and direct overseas enquiries to appropriate suppliers.

MARKETING

There were 163 applications for grants in England and Wales under the Marketing Development Scheme in 1995 and 94 were approved, representing £5.1 million in payments. In Scotland, 22 out of 28 applications, representing £800,000, were approved; and in Northern Ireland 4 out of 12 (£112,000). The scheme, directed at non-capital expenditure, aims to help industry develop the management skills to improve its marketing performance.

Agricultural goods are sold by individuals, private traders, and producers' co-operatives and special boards. The four statutory milk marketing schemes in Great Britain came to an end in November 1994. Producers are now free to sell their milk to whomever they wish. Dairy companies are now free to buy direct from producers. The Milk Marketing Boards (MMBs) no longer buy and sell milk, but exist in residuary form in order to deal with outstanding liabilities and dispose of retained assets.

Deregulation of the milk market in Britain, which frees a market worth over £3,000 million a year, was complete by March 1995, with the revocation of the Northern Ireland Milk Marketing Scheme. The Milk Development Council (MDC) was formed in 1995 to continue funding near-market R&D and other priority areas, such as enhancing the public image of milk, after the MMBs' abolition in 1994. Dairy farmers supported its formation in a referendum and its funding by a statutory levy on all milk production in Great Britain. Currently the levy is set at 0.04 pence a litre. The MDC also helps to fund the National Dairy Council, which provides nutritional guidance on milk and dairy products.

In 1995 awards totalling £20 million under the EU's Processing and Marketing grant covered some 90 projects throughout Britain. This scheme was discontinued in England after March 1996.

The Potato Marketing Scheme, and the Potato Marketing Board which administers it, will come to an end after the 1996–97 crop season. The non-regulatory functions of the Board (statistics, marketing and R&D) may be continued by a development council.

The British Wool Marketing Board retains its statutory powers to collect and sell Britain's wool clip (48 million kilograms in 1995) on behalf of 56,000 registered producers.

Co-operatives and other farmers' businesses handle much of the marketing of agricultural and horticultural produce, such as grain, fruit and vegetables; the Plunkett Foundation estimates that these had a turnover of some £2,400 million in 1995.

ROLE OF THE GOVERNMENT

Four government departments have joint responsibility for agriculture and fisheries matters—MAFF; the SOAEFD; the Welsh Office; and the Department of Agriculture for Northern Ireland.

Common Agricultural Policy

The original aims of the CAP were to increase agricultural productivity and efficiency, thus to ensure a fair standard of living for producers, to stabilise markets and to ensure supplies to consumers at reasonable prices. The main mechanisms for achieving this were a combination of support prices, import duties and market intervention. When prices of the main commodities fell below certain agreed levels, intervention authorities (in Britain the Intervention Board executive agency) bought the goods and stored them for later resale. Intervention stocks were exported or disposed of within the EU, where this could be done without disrupting internal markets. The market support system not only raised food prices for consumers but encouraged surplus production. Exports, either from the market or from intervention stocks, attracted export refunds (or an export tax) to fill the gap between EU and world prices.

Public Expenditure under the CAP by the Intervention Board and the Agricultural Departments

FORECAST 1995/96

2.5%
Other, inc. pigmeat
and oilseeds

47.4%
Arable area
payments
scheme

1.9%
Cereals

2.1%
Processed
goods

19.1%
Beef and
veal

15.8%
Sheepmeat

4.8% Sugar

6.4% Milk products

Although these price support mechanisms are still part of the CAP, the reforms of 1992 moved it away from supporting price levels and intervention arrangements were made less attractive. As a result, farmers now receive the most of their financial support in

the form of direct payments from the Exchequer under various arable and livestock schemes (see pp. 291–4) and much less now comes from the consumer through increased food prices. Certain conditions, in the form of quotas or obligations to 'set-aside' land, are placed on the producers who receive these payments, in order to control production. The Government funds expenditure in Britain on CAP measures and later claims reimbursement from the EU. Britain contributes to this reimbursement through payments to the EU budget, to which it is a net contributor.

All CAP support prices and direct subsidy payments are set in European Currency Units and are then converted into the currencies of the member states at special rates of exchange—so-called 'green rates'. These green rates are kept broadly in line with market rates in accordance with agreed rules. Partly as a result of sterling's depreciation, devaluations of the green pound during 1995 increased CAP support prices by 8.5 per cent. After the revaluation of Britain's green rate in June 1996, prices remained 5.6 per cent higher than in early 1995.

Nearly all the EU's expenditure on agricultural support is channelled through the European Agricultural Guidance and Guarantee Fund (EAGGF). The Fund's guarantee section (with a budget of £34,300 million in 1996) finances market support arrangements, including direct payments made under the CAP, while the guidance section (budget of £3,300 million in 1996) provides funds for structural reform—for example, farm modernisation and investment—and payments to assist certain farmers to change to alternative enterprises.

The Government has made clear its view that the CAP is too costly for consumers and taxpayers, and too restrictive for enterprising producers. It believes that radical reform of the CAP is necessary, involving progressive reductions in support prices and other production-related payments. The aim is the phasing-out of the artificial production controls like quotas and set-aside, which currently lead to bureaucratic burdens on

Table 18.5: Rates of Hill Livestock Compensatory Allowances 1996

	Severely disadvantaged LFA	Disadvantaged LFA
Breeding cows	£47.50	£23.75
Hardy breed ewes	£5.75	£2.65
Other ewes	£3.00	£2.65

Source: MAFF

producers. Removing these burdens would leave producers free to meet customers' demands. Not only is such reform desirable, the Government says, but it is inevitable if food mountains are not to reappear and grow rapidly as a result of surplus production. GATT restrictions on the levels of subsidised exports, which are likely to become tighter after the next World Trade Organisation (WTO) round of talks, will prevent these surpluses being sold on the world market. Future enlargement of the EU to the East will also be a significant pressure for change.

CAP Expenditure on Livestock in Britain

Beef Special Premium is paid up to twice in the life of male beef animals. In 1995, premium was worth £85.82 a head (before regional scale-back); this has risen to £93.11 a head in 1996. Estimated expenditure in respect of the 1996 scheme, including Extensification Premium, is £169 million in England and £328 million in Britain as a whole.

Suckler Cow Premium is paid on suckler cows rearing beef calves. In 1995, premium was worth £114.43 a head, which has risen to £124.12 a head in 1996. Estimated expenditure in respect of the 1996 scheme, including Extensification Premium, is £101 million in England and £258 million in Britain. Total suckler cow quota in England is some 710,000 head of cattle.

There was also support for beef prices through EU beef intervention and export subsidy schemes. The latter came to about £94 million in 1995–96; and intervention storage and other costs to about £2.2 million—a drop of 32 per cent on 1994–95. There was no intervention buying in 1995 and there were further reductions in British

and EU intervention stocks, which stood at 5,072 and 5,524 tonnes respectively at the end of the year—down to about 4 per cent of 1993 levels.

Sheep Annual Premium. Producers received a payment of £21.26 a ewe on eligible sheep under the 1995 Sheep Annual Premium Scheme. A supplement of £5.69 a ewe was paid in Less Favoured Areas (LFAs). Total payments in Britain in 1995–96 were £425 million, with a total quota of 19.62 million units.[2]

GATT Uruguay Round

On 1 July 1996 the EU implemented the second of the annual reductions in import protection and subsidised exports which are to happen each year until 2000 under the commitments which it made under the GATT Uruguay Round Agriculture Agreement. Britain participates in the WTO's Agriculture Committee and Committee on Sanitary and Phytosanitary [plant health] Measures, which monitor the implementation of the Uruguay Round commitments. The next round of multilateral negotiations on liberalising agricultural trade will start in 1999.

Price Guarantees, Grants and Subsidies

Expenditure in Britain in 1995–96 on CAP market regulation and on price guarantees, grants and subsidies was estimated at £2,753 million and £280 million respectively.

Farmers are eligible for grants aimed at environmental enhancement of their farms (see p.292).

---

[2] Quota is the number of cattle eligible for payments under a scheme.

In LFAs, where land quality is poor, farmers benefit from higher rates of grant and hill livestock compensatory allowances (HLCAs). These are headage payments on breeding cattle and sheep, and their purpose is to support the continuation of livestock farming in hills and uplands, thus conserving the countryside and encouraging people to remain in the LFAs.

In 1996 producers in the LFA (United Kingdom)[3] will receive direct livestock subsidy payments of £650 million, of which some £108 million comes from HLCAs (see Table 18.5).

Smallholdings and Crofts

In England and Wales county councils let smallholdings to experienced people who want to farm on their own account. Councils may lend working capital to them. At 31 March 1995 there were approximately 4,700 smallholdings in England and 840 in Wales. Land settlement in Scotland has been carried out by the Government, which, while seeking to dispose of holdings to its sitting tenants, still owns and maintains 105,677 hectares (260,977 acres) of land settlement estates, comprising 1,415 crofts and holdings.

In the crofting areas of Scotland— Highland, parts of Strathclyde, Western Isles, Orkney and Shetland—much of the land is tenanted by crofters (smallholders). They enjoy the statutory protection provided by crofting legislation and can benefit from government agriculture and livestock improvement schemes. Most crofters are part-time or spare-time agriculturalists, using croft income to supplement income from other activities. The Crofters Commission has a statutory duty to promote the interests of crofters and to keep all crofting matters under review. The Government, which owns over 100,000 hectares (247,000 acres) of crofting land, has proposed to transfer them to trusts which would give crofters more effective control over their land.

[3]Designation of LFA status is decided by the EU. The case for LFAs in Britain was submitted to the EU as covering all of Britain.

Agricultural Landlords and Tenants

About one-third of agricultural land in England and Wales is rented. The Agricultural Tenancies Act 1995 gives landlords and tenants in England and Wales greater freedom to decide the terms of new tenancy agreements taken up from September 1995. Full relief from inheritance tax on new tenancies from that date will also encourage landowners to offer tenancies.

In Scotland about 40 per cent of farmland is rented, partly reflecting the relatively large areas of land in crofting tenure, including common grazings.

Most farms in Northern Ireland are owner-occupied, but a practice known as 'conacre' allows occupiers not wishing to farm all their land to let it annually to others. Land let in this way—about one-fifth of agricultural land—is used mainly for grazing.

Agriculture and Protection of the Countryside

The White Papers on rural England and Scotland (see p. 281) set out new initiatives. The EU has agreed that land withdrawn from agricultural production under certain forestry or agri-environment schemes (where agriculture plays its part in protecting the countryside) can count towards a farmer's set-aside (arable land deliberately not used for agricultural purposes) obligation.

Since the mid-1980s the Government and its agencies have developed environmental land management schemes for the countryside which now make up Britain's programme under EC 'agri-environment' regulation 2078/92.

Environmentally Sensitive Areas

The ESA scheme (see Table 18.6) remains Britain's largest environmental scheme. Among the newest areas, designated in 1994, are the Shropshire Hills and Essex Coast in England, the Cairngorms Straths of Scotland and the Sperrins and Slieve Gullion in Northern Ireland. Farmers within the areas receive annual payments for carrying out farming practices which benefit nature

Table 18.6: ESAs as at 31 March 1996

	Number of ESAs	Farmers with agreements	Land designated	Areas covered by agreements	Payments to farmers in 1995–96
			'000 hectares ('000 acres)		(£ '000)
England	22	7,800	1,149 (2,839)	427 (1,055)	29,100
Wales	6	1,393	520 (1,284)	114 (281)	2,420
Scotland	10	1,094	1,439 (3,556)	374 (924)	2,500
Northern Ireland	5	2,599	220 (543)	90 (222)	1,609

Source: MAFF; Welsh Office; The Scottish Office; Northern Ireland Office

conservation, the landscape and conservation of historic features.

Participation in the scheme is voluntary. Farmers enter into 10-year agreements with the relevant agriculture department. An agreement specifies the agricultural management practices they will carry out. Each ESA has varying tiers of such practices, from basic care and maintenance to more extensive forms of management and environmental restoration. Details also vary, but participants may not convert grassland to arable and are subject to restrictions on fertiliser and chemical usage.

Most ESAs also restrict or control the numbers of stock on the land as well as the timing of cultivation. The annual payments (between £8 and £415 a hectare, depending on the needs of each tier) are designed to compensate for reduced profitability because of these less intensive production methods, and for the further work some management practices need. Additional payments are made for specific items, such as hedgerows and stone wall renewal, set out in conservation plans, and for allowing public access to suitable farmland.

Countryside Stewardship

Countryside Stewardship is to develop as the main government incentive scheme in England, with payments of £5 million a year in 1996 and 1997 (added to a current budget of £11.6 million), for the wider English countryside outside the ESAs. The scheme offers payments to farmers and landowners to improve the natural heritage under 10-year agreements. It targets chalk and limestone

grassland, lowland heath, waterside land, coast, uplands, historic landscapes, old orchards, and countryside around towns. Three new categories have been added:

- traditional field boundaries around farms, such as walls, ditches and hedgerows;

- old meadows and pastures—to maintain and increase biodiversity; and

- wildlife corridors created by uncropped margins in arable fields, and wild flowers and birds native to arable areas.

Other Schemes

In 1995 a further 6,500 hectares (16,000 acres), including 4,000 hectares (9,800 acres) of former pilot scheme land, entered the *Nitrate Sensitive Areas* (NSA; 32 areas in England). Annual payments, under five-year agreements, range from £65 a hectare for restrictions on nitrogen fertilisers to £590 a hectare for conversion of arable land to native species grassland. Total payments in 1995–96 were £3.6 million. Covering over 600,000 hectares (1,480,000 acres) in England and Wales, 68 *Nitrate Vulnerable Zones* have been designated in which farmers will in due course have to comply with mandatory rules relating to their farming practices.

There are four *Organic Aid Schemes* covering England, Northern Ireland, Scotland and Wales. These offer support for the conversion of land to organic production methods. In 1995–96, 4,015 hectares (9,920 acres) were entered into conversion under these schemes and payments totalling

£300,560 made. Land thus entered attracts payments for five years from the start of conversion. Payments are on a reducing scale starting at up to £70 a hectare. An additional £30 a hectare is payable on the first 5 hectares entered into a scheme.

In 1996 an Organic Conversion Information Service was launched in England. This provides free Helpline information and advisory visits to prospective organic farmers.

A programme of R&D worth about £1 million a year is also undertaken and support is given for the UK Register of Organic Food Standards, charged with overseeing standards of organic food production.

The *Arable Area Payments Scheme*, which gives area-based payments on cereals, oilseeds, protein and linseed crops, attracted 62,937 claims for 4.45 million hectares (11 million acres) in 1995. For the main scheme, growers must set aside part of the area on which they claim payment; for the simplified scheme, no set-aside is required, but the claim must not exceed 15.6 hectares (39.7 acres) in England or the equivalent elsewhere in Britain.

By the end of 1995 about 450 farmers had entered or applied to enter about 6,800 hectares (16,800 acres) in the four *British Habitat Schemes*. These aim to create, protect or enhance valuable wildlife habitats. Farmers, with management agreements for 10 or 20 years, earn from £125 to £525 a hectare.

To qualify for the *Moorland Schemes* farmers or crofters must enter at least 10 hectares (25 acres) in Wales or 20 hectares (49 acres) in England and Scotland, of heather moorland. Successful applicants must also reduce their sheep numbers, by at least ten animals (£25 a ewe), to specified densities for a five-year period. By the end of 1995, 6,358 hectares (15,710 acres) had come into the schemes.

Farmers made significantly fewer applications than expected under the *Countryside Access Scheme* for England and Wales—80 in 1994–95 and 50 in 1995–96. Agreements started in January 1995 have provided 60 km (37 miles) and 1,000 hectares (2,470 acres) of open space, with 29 per cent of guaranteed set-aside land accessible to the general public.

The *Farm Woodland Premium Scheme* encourages farmers to convert productive agricultural land to woodland by providing annual payments for 10 or 15 years to help offset agricultural income foregone. Payments are under review but currently go up to £250 a hectare and are in addition to the establishment grants available under the Woodland Grant Scheme (see p. 300). In 1995 over 1,100 applications for 6,600 hectares (16,300 acres) were approved for the whole of Britain.

Rural Economy

Eleven areas in Great Britain (including South West England, the English Northern Uplands, 70 per cent of the landmass of Wales and Dumfries and Galloway) have been designated eligible to receive funds under Objective 5b of the EU Structural Funds. Objective 5b aims to promote the welfare of rural areas by providing business advice, helping to develop infrastructure and environmental and conservation measures, and marketing local and regional products. Areas must have a low level of socio-economic development (assessed on the basis of GDP per inhabitant) and normally have a high share of agricultural employment in total employment, a low level of agricultural income and a low population density.

The EU has allocated £376 million in England for farm diversification, tourism and environmental management over the six years 1994–99. Of this, 15 per cent (£56 million) is to come from the EAGGF. With EU money to be match-funded (there must be an equal contribution from public funds), total EU and public expenditure specifically targeted at agriculture will be about £112 million.

Linked to Objective 5b is the LEADER II initiative, designed to help small-scale, innovative measures of benefit to local areas. The Commission has allocated almost £20 million to England for LEADER II measures. With matching national public funds, nearly £6 million is available to give direct support to agriculture. Other initiatives include Farmlink (to promote an understanding of agriculture by establishing links between farms and schools) and the Rural Stress Working Group.

Agricultural Training

ATB-Landbase Limited provides Industry Training Organisation (see p. 189) and other services for agriculture and commercial horticulture, as well as resources for the supply of instructors through local training, under contract to MAFF. The contract for 1996–97 is worth nearly £2 million. The agricultural colleges and other independent organisations also provide training.

Professional, Scientific and Technical Services

In England and Wales ADAS, an executive agency of MAFF and the Welsh Office, provides professional, business, scientific and technical services in the agriculture, food and drink, and environmental markets. Most advice and servicing are on a fee-paying basis. The Government gives free initial advice on conservation and the prevention of pollution. In England this advice is provided through ADAS and, in the case of conservation, also through the Farming and Wildlife Advisory Group. Similar services in Scotland come from the SOAEFD through the Scottish Agricultural College. In Northern Ireland they are available from the Department of Agriculture's agriculture and science services.

CONTROL OF DISEASES AND PESTS

Farm Animals

Britain maintains its animal health status by enforcement of controls on imports of live animals and genetic material, including checks on all individual consignments originating from outside the EU and frequent checks on those from other EU member states at destination points. Measures can be taken to prevent the importation of diseased animals and genetic material from regions or countries affected by disease. Veterinary checks also include unannounced periods of surveillance at ports.

> The number of new cases of BSE continues to decline—from a peak of 36,000 in 1992 to 15,600 in 1995. In spring 1996 suspect cases, at 2,998, were at the lowest level for five years. The total for 1995 was 41 per cent lower than in 1994.

A cattle passport system was introduced in Great Britain for all cattle born or imported from 1 July 1996. The Government is working on a computerised cattle recording and movement system for Great Britain. In Northern Ireland, the Department of Agriculture already operates such a system. Computerised cattle traceability will assist the control of BSE and other cattle diseases.

Professional advice and action on the statutory control of animal disease and the welfare of farm livestock are the responsibility of the State Veterinary Service. It is supported by the Veterinary Laboratories Agency, a primary supplier of specialist veterinary advice to MAFF, which offers its services to the private sector on a commercial basis. A similar service is provided in Scotland by the Scottish Agricultural College and in Northern Ireland by the Department of Agriculture's Veterinary Science Laboratories.

Rabies

Dogs, cats and certain other mammals are subject to import licence and six months' quarantine. Commercially traded dogs and cats from other EU countries which satisfy strict conditions are allowed entry without quarantine. There are severe penalties for breaking the law. No cases of rabies outside quarantine have occurred in Northern Ireland since 1923 and in Britain as a whole since 1970, except for an isolated stray insectivorous bat, which seemed to have come from continental Europe in 1996.

Fish

Controls to prevent the introduction and spread of serious diseases of fish and shellfish include restrictions on live fish imports and on the deposit of shellfish on the seabed, and movement restrictions on sites where outbreaks of notifiable diseases have been confirmed.

Plants

The agriculture departments apply statutory controls to implement the EU plant health regime, which is designed to prevent the introduction or spread of particularly harmful plant pests and disease. They also provide non-statutory services, including certification of exports to third countries and schemes for maintaining the health status of plant propagating material in Britain.

Pesticides

British legislation comprehensively controls pesticides so as to protect the health of humans, creatures and plants, safeguard the environment, and secure safe, efficient and humane methods of pest control. The Pesticides Safety Directorate, an executive agency of MAFF, is responsible for the evaluation and approval of agricultural pesticides in Great Britain. It also provides policy advice to MAFF in respect of the safety and effectiveness of pesticides and monitors pesticide usage, residues and wildlife incidents.

Veterinary Medicinal Products

The Veterinary Medicines Directorate is responsible to agriculture and health ministers for ensuring that authorised veterinary medicines meet standards of safety, quality and efficacy. Users of medicines, the health and welfare of treated animals, safety of consumers of food from treated animals, and the environment are all matters of concern. The independent Scientific Veterinary Products Committee advises the Government.

The Fishing Industry

The fishing industry provides 59 per cent by quantity of British fish supplies.

The fisheries departments are responsible for the administration of legislation concerning the fishing industry, including fish and shellfish farming, and for fisheries research. The safety and welfare of crews of fishing vessels are provided for under legislation administered by the Department of Transport.

The Sea Fish Industry Authority (SFIA) is an industry financed body. It undertakes R&D, provides training and encourages quality awareness. It also acts as an agent to pay government grants (£2.3 million in 1995–96) towards the cost of work necessary to obtain a Department of Transport vessel safety certificate.

Fish Caught

In 1995 demersal fish (caught on or near the bottom of the sea) accounted for 46 per cent by weight of total landings by British fishing vessels, pelagic fish (caught near the surface) for 40 per cent and shellfish for 15 per cent. Landings of all types of fish (excluding salmon and trout) by British fishing vessels totalled 704,000 tonnes compared with 669,000 tonnes in 1994. Cod and haddock represented 20 and 16 per cent respectively of the total value of demersal and pelagic fish landed, while anglerfish (8 per cent), mackerel and whiting (each with 6 per cent), plaice (5 per cent) and sole (4 per cent) were the other most important sources of earnings to the industry. The quayside value of landings of all sea fish, including shellfish, by British vessels in 1995 was £462 million.

Total allowable catches (TACs) for 1996 (see below) produced British quotas of 512,000 tonnes (expressed as cod equivalent), compared with 535,000 tonnes in 1993, 582,000 tonnes in 1994 and 547,000 tonnes in 1995. In addition British vessels have access to stocks where no allocation is made between member states.

The Fishing Fleet

The poor state of fish stocks, the severe pressure they are under and the size of fishing fleets have meant that fishing capacity has to be reduced. The pace at which it is done is limited not only by budgets but also by the impact on coastal communities and their economies. Under the EU's Multi-Annual Guidance Programme all member states have been set targets for reducing their fleets. Britain intended to achieve this objective through a combination of decommissioning and restrictions on time spent at sea. Although a legal challenge to restrictions has been dismissed by the European Court of Justice, the Government has not pursued restrictions. Some 7 per cent of tonnage has been removed in three tendering rounds: 4,755 gross registered tonnes (GRT) in 1993, 5,270 GRT in 1994—297 registered vessels for 1993–94—and 5,326 GRT in 1995, at a cost of some £28 million. At the end of 1995 the British fleet consisted of 9,313 registered vessels, including 454 deep-sea vessels longer than 24.4 m (80 ft). All commercial fishing vessels have to be licensed.

Fish Farming and Shellfish Production

Production of salmon and trout has grown from less than 1,000 tonnes in the early 1970s to 70,600 tonnes of salmon in Scotland and about 16,000 tonnes of trout in 1995. Scotland produces the largest amount of farmed salmon (with a first-sale value of £220 million) in the EU. Shellfish farming concentrates on molluscs such as oysters, mussels, clams and scallops, producing an estimated 4,500 tonnes a year.

The fish and shellfish farming industries, predominantly in the Highlands and Islands of Scotland, were estimated to have a combined wholesale turnover of some £254 million in 1995. Production in Great Britain is based on 932 businesses operating from 1,674 sites and employing more than 3,300 people.

Fishery Limits

British fishery limits extend to 200 miles or the median line (broadly halfway between the British coast and the opposing coastline of another coastal state), measured from baselines on or near the coast of Britain.

Common Fisheries Policy

The EU's CFP system for the conservation and management of fishing resources means that TACs are set each year in order to conserve stocks. TACs are then allocated between member states on a fixed percentage basis, taking account of traditional fishing patterns.

British vessels have exclusive rights to fish within 6 miles of the British coast. Certain other EU member states have historic rights in British waters between 6 and 12 miles. British vessels have similar rights in other member states' 6 to 12 mile belts. Between 12 and 200 miles EU vessels may fish wherever they have been allocated a share of the EU's TAC against agreed EU quotas. Non-EU countries' vessels may fish in these waters if they negotiate reciprocal fisheries agreements. Currently the only countries are Norway and the Faroes.

Technical conservation measures, crucial to the TAC regime, include minimum mesh sizes for nets and net configuration restrictions,

Table 18.7: Imports and Exports of Fish			*tonnes*
	1993	1994 provisional	1995 provisional
Imports			
Salt-water and shellfish	397,578	418,859	417,781
Freshwater fish	44,688	39,783	46,956
Fish meals	261,211	247,721	237,856
Fish oils	127,211	138,368	129,472
Exports and re-exports			
Salt-water fish and fish products	352,560	340,726	325,765
Freshwater fish	23,433	31,436	32,745
Fish meals	8,703	17,039	25,966
Fish oils	8,289	12,121	14,956

Sources: MAFF; The Scottish Office; Northern Ireland Office

minimum landing sizes and closed areas designed mainly to protect young fish.

Each member state is responsible for enforcement of CFP rules on its own fishermen and those of other member states in its own waters. EU inspectors monitor compliance.

After the full integration of Spain and Portugal into the CFP on 1 January 1996, new measures took effect to control fishing by all member states in Western waters. At the same time Spanish and Portuguese fishing vessels continue to be excluded from the North Sea, the Irish Sea and the Bristol Channel.

Quota Hoppers

Quota hoppers are British registered fishing vessels which are partly or wholly owned by foreign interests; which fish against British quotas; and land most of their catch abroad. There are more than 150 such vessels, accounting for some 22 per cent of the tonnage of Britain's offshore fishing fleet and 10 per cent of the catch of whitefish quota stocks. The Government is actively seeking EU Treaty changes through the Inter Governmental Conference that will allow individual member states to take appropriate action to ensure that their fishing communities and related industries derive real economic benefit from national quotas allocated under the CFP.

Fisheries Conservation Group

A review of the bass fishery has concluded that MAFF's conservation measures have increased stocks. MAFF has also published proposals to conserve scallops and considered provisions to conserve other shellfish. Of the stocks representing 85 per cent of British catches, only about 40 per cent are above the critical minimum stock size. Most stocks are at historically low levels, including some of the most important (for example, five different cod stocks and four plaice stocks).

MAFF and the agriculture departments set up the Fisheries Conservation Group in December 1995 to bring together representatives of the British industry, fisheries scientists and government experts. It has reappraised:

- types and mesh sizes of nets;
- areas for closure to protect juvenile fish; and
- minimum landing sizes for fish.

It has also looked into more selective catching techniques to conserve stocks. This work aims to help British negotiators when they deal with the EU technical conservation measures due to be adopted by the end of 1996.

Grant Schemes

In early 1996 the Government announced new grant schemes which will provide up to £27.8 million and attract between 5 and 30 per cent aid from the EU:

- the *Vessel Safety Improvement Scheme*—to improve safety on vessels and to cover projects costing £3,000 and over;
- the *Processing and Marketing Scheme*—for processing and marketing fisheries and aquaculture products;
- up to £6.1 million under the *Port Facilities Scheme* over three years for improvements to fishing ports;
- the *Freshwater Aquaculture Promotion Scheme*—grants to the freshwater industry; and
- up to £18 million under the *PESCA Scheme*—to help areas hitherto dependent on fishing to diversify into non-fishing activities.

Fisheries Agreements

CFP provisions are supplemented by a number of fisheries agreements between the EU and third countries, the most important for Britain being the agreements with Norway, Greenland and the Faroe Islands. EU catch quotas have also been established around Spitzbergen (Svalbard).

Fish and Shellfish Hygiene

Community legislation sets minimum hygiene standards for the production and placing on the market of fish and shellfish. All commercial shellfish beds producing bivalve molluscs are monitored for microbial contamination. Samples of water and shellfish flesh are tested for the presence of algal toxins. Periodic monitoring of fish and shellfish is carried out to check for the presence of contaminants. Other projects monitor shellfish and seawater for biotoxins and chemical contaminants.

Salmon and Freshwater Fisheries

Salmon and sea-trout are fished commercially in inshore waters around the British coast. Eels and elvers are also taken commercially in both estuaries and fresh water. Angling for salmon and sea-trout (game fishing) and for freshwater species (coarse fishing) is popular throughout Britain. There is no public right to fish in freshwater lakes and non-tidal rivers in Great Britain. In England and Wales those wishing to fish such waters must first obtain permission from the owner of the fishing rights and a licence from the Environment Agency. In Scotland salmon fisheries are managed locally by district salmon fishery boards. In Northern Ireland fishing is licensed by the Fisheries Conservancy Board for Northern Ireland and the Foyle Fisheries Commission in their respective areas, and 65 public angling waters, including salmon, trout and coarse fisheries, are accessible to Department of Agriculture permit holders.

Fisheries and Aquatic Environment

MAFF laboratories deal with marine and freshwater fisheries, shellfish, marine pollution, fish farming and disease. MAFF also commissions research work from the Natural Environment Research Council (NERC), the SFIA and a number of universities. It has two seagoing research vessels.

In Scotland the SOAEFD undertakes similar, and complementary, research, and also has two seagoing vessels.

The Department of Agriculture laboratories in Northern Ireland undertake research on marine and freshwater fisheries, and also have a seagoing research vessel.

Research

Departmental funding of R&D in agriculture, fisheries and food in 1996–97 amounts to about £181.7 million. This includes funding by MAFF, the SOAEFD, and the Department of Agriculture for Northern Ireland.

Agriculture and Food

Food safety research contributes to protecting the public, as do investigation of animal diseases, particularly those that may be transmitted to man, and flood and coastal defence. R&D also contributes to improving animal welfare, increasing the competitiveness of the agriculture, fishing and food industries, and protecting and enhancing the agricultural and marine environment. MAFF funding for research into transmissible spongiform encephalopathies has been increased to £10.4 million.

Research Bodies

The Biotechnology and Biological Sciences Research Council (BBSRC; see p. 332) is responsible for research in biological sciences that are vital for food and agriculture. The NERC is responsible for research on the environment, including agricultural aspects. These councils receive funds from the science budget through the Office of Science and Technology, and income from work commissioned by MAFF, by industry and by other bodies. They carry out research at research council sponsored institutes and in higher education institutions through their grant schemes.

ADAS carries out R&D, through regional centres and on clients' premises, under commission from MAFF and under contract for other bodies. There are research centres across England and Wales. MAFF receives scientific expertise and technical support from its other agencies, the Veterinary Laboratories Agency and the Central Science Laboratory, commissioning research from them as well as through open competition.

The five Scottish Agricultural and Biological Research Institutes, funded by the SOAEFD, cover areas of research complementary to those of the BBSRC institutes, while including work relevant to the conditions of northern Britain. The SOAEFD also funds agricultural research, education and advisory services at the Scottish Agricultural College, which operates from three centres. In Northern Ireland the Department of Agriculture does basic strategic and applied research in its specialist research divisions. It also has links with the Queen's University of Belfast and the Agricultural Research Institute of Northern Ireland.

Forestry

Woodland covers an estimated 2.4 million hectares (5.9 million acres) in Britain: about 7 per cent of England, 15 per cent of Scotland, 12 per cent of Wales and 6 per cent of Northern Ireland. This is about 10 per cent of the total land area and well below the 25 per cent average for the whole of Europe.

Britain's forestry programme protects forest resources and conserves woodland as a home for wildlife and for public recreation. It also promotes the market for home-grown timber.

The area of productive forest in Great Britain is 2.18 million hectares (5.39 million acres), 37 per cent of which is managed by the Forestry Commission. The rate of new planting in 1995–96 was 400 hectares (988 acres) by the Commission and 15,000 hectares (37,065 acres) by other woodland owners, with the help of grants from the Commission, mainly in Scotland. In 1995–96, 8,400 hectares (20,576 acres) of broadleaved trees were planted, a practice encouraged on suitable sites.

The forest area has doubled since 1919. Since 1987 nearly 170,000 hectares (420,070 acres) of new woodland have been created. (Over 7 million trees a year have been planted in Wales over the last five years.) Forestry employs more than 34,000 people. Britain's woodlands produce about 8 million cubic metres (282 million cubic feet) of timber a year—about 15 per cent of total consumption. The Government is spending £242 million to support the management of state and private forests and their expansion in the three years 1994–95 to 1996–97.

The volume of timber harvested on Commission lands in 1995–96 is estimated at 4 million cubic metres (141 million cubic feet).

The Commission's Woodland Grant Scheme pays grants to help create new woodlands and forests, and regenerate existing ones. Approval was given for 18,000 hectares (44,478 acres) of new planting in 1995–96, including 4,106 hectares (10,146 acres) of new natural regeneration. Three activities are eligible for woodland improvement grant under the scheme: helping to provide for public access to woodlands; restorative work on undermanaged woodlands; and supporting efforts in woodlands to conserve rare species such as the red squirrel, dormouse, capercaillie, and various bats and butterflies.

Annual payments to compensate farmers for agricultural income foregone are also available under the Farm Woodland Premium Scheme, administered by agriculture departments.

The Forestry Commission and Forestry Policy

The Forestry Commission, established in 1919, is the government department responsible for forestry in Great Britain. The Commissioners advise on forestry matters and are responsible to the Secretary of State for Scotland, the Minister of Agriculture, Fisheries and Food, and the Secretary of State for Wales.

Within the Commission, the Forestry Authority provides grants to private woodland owners for tree planting and woodland management, controls tree felling, and sets standards for the forestry industry as a whole. Forest Enterprise, a Next Steps agency of the Commission, develops and manages the Commission's forests and forestry estate, supplying timber and opportunities for recreation, and enhancing nature conservation and the forest environment.

With over a million hectares of land (2.5 million acres) the Forestry Commission is Britain's largest land manager and the biggest single provider of countryside recreation.

The Commission is financed partly by the Government and partly by receipts from sales of timber and other produce, and from rents.

Forestry Initiatives

Plans for 12 Community Forests[4] in England—for example, Thames Chase (east of London), Mercia (Staffordshire), Great North (Tyne and Wear), Mersey (close to Liverpool) and Bristol/Avon—have been approved. A new national forest in the English Midlands (500 sq km; 200 sq miles) is being established. In Wales, the Valleys Forest Initiative encourages local communities to participate in the development of 350 sq km (135 sq miles) of existing forest in the valleys of south Wales—about 20 per cent of the land area—which is owned by the Forestry Commission. Community forests are also being promoted and developed in Scotland and Northern Ireland.

Forestry Research

The Forestry Commission maintains two principal research stations, at Alice Holt Lodge, near Farnham (Surrey), and at Bush Estate, near Edinburgh, for basic and applied research into all aspects of forestry, on which it

---

[4]The Forestry and Countryside Commissions and local authorities plan to create Community Forests near certain towns as recreational and productive woodlands in areas that at present do not have them.

spends about £9 million a year. Aid is also given for research work in universities and other institutions.

The 1995 Forest Condition Survey showed that the overall condition of oak, Scots pine, Sitka spruce and Norway spruce has sustained an improvement since 1993. There was, however, a deterioration in the crown density of beech owing to a heavy nut crop.

Forestry in Northern Ireland

Woodland and forest cover about 80,000 hectares (197,500 acres) of Northern Ireland. State-owned forest constitutes 61,000 hectares (150,700 acres).

The Department of Agriculture for Northern Ireland is responsible for forestry through its Forest Service. It administers grant aid for private planting and woodland management, and spent £15 million during 1993–96 on private and state forest expansion. Additional supplements are available where the land is coming out of agriculture or provides recreation. Annual timber production is about 250,000 cubic metres (8.8 million cubic feet), 90 per cent from state forests. Receipts from sales of timber totalled £5 million in 1995–96. Forestry and timber processing employ 1,100 people.

Further Reading

Agriculture, Fisheries and Forestry, Aspects of Britain series, HMSO, 1993.

Agriculture in the United Kingdom 1995. HMSO.

Forestry Commission. Annual report. HMSO.

Ministry of Agriculture, Fisheries and Food and the Intervention Board. Departmental Report.

19 Transport and Communications

Transport	**302**	Shipping and Ports	313
Roads	303	Civil Aviation	316
Road Haulage	307	**Communications**	**319**
Passenger Services	308	Telecommunications	319
Railways	309	Postal Services	323
Inland Waterways	313		

Britain's transport and communications infrastructure is developing rapidly. The Channel Tunnel (see p. 311) has linked the rail transport system of Great Britain to that of the European mainland. Britain's road network is being improved, with the emphasis on upgrading existing routes rather than building new motorways. Investment at seaports and airports and in air traffic control equipment is expanding capacity and easing the international movement of people and goods. Britain's telecommunications infrastructure continues to develop, with several new entrants to the market since 1991.

Transport

There has been a considerable increase in passenger travel in recent years—in Great Britain it rose by 26 per cent between 1985 and 1995. Travel by car and van rose by 35 per cent and air travel rose substantially. However, travel by train remained much the same over the period and travel by motorcycle, pedal cycle and by bus and coach declined. In all, car and van travel accounts for 86 per cent of passenger mileage within Great Britain, buses and coaches for about 6 per cent, rail for 5 per cent and air 1 per cent. The amount of freight moved by road increased by 45 per cent between 1985 and 1995. Total motor traffic for 1995 is estimated at 430,900 million vehicle-km, up 2 per cent on 1994.

Car ownership has also risen substantially. In all, 69 per cent of households in Great Britain had the regular use of one or more cars in 1994; 24 per cent had the use of two or more cars. At the end of 1995 there were 25.4 million vehicles licensed for use on the roads of Great Britain, of which 21.4 million were cars; 2.2 million light goods vehicles; 421,000 other goods vehicles; 594,000 motorcycles, scooters and mopeds; and 74,000 buses and coaches.

Research on transport issues is undertaken by a number of public sector bodies and by industry, especially the motor, aviation, marine and oil industries. Research is also commissioned by the Department of Transport, the Civil Aviation Authority (CAA—see p. 317) and London Transport (LT—see p. 308). The Department of Transport commissions research from contractors, including the recently privatised Transport Research Laboratory, which was transferred to a non-profit-distributing foundation in March 1996. Other contractors include consulting engineers, universities, and institutes and laboratories of the research councils (see pp. 330–4). A £4 million initiative to encourage research on inland surface transport was launched by the Government in January 1996.

> The central message of a government Green Paper on transport in England, *Transport: the Way Forward*, published in April 1996, is that traffic growth is an issue that must be addressed in a more strategic way than in the past. It proposes more than 20 specific areas for action, including a new system of planning trunk roads and new powers for local authorities to manage traffic demand in their areas. Tougher emissions standards for new vehicles are also proposed.

ROADS

The total road network in Britain in 1994 was 389,200 km (241,800 miles). Trunk motorways[1] accounted for 3,200 km (2,000 miles) of this, less than 1 per cent, and other trunk roads for 14,400 km (9,000 miles), or 3.7

---

[1]That is, those motorways that are the direct responsibility of central government rather than of the local authority.

per cent. However, motorways carry 16 per cent of all traffic and trunk roads another 16 per cent. Combined, they carry over half of all goods vehicle traffic in Great Britain.

Management

Responsibility for trunk roads, including most motorways, rests in England with the Secretary of State for Transport, in Scotland with the Secretary of State for Scotland and in Wales with the Secretary of State for Wales. Central government meets most of the costs of construction and maintenance. The Highways Agency, an executive agency of the Department of Transport, is responsible for building, improving and maintaining motorways and trunk roads in England. Its total budget is £1,568 million in 1996–97.

A Road User's Charter, the second edition of which was published in March 1996, sets out the standards expected of the Highways Agency on motorways and trunk roads.

In Northern Ireland the Roads Service, an agency of the Department of the Environment for Northern Ireland, is responsible for the construction, improvement and maintenance of all public roads.

The main highway authorities for non-trunk roads in England are at present the county councils, the metropolitan district councils, the new unitary authorities (see pp. 75–6) and the London borough councils. In Wales and Scotland, the highway authorities are the unitary authorities (see p. 76).

Table 19.1: Road Length (as at April 1994)

kilometres

	Public roads	All-purpose trunk roads and trunk motorways	Trunk motorways[a]
England	279,073	10,412	2,700
Scotland	52,226	3,133	274
Wales	33,709	1,700	123
Northern Ireland	24,184	2,337[b]	111
Britain	**389,192**	**17,582**	**3,208**

Source: Department of Transport
[a]In addition, there were 44 km (28 miles) of local authority motorway in England and 31 km (20 miles) in Scotland.
[b]Class A road.

Road Programme

The recent transport Green Paper proposes a new system for trunk road planning which would bring it within the regional planning guidance system. This would give local authorities the chance to become involved at an early stage of the planning process. On present plans, Highways Agency capital spending on new roads will fall from £1,169 million in 1995–96 to £696 million in 1998–99, while spending on maintenance is expected to rise from £434 million to £490 million. In spring 1995, 53 motorway and trunk road schemes were under construction in England and 271 further schemes were in preparation.

> A total of 62 projects to encourage cycling are being promoted under the Government's Cycle Challenge scheme, at a cost of £2 million. The projects range from a £267,000 initiative to encourage people to cycle to work in York to a £1,250 scheme to promote bike trailer use in Devon.

Support for local authority road schemes is approved on a package basis, with local authorities being encouraged to submit bids for a package of measures covering both roads and public transport. For 1996–97, the Department of Transport has approved 53 package bids totalling £79 million, a £15 million increase over 1995–96 levels. A total of £236 million of government grant is available to support local authority spending on transport in England in 1996–97.

Road communications in Wales are benefiting from the second Severn Bridge, which opened in June 1996, the completion of the M4 motorway and improvements to the A55 and A465 roads. The A55 is now a dual carriageway across the Welsh mainland, and it is planned to extend this to Anglesey as soon as possible. The Welsh Office's trunk road and transport programme for 1996–97 will cost £155 million. A total of £100 million is also being made available in 1996–97 for local authority expenditure on roads and transport. This includes about £73 million under the transport grant arrangements.

The Government has committed £378 million between 1996–97 and 1998–99 to trunk road construction and improvement in Scotland. The main priorities within the trunk road programme are the upgrading to motorway standard of the Glasgow to Carlisle route, and the completion of the motorway network in central Scotland. These routes provide important links for commerce and industry to the south and to mainland Europe. The Government's strategy also includes a series of 'route action plans' designed to make significant improvements to safety and journey times on specific major routes. A total of £242 million was made available in 1995–96 for local authority capital expenditure on roads and transport schemes in Scotland; from April 1996 local authorities will receive a block capital allocation for all non-housing functions, giving them greater flexibility in the level of spending on transport.

In Northern Ireland the emphasis is on improving key strategic routes, constructing more bypasses, and improving roads in the Belfast area. There are plans to spend about £63 million in a five-year major works programme up to the year 2000.

> A pilot scheme to reduce congestion on part of the M25 London orbital motorway was introduced in August 1995. Overhead signs show lower speed limits when the road is heavily congested; by reducing 'stop-start' driving conditions, it is expected that average speeds will actually increase.

Private Finance

The Government is encouraging greater private sector involvement in the design, construction, operation and funding of roads. Privately funded schemes completed in recent years, being built or undergoing planning procedures include:

- a crossing of the River Thames at Dartford, which opened to traffic in 1991 and links into the M25;
- a bridge between the mainland of Scotland and Skye, which opened in 1995;

- a second crossing of the River Severn, which opened in June 1996; and
- a relief road north of Birmingham, a motorway which would be the first overland toll route in Britain, on which the report of a public inquiry is expected in mid-1997.

The Government is assessing the technology for the introduction of electronic tolls on the motorway network, which at present has no tolls except at a few river crossings. The Department of Transport has launched a series of competitions for contracts where private sector companies are invited to design, build, finance and operate roads ('DBFO' contracts), with remuneration from the Government principally related to usage ('shadow tolls'). Five contracts, with an estimated capital construction value of over £400 million, were awarded between January and May 1996, with three other projects under negotiation. A further tranche of five more DBFO projects was announced in 1995.

Licensing and Standards

The Driver and Vehicle Licensing Agency (DVLA) maintains official records of drivers and vehicles in Great Britain. At the end of 1995 it held records on 36.4 million drivers and 25.5 million licensed vehicles. New drivers of motor vehicles must pass a driving test before getting a full licence to drive; a written theory test on matters such as traffic signs and safety aspects of vehicles and driver attitude is being phased in, from July 1996 for new car drivers. The records for Northern Ireland are maintained by Driver and Vehicle Licensing Northern Ireland.

The Driving Standards Agency is the national driver testing authority in Great Britain. It also supervises professional driving instructors and the compulsory basic training scheme for learner motorcyclists. Minimum ages are:

- 16 for riders of mopeds, drivers of small tractors, and disabled people receiving a mobility allowance;
- 17 for drivers of cars and other passenger vehicles with nine or fewer seats

(including that of the driver), motorcycles and goods vehicles not over 3.5 tonnes permissible maximum weight;

- 18 for goods vehicles weighing over 3.5, but not over 7.5, tonnes; and
- 21 for passenger vehicles with more than nine seats and goods vehicles over 7.5 tonnes.

Before most new cars and goods vehicles are allowed on the roads, they must meet certain safety and environmental requirements, based primarily on standards drawn up by the EU. The Vehicle Certification Agency is responsible for ensuring these requirements are met through a process known as 'type approval'. It also provides a service to manufacturers wishing to obtain international vehicle system and component type approval in Great Britain.

The Vehicle Inspectorate is responsible for ensuring the roadworthiness of vehicles. It does this through the annual testing of vehicles, including heavy goods vehicles, light goods vehicles, public service vehicles, cars and motorcycles. It also ensures the compliance of drivers and vehicle operators with legislation through roadside and other enforcement checks.

In Northern Ireland the Driver and Vehicle Testing Agency (DVTA) is responsible for testing drivers and vehicles under statutory schemes broadly similar to those in Great Britain. Private cars four or more years old are tested at DVTA centres.

Road Safety

Although Great Britain has one of the highest densities of road traffic in the world, it has a good record on road safety, with the lowest road accident death rate in the EU. Figures for 1995 show that 3,621 people were killed on the roads (down 0.8 per cent on 1994 and the lowest annual figure since records began), 45,500 seriously injured (down 2.2 per cent) and 261,400 slightly injured (down 1.4 per cent). This compares with nearly 8,000 deaths a year in the mid-1960s. Several factors, such as developments in vehicle safety standards, improvements in roads, and the introduction of legislation on seat-belt wearing and drinking and driving, have contributed to the long-term decline in deaths and serious casualties.

Deaths on Britain's Roads 1926–1995

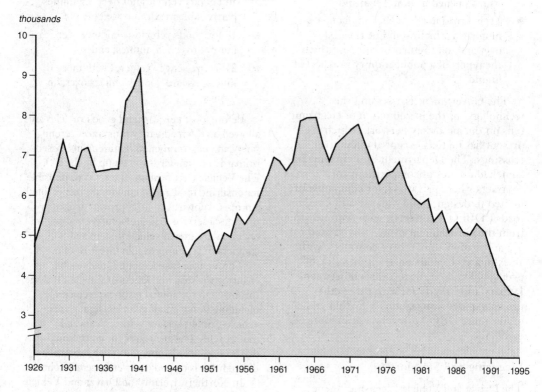

thousands

Source: Department of Transport

The Government's aim is to reduce road casualties by one-third by the end of the century, compared with the 1981–85 average. Priority is given to reducing casualties among vulnerable road-users (children, pedestrians, cyclists, motorcyclists and elderly people), particularly in urban areas, where about 75 per cent of road accidents occur. Strategies for reducing casualties focus on measures to combat speeding and drinking and driving, improvements in highway design, better protection for vehicle occupants and encouraging the use of cycle helmets. A study in west London has shown that automatic speed cameras have reduced road deaths in the area being studied by 70 per cent in two years. A total of £55 million has been set aside for spending on local road safety schemes in 1996–97, up by £5 million over 1995–96. Gloucester has been chosen in a Department of Transport competition as the site of the first

'Safe Town' initiative. It will receive £5 million over five years to implement a co-ordinated package of road safety measures. In Northern Ireland the target reduction relates to fatal and serious casualties only; a plan to achieve it was published in 1995.

Traffic in Towns

Traffic management schemes are used in many urban areas to reduce congestion, create a better environment and improve road safety. They include bus lanes, facilities for pedestrians and cyclists, and traffic-calming measures such as road humps to constrain traffic speeds in residential areas. Local authorities can introduce 20 mph (32 km/h) zones, subject to central government consent; monitoring has shown that on average these zones reduce accident casualties by 61 per cent and child pedestrian casualties by 67 per cent.

More than 270 had been authorised by June 1996.

Many towns have shopping precincts designed for the convenience of pedestrians, from which motor vehicles are excluded for all or part of the day. Controls over on-street parking are enforced through excess charges and fixed penalty fines, supported where appropriate by powers to clamp or remove vehicles.

Implementation is well under way on a 505-km (315-mile) network of priority 'red routes' in London. Marked by special signs and red lines at the kerb, these routes are subject to special stopping controls and other traffic management measures, strictly enforced with penalties higher than elsewhere. The Traffic Director for London is co-ordinating the introduction and operation of red routes throughout London, and the aim is to have the network fully operational by the year 2000. A pilot scheme in north and east London, introduced in 1991, led to significant falls in bus journey times and a more dependable service, with a consequent rise in passenger numbers. The Department of Transport is supporting the development of the London cycle network to make travel by bicycle much easier and safer.

> In the Government's transport strategy for London, published in May 1996, plans for future projects are presented as a rolling programme, including a package of possible new river crossings in east London.

ROAD HAULAGE

Road haulage traffic by heavy goods vehicles amounted to 144,000 million tonne-km[2] in Great Britain in 1995, 4 per cent more than in 1994. There has been a move towards larger and more efficient vehicles carrying heavier loads—about 80 per cent of the traffic, measured in tonne-km, is now carried by vehicles of over 25 tonnes gross weight.

---

[2]A tonne-km is equivalent to 1 tonne transported for 1 km.

Journey lengths are increasing, with the average haul now being 89 km (55 miles), 31 per cent longer than in 1980. Hauliers licensed to carry other firms' goods account for 74 per cent of freight carried in terms of tonne-km.

There were about 120,000 holders of an operator's licence in January 1996, with 432,000 large goods vehicles. Nearly 90 per cent of operators have fleets of five or fewer vehicles. The biggest in Great Britain are NFC plc, P & O Industrial Services Division, Ocean Group plc and Tibbet & Britten Group plc.

Licensing and Other Controls

In general, those operating goods vehicles or trailer combinations over 3.5 tonnes gross weight require a goods vehicle operator's licence. Licences are divided into restricted licences for own-account operators carrying goods connected with their own business, and standard licences for hauliers operating for hire or reward. Proof of professional competence, financial standing and good repute is needed to obtain a standard licence. In Northern Ireland own-account operators do not require a licence, although this is under consideration.

EC regulations prescribe maximum limits on driving times and minimum requirements for breaks and rest periods for most drivers of heavy goods vehicles over 3.5 tonnes. Drivers' activities are monitored automatically by a tachograph—a recording device in the cab. Separate British domestic rules govern the remainder. Under these, drivers are normally required to keep a written record of their activities. Speed limiters must also be fitted to heavy lorries. Large goods vehicles of over 12 tonnes maximum gross weight first used after January 1988 must have maximum powered speed limited to 56 mph (90 km/h).

International Road Haulage

International road haulage has grown rapidly and in 1995 about 950,000 road goods vehicles were ferried to mainland Europe. Of these, 486,000 were powered vehicles registered in Britain. In 1995 British vehicles carried almost 14 million tonnes internationally, about three times the amount for 1985. About 95 per cent of this traffic was with the

European Union. The largest commodity group carried is agricultural produce and foodstuffs, which accounted for 34 per cent of inward tonnage and 27 per cent of outward tonnage in 1995.

International road haulage within the EU was fully liberalised in 1993. 'Cabotage' (the operation of domestic road haulage within a member state by a non-resident) will be fully liberalised in 1998. Until then, quotas of permits are available which allow cabotage in most parts of western Europe. Haulage elsewhere takes place under bilateral agreements, most of which allow unrestricted numbers of British lorries into the country concerned, although some require permits. The European Conference of Transport Ministers issues a limited but increasing number of permits giving free access to, and transit across, several countries in Central and Eastern Europe.

PASSENGER SERVICES

Buses

Almost all bus services in Great Britain are provided by companies in the private sector, ranging from the three major groups with over 5,000 buses to small operators with fewer than five. The largest operators are Cowie British Bus, FirstBus and Stagecoach Holdings. Outside London, operators may provide services without restriction, although controls may be imposed on the number of vehicles operating if this would otherwise cause congestion or danger to other road users. While most local bus services are provided commercially, local authorities may subsidise the provision of services which are not commercially viable but which are considered to be socially necessary, after competitive tender. Local bus mileage outside London in 1994–95 was up 29 per cent on its 1985–86 pre-deregulation level.

The Government supports the privatisation of the remaining council-owned bus companies, of which there were 19 in England and Wales in March 1996. To encourage this, councils which sell shareholdings in bus companies before April 1997 will be able to spend three-quarters of the proceeds rather than being forced to keep back at least half to repay debt.

London Transport (LT) is a statutory corporation responsible for providing public transport in London. It no longer has its own buses, but organises about 700 bus routes through private sector companies operating under contract. LT completed the privatisation of its bus operating subsidiaries by the end of 1994. In the longer term deregulation of bus services in London is proposed. Provision would be made for operating socially necessary but uneconomic services and the continuation of a London-wide concessionary travel scheme. A London Bus Passenger's Charter sets service standards.

Bus priority measures, such as bus lanes and traffic light priority signalling, form an important element in many local authorities' package bids to the Department of Transport (see p. 304). The Department of Transport has been working with local authorities on developing an 800-km (500-mile) London bus priority network. This covers all heavily-used bus routes in London which are not covered by the red route network. It will give them priority at junctions, making buses quicker and more reliable. A further £9 million has been allocated in 1996–97 to continue development of the London bus priority network. New information systems are being provided to assist bus passengers in a number of cities.

In Northern Ireland subsidiaries of the publicly owned Northern Ireland Transport Holding Company supply almost all road passenger services. Citybus Ltd operates services in Belfast, and Ulsterbus Ltd runs most of the services in the rest of Northern Ireland. These companies have about 280 and 1,220 vehicles respectively. As well as the two major operators, there are about 75 small privately owned undertakings, often operating fewer than five vehicles.

Coaches

In Britain long-distance coach services are provided by companies in the private sector. There are no restrictions on routes served or the number of vehicles operated. A national network of routes is run by the National Express company, largely through franchised operations. Passenger comfort in coaches has improved in recent years, with, for example, the provision of refreshment facilities on some services.

> Coaches and minibuses carrying three or more children will have to be fitted with seatbelts on all seats from 1997. Regulations to fit seatbelts to all new coaches and minibuses will be introduced when the necessary agreement has been reached in the EU.

While all regular, and some shuttle, overseas coach services still require authorisation or permission from the authorities of the countries to or through which they travel, most tourist services within the EU have been liberalised. Operators no longer need prior permission to run either holiday shuttle services, where accommodation is included as part of the package, or occasional coach tours to, from or within another member state. In 1993 passenger cabotage was introduced for tours where a single vehicle carries the same group of passengers throughout a journey. Since January 1996, this has been extended to all non-regular services.

Taxis

There are about 58,000 licensed taxis in Great Britain, mainly in urban areas; London has about 18,000. In London and several other major cities taxis must be purpose-built to conform to strict requirements and new ones have to provide for people in wheelchairs. In many urban districts drivers must have passed a test of their knowledge of the area. At present, a local authority can only limit the number of licensed taxis if it is satisfied that there is no unfulfilled demand for taxis in its area. Private hire vehicles with drivers ('minicabs') may be booked only through the operator and not hired on the street. In most areas outside London private hire vehicles are licensed; there are about 52,000 in England

and Wales outside London. It is estimated that at least 40,000 minicabs operate in London.

Having reviewed the taxi licensing regime in England and Wales, in 1995 the Government announced that it intends to maintain the distinction between taxis and minicabs. It will introduce a licensing system for minicabs in London when legislative time permits. The power of local authorities to control numbers of taxis would be phased out.

There are about 4,000 licensed taxis in Northern Ireland. Licences are issued by the Department of the Environment for Northern Ireland on a broadly similar basis to that in Great Britain.

RAILWAYS

Railways were pioneered in Britain: the Stockton and Darlington Railway, opened in 1825, was the first public passenger railway in the world to be worked by steam power. The main railway companies in Great Britain were nationalised in 1948, coming under the control of the British Railways Board (BR). This rail network—consisting of track, stations, other infrastructure, locomotives and rolling stock—is now being privatised.

Privatisation

The Government's approach, enshrined in the Railways Act 1993, includes:

- the franchising of all BR's existing passenger services to the private sector;
- the transfer of BR's freight and parcels operations to the private sector;
- the creation of a new right of access to the rail network for private operators of both passenger and freight services;
- the separation of track from train operations, under which Railtrack is responsible for operating all track and infrastructure, with passenger services being run by BR until they are franchised;
- the privatisation of Railtrack;
- the appointment of a Rail Regulator to oversee the fair application of arrangements for track access and

charging, and a Franchising Director responsible for negotiating, awarding and monitoring franchises;

- opportunities for the private sector to lease stations; and
- improved grant arrangements for individual rail services or groups of services.

Railtrack was privatised in May 1996. Besides projects to maintain and renew the network, it expects to carry out improvements such as Thameslink 2000 (see below). Railtrack has also begun to let contracts for the modernisation of the West Coast Main Line.

BR has restructured its passenger services into 25 train operating units as a basis for the privatised railway network. The first two franchised services, South West Trains and Great Western, came into operation in February 1996. By June 1996 seven of the 25 franchises had been awarded, with all of the others advertised. The Franchising Director has announced that overall fare levels will not be allowed to rise above the rate of inflation for three years from January 1996. For the four years after that, they will be limited to the rate of inflation less 1 per cent. Key network benefits—such as through ticketing and discount cards—have been legally safeguarded as part of the franchising.

In all, by July 1996 some 60 former BR businesses had been sold. For example:

- BR's trainload freight companies, Transrail, Mainline and Loadhaul, were sold in February 1996 to North and South Railways, a consortium led by Wisconsin Central Ltd, and due to start operating under the name of English, Welsh and Scottish Railways;
- Red Star, the parcels business, was sold in September 1995;
- Rail Express Systems, the BR business which operates trains for the Royal Mail, including 22 Travelling Post Offices on which mail is sorted overnight by Post Office staff, was sold in December 1995; and
- Freightliner, which carries containers between major ports and inland terminals, was sold in May 1996.

In addition, a large number of infrastructure and maintenance businesses have been sold.

New regulations require rail operators to prepare a 'safety case' to demonstrate that safe practices will be followed at all times; these cases are validated by Railtrack. Railway employees who undertake work with safety implications are required to be fit and competent. The Railway Inspectorate, part of the Health and Safety Executive (see p. 201), is responsible for validating Railtrack's own safety case.

Operations

As part of the Citizen's Charter initiative, BR published a Passenger's Charter. Compensation is payable to passengers if performance falls by more than a small margin below the standards set in the Charter. Under the privatisation arrangements, franchisees are required to produce their own charters, which will include targets at least as demanding as BR's previous ones.

Investment

There has been substantial investment in Britain's railways in recent years. Railtrack expects to spend £8,125 million a year over five years maintaining and improving the network. Recent developments include a rail link serving Prestwick Airport near Glasgow, opened in 1994. Future improvements include the Thameslink 2000 project to increase greatly the capacity of the existing Thameslink service between north and south London. The government contribution is likely to be in excess of £100 million out of the total cost of £650 million.

Some of the passenger franchises have been let for longer than the usual seven-year period on condition that the franchisee provides new rolling stock. For example, the operator of the Gatwick Express service has been awarded a 15-year franchise, and plans to introduce completely new stock by 1999.

Passenger Services

The passenger network (see map facing inside back cover) comprises a fast inter-city network, linking the main centres of Great Britain; local stopping services; and commuter services in and around the large conurbations, especially London and south-east England. InterCity 125 trains, travelling at maximum sustained speeds of 125 mph (201 km/h), are the world's fastest diesel trains.

About 30 per cent of route-mileage is electrified, including the East Coast Main Line linking London and Edinburgh. A new generation of diesel multiple-unit trains has been introduced on regional services. The first of a new generation of electric trains entered service in Kent in 1992.

Freight

Nearly 90 per cent of rail freight traffic by volume is of bulk commodities, mainly coal, coke, iron and steel, building materials and petroleum. The opening of the Channel Tunnel has presented an important opportunity for non-bulk freight movement. The Government makes grants available to encourage companies to move goods by rail or water rather than road; over 150 schemes have benefited from freight facilities grant. The Department of Transport budget for such grants in 1996–97 is about £13 million. New freight operators have had rights of open access to the rail network since 1994, allowing services to be set up in competition with existing hauliers. National Power (see p. 269) and Direct Rail recently started services on their own account.

Northern Ireland

In Northern Ireland, the Northern Ireland Railways Company Ltd, a subsidiary of the Northern Ireland Transport Holding Company, operates the railway service on about 336 km (210 miles) of track. Its passenger charter includes a compensation scheme that operates if targets for punctuality and reliability are not met.

Channel Tunnel

The Channel Tunnel, the largest civil engineering project in Europe to be financed by the private sector, was opened to traffic in 1994. The project, which is estimated to have cost about £10,000 million, was undertaken by Eurotunnel, a British–French group which has a 65-year operating concession from the British and French governments.

Eurotunnel Services

Eurotunnel operates shuttle trains through twin one-way rail tunnels between the terminals near Folkestone and Calais, with the journey taking about 35 minutes from platform to platform. These trains provide a drive-on, drive-off service, with separate shuttle trains for passenger and freight vehicles. Car and coach passengers stay with their vehicles during the journey. Lorry drivers travel separately from their vehicles, in a carriage at the front of the shuttle. Eurotunnel runs passenger shuttle services every 15 minutes and freight shuttle services every 20 minutes at peak periods. In 1995, 391,000 trucks, 23,500 coaches and 1.2 million cars and other vehicles were carried through the tunnel.

Railway Services

About £1,400 million has been invested in new passenger and freight rolling stock and infrastructure improvements for Channel Tunnel services. More than 20 Eurostar high-speed trains run each day between the London terminal at Waterloo and Paris or Brussels. Daytime passenger services from the Midlands, northern England and Scotland to Paris and Brussels should begin operating in 1997. Overnight services from London and other parts of the country to continental Europe are also planned to start in 1997. A part-privately funded international station at Ashford in Kent opened in February 1996.

Freight services through the Channel Tunnel operate from a network of regional terminals to major industrial centres on the Continent. Four terminals—in London, Glasgow, Manchester and Birmingham —started operations when the tunnel opened. Because of infrastructure improvements and advanced wagon designs, over 90 per cent of standard continental 'swap-bodies' are able to travel over the lines between the tunnel and the British terminal network, even though the

British loading gauge is smaller than the continental gauge. The terminal facilities allow freight to be transferred easily between road and rail.

The Channel Tunnel Rail Link is a proposed private sector 108-km (67-mile) high-speed railway between London and the Channel Tunnel. Its London terminal will be at St Pancras, with intermediate stations at Stratford in east London, and Ebbsfleet and Ashford in Kent. The Government announced in February 1996 that London and Continental Railways, a private sector consortium, had won the competition to carry forward the £3,000 million scheme, scheduled for completion in 2003. The transfer to London and Continental of European Passenger Services, the operator of the British arm of the existing Eurostar services, took place in May 1996.

Other Railways in London

London Underground Ltd (LUL), a subsidiary of LT, operates services on 388 km (243 miles) of railway, of which about 170 km (106 miles) are underground. The system has 268 stations, with 468 trains running in the peak period. About 784 million passenger journeys were made on London Underground trains in 1995–96. LUL has a charter committing it to provide a certain level of service to passengers. It includes a compensation scheme that applies when delays of 15 minutes or more occur within LUL's control. In March 1996 LUL was set more demanding performance targets for the period to 1998–99, the first time it has had targets for a three-year period. Targets cover matters such as train reliability, escalators and lifts working, and station cleanliness.

Major investment in the Underground is under way or planned. Work started in 1993 on an extension of the Jubilee Line to Stratford (east London) via Docklands and the north Greenwich peninsula. The extension is scheduled to open in 1998. Total LUL investment in new lines will be £568 million in 1996–97, of which most will be spent on the Jubilee Line. LUL has also sought approval to build a northern extension to the East London Line to Dalston, where it would link with BR's North London Line.

The Docklands Light Railway (DLR), a 22-km (14-mile) route with 28 stations, connects the City of London with Docklands, Beckton and Stratford. An extension under the River Thames is planned to Greenwich and Lewisham, to be built by a private sector consortium. The DLR's operations will be franchised to the private sector for seven years from April 1997, the eventual aim being the sale of the railway to the private sector.

The Government has set aside funding for the Croydon Tramlink, a 28-km (18-mile) light rail network which would connect Croydon with Wimbledon, Beckenham and New Addington. This project would be a joint venture between LT and the private sector. Government financial support would be subject to satisfactory private sector bids; a preferred bidder was announced in April 1996.

Other Urban Railways

The Glasgow Underground, a heavy rapid transit system, operates on a 10-km (6-mile) loop in central Glasgow. The Tyne and Wear Metro is a 59-km (37-mile) light rail system connecting Newcastle upon Tyne with Gateshead, North and South Shields, Heworth and Jarrow. An extension to Sunderland is currently proposed by the Tyne and Wear Passenger Transport Executive. Two light railway systems have been constructed in recent years and are now in operation:

- the Greater Manchester Metrolink, connecting Altrincham and Bury with Manchester city centre on a 31-km (19-mile) route, to which further extensions are planned; and

- the South Yorkshire Supertram, which is a 29-km (18-mile) system connecting Meadowhall, Hillsborough and Halfway to Sheffield City Centre.

Construction work has now started on Midland Metro Line One in Birmingham. It is hoped that the system will commence operation in the summer of 1998. Other schemes with parliamentary approval include the Leeds Supertram and the Greater Nottingham Light Rapid Transit. There are also plans for a privately financed and run light railway between Caernarfon and Porthmadog in north Wales.

Traditional tramcars still operate in Blackpool, the Isle of Man and Llandudno.

Private Railways

There are over 100 small, privately owned passenger-carrying railways in Great Britain, mostly operated on a voluntary basis and providing limited services for tourists and railway enthusiasts. The prime aim of most is the preservation of steam locomotives. They generally run on old BR branch lines, but there are also several narrow-gauge lines, mainly in north Wales.

INLAND WATERWAYS

Inland waterways are popular for leisure and recreation and make a valuable contribution to the quality of Britain's environment. They also play an important part in land drainage and water supply, and some are used for carrying freight. The greatest amounts of seagoing freight are carried on the Rivers Thames, Forth, Humber and Mersey and the Manchester Ship Canal; the most important waterways for internal traffic are the Thames, the Aire and Calder Navigation, the Mersey and the Manchester Ship Canal.

British Waterways is responsible for 3,200 km (2,000 miles) of waterways in Great Britain, making up the greater part of the canal system. The majority of its waterways are primarily for leisure use, but about 620 km (385 miles) are maintained as commercial waterways. It is developing its built and natural heritage for tourism and recreational and commercial use, often in conjunction with the private sector. In 1995–96 British Waterways' revenue amounted to £92.9 million, including a government grant of £54.4 million to maintain its waterways to statutory standards.

SHIPPING AND PORTS

In March 1996 British companies owned 664 trading vessels of 100 gross tonnes or more, with a combined 12.5 million deadweight tonnes. Among the ships were 167 vessels totalling 6.6 million deadweight tonnes used as oil, chemical or gas carriers and 464 vessels totalling 5.8 million deadweight tonnes employed as dry-bulk carriers, container ships or other types of cargo ship. In all, 71 per cent of British-owned vessels are registered in Britain or British dependent territories such as Bermuda.

The tonnage of the British-registered trading fleet has been declining. In recognition of this, measures have been introduced to encourage British shipowners to register their vessels in Britain. These include the relaxation of officer nationality rules, which came into

Table 19.2: Traffic Through the Principal Ports of Great Britain				_million tonnes_
	1990	1991	1992	1993	1994
London	58.1	52.8	48.9	50.9	51.8
Forth	25.4	22.9	23.3	26.4	44.4
Tees and Hartlepool	40.2	42.9	43.4	42.7	43.0
Grimsby and Immingham	39.4	40.2	40.8	41.3	42.9
Sullom Voe	36.0	35.9	41.4	39.4	38.6
Milford Haven	32.2	35.7	35.6	35.7	34.3
Southampton	28.8	31.5	29.8	30.9	31.5
Liverpool	23.2	24.8	27.8	30.5	29.5
Felixstowe	16.4	16.1	18.0	20.3	22.1
Medway	13.6	16.1	14.3	13.6	14.7
Dover	13.0	12.0	13.1	13.8	14.1
Orkneys	8.6	9.2	8.5	11.9	14.1
Port Talbot	8.9	9.4	9.4	10.1	11.1

Source: Department of Transport

force in 1995. Except on 'strategic' ships, this opens positions to officers of any nation provided they hold British certificates of competency or equivalents. Fiscal changes announced in 1994 enable shipowners to carry forward tax charges resulting from ship sales to set against further investment within a six-year period. Assistance is also provided for seafarer training.

Cargo Services

About 95 per cent by weight (77 per cent by value) of Britain's foreign trade is carried by sea. In 1994 British seaborne trade amounted to 352 million tonnes (valued at £217,000 million). Tanker cargo accounted for 45 per cent of this trade by weight, but only 6 per cent by value.

Nearly all scheduled cargo-liner services from Britain are containerised. British tonnage serving these trades is dominated by a relatively small number of private sector companies. In deep-sea trades these usually operate in conjunction with other companies on the same routes in organisations known as 'conferences'. The object of these groupings is to ensure regular and efficient services with stable freight rates, to the benefit of both shipper and shipowner. Besides the carriage of freight by liner and bulk services between Britain and the rest of Europe, many roll-on roll-off services carry cars, passengers and commercial vehicles.

Passenger Services

In 1995 35 million international sea passenger movements took place between Britain and the rest of the world, compared with about 101 million international air passenger movements. Almost all passengers who arrived at or departed from British ports travelled to or from the continent of Europe or the Irish Republic. In 1995 about 207,000 people embarked on pleasure cruises from British ports. Traffic from southern and south-eastern ports accounts for a substantial proportion of traffic to the continent of Europe. The main British operators are Stena Sealink Line, P & O European Ferries and Hoverspeed, although not all their vessels are under the British flag.

Services are provided by roll-on roll-off ferries, hovercraft, hydrofoils and high-speed catamarans. There has been a trend towards using larger vessels, including new large high-speed vessels, in recent years as the ferry companies face competition from the Channel Tunnel.

Domestic passenger and freight ferry services also run to many of the offshore islands, such as the Isle of Wight, the Orkney and Shetland islands, and the islands off the west coast of Scotland. It is estimated that in 1994 there were about 39 million passengers on such internal services.

Merchant Shipping Legislation and Policy

The Government's policy is to promote open and competitive shipping markets. Regulations administered by agencies of the Department of Transport provide for marine safety and welfare, investigation of accidents and prevention and cleaning up of pollution from ships.

Britain plays a significant role in the formulation of shipping policy within the EU. All international services and most cabotage services within the EU have been liberalised. Full cabotage liberalisation will be achieved over the next ten years. Work is progressing to introduce a European programme to improve maritime safety and prevent pollution.

Ports

The Government's policy has been to:

- remove constraints preventing ports from operating efficiently;
- enable them to compete more fully on an equal footing; and
- expose the ports industry as a whole to the market.

There are about 80 ports of commercial significance in Great Britain, and in addition several hundred small harbours cater for local cargo, fishing vessels, island ferries or recreation. There are three broad types of port—trust ports owned and run by boards constituted as trusts, those owned by local authorities and company-owned ports. Most operate with statutory powers under private Acts of Parliament. Major ports controlled by trusts include Aberdeen, Dover, Ipswich, Milford Haven and Tyne. Local authorities own many small ports and a few much larger ports, including Portsmouth and the oil ports in Orkney and Shetland. The Ports Act 1991 facilitates the transfer of trust ports fully to the private sector; Clyde, Dundee, Forth, Medway, Tees and Hartlepool and the former Port of London Authority dock at Tilbury have already moved to the private sector. The Government has announced that the ports of Ipswich and Tyne will also be privatised.

Associated British Ports (ABP), Britain's largest port owner and operator, operates 22 ports, including Cardiff, Grimsby and Immingham, Hull, Newport, Southampton and Swansea. Together its ports handled 114 million tonnes of cargo in 1995. Other major ports owned by companies include Felixstowe, Liverpool, Manchester and a group of ferry ports, including Harwich (Parkeston Quay) and Stranraer.

Port Traffic

In 1995 traffic through major British ports amounted to 509 million tonnes. This comprised 171 million tonnes of exports, 179 million tonnes of imports and 159 million tonnes of domestic traffic (which included offshore traffic and landings of sea-dredged aggregates). The smaller ports handled an additional 39 million tonnes.

Britain's main ports, in terms of total tonnage handled, are shown in Table 19.2. Forth, Milford Haven and Sullom Voe (Shetland) mostly handle oil, while the main ports for non-fuel traffic are Dover, Felixstowe, Grimsby and Immingham, Liverpool, London, and Tees and Hartlepool.

Container and roll-on roll-off traffic in Britain has increased sixfold since 1970 to 108 million tonnes in 1994 and now accounts for 78 per cent of non-bulk traffic. The leading ports for container traffic are Felixstowe, London and Southampton. Those for roll-on roll-off traffic are Dover (Britain's leading seaport in terms of the value of trade handled),

Felixstowe, Grimsby and Immingham, Portsmouth and Ramsgate.

Northern Ireland has four fully-equipped ports, at Belfast, Larne, Londonderry and Warrenpoint, which handle worldwide trade. Belfast is the principal freight port, handling over half of all cargo through its modern roll-on roll-off facilities. It handled 12.3 million tonnes in 1995.

Development

Most recent major port developments have been at east- and south-coast ports. For example, at Felixstowe a £50 million extension to the terminal was completed in 1990; a new £100 million terminal on the River Medway caters for deep-sea container traffic; and Dover has started on a £100 million programme to develop its western docks to meet competition from the Channel Tunnel. A new cool store has been opened at Tees and Hartlepool, and there are plans for a new grain terminal. A 16-hectare (40-acre) car terminal has been built at Tyne. ABP invests about £50 million a year in developing its port facilities. Recent investments or development projects currently under way at ABP's ports include:

- deepening the main channel at Southampton, at a cost of £27 million, to allow better access by large container ships;

- the development of a new berth at Southampton's container port;

- the Nordic Terminal, a new £13.5 million four-berth roll-on roll-off facility at Immingham; and

- a £3 million animal feed terminal at Newport.

Purpose-built terminals for oil from the British sector of the North Sea have been built at Hound Point on the Forth, on the Tees, at Flotta and at Sullom Voe (one of the largest oil terminals in the world). Supply bases for offshore oil and gas installations have been constructed at several ports, notably Aberdeen, Great Yarmouth and Heysham.

Safety at Sea

The Department of Transport has two executive agencies concerned with safety at sea—the Coastguard Agency and the Marine Safety Agency (MSA). The former is responsible for HM Coastguard and the Marine Pollution Control Unit (see pp. 357–8). The MSA is responsible for marine safety and the prevention of pollution from ships. It carries out inspections on British and foreign ships using British ports to ensure that they comply with international safety, pollution prevention and operational standards. In 1995–96, 204 foreign-registered ships were detained by the MSA in British ports.

HM Coastguard is responsible for co-ordinating civil maritime search and rescue operations around the coastline of Britain. In a maritime emergency the coastguard calls on and co-ordinates facilities such as:

● Coastguard helicopters and cliff rescue companies;

● lifeboats of the Royal National Lifeboat Institution (a voluntary body);

● aeroplanes, helicopters and ships from the armed forces; and

● merchant shipping and commercial aircraft.

In 1995 HM Coastguard co-ordinated action in 12,220 incidents (including cliff rescues), in which 19,384 people were helped.

Some locations around Britain are hazardous for shipping. Measures are taken to reduce the risk of collision, including the separation of ships into internationally agreed shipping lanes. The traffic separation scheme in the Dover Strait, one of the busiest seaways in the world, is one such scheme. It is monitored by radar from the Channel Navigation Information Service near Dover. Ships are encouraged to report their movements and these are tracked. Those found contravening the regulations are identified and action is taken.

The number of British-registered merchant vessels involved in accidents has fallen in recent years—102 accidents involving vessels over 100 gross registered tonnage in 1994, compared with 183 in 1990.

Following pressure from Britain, international agreement was reached in February 1996 to improve safety regulations for roll-on roll-off ferries operating in north-west Europe and the Baltic. By October 2002 all ferries operating to and from Britain will have to meet the new standard for staying afloat even with water on the car deck.

The lighthouse authorities, which control about 370 lighthouses and other lights and buoys, are:

● the Corporation of Trinity House, which covers England, Wales and the Channel Islands;

● the Northern Lighthouse Board, for Scotland and the Isle of Man; and

● the Commissioners of Irish Lights for Northern Ireland and the Irish Republic.

They are funded mainly by light dues levied on shipping in Britain and Ireland. The Ports Act 1991 provided for the transfer of certain lights and buoys to harbour authorities where these are used mainly for local rather than general navigation. Responsibility for pilotage within harbours rests with harbour authorities under the Pilotage Act 1987.

CIVIL AVIATION

British aviation authorities are negotiating new international rights and improving facilities such as air traffic control. British airlines are entirely in the private sector, as are a number of the major airports.

Air Traffic

Total capacity offered on all services by British airlines amounted to 29,905 million tonne-km in 1995: 22,016 million tonne-km on scheduled services and 7,889 million tonne-km on non-scheduled services. British airlines carried 47.4 million passengers on scheduled services and 27.4 million on charter flights; 101 million passengers travelled by air (international terminal passengers) to or from Britain, a 5 per cent increase on 1994.

The value of Britain's overseas trade carried by air in 1995 was about £65,300 million. Air freight is important for the carriage of goods with a high value-to-weight ratio, especially where speed is essential.

British Airways

British Airways plc is one of the world's leading airlines. In terms of international scheduled services it is the largest in the world. During 1995–96 its turnover from airline operations was £7,760 million. The British Airways group carried 36.1 million passengers on scheduled and charter flights both within Britain and internationally.

British Airways' scheduled route network serves more than 300 destinations in 88 countries. Its main operating base is London's Heathrow airport, but services from Gatwick and regional centres such as Birmingham, Glasgow and Manchester have been expanding. Scheduled Concorde supersonic services operate from London Heathrow to New York and to Barbados, crossing the Atlantic in about half the time taken by subsonic aircraft. British Airways has a fleet of almost 300 aircraft, the largest in Western Europe, including seven Concordes, almost 70 Boeing 747s and four of the new Boeing 777s.

Other Airlines

Other major British airlines operating internationally include:

- Air UK;
- Britannia Airways, the world's biggest charter airline, which carried 8.0 million passengers in 1995 and has 29 aircraft;
- British Midland, which operates a large network of scheduled services and has 37 aircraft;
- Monarch Airlines; and
- Virgin Atlantic, which operates scheduled services between Britain, eight North American destinations, Athens, Dublin, Hong Kong, Johannesburg and Tokyo, with 18 aircraft.

Helicopters and Other Aerial Work

Helicopters are engaged on a variety of work, especially operations connected with Britain's offshore oil and gas industry. The main offshore operators in Britain are Bond Helicopters, British International Helicopters and Bristow Helicopters, with 43, 25 and 56 helicopters respectively in 1993. Light aircraft and helicopters are also used in other important commercial activities, such as charters, search and rescue services, load-lifting, aerial surveying and photography, and police and air ambulance operations.

Aviation Policy

The Government's civil aviation policy aims to maintain high standards of safety and security and to achieve environmental improvements by reducing noise and emissions from aircraft through international standards. It seeks to promote the interests of travellers by encouraging a competitive British industry, and is committed to encouraging more international services to and from regional airports. The Government has taken the lead in the EU and with bilateral partners in negotiating freer arrangements within which airline competition can flourish; arrangements within the European Economic Area (see p. 33) are now almost fully liberalised. New arrangements with an increasing number of countries are resulting in better provision of services at more competitive fares. The liberalisation of air services within the EU has seen the emergence of a number of low-cost airlines in Britain, such as Debonair and EasyJet.

Civil Aviation Authority

The CAA is an independent statutory body responsible for the economic and safety regulation of the industry and, through a wholly-owned subsidiary, National Air Traffic Services Ltd (NATS), for the provision of air navigation services. Its board members are appointed by the Secretary of State for Transport. The CAA's primary objectives are to ensure that British airlines provide air services to satisfy all substantial categories of public demand at the lowest charges consistent with a high standard of safety, and to further the reasonable interests of air transport users.

Air Safety

British airlines have a good safety record. In all but two of the 14 years to 1996, there were no passenger fatalities in accidents involving large commercially registered British aircraft in British airspace. During this period no crew or passenger fatalities associated with British-registered aircraft occurred in foreign airspace.

Every company operating aircraft used for commercial air transport purposes must possess an Air Operator's Certificate, which the CAA grants when it is satisfied that the company is competent to operate its aircraft safely. The CAA's flight operations inspectors, who are experienced civilian pilots, together with airworthiness surveyors, check that satisfactory standards are maintained. All aircraft registered in Britain must be granted a certificate of airworthiness by the CAA before being flown. In this and many other aspects of its work, the CAA is increasingly working to standards developed with its European partners in the Joint Airworthiness Authorities. New measures to increase inspections of foreign aircraft operating to Britain were announced by the Government in January 1996.

Each member of the flight crew of a British-registered aircraft, every ground engineer who certifies an aircraft fit to fly, and every air traffic controller must hold the appropriate official licence issued by the CAA. To qualify for a first professional licence, a pilot must undertake a full-time course of instruction approved by the CAA—or have acceptable military or civilian flying experience—and pass ground examinations and flight tests.

Air Traffic Control and Navigation Services

Civil and military air traffic control over Britain and the surrounding seas, including a large part of the North Atlantic, is carried out by NATS, working in collaboration with military controllers. NATS also provides air traffic control at most major British airports.

> Air traffic delays in Europe halved between 1992 and 1995. Average delays for flights from Britain were reduced from 14 to 4 minutes, despite a 5 per cent annual increase in traffic.

Britain plays a major role in European air traffic control developments through participation in a number of international forums. It has supported several European initiatives, including the establishment of a unit to manage traffic flows throughout Europe centrally, and a programme to harmonise and integrate European air traffic control. Within Britain, NATS has an investment programme running at around £75 million a year, which includes the construction near Southampton of a new air traffic control centre for England and Wales, due to become operational at the end of 1997. The Government has also approved a new air traffic control centre for Scotland at Prestwick to be designed, financed, built and maintained by the private sector.

Airports

Of the 142 licensed civil aerodromes in Britain, about one-fifth handle more than 100,000 passengers a year each. In 1995 Britain's civil airports handled a total of 130.9 million passengers (129.4 million terminal passengers and 1.5 million in transit), and 1.7 million tonnes of freight.

Heathrow is the world's busiest airport for international passengers and is Britain's most important airport for passengers and air freight, handling 54 million passengers (including transit passengers) and 1 million tonnes of freight in 1995. Proposals have been put forward for a fifth terminal at Heathrow, which could eventually cater for 30 million passengers a year. Gatwick is also one of the world's busiest international airports. The Government accepts that there is a strong case for further runway capacity in the south-east, but options for new runways at Heathrow or Gatwick will not be considered further.

Table 19.3: Passenger Traffic at Britain's Main Airports			*million passengers*		
	1991	1992	1993	1994	1995
London Heathrow	40.2	45.2	47.9	51.7	54.1
London Gatwick	18.7	20.0	20.2	21.2	22.3
Manchester	10.1	12.0	13.1	14.6	14.5
Glasgow	4.2	4.8	5.2	5.6	5.4
Birmingham	3.2	3.8	4.2	4.9	5.1
London Stansted	1.7	2.4	2.7	3.3	3.8
Edinburgh	2.3	2.7	2.9	3.1	3.2
Newcastle	1.5	2.0	2.1	2.5	2.4
Belfast International	2.2	2.3	2.2	2.1	2.3
Aberdeen	2.0	2.2	2.3	2.2	2.2
Luton	2.0	2.0	1.9	1.8	1.8
East Midlands	1.1	1.3	1.4	1.6	1.8
Bristol	0.8	1.0	1.1	1.3	1.4
Cardiff	0.5	0.7	0.8	1.0	1.0

Source: Civil Aviation Authority

Ownership and Control

Seven airports—Heathrow, Gatwick, Stansted and Southampton in south-east England, and Glasgow, Edinburgh and Aberdeen in Scotland—are owned and operated by BAA plc. Together they handle about 72 per cent of air passengers and 82 per cent of air cargo traffic in Britain.

Many of the other airports are controlled by local authorities, including Manchester, which is the third largest airport in Britain. A total of 12 major local authority airports now operate as companies. The Government is encouraging their privatisation. For example, East Midlands International Airport was sold by its local authority shareholders in 1993 and Cardiff Airport was sold in 1995. Councils which sell shareholdings in airports before April 1997 will be able to spend three-quarters of the proceeds on other capital projects.

The CAA has responsibility for the economic regulation of the larger airports. It has powers to take action to remedy practices considered to be unreasonable or unfair, in particular any abuse of an airport's monopoly position, and also to limit increases in charges to airlines at certain airports. All airports used for public transport and training flights must also be licensed by the CAA for reasons of safety. Stringent requirements, such as the provision of adequate fire-fighting, medical and rescue services, must be satisfied before a licence is granted.

Strict security measures are in force at Britain's airports; these were tightened in 1994 with the introduction of regulations requiring airlines to account for, and authorise for carriage, every item of hold baggage placed on board international flights originating in Britain. This has not only improved security but should also help reduce misrouted baggage.

Communications

The telecommunications industry is one of the most rapidly expanding sectors of the British economy. Despite the growth in electronic means of communication in recent years, postal services continue to be important. The volume of mail in Britain is increasing, with 14 per cent more letters delivered than five years ago.

TELECOMMUNICATIONS

In telecommunications, Britain has one of the most up-to-date networks in the world, with a great many recently licensed companies competing for business and investing heavily in digital fibre optic networks, radio–based networks and digital switching. The Government has sought to introduce competition into the market since 1981; it privatised the former monopoly operator British Telecommunications plc (BT) in 1984 and has encouraged the entry of many new companies providing a variety of telecommunications services.

In 1991 a major review of government telecommunications policy ended the 'duopoly' policy, under which only two companies, BT and Mercury Communications, were permitted to run nationwide fixed-link telecommunications systems. Other important points from the review were:

- greater freedom for existing mobile telecommunications operators and permission for cable television operators to provide telephone services in their own right;
- the introduction of 'international simple resale'[3] to destinations with equivalent freedom to Britain; and
- the establishment of a new regime for administering numbering, run by the Office of Telecommunications (OFTEL—see below), and the modification of operators' licences to allow for the introduction of number portability, whereby customers could retain the same number if they changed phone companies.

There is now already effective competition in most larger urban areas of Britain, especially in commercial centres such as the City of London, as new fixed link operators extend their networks. International calls have also opened up to competition as new operators offer cut-price services over lines leased from BT and Mercury. Many residential customers now have a choice of three fixed link operators: BT, Mercury or their local cable television operator (see p. 322). Total investment in the

telecommunications industry is expected to exceed £5,500 million in 1996.

Britain is pressing strongly for greater liberalisation in the world telecommunications market. Talks being held under the auspices of the World Trade Organisation (see p. 179) are due to be concluded by February 1997. Britain announced in June 1996 the liberalisation of the provision of international services by companies over their own facilities.

Office of Telecommunications

OFTEL, a non-ministerial government department, is the independent regulatory body for the telecommunications industry. It is headed by the Director General of Telecommunications, whose functions include:

- ensuring that licensees comply with the conditions of their licences;
- initiating the modification of licence conditions by agreement or a referral to the Monopolies and Mergers Commission (see p. 208);
- promoting effective competition in the telecommunications industry;
- providing advice to the President of the Board of Trade on telecommunications matters; and
- investigating complaints against public telecommunications operators.

In seeking to promote the interests of consumers, and to promote and maintain competition in the market, OFTEL is seeking to move away from regulation through detailed licence obligations towards acting as the telecommunications industry competition authority. OFTEL's proposal to make the 1997 price cap on some of BT's main services the last one (see p. 322) demonstrates its move towards less detailed regulation.

It is also looking towards the convergence of traditional telephone-based telecommunications with computer-based applications such as multimedia. In 1995 it published a consultative document which considered some of the published involved in the convergence of broadcasting, information technology and telecommunications.

---

[3] The use of international leased circuits connected with the public switched network at both ends.

TRANSPORT

The Airbus Industrie A321 typically seats 180 passengers, and is used on short to medium-range routes. British Aerospace designs and manufactures wings for all Airbus airliners.

Passenger rail services in Great Britain are being franchised to the private sector. The franchise for South West Trains is owned by Stagecoach; this class 442 electric train carries the company's livery.

London Taxis International, manufacturers of the Fairway taxi, pictured here, has announced a 17 per cent increase in sales of new London-style, purpose-built taxis over the past year. Taxis were also sold to seven new overseas customers, including France.

Major conservation and recreation areas

Orkney Islands

Shetland Islands

Legend:
- National Parks (Regional Parks in Scotland)
- Forest Parks
- Areas of Outstanding Natural Beauty (National Scenic Areas in Scotland)
- Heritage Coast (Coastal Conservation Zones in Scotland)
- National Trails - - - - -
- World Heritage Sites □

SCOTLAND

Speyside Way

West Highland Way

Southern Upland Way

NORTHERN IRELAND

Northumberland

North York Moors

Cleveland Way

Lake District

Wolds Way

Yorkshire Dales

Pennine Way

Peak District

Snowdonia

Offa's Dyke Path

Peddars Way and Norfolk Coast Path

The Broads (Special protected area)

WALES

ENGLAND

Pembrokeshire Coast

Brecon Beacons

Pembrokeshire Coast Path

Ridgeway

Thames Path

North Downs Way

South Downs Way

Exmoor

Dartmoor

South West Coast Path

South West Coast Path

0 20 40 60 80 100 km

0 20 40 60 miles

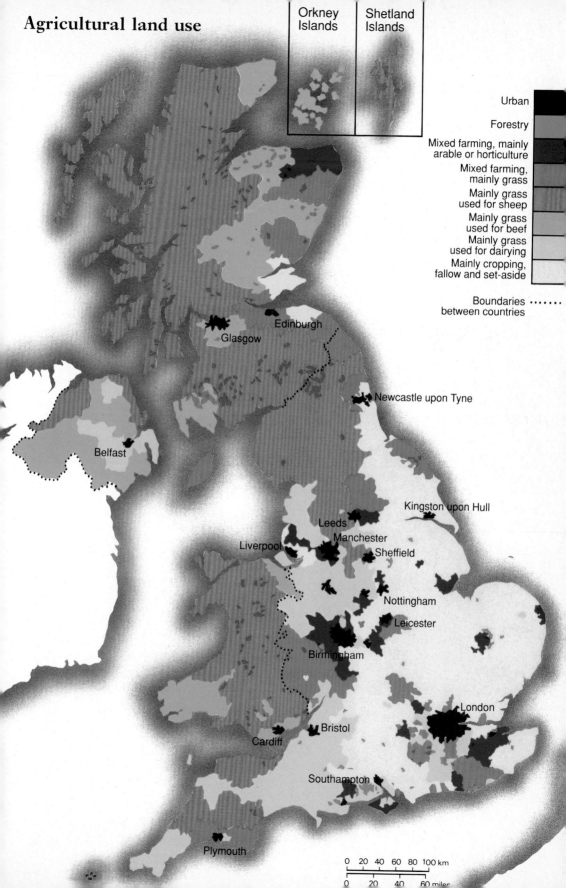

Agricultural land use

Orkney Islands

Shetland Islands

Urban

Forestry

Mixed farming, mainly
arable or horticulture

Mixed farming,
mainly grass

Mainly grass
used for sheep

Mainly grass
used for beef

Mainly grass
used for dairying

Mainly cropping,
fallow and set-aside

Boundaries ....
between countries

Glasgow

Edinburgh

Belfast

Newcastle upon Tyne

Kingston upon Hull

Leeds

Liverpool

Manchester

Sheffield

Nottingham

Leicester

Birmingham

London

Cardiff

Bristol

Southampton

Plymouth

0 20 40 60 80 100 km

0   20   40   60 miles

The Royal Mail's Railnet scheme, pictured here under construction, opened in 1996 in north London. The facility, one of the biggest and best equipped in Europe, is designed to get even more letters delivered on the first day after posting, and will take over the mail handling currently undertaken at the London rail termini.

The Royal Mail issues nine sets of special stamps each year, which are eagerly awaited by collectors. Here designer C. Walter Hodges completes a set showing London theatres of William Shakespeare's time.

Public Telecommunications Operators

There are about 150 licensed telecommunications operators in Britain. They include 125 licensed cable operators, 19 other regional and national public telecommunications operators (PTOs), and four mobile operators.

BT

BT runs one of the world's largest public telecommunications networks, including:

- 20.5 million residential lines;
- 6.5 million business lines;
- telex connections to about 20,000 British companies;
- over 132,000 public payphones; and
- a wide range of specialised voice, data, text and visual services.

BT handles an average of 103 million local, national and international telephone calls a day. The inland telephone and telex networks are fully automatic. International direct dialling is available from Britain to more than 200 countries, representing 99 per cent of the world's telephones. Following the sale of its shares in three tranches between 1984 and 1993, the Government has only a residual stake in BT to enable it to meet outstanding commitments under the bonus scheme which accompanied the privatisation.

BT has invested over £20,000 million since 1984 in the modernisation and expansion of its network to meet increasing demand and to introduce specialised services. The company has almost 3 million km (1.8 million miles) of optical fibre laid in its network in Britain. Modern digital electronic exchanges now serve nearly all telephone lines. The combination of digital exchange switching and digital transmission techniques, using optical-fibre cable and microwave radio links, is improving the quality of telephone services substantially. It also makes possible the provision of a wider range of services through the company's main network.

> Fibre optics can transform the capacity of a telephone network. According to BT Laboratories, an optical fibre has the capacity, in theory, to carry at one time all the conversations going on in the world twice over.

BT's services include:

- a free facility for emergency calls to the police, fire, ambulance, coastguard, lifeboat and air-sea rescue services;
- directory enquiries;
- various chargeable operator-connected services, such as reversed-charge ('collect') calls;
- an operator-handled 'Freefone' service and automatic Freefone and 'Lo-call' facilities that enable callers to contact organisations anywhere in Britain, either free or at local call rates;
- premium-rate services which allow callers to obtain information from independent providers; and
- select network services such as caller display, reminder calls, three-way calling, call waiting and call diversion, which are available to customers on digital exchanges.

Public payphone modernisation has included additional provision on sites convenient for travellers, such as train carriages, London Underground platforms and motorway service areas. Many BT public payphones now offer a choice of four methods of payment—coins, BT phonecards, BT chargecards and commercial credit or debit cards.

BT is the second largest shareholder in the International Telecommunications Satellite Organisation (INTELSAT), of which 125 countries are members, and is the largest investor in the European Telecommunications Satellite Organisation (EUTELSAT). It is also the second largest shareholder in the International Maritime Satellite Organisation (INMARSAT), with interests in a number of other consortia.

BT operates satellite earth stations in the London Docklands and at Goonhilly Downs (Cornwall), Madley (near Hereford), Aberdeen, and Mormond Hill (Grampian). In-flight operator-controlled telephone call facilities for passengers are provided via Portishead radio station near Bristol. Digital transmission techniques have been introduced for services to the United States, Japan, Hong Kong and Australia via the Madley and Goonhilly stations.

To increase its presence in the world market, BT has entered into several joint ventures with overseas firms: for example, MCI in the United States; the German industrial group VIAG; and Grupo Santander in Spain.

Under the regulatory regime, BT's prices are capped by OFTEL. What is intended to be the last cap, covering the period 1997 to 2001, will restrict the bills of low- to medium- spending residential customers and small businesses to rises in line with the Retail Prices Index minus 4.5 percentage points. This will only cover a quarter of BT's revenues; owing to the rapid development of competition in business and international calls OFTEL feels that regulation is no longer necessary in those areas.

Mercury Communications

Mercury Communications Ltd, which is part of the Cable & Wireless group and is 20 per cent owned by Bell Canada Enterprises, has constructed its own long-distance all-digital network. The network runs from the north of Scotland to the south coast, linking 90 cities and towns across Britain. Mercury now offers a service to all the population, both business and residential customers.

Major customers can have a direct digital link between their premises and the Mercury network. Routeing devices have also been developed to enable customers to use Mercury indirectly via their existing exchange lines. Businesses can take advantage of savings plans and automatic discounts as well. There are Mercury-compatible phones which connect the caller to the network at the push of a button. In addition, many customers are now able to use the Mercury network by dialling an access code.

International services are provided by satellite communications centres in London's Docklands, in Oxfordshire and at Brechin in Scotland, as well as by submarine cable links to continental Europe and the United States.

Other Operators

Other operators include Kingston Communications, which is the long-established network operator for the Kingston upon Hull area in the East Riding of Yorkshire. The 19 regional and national PTOs include:

- COLT, which focuses on business customers in the Greater London area;
- Energis, which is using the electricity infrastructure as a platform for installing new optical fibre networks;
- Ionica, which in May 1996 launched its service using radio to provide the final connection to customers, initially in East Anglia;
- Sprint, the third-largest long-distance telephone company in the United States, which is seeking to expand its domestic and international services in Britain; and
- Vodafone, the well-established mobile operator, which was granted a licence for fixed services in 1993.

Cable Television Franchises

Cable operators are now able to offer telephone services in their own right. In all, 102 of the 108 local cable television franchises in operation by April 1996 also offered voice telephony services. By then, the cable operators had installed 1.6 million telephone lines in Britain, compared with 2,200 lines in January 1991, and 5 million homes were passed by cable television networks.

Mobile Communications

The Government has encouraged the expansion of mobile telecommunications services, resulting in one of the most extensive networks in the world. Vodafone and Telecom Securicor Cellular Radio (Cellnet) run competing national cellular radio systems. Considerable investment has been made in establishing their networks to provide increased capacity for the growing numbers of mobile phone users (5.7 million by April 1996). The two companies also run the pan-European mobile system, known as GSM, in Britain.

Britain was the first country to offer personal communications network (PCN) services, which are intended to allow the same telephone to be used at home, at work and as a portable within the network's coverage. PCNs operate in the frequency range around 1.9 gigahertz. The Mercury One-2-One service started in 1993, and Hutchison Microtel's Orange service was launched in 1994.

National Band Three Ltd is licensed to offer a nationwide trunked radio service, while 33 licences have been awarded for London and regional services. Five licences to operate mobile data networks and another five to run nationwide paging networks have also been granted. Following a competition in 1995, licences are being awarded for two services serving remote rural areas and three national digital 'ISDN'[4] services.

Cable & Wireless

Cable and Wireless plc supplies a wide range of telecommunications services in over 50 countries worldwide. Its main business is the provision and operation, through the companies of the Cable & Wireless federation, of public telecommunications services in over 30 countries and territories, including Hong Kong, the United States and Japan, under franchises and licences granted by the governments concerned. It also supplies and manages telecommunications services and facilities for public and private sector customers, and undertakes consultancy work worldwide. It operates a fleet of ships and submersible vehicle systems for laying and maintaining submarine telecommunications cables. Its strategy is to build on its regional hubs in Asia, Western Europe and the Caribbean. It links these hubs through its worldwide network of cable and satellite communications.

Information Society Initiative

The Information Society initiative, launched in February 1996, seeks to increase awareness of the opportunities the 'information society' presents. A range of operators, including BT, are participating. Its comprehensive package of activities is designed to:

- bring forward the technologies and applications needed to service an information society;

- speed the development of creative programmes and ideas; and

- raise awareness among British companies of the business benefits of electronic working through local support centres aimed at business users.

POSTAL SERVICES

The Post Office, founded in 1635, pioneered postal services and was the first to issue adhesive postage stamps as proof of advance payment for mail.

The Royal Mail delivers to 26 million addresses, handling nearly 70 million letters and parcels each working day. This comes to more than 18,300 million items a year. Mail is collected from over 110,000 posting boxes, as well as from post offices and large postal users.

The Royal Mail has invested substantially in the latest mail-sorting technology, and mechanisation has been introduced at all stages of the sorting process. Automatic sorting utilises the information contained in the postcode; the British postcode system is one of the most sophisticated in the world, allowing mechanised sorting down to part of a street on a postman's round and, in some cases, to an individual address.

Britain has good international postal services, with prices among the cheapest. Royal Mail International dispatches 790 million items a year, including over 600 million by air. It has its own mail-handling centre at Heathrow, which handles about four-fifths of outward airmail. It uses 1,400 flights a week to send mail direct to over 300 destinations worldwide.

---

[4]Integrated services digital network.

Post Office Counters Ltd handles a wide range of transactions; it acts as an agent for the letters and parcels businesses, government departments, local authorities and Alliance & Leicester Giro—formerly Girobank, which was transferred to the private sector in 1990. In response to the government decision to grant it more commercial freedom, a number of new services have been developed, such as bureaux de change. There are just under 20,000 post offices, of which 700 are operated directly by the Post Office. The remainder are franchise offices or are operated on an agency basis by sub-postmasters.

Post Office Specialist Services

The Post Office offers a range of specialist services. Parcelforce 'Datapost', a door-to-door delivery service, provides overnight delivery throughout Britain and an international service to over 160 countries. 'Datapost Sameday' provides a rapid delivery within or between major cities in Britain. The Philatelic Bureau in Edinburgh is an important outlet for the Post Office's philatelic business, including sales to overseas collectors or dealers. The British Postal Consultancy Service offers advice and assistance on all aspects of postal business to overseas postal administrations, and over 50 countries have used its services since 1965.

Competition in Postal Services

The Post Office has a monopoly on the conveyance of letters within Britain. However, the Government has the power to suspend the monopoly in certain areas or for certain categories of mail and to license others to provide competing services. It has suspended the monopoly on letters subject to a minimum fee of £1.

In 1995 the Government announced a new business regime, which involves:

- removing existing capital financing limits;
- turning the main operating units into separate subsidiary limited companies;
- making full use of the Private Finance Initiative (see p. 162) to support moves into new markets; and
- allowing Post Office Counters to extend the range of services it provides.

The Government has made clear its commitment to:

- a universal letter and parcel service with a delivery to every address in Britain;
- a uniform and affordable tariff structure; and
- a nationwide network of post offices.

Private Courier and Express Service Operators

Private-sector couriers and express operators are allowed to handle time-sensitive door-to-door deliveries, subject to a minimum fee of £1. The courier/express service industry has grown rapidly and the revenue created by the carriage of these items is estimated at over £3,000 million a year. Britain is one of the main providers of monitored express deliveries in Europe, with London an important centre for air courier/express traffic.

Further Reading

Competition and Choice: Telecommunications Policy for the 1990s. Cm 1461. HMSO, 1991.

New Opportunities for the Railways. Cm 2012. HMSO, 1992.

Telecommunications. Aspects of Britain series, HMSO, 1994.

Transport and Communications. Aspects of Britain series, HMSO, 1992.

Transport Statistics Great Britain, annual report. HMSO.

Transport: the Way Forward. Cm 3234. HMSO, 1996.

20 Science and Technology

Introduction	325	Research in Higher Education	
Government Role	327	Institutions	339
Research Councils	330	Other Organisations	339
Government Departments	334	International Collaboration	342

Britain has a long tradition of research and innovation in science, technology and engineering in universities, research institutes and industry. Science and technology are critical elements in the innovation process, which is essential for competing successfully in domestic and international markets.

INTRODUCTION

British achievements in science and technology in the 20th century include fundamental contributions to modern molecular genetics through the discovery of the three-dimensional molecular structure of DNA (deoxyribonucleic acid) by Francis Crick, Maurice Wilkins, James Watson and Rosalind Franklin in 1953 and of cholesterol, vitamin D, penicillin and insulin by Dorothy Hodgkin.

Notable contributions in other areas over the past 25 years have been made by Stephen Hawking in improving the understanding of the nature and origin of the universe; Brian Josephson in superconductivity (abnormally high electrical conductivity at low temperatures); Martin Ryle and Antony Hewish in radio astrophysics; and Godfrey Hounsfield in computer-assisted tomography (a form of radiography) for medical diagnosis.

Other pioneering work includes the discovery in 1985 by British Antarctic Survey scientists of the hole in the ozone layer over the Antarctic. Researchers at the Laboratory of Molecular Biology, Cambridge, produced the first monoclonal antibodies, proteins produced by genetic engineering with enormous potential in the diagnosis and treatment of disease. More recently there have been several British breakthroughs in genetics research, including the identification of the gene in the Y chromosome responsible for determining sex, and the identification of other genes linked to diseases such as cystic fibrosis and a form of breast cancer. The world's first pig with a genetically modified heart has been bred by scientists at Cambridge University, an important milestone in breeding animals as organ donors for people.

With only 1 per cent of the world's population, Britain carries out 6 per cent of its total research and development (R & D). Britain has won more Nobel Prizes for Science—over 70—than any country except the United States. The most recent British winner is Professor Sir Harold Kroto of Sussex University, who shared the 1996 Chemistry prize with two US scientists for discovering the fullerene molecule.

Research and Development Expenditure

Total expenditure in Britain on scientific R & D in 1994 was £14,600 million, 2.2 per

Table 20.1: Company Investment in R & D

	R & D annual investment (£ million)	R & D as % of sales
Glaxo Wellcome	1,200	15.1
SmithKline Beecham	653	9.3
Unilever	585	1.9
Zeneca	549	11.2
Shell Transport and Trading	483	0.7
GEC	412	7.1
BT	271	2.0
Rolls-Royce	206	5.7
Reuters	191	7.1
ICI	185	1.8

Source: *The 1996 UK R & D Scoreboard*, DTI
Note: R & D expenditure includes expenditure overseas.

cent of gross domestic product. About 50 per cent of the funding was provided by industry and around 32 per cent by government. Significant contributions were made by private endowments, trusts and charities. Industry also funds university research and finances contract research at government establishments. Some charities have their own laboratories and offer grants for outside research. Contract research organisations carry out R & D for companies and are playing an increasingly important role in the transfer of technology to British industry.

Total spending on R & D in industry amounted to £9,500 million in 1994. Of this total, British industry's own contribution was 72 per cent, with 12 per cent from government and the rest from overseas. Since the ending of the Cold War, there has been a marked shift in the balance between civil and defence-related R & D, reflected, for example, in a reduction in real terms in aerospace R & D.

According to reports by listed British companies, there was a rise of 4.2 per cent in investment in R & D in 1995–96. The chemistry and biotechnology-based sectors—chemicals, pharmaceuticals and healthcare—account for 36 per cent of R & D spending by listed companies. Three of the four companies with the largest investment in R & D—Glaxo Wellcome, SmithKline

Beecham and Zeneca—are in these sectors (see Table 20.1). Electronics and aerospace are also areas of R & D strength. Some examples of recent notable R & D projects in these areas are given below.

Chemicals

Research carried out by the chemicals industry over the past few years has led to significant technological and commercial breakthroughs. Pharmaceuticals is the most research-intensive sector of the chemicals industry. British firms have been responsible for discovering and developing five of the world's 20 best-selling drugs (see p. 246). Research conducted by ICI, Glaxo Wellcome, SmithKline Beecham and Fisons led to the development of the first successful beta blockers, drugs used in the treatment of cardiovascular conditions; semi-synthetic penicillins; vaccines; and treatments for cancer, asthma, migraine and arthritis. More than 200 potential new medicines are currently under development in British laboratories.

Among a host of other research projects are the application of biotechnology to pharmaceuticals, disease resistant crops, new forms of food, plant science, and the development of advanced materials such as engineering plastics. The biotechnology sector continues to grow, with an increasing number of companies engaged in the development and manufacture of products using genetic modification techniques.

Electronics

British firms and research organisations, with government support, are leading in the development and application of the family of 'three-five' semiconductor materials (such as gallium arsenide). These materials have many uses, including lasers for optical fibre communications, microwave devices for satellite communications, and high efficiency solar cells.

BT (British Telecom) is in the forefront of the development of optical fibre cable and developed the first all-optical repeater. BT engineers are developing virtual reality techniques to transmit 3-D images on a television screen. Eventually, viewers will be able to experience, for example, the sensation of trying on clothes in a virtual shopping centre. In 1995–96 BT spent £271 million on R & D; up to 800 projects are being carried out at any one time, of which two-thirds are in software engineering.

Aerospace

Britain has led the world in many aspects of aerospace R & D over the past 80 years. Pioneering achievements include radar, jet engines, Concorde, automatic landing, vertical take-off and landing, flight simulators and ejector seats. British Aerospace, with Marconi and Dowty Boulton Paul, developed a system known as 'fly-by-wire', in which flying control surfaces are moved by electronic rather than mechanical means. British Aerospace is currently working with government and academic laboratories on the use of 'smart materials' in aircraft. These are structures within the aircraft which can continuously monitor for signs of damage or wear and communicate with the pilot via fibre optic cables. The technology will have applications in both military and civil aircraft, and is expected to improve safety and reduce maintenance costs.

GOVERNMENT ROLE

Science and technology issues as a whole are the responsibility of a Cabinet Minister, the President of the Board of Trade, acting on behalf of the Prime Minister. The Minister is supported by the Office of Science and Technology (OST)—which became part of the Department of Trade and Industry (DTI) in 1995. The OST is headed by the Government's Chief Scientific Adviser. It provides a central focus for the development of government policy on science and technology, both nationally and internationally, including strengthening the science base and maximising its contribution to economic performance and the quality of life. It co-ordinates science and technology policy across government departments.

The term 'science and engineering base' is used to describe the research and postgraduate training capacity based in the universities and colleges of higher education and in establishments operated by the research councils and government departments, together with the national and international central facilities (such as CERN—see p. 343) supported by the councils and available for use by British scientists and engineers. There are also important contributions from some private institutions, mainly those funded by charities. Universities and other institutions of the science and engineering base are the main providers of basic research and much of the strategic research (research likely to become applicable) carried out in Britain. They also increasingly collaborate with the private sector in the conduct of specific applied research. Nearly two-thirds of the Government's spending on civil R & D supports basic and strategic research carried out in the science and engineering base.

The OST has specific responsibility for the Science Budget and seven government-financed research councils (see pp. 330–4): the Engineering and Physical Sciences Research Council (EPSRC), the Medical Research Council (MRC), the Particle Physics and Astronomy Research Council (PPARC), the Natural Environment Research Council (NERC), the Biotechnology and Biological Sciences Research Council (BBSRC), the Economic and Social Research Council (ESRC) and the Council for the Central Laboratory of the Research Councils (CCLRC). OST funding provides assistance for research, through the research councils, in the following ways:

- by awarding grants and contracts to universities and other higher education establishments and to research units;
- by funding research council establishments;
- by supporting postgraduate study; and
- by subscribing to international scientific organisations.

The OST also supports universities (whose other main source of funding is the appropriate higher education funding council) through programmes administered through the Royal Society and the Royal Academy of Engineering (see p. 340).

Table 20.2: Planned Government Expenditure on Science, Engineering and Technology 1996–97

	£ million
Science Budget	1,312.0
of which: BBSRC	175.3
EPSRC	375.9
ESRC	63.1
MRC	281.9
NERC	164.7
PPARC	206.9
CCLRC	1.5
Royal Society	21.8
Royal Academy of Engineering	3.1
Higher education funding councils	981
Science and engineering base	**2,293**
Civil departments	1,098
British contribution to EU R & D	394
Total civil science, engineering and technology	**3,785**
Defence	2,188
Total expenditure on science, engineering and technology	**5,973**

Source: *Forward Look of Government-funded Science, Engineering and Technology*, 1996

Finance

Government finance goes to research establishments, higher education institutions and private industry, as well as collaborative research programmes. Total net government expenditure on science and technology (both civil and defence) in 1995–96 was £6,069 million, of which £3,883 million was devoted to civil science. The Science Budget (see Table 20.2) totals £1,312 million for 1996–97. Government funding for the science and engineering base has increased by over 10 per cent in real terms over the past ten years.

Among government departments, the Ministry of Defence (MoD—see p. 336) has the largest research budget. The main civil departments involved are the Department of Trade and Industry (see p. 334), the Ministry of Agriculture, Fisheries and Food (MAFF—see p. 336) and the Department of the Environment (see p. 337).

Strategy

The funding and organisation of British science and technology have changed considerably in recent years, in accordance with the principles set out in the White Paper, *Realising Our Potential: A Strategy for Science, Engineering and Technology*. Published in 1993, this was the first major review of science for over 20 years.

The White Paper aimed to create a closer partnership between government, industry and the scientific community in developing strengths in areas of importance to the future economic well-being of Britain. In particular, it established the Foresight Programme for the public and private sectors to work together to identify opportunities in markets and technologies likely to emerge over the next 10 to 20 years, and the actions which should be taken now to exploit them.

The programme is co-ordinated by a joint industry/academic steering group under the chairmanship of the Government's Chief Scientific Adviser. The steering group has identified seven cross-sectoral themes or priority areas:

- communications and computing power (with applications in all economic sectors);
- new organisms, products and processes from genetics (with applications in health, agriculture, food and environmental protection);
- materials science, engineering and technology;
- production processes and services;
- pollution monitoring and control technologies, and technologies for conserving energy and other resources;
- social trends (improving understanding of human factors involved in markets and scientific advance); and
- extending quality life (EQUAL) by examining the effects of lifestyle and diet on health and developing technologies to enhance the quality of life of an ageing population.

In March 1996 the Government published a further report which highlighted the considerable progress made under the

Foresight Programme. The report recommended some reorganisation of the 15 sector panels examining the opportunities in specific branches of science and technology; the number of panels has been increased to 16 with the addition of a panel for the marine sector.

The reports of the steering group and sector panels are being disseminated widely in order to:

- ensure that scientific excellence is sustained;
- increase collaboration between industry and academic institutions in areas of economic importance by building on links already forged;
- influence government priorities in science, engineering and technology programmes and in government regulation and training responsibilities; and
- help industry to develop more informed business and investment strategies.

Government departments, the universities and higher education funding councils, and the research councils are reflecting Foresight priorities in their research spending allocations. The private sector will be encouraged to take account of the priorities both in its participation in collaborative research programmes and in its strategic planning.

The Government is providing up to £30 million over four years for the first round of the Foresight Challenge Competition, to fund collaborative R & D projects to address priorities identified by the Foresight panels. Over 500 outline bids were received and some 60 consortia were then invited to submit full bids. The 24 projects selected directly address priorities in almost all the Foresight sectors. Funding from industry is contributing £62 million towards the total project costs of £92 million.

The 1993 White Paper also introduced the Realising Our Potential Award (ROPA) scheme, which focuses on researchers already working closely with industry and provides funding for separate 'curiosity-driven' research of their own choosing. Following a successful pilot project the scheme was extended to involve all the research councils. About 250

ROPAs, with a total value of £18 million, were awarded in 1996. In 1996–97 the expected funding for the scheme will be about £32 million. The Government also makes funds available through the research councils for the Co-operative Awards in Science and Engineering (CASE) scheme, which supports students on research projects jointly supervised with industry.

LINK

The LINK scheme provides a government-wide framework for collaborative research in support of wealth creation and improvement of the quality of life. LINK aims to promote partnerships in high-quality, commercially relevant research projects between industry and higher education institutions and other research base organisations. Under the scheme, government departments and research councils fund up to 50 per cent of the cost of research projects, with industry providing the balance. LINK is now operating through 54 programmes. More than 700 projects worth over £400 million have been started, involving over 1,100 companies and 130 research base institutions. The Government relaunched LINK in 1995, following a review which recommended improvements to make the scheme more flexible and effective in responding to the needs of industry and the research base. Since then 15 new programmes have been announced in response to priorities identified by the Foresight Programme.

Forward Look

The third *Forward Look of Government-funded Science, Engineering and Technology* was published in May 1996. It sets out the Government's policy and plans for publicly funded science, engineering and technology, presenting an overview of the programmes of individual government departments and research councils. It also describes measures being taken to achieve the objectives set out in the 1993 White Paper.

Public Awareness Campaign

A major policy initiative in the White Paper was the announcement of a campaign to promote the public awareness of science, engineering and technology. This seeks to:

- increase public awareness and appreciation of the contribution that science, engineering and technology make to Britain's economic wealth and quality of life; and

- raise levels of understanding of scientific terms, concepts and issues, so that public debate on controversial scientific and technological issues becomes better informed.

The Government also supports a number of programmes and events, such as the British Association's annual science festival and the National Science, Engineering and Technology Week. The third of these Weeks, held in March 1996, consisted of over 5,000 events in all parts of Britain. The year 1997 has been designated the Year of Engineering Success (YES). This initiative is intended to raise public awareness of the role of engineers in wealth creation and life enhancement and is supported by the engineering profession and industry.

Prior Options Review

The Government is conducting a programme of 'prior options' reviews of public sector research establishments. Each review examines whether the functions of the establishment are needed, the scope for greater involvement by the private sector (including the university sector) through privatisation or contracting out of work, and possibilities for rationalisation.

The reviews are being conducted in three rounds, with the aim of completing the major part of the work by the end of 1996. The results of some of the reviews have been announced. In a number of cases the Government has decided that a move away from the public sector is appropriate.

Career Development Initiatives

The 1993 White Paper recommended that postgraduate training should include broader skills and experience relevant to the needs of employers. Pilot schemes for two new qualifications, the engineering doctorate (EngDoc) and the research masters degree,

have been introduced to give this development further impetus.

A Development Unit was established in the OST in 1994 to promote the role of women in science, engineering and technology. It was set up in response to an independent report which found that women were under-represented in these sectors, and that there were too few women at senior levels; many women drop out of a science career after completing a PhD. From the experience of six major employers, the Unit has highlighted the economic and other benefits to business of measures which enable women scientists and engineers to combine a career and bringing up a family.

The research councils, the Royal Society and universities reached a formal agreement in 1996 on improving the career framework for research staff on short-term contracts.

RESEARCH COUNCILS

Each research council is an autonomous body established under Royal Charter, with members of its governing council drawn from the universities, professions, industry and government. Councils support research, study and training in universities and other higher education institutions, through their own institutes, and international research centres. They provide awards to about 15,000 postgraduate students in science, social sciences, engineering and technology. In addition to funding from the OST, the research councils receive income for research commissioned by government departments and from the private sector. Income from commissioned research is particularly important for the BBSRC and NERC.

Engineering and Physical Sciences Research Council

The EPSRC, the research council with the largest budget—about £376 million in 1996–97—has responsibility both for sustaining particular disciplines (chemistry, mathematics, physics and all branches of engineering) and for developing close links with the industries underpinned by these disciplines. The EPSRC has 14 programmes supporting research into core disciplines in the physical sciences and engineering, and in 'generic technologies'. These generic technologies and various sector-based initiatives are relevant to a wide range of industrial activities. Many of the generic technologies were a key concern of the Foresight panels. The work includes projects on information technology and computing science, engineering materials and design, and integrated production.

The EPSRC is a major participant in an industry-led collaborative programme with the ESRC, BBSRC and government departments. The Innovative Manufacturing Initiative is aimed at encouraging innovative business processes and technology in manufacturing industry, and focuses on specific sectors of industry. One key area for research highlighted by the Foresight Programme is in developing sophisticated new sensors for monitoring industrial processes.

The Council's environmental interests include its clean technology programme: the programme is co-ordinated with related activities in the DTI, the Department of the Environment, the BBSRC, NERC and ESRC. The programme aims to find ways of forestalling pollution in industrial processes rather than removing it at the 'end of the pipe'. Priority areas include cleaner synthesis, recycling and recovery, and sustainable cities.

A collaboration between EPSRC and the electronics company Sharp has produced a revolutionary new microwave oven that can choose the cooking times for different foods. Based on work by Dr Lionel Tarassenko at Oxford University's Department of Engineering, the oven contains sensors which detect the characteristic steam 'signature' produced by different foods when heated. The oven is the first of the company's products to be developed and manufactured outside Japan.

The EPSRC is also engaged in:

- supporting training in core disciplines at higher education institutions (involving some 8,000 students);

- encouraging technology transfer through collaboration between universities and industrial companies (for example, through the Teaching Company Scheme—see p. 335);

- providing access for British researchers to high-quality national and international facilities; and

- managing high-performance computer facilities for use by all the research councils.

Medical Research Council

The MRC, with a budget of £282 million in 1996–97, is the main source of public funds for medical research. It promotes and supports research and training aimed at maintaining and improving human health, advancing knowledge and technology, and providing well-trained staff to meet the needs of user communities, including the providers of healthcare and the biotechnology, food, healthcare, medical instrumentation, pharmaceutical and other biomedical-related industries.

About half the MRC's expenditure is made through its own institutes and units, which have close links with universities and medical schools, the rest going mainly on grant support of research in universities. The Council has two large institutes—the National Institute for Medical Research at Mill Hill in London and the Laboratory of Molecular Biology in Cambridge; it also runs the Clinical Sciences Centre at the Royal Postgraduate Medical School, London. It has about 40 research units and a number of smaller teams, and funds about 1,500 research grants.

Research funded by the MRC is conducted in the following broad areas:

- work on molecular structure and properties, cell biochemistry and physiology, and developmental biology;

- genetic blueprint and health—focusing on genome mapping and the study of the structure and functions of genes, this is looking at the enormous potential represented by genetics for the detection, prevention and treatment of disease;

- research examining interactions between the environment and the human body, including early childhood origins of adult disease, the consequences of clinical interventions, the health consequences of environmental pollution, and the effects on health of factors such as nutrition;

- basic and clinical research into viral, bacterial and parasitic diseases, and into the function and development of the immune system, and into allergy and the autoimmune system. This includes a significant research programme into HIV/AIDS;

- research aimed at improving the understanding of the central nervous system, covering the study of a wide range of mental diseases—including psychoses, dementia and addiction—and the development of better methods for their diagnosis, prevention and treatment;

- work on organ systems and cancer—the latter aiming to increase understanding of tumour biology and to develop methods of detecting cancers (including better methods of early detection and treatment); and

- research related to examining and testing the effectiveness of medical practice and healthcare—involving close liaison with the government health departments and the National Health Service.

Particle Physics and Astronomy Research Council

The main task of the PPARC, with a budget of £207 million in 1996–97, is to sustain and develop Britain's long tradition of excellence in research into fundamental physical processes. The PPARC maintains four research establishments: the Royal Greenwich Observatory at Cambridge, the Royal Observatory at Edinburgh and overseas observatories on La Palma in the Canary Islands and on Hawaii. The PPARC is a major source of funding for many leading university physics departments in Britain.

The PPARC supports research in three main areas:

- particle physics—theoretical and experimental research into elementary particles and the fundamental forces of nature;

- astronomy (including astrophysics and cosmology)—studying the origin, structure and evolution of the universe, and the life cycle and properties of stars; and

- planetary science (including solar terrestrial physics)—studying the origin and evolution of the solar system and the influence of the Sun on planetary bodies, particularly Earth.

The Council's work is in fields where international co-operation is particularly important: it makes substantial contributions to the European Space Agency (ESA) and the European Laboratory for Particle Physics (CERN—see p. 343), where the proposed Large Hadron Collider (LHC) is due to be completed by 2008. .

Through the PPARC, Britain is taking a leading role in the current largest international project in ground-based astronomy. The Gemini project involves building two 8m telescopes at Mauna Kea (Hawaii) and Cerro Pachon (Chile). These are due to be completed in 1999 and 2001 respectively . The other partners are the United States, Canada, Argentina, Brazil and Chile. Britain has a 25 per cent stake in the work, with major responsibility for the primary mirror support system and much of the control software.

Biotechnology and Biological Sciences Research Council

BBSRC, with a Science Budget allocation of £175 million in 1996–97, sustains a broad base of interdisciplinary research and training to underpin the biology-based industries, including biotechnology, pharmaceuticals, agriculture, agrochemicals and food.

Two potent naturally occurring insecticides have been isolated from *calceolaria andina*, a Chilean plant, by researchers at the Institute of Arable Crops Research in Rothamsted (Hertfordshire). The compounds, naphthoquinones, are effective against important insect pests such as whitefly, aphids and mites, including those resistant to many of the current commercial insecticides. Recently developed synthetic equivalents are particularly promising.

The research was part of an international project which also involved researchers at the University of Chile-Probio Ltd, the Royal Botanic Gardens, Kew, and the University of Southampton.

BBSRC operates programmes in both fundamental and strategic research. The scientific themes are biomolecular sciences, in conjunction with the EPSRC; genes and developmental biology; biochemistry and cell biology; plant and microbial sciences; animal sciences and psychology; and engineering and physical sciences. BBSRC has also developed a number of directed programmes in agricultural systems, chemicals and pharmaceuticals, and food to meet the needs of its principal industrial users. BBSRC supports research in eight research institutes and in universities.

BBSRC has an important role in training scientists and engineers; it has over 2,000 research studentships, including 600 funded through the CASE scheme (see p. 329), as well as an expanding postdoctoral fellowship scheme.

Natural Environment Research Council

In 1996–97 NERC will spend most of its Science Budget allocation of £165 million in the following areas:

- understanding and protecting biodiversity;

- environmental risks and hazards, including the release of genetically modified organisms, prediction of extreme events and rapid environmental assessments for operational needs;

- global change, including predictions on a range of time and space scales;

- natural resources—management of land, water and the coastal zone, the identification and exploitation of land, and freshwater- and marine-based resources and their sustainability;

- waste management, bioremediation (biological treatment of pollution), and land restoration; and

- pollution of air, land, sea and freshwater in relation to environmental and human health.

The Council supports research in its own and other research establishments as well as research and training in universities. It also provides a range of facilities for use by the environmental science community, including a marine research fleet. NERC establishments include the British Geological Survey, the British Antarctic Survey, the Centre for Coastal and Marine Sciences and the Centre for Ecology and Hydrology, together with a number of university-based units.

A new national centre for oceanographic science and technology, the Southampton Oceanography Centre, was officially opened in 1996. It is a national centre for research, training and support in oceanography, geology and aspects of marine technology and engineering. The Centre is a joint venture with Southampton University and incorporates the former NERC Institute of Oceanographic Sciences Deacon Laboratory, as well as some departments of the university. The NERC's Research Vessel Services are also located at the Centre.

NERC has a substantial external income from collaborative and contract research —about £40 million a year—and its staff provide a range of expert services. Many NERC programmes have important implications for sustainable development and environmental protection, and issues concerning the quality of life.

In March 1996 a NERC group completed

an investigation into the scientific aspects of the decommissioning of offshore oil and gas platforms. This independent international group of experts was established by NERC at the request of the Government following controversy over the planned disposal at sea of the Brent Spar platform in 1995. The report concluded that the global impact of deep sea disposal of a single large structure was likely to be small, similar to a large shipwreck. However, the cumulative effect of continued disposals should also be taken into consideration.

Economic and Social Research Council

ESRC, with an R & D provision of £63 million for 1996–97, supports high-quality research and training to meet the needs of its users and enhance Britain's economic competitiveness, the quality of life, and the effectiveness of public services and policy. All research funded by ESRC is conducted in higher education institutions or independent research institutes. The Council has eight priority themes:

- economic performance and development;
- environment and sustainability;
- governance and regulation;
- human communication and the social shaping of technology;
- innovation and business processes;
- knowledge and skill;
- lifespan, lifestyles and health; and
- social integration and exclusion.

The Council has already made significant investments in the area of innovation, organisations and business processes, launching three new centres in 1996–97:

- the Centre for Research on Innovation and Competitive Environments, in Manchester;
- the Centre for Organisation and Innovation in Manufacturing at the University of Sheffield; and
- the Complex Product Systems Innovation Research Centre at the Universities of Sussex and Brighton.

A Business Process Resource Centre has also been set up as part of the joint Innovative Manufacturing Initiative (see p. 331).

The Council devotes a substantial part of its expenditure to training that will develop and maintain a first-class research base in the social sciences. Over 1,000 postgraduate students are supported through research training awards, advanced course awards and fellowships. Through its participation in the Teaching Company Scheme (see p. 335), ESRC promotes partnerships between social scientists and business by placing graduates in companies for short-term projects.

Council for the Central Laboratory of the Research Councils

The CCLRC was established as an independent body with effect from April 1995. It promotes scientific and engineering research by providing facilities and technical expertise to meet the needs of the other research councils and their users. Its R & D budget for 1996–97 is £104.2 million, of which £82.4 million comes through agreements with the other research councils and the rest from contracts and agreements with other industries and organisations.

The CCLRC is responsible for two research establishments which were formerly part of the EPSRC: the Rutherford Appleton Laboratory at Chilton in Oxfordshire and the Daresbury Laboratory near Warrington in Cheshire. These centres provide facilities too large or complex to be housed by individual academic institutions. Among the facilities are the world's leading source of pulsed neutrons and muons, some of the world's brightest lasers and Britain's only source of synchrotron light (X-rays).

GOVERNMENT DEPARTMENTS

Department of Trade and Industry

Although most industrial R & D is financed by industry, the DTI gives assistance where there is a case for doing so. In 1995–96 its net expenditure on science and technology was estimated at £362 million, covering innovation and technology, aeronautics, space (see p. 338), and nuclear and non-nuclear energy.

In supporting these activities, the DTI's overall aim is to help companies to compete more effectively in global markets through improved innovation performance. It seeks to achieve this, in particular, by helping to improve the climate for business innovation, by encouraging industry to invest more in R & D, and by helping to develop partnerships between the academic base and industrial sectors in order to enhance the commercial exploitation of basic science.

Innovation and Technology

Innovation—the successful exploitation of new ideas—is vital in maintaining an economy based on competitive wealth creation. Through its Innovation Unit, which includes 15 seconded industrialists, the DTI seeks to influence the thinking of business, education, the media and government, as well as the public, towards innovation.

In Northern Ireland the Industrial Research and Technology Unit has a similar role to that of the DTI's Innovation Unit.

The DTI's innovation and technology programmes have shifted away from supporting technology generation towards concentrating on the exploitation and transfer of technology and the promotion of innovation. In particular, the DTI is:

- improving companies' access to local innovation services through Business Links (see p. 212);

- encouraging industry to collaborate with the science base in R & D and technology transfer projects under the LINK and Teaching Company schemes;

- putting more effort into helping firms of all sizes work together to undertake R & D projects, including those under the EUREKA initiative (see p. 343); and

- facilitating companies' access to best practice and technology from overseas and helping companies, especially small and medium-sized concerns, to identify technological opportunities and potential partners, both in Britain and overseas.

Academic–Business Partnerships

The Government supports the transfer of technology, knowledge and skills through partnerships between universities and business.

The Teaching Company Scheme (TCS) enables young graduates to work in industry for two years on technology transfer projects under the joint supervision of academic and company staff. In addition, there are 19 TCS Centres for Small Firms at selected universities. These help smaller businesses to obtain access to the technology and knowledge within the universities.

The Postgraduate Training Partnerships (PTP) scheme enables postgraduate students to undertake practical research in research and technology organisations under the joint guidance of academics and industrialists. There are eight PTPs, each recruiting up to ten PhD students a year.

The DTI recently funded a national technology transfer competition to reward effective partnerships between academic researchers and industry. In 1996 the £35,000 prize was won by UMIST Ventures Ltd, the technology transfer arm of the University of Manchester Institute of Science and Technology. The group developed Aromascan, an 'artificial nose' sensor for use in the food and drink industry. The technology has been shown to be more sensitive than expert wine tasters in recognising vintages and better than pigs at detecting truffles.

Aeronautics

The DTI's Civil Aircraft Research and Demonstration Programme (CARAD) supports research and technology demonstration in the aircraft and aero-engine industry, helping it to compete effectively in world markets. In 1996–97 the provision for aeronautics is about £20 million. The programme is part of a national aeronautics research effort, with over half of the research work supported being conducted in industry and the universities, and the remainder at the Defence Evaluation and Research Agency (see below). CARAD and earlier programmes have supported projects across the range of aero-engine technologies, including compressors, turbines, noise, nacelles and materials. These have helped Rolls-Royce to increase its share of the large civil engine market with its Trent 700 and 800 range of engines (see p. 252). Launch Aid is a means of providing government assistance for specific development projects in the aerospace industry.

Industrial Research Establishments

The DTI acts as the main customer, on behalf of all users of measurement (especially industry), for the development of new measurement standards under the National Measurement System (NMS—see p. 214) and materials metrology programmes. Most of the work of the National Physical Laboratory (NPL) is in support of these programmes; part of the work of the Laboratory of the Government Chemist (LGC) and the National Engineering Laboratory (NEL) also supports the NMS.

In common with other departments, the DTI reviewed the future of its laboratories, having previously established them as executive agencies, and in 1994 decided that their future would be in the private sector. In July 1995 a private sector contractor was appointed to run NPL for five years; NEL was sold to a private sector firm in October 1995; and LGC was established as an independent private sector company in March 1996.

Ministry of Defence

Ministry of Defence provision for R & D in 1996–97 is £2,188 million, of which about £595 million is for medium- and long-term applied research relevant to military needs. With the ending of the Cold War, the Government is committed to achieving a gradual reduction in real terms in spending on defence R & D.

The Defence Evaluation and Research Agency (DERA) is the largest single scientific employer in Britain. It was formed through a merger of the MoD's Defence Research

Agency with most of the Ministry's other non-nuclear science and technology establishments in 1995. Its role is to supply scientific and technical services primarily to the Ministry but also to other government departments. DERA has set up four dual-use technology centres in subjects ranging from structural materials to high-performance computing, to enhance the degree of collaboration between DERA, industry and the academic science base.

DERA subcontracts research to industry and universities, ensuring that their know-how is harnessed to meeting military requirements. It also works closely with industry in order to see that scientific and technological advances are taken forward at an early stage into development and production. This technology transfer is not just confined to the defence industry but has also led to important 'spin offs' into civil markets, in fields ranging from new materials and electronic devices to advanced aerodynamics. The latter in particular has been instrumental in giving Britain a leading role in civil aircraft design.

Ministry of Agriculture, Fisheries and Food

MAFF co-ordinates its research programme with The Scottish Office Agriculture, Environment and Fisheries Department, the Department of Agriculture for Northern Ireland and the research councils, particularly BBSRC. It also covers the research interests of the Welsh Office Agriculture Department.

The research programme reflects the Ministry's wide-ranging responsibilities for protecting and enhancing the rural and marine environment; protecting the public, especially in food safety and quality, flooding and coastal defence, and animal health and welfare; and improving the economic performance of the agriculture, fishing and food industries.

The budget for research expenditure in 1996–97 is £136 million, including support for the Royal Botanic Gardens, Kew (see p. 341). Research is contracted increasingly through open competition with research councils, the Ministry's agencies, non-departmental public bodies, higher education institutions and other organisations.

Department of the Environment

The Department of the Environment funds research in several policy areas: environmental protection, including radioactive substances; water; the countryside; planning and inner cities; local government; housing; building and construction; energy efficiency and environmental technology. The largest programmes are those on pollution-related climate change, regional and urban air quality, the safe disposal of radioactive waste, and best practice in energy efficiency. Total expenditure in 1996–97 is estimated at £114 million.

British scientific expertise is being made available in developing countries to protect threatened species of plants and animals as part of the Darwin Initiative (see p. 370). The Department has committed £12 million to 116 projects in more than 60 countries.

The new Environment Agency (see p. 355) has an R & D programme of £13.5 million in 1996–97.

Department of Health

The Department of Health's R & D strategy comprises two complementary programmes: the Policy Research Programme and the National Health Service R & D Programme. The Department also oversees the research programmes of the health-related non-departmental public bodies. Total expenditure on research in 1995–96, including expenditure by the non-departmental public bodies, was estimated at £69 million.

The strategy promotes strong links with the science base and with research councils, charities, industry and the European Union. The Department, together with the Medical Research Council, has helped to shape the EU's Biomedicine and Health Research Programme within the Fourth Framework Programme (see p. 342).

Overseas Development Administration

The Overseas Development Administration (ODA) commissions and sponsors technology development and research on topics relevant to those geographical regions designated as the primary targets of the aid programme and of benefit to the poorest people in those countries. Provision for R & D in 1996–97 is £81.4 million.

The ODA's support for R & D is organised into five main programmes, covering renewable natural resources and environment; engineering-related sectors (water and sanitation, energy efficiency and geoscience, urbanisation and transport); health and population; economic and social development; and education. R & D is also carried out as part of Britain's bilateral aid to particular countries. The ODA draws on a range of professional expertise in research councils, universities and the private sector.

The ODA also contributes to international centres and programmes undertaking R & D aimed at solving problems faced by developing countries. These contributions include support for the European Union's Science and Technology for Development programme, which sponsors research in renewable natural resources, agriculture, health and nutrition.

The Scottish Office

The Scottish Office both contracts and itself undertakes a wide range of R & D commissions. Total R & D planned expenditure in 1996–97 is £78.3 million in support of its policy responsibilities, which include agriculture, fisheries, health, the environment, education and home affairs. In many areas—medicine, agriculture and biological sciences, fisheries and marine science—public sector research in Scotland has an international reputation.

The Scottish Office Education and Industry Department encourages the development of science-based industry in a number of ways, for example, by promoting and administering government industrial R & D schemes, and promoting participation in, and dissemination of results from, EU R & D programmes.

The enterprise network in Scotland —Scottish Enterprise, Highlands and Islands Enterprise and LECs (see Chapter 14)—is addressing the need for innovation and technology transfer, both through grant support for product and process innovation and a wide range of initiatives. Scottish

Enterprise, together with the Royal Society of Edinburgh (see p. 341), has looked at how to improve the wealth-creating potential of academic research in universities and research institutes in Scotland, in particular by identifying practical means of converting research into wealth-creating products and processes. A strategy to achieve this was published in August 1996.

Space Activities

Britain's civil space programme is co-ordinated by the British National Space Centre (BNSC), a partnership between government departments and research councils. BNSC encourages the competitiveness of the space industry and the exploitation of opportunities in space, based on appraisal of project costs and potential technological and commercial benefits. Through BNSC, Britain spent over £200 million on space activities in 1995–96, with funding mainly from the DTI, the research councils, the Department of the Environment and the Meteorological Office. Around two-thirds of Britain's space expenditure was devoted to programmes shared with the European Space Agency (ESA). The remainder supported a programme of R & D in higher education institutions, government establishments and industry.

Around half of Britain's space programme is concerned with satellite-based Earth observation (remote sensing) for commercial and environmental applications. Britain has committed around £115 million to ESA's ERS-1 and ERS-2 satellites, which were launched in 1991 and 1995 respectively. It provided two of the instruments on both satellites: a Synthetic Aperture Radar and an Along Track Scanning Radiometer (ATSR). The radar is capable of supplying high resolution images of the Earth with 24-hour coverage irrespective of cloud cover conditions. The ATSR measures global sea surface temperature to a very high degree of accuracy. British-built remote sensing instruments are also at work on a number of other satellites, and BNSC promotes the commercial and scientific values of Earth observation data.

Britain is contributing £284 million to an important new Earth observation mission due to be launched in 1999 and known as ENVISAT-1. ENVISAT, carrying a new generation of ESA environmental instruments, including a new radar, will fly on the British-led Polar Platform. Britain is leading the development of ENVISAT's advanced radar, and an advanced version of the ATSR instrument that will measure infra-red emissions over land and sea.

The Earth Observation Data Centre at Farnborough (Hampshire), operated by the National Remote Sensing Centre, is one of ESA's four main processing and archiving facilities for storing and distributing ERS data for both scientific and commercial purposes.

Britain has a world-class reputation for its space science. A quarter of Britain's space budget is devoted to science, including astronomy, planetary science and geophysics. Science contributions have been made to missions ranging from the Hubble Space Telescope to the Ulysses solar space probe. Britain is contributing substantially to the SOHO mission to study the Sun, and to the Infrared Space Observatory. It is also participating in XMM, the ESA's X-ray spectroscopy mission, due to be launched in 1999.

There are bilateral agreements for scientific research between Britain and other countries, such as the United States through its National Aeronautics and Space Administration (NASA), Russia and Japan. British scientists developed, for example, the widefield camera for ROSAT (the German, British and US X-ray satellite), and a spectrometer for the Japanese-built Yohkoh satellite. They are also providing an X-ray telescope for the Russian Spectrum-X mission, expected to be launched in 1998.

A major area of British space expertise is satellite communications and navigation. In Europe, Britain is both a leading producer and user of satellite communications technology (see p. 253). It is contributing to preparations for future ESA satellite communications missions, including ARTEMIS, which will provide important communications links for the ENVISAT programme. Britain is also contributing to the development of a global navigation satellite system within Europe which will augment the United States GPS system to provide increased accuracy and reliability required for civil aviation global navigation.

RESEARCH IN HIGHER EDUCATION INSTITUTIONS

Universities carry out most of Britain's long-term strategic and basic research in science and technology. The higher education funding councils in England, Scotland and Wales (see p. 460) provide the main general funds to support research in universities and other higher education institutions in Great Britain. These funds pay for the salaries of permanent academic staff, who usually teach as well as undertake research, and contribute to the infrastructure for research. In Northern Ireland academic institutions are funded by the Department of Education for Northern Ireland. The quality of research performance of departments is a key element in the allocation of funding. In 1996 the funding councils carried out a research assessment exercise to assess the quality of research in each subject across all higher education institutions in Britain.

Basic and strategic research in higher education institutions are also supported by the research councils. Institutions undertaking research with the support of research council grants have the rights over the commercial exploitation of their research, subject to the prior agreement of the sponsoring research council. They may make use of technology transfer experts and other specialists, such as BTG (see below), to help to exploit and license commercially the results of their research.

The other main channels of support for scientific research in higher education institutions are industry, charities, government departments and the European Union. Institutions are expected to recover the full cost of commissioned research. The high quality of research in higher education institutions, and their marketing skills, have enabled them to attract more funding from a larger range of external sources, especially in contract income from industry and charities.

Science Parks

Science parks are partnerships between higher education or research centres and industry to promote commercially focused research and advanced technology. There are around 50 such parks in operation, and they are host to more than 1,200 companies. Most of these are engaged in computing, biotechnology, chemicals, electrical engineering and robotics. Technology transfer and R & D are the most common activities, rather than large-scale manufacturing.

A growing number of universities offer industry interdisciplinary research centres with exploitable resources. These include access to analytical equipment, library facilities and worldwide databases as well as academic expertise.

OTHER ORGANISATIONS

Industrial Research and Technology Organisations

Research and Technology Organisations (RTOs) are independent organisations carrying out commercially relevant research and other services on behalf of industry, often relating to a specific industrial sector. Britain has the largest RTO sector in Europe, consisting of around 70 organisations, which together employ over 10,000 people.

Charitable Organisations

Medical research charities are a major source of funds for biomedical research in Britain. Their combined contribution in 1996–97 will be about £342 million. The three largest contributors are the Wellcome Trust—the world's largest medical charity—with a contribution of £133 million, the Imperial Cancer Research Fund (£57 million) and the Cancer Research Campaign (£43 million).

BTG

BTG is among the world's leading technology transfer companies. It identifies commercially promising technology from universities, research institutions and companies worldwide; protects these technologies through patents; negotiates licences with industrial partners on a worldwide basis; and shares the net revenues with the sources of the inventions.

BTG holds over 9,000 patents and patent applications, covering more than 1,300 inventions with 478 current licence agreements. Its areas of activity include pharmaceuticals, agribusiness, automotive engineering, medical technology, electronics and telecommunications.

Professional Institutions and Learned Societies

There are numerous technical institutions and professional associations in Britain, many of which promote their own disciplines or the education and professional well-being of their members.

The Council of Science and Technology Institutes has seven member institutes representing biology, chemical engineering, chemistry, food science and technology, geology, hospital physics and physics.

The Engineering Council promotes the study of all types of engineering in schools and other organisations, in co-operation with its 200 industry affiliates, which include large private sector companies and government departments. Together with 39 professional engineering institutions, the Council accredits courses in higher education institutions. It also advises the Government on academic, industrial and professional issues.

More than 300 learned societies play an important role in advancing science and technology through meetings, publications and sponsorship.

Royal Society

The Royal Society, founded in 1660, is Britain's academy of science and has over 1,100 Fellows and more than 100 Foreign Members. Many of its Fellows serve on governmental advisory councils and committees concerned with research. The Society's estimated net expenditure on science and technology in 1996–97 is more than £29 million. Almost 80 per cent of the money which it distributes is derived from a grant

from the Government, the remainder coming from private sources.

The Society has a dual role, as the national academy of science and as the provider of a broad range of services for the scientific community in the national interest. Its activities are:

- recognising excellence in science and its application, for example, through election to the Fellowship and awarding medals and prizes;

- promoting independent advice, notably to government, on science and engineering-related matters;

- encouraging research and its application through research fellowships and grants to individual scientists, and disseminating the results of research through meetings, lectures, exhibitions and publications;

- fostering public understanding and awareness of science, and promoting science education;

- supporting international scientific relations, including exchange of scientists;

- providing resources for, and encouraging, research into the history of science; and

- acting as a forum for discussion of scientific issues.

Royal Academy of Engineering

The national academy of engineering in Britain is the Royal Academy of Engineering, founded in 1976. The Academy has 1,036 Fellows, 68 Foreign Members and 14 Honorary Fellows. It promotes excellence in engineering for the benefit of society. In 1996–97 it is receiving a grant of £3.1 million from the OST and plans to raise over £6.5 million from other sources.

The Academy's programmes are aimed at attracting first-class students into engineering, raising awareness of the importance of engineering design among undergraduates, developing links between industry and higher education, and increasing industrial investment in engineering research in higher education institutions.

In 1996 the Academy launched the Engineering Foresight Awards Scheme to enable British engineers to take part in short-term R & D projects overseas on subjects identified in the Foresight Programme.

Other Societies

In Scotland the Royal Society of Edinburgh, established in 1783, promotes science by running postdoctoral research fellowships and studentships, awarding prizes and grants, organising meetings and symposia, and publishing journals. It has been involved with Scottish Enterprise in developing a strategy to increase the extent of commercial use of the products of the Scottish research base (see p. 338) and has been active in the Foresight process. It also acts as a source of independent scientific advice to the Government and others.

Three other major institutions publicise scientific developments by means of lectures and publications for specialists and schoolchildren. Of these, the British Association for the Advancement of Science (BAAS), founded in 1831, is mainly concerned with science, while the Royal Society of Arts, dating from 1754, deals with the arts and commerce as well as science. The Royal Institution, which was founded in 1799, also performs these functions and runs its own research laboratories.

The Committee on the Public Understanding of Science (COPUS), set up in 1986 by the Royal Society, the BAAS and the Royal Institution, acts as a focus for a wide-ranging programme to improve public awareness of science and technology.

Zoological Gardens

The Zoological Society of London, an independent conservation, science and education body founded in 1826, runs London Zoo, which occupies about 15 hectares (36 acres) of Regent's Park, London. The Society is responsible for the Institute of Zoology, which carries out research in support of conservation. The Institute's work covers a broad range of topics, including ecology, behaviour, reproductive biology and conservation genetics. The Society also operates in field conservation and consultancy, and is concerned with practical field conservation, primarily in East and Southern Africa, the Middle East and parts of Asia.

Whipsnade Wild Animal Park near Dunstable (Bedfordshire) is also owned by the Society. Other well-known zoos include those in Edinburgh, Bristol, Chester, Dudley and Marwell (near Winchester).

Botanic Gardens

The Royal Botanic Gardens, Kew, founded in 1759, covers 121 hectares (300 acres) at Kew in west London and a 187-hectare (462-acre) estate at Wakehurst Place, Ardingly, in West Sussex. They contain the largest collections of living and dried plants in the world. Research is conducted into all aspects of plant life, including physiology, biochemistry, genetics, economic botany and the conservation of habitats and species. Kew is to build a seed bank containing the world's most comprehensive collection of plants at Wakehurst Place. In 1996 it was allocated £21 million by the Millennium Commission towards the estimated £76 million cost of the project. Staff are also active in programmes to return endangered plant species to the wild. Kew participates in joint research programmes in more than 50 countries.

The Royal Botanic Garden in Edinburgh, founded in 1670, is a centre for research into taxonomy (classification of species), for the conservation and study of living plants and for horticultural education.

A national botanic garden and research centre for Wales is to be developed on a 230-hectare (570-acre) site on the Middleton Hall estate at Llandeilo, near Swansea. The £43 million project is backed by a consortium of public and private organisations and individuals. The project has been awarded £21.7 million by the Millenium Commission.

Scientific Museums

The Natural History Museum has 68 million specimens, ranging from a blue whale skeleton to minute insects. It is one of the world's principal centres for research into natural history, offering an advisory service to institutions all over the world.

The Science Museum promotes understanding of the history of science, technology, industry and medicine. Its extensive collection of scientific instruments and machinery is complemented by interactive computer games and audio-visual equipment for visitors to use. In this way, the museum explains scientific principles to the general public and documents the history of science, from early discoveries to space age technology. These two museums are in South Kensington, London. Other important collections include those at the Museum of Science and Industry in Birmingham, the Museum of Science and Industry in Manchester, the Museum of the History of Science in Oxford, and the Royal Scottish Museum, Edinburgh.

Science Festivals

Science festivals are a growing feature of local co-operative efforts to further understanding of the contribution made by science to everyday life. Schools, museums, laboratories, higher education institutions and industry contribute to a large range of special events.

The oldest and most widely publicised science festival is the British Association Annual Festival of Science, held at a British university. The BAAS is also involved in organising the National Science, Engineering and Technology Week (see p. 330). The largest science festival in one place is the annual Edinburgh International Science Festival; in 1996 it included 265 events and attracted about 155,000 visitors. A centre housing a permanent exhibition is due to open in 1998. The £1.2 million project is backed by the City of Edinburgh, the Millennium Commission and a group of private sponsors.

INTERNATIONAL COLLABORATION

Britain has a key role in a wide variety of major international scientific facilities and research programmes.

European Union

Since 1984 the EU has run a series of R & D framework programmes in several strategic sectors, with the aim of strengthening the scientific and technological basis of European industry and supporting the development of EU policies more broadly.

The Fourth Framework Programme runs from 1994 to 1998. It has a budget of 13,000 million ECUs (about £10,900 million) and provides funds for international collaborative research in fields such as biotechnology, industrial materials and information technology. Britain played a significant role in shaping its structure and priorities. It also helped secure agreement that the EU should develop 'generic' technologies with a broad range of industrial applications, rather than funding research projects to meet the needs of specific industrial sectors. The EU has also agreed that more resources should be devoted to disseminating technology from research projects to small and medium-sized enterprises.

Two examples of the many EU research activities involving British organisations, both of which are part of the Fourth Framework Programme, are:

- the EU's Information Technology Programme, which is a shared cost collaborative programme designed to help build the services and technologies that underpin the information society. The programme is open to companies, academic institutions and research bodies. Britain is currently participating in 369 projects in the programme; and

- the Training and Mobility of Researchers (TMR) programme, which aims to develop human resources for science and technology through promoting high-level training for researchers and encouraging their mobility across the community. Britain is the most popular destination under the programme, with over 30 per cent of TMR fellows opting to train in British laboratories.

Other International Activities

Over 700 British organisations have taken part in EUREKA, an industry-led scheme to encourage European co-operation in developing and producing advanced products and processes with worldwide sales potential. Britain is involved in 300 projects, including research into the factory of the future and a sub-programme to generate projects with an environmental theme. There are 25 members of EUREKA, including the 15 EU countries and the European Commission. Britain currently holds the Presidency of EUREKA until June 1997.

The COST (European Co-operation in the field of Science and Technical research) programme encourages co-operation in national research activities across Europe, with participants from industry, academia and research laboratories. Transport, telecommunications and materials have traditionally been the largest areas supported. New areas include physics, chemistry, neuroscience and the application of biotechnology to agriculture, including forestry. There are currently 25 member states and Britain takes part in almost all of about 125 current COST actions.

Other examples of international collaboration include the European Space Agency (see p. 338) and CERN, the European Laboratory for Particle Physics, based in Geneva. Scientific programmes at CERN aim to test, verify and develop the 'standard model' of the origins and structure of the universe. There are 19 member states. Britain's programme is co-ordinated through the CCLRC and the subscription is paid by the PPARC.

Contributions to the high-flux neutron source at the Institut Laue-Langevin and the European Synchrotron Radiation Facility, both in Grenoble, are paid by the EPSRC. The PPARC is a partner in the European Incoherent Scatter Radar Facility within the Arctic Circle, which conducts research on the ionosphere.

Through the MRC, Britain participates in the European Molecular Biology Laboratory (EMBL), based in Heidelberg, Germany. Britain was chosen as the location for the European Bioinformatics Institute, an outstation of the EMBL. The Institute, based in Cambridge, provides up-to-date information on molecular biology and genome sequencing for researchers throughout Europe. It became fully operational in 1995.

The MRC pays Britain's contribution to the Human Frontier Science programme, which supports international collaborative research into brain function and biological function through molecular level approaches. It also pays Britain's subscription to the International Agency for Cancer Research.

NERC has a major involvement in international programmes of research into global change organised through the World Climate Research Programme and the International Geosphere–Biosphere Programme. NERC also supports Britain's subscription to the Ocean Drilling Program and is involved in a wide range of other international activities.

Britain is a member of the science and technology committees of international organisations such as the OECD and NATO, and of various specialised agencies of the United Nations. Among non-governmental organisations, the research councils, the Royal Society and the British Academy are members of the European Science Foundation, and a number of British scientists are involved in its initiatives.

The British Government also enters into bilateral agreements with other governments to encourage closer collaboration on science, engineering and technology. Such agreements were signed, for example, with South Africa in 1995 and with India and the Russian Federation in 1996. Staff in British Embassies and High Commissions conduct government business on, and promote contacts in, science, engineering and technology between Britain and overseas countries; and help to inform a large number of organisations in Britain about science, engineering and technology developments and initiatives overseas. There are science and technology sections in British Embassies in Paris, Bonn, Washington, Tokyo, Moscow and Peking. A number of other posts have officers whose responsibilities include science, engineering and technology.

The British Council (see p. 140) promotes better understanding and knowledge of Britain and its scientific and technological achievements. It encourages exchange of specialists, supplies specialised information, and fosters co-operation in research, training and education. The Council also identifies and manages technological, scientific and educational projects in developing countries.

The research councils maintain, with the British Council, a joint office in Brussels to promote European co-operation in research.

Further Reading

Forward Look of Government-funded Science, Engineering and Technology 1996. HMSO, 1996.

A Guide to the Governmental Organisation of Science and Technology in Britain. British Council, 1995.

Progress through Partnership: First Progress Report on the Technology Foresight Programme 1996. HMSO, 1996.

Realising Our Potential: A Strategy for Science, Engineering and Technology. Cm 2250. HMSO, 1993.

Science and Technology. Aspects of Britain series, HMSO, 1995.

The
Environment

21 Sustainable Development

Government Strategy	347	Business and Consumer Involvement	351
Indicators of Sustainable Development	348	Environmental Research	353

Sustainable development can be defined as development that meets the needs of the present without compromising the ability of future generations to meet their own needs. The Government's strategy on sustainable development was published in 1994, as one of the documents that arose from the Rio de Janeiro 'earth summit'. A further major report setting out key indicators of progress towards sustainable development in Britain was published in March 1996. The most recent edition of *This Common Inheritance*, the Government's annual White Paper on the environment, was published in March 1996.

Government Strategy

The Government published its national strategy on sustainable development in 1994. It was one of the documents that came out in response to the agreements signed at the 1992 Rio de Janeiro 'earth summit', the United Nations Conference on Environment and Development (UNCED). The other documents, published at the same time, cover biodiversity (see p. 370), climate change (see pp. 359–60), and forestry.

The national strategy included the establishment of three bodies to assist policy on sustainable development:

- an independent panel, which advises on issues of major strategic importance to sustainable development;
- a round table, which brings together interests such as business, local government and academics to discuss these matters with ministers; and
- 'Going for Green', an independent committee which seeks to persuade

individuals and groups to commit themselves to sustainable development.

In January 1996 the Government Panel on Sustainable Development produced its second annual report, which concentrated on environmental accounting, biotechnology, forestry and the disposal of radioactive waste. The Government published its response in March 1996. The Panel is currently looking at biodiversity and agriculture in Britain; government procurement; carbon dioxide emissions and energy; and subsidies. Its next report is due to be published in January 1997.

The UK Round Table on Sustainable Development consists of about 30 members, drawn from central and local government, business, environmental organisations and other sectors of the community. It published its first report in April 1996, detailing its work in the preceding year. Its priorities in that year included transport and energy, although it also made recommendations on the new landfill tax (see p. 166) and environmental trusts. The

Government has welcomed the report. The Round Table also keeps in close touch with similar bodies promoting sustainable development in other countries.

In March 1996 the Government published *This Common Inheritance: UK Annual Report 1996*, which sets out progress during 1995 on the commitments in the strategy and in previous White Papers. It also highlights quantified targets and spells out government priorities for the year ahead.

The Environment Act 1995 set up the Environment Agency (see p. 355), covering England and Wales, and the Scottish Environment Protection Agency. The Government is giving the Environment Agency statutory guidance on the contribution it can make to sustainable development.

Indicators of Sustainable Development

The Government's report on indicators of sustainable development was published in March 1996. It lists 118 indicators, grouped into 21 broad headings. The broad headings are:

- the economy;
- transport use;
- leisure and tourism;
- overseas trade;
- energy;
- land use;
- water resources;
- forestry;
- fish resources;
- climate change;
- ozone layer depletion;
- acid deposition;
- air;
- freshwater quality;
- marine;
- wildlife and habitats;
- land cover and landscape;
- soil;
- minerals extraction;
- waste; and
- radioactivity.

Where possible, the indicators track trends over the last 20 to 25 years. Their publication makes Britain one of the first countries in the world to construct indicators which explicitly try to link environmental and development concerns.

The Economy

One of the key aims of sustainable development is to promote a healthy economy in order to generate the resources needed to meet people's needs and improve environmental quality. This in turn can further the protection of human health and the natural environment. Britain's economy is extensively described in the Economic Affairs section of *Britain 1997*, the chapters of which between them cover a number of different aspects of the economy. The key sustainable development indicators chosen for tracking the economy include gross domestic product, consumer spending, inflation and employment. Also under this heading are two indicators that look at human health in Britain: infant mortality and life expectancy.

Transport Use

Transport has an important bearing on the environment, and a key aim of sustainable development is therefore to strike a balance between the ability of transport to serve economic development and the need to protect the environment and sustain the quality of life, both now and in the future. A broad picture of Britain's transport infrastructure and policies is given in Chapter 19; policies to reduce transport-related pollution are looked at on pp. 361–2. The key sustainable development indicators which the Government has selected on transport use include total passenger miles travelled, numbers of short journeys, the volume of freight traffic, and real change in the cost of different modes of transport.

Leisure and Tourism

The growth of leisure and tourism in recent decades has put some stress on the environment, especially where large numbers of people wish to visit wild places (see the special Introduction, pp. vii–xv). The aim is to maintain the quality of the environment in which leisure takes place. If the environment were allowed to deteriorate, an essential part of Britain's attractiveness to tourists would be lost. A number of initiatives have been taken to help reconcile the needs of tourism and leisure with those of the environment: for example, in 1994 the English Tourist Board published *Getting it Right—A Guide to Visitor Management*. This booklet, produced jointly with the English Historic Towns Forum and a firm of chartered surveyors, is a guide to the management of visitors in historic towns and draws on the experiences of 12 towns that have drawn up such plans. The key indicators for this sector include the number of leisure journeys and air travel to and from Britain.

Overseas Trade

The aim is to ensure that Britain's trading activities contribute to sustainable development, both at home and abroad. Britain's overseas trading patterns are covered in detail in Chapter 12. The indicators that have been chosen are imports and exports in certain categories, including food, basic materials including fuel, and manufactured goods.

Energy

Energy is vital to a developed economy such as Britain's. The key objectives are to ensure the supply of energy at competitive prices, reduce adverse consequences of energy use and encourage consumers to meet their needs with less energy through energy efficiency. Energy conservation is also closely linked to the prevention of global climate change, as the consumption of fossil fuels can lead to the emission of greenhouse gases (see pp. 359–60). Energy use in Britain is covered in Chapter 17; this includes energy efficiency measures (see pp. 261–2) and new and renewable sources of energy (see pp. 274–5). Key indicators selected for energy include primary and final energy consumption for Britain, fuel prices, the depletion of fossil fuels, nuclear and renewable fuel capacities and energy consumption by various key sectors.

Land Use

A key objective is to balance the competing demands for the finite amount of land available. The main issues are to minimise the loss of rural land to development and to maintain the viability of town centres, with people living near where they work. The Government has taken various steps to promote this—for example, strengthening planning controls so as to promote the viability of town centres (see p. 383), as well as spending heavily over many years on urban regeneration (see pp. 375–81). The key indicators selected here include the percentage of Britain's land area covered by urban development, the reclamation of derelict land, the re-use of urban land for development, the amount of land taken for new roads, out-of-town retail floorspace, average journey lengths, and spending on regeneration.

Water Resources

The aim is to ensure that there is sufficient water to meet consumers' needs, including those of agriculture and industry, while protecting the aquatic environment from damage caused by over-abstraction. Britain's water industry is covered in pp. 278–80. Key indicators include licensed abstractions compared with rainfall levels in drought years, abstractions for irrigation, and the level of public water supply.

Forestry

Forests play a vital role in the world's ecosystem, and were another of the areas selected for special attention at the UNCED conference. Britain produced its forestry programme in 1994, following on from the conference. Britain's forestry industry is covered in Chapter 18; for information on the programme for the new National Forest and 12 community forests see p. 367. Key indicators for forestry include forest cover, the amount of ancient semi-natural woodland, and tree health.

Fish Resources

In order to sustain the fishing industry, it is necessary to protect fish stocks in British waters. This is being done in the context of the EU Common Fisheries Policy—see pp. 297–8 for the conservation measures being used to protect fish stocks. Key indicators include fish stocks and catches.

Climate Change

Man-made emissions of 'greenhouse gases' are believed to be changing the world's climate, with potentially very serious consequences for the future habitability of large parts of the world. Climate change was therefore one of the areas to be tackled at the UNCED conference, and Britain has developed an action plan to meets its commitments. This is covered on pp. 359–60. Key indicators include British emissions of greenhouse gases and global temperature change.

Ozone Layer Depletion

Scientists have discovered thinning of the stratospheric ozone layer, caused by various ozone-depleting chemicals released into the atmosphere by human activities. International action has been taken to phase out the main substances causing the problem and replace them with less harmful alternatives. These measures are described in more detail on p. 360. Indicators include the atmospheric loading of chlorine, the observed depletion of ozone over Britain and the consumption of chlorofluorocarbons.

Acid Deposition

Britain has accepted very challenging targets to reduce acidifying emissions, principally sulphur dioxide (SO_2) and oxides of nitrogen (NO_x). There have already been significant reductions in some acidifying emissions, and benefits from this have been observed in lower acidity levels in some Scottish lochs (see pp. 360–1). Key indicators in this sector include the extent to which 'critical loads' in soils and freshwaters are being exceeded, emissions of SO_2 and NO_x from power stations, and emissions of NO_x from road transport.

Air

The key aim is to control air pollution in order to reduce the risks of adverse effects on natural ecosystems, human health and the quality of life. The reduction of emissions, especially in urban areas, is very important. Legislation has made important strides in recent decades in the control of air pollution (see pp. 358–62), while the Government has introduced extensive monitoring of pollution levels. Key indicators include emissions and concentrations of various pollutants and expenditure on air pollution abatement.

Freshwater Quality

The quality of Britain's freshwaters is generally good, especially in Scotland and Northern Ireland. The aim is to maintain and improve that record in order to sustain the aquatic environment. Large-scale investment is being made by the water companies to improve standards at water treatment plants, and the Government is introducing a system of statutory water quality objectives (see pp. 356–7). Key indicators include chemical and biological river quality, the levels of nitrates and phosphorus in rivers, pesticides in rivers and groundwaters, the number of pollution incidents, the proportion of discharge consents that are being complied with, and expenditure on water abstraction, treatment and distribution.

Marine

The key issue is to prevent pollution from human activities reaching the sea, especially pollution from toxic substances that persist in the marine environment. Britain has made considerable progress on reducing the input of dangerous substances into its coastal waters, and there have been significant improvements in the quality of its bathing waters (see p. 357). Important indicators here include estuarial water quality, concentrations of key pollutants, bathing water quality, the concentration of contaminants in fish, and the amount of oil spilled or discharged into the sea.

Wildlife and Habitats

It is important that the variety of wildlife in Britain is conserved as far as possible, and that commercially exploited species are managed in a sustainable way. Many species of plant and animal wildlife in Britain are protected by law, and there are active programmes to support or reintroduce certain species (see p. 366). Key indicators include the number of native species at risk in Britain, plant diversity, and the number of lakes and ponds.

Land Cover and Landscape

A key sustainable development issue is to balance the protection of the countryside's landscape and habitats of value for wildlife with the maintenance of an efficient food supply. Programmes such as the Environmentally Sensitive Areas scheme (see pp. 292–3) help ensure that farming is carried out in an environmentally acceptable way, while various designations and other schemes assist the protection of important habitats (see pp. 365–6). Key indicators include rural land cover, nitrogen and pesticide usage, agricultural productivity, the number of sites covered by important designations and length of linear landscape features.

Soil

Soil is a limited resource, vital both for the production of food and as an ecosystem for various organisms. Problems can include the acidification of soils as alkaline nutrients leach out, and contamination with heavy metals. The key indicators for sustainability in this area include soil quality and concentrations of heavy metals in soils.

Minerals Extraction

Britain has many mineral resources (see Chapter 17). However, increasingly there are limitations on sources of supply which are free from environmental constraints. The key aims for sustainable development are to conserve minerals as far as possible while ensuring an adequate supply, to minimise waste production and to encourage the efficient use of materials.

The key indicators for this sector include the output of aggregates, the area of land worked for minerals, and the reclamation of mineral workings.

Waste

Britain is seeking to reduce the amount of waste produced, to make best use of waste which is produced, and to minimise pollution from waste. Recycling schemes are important in this, and the Government has set some ambitious targets in its recent waste strategy (see p. 356). Key indicators include the quantities of household, industrial and commercial waste created, the recycling of household waste and materials, and the amount of energy produced from waste.

Radioactivity

Radioactive materials, used properly, can bring many benefits in a wide range of fields. However, care must be taken to ensure that exposure of the public to radiation is minimised and that radioactive wastes are properly treated. Britain's nuclear power programme is covered on pp. 273–4; the tackling of waste and other problems, such as naturally occurring radon gas, is looked at on pp. 363–4. The key indicators include radiation exposure, discharges from nuclear power stations and the quantities of radioactive waste created.

Business and Consumer Involvement

The Government has launched a number of initiatives to help business improve its environmental performance, ensure business concerns are taken into account when policy is made, and help consumers assess firms' environmental credentials. For example, the Environmental Technology Best Practice Programme promotes better environmental practices that reduce business costs for all areas of industry and commerce, with information and advice on environmental techniques. It also provides an environmental helpline. In 1995 the Government announced the establishment of the Small Company Environmental and Energy Management

Assistance Scheme (SCEEMAS), which makes grants to small companies to improve their environmental performance.

Advisory Committee on Business and the Environment

The Advisory Committee on Business and the Environment is made up of 26 business leaders, appointed by the Government and serving in a personal capacity. Its roles are:

- advising the Government on environmental issues of concern to business;

- providing a link with international business initiatives on the environment; and

- helping to mobilise the business community through demonstrating good environmental practice.

Much of the Committee's work is carried out through working groups which concentrate on a particular area.

British Standard on Environmental Management

In 1994 the British Standards Institution (see p. 214) published BS7750, the world's first standard for environmental management systems. Having been tested in a wide range of businesses and other bodies, the standard can be used by any organisation. BS7750 shares many features of the widely used BS EN ISO 9000—formerly BS5750—quality management standard. The first BS7750 certificates were awarded in 1995.

Eco-management and Audit

In 1993 the European Union adopted a regulation setting up a voluntary eco-management and audit scheme, which became operational throughout the EU in 1995. Although it is intended primarily for the manufacturing, power and waste disposal sectors, its use can be extended to other sectors on an experimental basis. The first such adaptation was the British scheme for local government. Registration covers individual sites[1] rather than companies' entire operations.

An essential component is an environmental management system, such as one certified under BS7750. Applicants must also prepare and publish an environmental statement which, together with the management system, needs to be verified by an accredited independent body. A full cycle of review and verification has to be conducted at least once every three years.

In 1995 five companies in Britain—Akzo Nobel, Ciba Clayton, Design to Distribution, National Power and NOR Systems—became the first in Europe to register sites under the scheme. Government grants are available to help small businesses meet the cost of employing environmental experts to assist with registration.

Ecolabelling

Increasingly consumers wish to take environmental considerations into account when buying goods. Britain has played a leading role in developing the EC ecolabelling scheme. This voluntary scheme aims to help consumers identify those products which are less harmful to the environment over their whole lifecycle. In 1993 Britain awarded the

The European Ecolabel

---

[1] Or 'operational units', in the case of local authorities.

first European ecolabels to Hoover Ltd for washing machines in its 'New Wave' range. Since then, other products have started to carry the labels, including brands of kitchen towels, toilet paper and paints.

Environmental Research

Research into environmental protection is essential to the formulation of the Government's environmental policies. Total spending on environmental research and development in 1995–96 was substantial, running into hundreds of millions of pounds. The Department of the Environment alone commissioned research worth a total of £25 million in 1995–96, looking into subjects such as:

- climate change;
- atmospheric pollution and its monitoring;
- toxic chemicals and genetically modified organisms;
- waste disposal; and
- water quality and health.

Other departments have substantial programmes, notably the Ministry of Agriculture, Fisheries and Food, The Scottish Office Agriculture and Fisheries Department and other official bodies such as the Environment Agency and the Meteorological Office, including the Hadley Centre (see p. 359). The Natural Resources Institute (see p. 140) also has an important role in environmental research,

as do many of Britain's universities. For example, the Climatic Research Unit at the University of East Anglia is regarded as the most important of its kind in the world. Nearly 100 British universities and colleges now run courses on environmental studies or natural resource management.

Research Councils

Basic and strategic research is carried out by government-funded research councils (see pp. 330–4). Most have a role in environmental protection research, but particularly important is the Natural Environment Research Council (NERC), which had a Science Budget allocation of £165 million in 1996–97, plus contracts of £40 million. NERC undertakes and supports research in the environmental sciences and funds postgraduate training. Its programmes encompass the marine, earth, terrestrial, freshwater, polar and atmospheric sciences. NERC puts particular emphasis on international collaborative work on global environmental issues. For example, it is helping to develop global atmospheric climate models and strengthening atmospheric research in the Arctic. A major research programme, the Terrestrial Initiative in Global Environmental Research, aims to assess the likely impact of climate change on Britain and elsewhere and was scheduled to be completed in 1996. NERC also co-ordinates the development and operation of the Environmental Change Network.

Further Reading

Digest of Environmental Statistics. Annual report. HMSO.

Indicators of Sustainable Development for the United Kingdom. HMSO, 1996.

Making Waste Work: A Strategy for Sustainable Waste Management. HMSO, 1996.

Sustainable Development: The UK Strategy. HMSO, 1994.

This Common Inheritance: UK Annual Report 1996. HMSO.

22 Environmental Protection

Pollution Control	354	Genetically Modified	
Administration	354	Organisms	364
Integrated Pollution Control	355	**Conservation**	364
Land	355	The Countryside and Nature	
Water	356	Conservation	364
Air	358	Environmental Improvement	371
Noise	362	Buildings and Monuments	371
Radioactivity	363	World Heritage Sites	373

Britain engages fully in international co-operation on matters of environmental protection. It develops much of its legislation on pollution control and the conservation of wildlife in collaboration with its partners in the European Union (EU) and organisations such as the Organisation for Economic Co-operation and Development and the United Nations (UN). The built environment is also protected by the designation of conservation areas and the listing of buildings of interest. Several important agreements were reached at the United Nations Conference on Environment and Development (UNCED), popularly known as the 'earth summit', held in Rio de Janeiro in 1992.

Pollution Control

The Government's commitment to pollution control is demonstrated by the important role it plays in the regulation of industry. The production industries are estimated to have spent £2,300 million on protecting the environment in 1994, while large sums were spent by local authorities on the proper disposal of household waste.

Administration

Executive responsibility for pollution control is divided between local authorities and central government agencies. Central government makes policy, promotes legislation and advises pollution control authorities on policy implementation. The Secretary of State for the Environment has general responsibility for co-ordinating the work of the Government on environmental protection. In Scotland and Wales the respective Secretaries of State are responsible for co-ordinating pollution control within their countries. In Northern Ireland, this responsibility rests with the Department of the Environment for Northern Ireland. Local authorities also have important duties and powers. They are responsible for such matters as:

- collection and disposal of domestic wastes;
- keeping the streets clear of litter;

- control of air pollution from domestic and from many industrial premises; and

- noise and general nuisance abatement.

The Environment Agency (EA), a new non-departmental public body combining the functions of the former National Rivers Authority, Her Majesty's Inspectorate of Pollution and the waste regulation authorities, began operation in England and Wales in April 1996. Through the mechanism of 'integrated pollution control' (IPC—see below), it has a central role in the control of particular industrial emissions to land, air and water. Other discharges to water are subject to discharge consents (see p. 356).

The Scottish Environment Protection Agency (SEPA) was set up at the same time to combine the functions formerly carried out by Her Majesty's Industrial Pollution Inspectorate and the Scottish river purification authorities. The waste regulation and some of the air pollution functions of the district and islands councils also were taken over by the SEPA.

In Northern Ireland, water quality is monitored by the Environment and Heritage Service of the Department of the Environment for Northern Ireland.

An independent standing body, the Royal Commission on Environmental Pollution, advises the Government. It has produced 19 reports on a variety of topics, the latest being on the sustainable use of soil.

Integrated Pollution Control

Under the Environmental Protection Act 1990, a system of 'integrated pollution control' (IPC) has been phased in to control certain categories of industrial pollution. The potentially most harmful processes are specified for IPC, and require authorisation, in England and Wales from the EA. Emissions to air from more minor processes are controlled by local authorities under a parallel system of local air pollution control (LAPC). In granting authorisation for releases under IPC, the EA requires the use of the best available techniques not entailing excessive cost to prevent or minimise polluting emissions and to ensure that any releases are made harmless.

In Scotland, IPC and LAPC are administered by the SEPA. In Northern Ireland broadly similar controls are exercised by the Environment and Heritage Service, and proposals are being formulated for the introduction of a system of pollution control similar to IPC. The Government has secured agreement to the introduction of IPC on the British model within the European Community (EC), where a directive on integrated pollution prevention and control is expected to be adopted shortly.

Land

Certain local authorities are designated as waste collection or waste disposal authorities, responsible for different parts of the process of dealing with controlled wastes. Waste regulation, formerly a local authority responsibility, now rests with the EA and the SEPA. A licensing system regulates waste disposal sites, treatment plants and storage facilities receiving controlled wastes. 'Special'—that is, hazardous—wastes are subject to additional controls, which have been tightened with new regulations that came into force in September 1996. Responsibility for proper handling of waste falls on everyone who has control of it from production to final disposal or reclamation. Operators of landfill sites now remain responsible for them, even after closure, until the EA is satisfied that no future hazard is likely to arise.

In Scotland, the new unitary councils (see p. 76) are responsible for the collection and disposal of refuse, with the SEPA acting as waste regulation authority. In Northern Ireland, responsibility for the collection, disposal and regulation of waste currently rests with the district councils. However, the centralisation of waste regulation is proposed.

The Government has introduced a landfill tax (see p. 166), which provides a fiscal incentive for waste minimisation and recycling.

Litter and Dog Fouling

It is a criminal offence to leave litter in any public place in the open air or to dump rubbish except in designated places. The maximum fine is £2,500. Local authorities have a duty to keep their public land as free of litter and refuse (including dog faeces) as practicable. Members of the public have powers to take action against authorities which fail to comply with their responsibilities. Local authorities also have powers to make it an offence not to clear up after one's dog in specified places.

To help counteract the problem of litter, financial support from the Department of the Environment—which will total £2.7 million in 1997–98—is given to the Tidy Britain Group, which is recognised as the national agency for tackling litter. It provides a comprehensive anti-litter programme in collaboration with local authorities and the private sector.

Recycling and Materials Reclamation

The Government encourages the reclamation and recycling of waste materials whenever this is the best practicable environmental option; its target is for 25 per cent of all recyclable household waste to be recycled or composted by 2000. Local authorities have to make plans for the recycling of waste. Waste disposal authorities in England must pay 'recycling credits' to waste collection authorities when they collect and return household waste for recycling. These credits are based on savings in disposal costs that have been avoided. In Wales and Scotland, the same authorities handle waste collection and disposal, so that the need for payments does not arise. The Environment Act 1995 gives the Government reserve powers to place an obligation on businesses to re-use, recover or recycle products and materials. Draft regulations would require certain businesses in the packaging chain to recover and recycle specified tonnages of packaging waste by 2001, in line with targets set down in an EC directive. Subject to parliamentary procedures, these regulations will come into effect in January 1997.

The Government has supported pilot recycling initiatives in Sheffield, Cardiff, Dundee and the county of Devon, which have tested a variety of collection and sorting methods. For some time now, members of the public have been able to deposit used glass containers for recycling in bottle banks. There are over 9,000 such banks in Britain, and about 6,600 can banks. There are also over 6,000 paper banks and plastics banks. A variety of other materials, such as textiles, are also recycled.

> The Government published its draft strategy for sustainable waste management in England and Wales in 1995. The key new targets it set were to: reduce the proportion of controlled waste going to landfill to 60 per cent of the total by 2005; recover 40 per cent of municipal waste by 2005; have 40 per cent of domestic properties with a garden carrying out home composting by 2000; and have easily accessible recycling facilities for 80 per cent of households by 2000. The SEPA is preparing a waste strategy for Scotland.

Water

All discharges to water in Britain require the consent of the regulatory authority. In England and Wales the EA's principal method of controlling water pollution is through the regulation of all effluent discharges into groundwaters, inland and coastal waters. The EA maintains public registers containing information about water quality, discharge consents, authorisations and monitoring. Similar arrangements apply in Scotland, where control is exercised by the SEPA. In Northern Ireland the Environment and Heritage Service is responsible for controlling water pollution.

The Government introduced regulations for a new system of classifying water quality in England and Wales in 1994. This system will provide the basis for setting statutory water quality objectives (SWQOs), which will specify for each individual stretch of water the standards that should be reached and the target date for achieving them. The system of SWQOs will provide the framework for the EA to set discharge consents. Once objectives are set, the EA will be under a duty to use its powers to ensure that they are met. In March 1996 the EA began consultations on a small batch of pilot SWQOs. The experience gained from these will be valuable in determining whether to proceed in other water catchment areas.

More than 95 per cent of the population in Britain live in properties connected to a sewer, and sewage treatment works serve over 80 per cent of the population. In England and Wales the water industry is committed to an investment programme of some £11,000 million over ten years for improvements to water quality. Progressively higher treatment standards for industrial waste effluents and new measures to combat pollution from agriculture are expected to bring further improvements in water quality. In Scotland, sewage treatment and disposal come within the water and sewerage programme, which is planned to be £220 million in 1996–97.

> In March 1996 the Government announced the designation of 68 Nitrate Vulnerable Zones in England and Wales. The aim of the zones is to protect water against pollution caused by nitrates used in agriculture; within these areas farmers can be required to change their farming practices to reduce the risk from nitrates, for example by limiting the application of fertilisers at certain times of year.

Over the past 30 years, notable progress has been made in cleaning up the previously heavily polluted major estuaries of the east coast of Britain, including the Forth, Tees, Thames and Tyne. The 1995–2000 price controls on the water companies, announced in 1994, made provision for an extra £522 million of spending on river quality in England and Wales. Results from the monitoring of inland waters there indicate good progress in maintaining and improving quality, with over 90 per cent of rivers and canals now of good or fair quality.

Bathing Waters and Coastal Sewage Discharges

The water industry is investing roughly £2,000 million to provide treatment of coastal sewage discharges and improve the quality of Britain's bathing waters. In the 1995 tests of bathing water quality, 89 per cent of identified bathing waters (413 out of 464) in Britain met the mandatory coliform bacteria standards of the EC bathing water directive, compared with 66 per cent of beaches in 1988. The majority of the schemes in the improvement programme are complete. Sea dumping of sewage sludge will cease by the end of 1998.

Marine Environment

In 1992 a new Convention for the Protection of the Marine Environment of the North East Atlantic was agreed in Paris. It covers inputs and discharges from both land and sea, sets targets for the introduction of additional safeguards for the area, and requires contracting parties to take all possible steps to prevent or eliminate pollution through an action plan subject to annual review. Britain is also a leading participant in the series of North Sea Conferences, an international forum of countries bordering the North Sea, the most recent of which was held in Denmark in 1995. Good progress is being made in meeting North Sea Conference targets for reducing the input of dangerous substances into the sea. For example, direct and riverine inputs of cadmium, lead and mercury to coastal waters were more than halved between 1985 and 1993.

International action on the prevention of pollution from ships is taken through the International Maritime Organization (IMO). Britain applies international requirements to all ships in British waters and to British ships wherever they are. Enforcement is undertaken by the Department of Transport.

The Marine Pollution Control Unit (MPCU), part of the Coastguard Agency, is responsible for dealing with spillages of oil or other hazardous substances from ships at sea. The Government's national contingency plan, which is developed and maintained by the MPCU, sets out arrangements for dealing with pollution. The Unit has at its disposal various counter-pollution facilities, including:

- remote sensing surveillance aircraft;
- aerial and seaborne spraying equipment;
- stocks of oil dispersants;

- mechanical recovery and cargo transfer equipment; and
- specialised beach cleaning equipment.

The most recent major incident in which these capabilities were put to the test was when the tanker *Sea Empress* ran aground off Milford Haven in south Wales in February 1996.

Licences for oil and gas exploration include special conditions designed to protect the environment. Applicants for licences in sensitive areas must demonstrate that they have addressed the environmental concerns when developing their work programme. Before commencing offshore operations, the operators are required to have approved oil spill contingency plans in place. In addition, all discharges that contain oil are controlled under the Prevention of Oil Pollution Act 1971, and limits are set for the permissible level of oil discharged. In response to commitments made at the North Sea Conference, progressively tighter limits on oil discharged with drill cuttings have been set. This has resulted in the quantity of oil discharges from this source from installations in British waters falling from 18,500 tonnes in 1988 to 3,180 tonnes in 1995.

Britain ended the dumping of industrial waste at sea in 1992. Waste has not been licensed for incineration at sea since 1990. The dumping at sea of most types of waste will be phased out over the next few years. In 1994 Britain announced that it was accepting an internationally agreed indefinite ban on the sea dumping of low- and intermediate-level radioactive waste—the sea dumping of high-level waste was already prohibited. After the phasing out of sewage sludge dumping in 1998, the only category of waste which Britain will routinely dump at sea will be dredged material from ports, harbours and the like. This will only be approved for dumping at sea if no beneficial use for the material is available.

Air

Air quality in Britain has improved considerably in the last 30 years. Total emissions of smoke in the air have fallen by over 85 per cent since 1960. London and other major cities no longer have the dense smoke-laden 'smogs' of the 1950s and in central London winter sunshine has increased by about 70 per cent since the late 1950s. However, new concerns have arisen, especially over the emissions from the growing number of motor vehicles and their possible impact on health. Measures have consequently been adopted to reduce substantially emissions from new vehicles (see p. 361).

The Environment Act 1995 provides a new framework for air quality management, including the publication by the Government of a national strategy which will set air quality standards and targets for the pollutants causing the most concern. This was issued for consultation in August 1996, containing air quality targets for the year 2005. The Act also places new duties on local authorities to assess air quality in their boundaries and to prepare action plans where standards are not met or are unlikely to be met in future. Pilot schemes are being taken forward in 14 areas before full implementation in April 1997. Earlier legislation allows local authorities to declare 'smoke control areas' within which the emission of smoke from chimneys is an offence. About two-thirds of the dwellings in conurbations are covered by smoke control orders—around 6,340 are in force.

Those industrial processes with the greatest potential for harmful emissions are controlled under the Environmental Protection Act 1990, enforced in England and Wales by the EA, and are subject to IPC. Processes with a significant but lesser potential for air pollution require approval, in England and Wales from local authorities. Local authorities also control emissions of dark smoke from trade and industrial premises.

In 1994 the Government announced funding of £5 million for a co-ordinated programme of research on air pollution and respiratory disease. Ten key areas are being addressed, including the short- and long-term effects of exposure to air pollutants, and the development of methods for measuring personal exposure to air pollutants. An expert panel is recommending standards for maximum levels of various pollutants, which the Government aims to meet or exceed by 2005. Britain's automatic air quality monitoring network is being extended and upgraded at a cost of over £4 million a year, while local authority sites are being integrated into the national network. By the end of 1996, the automated urban network is scheduled to include over 100 sites.

Since 1990, the Department of the Environment's Air Quality Bulletins have made daily air pollution data from the monitoring network available to the public. These give the concentrations of the main pollutants, together with an air pollution forecast—and grade air quality on a scale between 'very poor' and 'very good'. The information features in television and radio weather reports, and appears in many national and local newspapers. Information, updated hourly from the automatic monitoring sites, is also available directly on a special free telephone number, on videotext systems and on the Internet.

Climate Change

Several gases naturally present in the atmosphere keep the Earth at a temperature suitable for life by trapping energy from the sun—the so-called 'greenhouse effect'. Emissions from human activities are increasing the atmospheric concentrations of several important 'greenhouse gases'. This is believed to be leading to additional global warming. The most significant greenhouse gases include water vapour, carbon dioxide (CO_2), methane and wholly man-made substances such as chlorofluorocarbons (CFCs).

The Intergovernmental Panel on Climate Change (IPCC) was established in 1988 to consider climate change and possible responses to it. The IPCC's second assessment report was published in spring 1996. One of its key conclusions was that the balance of evidence suggested a discernible human influence on global climate. It suggested that between 1990 and 2100 there might be an increase in global mean surface temperatures of about 2°C—a greater average rate of warming than any seen in the last 10,000 years.

Britain is conducting extensive research into climate change. The research programme includes the construction of an advanced climate change detection instrument for launch on a satellite towards the end of the 1990s, and

the work of the Hadley Centre for Climate Prediction and Research. A July 1996 report from the UK Climate Change Impacts Review Group suggested that the effect of climate change in Britain over the next 30 years could be to push the climate zones northwards by as much as 200 km (120 miles). The north-west could become wetter, while the south-east could be more prone to drought.

The Framework Convention on Climate Change was signed by more than 150 nations at the 1992 'earth summit' in Rio de Janeiro (see p. 347). Its objective is to achieve stabilisation of greenhouse gas concentrations in the atmosphere at a level which would prevent dangerous man-made interference with the climate system.

Britain is one of a handful of developed countries on course to meet its Convention commitments to return emissions of greenhouse gases to below 1990 levels by the year 2000. Its CO_2 emissions are expected to be 4 to 8 per cent below 1990 levels, reflecting the impact of Britain's climate change programme, published in 1994. The programme aims to ensure that both individuals and organisations exploit the scope for taking measures that are cost-effective in their own right. Britain's national programme for combating the threat of global climate change includes:

- the removal of subsidies on the use of fossil fuels;

- an annual increase in road fuel duties of 5 per cent in real terms;

- the introduction of value added tax on domestic fuel;

- the promotion of new and renewable sources of energy to enable them to compete in energy markets;

- programmes to improve industrial, commercial and domestic energy efficiency; and

- the adoption of EU minimum efficiency standards for electrical appliances.

In 1995 the first conference of parties to the Convention met in Berlin and set in hand a process for agreeing new commitments for the period beyond 2000. The so-called 'Berlin Mandate' is aimed primarily at strengthening commitments from developed nations.

Another meeting is due to be held in Kyoto, Japan at the end of 1997, where a protocol should be agreed to fulfil the Berlin Mandate. Britain is proposing that developed countries should aim to reduce their total emissions of greenhouse gases from 1990 levels by up to 10 per cent by the year 2010.

Stratospheric Ozone Layer

Stratospheric ozone forms a layer of gas about 10 km to 50 km (6 to 30 miles) above the Earth's surface, protecting it from the more harmful effects of solar radiation. However, there is evidence for ozone losses over much of the globe, including a 'hole' in the ozone layer over Antarctica, first discovered by British scientists in 1985. Ozone depletion is caused by man-made chemicals containing chlorine or bromine, such as CFCs or halons.

The Government is committed to the earliest possible phasing out of all ozone-depleting substances. Britain was one of the first 25 signatories to the 1987 Montreal Protocol, which deals with the protection of the stratospheric ozone layer. The Protocol required the phasing out of the production of halons by the end of 1993, and the phasing out of CFCs, 1,1,1 trichloroethane and carbon tetrachloride by the end of 1995 in all developed countries. This has been substantially achieved in Britain apart from exemptions for a small number of essential uses, for example in medical inhalers. The Protocol has also placed controls on hydrochlorofluorocarbons, which are transitional substances with much lower ozone-depleting potential than CFCs. They are needed in a number of areas to allow industry to cease using CFCs more quickly, but must be phased out in new equipment by 2020. Production and consumption of methyl bromide must be phased out by 2010. EC regulations impose even tighter requirements on member states.

The Montreal Protocol also imposes controls on developing countries, which are committed to phasing out CFCs by 2010. A multilateral fund has been established to assist developing countries to comply with the controls on ozone-depleting substances; Britain contributes towards this.

Emissions of Sulphur Dioxide and Oxides of Nitrogen

Sulphur dioxide (SO_2) and oxides of nitrogen (NO_x) are the main gases that lead to acid rain. The principal sources are combustion plants that burn fossil fuels, such as coal-fired power stations, and, for NO_x, road transport. National SO_2 emissions have fallen by over 40 per cent since 1970 and a substantial programme seeks to ensure that this fall continues. For example, under an EC directive on the control of emissions from large combustion plants, the Government has published a national plan setting out phased reductions in emissions from existing plants of NO_x by 30 per cent by 1998 and of SO_2 by 60 per cent by 2003, in both cases compared with the level in 1980. The latest figures, for 1994, show that Britain had achieved a reduction of 49 per cent in both cases. Britain has also met the targets set in the first United Nations Economic Commission for Europe (UNECE) protocol on NO_x. Britain is currently involved in development of a new UNECE protocol on NO_x, and in 1994 signed the second UNECE sulphur protocol. It agreed to secure a reduction of at least 80 per cent in SO_2 emissions from all sources by 2010. The Government recently issued a consultation paper on its proposed strategy.

Tougher authorisations for power stations belonging to the two main operators, National Power and PowerGen, were issued in March 1996. These set stringent SO_2 emission reduction targets—an 85 per cent cut from 1991 levels of SO_2 emissions by 2005—but allow the operators freedom to determine the means to meet the requirements. This might include fitting abatement equipment, switching to low-sulphur fuel or reducing the operating periods of particular stations.

The damaging effect of acid depositions from combustion processes on freshwaters and soils has been demonstrated by scientific research. Lower emissions of SO_2 over the past

Emissions of Sulphur Dioxide

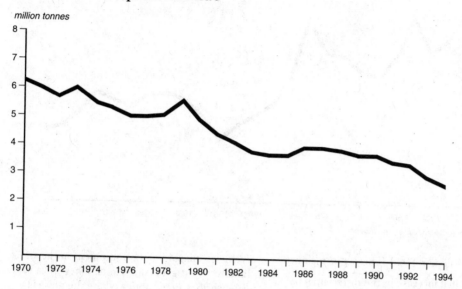

million tonnes

Source: Department of the Environment

20 years (see graph) have, however, led to the first signs of a decrease in acidification in some lochs in south-west Scotland.

Vehicle Emissions

Stringent emission standards for passenger cars were introduced at the end of 1992, which effectively require new petrol-engined cars to be fitted with catalytic converters. These typically reduce emissions by over 75 per cent. Diesel cars are also subject to strict controls on particulate emissions. Since 1994, vans have had to meet the same limit as cars. Stricter controls for heavy diesel vehicles, including lorries and buses, were introduced in 1993. Further cuts in permitted emission levels are being introduced in 1996 and 1997.

Compulsory tests of emissions from vehicles in use are a key element in Britain's strategy for improving air quality. Britain has introduced metered emission tests and smoke checks into the annual 'MoT' roadworthiness test. In 1995, limits for vehicles in service were further tightened, and special tests were applied to catalyst-fitted vehicles from January 1996.

Enforcement checks carried out at the roadside or in operators' premises also include at least a visual check for excessive smoke. Wherever possible, a smoke meter is used for borderline cases. The Vehicle Inspectorate (see p. 305) carried out more than 110,000 roadside enforcement checks in 1995–96.

As a result of these measures, a marked and progressive decline in regulated pollutants is expected, which will continue until well into the first decade of the 21st century.

The November 1995 Budget contained a government commitment to look into ways of using vehicle excise duty to encourage low-emission vehicles. It also reduced the duty on liquid petroleum gas and compressed natural gas, as studies have shown that these are relatively clean fuels.

Sales of unleaded petrol have risen from virtually nothing in the mid-1980s to over 65

Emissions of Carbon Dioxide

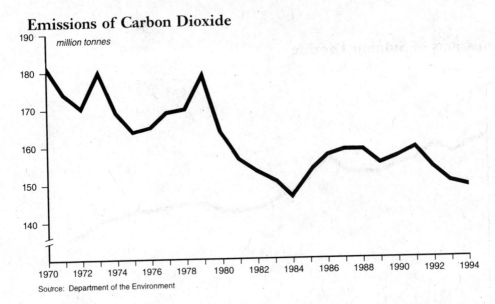

Source: Department of the Environment

per cent of all petrol sold. This is due mainly to:

- a gradual increase in the differential in duty between leaded and unleaded petrol;
- the requirement for all new cars from October 1990 onwards to be capable of running on unleaded petrol; and
- the necessity for cars fitted with catalytic converters to use unleaded petrol.

These measures have contributed to a 70 per cent reduction of lead in the air.

Regulations were introduced in 1994 which for the first time set compulsory limits to the volatility of petrol. The expected benefits include a reduction in volatile organic compounds given off. The regulations also introduce a new EC standard for low sulphur diesel fuel, which will further reduce particulate emissions from all diesel vehicles from 1996.

Internationally developed standards have also been implemented in Britain to control the emission of smoke, vented fuel and unburned hydrocarbons from civil aircraft. International standards to control NO_x and carbon monoxide will be incorporated into domestic legislation.

Noise

Local authorities have a duty to inspect their areas for noise nuisance from premises and

vehicles, machinery or equipment in the street, and to investigate complaints. They must serve a noise abatement notice where the noise is judged to be a statutory nuisance. They can also designate 'noise abatement zones' within which registered levels of noise from certain premises may not be increased without their permission. There are also specific provisions in law to:

- control noise from construction and demolition sites;
- control the use of loudspeakers in the streets; and
- enable individuals to take independent action through the courts against noise nuisance.

The Government believes that, wherever possible, attempts should be made to resolve problems informally. It promotes increased public awareness of neighbour noise issues and also encourages the use of community mediation, funding the umbrella organisation Mediation UK. However, informal resolution may not always be possible, and so it supported the Noise Act 1996, which was passed as a Private Member's Bill and strengthens the law in England and Wales on noisy neighbours. The Housing Act 1996 (see p. 385) includes new powers for local authorities to deal with anti-social behaviour by tenants, which includes noise nuisance.

Regulations set out the permissible noise levels for various classes of new vehicle, and a new EC noise directive is due to be implemented by October 1996. Compensation may be payable for loss in property values caused by physical factors, including noise from new or improved public works such as roads, railways and airports. Regulations also require highway authorities to make grants available for insulation of homes that would be subject to specified levels of increased noise caused by new or improved roads. Noise insulation may also be provided where construction work for new roads will seriously affect nearby homes for a substantial period of time. Equivalent regulations for new railways have been introduced.

Britain has played a leading role in negotiations aimed at phasing out older, noisier subsonic jet aircraft. The phased implementation of a complete ban on the operation of 'Chapter 2' aircraft (noisier planes, as classified by international agreement) began in 1995, and it is intended to phase out all these types by 2002. Various operational restrictions have been introduced to reduce noise disturbance further at Heathrow, Gatwick and Stansted, where the Secretary of State for Transport has assumed responsibility for noise abatement. These measures include:

- restrictions on the type and number of aircraft operating at night;

- the routeing of departing aircraft on routes chosen to minimise noise nuisance; and

- quieter take-off and landing procedures.

The Government has introduced a control system for night flights combining a noise quota with a ceiling on the total number of movements. The population disturbed by aircraft noise[1] at Heathrow fell from 591,000 in 1988 to 372,000 in 1992, even though the number of air transport movements increased.

This was largely because of the phasing out of older, noisier aircraft.

Radioactivity

Man-made radiation represents only a small fraction of that to which the population is exposed; most is naturally occurring. A large proportion of the man-made radioactivity to which the public is exposed comes from medical treatments, such as X-rays. Nevertheless, man-made radiation is subject to stringent control. Users of radioactive materials must be registered by the EA in England and Wales or its equivalents in Scotland and Northern Ireland; authorisation is also required for the accumulation and disposal of radioactive waste. The Health and Safety Executive (see p. 201), through its Nuclear Installations Inspectorate, is responsible for granting nuclear site licences for major nuclear installations. No installation may be constructed or operated without a licence granted by the Executive.

The National Radiological Protection Board (NRPB) provides an authoritative point of reference on radiological protection. In 1987 the Government announced measures to deal with the problem of radon, a naturally occurring radioactive gas which can accumulate in houses. These included a free survey by the NRPB for householders living in areas mostly likely to be affected by radon. Cornwall, Devon, Derbyshire, Northamptonshire and Somerset have been found to have the highest numbers of homes over the recommended action level. However, other areas with above-average number of houses likely to be affected by radon have now been identified. As a result of earlier surveys, the NRPB can now predict with much greater accuracy the areas most likely to have substantial numbers of homes above the action level. Free tests are therefore being offered by invitation to householders in those areas.

Radioactive Waste Disposal

Radioactive wastes vary widely in nature and level of activity, and the methods of disposal reflect this. Some wastes can be disposed of safely in the same way as other industrial and household wastes. UK Nirex is responsible for

---

[1]That is, living within the 57 Leq noise contour, which is generally regarded as the onset of disturbance. Using the older, broadly comparable, 35 NNI measure, about 1.6 million people were affected in 1979.

developing a deep disposal facility for solid low-level and intermediate-level radioactive waste. It is concentrating detailed geological investigations on an area near the British Nuclear Fuels site at Sellafield, in Cumbria. As part of these studies, Nirex has applied for planning permission for an experimental underground rock laboratory, known as a 'rock characterisation facility', and a public inquiry has been held into this.

The Department of the Environment is developing a research strategy into the disposal of high-level or heat-generating waste. This waste will first be stored in vitrified form for at least 50 years to allow the heat and radioactivity to decay.

All contracts for reprocessing spent nuclear fuel from overseas entered into since 1976 include provisions for the resulting waste to be returned to the country of origin. The government has announced that it will accept 'waste substitution' in such cases, provided there are appropriate disposal arrangements in Britain for the substituted waste.

Genetically Modified Organisms

Genetically modified organisms (GMOs) have many potentially beneficial uses, such as better and increased supplies of food and advances in health care. As with any new technology, however, it is important to make sure that there are no significant risks to mankind or the environment. This is done through the Environmental Protection Act 1990 and subsequent regulations. Advice on all applications to release or market GMOs is provided by a statutory advisory committee. Britain participated in drawing up draft international guidelines on safety in biotechnology, which were adopted by the United Nations Environment Programme in 1995. It also supports the development of a safety protocol to the Convention on Biological Diversity (see p. 370), which would focus on transboundary movements of living modified organisms.

Conservation

Britain has a long tradition of conservation, and for many years has had policies and laws designed to protect both its natural environment and its built heritage. A wide variety of designations are used to protect areas, sites and monuments that are of special interest, and various organisations work towards the conservation of different aspects of Britain's national heritage.

Among the agreements reached at the 'earth summit' were a convention on biodiversity (see p. 370) and a declaration for the management of forests. In 1994, Britain published its national strategies for biodiversity (see p. 370) and forestry.

The Department of the Environment is responsible for countryside policy and environmental protection in England; the Department of National Heritage has responsibility for the listing of buildings and for scheduled ancient monuments in England. The Welsh Office, The Scottish Office and the Department of the Environment for Northern Ireland have broadly equivalent responsibilities. Agencies such as English Nature, English Heritage, the Countryside Commission and their equivalents carry out many functions on behalf of the Government. In addition, local authorities and a wide range of voluntary organisations are actively involved in environmental conservation and protection.

The Countryside and Nature Conservation

Four government agencies are responsible for countryside policy and nature conservation in Great Britain:

- the Countryside Commission and English Nature, which both act in England, the former being responsible for countryside policy and the latter for nature conservation;
- the Countryside Council for Wales (CCW); and
- Scottish Natural Heritage (SNH).

The Joint Nature Conservation Committee (JNCC) is the mechanism through which the three nature conservation agencies in England, Wales and Scotland fulfil their responsibilities for international nature conservation matters and those affecting Great Britain as a whole.

The JNCC also undertakes research in connection with these responsibilities and sets standards for data, monitoring and other matters connected with nature conservation. It includes representatives from Northern Ireland and independent members, and has a supporting specialist staff.

Countryside Agencies

The Countryside Commission, the CCW and SNH are responsible for promoting the enhancement of the natural beauty and amenity of the countryside and encouraging the provision of facilities for open-air recreation. They are expected to respect the needs of those who live and work in the countryside. Activities undertaken by these bodies include:

- advising the Government on countryside matters;
- assisting the provision by local authorities and others of facilities for recreation in the countryside, often within easy reach of towns;
- designating and improving recreational rights of way;
- undertaking research projects; and
- ensuring the protection of special landscapes.

Total funding for the countryside agencies in 1996–97 is £26 million for the Countryside Commission, £22 million for the CCW and £37 million for SNH.

The Countryside Commission recognises over 210 country parks and over 230 picnic sites in England. A further 35 country parks and about 30 picnic sites in Wales are recognised by the CCW. In Scotland there are 36 country parks, and many local authority and private sector schemes for a variety of countryside facilities have been approved for grant aid by SNH.

In Wales the Tir Cymen scheme, administered by the CCW, rewards farmers who make agreements to manage their farms in an environmentally friendly manner.

Nature Conservation Agencies

English Nature, the CCW and SNH are the Government's statutory advisers on nature conservation in their areas. Their work includes:

- establishing and managing national nature reserves and encouraging the establishment of local nature reserves;
- advising the Government;
- identifying, notifying and monitoring Sites of Special Scientific Interest (SSSIs);
- providing general nature conservation information and advice;
- giving grants; and
- supporting and conducting research.

English Nature's funding for 1996–97 is £39 million.

There are over 300 national nature reserves covering some 190,000 hectares (468,000 acres) in Great Britain, and two statutory marine nature reserves, surrounding the islands of Lundy, off the Devon coast, and Skomer, off the coast of Wales. About 6,700 SSSIs have been notified in Great Britain for their plant, animal, geological or physiographical features. Some are of international importance and have been designated for protection under the EC Birds Directive or the Ramsar Convention (see p. 370). Local authorities have declared about 395 local nature reserves in England, 23 in Scotland and 26 in Wales.

In England, to assist those who have an interest or involvement in environmental planning and conservation action, English Nature and the Countryside Commission have jointly mapped and are describing areas of distinct landscape and ecological character. This framework will underpin the separate programmes of the two agencies. English Nature's 'Natural Areas' have a distinctive character that derives from the underlying geology, land forms, flora and fauna, and the land uses and settlement patterns of the area. The Natural Areas framework has been subject to public consultation, and potential links with the Countryside Commission's Countryside Character Programme are currently being explored. This latter programme will use the map and description to help guide countryside policies and programmes.

English Nature enters into land management agreements with owners and occupiers of SSSI land, increasingly to support management that is beneficial for its wildlife and natural features. Payments made under these agreements totalled £5.6 million in 1994–95. Overall, English Nature's grant schemes provide more than £2 million a year to assist local action to sustain biodiversity and geodiversity. SNH and the CCW also enter into land management agreements.

The Department of the Environment for Northern Ireland has responsibility for both nature and countryside conservation. The Council for Nature Conservation and the Countryside advises the Department on nature conservation matters, including the establishment and management of land and marine nature reserves and the declaration of Areas of Special Scientific Interest. In all, 72 Areas of Special Scientific Interest had been declared by March 1995, covering 75,000 hectares (185,000 acres), and 47 statutory nature reserves had been established.

County wildlife trusts, urban wildlife trusts and the Royal Society for the Protection of Birds (RSPB) play an important part in protecting wildlife throughout Britain, having established between them over 2,000 reserves. The county and urban trusts are affiliated to a parent organisation, RSNC The Wildlife Trusts. The RSPB is the largest voluntary wildlife conservation body in Europe.

Wildlife Protection

The principal piece of legislation protecting wildlife in Great Britain is the Wildlife and Countryside Act 1981. This has:

- extended the list of protected species;
- restricted the introduction into the countryside of animals not normally found in the wild in Britain; and
- afforded greater protection for SSSIs than previously and made provision for marine nature reserves.

There is also provision for reviews of the list of protected species to be conducted by the three official nature conservation agencies, acting jointly through the JNCC, every five years, and for recommended changes to be submitted to the Secretary of State for the Environment. In Northern Ireland separate legislation on species and habitat protection is in line with the rest of Britain.

Species Recovery and Reintroduction

Extensive research and management are carried out to encourage the recovery of populations of species threatened with extinction. The three nature conservation agencies have also set up recovery programmes for a number of threatened species of plants and animals. English Nature's programme covers 43 species, including the dormouse, the Plymouth pear and the fen raft spider. The aim is to ensure the survival of self-sustaining populations of these threatened species in the wild. SNH has a programme initially covering 17 species, and the CCW one covering 15 species.

Schemes have been devised to reintroduce species into areas in which they used to be found. For example, the red kite had died out in England and Scotland, although it was still found in Wales and mainland Europe. An international project was successfully co-ordinated by the JNCC and the RSPB to bring adult birds from Sweden and Spain and release them into the wild in areas which the species no longer inhabited. Other species reintroduced in recent years include the white-tailed sea eagle and the large blue butterfly. The Royal Botanic Gardens at Kew holds seeds from about 3,000 plant species which are extinct or under severe threat in the wild, and has had some success with reintroduction projects. The Royal Botanic Gardens in Edinburgh also plays a significant role.

Tree Preservation and Planting

Tree preservation orders enable local authorities to protect trees and woodlands in the interests of amenity. Once a tree is protected, it is in general an offence to cut down, reshape or generally wilfully destroy it without permission. The courts can impose substantial fines for breaches of such orders. Where protected trees are felled in contravention of an order or are removed because they are dying, dead or dangerous, replacement trees must be planted. Local authorities have powers to enforce this.

Broadleaved Tree-planting 1980–81 to 1994–95

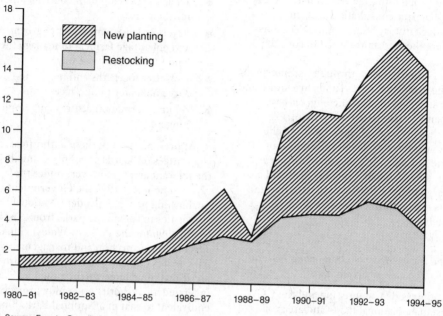

Thousands of hectares

Source: Forestry Commission

Tree planting is encouraged through various grant schemes. The planting of broadleaved trees has increased more than tenfold since 1985. Major afforestation projects involving the Countryside Commission include the creation of a new national forest in the Midlands, and 12 community forests near major cities. The Woodland Trust is a voluntary body which protects existing woodland and plants new trees for the future. It now owns about 800 woods across Britain, and has planted well over a million trees in the past ten years or so.

The Coast

Local planning authorities are responsible for planning land use at the coast; they also aim to safeguard and enhance the coast's natural attractions and preserve areas of scientific interest. The protection of the coastline against erosion and flooding is administered centrally by the Ministry of Agriculture, Fisheries and Food, the Welsh Office and The Scottish Office. Operational responsibility lies with local authorities and the EA (see p. 355). New measures to improve the management of the coast of England were announced by the Government in 1994. These include the establishment of a standing forum on coastal issues and a review of by-laws relating to coastal management. Certain stretches of undeveloped coast of particular beauty in England and Wales are designated as heritage coast; jointly with local authorities, the countryside agencies have designated 45 heritage coasts, protecting 1,525 km (948 miles), about 35 per cent of the total length of coastline.

English Nature, through its Campaign for a Living Coast, provides funds for groups setting up voluntary marine nature reserves or producing management plans for England's estuaries. So far, 11 reserves have been grant–aided and 20 estuary management plans produced, covering more than 85 per cent of England's total estuarine area. There are 29 informal marine consultation areas in Scotland. Statutory bodies taking decisions that affect these areas are asked to consult SNH.

The National Trust, through its Enterprise Neptune campaign, raises funds to acquire and protect stretches of coastline of great natural beauty and recreational value. About £22 million has been raised since 1965 and the Trust now protects 893 km (555 miles) of coastline in England, Wales and Northern Ireland. The National Trust for Scotland also owns large parts of the Scottish coastline and protects others through conservation agreements.

National Parks, Areas of Outstanding Natural Beauty and National Scenic Areas

The Countryside Commission and the CCW can designate National Parks and areas of outstanding natural beauty (AONBs), subject to confirmation by the Secretaries of State for the Environment and for Wales respectively.

Ten National Parks have been established in England and Wales. Their aim is first to provide protection for the outstanding countryside they contain and secondly to provide opportunities for access and outdoor recreation. They are 'national' in the sense that they are of special value to the nation as a whole. However, most of the land remains in private hands. These areas are administered by individual National Park authorities. Among other things, they:

● act as the development control authority for their areas;

● negotiate land management agreements and encourage farmers to manage their land in the traditional way;

● look after footpaths and negotiate agreements for public access; and

● set up information centres and employ rangers.

At present, most of these authorities are committees or boards of county councils for the relevant areas. However, under the Environment Act 1995 the Government is establishing new independent National Park authorities to run all the parks from April 1997 (April 1996 for the Parks in Wales). This will allow better protection and management of the park areas. The Norfolk and Suffolk Broads are also administered by their own independent authority and enjoy protection equivalent to that of a National Park. Since 1994 the planning policies that apply to the National Parks have also applied to the New Forest area in Hampshire.

A total of 41 AONBs have been designated, covering around 20,400 sq km (7,900 sq miles) in England and 830 sq km (320 sq miles) in Wales. They comprise parts of the countryside which lack extensive areas of open country suitable for recreation and hence National Park status, but which nevertheless have an

Table 22.1: National Parks and Other Designated Areas, December 1995

	National Parks area (sq km)	Percentage of total area	Areas of Outstanding Natural Beauty[a] (sq km)	Percentage of total area
England	9,934	7	20,393	16
Wales	4,098	20	832	4
Scotland	–	–	10,018	13
Northern Ireland	–	–	2,849	20

Sources: Countryside Commission, Countryside Council for Wales, Scottish Natural Heritage, Department of the Environment for Northern Ireland
[a]National Scenic Areas in Scotland.

important landscape quality. Local authorities are encouraged to give special attention to AONBs in their planning and countryside conservation work.

In Scotland there are four regional parks and 40 National Scenic Areas, covering more than 11,000 sq km (4,300 sq miles), where certain kinds of development are subject to consultation with SNH and, in the event of a disagreement, with the Secretary of State for Scotland. Working parties have made recommendations for the management of the Cairngorms and for Loch Lomond and the Trossachs, two areas of outstanding natural importance in Scotland. For the former, the Government has established a Cairngorms Partnership, as recommended by the working party. In the latter case, the new local authorities are establishing a joint committee for the area. In the wider countryside SNH provides grants for a range of countryside projects.

In Northern Ireland the Council for Nature Conservation and the Countryside advises the Department of the Environment for Northern Ireland on the preservation of amenities and the designation of areas of outstanding natural beauty. In all, nine such areas have been designated, covering over 2,800 sq km (1,100 sq miles); seven areas are being managed as country parks and one as a regional park.

There are 11 forest parks in Great Britain, covering some 2,400 sq km (950 sq miles) and administered by the Forestry Commission. There are nine in Northern Ireland, where they are administered by the Forest Service of the Department of Agriculture.

Public Rights of Way and Open Country

County and metropolitan district councils in England and Wales are responsible for keeping public rights of way signposted and free from obstruction. Public paths are usually maintained by these highway authorities, which also supervise landowners' duties to repair stiles and gates. In Scotland, planning authorities are responsible for asserting and protecting rights of way. Local authorities in Great Britain can create paths, close paths no longer needed for public use and divert paths to meet the needs of either the public or

landowners. Farmers in England and Wales are required by law rapidly to restore public paths damaged by agricultural operations. In England and Wales there are some 225,000 km (140,000 miles) of rights of way.

There are ten approved national trails open in England, stretching about 2,800 km (1,740 miles), two in Wales, and three approved-long-distance routes in Scotland, covering about 550 km (345 miles). Approval for a new national trail along the line of Hadrian's Wall was announced in 1994, and in 1995 a new Pennine Bridleway, designed for horseriders and mountain bikers, was approved. Formal consultations are under way into the designation of the Cotswold Way as a national trail in England, and Glyndŵr's Way in Wales. In Scotland, a new Great Glen Way is at an advanced stage of planning.

The Countryside Commission intends to help authorities bring all rights of way in England into good order by the end of the century, and a Parish Path Partnership scheme has been introduced, which is designed to stimulate local involvement and improvement. The CCW is also establishing a network of public rights of way in Wales, and a Public Paths Campaign has been introduced. In Scotland a major new 'Paths for All' initiative has been started by SNH to promote better access to countryside close to towns and cities.

There is no automatic right of public access to open country, although many landowners allow it more or less freely. A scheme to encourage farmers to open 'set-aside' land (see p. 292) to the public was launched in 1994. Local planning authorities in England and Wales can secure access by means of agreements with landowners. If agreements cannot be reached, authorities may acquire land or make orders for public access. Similar powers cover Scotland and Northern Ireland; in Northern Ireland the primary responsibility lies with district councils. In Scotland there is a tradition of freedom to roam, based on tolerance between landowners and those seeking reasonable recreational access to the hills.

Common land totals an estimated 600,000 hectares (1.5 million acres) in England and Wales, but a legal right of public access exists for only one-fifth of this area. Common land is usually privately owned, but people other than the owner may have various rights over it, for example, as pasture land. Commons are protected by law and cannot be built on or enclosed without the consent of the Secretaries of State for the Environment or Wales. There is no common land in Scotland or Northern Ireland.

> The Millennium Commission (see p. 43) has agreed in principle to award up to £10 million to the Countryside Commission towards a £20 million programme that will enable at least 250 communities in England to have their own millennium greens by the year 2000. A millennium green would be an area of open space—large or small—to be enjoyed permanently by the local community, designed to be in easy walking distance of people's homes.

Voluntary Sector

Many voluntary organisations are concerned to preserve the amenities of the countryside, including the Council for the Protection of Rural England, the Campaign for the Protection of Rural Wales, the Association for the Protection of Rural Scotland and the Ulster Society for the Preservation of the Countryside.

International Action

Britain plays a full part in international action to conserve wildlife. Its international obligations include the Berne Convention on the conservation of European wildlife and natural habitats, and EC directives on the conservation of wild birds (the Birds Directive) and of natural habitats and wild fauna and flora. The implementation of the latter directive, which came into force in 1994, entails the designation of Special Areas of Conservation (SACs). Together with Special Protection Areas (SPAs) designated under the Birds Directive, the SACs contribute to a EU-wide network of protected sites known as 'Natura 2000'. Britain is also party to the Ramsar Convention on wetlands of international importance.

Britain is a party to the Convention on International Trade in Endangered Species of Wild Fauna and Flora, which strictly regulates trade in endangered species by means of a permit system. Britain has taken new measures to improve the enforcement of the Convention.

The Convention on Biological Diversity was signed by over 150 countries, including Britain, at the 'earth summit'. It requires countries to develop national strategies for the conservation and sustainable use of biological diversity. Britain published its biodiversity action plan in 1994. In 1995 the Biodiversity Steering Group, with representatives from a range of sectors, published a report advising the Government on:

- the development of a range of specific costed targets for key species and habitats for the years 2000 and 2010;

- improving accessibility and co-ordination of existing biological data, providing common standards for future recording; and

- increasing public awareness of, and involvement in, the conservation of biodiversity.

The Government published its response to the report in May 1996, welcoming the objectives and targets put forward by the Group as relevant benchmarks against which future success in conserving individual species and habitat types can be assessed.

> The 1995 Biodiversity Steering Group report contained costed action plans for 116 of Britain's most threatened species and 14 key habitats. It recommended that a further 286 species and 24 key habitat action plans be prepared within three years. It also contains guidance for preparing local biodiversity action plans, which will enable people to express their views on what wildlife they consider to be important and locally distinctive.

The Darwin Initiative forms part of the measures announced by Britain at the

UNCED meeting. It is intended to make British experience available to developing countries with important biological resources, with the aim of assisting the conservation and sustainable use of species there. A committee of distinguished experts advises the Government on the Initiative. By March 1996, 116 projects, totalling over £12 million, had been approved.

Environmental Improvement

The Government assists local voluntary organisations to promote projects such as creating parks, footpaths and other areas of greenery in cities; conserving the industrial heritage and the natural environment; and recycling waste. The Department of the Environment makes grants through the Environmental Action Fund, worth over £4 million in 1996–97, to support projects which actively assist in tackling environmental problems. The Civic Trust (see p. 373) manages a Local Projects Fund for the Department.

The Scottish Office Environment Department made £430,000 available in 1995–96 to 46 environmental organisations under its Special Grants (Environmental) Programme to help them carry out environmental conservation, improvement and education work. Scottish Enterprise and Highlands and Islands Enterprise (see p. 215) are responsible for environmental improvement and land reclamation in Scotland. The Government's programme of Environmentally Sensitive Areas (see p. 292) supports environmentally sensitive farming practices that protect and enhance the countryside.

Buildings and Monuments

Lists of buildings of special architectural or historical interest are compiled by the Government, in England with the advice of English Heritage. In Scotland and Wales, buildings are listed by Historic Scotland and Cadw: Welsh Historic Monuments, executive agencies of the Scottish and Welsh Offices respectively. It is against the law to demolish, extend or alter the character of any 'listed' building without prior consent from the local planning authority or the appropriate Secretary of State. The local planning authority can issue 'building preservation notices' to protect for six months unlisted buildings that are at risk, while the Government considers whether they should be listed. In Northern Ireland, the Environment and Heritage Service is directly responsible for the listing of buildings.

Ancient monuments are similarly protected through a system of scheduling. English Heritage, the government agency responsible for the conservation of historic remains in England, has embarked upon a programme to evaluate all known archaeological remains in England. This is expected to result in a significant increase in the number of scheduled monuments. A similar effort is being made to increase the number of listed buildings and scheduled monuments in Wales. A resurvey of buildings is also beginning in Northern Ireland, and the number of scheduled monuments there is expected to rise.

Many of the royal palaces and parks are open to the public; their maintenance is the responsibility of the Secretaries of State for National Heritage and for Scotland. Historic Royal Palaces and the Royal Parks Agency are

Table 22.2: Scheduled Monuments and Listed Buildings

	Listed buildings	Scheduled monuments
England	447,400	15,300[a]
Wales	18,600	2,900
Scotland	42,200	6,700
Northern Ireland	8,600	1,200

Source: Department of Natural Heritage, Welsh Office

[a] This is the number of register entries, some of which cover more than one side. There are approximately 22,000 individual sites in England.

the executive agencies which carry out this function.

English Heritage cares for over 400 properties on behalf of the Secretary of State for National Heritage, advises the Government on certain categories of applications for consent to alter or demolish scheduled monuments and listed buildings, and gives grants for the repair of ancient monuments and historic buildings in England. Many of the properties in its care are now being managed locally; 107 agreements for local management had been made by the end of 1995–96. Most of its monuments are open to the public. Core government funding for English Heritage is £107 million in 1996–97.

In Scotland and Wales, Historic Scotland, which cares for 330 monuments, and Cadw, with 132, perform similar functions. Both agencies are advised by an Ancient Monuments Board and an Historic Buildings Council. The Department of the Environment for Northern Ireland has 181 historic monuments in its care, managed by the Environment and Heritage Service. It too is advised by a Historic Buildings Council and a Historic Monuments Council.

Local planning authorities have designated more than 9,000 'conservation areas' of special architectural or historic interest in England; there are 469 in Wales, 674 in Scotland and 53 in Northern Ireland, designated by the Department of the Environment for Northern Ireland. These areas receive additional protection through the planning system, particularly over the proposed demolition of unlisted buildings. In 1995 the Government strengthened the ability of local planning authorities in England and Wales to protect conservation areas.

The National Heritage Memorial Fund helps towards the cost of acquiring, maintaining or preserving land, buildings, works of art and other items of outstanding interest which are also of importance to the national heritage. Government funding totals £8 million in 1996–97. The Fund also acts as the distributing body for the heritage share of the proceeds from the National Lottery (see p. 42).

Industrial, Transport and Maritime Heritage

Britain was the first country in the world to industrialise on a large scale, and many advances in manufacturing were invented in Britain. This has resulted in a large industrial heritage, the importance of which is being increasingly recognised. Key sites are scheduled or listed; one of the most important, the Ironbridge Gorge, where Abraham Darby (1677–1717) first smelted iron using coke instead of charcoal, has been designated a World Heritage Site (see p. 373). Other museums devoted to the preservation of industrial buildings and equipment have also been set up.

Britain, which pioneered railways, has a fine heritage of railway buildings and structures, and there is an active movement to preserve it, with many volunteers. A large number of disused railway lines have been bought by railway preservation societies, and several railway museums have been established.

Reminders of Britain's maritime past are also preserved. At Portsmouth are preserved HMS *Victory*, Nelson's flagship, HMS *Warrior*, the world's first iron battleship, and the remains of the *Mary Rose*, an early 16th-century warship, raised from the seabed in 1982. The Imperial War Museum has opened the cruiser HMS *Belfast* to the public in the Pool of London. Isambard Kingdom Brunel's SS *Great Britain*, the world's first large screw-driven ship, is preserved in Bristol. A voluntary body, the Maritime Trust, has been established to preserve vessels and other maritime items of historic or technical interest. The Trust's vessels include the clipper *Cutty Sark* at Greenwich. In all, it is estimated that some 400 historic ships are preserved in Britain, mostly in private hands.

Voluntary Sector

Among the organisations which campaign for the preservation and appreciation of buildings are:

- the Society for the Protection of Ancient Buildings;

- the Ancient Monuments Society;

- the Georgian Group;

- the Victorian Society;

- the Twentieth Century Society;

- the Architectural Heritage Society of Scotland;

- the Ulster Architectural Heritage Society;

- the Architectural Heritage Fund; and

- the Council for British Archaeology.

While funded largely by private donations, some of these amenity societies have statutory responsibilities, in recognition of which they receive government support.

The National Trust (for Places of Historic Interest or Natural Beauty), a charity with over 2.3 million members, owns and protects 320 properties open to the public, in addition to over 265,000 hectares (655,000 acres) of land in England, Wales and Northern Ireland. Scotland has its own National Trust, which owns 35 historic houses and 74,800 hectares (184,700 acres) of land.

The Civic Trust, a voluntary body, makes awards for development and restoration work which enhance surroundings. It undertakes urban regeneration projects and acts as an umbrella organisation for nearly 1,000 civic societies. There are associate trusts in Scotland, Wales and north-east England.

World Heritage Sites

Britain is well represented in the World Heritage List, which was established under the World Heritage Convention to identify and secure lasting protection for those parts of the world heritage of outstanding universal value. So far 14 sites in Britain have been listed. These are:

- Canterbury Cathedral, with St Augustine's Abbey and St Martin's Church, in Kent;

- Durham Cathedral and Castle;

- Studley Royal Gardens and Fountains Abbey, in North Yorkshire;

- Ironbridge Gorge, with the world's first iron bridge and other early industrial sites, in Shropshire;

- the prehistoric stone circles at Stonehenge and Avebury, in Wiltshire;

- Blenheim Palace, in Oxfordshire;

- the city of Bath, in Avon;

- Hadrian's Wall, the former Roman frontier in northern England;

- the Tower of London;

- the Palace of Westminster, Westminster Abbey and St Margaret's, Westminster, also in London;

- the islands of St Kilda, in Scotland;

- Edinburgh Old and New Towns;

- the castles and town walls of King Edward I, in north Wales; and

- the Giant's Causeway and Causeway Coast, in Northern Ireland.

Support for these sites under various programmes can be considerable. For example, Durham Cathedral received £95,000 in government repair grant in 1994–95.

In June 1996 the Government announced that it has put forward the centre of Greenwich for consideration as a World Heritage site. The area proposed for designation includes the old Royal Observatory, the National Maritime Museum and the Royal Naval College.

Further Reading

Conservation. Aspects of Britain series, HMSO, 1993.
Pollution Control. Aspects of Britain series, HMSO, 1993.
Digest of Environmental Statistics. Annual report. HMSO.
The UK Environment. HMSO, 1992.
This Common Inheritance: UK Annual Report 1996. HMSO, 1996.

23 Local Development

Regeneration	375	Wales, Scotland and Northern	
Single Regeneration Budget	375	Ireland	379
Other Measures	377	Public Sector Land	381
Enterprise and Simplified		Planning	381
Planning Zones	378	Development Plans	382
European Union Programmes	378	Development Control	383
Rural Development	378	Architectural Standards	384

Economic trends in recent decades have altered traditional patterns and locations of employment and brought profound changes to local economies. Many inner-city areas have suffered from long-established industries moving out or closing down, leaving problems of dereliction and unemployment. Unemployment also affects the countryside, where rural areas have had to diversify away from farm production. The Government is addressing these problems with a variety of regeneration programmes to stimulate business, employment and physical renewal. It seeks to balance the demands for land from business, housing, transport, farming and leisure, and to protect the environment, by means of a statutory system of land-use planning and development control.

REGENERATION

The Government is seeking to overcome urban problems in England using a Single Regeneration Budget (SRB), which brought together 20 previous programmes from five government departments. Several of the more important programmes are described below. Urban problems in Scotland, Wales and Northern Ireland are being tackled by Partnerships, the Programme for the Valleys and the Making Belfast Work initiative respectively, as well as by many other government programmes (see pp. 379–81). Other programmes and policies are directed at addressing the needs of rural areas.

Single Regeneration Budget

The Secretary of State for the Environment has overall responsibility for the SRB, which came into operation in 1994–95. The aim is to promote more flexible and locally responsive forms of regeneration, building on the approach pioneered with the City Challenge initiative (see p. 376). The 1996–97 allocation is £1,318 million. The main programmes funded by the SRB are administered by the integrated Government Offices for the Regions (GORs), which combine the former regional offices of the Departments of the Environment, Employment, Trade and Industry, and Transport. The SRB Challenge

Fund was launched in 1995 to support bids for local regeneration initiatives. The first two bidding rounds, for schemes starting in April 1995 and April 1996 respectively, resulted in 372 schemes being approved. These are expected to create or safeguard 500,000 jobs, support over 80,000 new businesses, complete or improve nearly 170,000 homes and support over 20,000 voluntary or community groups. On average, every £1 of Challenge Fund money attracts £2.50 of private investment in the projects supported. A third round of bidding is being held for schemes to start in April 1997.

City Challenge

Under the City Challenge initiative, launched in 1991, local authorities were invited, in partnership with the private and voluntary sectors, local communities and government agencies, to submit imaginative and comprehensive plans for regenerating key neighbourhoods by tackling problems of physical decay, lack of economic opportunity and poor quality of life. The best of these proposals are receiving government funding of £37.5 million each over five years, subject to satisfactory progress being made towards achieving agreed targets and objectives.

There have been two rounds of the City Challenge competition. In the first pilot round, 11 local authorities in England were selected to draw up detailed action plans, which commenced in 1992 and are due to be fully implemented by March 1997. The 20 authorities successful in the second round competition began work on their five-year programmes in 1993. In the six-year period to 1997–98, £1,163 million of City Challenge money is expected to attract over £3,500 million of private sector investment.

Urban Development Corporations

Twelve urban development corporations (UDCs) were set up in England by the Government to reverse large-scale urban decline. The first two, London Docklands and Merseyside, started operations in 1981. Ten others were subsequently established: Birmingham Heartlands, Black Country (West Midlands), Bristol, Leeds, Central Manchester, Plymouth, Sheffield, Trafford Park (Greater Manchester), Teesside, and Tyne and Wear. At their peak, the UDCs covered about 16,000 hectares (about 40,000 acres). The Bristol and Leeds development corporations were wound up in 1995, and Central Manchester in March 1996. All the other UDCs are scheduled to be wound up by March 1998. Public expenditure on the programme will be £208 million in 1996–97, including spending on the Docklands Light Railway (see p. 312).

Task Forces

Task Forces, first set up in 1986, are small teams of five or six people drawn from government departments, local authorities and the private and voluntary sectors, which operate in the most deprived urban areas in England. Task Forces concentrate on the economic regeneration of designated inner-city areas by:

- improving local people's employment prospects;
- supporting training and education initiatives; and
- identifying and removing barriers to employment.

They also aim to stimulate enterprise and strengthen the capacity of communities to meet local needs. Task Forces have a limited life: an important part of their work is to build up local organisations to which they can hand over as they withdraw. Since 1986 Task Forces have spent over £148 million, which has helped to provide over 37,000 jobs and more than 17,000 training places, and supported over 44,000 businesses.

English Partnerships

English Partnerships, a government regeneration agency, promotes the development of vacant, derelict and contaminated land throughout England. Its key objectives are to:

- stimulate local enterprise;
- create job opportunities; and
- improve the environment.

These objectives are being addressed in partnership with other public bodies and the private and voluntary sectors. In 1994–95 more than 250 new projects were approved, creating 13,200 jobs, reclaiming over 1,600 hectares (4,000 acres) and attracting £300 million in private finance. English Partnerships' planned gross expenditure for 1996–97 is about £207 million. It is also eligible for assistance from the European Regional Development Fund (see p. 127).

Safer Cities

Higher than average crime rates, and the fear of crime, are particular problems in inner-city areas. Safer Cities projects bring together all sections of the local community to combat crime and the fear of crime. Since the programme's launch in 1988 almost 4,500 crime prevention and community safety measures have been initiated, with funding of £26 million. Results from the first phase of the programme are being evaluated, and a second phase is under way. Examples of help include providing activities for young people who might be tempted to commit crime, and fitting good quality locks to houses on estates which have a high burglary rate. Successes include a 40 per cent reduction in burglaries on a Wolverhampton estate and a 60 per cent reduction in car crime in a Bradford car park.

Compacts

School/industry 'Compacts' have been introduced since 1988 in urban areas in England. Employers work with schools to guarantee a job with training for all school-leavers aged 16 to 18 who meet agreed targets for motivation and achievement.

Regional Enterprise Grants

The Regional Enterprise Grant programme (see pp. 214–6), which has also been brought within the SRB, supports investment and innovation projects in small firms in designated areas. A total of £13.7 million was allocated to small businesses in 1995–96.

Other Measures

The first of a network of City Technology Colleges was opened near Birmingham in 1988; 15 are currently operating. Intended to raise educational standards, the colleges have been established jointly by government and industry.

Training programmes such as Youth Training (see p. 191) and Training for Work (see p. 190) are helping many people in the inner cities. About one-third of young people participating in Youth Training are from inner cities. In addition, over 100 Employment Service 'outreach' staff are based in, or regularly visit, inner-city areas, where they help unemployed people look for jobs and encourage them to participate in employment and training programmes. This activity supplements normal jobcentre services. In 1992–93 there were about 500 inner-city Jobclubs, many catering for people with literacy and numeracy or language difficulties.

The Government encourages tourism as a force for improving inner-city areas, and several major projects which create a cultural and artistic focus for inner-city regeneration have been undertaken. Examples include the development of the Royal Armouries Museum at Clarence Dock in Leeds, which opened in March 1996 at a cost of £42.5 million, and the International Convention Centre in Birmingham. The English Tourist Board and regional tourist boards encourage promotional activities in inner-city areas through local initiatives bringing together tourist boards, local authorities, the private sector and other agencies.

In 1994 the Government launched the Urban Forum, a new national body that brings together voluntary organisations engaged in urban policy and regeneration. Its aims are to act as a communication channel between the voluntary sector and the Government; develop new ideas; and encourage local communities and voluntary groups to engage in regeneration partnerships.

Groundwork Trusts

Groundwork trusts seek to alleviate environmental problems arising from dereliction and vandalism and to increase public awareness of opportunities to change and improve local environments. They work in partnership with public bodies, the private sector, voluntary organisations and individuals. Traditionally, the trusts have tended to concentrate on fringe urban or suburban areas, but increasingly they are also becoming involved in inner-city areas. For example, a trust has recently been set up in the Hackney area of inner London. Government funding for Groundwork in 1996–97 is £6.9 million in England. The Groundwork Foundation is a national body providing the trusts with advice and support.

Enterprise and Simplified Planning Zones

Since 1981 the Government has established 28 enterprise zones, including four extensions. Each zone runs for a period of ten years from designation; most have, therefore, already reached the end of their lives. Benefits available in the zones include:

- exemption from the national non-domestic rate (the local property tax payable by non-domestic property owners—see p. 171);

- 100 per cent allowances for corporation and income tax purposes for capital expenditure on industrial and commercial buildings; and

- a simplified planning system.

At present it is not generally intended to extend the enterprise zone scheme by designating any further sites. However, the Government has retained the option of establishing further zones in exceptional circumstances; for example, a new zone is likely to be designated in 1996 in Newcastle upon Tyne to help address the loss of jobs in shipbuilding.

Simplified planning zones (SPZs) are designed to help local authorities to secure development in their areas. An SPZ scheme, which also lasts for ten years, provides full planning permission for specified types of development. Like enterprise zones, from which the concept was derived, SPZs can act as part of an overall package to generate private sector interest in an area.

European Union Programmes

Run-down areas in Britain benefit from EU Structural Funds (see p. 127). These come mainly from the European Regional Development Fund (ERDF), which finances infrastructure projects and support for industry, among other things. Objectives for the Funds include regenerating areas affected by industrial decline and combating long-term unemployment. The Department of the Environment is responsible for co-ordinating ERDF programmes in England. About £1,195 million has been allocated to declining industrial regions in England during the period 1994–96.

Following a review of the Structural Funds, Merseyside qualified for 'Objective 1' support.[1] This attracts the highest level of Structural Funds support. Merseyside stands to receive about £633 million from the Funds between 1994 and 1999.

In 1995 it was announced that six non-Objective 1 urban areas in England were to receive funding of £37 million under the URBAN Community Initiative, an EU-wide scheme to promote urban regeneration that complements domestic programmes.

Rural Development

The British countryside is facing considerable change. Agricultural reform (see p. 290), together with a reduction of jobs in defence establishments, is creating a need for more diversified employment opportunities. The movement of people into the countryside has increased the demand for housing and local services and, with a major projected growth in the number of

---

[1] The aim of Objective 1 is to promote economic development in underdeveloped regions.

households, is likely to continue. Rural areas generally have been successful in recent years, with strong growth in employment, especially in high-technology industries. Continuing technological change will provide new opportunities for industry to overcome problems of remoteness stemming from a rural location.

The Government's 1995 White Paper, *Rural England: A Nation Committed to a Living Countryside*, set out the policy framework for rural areas. Proposals to promote sustainable development in the countryside include an expansion of the Countryside Stewardship scheme (see p. 293), new planning treatment for rural businesses, new powers for parish councils in community transport, larger grants to housing associations in recognition of the higher costs of developing small schemes in villages, and a new rate relief scheme targeted at general stores and post offices. Separate White Papers have been published for Scotland and Wales (see pp. 380–1).

The Rural Development Commission is the government agency concerned with the economic wellbeing of the people who live and work in rural England. During 1996–97 the Commission is expected to spend £44 million. The bulk of this money is targeted at 312 Rural Development Areas (RDAs), which cover 35 per cent of the land area of England and 2.75 million people. Expenditure within the RDAs seeks to diversify the rural economy and strengthen rural communities through grants and advice to business, the provision of workspace and support for projects developed in partnership with the private, public and voluntary sectors.

Wales, Scotland and Northern Ireland

Wales

A new Strategic Development Scheme (SDS) was launched in Wales in 1994, into which the previous Urban Programme was subsumed. Projects costing almost £63 million were approved for 1996–97, which are expected to generate more than £80 million of private investment; 76 new major projects will be started as a result. In 1996–97, local authorities were for the first time given freedom to allocate part of the SDS budget themselves, without prior approval of the Welsh Office; some £13 million of the total has been passed to local authorities, of which £9 million was available for them to allocate to projects. In addition, Urban Investment Grant encourages private sector developments on derelict and run-down sites in urban areas; the 1996–97 budget is £6.8 million.

As part of its area development activities, the Welsh Development Agency (WDA— see p. 26), in conjunction with local authorities and the private sector, is regenerating and revitalising towns and cities throughout Wales. In urban areas, through infrastructure and environmental improvement schemes, it has brought in £115 million of private sector investment in two years. Its other capital development programmes have also played a vital role in the development of the economy. For example, its property development programme provides readily available industrial premises, both for local businesses and for inward investment projects. Its budget in 1996–97 for area development is almost £88 million. Development is also encouraged by the Land Authority for Wales, a statutory body with powers to make land available for development in circumstances where the private sector would find this difficult or impossible. It is a self-financing trading body which ploughs back its profits for future investment.

The first Programme for the Valleys, which ran from 1988 to 1993, was an extensive scheme of economic and urban regeneration, covering an area of about 2,200 sq km (860 sq miles) in the south Wales valleys. In 1993 the Government launched a new five-year Programme, which builds on the first Programme and introduces new initiatives for the social, economic and environmental regeneration of the Valleys. The aims of the new Programme are to:

- create more, better-quality jobs;
- improve training, education and transport;
- improve the quality of the environment;
- improve the quality and choice of housing; and
- improve the health of local people.

It is expected that in 1995–96, 5,000 homes will have been renovated, over £23 million spent on land reclamation by the WDA, and £170 million of new roads started or completed.

The Cardiff Bay Development Corporation was set up in 1987 to promote redevelopment in part of south Cardiff, once its commercial centre. Government support for the Corporation will be £58 million in 1996–97. The Corporation's regeneration strategy includes a £191 million barrage project which will create a large freshwater lake within Cardiff Bay and 12 km (7 miles) of waterside frontage. Work commenced on its construction in 1994 and is scheduled to be completed in 1998. It is expected that more than 25,000 new jobs will be created in the Cardiff Bay area, 6,000 new homes will be built and over £1,175 million of private investment will be attracted.

The Government published a White Paper, *A Working Countryside for Wales*, in March 1996. Its proposals include:

- a new rate relief scheme for village shops and post offices;
- the development of a strategy to promote the Welsh food industry;
- the transfer of funding for rural schemes from the WDA to local authorities;
- improvements for basic services such as health and transport; and
- continuing support for the Welsh language.

Scotland

The Government set out its strategy for improving the quality of life in the most deprived urban areas in Scotland in the 1995 policy statement *Programme for Partnership*. In April 1996 it formally invited councils and other bodies to form partnerships and bid for

Urban Programme funding under the framework set out in the policy statement. It is expected that by autumn 1996 the Government will have designated the first Priority Partnership Areas, in each of which a broadly-based partnership will undertake comprehensive regeneration. Of the available resources—over £81 million in 1996–97—the larger part will be directed towards the Priority Partnerships Areas. The partnerships there will receive a block allocation of money from the Urban Programme, leaving detailed decisions about regeneration projects to be taken by the partnerships themselves. Remaining funds will go to other areas eligible for Urban Programme support, to assist regeneration activity put forward by local councils or partnerships.

The strategy builds on the experience gained from four Partnerships in areas of Dundee, Edinburgh, Glasgow and Paisley. Set up in 1988, three of these are still operational, led by The Scottish Office and involving other bodies and groups, including Scottish Enterprise (see p. 216), Scottish Homes (see p. 389), local authorities, the private sector and local communities. Their objectives include plans to:

- improve the quality and tenure mix of housing available to local people;
- improve employment prospects by providing more opportunities for training and further education; and
- tackle social and environmental problems on the estates.

Local Enterprise Companies (LECs—see p. 189), working under contract to Scottish Enterprise, have substantial budgets and a range of powers and functions to improve the environment and encourage business and employment in their areas. Responsibility for derelict land reclamation also rests with Scottish Enterprise, LECs and Highlands and Islands Enterprise. They may acquire and reclaim land either by agreement or compulsorily; increasingly they seek to work with the private sector to bring land back into use.

The Compact scheme (see p. 377) has also been introduced in Scotland, where nine

Compacts are in operation. Many employers and business organisations participate in Education Business Partnerships in Scotland. The Training and Employment Grants scheme is designed to increase access to employment opportunities for young and long-term unemployed people.

A rural White Paper covering Scotland, launched in December 1995, announced a new £2.4 million Partnership Fund to support rural partnerships of government departments and agencies, private sector bodies and voluntary groups with responsibilities in rural areas. A National Rural Partnership has been established to encourage the formation of such local partnerships and to advise on spending priorities for the Partnership Fund. The Government's target is for 20 rural partnerships to be set up by March 1997.

Northern Ireland

Urban Development Grant is the principal urban regeneration measure in Northern Ireland. Its objective is the economic and physical regeneration of inner-city areas of Belfast and Londonderry by encouraging private enterprise and investment in property development, leading to job creation and improvement of the environment. Projected expenditure for 1996–97 is £5.4 million.

A comprehensive development programme aims to revitalise run-down areas of Belfast, with anticipated spending of £1.8 million in 1996–97. The Making Belfast Work initiative's strategy for 1995–97 aims to increase employment opportunities and quality of life in the most disadvantaged areas of Belfast. The development of area partnerships is now a major policy priority. In addition to extensive funding already allocated to mainstream departmental programmes, Making Belfast Work provided a further £170 million between 1988 to 1996. An additional £25 million has been allocated in 1996–97. The Laganside Corporation was established in 1989 to regenerate Belfast's riverside area. Its government grant in 1996–97 is £7.6 million.

The Londonderry Initiative was established in 1988 to address various problems of urban decline in the area. Its main aims include

attracting private sector investment to the city, helping people to secure jobs and refurbishing the physical environment. By March 1996 nearly £21 million had been allocated to the Initiative.

The Community Regeneration and Improvement Special Programme is jointly funded by the Department of the Environment for Northern Ireland and the International Fund for Ireland (see p. 16). A total of 44 small towns, as well as Londonderry, Newry, Strabane, Portadown and Craigavon, have been assisted at a cost to the Government of £26 million since the programme was started in 1990. The urban regeneration sub-programme of the Special Support Programme for Peace and Reconciliation aims to promote peace and reconciliation by renewing urban areas affected by deprivation. Introduced in 1996, it has a budget of about £16 million over the period to 1999 and covers the main urban areas of Northern Ireland, including Belfast and Londonderry.

Public Sector Land

The Department of the Environment promotes the sale and development of vacant and under-used public sector land in England. Information is being assembled on key sites with development potential and, where there are no firm plans to market or develop land, action will be taken to promote the sale of sites. Under the 'Public Request to Order Disposal' scheme, members of the public are encouraged to ask the Government to order public bodies to dispose of vacant or under-used land on the open market. In 1994 the rules governing the way local authorities can spend the proceeds of asset sales were altered to encourage the sale of surplus land.

PLANNING

Direct responsibility for land-use planning in Great Britain lies with local authorities. The Secretaries of State for the Environment, Wales and Scotland have overall responsibility for the operation of the system. The Department of the Environment brings together the major responsibilities for land-use planning, housing and construction, countryside policy and environmental protection in England. The Welsh and Scottish Offices have broadly equivalent responsibilities, which also extend to transport. In Northern Ireland the Department of the Environment for Northern Ireland is responsible for planning matters, working closely with the district councils.

In England, the Department of the Environment provides national and regional guidance on planning, while strategic planning is the responsibility of the county councils and unitary district authorities. At present, most district councils are responsible for local plans and development control, except for minerals and waste, which are dealt with by the county and unitary district councils. In London and the metropolitan counties, and in some non-metropolitan unitary areas, districts prepare unitary development plans and are responsible for development control.

In Wales and Scotland, planning responsibilities now rest with the new unitary authorities (see p. 76).

Development Plans

Development plans have a central role in shaping development patterns in an area, as planning decisions must be made in accordance with the development plan unless 'material considerations' indicate otherwise. In England and Wales, the preparation of a district-wide development plan is mandatory. In March 1996 the Government consulted on measures to speed up the adoption of development plans.

The present development plan system in England comprises structure, local and unitary development plans:

- structure plans, setting out broad policies for the development and use of land, are adopted by county councils and some unitary councils;

- local plans, prepared in general conformity with the adopted structure plan, and providing detailed guidance for development, are adopted by most district

councils and National Park authorities; and

- unitary development plans, setting out both strategic and detailed land-use and development policies, are adopted by metropolitan districts, London boroughs and some non-metropolitan unitary authorities.

County councils and unitary councils also draw up local plans for minerals and waste.

Following local government reorganisation (see pp. 75–6), some district councils in England have acquired unitary status or will do shortly. Unless these are given a unitary development plan function, they become the structure plan authority for their area. In most cases the Government expects these unitary authorities to work with the surrounding county council or with neighbouring unitary authorities on a joint structure plan corresponding to the original county area.

In Wales, the new councils have taken over responsibility for plan preparation and will be drawing up unitary development plans for their areas. It is intended to have these plans in place by the year 2000. In Scotland the new councils have also undertaken responsibility for plan preparation. In some cases, structure may be taken forward by a joint committee of more than one council. Under Northern Ireland's single-tier system, plans are prepared by the Department of the Environment for Northern Ireland.

Members of the public are encouraged to become involved in the formulation of plan policies and proposals. They can formally object and, in the case of local and unitary development plans, make their case in public to an independent inspector (reporter in Scotland). When formulating plans, planning authorities must take account of any strategic or regional guidance issued by the Government.

An important element of the Government's strategy for sustainable development (see Chapter 21) is for full use to be made of urban land in existing towns and cities, while having regard to the quality of the urban environment, in order to avoid the need to develop 'green field' sites and to reduce transport demands.

The Government announced new planning guidance in June 1996 aimed at revitalising town centres in England. It encourages a plan-led approach to promoting development in town centres, lays emphasis on the importance of a coherent town centre parking strategy in maintaining urban vitality, and requires clearer assessment of retail proposals that could have an impact on the viability of town centres. When putting forward out-of-centre retail proposals, developers will be expected to demonstrate that they have first thoroughly examined more central sites. Broadly similar guidance for Scotland had been issued in April 1996.

Green Belts

'Green Belts' are areas of land intended to be left open and free from inappropriate development. Their purposes are to:

- check the sprawl of large built-up areas;
- safeguard surrounding countryside from encroachment;
- prevent neighbouring towns from merging;
- preserve the special character of historic towns; and
- assist in urban regeneration by encouraging the re-use of derelict and other urban land.

Green Belts have been established around major cities and conurbations, including London, Aberdeen, Edinburgh, Glasgow, Merseyside, Greater Manchester and the West Midlands, as well as several smaller towns. Some 1.5 million hectares (3.8 million acres) are designated as Green Belt in England and 155,000 hectares (380,000 acres) in Scotland. The Government attaches great importance to the protection of Green Belts, which have been a cornerstone of the planning system for over 40 years. Planning guidance on Green Belts in England was revised in 1995 to strengthen

further the strict controls over development and to secure greater benefits for the environment. In Scotland, Green Belt policy has also been updated, and guidance on Green Belts in Wales was introduced in May 1996.

Development Control

Most development requires specific planning permission. Applications are dealt with in the light of development plans and other relevant planning considerations, including national and regional guidance. In 1995–96 about 457,000 applications for planning permission were received by district councils in England; in total, about 363,000 applications were granted in this period. The Government has set local authorities in England and Wales a target of deciding 80 per cent of applications within eight weeks.

Local planning authorities in England and Wales are required to publicise planning applications locally. Methods commonly used include site notices, newspaper advertising and notifying neighbours. In Scotland applicants are required to notify owners, occupiers and, in some cases, lessees of neighbouring land and buildings when an application is submitted to the planning authority. Newspaper advertising is required for certain types of development.

Applicants have a right of appeal to the relevant Secretary of State if a local authority refuses planning permission, grants it with conditions attached, or fails to decide an application within eight weeks[2] (or whatever longer period is agreed with the applicant). The majority of appeals are decided on the basis of written submissions. However, either party has the right to be heard by an inspector at a public local inquiry or at a hearing. A local inquiry is usually held for more complicated or controversial applications. Similar provision is made in Northern Ireland.

The Secretaries of State can direct that a planning application be referred to them for decision. They generally only use this power to 'call in' proposals which raise planning issues of national or regional importance. In such circumstances, applicants and local planning

---

[2]Two months in Scotland.

authorities have the right to be heard by a person appointed by the Secretary of State, and a public inquiry will normally be held. In Northern Ireland, major planning applications can be referred to a public inquiry in certain circumstances.

Environmental Impact Assessment

Planning applications for certain types of development must be accompanied by an environmental statement. This should describe the likely environmental effects and measures to minimise them. These statements are available to the public and to statutory bodies such as the Countryside Commission and English Nature (see pp. 364–5). Planning authorities must consider the environmental statement, and any representations received on it, before granting planning permission. The Government published a good practice guide on preparing environmental statements in 1995.

Architectural Standards and the Built Environment

The Government emphasises the importance of good design and quality, both in individual buildings and in the built environment as a whole. It advises that the appearance of new developments, and their relationship to their surroundings, are issues that should be addressed through the design of individual buildings and through urban design. While local planning authorities should reject designs which are out of scale or character with their surroundings, the Government's view is that they should not seek to control the detailed design of buildings unless the sensitive character of their location justifies it, nor should they seek to impose a particular architectural taste or style arbitrarily. Guidance on architectural competitions is being updated in 1996 by the Department of the Environment and the Department of National Heritage.

The Royal Fine Art Commissions for England, Wales and Scotland advise government departments, local planning authorities and other public bodies on questions of quality, public amenity and artistic importance.

The new Architects Registration Board, together with the architects' professional bodies—the Royal Institute of British Architects, the Royal Incorporation of Architects in Scotland and the Royal Society of Ulster Architects—exercises control over standards in architectural training and encourages high standards in the profession. The Royal Town Planning Institute carries out similar functions for the planning profession.

Further Reading

Assessing the Impact of Urban Policy. HMSO, 1994.

Environmental Appraisal of Development Plans: A Good Practice Guide. HMSO, 1993.

Planning. Aspects of Britain series, HMSO, 1992.

Urban Regeneration. Aspects of Britain series. HMSO, 1995.

COSTUMES AND FABRICS

Angels & Bermans, London, who claim to be the oldest and largest costume company in the world, have doubled their exports in the last few years. They have supplied costumes for many internationally successful films, including *Four Weddings and a Funeral* and *The Madness of King George*.

Old documents, paintings and brocades have all inspired British fabric designer John Crowell. His love of antique textiles and research into (and restoration of) buildings, led him to establish a design company in Chelsea which now carries out commissions around the world.

CHARITIES

A child and carer at Barnados, which helps children, young people and their families through over 150 community-based projects. These include day care centres, intermediate treatment for young drug abusers, working with young offenders and helping young people leaving care to cope with life outside an institution.

ACTIONAID works in 20 countries in Africa, Asia and Latin America, helping to reduce poverty and improve the quality of life for people living in the world's poorest communities. Pictured here are women at a well in The Gambia, where in one year alone the charity provided almost 15,000 people with access to safe water.

Age Resource, part of the charity Age Concern, provides recognition, encouragement and support to groups of older people who are committed to an active and fulfilling life and at the same time use their skills and experience to make a contribution to the community, either locally or nationally. Pictured here are volunteers from the Radnorshire Wildlife Trust, who won an Age Resource award for their restoration work on a 16th-century Welsh longhouse on the Gilfach Farm Nature Reserve, Powys, Wales.

The Imperial Cancer Research Fund aims to find better ways to avoid, detect and treat all forms of cancer. Here a researcher is at work in the Fund's laboratory at St Thomas' Hospital, London.

CONTEMPORARY MUSIC

Oasis, one of Britain's most popular contemporary bands, enjoys worldwide success.

Jazz music has a large following in Britain; saxophonist Courtney Pine has established an international reputation.

24 Housing

Administration	385	Improving Existing Housing	391
Home Ownership	386	Homelessness	392
Privately Rented Housing	388	Housing Advice	394
Social Housing	388		

Increasing home ownership and choice in renting are key themes in the Government's housing policies. Strategies to enhance both urban and rural environments include improvements to housing and diversification of tenure. Further measures are being taken to reduce homelessness.

In all, 189,000 new dwellings were completed in Great Britain in 1995, a rise of 3.6 per cent on 1994. Growth in owner-occupation has been particularly marked, increasing from 50 per cent in 1971 to 67 per cent at the end of 1995. Both the public and the private sectors build housing, but about four-fifths of new dwellings are built by the private sector for sale to owner-occupiers.

Local authorities are encouraged to see their housing role as an enabling one, working with housing associations and the private sector to increase the supply of low-cost housing for sale or rent without necessarily providing it themselves. Housing associations are now the main providers of new 'social housing' —housing provided at rents affordable to people on low incomes, usually substantially below market rents. This allows local authorities to focus on improving the management of their own stock. Rents on new private sector lettings in Great Britain were deregulated (freed from controls) in 1988, with the aim of stimulating the private rented sector, which had been declining for most of this century. These policies have been taken forward with the Housing Act 1996.

Administration

The Secretary of State for the Environment in England and the Secretaries of State for Wales, Scotland and Northern Ireland are responsible for formulating housing policy and supervising the housing programme.

The construction and structural alteration of housing are subject to building regulations laid down by the Government. In addition, warranty arrangements provided by the National House-Building Council cover many new houses. This body sets standards and enforces them by inspection, providing cover against major structural defects for at least ten years.

Housing Act 1996

In 1995 the Government set out its housing policies for England and Wales in a White Paper, *Our Future Homes*. It included commitments to a sustainable expansion in home ownership, based on economic stability, stable house prices and low interest rates; further funding to ensure there is no necessity for people to sleep rough (outside in the street); and a target to build half of all new homes on re-used sites. It also envisaged the creation of a new framework for social rented housing with rents remaining affordable to tenants in low-paid work, a greater diversity of social landlords, more transfers of local authority housing to new landlords outside the public sector, and commercial organisations competing alongside housing associations for grants to provide social housing. Many of the proposals have been enacted in the Housing Act 1996, which applies mostly to England and Wales. Key features of the Act include:

- a new purchase grant scheme to help housing association tenants to buy the homes they are currently renting;

- a fairer system for allocating social housing, with the retention of a 'safety net' for families and vulnerable people who lose their homes through no fault of their own;

- a right for council tenants to vote for new types of social landlord who could bring in private money to improve their estates;

- stronger powers for landlords to act against tenants engaged in anti-social behaviour;

- better protection against unscrupulous landlords who, for example, make excessive service charges; and

- improved safety standards for people in 'bedsits' and hostels.

The White Paper proposal to create housing investment trusts in order to encourage financial institutions to invest in private rented housing was embodied in the Finance Act 1996.

Home Ownership

The number of owner-occupied dwellings in Great Britain amounted to 16 million at the end of 1995, compared with 4.1 million in 1950.

Mortgage Loans

Most people buy their homes with a mortgage loan, using the property as security. These are obtained through building societies, banks or other financial institutions such as specialist mortgage lenders. Additionally, some companies grant loans for house purchase to their employees. The amount that lenders are prepared to advance to a would-be house purchaser is generally calculated as a multiple of his or her annual income, typically up to two-and-a-half or three times earnings, and the term of the loan is commonly 25 years. Owner-occupiers get tax relief on interest payments on the first £30,000 of their mortgages on their main home.

In the recession in the early 1990s, many homeowners saw a fall in the value of their homes, and some have had trouble keeping up with mortgage payments. The Government's policies to overcome these problems have been based on maintaining a healthy economy, low interest rates and stable house prices in order to help keep home ownership affordable. The number of repossessions in the first half of 1996 was down 38 per cent from its peak of 38,900 in the second half of 1991. The first half of 1996 saw a continued recovery in house prices.

Tenure in Great Britain

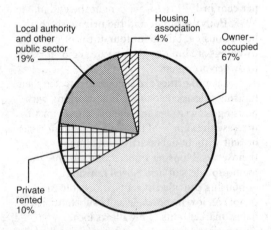

Source: *Department of the Environment*

Right to Buy and Low-Cost Ownership

With a few exceptions, in England and Wales public tenants with secure tenancies of at

House prices 1983–1994

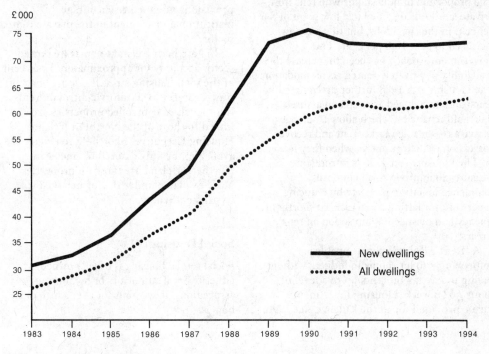

£ 000

Source: *Housing and Construction Statistics*

least two years' standing are entitled to buy their house or flat at a discount dependent upon the length of the tenancy. Similar provisions apply in Scotland and Northern Ireland. A total of 2.1 million council, housing association or New Town development corporation houses were sold into owner-occupation in Great Britain between 1979–80 and the end of 1995. Sales are continuing at a rate of about 60,000 a year.

Other schemes to encourage the availability of low-cost home ownership include shared ownership schemes[1] and discounted sales of empty properties owned by local authorities. Some £60 million is being made available to local authority

tenants in England under the Cash Incentive Scheme, under which tenants of social housing are given cash help to buy in the private sector. Over 5,000 local authority tenants a year are given help in this way, thereby opening up new lettings for those in greatest need.

In Wales, local authorities and housing associations operate a low-cost home ownership scheme which allows purchasers to buy a home for 70 per cent of its value, the balance being secured as a charge on the property. Scottish Homes operates a scheme to encourage private developers to build for owner-occupation in areas they would not normally consider. In 1996–97 planned investment in the scheme is about £21 million. A shared ownership scheme in Northern Ireland is administered by the Northern Ireland Co-ownership Housing Association.

[1] These involve the homeowner buying a share of a property from a housing association and paying rent for the remainder.

Privately Rented Housing

The proportion of households who rent from private landlords declined to a low point of 8.6 per cent in the late 1980s, but this has now increased to over 10.0 per cent. The Government's policy has been to increase the availability of privately rented accommodation. The Housing Act 1988 further deregulated rents, and introduced assured and assured shorthold tenancies, which allow landlords to charge a reasonable market rent and recover possession of their property when they need to. The Housing Act 1996 is introducing measures to improve small landlords' confidence in letting property by reducing paperwork for letting on an assured shorthold tenancy and by speeding up action on rent arrears.

A 'Rent a Room' scheme enables homeowners to let rooms to lodgers without having to pay tax on rents up to a level of about £62 a week. Housing investment trusts, provided for in the Finance Act 1996, will be companies set up to own residential property for rent. They will benefit from tax provisions designed to encourage institutional investment in the private rented sector.

In Northern Ireland the private rented sector accounts for approximately 5 per cent of the total housing stock. Less than half of this is subject to statutory control on rents. Rent levels of controlled properties are linked to those of the Northern Ireland Housing Executive. Shorthold tenancies are available; the only assured tenancies in Northern Ireland are those on properties made available under the former Business Expansion Scheme.

Social Housing

Social rented housing is usually owned either by local authorities or by housing associations. It accounts for over a fifth of all homes.

Type of Accommodation Occupied

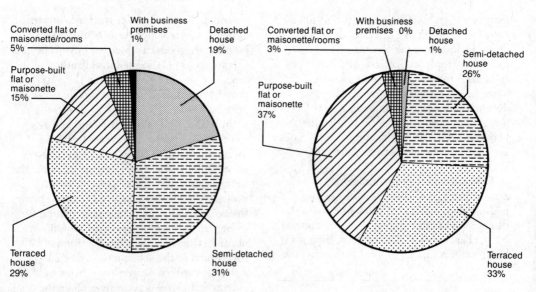

All households

Converted flat or maisonette/rooms 5%
With business premises 1%
Detached house 19%
Purpose-built flat or maisonette 15%
Terraced house 29%
Semi-detached house 31%

Local authority tenants

Converted flat or maisonette/rooms 3%
With business premises 0%
Detached house 1%
Semi-detached house 26%
Purpose-built flat or maisonette 37%
Terraced house 33%

Source: *General Household Survey 1993*

388

Public Housing

Most social housing in Great Britain is provided by local housing authorities.[2] At present these are:

- district councils, in those parts of England with two-tier local government;

- London borough councils, metropolitan districts and unitary authorities, in areas with single-tier local government; and

- the new unitary councils in Scotland and Wales, plus the Scottish islands councils.

Public housing is also provided by Scottish Homes, which currently has a stock of about 36,000 houses. It is, however, in the process of transferring its houses to alternative landlords such as housing associations. The Northern Ireland Housing Executive is responsible for the provision and management of public housing there. The Development Board for Rural Wales also used to provide housing, but transferred all its 1,200 houses to other social landlords in April 1996.

Public housing authorities in Great Britain own about 4.6 million houses and flats; the Northern Ireland Housing Executive owns about 145,000 homes. Since 1988, a number of local authorities have transferred all their housing stock to housing associations and others are considering doing so. This has the advantage of bringing in new sources of funding and types of management. By July 1996, 51 authorities had transferred their stock, involving over 220,000 properties and raising more than £3,600 million.

Local authorities meet the capital costs of modernising their stock by:

- borrowing from the Public Works Loan Board (an independent statutory body set up to make loans to local authorities) or on the open market;

- using part of the proceeds from the sale of local authority houses and other assets;

- drawing on their revenue accounts; or

- using grants from central government.

[2]The reorganisation of local government in England (see pp. 75–6) will change these arrangements as new local authorities take over in some areas.

Councils must maintain housing revenue accounts on a 'ring-fenced' basis to keep them separate from other council funds. The Government grants local authorities in England and Wales Housing Revenue Account Subsidy. This is worth £3,834 million in England and £193 million in Wales in 1996–97. In Scotland, Housing Support Grant of about £20 million is available in 1996–97 for those authorities which are in deficit on their housing revenue accounts.

Local authorities in England will be able to borrow £1,213 million in 1996–97 for their housing investment programmes. In Scotland, local authorities have received capital allocations amounting to £341 million for investment in council homes. In Northern Ireland, the Housing Executive's capital programme is financed mainly by borrowing from government and receipts from house sales. In 1996–97 borrowing will total £70 million. Revenue expenditure is funded from rental income and by a government grant, which in 1996–97 is about £139 million.

Housing Associations

Housing associations, which are non-profit-making, are now the main providers of new low-cost housing for rent and for sale to those on low incomes and in the greatest housing need. Some specialise in providing supported housing to meet the special needs of those with, for example, learning difficulties (mental handicap), drug and alcohol problems, young people at risk and frail elderly people. Associations own, manage and maintain over 950,000 homes and about 65,000 hostel and special-needs bed-spaces in Great Britain, providing homes for well over 1 million people.

In Great Britain new housing schemes carried out by associations may qualify for Housing Association Grant if the association concerned is one of about 2,200 registered with the Housing Corporation (in England), Scottish Homes or Housing for Wales. These three organisations are statutory bodies which supervise and pay grant to housing associations in their respective parts of Great Britain. Broadly similar assistance is available to associations in Northern Ireland.

The Housing Corporation's approved development programme provides for about £1,060 million in grants in 1996–97. This is supplemented by private finance attracted by housing associations, thereby allowing more homes to be built with available public resources. In 1996–97, Housing Corporation funding will make possible an additional 43,000 lettings for rent or shared ownership.

For 1996–97, expenditure on Scottish Homes' development funding programme, which includes grants to private developers and landlords, is £280 million, while the target for the amount of private finance attracted is estimated to be £160 million. Housing for Wales is managing a net capital programme of £85 million in 1996–97, with a target of making over 3,000 new homes available. Government provision to the housing association movement in Wales was almost £500 million between 1992–93 and 1995–96. Private sector finance generated over the same period reached almost £275 million.

Northern Ireland's registered housing associations are expected to start 1,250 units of accommodation in 1996–97. They now have a stock of about 19,000 units for rent. The budget for building for rent is £36 million in 1997–98, which, with an additional £11 million of private finance, will provide a further 1,100 units of rented accommodation. Government plans allow for total funding of £238 million over the period 1993–94 to 1997–98.

Tenants' Rights

Local authority tenants in England, Scotland and Wales have security of tenure and other statutory rights, which are set out in a Council Tenant's Charter. In addition to the right to buy (see p. 386), these include the right to get certain urgent repairs done quickly at no cost to themselves and the right to be paid when they move home for certain improvements they have made.

Compulsory competitive tendering is being introduced for council house management; tenants must be kept closely involved in the process of letting the tenders to manage council estates. Tenants also have the right to take over the running of their estates through tenant management organisations (TMOs). Over 100 TMOs are operational and about 100 more are in the process of development.

> The 100th tenant management organisation (TMO), on the Stockwell Park estate in Brixton, south London, was set up in November 1995. The first borough-wide TMO, also in London, was established in Kensington and Chelsea in April 1996. This TMO, directed by a board composed mostly of tenants, now manages 8,660 dwellings.

In England and Wales the rights of housing association tenants are protected under Tenants' Guarantees, which are issued by the Housing Corporation and Housing for Wales. They cover matters such as tenancy terms, principles for setting rent levels and the allocation of tenancies. Under these guarantees, tenants receive contractual rights in addition to their basic statutory rights, and associations are required to set and maintain rents at levels affordable by those in low-paid employment. Similar non-statutory guidance, based on arrangements agreed between Scottish Homes and the Scottish Federation of Housing Associations, has been implemented in Scotland. In Northern Ireland, the Department of the Environment for Northern Ireland has issued a Tenants' Guarantee, similar to the English and Welsh versions, for tenants of registered housing associations.

Following a Citizen's Charter commitment, the Government launched a Housing Association Tenants' Ombudsman Service in 1993, under the auspices of the Housing Corporation. The scheme, which covers England, allows independent investigation of tenants' complaints against their housing association, giving them a right similar to that for council tenants through the local government ombudsman (see p. 80). Provision to make the service statutorily independent is included in the Housing Act 1996. Similar schemes have been launched in Scotland and Northern Ireland.

Housing for Older People

Sheltered housing provides specialised facilities for elderly people, such as common and laundry rooms, alarm systems and resident or non-resident warden support. Increasing emphasis is being placed on schemes to help them to continue to live in their own homes by, for example, adapting their present homes to meet their particular needs. In England, government-funded home improvement agencies help elderly people, people with disabilities and those on low incomes to carry out repairs and improvements to their properties. Almost £4.4 million of government help will go to support 142 home improvement agencies in 1996–97. Care and Repair Ltd is the national co-ordinating and monitoring body. Similar arrangements apply in Wales, where in 1996–97 more than £895,000 in government help will go to support 24 home improvement agencies. Corresponding provision is made for Scotland under the Care and Repair scheme co-ordinated by Scottish Homes.

Rural Housing

Where there is an identified need for low-cost housing in rural areas, local authorities can permit housing in areas where development would not normally be allowed, so long as the new housing can be reserved to meet that need. The Housing Corporation also funds a special rural programme to build houses in small villages; between 1989–90 and 1995–96 it approved funding for the building of over 12,000 such homes.

Housing for Wales has a major role in rural housing provision, with at least a quarter of its programme devoted to rural areas. The Welsh Office also supports low-cost schemes for rural housing. In Scotland, considerable progress is being made through a range of initiatives launched in 1990 as part of the Scottish Homes Rural Strategy. Scottish Homes has invested over £360 million in rural areas since 1989–90, providing more than 12,000 homes. In 1996–97 it will spend more than £53 million in rural areas, making 1,500 homes available. The Northern Ireland Housing Executive operates a rural strategy; this involves action both in public housing and also in the house

renovation grant scheme for private housing, which it administers.

Improving Existing Housing

In urban areas of Britain, slum clearance and redevelopment used to be major features of housing policy, but there has been a trend in recent years towards the modernisation and conversion of sub-standard homes in order to help maintain existing communities. Housing conditions have improved considerably, but problems remain in some areas where there are concentrations of dwellings requiring substantial repairs. In some cases, however, clearance may still be the most satisfactory course of action. To help overcome objections to clearance, the Housing, Grants, Construction and Regeneration Act 1996 has recently allowed local authorities to pay a new discretionary relocation grant to those displaced by clearance to help them purchase at least a part share in a new home in the same area.

Social Housing

Over the next ten years, the Government plans to tackle the problems of the most deprived housing estates by:

- improving the physical quality of the estates;
- encouraging diversity of tenure by increasing home ownership and renting from private social landlords; and
- improving economic and social conditions.

Run-down estates will be improved through the Single Regeneration Budget (SRB—see p. 375) Challenge Fund, which encourages local partnerships in England to tackle social and economic problems, including housing improvements. A high proportion of successful bids for Challenge Fund support include improvements to housing. A new £314 million Estate Renewal Challenge Fund is being made available over three years to help improve the remaining poor-quality estates by speeding their transfer to housing associations and other new landlords.

There are a number of estates in poorer condition which would benefit from the investment that transfer to a social landlord (see p. 389) can bring, but which are unable to attract funding for a transfer because of low or negative revenue valuations (generally where the cost of upkeep over the next 30 years will be more than the rental income). The Estates Renewal Challenge Fund was set up by the Government in 1995 to provide an injection of money to facilitate transfers where they would not have been viable otherwise and where such support represents good value for money in the long term. In the first round, 11 local authorities received a total of £174 million. It is expected that this will generate over £250 million of private investment for the transferred homes.

On six estates, tenants have voted for housing action trusts to take over their housing from the local authority; the aim is to provide new solutions to the physical, social, economic and environmental problems of the areas.

In Wales, Estate Partnership funding is available to tackle the problems of selected estates; £10.6 million of central government support has been allocated for this in 1996–97 to supplement local authority and private sector contributions.

In Scotland, the Government's approach to urban regeneration is based on the partnership approach. In the urban Partnerships in parts of Dundee, Edinburgh, Glasgow and Paisley (see p. 380), more than 2,000 new houses have been built and another 5,500 refurbished. More choice of housing type and tenure is now available, and home ownership has been increased.

Private Housing

The Government offers help through house renovation grants to owners of private housing who are on low incomes and unable to afford necessary repairs and improvements. Specific help is available to disabled people needing adaptations to their homes. Since 1990, house renovation grants, disabled facilities grants, and minor works assistance grants have provided up to 100 per cent support for essential repairs and improvements to the poorest homeowners. In all 460,000 grants were made in England between 1991–92 and 1995–96, totalling almost £2,200 million.

The Government has recently legislated in the Housing, Grants, Construction and Regeneration Act 1996 to reform the renovation grant system in order to give local authorities greater discretion in deciding applications for renovation grant. The aim is to enable local authorities to target more resources towards:

● renewal areas declared by the local authority;

● improving the housing conditions of vulnerable people; and

● supporting community care policies (see Ch. 25) and enabling elderly, ill or disabled people to continue to live independently.

In Scotland, local authorities award grants for improvement and repair. Scottish Homes also has the power to provide grants to complement the role of local authorities in private house renewal. In Northern Ireland, grants are allocated on a similar basis to that in England and Wales through the house renovation grants scheme, administered by the Northern Ireland Housing Executive. In isolated rural areas, a grant to replace dwellings which cannot be restored is also available through this scheme.

Homelessness

Local authorities have a legal duty to secure accommodation for households which are eligible for assistance and which they accept are unintentionally homeless and in priority need. The latter category includes

Table 24.1: Households in England Accepted as Homeless	
1989[a]	122,180
1990[a]	140,350
1991[a]	144,780
1992	142,890
1993	132,380
1994	122,660
1995	120,810

Source: Department of the Environment
[a]1989, 1990 and first quarter 1991 figures are based on estimates in line with a new definition introduced in the second quarter of 1991.

pregnant women, people with dependent children, and those who are vulnerable because of old age, mental or physical handicap or other special reasons. Visitors to Britain, and certain other groups of people who require leave to enter the country, are not eligible for homelessness assistance or to be allocated council housing. The number of households accepted as homeless has fallen since 1991 in England (see Table 24.1) and since 1993 in Wales.

Provisions in the Housing Act 1996, which will come into force in January 1997, will reform the law on homelessness and the allocation of council housing. This will ensure fairer access to long-term social housing by creating a single route to such accommodation—the local authority housing register—while ensuring a safety net for families and vulnerable people who lose their home through no fault of their own. In Scotland, where the number of homeless households continued to rise until 1993–94, the policy on homelessness is under review following consultations in 1994. In Northern Ireland, where the number of households accepted as homeless has remained stable since the homelessness legislation was extended there in 1989, consideration is being given to the most appropriate way to effect the reforms provided for in the Act.

Most people accepted as homeless have some form of accommodation, even though this may be temporary, overcrowded or otherwise unsatisfactory. Those entitled to rehousing are found accommodation by local authorities. Only a small proportion of the homeless are 'roofless'—that is, literally without accommodation.

In 1990 the Government established the Rough Sleepers Initiative to tackle the problem in central London, with resources of £182 million in its first six years. This provided about 950 new places in short-term hostels and at least 3,300 permanent and 700 leased places in 'move-on' accommodation for hostel dwellers. A voluntary sector count, held in May 1996, found that 288 people were sleeping rough in central London, compared with estimates of over 1,000 before

the Rough Sleepers Initiative began (see Table 24.2).

The third phase of the Initiative was announced in March 1996, involving the provision of:

- at least 250 new permanent homes;
- up to 200 new beds in basic hostel accommodation;
- up to 40 beds in permanent high-care accommodation; and
- up to 30 beds in a new 'wet' hostel for people sleeping rough who have drink problems.

The Initiative was also extended to Bristol (see panel), and the extent of the problem in 23 other areas in England is being evaluated.

Details of help for rough sleepers in Bristol were announced in June 1996. The £7.5 million package includes at least 150 new permanent homes, 24 beds in permanent high-care accommodation for mentally ill people, and the employment of additional resettlement workers to help people adjust to life in new accommodation.

Since 1990 more than £23 million has been spent by the Department of Health on the Homeless Mentally Ill Initiative, a programme to supply accommodation and psychiatric care for mentally ill people who have been sleeping

Table 24.2: Rough Sleepers Counted in Central London

Month and Year	Number
March 1992	440
November 1992	419
June 1993	358
November 1993	287
May 1994	268
November 1994	288
May 1995	270
May 1996	288

Source: Department of the Environment

rough in central London. The Department has a long-term commitment to help with the running costs of the accommodation. It also funds health care projects designed to ensure that homeless people have access to health services. The Government announced in March 1996 that the amount spent each year by the Department of Health on the Initiative would be almost doubled to £4.2 million. From 1996–97 it is being expended in tandem with the Rough Sleepers Initiative in London and to Bristol.

The Government is giving £7.8 million in 1996–97 to voluntary groups helping single homeless people in England. Grants of over £400,000 for 1996–97 have been made to voluntary organisations tackling homelessness in Scotland, £523,000 in Wales and £335,000 in Northern Ireland. Research is being carried out into rooflessness in Scotland to inform future policy, and this was expected to be published by the end of 1996.

Further Reading

Housing. Aspects of Britain series. HMSO, 1993.
Our Future Homes. HMSO, 1995.

Annual Reports
Building Societies Commission. HMSO.
Housing and Construction Statistics. HMSO.
The Housing Corporation. Housing Corporation.

Housing Advice

As well as housing associations, other voluntary sector bodies have a role to play in housing matters. Such groups undertake a number of roles, for example advising people about their rights under housing law or encouraging energy efficiency in the home. The Government allocates grants to assist the work of such bodies. In England the largest project currently funded is the Homelessness Advice Service, with £1.8 million in 1996–97; in Scotland aid of over £1 million in 1996–97 is being given to about 20 voluntary bodies for work on homelessness and other housing matters. In Northern Ireland, the government is providing about £200,000 in 1996–97 to the Housing Rights Service, a voluntary organisation which provides advice on all aspects of housing, and £182,000 to the Northern Ireland Tenants Action Project, which promotes the participation of tenants in the management of their homes.

Social and
Cultural Affairs

25 Health and Social Services

Major Policy Developments	398	Safety of Medicines	419
The National Health Service	**400**	Research	419
Administration	401	The Health Professions	419
Family Health Services	405	Health Arrangements with	
Hospital and Specialist		Other Countries	421
Services	407	**Personal Social Services**	**421**
Environmental Health	418		

Total spending on health and social services in 1996–97 is expected to be £41,224 million: £40,793 million on health and £431 million on social services. Key elements of the Government's spending plans include: continued expansion of primary care (family health services); improvements in the mental health services; research and development; and education and training in the National Health Service.

The National Health Service (NHS) provides a full range of medical services which are available to all residents, regardless of their income. Local authority personal social services and voluntary organisations provide help and advice to the most vulnerable members of the community. These include elderly, physically disabled and mentally ill people, those with learning disabilities (mental handicap) and children in need of care.

Central government is directly responsible for the NHS, which is administered by a range of local health authorities and health boards throughout Britain. Personal social services are administered by local authorities but central government is responsible for establishing national policies, issuing guidance and overseeing standards. Joint finance and planning between health and local authorities aims to prevent overlapping of services and to encourage the development of community services.

Spending on the health service has increased substantially in real terms since 1980, reflecting the priority given to this sector, and it is planned to grow further over the next two years. More patients are being treated than ever before.

The Health Programme is funded mainly by central government and consists of:

- Hospital and Community Health Services (HCHS), providing all hospital care and a range of community services;

- Family Health Services (FHS), providing general medical, dental, pharmaceutical and some ophthalmic services, and covering the cost of medicines prescribed by general practitioners (GPs);

- Central Health and Miscellaneous Services (CHMS), providing services most effectively administered centrally, such as welfare food (which includes free milk and vitamins to families with children under five, and pregnant women, on Income Support) and support to the voluntary sector; and

- the administrative costs of the health departments.

The Government has targeted four priority areas in allocating funds to the health authorities in England for 1996–97. These are: primary care; research and development; education and training in the NHS; and mental health services.

The Personal Social Services programme consists largely of spending by local authorities. The programme is financed in part by central government but most local authority personal social services revenue spending depends on decisions by individual local authorities on how to spend the resources available to them.

Major Policy Developments

Reforms in Management

The NHS and Community Care Act 1990 introduced wide-ranging reform in management and patient care in the health and social care services. The NHS reforms, which came into effect in 1991, aim to give patients, wherever they live in Britain, better health care and greater choice of service:

1. Health authorities and health boards have been given a new role as purchasers of health care for their local residents, and are responsible for assessing local health care needs and ensuring the availability of a full range of services to meet identified health needs. They ensure that those needs are met within existing resources.

2. Each health authority/health board is funded to buy health care for its local residents through arranging contracts with hospitals and other health service units in either the public or the private sector. Hospitals are now directly funded for the number of patients they treat.

3. The contracts agreed between health authorities/health boards, GP fundholders (see below), and hospitals set out the quality, quantity and cost of the services to be delivered during the year. The contracts

secured by each health authority are based on wide consultation with all local GPs.

4. Hospitals may apply to become self-governing NHS Trusts (see p. 408), independent of local health authority control but remaining within the NHS. They are accountable to the relevant health department, and are funded largely through general taxation, under contracts with health authorities. NHS Trusts provide the services that health authorities/health boards and GP fundholders (see below) wish to buy.

5. GPs from larger medical practices may apply to join the general practitioner fundholding scheme (see p. 406), under which they receive an annual budget directly from the health authority/health board, enabling them to buy certain hospital services for their patients.

The reforms in community care provision, which came into force between 1991 and 1993, establish a new financial and managerial framework which aims to secure the delivery of good quality services in line with national objectives. They are intended to enable vulnerable groups in the community to live as independently as possible in their own homes for as long as they are able and wish to do so, and to give them a greater say in how they live and how the services they need should be provided. (For fuller details see p. 422.)

Broadly similar changes were introduced under separate legislation in Northern Ireland, where health and personal social services are provided on an integrated basis by health and social services boards.

Patient's Charters

Patient's Charters are part of the health departments' response to the Government's Citizen's Charter programme (see p. 69). The Charters support the objectives of the NHS reforms: to improve standards of health care and sensitivity to patients in the NHS. They set out for the first time the rights of patients and the standards of service they can expect to receive from the NHS. The responsibility for implementing the Patient's Charters rests with all parts of the NHS, English regional offices (see p. 402), purchasers and providers of services (see above).

The original Patient's Charter in England came into force in 1992. An expanded and updated Patient's Charter was issued in 1995, covering dental, optical and pharmaceutical services and the hospital environment, including cleanliness and security.

In England the Patient's Charter also sets national charter standards, which are not legal rights but specific standards of service that the NHS aims to provide. These cover respect for the individual patient; waiting times for ambulances, clinical assessment in accident and emergency departments and appointments in out-patient clinics; and cancellation of operations. Also included are local charter standards of service which health authorities aim to provide (see below).

Separate but similar Patient's Charters have been developed for Scotland, Wales and Northern Ireland.

In England a maternity services charter, describing key standards and rights, was published in 1994, a blood donor's charter was issued in 1995, and a patient's charter for children and young people was issued in March 1996. The last mentioned covers hospital and community services and sets out the services available to healthy children, and the health checks available for babies and pre-school aged children.

All health authorities in England and health boards and NHS Trusts in Scotland have produced local charters, which include statements of the standards of service patients can expect to receive from them. Staff in GP practices are being encouraged to produce their own practice charters, setting out the standards of service they offer their patients. By September 1995, 80 per cent of GP practices in England had, or were developing, charters.

Openness in the NHS

The Code of Practice on Openness in the NHS came into force in 1995. Designed to make NHS organisations more accountable and provide greater public access to information, the Code applies to NHS Trusts, health authorities and local health practitioners such as GPs, dentists and pharmacists. It sets out the information that NHS Trusts and health authorities/health boards should publish or otherwise make available.

The NHS Code of Practice on Openness contains, among other things:

- information about what services are provided, the targets and standards set and results achieved, and the costs and effectiveness of the service;

- details of important proposals on health policies or proposed changes in the way the services are delivered; and

- information about how people can have access to their own personal health records.

A Code of Practice on Openness in the Health and Personal Social Services is being developed for Northern Ireland.

Developing Health Strategies

The Government emphasises the importance of promoting health as well as treating illness. Preventive health services such as health education, and the responsibility that individuals have for their own health, play a major part in this. While great progress has been made in eliminating infectious diseases such as poliomyelitis, there is still scope for greater success in controlling the major causes of early death and disability.

The White Paper *The Health of the Nation*, published in 1992, sets out a strategy for improving health in England; its long-term aim is to enable people to live longer, healthier lives. It set targets for improvements in the following areas:

- coronary heart disease and stroke (the major causes of premature death in England);

- cancers (now the biggest cause of death across all ages);

- accidents (the commonest cause of death in those under 30);

- mental illness (a leading cause of ill-health and also a cause of many suicides); and

- HIV/AIDS and sexual health (there is

much scope for reducing sexually transmitted diseases and unwanted pregnancies, especially among teenagers).

Targets were set for:

- reducing death rates (for example, from coronary heart disease and stroke in those under 65 by at least 40 per cent by the year 2000);
- reducing ill-health (such as the incidence of invasive cervical cancer by at least 20 per cent by 2000); and
- reducing risk behaviour (for example, the percentage of smokers to no more than 20 per cent of the population by 2000).

In most areas there has been steady progress towards the targets but in a few cases, such as teenage smoking, obesity and lung cancer deaths among women under 75, figures are on the increase. While the NHS has a central role in working towards the targets, the strategy also emphasises that there is a role for everyone in improving the nation's health.

Strategies have also been developed for Scotland, Wales and Northern Ireland which reflect the health variations in the different parts of Britain. In Wales, where the first of Britain's four national health strategies was published in 1990, areas for improvement include, among others: cancers, cardiovascular disease, maternal and early child health, physical disability, mental handicap and mental health, and injuries. Scotland's national strategy, first issued in 1991, places special emphasis on coronary heart disease, cancer, HIV/AIDS, accidents, dental and oral health, smoking, alcohol and drug misuse. Northern Ireland's strategy, also published in 1991, sets targets for improvements in a number of key areas, which include circulatory diseases, cancers, respiratory diseases, child and maternal health, and mental health. (For publication details of all these, see Further Reading.)

National activity in England includes, for example, interdepartmental taskforces on accident prevention, smoking, the workplace and physical activity, work with professional and voluntary bodies, and the provision of guidance setting out a range of possible actions for each tier of the NHS. At local level, the NHS is being encouraged to form 'healthy alliances' with agencies ranging from the voluntary sector through to industry and the media. Progress towards the targets is monitored regularly and formally reviewed, and periodic progress reports are published. Similar initiatives are being taken in Scotland, Wales and Northern Ireland.

The Government is working closely with the World Health Organisation (WHO) in presenting *The Health of the Nation* as one possible approach for other countries wishing to develop a strategic approach to improving health.

The Government is to commission an independent interim review of *The Health of the Nation* strategy. A report is expected in early 1998.

The National Health Service

The NHS is based upon the principle that there should be a full range of publicly provided services designed to help the individual stay healthy. The services are intended to provide effective and appropriate treatment and care where necessary while making the best use of available resources. All taxpayers, employers and employees contribute to its cost so that those members of the community who do not require health care help to pay for those who do. Some forms of treatment, such as hospital care, are provided free; others (see p. 402) may be charged for.

Growth in real spending on the health service is being used to meet the needs of increasing numbers of elderly people and to take full advantage of advances in medical technology. It is also used to provide more appropriate types of care, often in the community rather than in hospital, for priority groups such as elderly and mentally ill people and those with learning disabilities. Increased spending has, in addition, been allocated to combat the growing problems arising from alcohol and drug misuse; and to remedy disparities in provision between the regions of Britain.

In 1995 the Government announced six national priorities for the NHS in England over the next three to six years. These are:

- further developing a primary care-led NHS;
- securing a comprehensive range of secure, residential, in-patient and community services for people with mental illness;
- improved cost-effectiveness;
- giving greater voice to the users of services, and their carers;
- securing better services to meet the continuing health care needs of elderly, disabled or vulnerable people; and
- developing NHS organisations as good employers.

Similar priorities have been identified in Scotland, Wales and Northern Ireland.

The Voluntary Sector

Government grant aid to voluntary organisations working in health and personal social services in England (£50 million in 1995–96) goes primarily to national organisations dealing with children, elderly people, carers and people from ethnic minorities, as well as those looking after people with mental illness, physical or learning disabilities, or suffering from the effects of HIV/AIDS or the misuse of alcohol or drugs. In Scotland central government grants to voluntary organisations in social welfare amount, in 1996–97, to almost £9 million. In Northern Ireland the Department of Health and Social Services plans to spend £6.4 million in support of a wide range of voluntary activity during 1996–97.

Health authorities and boards and local authorities have similar powers to make grants to local organisations.

ADMINISTRATION

The Secretary of State for Health in England and the Secretaries of State for Scotland, Wales and Northern Ireland are responsible for all aspects of the health services in their respective territories. The Department of Health is responsible for national strategic planning in England. Within the Department of Health the NHS Executive is responsible for developing and implementing policies for the provision of high quality health services. The Scottish Office Department of Health, the Welsh Office and the Department of Health and Social Services in Northern Ireland have similar responsibilities.

Table 25.1: Clients of selected advisory and counselling services, Britain

	1971	1981	1991	Thousands 1994
Citizens Advice Bureaux	1,500	4,515	8,278	–[1]
Samaritans	–	1,700	2,500	3,748
Law Centres Federation	1	155	452	525
Youth Access	–	30	113	250
Disablement Information and Advice Lines	–	40	75	137
Childline	–	–	69	90
Relate (marriage guidance)	22	38	70	70
Alcoholics Anonymous	6	30	45	48
Cruse Bereavement Care	–	–	55	97
Turning Point (for people suffering from the misuse of drugs or alcohol and for those with mental illness)	–	–	–	27
Catholic Marriage Advisory Council	3	3	17	10
Al-Anon Family Groups	1	7	13	11

Source: *Social Trends*
[1]The Citizens Advice Bureaux introduced a new recording system in 1994. This now records problems rather than enquiries; a single problem may involve more than one enquiry. The figure for 1994 is 7.1 million problems.

Health authorities in England and Wales (see below) and health boards in Scotland are responsible for securing hospital and community health services in their areas. They also arrange for the provision of services by doctors, dentists, pharmacists and opticians, as well as administering their contracts. The health authorities and boards co-operate closely with local authorities responsible for social work, environmental health, education and other services. There are community health councils (local health councils in Scotland) for each district, representing local opinion on the health services provided.

In Northern Ireland health and social services boards are responsible as agents of the Department of Health and Social Services for assessing the health and social care needs of their resident populations. The representation of public opinion on these services is provided for by area health and social services councils.

Recent Changes in England and Wales

In April 1996 further changes to streamline the administrative structure of the NHS in England and Wales were fully implemented:

- the former district health authorities and family health services authorities were replaced by new single all-purpose health authorities. The new authorities are responsible for the whole range of health issues and health services for the areas they serve. Their role is to assess the needs of their population, draw up strategies with local GPs, hospitals, community health services, local authorities and local people, and buy services to meet those needs. The boundaries of the new health authorities, which largely reflect previous district health authority boundaries, have populations of between 125,000 and 1 million; and

- the 14 former regional health authorities in England, previously responsible for planning, resource allocation, major capital building work and certain specialised hospital services, were abolished and replaced with eight regional offices of the NHS Executive, keeping more of a distance from day-to-day operational matters.

These changes build on the 1990 NHS reforms (see p. 398) and continue the devolution of responsibilities and decision-making in the NHS to local level. By 1997–98, when the new structure is fully implemented, savings will rise to nearly £150 million a year, and will be retained by the NHS and reinvested in patient care.

Finance

About 82 per cent of the cost of the health service in Great Britain is paid for through general taxation. The rest is met from:

- the NHS element of National Insurance contributions (see p. 431), paid by employed people, their employers, and self-employed people (12.1 per cent);

- charges towards the cost of certain items such as drugs prescribed by family doctors, and general dental treatment (2.3 per cent); and

- other receipts, including land sales and the proceeds of income generation schemes (0.9 per cent).

Health authorities may raise funds from voluntary sources. Certain hospitals increase revenue by taking private patients, who pay the full cost of their accommodation and treatment.

In 1996–97 an estimated 85 per cent of medical prescription items are being supplied free. Prescription charges are not paid by:

- children under 16 years (or young people under 19 who are in full-time education);

- pregnant women and women who have had a baby in the past year;

- people aged 60 and over;

- patients with certain medical conditions;

- war and armed forces disablement pensioners (for prescriptions which relate to the disability for which they receive a war pension); and

- people in families who are receiving Income Support, income-based Jobseeker's Allowance or Disability Working Allowance (see Ch. 26); and people or families with low incomes.

Health Service Expenditure in England

NHS Gross Expenditure 1995–96

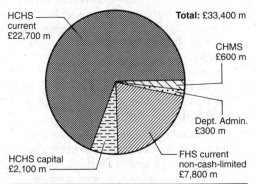

HCHS current £22,700 m

Total: £33,400 m

CHMS £600 m

Dept. Admin. £300 m

FHS current non-cash-limited £7,800 m

HCHS capital £2,100 m

Hospital and Community Health Services Gross Current Expenditure by Sector 1993–94

Total: £21,361 m

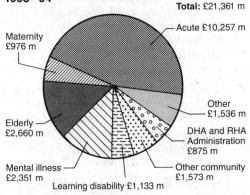

Maternity £976 m

Acute £10,257 m

Other £1,536 m

Elderly £2,660 m

DHA and RHA Administration £875 m

Mental illness £2,351 m

Other community £1,573 m

Learning disability £1,133 m

1. Other community services include health visiting, immunisation, screening, health promotion and community dental services.

2. Other services include ambulances, the blood transfusion service, mass radiography and the Service Increment for Teaching and Research (SIFTR).

Non-cash-limited Family Health Services Gross Expenditure 1994–95

Total: £7,324 m

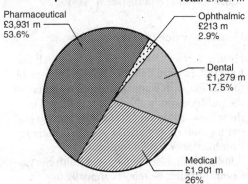

Pharmaceutical £3,931 m 53.6%

Ophthalmic £213 m 2.9%

Dental £1,279 m 17.5%

Medical £1,901 m 26%

Source: *Department of Health. The Government's Expenditure Plans 1996–97 to 1998–99.*

Note: Differences between totals and the sums of their component parts are due to rounding.

In 1995 nearly 473 million prescriptions were dispensed in England, almost 20 per cent more than in 1985. The cost of dispensing prescriptions was £3,681 million—an increase of 17 per cent in real terms over 1985.

There are proportional charges for most types of NHS dental treatment, including examinations. However, women who begin a course of treatment while pregnant or within 12 months of having a baby, children up to 18, students under 19, those who receive, or whose partners receive, Jobseeker's Allowance, Income Support or Disability Working Allowance are entitled to free treatment. Others on low incomes may be entitled to free treatment or to help with charges.

Sight tests are free to children, full-time students under the age of 19, people in families receiving Income Support, income-based Jobseeker's Allowance or Disability Working Allowance and those with specified medical needs. A voucher to help with the cost of spectacles is also available for children, full-time students under the age of 19, people receiving the above benefits and those requiring certain complex lenses. Other people on low incomes may apply for help under the NHS Low Income Scheme.

Hospital staff are salaried and may be employed full-time or part-time. Family practitioners (doctors, dentists, optometrists and community pharmacists) are self-employed or, in the case of pharmacists, employed by a pharmacy company, and have contracts with the NHS. GPs are paid by a system of fees and allowances designed to reflect responsibilities, workload and practice expenses. Dentists providing treatment in their own surgeries are paid by a combination of capitation fees for treating children, continuing care payments for adults registered with the practice, and a prescribed scale of fees for individual treatments. Community pharmacists dispense from their own or their company's premises and are refunded the cost of the items supplied, together with professional fees. Ophthalmic medical practitioners and ophthalmic opticians taking part in the general ophthalmic service receive approved fees for each sight test carried out.

Private Finance Initiative

The Private Finance Initiative (PFI) was launched in 1992 to promote partnership between the public and private sectors on a commercial basis (see p. 162). In the health service it involves the use of private finance in NHS capital projects for the design, construction and operation of buildings and support services. Since 1992 over 50 NHS schemes in England alone have been approved, with a total capital value of £500 million. Plans are in progress for a further 40 major schemes, costing over £1,500 million, for a new generation of NHS hospitals designed, built and maintained by the private sector.

Schemes already announced include a £50 million project which will provide a new paediatric wing, a private unit, and a medical science park for research and biotechnology at St James's University Hospital NHS Trust in Leeds, and a new £170 million district general hospital for the Norfolk and Norwich NHS Trust. PFI schemes must have the full support of local health authorities (see p. 402) and other purchasers of clinical services.

The Government considers that the Private Finance Initiative reinforces the principle of health care based on clinical need without regard to the ability to pay, delivering a modern and efficient service, while freeing the NHS to make clinical decisions for patients.

Staffing

The NHS is one of the largest employers in the world, with a workforce of nearly 1 million people. Staff costs account for approximately 64 per cent of current spending on hospitals and community health services. Between 1984 and 1994:

- the number of hospital medical and dental staff in Great Britain rose by 20 per cent to 65,000, while the number of hospital medical consultants grew by 28 per cent to 20,400.
- The number of professional and technical staff in England rose by 27.7 per cent to 92,800.

- The number of nursing and midwifery staff, who make up 46 per cent of the NHS workforce in England, decreased by 11 per cent to 353,100. This reflects the growth in bursaried students under the Project 2000 nurse training scheme—see p. 420. (Project 2000 trainees have full student status and are not NHS employees.) The change masks an underlying trend of an increase of 5 per cent in the number of qualified nursing and midwifery staff since 1984.

- The number of general and senior managers has risen in recent years; this reflects the progressive introduction of management posts in a series of phased stages since 1986. In England general and senior managers numbered 23,000 in 1994, accounting for 3 per cent of the total NHS workforce and 4.4 per cent of total NHS spending on salaries and wages; in Scotland general and senior managers numbered 1,720 in 1994, just over 1.5 per cent of the total workforce.

- The sharp falls in the numbers of directly employed ancillary staff and of maintenance and works staff reflect the continuing effect of competitive tendering (see p. 78). Many of these jobs are now carried out by the private sector.

The Government's aim throughout the service is progressively to introduce greater pay flexibility to allow managers to relate pay to local markets and reward individual performance. A number of measures are being taken to provide a more effective workforce through better management development, education and training (see p. 419).

Health Service Commissioners

Health Service Commissioners (one each for England, Scotland and Wales) are responsible for dealing with complaints from members of the public about health service bodies. The three posts are at present held by one person (with a staff of 80), who is also Parliamentary Commissioner for Administration (Ombudsman—see p. 63). As Health Service Commissioner, he reports annually to Parliament. In Northern Ireland the

Commissioner for Complaints has a similar role.

The Health Service Commissioner can investigate complaints that a person has suffered injustice or hardship as a result of:

- a failure in a service provided by a health service body;
- a failure to provide a service which the patient was entitled to receive; or
- maladministration by an NHS authority—that is, something that the NHS authority failed to do or did in the wrong way.

Complaints must be sent to the Ombudsman in writing, and the health service body concerned should first have been given a reasonable opportunity to respond.

New NHS Complaints System

Legislation passed in April 1996 extends the Health Service Ombudsman's jurisdiction to include complaints against all family health service practitioners and their staff, and about the exercise of clinical judgment.

Following an independent review of NHS complaints procedures, the Government introduced a new complaints system in Britain in April 1996. Under this, complaints about all NHS-funded services are dealt with in a similar fashion at two distinct levels. The new procedures aim to resolve complaints speedily at a *local level*; where complainants are dissatisfied with the response at local level, a new system of *review by an independent panel* is an option.

Patients can refer complaints to the Health Service Ombudsman if they are dissatisfied with the response from the NHS.

FAMILY HEALTH SERVICES

The family health services are those given to patients by doctors (GPs), dentists, opticians and pharmacists of their own choice. They remain the first point of contact most people have with the NHS. Every year there are about 250 million consultations with GPs and about 6 million people visit a pharmacy every day. Often those who visit their GP or dentist need no clinical treatment but healthy lifestyle counselling and preventive health care advice instead. The Government's longstanding policy has been to build up and extend these services in order to improve health and relieve pressure on the far more costly secondary care sector (that is, hospital and specialist services).

GPs provide the first diagnosis in the case of illness, give advice and may prescribe a suitable course of treatment or refer a patient to the more specialised services and hospital consultants. About four-fifths of GPs in Britain work in partnerships or group practices. Primary health-care teams also include health visitors and district nurses, midwives, and sometimes social workers and other professional staff employed by the health authorities. Most GPs in Great Britain and about 50 per cent in Northern Ireland work in health centres. As well as providing medical and nursing services, health centres may also have facilities for health education, family planning, speech therapy, chiropody, assessment of hearing, physiotherapy and remedial exercises. Dental, pharmaceutical and ophthalmic services, hospital out-patient and supporting social work services may also be provided.

There have been substantial increases in primary health care staff in recent years. For example, between 1985 and 1995 the number of GPs in England increased by 11.1 per cent (to over 26,500); and average patient list size fell by 8.8 per cent (to just under 1,900). The wholetime equivalent number of GP practice nurses increased fourfold—to 9,100—and the number of opticians increased by over 14.9 per cent (to 6,778).

Special funds have been earmarked by the Government for improving the quality of primary health care in some inner city areas.

Ethnic Minority Health

Efforts have also been made to improve health services for ethnic minority communities. The NHS Ethnic Health Unit was set up in 1994 for three years to work with health authorities,

NHS Trusts and GPs to ensure that people from different ethnic backgrounds derive full benefit from the *Health of the Nation* strategy (see p. 399), local health purchasing policies, the Patient's Charter (see p. 398), the Care in the Community initiatives and the developing role of primary care. The Unit has achieved this through a number of initiatives and project funding, which aim to give local people a greater say in shaping health services over the three years. Funding of over £2.5 million has supported local initiatives, including those in primary health care, in more than half of the health authorities in England.

Recent Developments

GP Fundholders

In England and Northern Ireland GP practices with 5,000 patients or more may apply for fundholding status. The corresponding figure in Wales and Scotland is 4,000. This is a voluntary scheme which gives larger medical practices the opportunity to manage NHS money for the benefit of their patients. It aims to improve services for patients and enable GPs to explore more innovative methods of providing health care. GP fundholders are responsible for part of their own NHS budgets, enabling them to buy certain non-urgent hospital services. NHS costs of prescription charges and part of the cost of running the practice are also covered. Fundholders may negotiate for services directly with hospitals from both public and private sectors in any health authority or health board in Britain. GP fundholders may buy NHS community nursing services for their patients, including district nursing and health visiting services and (except in Northern Ireland) community psychiatric and community mental handicap nursing.

A new option—community fundholding—has been introduced for small practices or as a stepping stone for larger ones who are not yet ready to become standard fundholders. (In England only there is a minimum list size requirement of 3,000 patients.) By April 1996 some 14,000 GPs in almost 3,300 practices in Britain had become fundholders, covering 47 per cent of the population.

Contracts

The performance-related contract for GPs, introduced in 1990, is designed to raise standards of care, extend the range of services available to patients and improve patient choice. The changes are intended to make it easier for patients to see their GP at times convenient to them; or to change doctors; and to encourage doctors to practise more preventive medicine.

The contract for dentists, introduced in 1990, aims at improving care and providing more information to patients about general dental services. As a result NHS dental care now includes preventive care as well as restorative treatment. All adults and children have a period of continuing care following treatment. There are also incentives for dentists to undertake further training and to move to areas which are less well served.

Recent improvements to the contract for NHS dentists include reinforcing the priority given to children's oral health by introducing fees for individual items of treatment in addition to the monthly capitation payment made to dentists for each child registered.

In the longer term the Government plans to introduce a system of local contracting by health authorities for primary care dentistry. This will be similar to the system operating in other areas of the health service.

GP/Health Authority Links

Electronic links between GPs and health authorities are replacing paper-based systems with the interchange of electronic data. The main benefits are: speedier processing of claims; faster transfer of patient medical records; reduced clerical effort; and the elimination of the risk of losing paperwork in transit.

Community Pharmacists

The Government has funded a number of initiatives aimed at raising standards within pharmacies and making fuller use of pharmacists' skills. These include the development of a comprehensive programme of continuing education and training, and a number of audit initiatives to promote community pharmacists' participation in clinical audit (see below).

Since 1992–93 additional funding has been made available to encourage participation by pharmacists in local needle exchange schemes for drug misusers and in the safe disposal of unwanted medicines. Around £1 million was made available in 1995–96 for local projects to examine the contribution community pharmacists can make to improving the quality and cost effectiveness of GP prescribing.

At the local level a large number of health authorities have involved pharmacists in a range of service developments. These include participation in health promotion campaigns and in home visits.

Midwives, Health Visitors and District Nurses

Midwives provide care and support to women throughout pregnancy, birth and the postnatal period (up to 28 days after the baby is born). Midwives work in both hospital and community settings.

Under a number of pilot schemes in England and Scotland district nurses and health visitors are able to prescribe from a limited list of drugs and medical appliances. These schemes are based in GP fundholding practices and are intended to reduce significantly the time patients have to wait for relief of their symptoms.

Health visitors are responsible for the preventive care and health promotion of families, particularly those with young children. They have a public health role, identifying local health needs and working closely with GPs, district nurses and other professions. District nurses give skilled nursing care to people at home or elsewhere outside hospital; they also play an important role in health promotion and education.

HOSPITAL AND SPECIALIST SERVICES

District general hospitals offer a broad range of clinical specialities, supported by a range of other services such as anaesthetics, pathology and radiology. Almost all have facilities for the admission of emergency patients, either through Accident and Emergency Departments or as direct referrals from GPs. Treatments are provided for in-patients, day cases, out-patients and patients who attend wards for treatment such as dialysis. In England some hospitals also provide specialist services which cover more than one regional district. These are known as supra-regional or supra-district services covering, for example, heart and liver transplants, and craniofacial services and rare eye and bone cancers. (In Scotland similar services are contracted for centrally.) There are also specialist hospitals such as the world-famous Hospital for Sick Children at Great Ormond Street, Moorfields Eye Hospital, and the National Hospital for Neurology and Neurosurgery, all in London. These hospitals combine specialist treatment facilities with the training of medical and other students, and international research.

Many of the hospitals in the NHS were built in the 19th century; some trace their origins to much earlier charitable foundations. Much has been done to improve and extend existing hospital buildings and many new hospitals have been or are being opened. Recent policy has been to provide a balanced hospital service centred around a district general hospital, complemented as necessary by smaller, locally based hospitals and facilities.

The hospital service is now treating more patients a year than ever before. In England between 1990–91 and 1994–95 the total number of operations rose by 29 per cent to nearly 5.8 million, with heart bypass operations up by 70 per cent to 22,000. Over the same period, the number of hip operations rose by 26 per cent to over 62,000, and eye lens operations went up by 54 per cent to 152,000.

Waiting Times

Over the last few years there have been substantial reductions in the number of patients waiting more than 12 months for in-patient or day case treatment. In March 1996:

- fewer than 5,000 patients in England had been waiting over a year for hospital treatment, compared with more than 200,000 in 1990. There are now very few patients waiting more than 18 months for treatment.

- the number of patients in Scotland waiting over a year for hospital treatment had fallen to fewer than 150, while nobody had waited for over 18 months.

NHS Trusts

Under the NHS and Community Care Act 1990 hospitals and other health service units (for example, ambulance services and community health services) may apply to become independent of direct local health authority control and establish themselves as self-governing NHS Trusts. Parallel legislation was introduced in Northern Ireland to create Health and Social Services Trusts, which, because of the integrated nature of the service there, carry a much wider workload than their counterparts in Great Britain. The Trusts remain within the NHS, accountable to the appropriate Secretary of State and finally to Parliament. Trusts are required to publish their business plans and annual reports and accounts, and to hold at least one public meeting a year. Since September 1995 all annual reports have been required to provide information about management costs.

Each Trust is run by a board of directors. Trusts are free to employ their own staff and set their own rates of pay, although staff transferring to Trust employment retain their existing terms and conditions of service. Trusts are also free to carry out research and provide facilities for medical education and other forms of training. They derive their income mainly from NHS contracts to provide services to health authorities and GP fundholders. They may treat private patients to generate income provided this does not interfere with NHS obligations. By mid-1996 over 520 Trusts in Britain were delivering almost all NHS hospital and community health services.

Organ Transplantation

The United Kingdom Transplant Support Service Authority provides a centralised organ matching and allocation service. During 1995, 1,802 kidney transplants were performed. A similar service exists for corneas and, in 1995, 2,424 were transplanted. By 1996 there were 15,000 kidney transplant patients alive in Britain, more than in any other European country.

Heart transplant operations have been conducted at Papworth Hospital in Cambridgeshire and Harefield Hospital in London since 1979. There are six other designated heart transplant centres in England, and one in Scotland. Programmes for lung and combined heart and lung transplantation are in progress and in 1995, 319 heart, 113 lung, and 58 heart/lung transplants were performed. The world's first combined heart, lungs and liver transplant operation was carried out at Papworth in 1987. There are six designated liver transplant units in England and one in Scotland. In 1995, 669 liver transplants were performed.

> A voluntary organ donor card system enables people to indicate their willingness to become organ donors in the event of their death. The NHS Organ Donor Register, a computer database, was launched in 1994. By October 1996 it contained over 3.5 million names.

Commercial dealing in organs for transplantation is illegal.

Blood Transfusion Services

Blood transfusion services are run by the National Blood Authority in England, the Scottish National Blood Transfusion Service, the Welsh Health Common Services Agency in Wales and the Northern Ireland Blood Transfusion Agency. Britain is self-sufficient in blood and blood products.

In England alone around 2.4 million donations are given each year by voluntary unpaid donors and separated into many different life-saving products for patients. Red cells, platelets and other products with a limited 'shelf life' are prepared at blood centres. The production of plasma products is undertaken at the Bio Products Laboratory in Elstree (Hertfordshire) and the Protein Fractionation Centre in Edinburgh.

Each of the four national bodies co-ordinates programmes for donor recruitment, retention and education, and donor sessions are organised regionally, in towns, villages and workplaces. Donors are normally aged between 18 (17 in Scotland) and 65. Blood centres are responsible for blood collection, screening, processing and supplying hospital blood banks. They also provide wide-ranging laboratory, clinical, research, teaching and advisory services and facilities. These are subject to nationally co-ordinated quality audit programmes.

Ambulance and Patient Transport Services

NHS emergency ambulances are available free of charge for cases of sudden illness or collapse, for accidents and for doctors' urgent calls. Rapid response services, in which paramedics use cars and motor cycles to reach emergency cases, have been introduced in a number of areas, particularly London and other major cities with areas of high traffic density. Helicopter ambulances serve many parts of England and an integrated air ambulance service is available throughout Scotland.

Non-emergency patient transport services are available free of charge to NHS patients considered by their doctor (or dentist or midwife) to be medically unfit to travel by other means. The principle applied is that each patient should be able to reach hospital in a reasonable time and in reasonable comfort, without detriment to his or her medical condition. In many areas the ambulance service organises volunteer drivers to provide a hospital car service for non-urgent patients.

Patients in families whose heads are on Income Support or Disability Working Allowance automatically have their travelling expenses to hospital reimbursed. People on low incomes may also be eligible.

Rehabilitation

Rehabilitation services are available for elderly, young, and mentally ill people, and for those with physical or learning disabilities who need such help to resume life in the community. These services are offered in hospitals, centres in the community and in people's own homes through co-ordinated work by a range of professionals.

Medical services may provide free artificial limbs and eyes, hearing aids, surgical supports, wheelchairs, and other appliances. Following assessment, very severely physically disabled patients may be provided with environmental control equipment which enables them to operate devices such as alarm bells, radios and televisions, telephones, and heating appliances. Nursing equipment may be provided on loan for use in the home.

Local authorities may provide a range of facilities to help patients in the transition from hospital to their own homes. These include the provision of equipment; help with cleaning, shopping and cooking; care from domestic help workers; and professional help from occupational therapists and social workers. Voluntary organisations also provide services, complementing the work of the statutory agencies and widening the range of services.

Hospices

A number of hospices provide care for terminally ill people (including children), either directly in in-patient or day-care units or through nursing and other assistance in the patient's own home. Control of symptoms and psychological support for patients and their families form central features of the modern hospice movement, which started in Britain in 1967 and is now worldwide. Some hospices are administered entirely by the NHS; the rest are run by independent charities, some receiving support from public funds. The number of voluntary hospices has more than doubled in the past ten years. There are 183 hospices in England and Wales, providing over 2,710 beds; in Scotland 12 independent voluntary hospices provide 173 beds; and in Northern Ireland there are 4 independent hospices providing 63 beds.

The National Council for Hospice and Specialist Palliative Care Services covers England, Wales and Northern Ireland; its Scottish counterpart is the Scottish Partnership Agency for Palliative and Cancer Care.

Private Medical Treatment

The Government's policy is to welcome cost-effective co-operation between the NHS and the independent sector in meeting the nation's health needs. It believes that this will benefit the NHS by adding to the resources devoted to health care and offering flexibility to health authorities in the delivery of services. Some health authorities share expensive facilities and equipment with private hospitals, and NHS patients are sometimes treated (at public expense) in the private sector to reduce waiting lists. The scale of private practice in relation to the NHS is, however, very small.

An estimated three-quarters of those receiving acute treatment in private hospitals or NHS hospital pay-beds are covered by health insurance schemes, which make provision for private health care in return for annual subscriptions. Over 3 million people subscribe to such schemes, half of them within group schemes, some arranged by firms on behalf of employees. Subscriptions often cover more than one person (for example, members of a family); about 12 per cent of the population in Britain is covered by private medical insurance. A survey carried out in 1994 showed that 36 per cent of households with an annual gross income of £26,000 or more had private medical insurance, compared with only 3 per cent of those with an annual gross income of less than £8,000. Those on higher incomes were also more likely to have the majority of the costs of their private medical insurance met by their employer.

Tax relief on private health insurance premiums paid by people aged 60 and over is designed to allow people of retirement age to retain their insurance at a time when premiums increase and their incomes decrease. Provisional figures for 1995–96 show that approximately 550,000 people aged over 60 received this tax relief at the cost of £110 million.

Many overseas patients come to Britain for treatment in private hospitals and clinics, and Harley Street in London is an internationally recognised centre for medical consultancy.

Parents and Children

Special preventive services are provided under the NHS to safeguard the health of pregnant women and of mothers with young children. Services include free dental treatment; health education; and vaccination and immunisation of children against certain infectious diseases (see p. 416).

Since 1994 government policy has been to offer women more choice in maternity care provision and to move towards greater community-based care. A woman is entitled to care throughout her pregnancy, the birth and the postnatal period. Care may be provided by a midwife, a community-based GP, a hospital-based obstetrician, or a combination of these. The birth may take place in a hospital maternity unit, a midwife/GP-led unit, or at home. After the birth, a midwife will visit until the baby is at least ten days old and after that a health visitor's services are available. Throughout her pregnancy and for the first year of her baby's life, a women is entitled to free prescriptions and dental care.

A comprehensive programme of health surveillance is provided for pre-school children in clinics run by the community health authorities, and increasingly by GPs. This enables doctors, dentists and health visitors to oversee the physical and mental health and development of pre-school children. Information on preventive services is given and in some clinics welfare foods are distributed. The school health service offers health care and advice for schoolchildren, including medical and dental inspection and treatment where necessary.

Child guidance and child psychiatric services provide help and advice to families and children with psychological or emotional problems.

In recent years special efforts have been made to improve co-operation between the community-based child health services and local authority social services for children. This is particularly important in the prevention of child abuse and for the health and welfare of children in care (see p. 427).

Human Fertilisation and Embryology

The world's first 'test-tube baby' was born in Britain in 1978, as a result of the technique of *in vitro* fertilisation. This opened up new horizons for helping with problems of infertility and for the science of embryology. The social, ethical and legal implications were examined by a committee of inquiry under Baroness Warnock (1984) and led eventually to the passage of the Human Fertilisation and Embryology Act 1990, one of the most comprehensive pieces of legislation on assisted reproduction and embryo research in the world.

This Act set up the Human Fertilisation and Embryology Authority (HFEA) to license and control centres providing certain infertility treatments, undertaking human embryo research or storing gametes or embryos. The HFEA maintains a code of practice giving guidance about licensed centres, and reports annually to Parliament.

Legislation was passed in 1996 to extend from 5 to 10 years the storage period for human embryos. The use of fetal ovarian tissue in fertility treatment was banned in 1994. Commercial surrogacy agencies and advertising of, or for, surrogacy services are also prohibited.

Family Planning

Free family planning advice and treatment is available from GPs or from family planning clinics. Clinics are also able to provide condoms free of charge. The *Health of the Nation* White Paper contains the objective of ensuring the provision of effective family planning services for those who want them.

Abortion

Under the Abortion Act 1967, as amended, a time limit of 24 weeks applies to the largest category of abortion—risk to the physical or mental health of the pregnant woman—and also abortion for similar risk to any existing children of her family. There are three categories in which no time limit applies: to prevent grave permanent injury to the physical or mental health of the woman; where there is a substantial risk of serious fetal handicap; or where continuing the pregnancy would involve a risk to the life of the pregnant woman greater than if the pregnancy were terminated. The Act does not apply in Northern Ireland.

In 1994:

- the number of legal abortions in England and Wales fell by 1.1 per cent to 166,876 compared with 168,714 in 1993—the fourth successive annual decrease;

- just over 4 million abortions were carried out in England and Wales between the introduction of the Abortion Act in 1968 and the end of 1994, of which 83 per cent were carried out on resident women;

- nearly 89 per cent of abortions on resident women were performed at less than 13 weeks gestation, compared with 75 per cent in 1971.

Drug Misuse

The misuse of drugs, such as heroin, cocaine and amphetamines, is a serious social and health problem, and the Government has made the fight against such misuse a major priority. (See p. 86 for details of the Government's comprehensive drugs strategy for 1995–98).

Research on various aspects of drug misuse is funded by several government departments. The Government is advised on matters relating to drug misuse and connected social problems by the Advisory Council on the Misuse of Drugs (in Scotland the Scottish Advisory Committee on Drug Misuse).

Prevention

The Government has run national mass media publicity campaigns since 1985 to persuade young people not to take drugs, and to advise parents, teachers and other professionals on how to recognise and combat the problem. Since 1991–92 the focus has changed to give greater emphasis to locally-based campaigns and includes work on solvent misuse. In late

1995 the Department of Health launched a £5 million–a–year publicity campaign, to run for three years. This aims to increase public awareness of the risks of drug taking.

The Home Office Drugs Prevention Initiative provides funding for local drugs prevention teams in 12 areas in England. The teams aim to strengthen community resistance to drug misuse by supporting a wide range of drugs prevention activities. Since the Initiative began in 1990 some 1,800 projects have been supported. The 1996–97 budget for the Initiative is £5.9 million and funding will continue until March 1999. The main objective will be to assess the outcomes of the various community-based approaches to drugs prevention.

The Government makes funds available through local education authorities in England and Wales to provide in-service training for teachers involved in drug-prevention work in schools. As part of the National Curriculum in England and Wales (see p. 451), children in primary and secondary schools receive education on the dangers of drug misuse. A circular on drug prevention and schools, containing guidance to help schools provide effective drug education programmes, was launched in 1995.

Separate measures have been introduced in Scotland to discourage drug misuse through publicity campaigns and action in the education service and the community. Some £1 million has been made available to the Scotland Against Drugs Campaign, launched in May 1996. This aims to attract support at a local level in tackling the drugs misuse problem in Scotland.

National Drugs Helpline

A national drugs and solvents telephone helpline provides a 24-hour free confidential advice, counselling and information service throughout Britain to anyone concerned about the health implications of drugs or solvent misuse.

Treatment and Rehabilitation

Treatment for drug dependence includes: residential detoxification and rehabilitation; community drug dependency services; needle and syringe exchange schemes to combat the spread of HIV/AIDS and other blood-borne infections; advice and counselling; and after-care and support services. Facilities are provided by both statutory and independent agencies.

A task force set up to review the effectiveness of treatment services for drug misusers in England reported in May 1996. It recommended that:

- services which are a first point of contact for drug misusers should offer basic health checks;

- the process of 'shared care' with appropriate support for GPs should be made available as widely as possible;

- steps should be taken to ensure drug misusers who inject or are at risk of injecting have better access to Hepatitis B vaccinations; and

- counselling and support services should be recognised as core components of drug treatment and not as subsidiary to other treatments.

The total amount available to health authorities in England for drug treatment services in 1996–97 is over £27.5 million. An additional £6 million is being made available to improve services for young people and to develop methadone programmes. In addition, a grant is payable each year to local authorities to enable them to support voluntary organisations providing services to drug and alcohol misusers. In Scotland, £24.5 million is being made available in 1996–97 for the support of drug misuse/ HIV/AIDS services.

An increasing number of GPs treat drug misusers, but only a limited number of doctors are licensed to prescribe certain controlled drugs such as heroin and cocaine to drug misusers. (However, any doctor may prescribe these drugs for the treatment of organic injury or disease, and any doctor can prescribe methadone as a substitute drug for drug misusers.) All doctors must notify the authorities of any patient they consider to be addicted to certain controlled drugs, and guidelines on good medical practice in the treatment of drug misuse have been issued to doctors.

Other Services

A number of non-statutory agencies work with, and complement, health service provision. Advice and rehabilitation services, including residential facilities, for example, are provided by many voluntary organisations. Support in the community is provided by the probation service and local social services departments (social work departments in Scotland). In April 1996 the Government announced grants totalling £1 million for voluntary organisations which help drug misusers.

Solvent Misuse

Government policy aims to prevent solvent misuse through educating young people, parents and professionals and, where practicable, restricting the sales of solvent-based liquefied gas and aerosol products to young people. National television and press publicity campaigns, targeted at parents, were run in 1992 and 1994.

In England, Wales and Northern Ireland it is an offence to supply such substances to children under 18 if the supplier knows or has reason to believe they are to be used to induce intoxication. In Scotland proceedings can be taken under the common law.

The Department of Health funds a hospital-based unit in London to collect and publish annually the mortality statistics associated with solvent misuse. The statistics for 1994 show the number of deaths having fallen to 57, the lowest figure for 13 years.

Alcohol Misuse

Alcohol is consumed by over 90 per cent of the adult population. It is estimated that about 7.8 million people over 16 in England and Wales (26 per cent of men and 11 per cent of women) drink more than the currently recommended sensible levels and that 1.5 million people drink at a dangerous level. An estimated 9 million working days each year are lost through alcohol-related absence. The costs of

alcohol misuse to the NHS have been estimated (at 1990 prices) at £149 million a year, and the total annual cost to society at £2,500 million.

The Government recognises the harm that results from the misuse of alcohol; its approach is to encourage people who wish to drink to confine their drinking to sensible levels and to appropriate occasions. It considers that education about sensible drinking helps individuals to make informed choices about their drinking. It seeks to tackle alcohol-related problems through a co-ordinated programme of action across government departments, and involving health and local authorities, the independent sector, employers and the alcohol industry.

In reports published in 1986 and 1987 the British medical profession advised that sustained drinking above 21 units of alcohol a week by men and 14 units a week by women progressively increased the risk to health.[1] The Government incorporated this advice in the *Health of the Nation* targets relating to alcohol. However, in 1996 the government body set up to review the sensible drinking message in the light of the latest scientific and medical research issued its first report, which recommended a small increase in the present recommended levels. The report:

- cited evidence that drinking one or two units of alcohol a day gives a significant health benefit in reducing the risk of coronary heart disease for men over 40 and post-menopausal women;

- concluded that men who drink more than 3 to 4 units a day and women who drink more than 2 to 3 units a day run an increasingly significant risk of illness and death from a number of conditions, including stroke, some cancers, accidents and hypertension.

As a result the Government is to reappraise the place of alcohol in the *Health of the Nation* strategy and is to commission a new health

---

[1] A unit is 8 grammes of pure alcohol: roughly equivalent to half a pint of ordinary strength beer or lager, or a glass of wine, or—in England, Scotland and Wales—a pub measure of spirits. (In Northern Ireland a pub measure of spirits is bigger than in the rest of Britain and is measured as one and a half units.)

promotion campaign based on the report's findings.

Part of the funds of the Health Education Authority (see p. 417) are for promoting the sensible drinking message in England, and equivalent bodies are similarly funded in other parts of Britain. At a local level this requires co-ordinated action by a wide range of organisations with an interest in the use or misuse of alcohol.

Treatment and rehabilitation within the NHS include in-patient and out-patient services in general and psychiatric hospitals and specialised alcoholism treatment units. Primary care teams (GPs, community psychiatric nurses and social workers) and voluntary organisations providing treatment and rehabilitation in hostels, day centres and advisory services also play an important role.

The development of services to help problem drinkers and their families is being taken forward within the framework of community care. Local authorities are required to identify the need for alcohol misuse services in their area, and to list the services provided in their community care plans (see p. 422). They are then responsible for arranging for the needs of individuals with alcohol problems to be assessed, and for buying an appropriate course of care.

There is close co-operation between statutory and voluntary organisations. In England the voluntary agency Alcohol Concern plays a prominent role in improving services for problem drinkers and their families; increasing public awareness of alcohol misuse and harm-free drinking; and improving training for professional and voluntary workers.

Between 1990–91 and 1997–98 a total government contribution of £9 million is being allocated to Alcohol Concern for improving and extending the network of care, advisory and counselling services. In addition, a grant of £2.5 million is being paid to local authorities during 1996–97 to help voluntary agencies improve and extend provision for alcohol and drug misusers in England. The Scottish Council on Alcohol undertakes similar work in Scotland, with the help of a government grant (£150,000 in 1996–97). Research and surveys on various aspects of alcohol misuse are funded by several government departments.

Smoking

Cigarette smoking is the greatest preventable cause of illness and death in Britain. It is associated with around 110,000 premature deaths and an estimated 50 million lost working days each year, and costs the NHS an estimated £610 million a year for the treatment of related diseases (for example, heart disease, lung cancer and bronchitis). In Scotland alone, for example, over 10,600 people die each year as a result of their smoking—that is, one in six of all deaths in Scotland. In addition, smoking by pregnant women is associated with low birth weight in infants. The Government's health education policy is supported by voluntary agreements with the tobacco industry (see below) aimed at reducing the level of smoking.

The Government aims to reduce smoking in England from the present 30 per cent of adults to 20 per cent by the year 2000. Smoking is also being tackled as a priority in Wales, Scotland and Northern Ireland and similar targets have been set.

A three-year national campaign in England, aimed at adult smokers and costing a total of £13.5 million a year, started in 1994. A new three-year education campaign for teenagers will be commissioned later in 1996. Education on the harmful effects of smoking is included in the National Curriculum for all pupils in publicly maintained schools in England and Wales. In Scotland the Health Education Board for Scotland (see p. 417) operates a free telephone helpline, 'Smokeline', which has received over 329,500 calls since 1992 and has been successful in helping a large number of people to stop smoking. The Board is spending some £588,000 on smoking initiatives in 1996–97.

The Government also supports the work of the voluntary organisation Action on Smoking and Health (ASH), whose services include a workplace services consultancy, offering advice and help to employers in formulating anti-smoking policies. The Government is committed to creating a smoke-free environment, with facilities where appropriate for those who wish to smoke, and has published a code of practice on smoking in public places. Health authorities have been asked to promote non-smoking as the normal practice in health service buildings and to give help and advice to people who want to give up smoking. It is estimated that passive smoking may cause a number of deaths through lung cancer every year.

The Tobacco Control Alliance, founded in 1994 and supported by over 40 organisations, calls for a concerted effort to eliminate tobacco use in Britain, to create an environment where children are relieved of the pressure to start smoking, and to encourage and help smokers to stop.

A new agreement with the tobacco industry on the use of additives is to be introduced.

Tobacco Advertising and Promotion Controls

All tobacco advertising is banned on television, and cigarette advertisements are banned on radio. Other forms of advertising and promotion of tobacco products are regulated by two voluntary agreements between the Government and the tobacco industry.

- The first agreement bans tobacco advertising in cinemas and in young women's magazines. It also prohibits outdoor poster advertising within 200 metres of schools; places an upper limit on poster advertising expenditure; and requires the tobacco industry to remove all permanent shopfront advertising by the end of 1996. It also requires that government health warnings appear on all tobacco advertising, alerting the consumer to the risks associated with smoking.

- The voluntary agreement on sports sponsorship covers levels of spending, restrictions on sponsorship of events chiefly for spectators under 18 years, and controls over the siting of advertising at televised events.

The health warnings which appear on packets of tobacco products are governed by law and not by voluntary agreement. Packets of cigarettes and rolling tobacco must carry one of the following warnings:

- Smoking kills.

- Smoking causes heart disease.
- Smoking causes fatal diseases.
- Smoking causes cancer.
- Smoking when pregnant harms your baby.
- Protect children: don't make them breathe your smoke.

All tobacco products must also carry the warning 'tobacco seriously damages health'.

AIDS

Up to the end of June 1996 a total of 12,976 cases of AIDS had been reported in Britain, of whom 9,148 (70 per cent) had died; the total number of recognised HIV infections was 27,088. The latest projections (published in January 1996) show that new cases of AIDS among homosexual and bisexual men are expected to fall from the 1994 level, but that new cases of AIDS from heterosexual contact are expected to increase. Levels among intravenous drug users are now low, but there may be a slight increase among this group. The total number of people with AIDS and HIV infections at the end of each year is expected to increase to reach more than 8,000 by the end of 1999.

Government Strategy

Key elements of the Government's strategy include:

- encouraging appropriate behaviour change by increased targeting of sections of the population at particular risk, including homosexual and bisexual men and drug misusers;

- sustaining and improving general public awareness;

- continuing to make HIV testing facilities more widely known, and encouraging health authorities to commission additional accessible HIV testing sites; and

- continued funding for the voluntary sector.

The Government's commitment to policies in this area is demonstrated by its inclusion of

HIV/AIDS with sexual health as one of the five key areas in the *Health of the Nation* White Paper. HIV/AIDS has also been identified as a health priority in Scotland. A concerted approach is being maintained, spanning government, the NHS, local authorities and the voluntary sector (including women's groups, religious communities and organisations working with ethnic minorities).

In England NHS funding for HIV/AIDS and drug-related services amounted to £270 million in 1996–97, and local authority funding amounted to £13.7 million. In Scotland a record £25 million has been made available to health boards for HIV/AIDS and drug misuse in 1996–97, in addition to their general allocations for HIV/AIDS-related purposes. Within local authority grant-aided expenditure around £1.3 million has been identified for AIDS-related work. Details of Britain's contribution to international co-operation on AIDS are given in Chapter 9.

Voluntary Organisations

Voluntary agencies concerned with HIV/AIDS include the Terrence Higgins Trust, London Lighthouse, Body Positive and the National AIDS Trust. Both London Lighthouse and the Mildmay Mission Hospital, in London, provide hospice care and community support. The Government will continue distributing grants on a yearly basis, taking into account developing health priorities and the ability of voluntary bodies to raise funds from other sources for HIV/AIDS work.

Infectious Diseases

Health authorities/health boards carry out programmes of immunisation against diphtheria, measles, mumps, rubella, poliomyelitis, tetanus, tuberculosis and whooping cough. Immunisation is voluntary, but parents are encouraged to protect their children. The proportion of children being vaccinated has been increasing since 1978. GPs who achieve targets of 70 and 90 per cent uptake of child immunisation receive special payments.

A £20 million nationwide campaign to immunise all children between 5–16 (5–18 in Scotland and Northern Ireland) with measles and rubella vaccine was launched in 1994—the largest immunisation campaign yet mounted in Britain.

A new immunisation, 'Hib', was introduced in 1992, offering protection against invasive haemophilus disease, a major cause of meningitis in children under five years. As a result, notifications of Hib infections in England and Wales fell by 87 per cent between October–December 1992 and October–December 1993.

The Public Health Laboratory Service aims to protect the population from infection through the detection, diagnosis, surveillance, prevention and control of communicable diseases in England and Wales. Similar facilities are provided in Scotland by the Scottish Centre for Infection and Environmental Health and, in Northern Ireland, by some hospital laboratories.

In response to the worldwide resurgence of TB (tuberculosis) in recent years, the Government has set up a working group to consider policies for TB control.

Cancer Care

Controlling cancer forms an enormous part of the NHS's work, consuming nearly 10 per cent of its total budget. In 1995 the Government outlined proposals for reorganising the provision of cancer services in England and Wales. It proposes care at three levels:

- *primary care*, with detailed discussions between GPs and the hospital service to clarify patterns of referral and follow-up;
- *designated cancer units*, which will be created in many district hospitals and will be large enough to support multi-disciplinary clinical teams, with sufficient expertise and facilities to manage the more common cancers; and
- *designated cancer centres*, which will treat less common cancers, as well as providing more specialised treatments that are too technically demanding, or require too much specialised equipment to be provided for the cancer units.

The reduction of deaths and illness from cancer is a key area in the Government's *Health of the Nation* White Paper. The targets set are:

- to reduce breast cancer deaths among women invited for screening by at least 25 per cent by the year 2000;
- to reduce the incidence of invasive cervical cancer by at least 20 per cent by the year 2000;
- to halt the year-on-year increase in the incidence of skin cancer by 2005; and
- to reduce the death rate for lung cancer under the age of 75 by at least 30 per cent in men and by at least 15 per cent in women by 2010.

Cancer Screening

Breast cancer is recognised as a major health problem in Britain. In England and Wales some 13,000 women die from it each year and 1 in 12 women in England will develop it. Britain was the first country in the European Union to introduce a nationwide breast screening programme, under which women aged between 50 and 64 are invited for mammography (breast X-ray) every three years by computerised call and recall systems.

The nationwide cervical screening programme aims to reduce death from cancer of the cervix by inviting women aged between 20 and 64 (20 and 60 in Scotland) to take a free smear test at least every five years. Health authorities must ensure that the results of a smear test are returned from the laboratory to the patient within a month.

Special payments are made to GPs who achieve targets of 50 and 80 per cent for the uptake of smear tests. The Government estimates that over 98 per cent of GPs now earn bonus payments for meeting cervical screening targets.

Deaths from cervical cancer in England and Wales have fallen since the programme began, dropping from 1,942 in 1988 to 1,369 in 1994.

Health Education

Responsibility for health education in Britain lies with four separate health education authorities, which work alongside the national health departments. All four authorities form part of the NHS. They are the Health Education Authority; Health Promotion Wales; The Health Education Board for Scotland; and the Health Promotion Agency for Northern Ireland. All have broadly similar responsibilities. Their aims are:

- to provide information and advice about health directly to members of the public;
- to support other organisations and health professionals who provide health education to members of the public; and
- to advise the Government on health education.

In addition, the Health Education Authority has the major executive responsibility for public education in Britain about AIDS. It also assists in the provision of training for HIV/AIDS workers, and provides a national centre of information and advice on health education. Major campaigns carried out by the health education authorities include those focusing on coronary heart disease, cancer, smoking and alcohol misuse.

Almost all NHS health authorities/health boards have their own health education service, which works closely with health professionals, health visitors, community groups, local employers and others to determine the most suitable local programmes. Increased resources in the health service are being directed towards health education and preventive measures. GPs receive special payments for health promotion programmes.

Healthier Eating

There has been growing public awareness in recent years of the importance of a healthy diet. Medical research has shown that a diet which is low in fats, especially saturates, and rich in fruits, vegetables and starchy foods contributes to good health and can reduce the risk of certain serious illnesses, such as coronary heart disease and stroke.

The *Health of the Nation* White Paper followed the recommendations of the Committee on the Medical Aspects of Food and Nutrition Policy (COMA) that people should reduce their average intakes of total fat and saturated fatty acids and avoid obesity in order to reduce cardiovascular disease. It contained dietary targets for reducing these two nutrients and for reducing adult obesity, and the Nutrition Task Force was established in 1992 to devise a programme to achieve them. The programme was implemented through a number of project teams in information and education, catering, the NHS and the food chain. The Task Force published its final report in April 1996.

In July 1996 the Scottish Diet Action Group published an action plan designed to deliver, over 10 years, the changes recommended in a 1993 working party report on the improvements required in the Scottish diet. The plan highlights the steps that the food industry and other interests can take voluntarily to improve the Scottish diet. The Food and Nutrition Strategy Group is developing a plan for Northern Ireland.

Nutritional labelling indicating the energy, fat, protein and carbohydrate content of food is being encouraged on a voluntary basis. The major supermarket chains and most food manufacturers have already introduced voluntary labelling schemes. Nutrition labelling is compulsory on products for which a nutritional claim is made. The food industry is exploring ways of making the labelling information easier to understand.

ENVIRONMENTAL HEALTH

In Britain there is no single government department responsible for environmental health as a whole, although the Department of Health advises other government departments on the health implications of their policies. The role of central government departments includes the formulation of policy, drafting and processing of legislation on environmental health services, provision of guidance on the legislation, and, in some areas, enforcement. Environmental health services are mainly operated at local level through regional and district local government units.

Professionally trained environmental health officers are mainly employed by district councils. They are concerned with inspection, health education and regulation.

In Northern Ireland district councils are responsible for noise control; collection and disposal of refuse; clean air; and food composition, labelling and hygiene.

The Institute for Environment and Health, a public body established by the Medical Research Council (see below) in 1993, is concerned mainly with the chemical hazards to which people may be exposed through the environment. In Scotland the Scottish Centre for Infection and Environmental Health provides surveillance and advisory services on environmental health matters.

Safety of Food

Under the Food Safety Act 1990 it is illegal to supply food unfit for human consumption or falsely or misleadingly labelled. Treatments or processes must not make food harmful to health. Places where food or drink is prepared, handled, stored or sold must comply with hygiene provisions. Local authorities enforce food law and environmental health officers may take away for examination samples of food sold for human consumption. Specific regulations lay down hygiene requirements for milk and milk products, meat and meat products, eggs, fish products and shellfish, and cover labelling, composition, additives and contaminants. The Department of Health and the Ministry of Agriculture, Fisheries and Food, along with their counterparts in Scotland and Northern Ireland, are concerned with the safety and quality of Britain's food. Departments work closely with industry, local environmental health and trading standards departments and consumer bodies to help ensure protection of public health.

CJD and Public Health

In March 1996 a government scientific advisory committee announced the discovery of a new variant of CJD (Creutzfeldt-Jakob disease), an extremely rare spongiform encephalopathy in humans. The Committee concluded that the most likely explanation, in the absence of any credible alternative, is that these cases are linked to exposure to the cattle disease BSE (bovine spongiform encephalopathy) through the eating of bovine products, which may have been contaminated by BSE-infected brain and spinal cord before the introduction of the ban on specified bovine offals in 1989.

While there remains no unequivocal scientific evidence that CJD is linked to BSE, the Government is providing additional funding for research into CJD and BSE, including for that carried out at the national CJD Surveillance Unit in Edinburgh, which monitors the incidence of the disease.

See Chapter 18 for details of government measures to control the spread of BSE.

SAFETY OF MEDICINES

Only medicines that have been granted a product licence may be sold or supplied to the public. Licences are issued following scientific assessment by the Medicines Control Agency of the Department of Health. (The Veterinary Medicines Directorate of the Ministry of Agriculture, Fisheries and Food is similarly responsible for animal medicines.)

A number of committees provide independent advice to Ministers. The Medicines Commission advises on matters connected with the safety of human and veterinary medicines; its duties also include hearing appeals from companies against advice that a product licence should not be granted. The Committee on Safety of Medicines advises on the safety, quality and efficacy of medicinal products for human use and promotes the collection and investigation of information relating to adverse reactions.

RESEARCH

The Department of Health's Research and Development (R&D) strategy comprises two complementary programmes:

- The Policy Research Programme provides a base for the development of policy for the health service, social services and public health. Research is focused on a range of strategic programmes that cover the department's central responsibilities. Priorities are set in relation to the goals, aims and objectives of the Department; the feasibility of research; the likely return

on the investment in research; and the appropriateness and availability of other research budgets.

- The NHS R&D Programme aims to secure a health service in which clinical, managerial and policy decisions are based on sound information about research findings and scientific developments. The setting of priorities is based on widespread consultation. Over 300 studies have been funded in areas including mental health, physical and complex disabilities, and cardiovascular disease and stroke. Health technology assessment, which evaluates new, as well as existing, technologies, is the largest single body of research in the programme.

Two major centres for disseminating and implementing research have been established: the UK Cochrane Centre and the NHS Centre for Reviews and Dissemination.

From April 1998 funding for R&D in the NHS will be provided from a single budget raised by a levy on all purchasers of NHS services.

See Chapter 20 for information on the work of the Medical Research Council (the main government agency for the support of biomedical and clinical research).

THE HEALTH PROFESSIONS

Doctors and Dentists

Only people on the medical or dentists' registers may practise as doctors or dentists in the NHS. University medical and dental schools are responsible for undergraduate teaching; the NHS provides hospital facilities for training. Full registration as a doctor requires five or six years' training in a medical school and hospital, with a further year's experience in a hospital. For a dentist, five years' training at a dental school is required.

An extensive review of specialist medical training was carried out in 1992–93 and plans for implementing its recommendations are in progress. These are expected to have a major impact on the way in which training is carried out in the NHS and on the role and responsibilities of hospital doctors. They will include more intensive and better structured training programmes which, together with the reduction from three to two training grades, will shorten the minimum training time for most hospital specialists. The changes, together with other policies to increase consultant numbers and reduce junior doctors' hours, are expected to increase the amount of service provided to NHS patients by consultants.

The regulating body for the medical profession is the General Medical Council and, for dentists, the General Dental Council. The main professional associations are the British Medical Association and the British Dental Association.

Nurses, Midwives and Health Visitors

There are two routes to registration as a nurse or midwife: either through a higher education diploma or through a degree course.

Most students undertake the pre-registration Diploma in Higher Education (Project 2000) programme, which emphasises health promotion as well care of the sick and enables students to work either in hospitals or in the community. The course lasts three years and consists of periods of college study combined with practical experience in hospitals or in the community. The first half of the course comprises a common foundation programme; the second half comprises one of the following specialist branches: adult nursing, mental health nursing, learning disability nursing, and children's nursing.

Midwifery training for registered general nurses or registered general nurses (adult) takes 18 months, but for others the training lasts three years.

Health visitors are registered general nurses who have completed a course in health visiting. In 1995 new standards were introduced and by 1998 all courses will be at degree rather than at diploma level.

District nurses are registered general nurses who provide care for clients in the community. As with health visitors, new standards were introduced in 1995. By 1998 all courses will be at degree rather than at diploma level. In Northern Ireland health visitors, district nurses and schools nurses, community

psychiatric, community mental handicap and occupational health nurses undertake a one-year diploma course.

The United Kingdom Central Council for Nursing, Midwifery and Health Visiting is responsible for regulating and registering these professions. Four National Boards—for England, Wales, Scotland and Northern Ireland—are responsible for ensuring that the education and training policies of the Council are carried out. The main professional associations are the Royal College of Nursing and the Royal College of Midwives.

Pharmacists

Only people on the register of pharmaceutical chemists may practise as pharmacists. Registration requires three or four years' training in a school of pharmacy, followed by one year's practical experience in a community or hospital pharmacy approved for training by the Royal Pharmaceutical Society of Great Britain or the Pharmaceutical Society of Northern Ireland (regulatory bodies for the profession).

Opticians

The General Optical Council regulates the professions of ophthalmic optician and dispensing optician. Only registered ophthalmic opticians (or registered ophthalmic medical practitioners) may test sight. Training of ophthalmic opticians takes four years, including a year of practical experience under supervision. Dispensing opticians take a two-year full-time course with a year's practical experience, or follow a part-time day-release course while employed with an optician.

Other Health Professions

Chiropodists, dieticians, medical laboratory scientific officers, occupational therapists, orthoptists, physiotherapists and radiographers may, on qualification, apply for state registration. Each profession has its own board under the general supervision of the Council for Professions Supplementary to Medicine.

Applications for a further two boards have been made from art, drama and music therapists, and from orthotists and prosthetists. State registration is mandatory for employment in the NHS and local authorities and is highly recommended in other public services and the private sector.

Following the report of an independent review of the legislation governing the regulation of these key health professionals—*The Regulation of Health Professions*—published in July 1996, the Government proposes to introduce legislation to streamline existing arrangements.

Dental therapists and dental hygienists are almost exclusively recruited from certified dental nurses who have taken at least one year's training. Dental therapists then take a 2–3 year training course and dental hygienists take a two-year training course; both carry out simple dental work under the supervision of a registered dentist.

National and Scottish Vocational Qualifications (NVQs and SVQs—see p. 458) have been developed for health care support workers, ambulance personnel, operating department practitioners, physiological measurement technicians and administrative and clerical staff.

Complementary Medicine

Complementary medicine (or complementary therapies) can cover a range of therapies and practices, the best known being osteopathy, chiropractic, homoeopathy, acupuncture and herbalism.

Complementary medicine, with the exception perhaps of homoeopathy, is usually available only outside the NHS and is not commonly included in private health insurance schemes.

HEALTH ARRANGEMENTS WITH OTHER COUNTRIES

The member states of the European Economic Area (see p. 127) have special health arrangements under which EEA nationals resident in a member state are entitled to receive emergency treatment, either free or at a reduced cost, during visits to other EEA countries (in most cases on the production of a completed Form E111, which visitors should obtain before travelling). There are also arrangements for people who go to another EEA country specifically for medical care, or who require continuing treatment for a pre-existing condition. In addition, there are arrangements where any visitor to Britain can receive immediate treatment for an emergency condition arising during their stay. Visitors are generally expected to pay if the purpose of their visit is to seek medical treatment. Visitors who are not covered by reciprocal arrangements must pay for any medical treatment they receive.

Personal Social Services

Personal social services help elderly people, disabled people, children and young people, people with mental illness or learning disabilities, their families and carers. Major services include skilled residential and day care, help for people confined to their homes, and the various forms of social work. The statutory services are provided by local government social services authorities in England and Wales, social work departments in Scotland, and health and social services boards in Northern Ireland. Alongside these providers are the many and varied contributions made by independent private and voluntary services. Much of the care given to elderly and disabled people is provided by families and self-help groups. There are an estimated 7 million informal carers in Britain, at least 1.5 million of whom provide over 20 hours of care a week. Legislation which came into force in April 1996 gives carers who provide (or intend to provide) substantial care on a regular basis the right, on request, to an assessment of their ability to provide care.

Demand for personal social services is rising because of the increasing number of elderly people, who, along with disabled and mentally ill people, or those with learning disabilities, can lead more normal lives in the community, given suitable support and facilities.

In response to the piecemeal way regulation in social services has developed, in September 1995 the Government launched a wide-ranging review of the regulation and inspection of children's and adult personal social services.

Management Reforms

New policies on community care in England, Wales and Scotland have been implemented in stages under the NHS and Community Care Act 1990. In Northern Ireland similar arrangements were introduced in 1993 under equivalent legislation. Many of the procedures which local authorities have implemented correspond to similar procedures recently introduced in the NHS (see p. 398).

Local authorities increasingly act as enablers and commissioners of services, rather than as the actual providers, after assessing their populations' needs for social care. They are now responsible for funding and arranging social care in the community for people who require public support. This includes the provision of home helps or home care assistants to support people in their own homes, and making arrangements for residential and nursing home care for those no longer able to remain in their own homes. Previously, residents of these homes who obtained public funding received help principally through special higher levels of Income Support (see p. 437).

Local authorities published their first local community care charters in April 1996. These give local people more information about the services and standards they can expect under the community care reforms. At the same time new community care plans were also published. In Scotland the timetable for introduction is longer because of the reorganisation of local government which took effect in April 1996 (see p. 76).

Recent figures for services provided or bought by local authorities for people being cared for at home show that during a survey week in England between 1994 and 1995:

- the number of hours of home help and home care provided rose by just under 8

per cent (to 2.4 million), although the number of households receiving services decreased by 5 per cent (to 512,000);

- places provided at day centres increased by 6 per cent (to 602,000), while attendances increased by 3 per cent (to 464,000); and

- the number of meals provided at home or in lunch clubs increased by almost 3 per cent (to 815,000), although the number receiving meals decreased by over 11 per cent (to 266,000).

All of the growth in home help and home care was in the independent sector, where provision in 1995 amounted to 29 per cent of the total provided, compared with less than 19 per cent in 1994.

Finance

In 1993–94 almost 50 per cent of local authorities' spending on personal social services was on older people (see Table 25.1). The biggest single item of expenditure was care for older people, which accounted for just under half of all gross spending in this area. Although most of this expenditure related to residential care provided by local authorities, the balance is expected to change as, under the community care reforms, more services are bought from the independent sector.

During the same period the greater part of local authorities' spending on children's services involved the provision of community homes (£300 million), fostering (£245 million) and field social work (£325 million).

Legislation was passed in July 1996 to enable local authorities to give certain people cash payments as an alternative to community care services, so that individual recipients will be able to choose how to buy their services rather than having to accept the direct provision from a local authority. The legislation is not yet in force.

In April 1996 the Government announced new measures to subject local social services authorities to closer scrutiny of their cost-effectiveness and quality of service. In England and Wales future councils will be subject to review by the Social Services

Inspectorate and the Audit Commission (see p. 80). In Scotland the Social Work Services Inspectorate and the Accounts Commission will continue to monitor and evaluate services.

Elderly People

Older people represent the fastest growing section of the community. The proportion of the population aged 75 and over has risen from 4.7 per cent 25 years ago to 7.1 per cent in 1996. In this period the proportion of those over 85 has doubled from 0.9 per cent to 1.8 per cent of the population.

Services for elderly people are designed to help them live at home whenever possible. These services may include advice and help given by social workers, domestic help, the provision of meals in the home, sitters-in, night attendants and laundry services as well as day centres, lunch clubs and recreational facilities. Adaptations to the home can overcome a person's difficulties in moving about, and a wide range of equipment is available for people with difficulties affecting their hearing or eyesight. Alarm systems have been developed to help elderly people obtain assistance in an emergency. In some areas 'good neighbour' and visiting services are arranged by the local authority or a voluntary organisation. Elderly people who live in residential care homes or nursing homes are subject to charging with a means test. Those who cannot afford to pay have their costs met by the State. Local authorities may also levy charges for domiciliary services.

In May 1996 the Government issued a consultation paper on financial provision for long-term care.[2] The main proposal is to set up a scheme for people who have financed some of their long-term care costs through an insurance policy or an annuity. These people would receive extra protection for their assets when assessed by a means test for residential care applied by local authorities. The Government intends to introduce legislation in time for the partnership scheme to be in force from 1997.

The most marked trend in residential care provision over recent years has been the continuing increase in the number of places provided in the private and voluntary sector and the corresponding fall in the number provided in local authorities' own homes. Independent sector homes generally have lower costs. Their use is encouraged by central government finance, which requires a high proportion of each year's new community care finance to be spent in the private sector.

New rules for assessing the amount to be contributed by people in residential care or nursing homes came into force in April 1996. Under these, the amount of capital wholly disregarded by the means test has more than trebled from £3,000 to £10,000 and the level of capital above which people are asked to meet their own care costs in full has doubled from £8,000 to £16,000.

As part of their responsibility for public housing, local authorities provide homes designed for elderly people ('sheltered accommodation'); some of these developments have resident wardens. Housing associations

---

[2] *A New Partnership for Care in Old Age.* Cm 3242, HMSO, £9.40.

Table 25.3: Hospital and local authority expenditure on elderly people in England

	1986–87	1991–92[1]	£ million at 1993–94 prices 1993–94
Hospitals	7,295	8,377	8,935
Local authority:			
Residential	1,089	1,163	1,322
Non-residential	1,072	1,310	1,560

Source: *Social Trends*

and private builders also build such accommodation.

Many local authorities provide free or subsidised travel for elderly people within their areas.

Disabled People

Britain has an estimated 6 million adults with one or more disabilities, of whom around 400,000 (7 per cent) live in communal establishments. Over the past ten years there has been increasing emphasis on rehabilitation and on the provision of day, domiciliary and respite support services to enable disabled people to live independently in the community wherever possible.

Local social services departments help with social rehabilitation and adjustment to disability. They are required to identify the number of disabled people in their area and to publicise services. These may include advice on personal and social problems arising from disability, as well as on occupational, educational, social and recreational facilities, either at day centres or elsewhere. Other services provided may include adaptations to homes (such as ramps for wheelchairs, stairlifts and ground-floor toilets), the delivery of cooked meals, and help with personal care at home. In cases of greatest need, help may be given with installing a telephone or a television. Local authorities and voluntary organisations may provide severely disabled people with residential accommodation or temporary facilities to allow their carers relief from their duties. Special housing may be available for those able to look after themselves.

The Independent Living (1993) Fund is an independent and discretionary trust which provides financial help to very severely disabled people of working age to enable them to live independently in the community. The Fund works in partnership with local authorities, which are expected to make a contribution in the form of services equivalent to what they would have spent on residential or nursing care.

Some authorities provide free or subsidised travel for disabled people on public transport, and they are encouraged to provide special means of access to public buildings. Special government regulations cover the provision of access for disabled people in the construction of new buildings.

The Disability Discrimination Act 1995 is designed to tackle discrimination against disabled people in Britain by providing them with a more accessible environment. The Act:

- provides a right for disabled people in employment and places a duty on employers with 20 or more staff to consider reasonable adjustments to the terms on which they offer employment where these would help to overcome the practical effects of a disability;

- provides a right of access to goods and services which will make it unlawful to refuse to serve a disabled person and may require service providers to make reasonable adjustments to their services to make them more accessible; and

- establishes the National Disability Council to advise the Government on eliminating discrimination against disabled people. The Council has already prepared its proposals for a code of practice on the rights of access to goods, facilities and services; this is currently the subject of public consultation.

The Government plans to implement the new employment rights and the initial rights of access to goods, facilities and services by the end of 1996.

People with Learning Disabilities (Mental Handicap)

The Government's policy is to encourage the development of local services for people with learning disabilities and their families through co-operation between health authorities, local authorities, education and training services and voluntary and other organisations.

Local authority social services departments are the leading statutory agency for planning and arranging services for people with learning disabilities. They provide or arrange short-term care, support for families in their own homes, residential accommodation and support for various types of activities outside the home. The main aims are to ensure that as far as possible people with learning disabilities can lead full lives in their communities and are admitted to hospital only when it is necessary on health grounds. People with learning disabilities form the largest group for local authority-funded day centre places and the second largest group in residential care.

The NHS provides for the primary health care needs of people with learning disabilities as it does for the general population. It also provides specialist services when the ordinary NHS services cannot meet health care needs. Residential care is provided for those with severe or profound disabilities whose needs can only effectively be met by the NHS.

Mentally Ill People

Government policy aims to ensure that people with mental illnesses should have access to all the services they need as locally as possible. The cornerstone of community care policy for mentally ill people is the Care Programme Approach. Under this, each patient in contact with the specialist services should receive an assessment and a care plan, have a key worker appointed to keep in touch with him or her, and be given regular reviews. Implementation of this approach is being closely monitored by the NHS Executive.

While the total number of places for mentally ill people in the large hospitals has continued to fall, this has been matched by increasing provision of alternative places in smaller NHS hospitals, local authority accommodation and private and voluntary sector homes.

Arrangements made by social services authorities for providing preventive care and after care for mentally ill people in the community include day centres, social centres and residential care. Social workers help patients and their families with problems caused by mental illness. In some cases they can apply for a mentally disordered person to be compulsorily admitted to and detained in hospital under the Mental Health Act 1983 or, in Scotland, the Mental Health (Scotland) Act 1984. In England and Wales the Mental Health Act Commission provides important safeguards for patients to ensure that the Act is

used appropriately. The Mental Welfare Commission for Scotland performs similar functions. Different arrangements apply in Northern Ireland.

A grant of £58.3 million for 1996–97 to local authorities in England is designed to encourage them to increase the level of social care available to mentally ill patients, including those with dementia who need specialist psychiatric care in the community.

The Mental Health (Patients in the Community) Act 1995 aims to ensure more effective care and supervision for people with severe mental illness. The legislation, which came into force in April 1996, introduces a new power of 'supervised discharge' for patients in England and Wales who need special supervision after they leave hospital. Similar arrangements, called Community Care Orders, have been introduced in Scotland under the same legislation. Under these provisions patients who do not receive the services they need or do not comply with any requirements placed on them must have their care plans reviewed; where appropriate their compulsory readmission to hospital may be considered.

In addition supervision registers for discharged patients most at risk were introduced in 1994, maintained by the providers of services for mentally ill people and allow hospital staff to keep track of discharged patients. For details of the Government's homeless mentally ill initiative, see p. 393.

The first government-backed national survey of mental illness was carried out in 1993–94. The survey, which covers adults aged 16 to 64 living in communal establishments as well as those living in private households, aims to provide up-to-date information on mental illness among adults, as well as on associated social disabilities. It also examined the varying use of health, social and voluntary care services, and the risk factors associated with mental illness. The results of the survey have been published in a series of eight reports, the last four of which were issued in May 1996.[3]

There are many voluntary organisations concerned with those suffering from mental illness or learning disabilities, and they play an important role in providing services for both groups of people.

Help to Families

Social services authorities, through their own social workers and others in the voluntary sector, give help to families facing special problems. This help takes the form of services for families with children in need or at risk of harm or neglect, including some who may need care away from their own families; and support for family carers who look after elderly and other family members, in order to give them relief from their duties. There is also help for single parents. Local authorities or voluntary organisations now run many refuges for women, often with young children, whose home conditions have become intolerable. The refuges provide short-term accommodation and support while attempts are made to relieve the women's problems. Many authorities also contribute to the cost of support and counselling for families (such as marriage guidance) carried out by voluntary organisations.

Day Care for Children

Day care facilities for children under five are provided by local authorities, voluntary agencies and privately. In allocating places in their day nurseries and other facilities, local authorities give priority to children with special social, learning or health needs. Local authorities also register and inspect childminders, private day nurseries and playgroups in their areas and provide support and advice services.

Day care figures for England up to the end of March 1995 show:

- nearly 5,500 day nurseries with 161,000 places—an increase of 9 per cent over 1994;
- 97,000 registered childminders, providing 374,000 places—an increase of 5 per cent over 1994; and
- 17,000 playgroups providing about 411,000 places.

In 1993 the Government launched a £45 million scheme to help create childcare facilities in Great Britain for children over five after school hours and during the holidays (see p. 39).

Child Protection

Cases of child abuse are the joint concern of a number of different agencies and professions. Area child protection committees provide forums for discussion and co-ordination and draw up policies and procedures for handling these cases. The Government's central initiative on child abuse has provided funding for a variety of projects, including training for health visitors, school nurses, and local authority social services staff. In Scotland the Government provides support for child protection training at the University of Dundee and through a grant scheme for local authorities. The results of a wide-ranging research programme into child abuse in Great Britain were published in June 1995.[4] Among its findings were that:

- about 160,000 children a year were being referred into the protection system. A third came from lone parent families, and two-thirds were living in a household that lacked a wage earner. Domestic violence and mental illness were features in 15 per cent of cases. One in seven of the parents had themselves been abused as children.
- about 40,000 enquiries ended without any action being taken after professionals had made informal checks. In a further 80,000 cases matters were quickly allowed to rest after parents had been interviewed;

---

[3]Surveys of Psychiatric Morbidity in Great Britain. Report 5: *Physical Complaints, Service Use and Treatment of Residents with Psychiatric Disorders*. HMSO, £15. Report 6: *Economic Activity and Social Functioning of Residents with Psychiatric Disorders*. HMSO, £15. Report 7: *Psychiatric Morbidity among Homeless People*. HMSO, £21. Report 8: *Adults with a Psychotic Disorder Living in the Community*. HMSO, £15.

[4]*Child Protection: Messages from Research*. HMSO, £14.

- in the comparatively small number of cases where abuse was established, 96 per cent of children involved stayed at home, and where they were removed, 70 per cent returned home within six months.

Children in Care

Local government authorities must provide accommodation for children who have no parent or guardian, have been abandoned, or whose parents are unable to provide for them.

The Children Act 1989, which came into effect in England and Wales in 1991, recast the legislative framework for children's services, care and protection into a single coherent structure. It placed new duties on local authorities to safeguard and promote the welfare of children. Under the Act parents of children in care retain their parental responsibilities but act as far as possible as partners with the authority. There is a requirement for local authorities to prepare a child for leaving their care and to continue to advise him or her up to the age of 21. Local authorities are required to have a complaints procedure with an independent element to cover children in their care.

The number of children looked after by local authorities continues to decline as local authorities respond to the Act's requirement that wherever possible children should remain at home with their families.

By the end of March 1995, provisional figures for England show:

- there were 49,000 children looked after by local authorities, similar to the previous year's figure;
- 65 per cent of children were placed with foster parents, compared with 63 per cent in 1994, reflecting a continued decline in the numbers in other types of accommodation.

In England and Wales a child may be brought before a family proceedings court if he or she is neglected or ill-treated, exposed to moral danger, beyond the control of parents, or not attending school. The court can commit children to the care of a local authority under a care order. Under the Children Act 1989 certain preconditions have to be satisfied to justify an order. These are that the children are suffering

or are likely to suffer significant harm because of a lack of reasonable parental care or because they are beyond parental control. However, an order is made only if the court is also satisfied that this will positively contribute to the children's well-being and be in their best interests. In court proceedings children are entitled to separate legal representation and the right to have a guardian to protect their interests.

All courts have to treat the welfare of children as the paramount consideration when reaching any decision about their upbringing.

Recent concerns over standards of care in certain local authority children's homes prompted a number of official inquiries between 1992 and 1993; their recommendations are now being implemented.

In September 1996, as part of the Government's response to incidents of child abuse in North Wales in the 1970s and 1980s, a review began of the safeguards introduced by the Children Act in 1991 and after, for children living away from home in England and Wales. A parallel review is in progress in Scotland.

In Scotland children who have committed offences or are in need of care and protection may be brought before a children's hearing, which can impose a supervision requirement on a child if it thinks that compulsory measures are appropriate. Under these requirements most children are allowed to remain at home under the supervision of a social worker, but some may live with foster parents or in a residential establishment while under supervision. Supervision requirements are reviewed at least once a year until ended by a children's hearing. The Children (Scotland) Act 1995, whose major provisions come into force between November 1996 and April 1997, contains major reforms of both public and private law and places the child at the centre of decision-making. It maintains and strengthens the children's hearings system, introduces new child protection procedures and places wide duties on local authorities to promote the welfare of children.

In Northern Ireland the juvenile court may place children who are in need of care, protection or control into the care of a fit person (including a health and social services board or trust), or may make them subject to a supervision order. The Children (Northern Ireland) Order 1995 provides Northern Ireland with legislation broadly equivalent to the Children Act 1989 in England and Wales and creates a separation between the treatment of children in need of care and young offenders. The legislation is expected to come into force in October 1996.

Fostering and Children's Homes

When appropriate in England and Wales, children in care are placed with foster parents, who receive payments to cover living costs. Alternatively, the child may be placed in a local authority, voluntary or private children's home or other suitable residential accommodation, including boarding school. In Scotland local authorities are responsible for placing children in their care in foster homes, in local authority or voluntary homes, or in residential schools. Similar provisions apply in Northern Ireland. Regulations concerning residential care and the foster placement of children in care are made by central government.

Adoption

Local authority social services departments are required by law to provide an adoption service, either directly or by arrangement with approved voluntary adoption societies. Agencies may offer adoptive parents an allowance in certain circumstances if this would help to find a family for a child. Under adoption law it is illegal to receive an unrelated child for adoption through an unapproved third party. The Registrars-General keep confidential registers of adopted children. Adopted people may be given details of their original birth record on reaching the age of 18, and counselling is provided to help them understand the circumstances of their adoption. An Adoption Contact Register enables adopted adults and their birth parents to be given a safe and confidential way of making contact if that is the wish of both parties. A person's details are entered only if they wish to be contacted.

The number of children, babies in particular, who are available for adoption is far exceeded by those people wishing to adopt. In recent years fewer than 7,000 children have been adopted annually. Of those, about half are adopted by one legal parent and a new partner, following marriage or remarriage.

A draft adoption Bill was issued in March 1996, proposing new safeguards for children being adopted and updating adoption law and practice in England and Wales. It includes proposals to allow children aged 12 or over to agree to the making of their adoption order and to have the right to apply to take part in their own adoption proceedings; simpler alternatives to adoption for step-parents, relatives or long-term foster parents; and streamlined arrangements for adopting from overseas.

In Scotland a number of significant changes in adoption law were introduced in the Children (Scotland) Act 1995.

Social Services Staff

The effective working of the social services depends largely on professionally qualified social workers. Training programmes leading to a Diploma in Social Work (DipSW) are provided by partnerships between educational institutions (universities and colleges of higher and further education) and employing agencies. The Central Council for Education and Training in Social Work (CCETSW) is the statutory body responsible for promoting and regulating social work training. Since 1989, CCETSW has been implementing a programme of improvements to training and qualifications. The range of qualifications now available include National Vocational Qualifications (NVQs and, in Scotland, SVQs), the DipSW and two further awards—the Post Qualifying Award in Social Work and the Advanced Award in Social Work. The range of qualifications is relevant for staff working in all sectors, including those in residential, day and domiciliary care service.

Professional social workers (including those

in the NHS) are employed mainly by the social services departments of local authorities (local authority social work departments in Scotland and Health and Social Services Trusts in Northern Ireland). There is also a growing independent sector.

The Government is committed to improving social work training and each of the four countries of Britain has a personal social services training strategy whose objectives include increasing the supply of qualified social workers, improving the quality of qualifying training and the training of the existing workforce.

A government consultation paper on proposals for improving the professional regulation of social services is to be issued later in 1996.

Further Reading

Health Education in Scotland: A National Policy Statement. The Scottish Office, 1991.

Health for All in Wales: Strategies for Action. Health Promotion Authority for Wales, 1990.

The Health of the Nation: A Strategy for Health in England. Cm 1986. HMSO, 1992.

A Regional Strategy for the Health and Personal Social Services in Northern Ireland 1992–97. Northern Ireland Department of Health and Social Services, 1992.

Scotland's Health: A Challenge to Us All. The Scottish Office, 1992.

Social Welfare (2nd edn.). Aspects of Britain series, HMSO, 1995.

The Informability Manual. Offers basic guidelines to providers of services, in both the public and private sectors, on the techniques and media to be used in making information more accessible to people with disabilities. HMSO, 1996.

Annual Publications

Health and Personal Social Services Statistics for England. HMSO.

A Regional Strategy for Health and Social Wellbeing 1997–2000. Northern Ireland Department of Health and Social Services.

Scotland Getting Better: The NHS in Scotland Annual Report. The Scottish Office.

Scottish Health Statistics. The Scottish Office.

Welsh Health: Annual Report of the Chief Medical Officer. The Welsh Office.

On the State of the Public Health. The Annual Report of the Chief Medical Officer of the Department of Health. HMSO.

26 Social Security

Administration	430	Arrangements with Other	
Contributions	431	Countries	441
Benefits	432		

Social security is the Government's largest expenditure programme. Planned spending in 1996–97 is almost one-third of public expenditure (see pp. 161–2). Recent developments include the reform of benefits for unemployed people, measures to improve incentives for unemployed people to find work, changes in the provision for people of working age unable to work because of illness or disability, and measures to curb the growth in benefit payments for housing costs.

The social security system is designed to secure a basic standard of living for people in financial need by providing income during periods of inability to earn (including periods of unemployment), help for families and assistance with costs arising from disablement.

As part of its long-term review of public spending (see pp. 163–5), the Government is examining the social security programme and reforming the structure of the present system to ensure it involves:

- better targeting of those in need;
- encouraging more self-provision; and
- providing more incentives to work.

There are three broad categories of social security benefit:

- **contributory benefits**, where entitlement depends on a satisfactory record of payment of contributions to the National Insurance Fund,[1] from which benefits are paid;

- **income-related benefits**, available to people whose income falls below a certain level; and
- **other benefits**, which depend on qualifying conditions such as disability or family needs.

Contributory benefits account for about one half of programme expenditure, income-related benefits for almost a third, and other non-contributory benefits about a sixth. General taxation provides over half the income for the social security programme, with employers' National Insurance contributions around a quarter and employees' National Insurance contributions about a fifth. Appeals about claims for benefits are decided by independent tribunals.

ADMINISTRATION

Administration in Great Britain is handled by five separate executive agencies of the Department of Social Security, together employing a total of some 90,000 staff:

- the Benefits Agency administers and delivers the majority of benefits;

---

[1] The National Insurance Fund is a statutory fund into which all National Insurance contributions payable by employers, employees and self-employed people are paid and from which expenditure on contributory benefits is met.

- the Child Support Agency assesses and collects maintenance payments for children (see p. 435);
- the Contributions Agency handles National Insurance contributions;
- the Information Technology Services Agency computerises the administration of social security; and
- the War Pensions Agency delivers services to war pensioners.

The Employment Services Agency of the Department for Education and Employment pays benefits to unemployed people on behalf of the Benefits Agency. The housing and council tax benefit schemes are administered by local authorities, which recover most of the cost from the Government.

In Northern Ireland National Insurance contributions and social security benefits are administered by the Social Security Agency. The housing benefit scheme is administered by the Northern Ireland Housing Executive and the Rate Collection Agency; council tax does not apply in Northern Ireland, where domestic 'rates' are still collected.

A major programme to improve quality and customer service is in progress. The Benefits Agency, for example, is moving towards one-stop service delivery (a single contact point to handle each customer's business with the Agency).

The Benefits, Contributions and War Pensions Agencies publish customer charters.

Anti-fraud Measures

Further measures are being introduced to improve the prevention and detection of social security fraud. These include:

- greater financial incentives to local authorities to prevent and detect fraud in the benefits they administer;
- better use of information technology; and
- better targeting of resources, and additional resources where necessary.

In 1994–95 £717.6 million of fraud was identified and stopped. In the four years since its formation, the Benefits Agency has saved over £2,000 million through anti-fraud work.

Advice about Benefits

The demand for advice about benefits is partly met by the Freeline Social Security Service, which handles over 1 million calls each year. The Ethnic Freeline Service provides information on social security in Urdu, Punjabi and Chinese. There is also a freeline service in Welsh.

The Department of Social Security produces a range of leaflets and posters providing general information on entitlement and liability. These are available in English and a number of other languages.

CONTRIBUTIONS

Entitlement to National Insurance benefits such as Retirement Pension, Incapacity Benefit, Unemployment Benefit, Maternity Allowance and Widow's Benefits, is dependent upon the payment of contributions. There are five classes of contributions. **The rates given below are effective from April 1996 to April 1997:**

- Class 1—paid by employees and their employers. Employees with earnings below £61 a week do not pay Class 1 contributions. Contributions on earnings of £61 a week and over are at the rate of 2 per cent of the first £61 of total earnings and 10 per cent of the balance, up to the upper earnings limit of £455 a week. Employers' contributions are subject to the same threshold. On earnings above the threshold, contributions rise in stages from 3 per cent of total earnings up to a maximum of 10.2 per cent when earnings are £210 or more a week; there is no upper earnings limit. The contribution is lower if the employer operates a 'contracted-out' occupational pension scheme (see p. 434).
- Class 1A—paid by employers who provide their employees with fuel and/or a car for private use. A Class 1A contribution is payable on the cash equivalent of the benefit provided.
- Class 2—paid by self-employed people. Class 2 contributions are at a flat rate of £6.05 a week. The self-employed may claim exemption from Class 2

contributions if their profits are expected to be below £3,430 for the 1996–97 tax year. Self-employed people are not eligible for unemployment and industrial injuries benefits.

- Class 3—paid voluntarily to safeguard rights to some benefits. Contributions are at a flat rate of £5.95 a week.

- Class 4—paid by the self-employed on their taxable profits over a set lower limit (£6,860 a year), and up to a set upper limit (£23,660 a year) in addition to their Class 2 contribution. Class 4 contributions are payable at the rate of 6 per cent.

Employees who work after pensionable age (60 for women and 65 for men) do not pay contributions but the employer continues to be liable. Self-employed people over pensionable age do not pay contributions.

A one-year National Insurance Contribution Holiday for employers was introduced in April 1996 to encourage employers to take on people who have been unemployed for two years or more. This enables employers to claim back an amount equivalent to their share of the National Insurance contribution for each qualifying employee for up to a year.

BENEFITS

For most contributory benefits there are two conditions. First, before benefit can be paid at all, a certain number of contributions must have been paid. Second, the full rate of benefit cannot be paid unless contributions have been paid or credited to a specific level over a set period. A reduced rate of benefit is payable dependent on the level of contributions paid or credited. For example, a great many of those receiving retirement pensions and widows' benefits receive a percentage-based rate of benefit. Benefits are increased annually in line with percentage increases in retail prices. The main benefits (payable weekly) are summarised on pp. 433–40. **Rates given are those effective from April 1996 until April 1997.**

Social Security Expenditure: Great Britain 1995–96

Analysis of planned expenditure 1995–96

Percentage of expenditure by broad groups of beneficiaries 1995–96

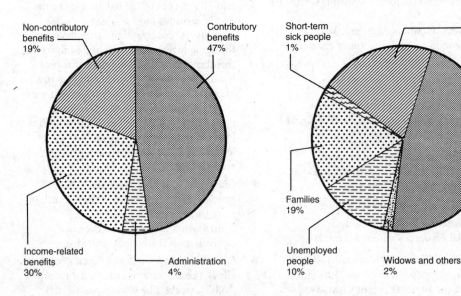

Non-contributory benefits 19%

Contributory benefits 47%

Income-related benefits 30%

Administration 4%

Short-term sick people 1%

Long-term sick and disabled people 24%

Families 19%

Unemployed people 10%

Widows and others 2%

Elderly people 44%

Source: *Social Security Departmental Report: The Government's Expenditure Plans 1996–97 to 1998–99.*

Retirement Pension

A state **Retirement Pension** is payable, if the contribution conditions have been met, to women at the age of 60 and men at the age of 65. The Sex Discrimination Act 1986 protects employees of both sexes in a particular occupation from being required to retire at different ages. This, however, has not affected the payment of the state retirement pension at different ages for men and women.

Legislation was introduced in 1995 to equalise the state pension age for men and women at 65. The change will be phased in over ten years, starting from April 2010. Women born before 6 April 1950 will not be affected; their pension age will remain at 60.

The new pension age of 65 will apply to women born on or after 6 April 1955. Pension age for women born between these dates will move up gradually from 60 to 65.

The state pension scheme consists of a basic weekly pension of £61.15 for a single person and £97.75 for a married couple, together with an additional earnings-related pension. Pensioners may have unlimited earnings without affecting their pensions. Those who have put off their retirement during the five years after state pension age may earn extra pension. A non-contributory retirement pension of £36.60 a week is payable to people over the age of 80 who meet certain residence conditions, and who have not qualified for a

Table 26.1: Estimated Numbers Receiving Benefits[a] in Great Britain 1995–96 (forecast)

Benefit	Contributory (C) or non-contributory (NC)	Thousands
Retirement Pension	C	10,322
Widows' Benefit	C	291
Unemployment Benefit[b]	C	390
Incapacity Benefit	C	1,881
Maternity Allowance	C	12
Non-contributory Retirement Pension	NC	29
War Pension	NC	331
Attendance Allowance	NC	1,162
Disability Living Allowance	NC	1,771
Disability Working Allowance	NC	8
Invalid Care Allowance	NC	339
Severe Disablement Allowance	NC	368
Industrial Injuries Disablement Benefit[c]	NC	231,000
Reduced Earnings Allowance[c]	NC	143,000
Industrial Death Benefit	NC	21
Income Support	NC	5,601
Child Benefit	NC	
number of children		12,993
number of families		7,125
One Parent Benefit	NC	1,067
Family Credit	NC	658
Housing Benefit	NC	
rent rebate		2,918
rent allowance		1,870
Council Tax Benefit	NC	5,735

Source: *Social Security Departmental Report: The Government's Expenditure Plans 1996–97 to 1998–99.*
[a] Figures are for beneficiaries at any one time.
[b] From 1996–97 Unemployment Benefit has been replaced by contributory-based Jobseekers Allowance.
[c] Figures refer to the number of pensions and in payment, and not to the number of recipients.

contributory pension. People whose pensions do not give them enough to live on may be entitled to Income Support (see p. 437). Over 10.2 million people in Great Britain received a basic state pension in 1995.

Rights to basic pensions are safeguarded for people whose opportunities to work are limited while they are looking after a child or a sick or disabled person. Men and women may receive the same basic pension, provided they have paid full-rate National Insurance contributions when working. From April 1999 the earnings-related pension scheme will be based on a lifetime's revalued earnings instead of on the best 20 years. It will eventually be calculated as 20 per cent rather than 25 per cent of earnings, to be phased in over ten years from 1999. The pensions of people retiring this century will be unaffected.

Occupational and Personal Pensions

Employers may 'contract out' their employees from the state scheme for the additional earnings-related pension and provide their own occupational pension instead. Their pension must be at least as good as the state additional pension. Joining an employer's contracted-out scheme is voluntary: employers are not free to contract out employees from the earnings-related pension scheme without the employees' consent. The State remains responsible for the basic pension.

Occupational pension schemes cover about half the working population and have nearly 11 million members. The occupational pension rights of those who change jobs before pensionable age, who are unable or who do not want to transfer their pension rights, are now offered some protection against inflation. Workers leaving a scheme have the right to a fair transfer value. The trustees or managers of pension schemes have to provide full information about their schemes.

Increasing numbers of pensioners receive income from occupational pensions and investment income. Around two-thirds of all pensioners now receive an occupational pension worth, on average, over £70 a week, while more than three-quarters have some form of income from their investments, receiving an average of over £37 a week.

As an alternative to their employers' scheme or the state additional earnings-related pension scheme, people are entitled to choose a personal pension available from a bank, building society, insurance company or other financial institution. In 1993–94, 5.7 million people contracted out of the state earnings-related pension scheme and took out personal pensions. Legislation passed in 1995 requires occupational schemes to provide equal treatment between men and women and to make personal pensions more flexible and attractive to a broader age range.

A Pensions Ombudsman deals with complaints about maladministration of pension schemes and adjudicates on disputes of fact or law. A pensions registry helps people trace lost benefits.

Parents and Children

Most pregnant working women receive **Statutory Maternity Pay** directly from their employer. It is paid for a maximum of 18 weeks to any woman who has been working for the same employer for 26 weeks and who earns on average at least £61 a week. She will receive 90 per cent of her average weekly earnings for the first six weeks and a lower rate of £54.55 a week for the remaining 12 weeks. Women who are not eligible for Statutory Maternity Pay because, for example, they are self-employed, have recently changed jobs or given up their job, may qualify for a weekly **Maternity Allowance**, which is payable for up to 18 weeks. This amounts to £54.55 a week for employees and £47.35 a week for the self-employed and those not in work.

All pregnant employees have the right to take 14 weeks' maternity leave.

A payment of £100 from the Social Fund (see p. 440) may be made if the mother or her partner receive Income Support, income-related Jobseeker's Allowance, Family Credit or Disability Working Allowance (see pp. 436–9). It is also available if a woman adopts a baby.

Non-contributory **Child Benefit** of £10.80 a week for the eldest qualifying child and £8.80 for each other child is the main social security benefit for children. Tax-free and normally paid to the mother, Child Benefit is payable for children up to the age of 16 and for those up to 19 if they continue in full-time non-advanced education. In addition, **One Parent Benefit** of £6.30 a week is generally payable to certain people bringing up one child or more on their own, whether as their parents or not. A non-contributory **Guardian's Allowance** of £11.15 a week for an orphaned child is payable to a person who is entitled to Child Benefit for that child. This is reduced to £9.15 if the higher rate of Child Benefit is payable for the child. In exceptional circumstances a Guardian's Allowance may be paid on the death of only one parent.

At the end of 1995 Child Benefit was paid for 12,780,000 children, an increase on the previous year of 80,000.

Child Support Agency

An estimated 1.4 million lone parents bring up over 2 million children in Britain. The Child Support Agency (CSA), which started work in April 1993, is gradually replacing the court system for obtaining basic child maintenance. The CSA is responsible for assessing, collecting and enforcing child maintenance payments and for tracing absent parents. Assessments are made using a formula which takes into account each parent's income and essential outgoings.

Changes to the child support arrangements were introduced in 1994 to take account of the concerns of members of the public and MPs. The Government believes that the formula approach to assessment of maintenance is appropriate for most separated parents. However, a case has been made for further changes. Legislation passed in 1995 introduces a system of departures from the formula assessment of child support to allow the amount of maintenance payable to be varied in a small proportion of cases from 1996–97. Other measures are designed to improve the review process in child support and to introduce a child maintenance bonus worth up to £1,000 when the parent with care of the child returns to work.

In Northern Ireland the child support maintenance scheme is operated by the Northern Ireland Child Support Agency, established at the same time as the CSA.

Childcare Charges

Families claiming Family Credit (see p. 439), Disability Working Allowance (see p. 436), Housing Benefit and Council Tax Benefit (see pp. 438–9), and who pay for childcare for children aged under 11, can have up to £60 a week in childcare charges offset against their earnings when their benefit entitlement is worked out. This help is for lone parents, and families where both partners work or where one partner is disabled, who use formal childcare through registered childminders and day nurseries. Many families are expected to take up work as a direct result of the change.

Widows

Widows under the age of 60, or those over 60 whose husbands were not entitled to a state retirement pension when they died, receive a tax-free single payment of £1,000 following the death of their husbands, provided that their husbands had paid a minimum number of National Insurance contributions. Women whose husbands have died of an industrial injury or prescribed disease may also qualify, regardless of whether their husbands had paid National Insurance contributions.

A widowed mother with at least one child for whom she is getting Child Benefit receives a **Widowed Mother's Allowance** of £61.15 a week, with a further £9.90 for a child for whom the higher rate of Child Benefit is payable and £11.15 for each subsequent child. A widow's basic pension of £61.15 a week is payable to a widow who is 55 years or over when her husband dies or when her entitlement to Widowed Mother's Allowance ends. A percentage of the full rate is payable to widows who are aged between 45 and 54 when their husbands die or when their entitlement to Widowed Mother's Allowance ends. Special rules apply for widows whose husbands died before 11 April 1988. Entitlement continues until the widow remarries or begins drawing retirement pension. Payment ends if she lives with a man as his wife. Widows also benefit under the Industrial Injuries scheme (see p. 437).

A man whose wife dies when both are over pension age inherits his wife's pension rights just as a widow inherits her husband's rights.

Sick and Disabled People

Statutory Sick Pay and Incapacity Benefit

A variety of benefits are available for people unable to work because of sickness or disablement. Employers are responsible for paying **Statutory Sick Pay** to employees from the fourth day of sickness for up to a maximum of 28 weeks. There is a single rate of Statutory Sick Pay for all qualifying employees provided their average weekly earnings are at least equivalent to the lower earnings limit for the payment of National Insurance contributions. The weekly rate is £54.55.

Entitlement to **Incapacity Benefit** begins when entitlement to Statutory Sick Pay ends or, for those who do not qualify for Statutory Sick Pay, from the first day of sickness. The benefit has three rates:

- a lower rate of £46.15 a week for the first 28 weeks (for those not entitled to statutory sick pay);
- a higher rate of £54.55 a week between the 29th and 52nd week; and
- a long-term rate of £61.15 a week from the 53rd week of incapacity.

Extra benefits may be paid for adult and child dependants. Incapacity Benefit is taxable from the 29th week of incapacity.

A new, more objective medical test of incapacity for work has been introduced for Incapacity Benefit as well as for other social security benefits paid on the basis of incapacity for work. The new test usually applies after 28 weeks' incapacity for work and assesses ability to perform a range of work-related activities rather than the ability to perform a specific job.

Severe Disablement Allowance

A **Severe Disablement Allowance** of £36.95, plus additions of up to £12.90 a week depending on the person's age and when they became incapable of work, may be payable to people who have not been able to work for at least 28 weeks because of illness or disability and who cannot get Incapacity Benefit because they have not paid enough National Insurance contributions. Claims may be made by people aged between 16 and 65. Once a person has qualified for the allowance, there is no upper limit for receipt. Additions for adult dependants and for children may also be paid. Since April 1995 new claimants have had to satisfy the same incapacity test as that used in Incapacity Benefit (see above).

People who become incapable of work after their 20th birthday must also be medically assessed as at least 80 per cent disabled for a minimum of 28 weeks. People already in receipt of certain benefits, such as the middle or higher rate of Disability Living Allowance, will automatically be accepted as 80 per cent disabled.

Other Benefits

Disability Living Allowance is a non-contributory tax-free benefit for people disabled before the age of 65 who need help with personal care or with mobility. It has two components: a care component which has three weekly rates—£48.50, £32.40 and £12.90; and a mobility component which has two rates—£33.90 and £12.90.

A non-contributory, tax-free **Attendance Allowance** of £32.40 or £48.50 a week may be payable to people severely disabled at or after age 65, who have personal care needs, depending upon the amount of attention they require. The higher rate of Attendance Allowance and/or Disability Living Allowance may be paid to people who are terminally ill.

A non-contributory **Invalid Care Allowance** of £36.60 weekly may be payable to people between 16 and 65 who cannot take up a paid job because they are caring for a person receiving either Attendance Allowance or the higher or middle care component of Disability Living Allowance. An additional carer's premium may be paid if the recipient is also receiving Income Support, income-related Jobseeker's Allowances, Housing Benefit or Council Tax Benefit. An estimated 1.5 million adults in Great Britain care for a disabled person for at least 20 hours a week.

Disability Working Allowance is an income-related tax-free benefit which helps some disabled people aged 16 or over who work an average of 16 hours a week or more and have an illness or disability which puts them at a disadvantage in getting a job. Awards are for fixed periods of six months. To qualify a person must either:

- be getting Disability Living Allowance, or an analogous benefit, such as Constant Attendance Allowance under the War Pensions or Industrial Injuries Disablement scheme; or

- have an invalid three-wheeler or other vehicle under the NHS Act 1977; or

- have been entitled to one of the following in at least one of the 56 days before the date of claim: higher rate short-term Incapacity Benefit; long-term Incapacity Benefit; Severe Disablement Allowance; or the disability premium or higher pensioner premium with Income Support, Housing Benefit or Council Tax Benefit.

The allowance is available to single people, lone parents and couples. The rate depends on the person's income and size of family, and the ages of any children. The allowance is not payable if capital or savings exceed £16,000.

Motability, an independent charitable organisation, helps disabled drivers to obtain vehicles or powered wheelchairs on favourable terms by using the higher rate mobility component of Disability Living Allowance or the War Pension mobility supplement. Almost 5 per cent of all new cars registered in Britain in 1994 were bought under the Motability scheme, which currently has more than 200,000 customers.

Industrial Injuries Disablement Benefits/ Reduced Earnings Allowance

Various benefits are payable for disablement caused by an accident at work or a prescribed disease caused by a particular type of employment. The main benefit is **Industrial Injuries Disablement Benefit**: up to £99 a week is usually paid after a qualifying period of 15 weeks if a person is 14 per cent or more physically or mentally disabled as a result of an industrial accident or a prescribed disease.

Basic Disablement Benefit can be paid in addition to other National Insurance benefits, such as Incapacity Benefit. It can be paid whether or not the person returns to work and does not depend on earnings. The degree of disablement is assessed by an independent adjudicating medical authority and the amount paid depends on the extent of the disablement and on how long it is expected to last. Except for certain progressive respiratory diseases, disablement of less than 14 per cent does not attract Disablement Benefit. In certain circumstances additional allowances, such as **Constant Attendance Allowance** and **Exceptionally Severe Disablement Allowance**, may be payable. In some cases **Reduced Earnings Allowance** may be payable.

Income Support

From 7 October 1996 **Income Support** is payable only to certain people who are not required to be available for work, and whose financial resources are below certain set levels. They include lone parents, pensioners, carers and long-term sick and disabled people. Income Support is made up of a personal allowance based on age and on whether the claimant is single, a lone parent or has a partner; age-related allowances for dependent children and additional sums known as premiums, and housing costs. From this total amount other income, including other social security benefits, is deducted.

The Income Support scheme sets a limit to the amount of capital a person may have and still remain entitled to claim it. People with savings or capital worth more than £8,000 are ineligible; savings between £3,000 and £8,000 will reduce the amount received. Since April 1996 there have been new capital limits for people living permanently in residential care or a nursing home.

Until 7 October 1996 Income Support was also available to unemployed people on low incomes, capable of, available for, and actively seeking work. These people now qualify for assistance under the Jobseeker's Allowance (see below).

Jobseeker's Allowance

Up to 7 April 1996 Unemployment Benefit of £46.45 a week for a single person or £75.10 for a couple was payable for up to a year in any one period of unemployment. Another benefit, Income Support (see above), was payable to people whose income fell below certain set levels and who were not working for more than 16 hours a week. A new benefit, **Jobseeker's Allowance**, was introduced on 7 October 1996, replacing the former Unemployment Benefit and Income Support for unemployed people with a single allowance paid at standard rates. Since October 1996 all unemployed people have been required to enter into a Jobseeker's Agreement, setting out a plan of action to seek work. Most recipients qualify through a means test, and the benefit is paid at rates determined by family circumstances on a basis similar to Income Support (see p. 436).

- *Contribution-based Jobseeker's Allowance*: those with a sufficient National Insurance contribution record are entitled to a personal Jobseeker's Allowance for up to six months, regardless of any savings or partner's income.
- Income-based Jobseeker's Allowance: those on a low income are entitled to an income-based Jobseeker's Allowance, payable for as long as the jobseeker requires support and continues to satisfy the qualifying conditions. The amount a claimant receives comprises an age-related personal allowance, allowances for dependent children, premium payments for those with children or special needs, and mortgage interest payments.

Back to Work Bonus

To enhance incentives to take up or keep part-time work, and encourage people to move off benefit and into employment, recipients of Jobseeker's Allowance and people aged under 60 who receive Income Support can benefit from a **Back to Work Bonus**. People who have been unemployed for three months or more and are working part-time may keep the first £5 of their earnings (£10 for couples, £15 for lone parents, disabled people and some people in special occupations) in any week in which they work while receiving benefit. An amount equal to half of any earnings above that level counts towards the build-up of a bonus amount. When the unemployed person moves

off benefit and into employment, he or she will be able to claim a tax-free lump sum of up to a £1,000. The part-time (up to 24 hours a week) earnings of a partner can also contribute towards building up a Back to Work Bonus, which can be paid if the couple leave benefit as a result of the partner moving into work.

Government Aims

The Government's three main aims in introducing Jobseeker's Allowance are:

- to improve the operation of the labour market by helping people in their search for work, while ensuring they understand and fulfil the conditions for receipt of benefit;
- to secure better value for money for the taxpayer by a streamlined administration, closer targeting on those who need financial support and a regime which more effectively helps people back into work;
- to improve the service to unemployed people themselves by a simpler, clearer, more consistent benefit structure, and by better service delivery, wherever possible from a single office.

The introduction of Jobseeker's Allowance is expected to reduce expenditure on benefits by around £300 million between 1996–97 and 1997–98.

Housing Benefit

The **Housing Benefit** scheme assists people who need help to pay their rent (rent and/or domestic rates in Northern Ireland), using general assessment rules and benefit levels similar to those for Income Support (see p. 437). Unlike Income Support, the Housing Benefit scheme sets a limit of £16,000 on the amount of capital a person may have and still remain entitled to claim benefit.

Since January 1996 Housing Benefit for most private sector tenants has been calculated by reference to the general level of rents for properties with the same number of rooms in the locality. The new measures are designed to ensure that private sector tenants receiving benefit have an incentive to choose better value accommodation at the outset of a tenancy.

In 1995–96 a total of £10,800 million of Housing Benefit was claimed. An average 4.8 million people claimed.

Recent Changes

Since October 1996 most single people under 25 who are not lone parents and who are renting privately have had their Housing Benefit limited to the average cost of non-self-contained accommodation in the locality. This is intended to reduce disincentives to work, and to discourage young people from leaving home before they can afford to do so.

Council Tax Benefit

Council Tax Benefit helps people to meet their council tax payments. The scheme offers help to those claiming Income Support and income-based Jobseeker's Allowance and others with low incomes. Subject to rules broadly similar to those governing the provision of Income Support and Housing Benefit (see above), people may receive rebates of up to 100 per cent of their council tax. At present over 5 million households receive such help. A person who is solely liable for the council tax may also claim benefit (called 'second adult rebate') for a second adult who is not liable to pay the council tax and who is living in the home on a non-commercial basis.

In 1995–96 the total amount of Council Tax Benefit claimed was £2,100 million. An average 5.7 million people claimed.

Benefit Controls on People from Abroad

Residence Test

A new residence test, which came into force in August 1994, requires claimants to establish that they are habitually resident in Britain before a claim for income-based Jobseeker's Allowance, Housing Benefit or Council Tax Benefit can be paid. The test brings Britain into line with most other European countries, which already limit access to their benefit systems to those who have lived in the country for some time.

Asylum Seekers

Since February 1996 people who claim asylum on arriving in Britain have had their

entitlement to Income Support (income-based Jobseeker's Allowance from October 1996), Housing Benefit and Council Tax Benefit restricted. They now cease to be eligible for benefits if their asylum claim is refused by the Home Office rather than, as before, from the time their appeal was rejected. People who claim asylum after they have arrived in Britain are no longer entitled to benefit.

Family Credit

Family Credit is payable to low-paid employed and self-employed working families with children. It is payable to couples or lone parents. At least one parent must work for a minimum of 16 hours a week. The amount payable depends on a family's net income (excluding Child Benefit) and the number and ages of the children in the family. A maximum award, consisting of an adult credit, plus a rate for each child varying with age, and an extra credit if the parent works more than 30 hours a week, is payable if the family's net income does not exceed £72.50 a week. The award is reduced by 70 pence for each pound by which net income exceeds this amount. In certain cases where children under 11 have formal childcare arrangements, up to £60 a week can be deducted from net income before Family Credit is assessed. People with savings or capital worth more than £8,000 are ineligible; savings between £3,000 and £8,000 will reduce the amount received.

The processing of Family Credit claims has been speeded up to eliminate gaps in income on moving into work, and by July 1996 most claims were being cleared within five days.

In 1993–94 the total amount of family credit claimed was £990 million; total amount unclaimed was £230 million. The average number of people claiming was estimated at 440,000 and the average number not claiming although entitled was 180,000.

Earnings Top-up

While Family Credit (see above) helps people with dependent children to be better off in work, there has been no similar provision for single people and couples without children. In October 1996 a new benefit—Earnings Top-up—was introduced on a pilot basis to test whether topping up wages for workers without dependent children helps them get jobs and stay in work. The new benefit is tested at two different levels, with different rates for couples and single people. It is payable in eight pilot areas only and is the first social security benefit to be introduced on a pilot basis. A decision on possible national introduction will be made after full research and evaluation has been carried out.

Social Fund

The **Social Fund** consists of regulated payments, which do not have limited resources, and discretionary payments, which are paid out of an annual budget (£141.5 million in 1996–97).

The regulated payments are:

- maternity payment—£100 for each baby born or adopted. Payable to those on Income Support, income-based Jobseeker's Allowance, Family Credit or Disability Working Allowance;
- funeral payment—includes up to £500 for specified funeral directors' charges, plus the reasonable costs of all burial or cremation expenses. Available to those on Income Support and income-based Jobseeker's Allowance, Family Credit, Housing Benefit, Council Tax Benefit or Disability Working Allowance; and
- cold weather payment—£8.50 a week towards the extra cost of heating in very cold weather from November to March. Payable to those on Income Support who are elderly, disabled or have children under five years.

The discretionary payments are:

- community care grants to help, for example, people resettle into the community from care, or to remain in the community, and to ease exceptional pressure on families. Available to those on Income Support or income-based Jobseeker's Allowance;
- budgeting loans for important intermittent expenses after 26 weeks on Income Support or income-based Jobseeker's Allowance; and

- crisis loans to help people in an emergency or as a result of a disaster where there is a serious risk to health or safety. There is no qualifying benefit for this loan.

War Pensions and Related Services

Pensions are payable for disablement as a result of service in the armed forces or for certain injuries received in the merchant navy or civil defence during wartime, or to civilians injured by enemy action. The amount paid depends on the degree of disablement: the pension for 100 per cent disablement is £105 a week.

There are a number of extra allowances. The main ones are for unemployability, restricted mobility, the need for care and attendance, the provision of extra comforts, and as maintenance for a lowered standard of occupation. An age allowance of between £7.00 and £21.60 is payable weekly to war pensioners aged 65 or over whose disablement is assessed at 40 per cent or more.

Pensions are also paid to war widows and other dependants. (The standard rate of pension for a private's widow is £79.35 a week.) Until 1995 the War Widow's Pension was withdrawn on remarriage and a lump sum worth one year's pension was awarded. Legislation passed in July 1995 has restored the pension where the former war widow has remarried and then become widowed again, divorced or legally separated.

The War Pensions Agency maintains a welfare service for war pensioners, war widows and other dependants. It works closely with ex-Service organisations and other voluntary bodies which give financial aid and personal support to those disabled or bereaved as a result of war.

Concessions

Other benefits for which unemployed people and those on low incomes may be eligible include exemption from health service charges (see p. 402), grants towards the cost of spectacles, free school meals and free legal aid (see pp. 112–3).

People on low incomes, as well as all pensioners, widows and long-term sick people on Incapacity Benefit, receive extra help to meet the cost of VAT on their fuel bills. In 1996–97 some

Table 26.2: Tax Liability of Social Security Benefits

Not Taxable	*Taxable*
Attendance Allowance	Incapacity Benefit
Child Benefit	(long term or short term higher rate)
Child's Special Allowance	Industrial Death Benefit Pensions
Council Tax Benefit	Invalid Care Allowance
Disability Living Allowance	Jobseeker's Allowance[a]
Family Credit	Retirement Pension
Guardian's Allowance	Statutory Maternity Pay
Housing Benefit	Statutory Sick Pay
Incapacity Benefit (short term lower rate)	Widowed Mother's Allowance
Income Support	Widow's Pension
Industrial Disablement Benefit/Reduced	(Income Support paid in certain trade
Earnings Allowance	dispute cases)
Maternity Allowance	
One Parent Benefit	
Severe Disablement Allowance	
War Disablement Pension	
War Widow's Pension	

Source: *Inland Revenue*

[a] That part of the Jobseeker's Allowance equivalent to the individual or couple rate of personal allowance, as appropriate.

15 million people will have benefited, at a cost in this year alone of £710 million.

Reduced charges are often made to unemployed people, for example, for adult education and exhibitions, and pensioners are usually entitled to reduced transport fares.

Taxation

The general rule is that benefits which replace lost earnings are subject to tax, while those intended to meet a specific need are not (see Table 26.2). Various income tax reliefs and exemptions are allowed on account of age or a need to support dependants.

ARRANGEMENTS WITH OTHER COUNTRIES

As part of the European Union's efforts to promote the free movement of labour, regulations provide for equality of treatment and the protection of benefit rights for employed and self-employed people who move between member states. The regulations also cover retirement pensioners and other beneficiaries who have been employed, or self-employed, as well as dependants. Benefits covered include Child Benefit and those for sickness and maternity, unemployment, retirement, invalidity, accidents at work and occupational diseases.

Britain has reciprocal social security agreements with a number of other countries which also provide cover for some National Insurance benefits and family benefits.

In 1995 750,000 British National Insurance pensions were paid overseas, at a cost of some £940 million.

Further Reading

Social Security Statistics 1996. HMSO, 1996.

Social Welfare (2nd edn.). Aspects of Britain series, HMSO, 1995.

The Government's Expenditure Plans 1996–97 to 1998–99. Department of Social Security. Cm 3213. HMSO, 1996.

27 Education

History	442	Education and Training after 16	456
Administration	443	Links with Other Countries	463
Schools	443	The Youth Service	464

Over half a million teachers are employed in Britain's 29,000 state,[1] 2,000 special and 2,400 fee-paying independent schools, which are attended by over 9 million pupils. About 71 per cent of pupils continue studying after the age of 16. The proportion of young people entering universities and colleges has risen from one in eight in 1980 to almost one in three. Continuing education for adults is provided by a variety of colleges and institutions, including universities. Expenditure on education was £26,846 million in 1993–94.

HISTORY

England and Wales

Although government grants for education were first made in 1833, it was the 1870 Education Act in England and Wales which embodied the principle of compulsory elementary education with government aid. There were two types of elementary school—church voluntary schools and state schools provided by school boards. Attendance at school became compulsory in 1880 for children aged between five and ten, and the school leaving age was progressively raised to 14 by 1918.

A co-ordinated national system of education was introduced for the first time by the 1902 Education Act, and local government became responsible for state education and for helping to finance the voluntary schools. The system was supervised by the Board of Education.

In 1944 a new Education Act raised the school leaving age to 15, and schools were divided into primary and secondary. All children were given a secondary education, and the newly created Ministry of Education was empowered to develop a national education policy. Local government remained responsible for administering the system.

Children were allocated to different secondary schools—grammar, secondary technical or secondary modern—on the basis of selection tests taken at the age of 11. The local education authorities were required to prepare and submit to the Minister of Education development plans covering the whole process of primary and secondary education, while proceeding with the planned development of technical and adult education through schemes of further education.

In the 1960s and 1970s the selective system was gradually replaced by comprehensive schools, which take pupils of all abilities. The school leaving age was raised to 16 in 1972–73.

---

[1] For ease of reference the term 'state school' is used to cover schools maintained from public funds.

Scotland

An Act passed in 1872 transferred responsibility for Scottish education from the churches to elected school boards, which provided compulsory education for children between the ages of five and 13, and evening schools for young people over 13. The working of the new system was supervised by a central government department (now the Scottish Office Education and Industry Department) which also administered the distribution of the parliamentary grant.

In 1901 the school leaving age was raised to 14. An Act passed in 1918 replaced the boards with local government authorities and made the provision of secondary education mandatory for all children wanting it. Church schools were transferred to education authorities, while preserving their denominational character. The school leaving age was raised to 15 in 1947 and to 16 in 1972–73.

Northern Ireland

Education in Northern Ireland was brought into a single system by legislation passed in 1923, under which local government took over responsibility for its administration, supervised by the Ministry of Education. Children were required to receive 'elementary' education between the ages of six and 14. Secondary education remained largely in the hands of voluntary bodies, with assistance provided from public funds. Technical education was provided almost entirely by the local education authorities. The school leaving age was raised to 15 in 1947 and to 16 in 1972–73.

Reform

During the 1970s concern arose about the quality of education provided by Britain's schools and the lack of a formal national school curriculum. Since then major reforms have taken place in the three education systems, including the introduction of various forms of national curriculum (see p. 451), more choice of school for parents, and the provision of much more information about school performance.

ADMINISTRATION

The Secretary of State for Education and Employment has overall responsibility for school and post-school education in England. The Secretaries of State for Scotland, Wales and Northern Ireland exercise similar responsibilities in those countries. These are exercised through the Department for Education and Employment in England, The Scottish Office Education and Industry Department, the Welsh Office Education Department, and the Department of Education for Northern Ireland.

Most state school education is provided by local government education authorities and the rest by self-governing grant-maintained (GM) schools (see p. 444). In Northern Ireland the education service is administered locally by five education and library boards; in June 1996 the Government announced that the number of boards would be reduced to three.

SCHOOLS

Finance

LEA-maintained Schools

Central government annually determines an appropriate level of spending by local education authorities (LEAs) in England and Wales on all their services, including within that total an amount for education. This spending is funded from a number of sources, including Revenue Support Grant direct from the Government, non-domestic rates paid by business and commerce, and local taxes. LEAs themselves, however, decide how much of their resources should be spent on education or on their other services.

LEAs also receive some resources through central government grants. These focus mainly on training to improve school performance in literacy and numeracy and on support for information technology. Extra resources also go to inner city schools facing particularly severe problems. Additional government grants are made for capital expenditure at voluntary-aided schools (see p. 444).

Grant-maintained Schools

State grant-maintained (GM) self-governing schools are not financed by LEAs, as they have chosen to opt out of LEA control (see below). Instead, the Funding Agency for Schools in England calculates and pays grants to GM schools from public funds. Grant-maintained schools in Wales are funded by the Welsh Office.

Scotland and Northern Ireland

In Scotland most state schools are provided by local government education authorities; self-governing schools are funded directly by the Government. The education authorities are financed in a similar way to those in England and Wales.

The costs of the education and library boards in Northern Ireland are met by the Department of Education.

School Management

England and Wales

There are four kinds of state school that are wholly or mainly supported from public funds:

- LEA owned and funded county schools;
- voluntary schools, mostly established by religious denominations and grant-aided by LEAs; the governors of some types of voluntary school contribute to capital costs;
- special schools for pupils with special educational needs; and
- self-governing GM schools (see below).

LEA-financed Schools

Each LEA-maintained county, voluntary and special school has a governing body which includes governors appointed by the LEA, elected teacher and parent governors, and people co-opted from the local community. Voluntary schools also have governors from the church associated with the school.

All county, voluntary schools and special schools manage their own budgets. LEAs allocate funds to the schools, largely on the basis of pupil numbers. The school governing body is responsible for overseeing spending and for most aspects of staffing, including appointments and dismissals.

Grant-maintained Status

Some 18 per cent of secondary schools in England are grant-maintained (GM) self-governing schools. In Wales the proportion is approximately 5 per cent. GM status is achieved if the school's parents support the idea in a ballot and if the Secretary of State approves the school's proposals for GM status. The governing bodies of non-GM state schools must consider each year whether or not to hold a ballot on GM status. If they decide not to do so, they must tell parents why.

The governing body for GM schools consists of parents, teachers and people from the community served by the school. Governors take all decisions about school management, employ and pay staff, are responsible for school premises, and may acquire or dispose of land. GM schools are entitled to borrow money on the commercial market for capital investment.

City Technology Colleges

The 15 city technology colleges are non-fee-paying independent schools created by a partnership of government and private sector sponsors. The promoters own or lease the schools, employ teachers and other staff, and make substantial contributions towards the costs of building and equipment. There is no LEA involvement. The colleges teach the National Curriculum but with an emphasis on mathematics, technology and science.

Specialist Schools

The specialist schools programme was launched in 1993 with the creation of technology colleges. These are state secondary schools which teach the National Curriculum but with a special emphasis on technology, science and mathematics. A national network of language colleges concentrates on teaching modern foreign languages while continuing to deliver the full National Curriculum. Two similar schemes, one for the arts and the other for sports, were announced in June 1996.

A school must have the backing of a private-sector sponsor if it wishes to become specialised. Capital and annual grants are available from public funds to complement business sponsorship. There are 151 technology colleges and 31 language colleges in England.

Selection of Pupils

Under Government proposals for England and Wales published in June 1996, secondary schools would be given powers to select more of their pupils on grounds of aptitude and academic ability. Grant-maintained schools would be able to select up to 50 per cent of pupils, technology and language colleges up to 30 per cent in their specialist subjects, and other schools up to 20 per cent without having to publish statutory proposals. New grammar schools would also be encouraged and promoted by the Funding Agency for Schools.

Scotland

In Scotland most schools have school boards consisting of elected parent and staff members as well as co-opted members. They are required to promote contact between parents, the school and the community, and are involved in the appointment of senior staff and the community use of school premises.

Devolved management (from the local education authority to the school) is in place in primary and secondary schools. By April 1997 this will be extended to special schools.

Parents of children at state schools can opt for self-governing status following approval by a ballot; the school then receives funding directly from central government instead of the education authority. There are two self-governing schools in Scotland.

Northern Ireland

The main categories of school supported by public funds are:

- controlled schools, which are owned by the education and library boards and wholly financed from public funds;
- voluntary maintained schools, most of which are owned by the Roman Catholic Church; the majority of these schools are wholly financed from public funds;
- voluntary grammar schools, which may be owned by denominational or non-denominational bodies and are largely financed from public funds; and
- grant-maintained or controlled integrated schools, taking both Protestant and Roman Catholic pupils.

All publicly financed schools are managed by boards of governors, which include elected parents and teachers among their members.

Although all schools must be open to pupils of all religions, most Roman Catholic pupils attend Catholic maintained schools or Catholic voluntary grammar schools, and most Protestant children are enrolled at controlled schools or non-denominational voluntary grammar schools.

The Government has a statutory duty to encourage integrated education as a way of breaking down sectarian barriers. There are 32 integrated schools and pupil numbers are expected to rise to over 6,000 (about 2 per cent of the school population) by 1997. Integrated schools are financed by the Government. Existing controlled, maintained and voluntary grammar schools can apply to become integrated following a majority vote by parents.

All nursery, primary and secondary schools are financed on a basis which relates a major part of each school's resources to the number of pupils it can attract. All secondary schools have delegated budgets under which school governors decide spending priorities. Nursery and primary schools have partially delegated budgets with responsibility for the non-staff elements of their budgets. Most primary schools have full delegation of budgets on a voluntary basis.

School Places

Education authorities are responsible for providing school places, with the exception of

GM schools in England and Wales, where governing bodies are responsible.

Under the 1993 Education Act the Funding Agency for Schools in England may take on some responsibility for securing enough school places in individual LEA areas. In areas where between 10 and 75 per cent of pupils are being educated in GM primary or secondary schools, the LEA and the Agency may be jointly responsible. Once 75 per cent of primary or secondary pupils are in GM schools, the Agency may be solely responsible for the provision of school places. The Agency can only be involved in the provision of school places if the Secretary of State makes an order to that effect.

Pupils

Parents are required by law to see that their children receive efficient full-time education, at school or elsewhere, between the ages of five and 16 in Great Britain and four and 16 in Northern Ireland. About 94 per cent of pupils receive free education financed from public funds, while the others attend independent schools financed by fees paid by parents.

Boys and girls are taught together in most primary schools. Almost 90 per cent of pupils in state secondary schools in England and Wales and about 63 per cent in Northern Ireland attend mixed schools. In Scotland virtually all state secondary schools with one exception are mixed. Most independent schools (see p. 449) for younger children are mixed; the majority providing secondary education are single-sex, but the number of mixed secondary schools is growing.

Nursery Schools

Nearly 57 per cent of three- and four-year-olds in Britain attend nursery schools, nursery classes or reception classes in primary schools. In addition, many children attend pre-school playgroups, most of which are organised by parents.

In July 1995 the Government launched a voucher scheme to provide over time a nursery place for every child in the pre-school year in Britain whose parents wish to take it up. The first phase of the scheme began in April 1996 in four volunteer local authorities in England, and it will become fully operational throughout the rest of England in April 1997.

Both public and private providers of nursery education under the scheme will be required by the Government to meet certain minimum standards regarding literacy, numeracy and personal and social skills. Schools will be inspected regularly.

Similar arrangements will apply in Wales, Scotland and Northern Ireland.

Primary Schools

Compulsory education starts in infant primary schools or departments; at seven many transfer to separate junior primary schools or departments. The usual age for transfer from primary to secondary schools is 11 in England, Wales and Northern Ireland, but some local authorities in England have established first schools for pupils aged five to eight, nine or ten, and middle schools for age-ranges between eight and 14. In Scotland primary schools take children from five to 12, when they transfer to secondary schools. In Northern Ireland, children transfer to secondary school at the age of 11. For information on independent schools, see p. 449.

Secondary Schools

Around nine-tenths of the state secondary school population in Great Britain attend comprehensive schools. These mostly take pupils without reference to ability or aptitude and provide a wide-ranging secondary education for all or most of the children in a district. Schools in England and Wales can be organised in a number of ways. They include:

- those taking the 11 to 18 age-range;
- middle schools (see above); and
- schools with an age-range of 11 or 12 to 16.

Most other state-educated children attend grammar or secondary modern schools, to which they are allocated after selection procedures at the age of 11.

Scottish secondary education is almost

completely non-selective; the majority of schools are comprehensives covering the age-range 12 to 18.

In Northern Ireland secondary education is organised largely along selective lines, the 71 grammar schools admitting some 61,000 pupils on the basis of tests in English, maths and science. Over 90,000 pupils attend non-grammar secondary schools. Some secondary schools are run on a non-selective basis.

Table 27.1: School Pupils by Type of School in Britain	
	1993–94
All public sector[a]	8,647,000
Nursery schools	62,000
Primary schools	4,998,000
Secondary schools	3,588,000
Independent schools	591,000
Special schools[b]	114,000
Total pupils	**9,352,000**

Sources: Department for Education and Employment, Welsh Office, The Scottish Office Education and Industry Department and Department of Education for Northern Ireland
Note: Differences between totals and the sums of their component parts are due to rounding.
[a]Excludes public sector special schools.
[b]Includes state schools and those run by charities.

Rights of Parents

Parents must be given general information about a school through a prospectus and the school's annual report or, in Scotland, the school's handbook. They also have a statutory right to express a preference for a particular school for their child, and there is an appeal system if their choice is not met.

In England and Wales parents choosing a local secondary school have the right to see:

- national performance tables showing the latest public examination results, vocational qualification results and rates of absence on a school-by-school basis; and

- information in each local school's prospectus on its public examination results, vocational qualification results, attendance rates and the destinations of school leavers.

In England parents will also be able to see primary school performance tables based on National Curriculum assessment results.

Summaries of school inspection reports (see p. 455) are given to parents.

All state schools in England and Wales have to give parents a written annual report on their child's achievements, containing details about:

- the child's progress in all subjects and activities;

- the child's general progress and attendance record;

- the results of National Curriculum assessments and of public examinations taken by the child;

- comparative results of pupils of the same age in the school and nationally; and

- the arrangements for discussing pupils' school reports with teachers.

All parents are invited to an annual meeting to discuss the governors' annual report.

School performance tables for England are available on the Internet.

In Scotland information is published for parents on school costs, examination results, pupil attendance and absence, and the destinations of school leavers. Inspection reports are published for parents. National guidelines to schools on reporting to parents advise that they should provide them with information about their children's attainment in the various subjects, teachers' comments on their progress and details about steps to build on success or overcome difficulties. One main school report each year is advised, together with one brief update report.

The Northern Ireland system for reporting to parents is broadly similar to that in England and Wales.

Failing Schools

If school inspectors in England and Wales identify a school failing to give its pupils an acceptable standard of education, the LEA can appoint new governors and withdraw delegated management from the school. As an alternative, central government can put the school under new management until its performance reaches a satisfactory level. The new management is financed from central government. After further visits from the schools inspectorate (see p. 455), the Secretary of State decides whether the school has made sufficient progress. If it has, it becomes grant-maintained; if it has not, the school closes. This process takes about two years.

Ethnic Minority Children

Most school-aged children from ethnic minorities were born in Britain and tend to share the interests and aspirations of children in the population at large. Nevertheless, a substantial number still have particular needs arising from cultural differences, including those of language, religion and custom.

The education authorities have done much to meet these needs. English language teaching continues to receive priority for some 450,000 pupils for whom English is an additional language. Schools may teach the main ethnic minority community languages at secondary level in England and Wales as part of the National Curriculum. Schools have to take account of the ethnic and cultural backgrounds of pupils, and curricula should reflect ethnic and cultural diversity. Measures have been taken to improve the achievement of ethnic minority pupils, and to prepare all children, not just those of ethnic minority origin, for living in a multi-ethnic society.

From 1996 the annual school census in England will include new questions about the ethnic backgrounds of pupils in order to ensure that all pupils have equal opportunities to achieve their full potential.

Special Educational Needs

Special educational needs comprise learning difficulties of all kinds, including mental and physical disabilities which hinder or prevent learning. LEAs in England and Wales must identify children whose learning difficulties are very severe or complex, assess and meet their needs, and involve parents in decisions about their child's special education.

If the LEA believes that it should determine the education for the child, it must draw up a formal statement of the child's special educational needs and the action it intends to take to meet them. There are statutory time limits governing this procedure.

A state school named in the statement is required to admit the child.

In England and Wales parents have a right of appeal to the Special Educational Needs Tribunal if they disagree with the LEA decisions about their child's special educational needs. The Tribunal's verdict is final and binding on all parties.

Wherever possible, children with special educational needs are educated in ordinary schools, where placement must be compatible with the needs of the child and with the provision of efficient education for the other children in the school. The LEA is required to comply with parents' choice of school unless this is inappropriate for the child, involves an inefficient use of resources or is incompatible with the efficient education of other children.

A Government Code of Practice offers practical guidance to all LEAs and state schools in England and Wales on how to identify, assess and monitor all pupils with special educational needs.

Each school in England and Wales must formulate a policy on pupils with special educational needs and publish information about that policy. Annual reports to parents must report on the success of these policies.

In Scotland the choice of school is a matter for agreement between education authorities and parents. A 1995 report by school inspectors sets out clear basic principles which emphasise the importance of partnership between all involved in meeting special educational needs.

In Northern Ireland legislation has been passed under which similar arrangements to those in England and Wales, including an appeal system, will be introduced.

There are nearly 2,000 special schools (both day and boarding) in Britain for pupils with special educational needs. Some of these are run by voluntary organisations and some are established in hospitals. They cater for some 114,000 pupils. The pupil/teacher ratio in special schools is 5.9 to 1 compared with 18.9 to 1 in mainstream state schools.

The Government has published guidance for parents of children with special needs in England, Wales and Scotland which sets out the rights and responsibilities of parents in their child's education.

Health and Welfare of Schoolchildren

Physical education, including organised games, is part of the curriculum of all state schools. In England and Wales playing fields must be available for pupils over the age of eight. Most secondary schools have at least one gymnasium.

Government health departments are responsible for the medical inspection of schoolchildren and for advice on, and treatment of, medical and dental problems. The education service seeks to help prevent and deal with juvenile drug misuse and to help prevent the spread of AIDS. In England government funds support the training of teachers with responsibility for anti-drug education.

The Government has also issued guidance on drug prevention in England's schools, outlining how to teach pupils about the dangers of drug misuse, advising schools on drug education and prevention, and giving advice on how to deal with drug-related incidents on school premises. In Scotland similar curriculum advice is made available to every school. School drug education programmes are subject to inspection by school inspectors.

In Northern Ireland a drug education, advice and resource pack has been issued to all schools and colleges. It includes guidance on drug education policies and procedures for the handling of drugs incidents in schools. All schools must have a drug education policy and publish details about it in their prospectus.

LEAs and GM schools are responsible for providing school meals for pupils. They make their own decisions on the nature of the meals service, taking account of local circumstances. In Northern Ireland school meals must be provided for primary, special and grant-aided nursery school pupils.

Free meals must be provided for children whose parents receive a social security benefit called income support or another known as income-based Jobseekers' Allowance; all other pupils have to be charged for meals. Although LEAs and GM schools do not have to provide milk to any pupil, they may provide free milk to pupils of parents in receipt of either of the above social security benefits; they can also offer subsidised milk to other pupils.

LEAs must provide free of charge the transport they consider necessary to enable pupils living in their area to attend school and they may help other pupils with their fares. LEAs must publish annually their policy on free and assisted transport.

Corporal punishment is prohibited by law in state schools in Britain, and for pupils in independent schools whose fees are met wholly or partly from public funds under the Assisted Places Scheme (see below).

Independent Schools

Fee-paying independent schools providing full-time education for five or more pupils of compulsory school age must register by law with the Department for Education and Employment and are subject to inspection. They can be required to remedy serious shortcomings in their accommodation or teaching and, in the case of boarding schools, welfare of pupils. They must exclude anyone regarded as unsuitable to teach in, or own, a school. About 6 per cent of school children attend independent schools.

There are about 2,400 independent schools in Britain educating 600,000 pupils of all ages. They charge fees varying from around £300 a term for day pupils at nursery age to over £4,000 a term for senior boarding pupils. Many offer bursaries to help pupils from less well-off families. Such pupils may also be helped by the Government's Assisted Places Scheme, under which financial assistance is given according to parental income. Over 38,000 places are offered in England, Wales and Scotland under the scheme, which the Government is going to double in size. The Government also gives income-related help with fees to pupils at eight music and ballet schools; there are a limited number of similar scholarships at cathedral choir schools.

Independent schools range from small kindergartens to large day and boarding schools, and from new and, in some cases, experimental schools to ancient foundations. The 600 boys', girls' and mixed preparatory schools prepare children for entry to senior schools. The normal age-range for these preparatory schools is from seven-plus to 11, 12 or 13, but many have pre-preparatory departments for younger children. A number of independent schools have been established by religious orders and ethnic minorities.

Independent schools for older pupils—from 11, 12 or 13 to 18 or 19—include about 550 which are often referred to as 'public schools'. These are members of the Headmasters' and Headmistresses' Conference, the Governing Bodies Association, the Society of Headmasters and Headmistresses of Independent Schools, the Girls' Schools Association and the Governing Bodies of Girls' Schools Association.

In Northern Ireland the 21 independent schools, educating about 1,000 pupils, are subject to inspection by the Department of Education for Northern Ireland.

Teachers

England and Wales

Teachers in state schools in England and Wales are appointed by LEAs or school governing bodies. They must hold qualifications approved by the Government.

Almost all entrants to teaching in state schools in England and Wales complete an approved course of teacher training. These courses are offered by university departments of education as well as other higher education establishments (see p. 459) and groups of schools. One of the two main qualifications is the four-year Bachelor of Education (BEd) honours degree. The other is the successful completion of a three-year degree course, topped up by a one-year Postgraduate Certificate in Education (PGCE) course.

> Formal teacher appraisal has been introduced in English and Welsh schools in order to assist professional development, strengthen the management of schools and improve the quality of education for pupils.

Reform of Initial Teacher Training

Under new government reforms in England and Wales, schools play a much larger part in initial teacher training by taking on more responsibility for planning and managing courses and for the selection, training and assessment of students, usually in partnership with institutions. The reforms enable schools to train students to teach their specialist subjects, assess pupils and manage classes.

The reforms allow consortia of schools to run courses for postgraduate students if they wish to do so. Other courses, including all undergraduate courses, are run by universities and colleges in partnership with schools.

The Teacher Training Agency is responsible for accrediting training providers, financing initial teacher training courses, ensuring that national standards are met and promoting teaching. In 1995 the Government asked the Agency to introduce a new professional qualification for headteachers. In 1996 the Government requested the Agency to develop a national curriculum for initial teacher training covering the core subjects of English, mathematics and sciences. It has also asked the Agency to produce a professional framework for teacher training which would set out standards and qualifications at key stages in the profession.

In Wales, initial teacher training is funded by the Higher Education Funding Council for Wales, which also accredits institutions and schools providing courses.

Other Training

Under the Licensed Teacher Scheme, a trainee teacher is appointed to a school, which then provides training and pays a salary; on successful completion of a two-year period of in-service training, qualified teacher status is granted. The Scheme and other employment-based routes into teaching are presently under review. Qualified teachers from other European Union countries are usually granted qualified teacher status.

Scotland

All teachers in education authority schools must be registered with the General Teaching Council (GTC) for Scotland. The GTC is responsible for disciplinary procedures under which teachers guilty of professional misconduct may be removed permanently or temporarily from the register. Advice is given by the GTC to the Secretary of State on teacher supply and the professional suitability of teacher training courses.

All entrants to the teaching profession are graduates. New primary teachers qualify either through a four-year BEd course or a one-year postgraduate course at a higher education teacher training institution. Teachers of academic subjects at secondary schools must hold a degree with at least two passes in each subject which they wish to teach. Secondary school teachers must undertake a one-year postgraduate training course or an undergraduate course combining subject studies, study of education and school experience.

Guidelines for initial teacher training courses, issued in 1993, stress the importance of partnership between teacher training institutions and schools, and the competences required in the classroom for teachers beginning their careers.

All pre-service courses must be approved by The Scottish Office Education and Industry Department. They must also be validated by a higher education institution and accredited by the GTC as leading to registration. Education authorities have developed schemes to implement national guidelines for staff development and appraisal.

Northern Ireland

Teacher training is provided by Queen's University, in Belfast, the University of Ulster, two colleges of education and the Open University (OU—see p. 461). The principal courses are BEd Honours (four years) and the one-year Postgraduate Certificate of Education. The OU course is part-time and lasts 18 months. Education and library boards have a statutory duty to ensure that teachers are equipped with the necessary skills to implement education reforms and the Northern Ireland school curriculum.

School Curriculum

England and Wales

The National Curriculum consists of core subjects, which are compulsory for five- to 16-year-olds, and foundation subjects, which must be studied to the age of 14 at least. In England the core subjects of the curriculum are English, mathematics and science, and the foundation subjects are technology (design and technology, and information technology), history, geography, music, art, physical education and, for secondary school pupils, a modern foreign language.

This is also the case in Wales but, in addition, Welsh is a core subject in Welsh-speaking schools and a foundation subject in non-Welsh speaking schools. Nearly all primary schools in Wales teach Welsh as a first or second language and about a quarter use Welsh as the sole or main medium of instruction. In secondary schools, Welsh is compulsory for pupils aged 11 to 16 in Welsh-speaking schools and for pupils aged 11 to 14 in other schools. By August 1999 Welsh will be compulsory for almost all 11- to 16-year-old pupils.

There is more choice in the curriculum for pupils aged 14 to 16. History, geography, art and music are all optional subjects, as are technology and a modern foreign language in Wales. In England a modern foreign language and technology became compulsory subjects for 14- to 16-year-olds in September 1996.

Religious education is required for all pupils as part of the basic curriculum and all secondary schools must provide sex education. Parents have a right to withdraw their children from these subjects (see p. 453).

A revised National Curriculum was introduced for five- to 14-year-olds in September 1995 and for 14- to 16-year-olds in September 1996. This places greater emphasis on literacy and numeracy. For each subject programmes of study lay down what pupils should be taught, with attainment targets setting out the expected standards of pupils' performance. Schools are also required to provide pupils with the opportunity to develop information technology skills across all National Curriculum subjects.

In the summer of 1997 pupils' performance at the ages of 7, 11 and 14 will be assessed by their teachers in the core subjects of English, mathematics and science. Fourteen-year-olds will also be assessed in the foundation subjects of the National Curriculum. In addition, all

7-year-olds will take National Curriculum tests in English and mathematics and most 11- and 14-year-olds will take tests in the core subjects. In Welsh-speaking schools the three age groups are tested in Welsh.

The General Certificate of Secondary Education (GCSE) is the major qualification taken by pupils at the end of compulsory schooling at the age of 16. The proportion of pupils with five or more GCSEs at grades A to C has risen significantly in recent years. In England, the proportion rose from nearly 33 per cent in 1988–89 to 43 per cent in 1994–95.

General supervision of examination standards rests jointly with the School Curriculum and Assessment Authority in England and the Curriculum and Assessment Authority for Wales.

The Independent Appeals Authority for School Examinations hears appeals against grades awarded in GCSE and GCE A level and AS examinations (see p. 457) when the appeals procedures of the examining body concerned have been exhausted.

A new vocational course for pupils aged 14 to 16 is being piloted. The new Part One General National Vocational Qualification (GNVQ) is broadly equivalent to two GCSE courses and is available in six subject areas—business; health and social care; manufacturing; art and design; information technology; and leisure and tourism. Engineering will be introduced in September 1997.

New GCSE (Short Course) qualifications were introduced from September 1996. These take half the time typically allotted to a GCSE and are available in modern foreign languages, physical education, religious education, geography, history, design and technology, and information technology. For schools in Wales a GCSE (Short Course) qualification is available in Welsh as a second language.

A new vocational qualification for 14- to 16-year-olds in foreign languages will provide an alternative way to assess short course requirements in languages.

Scotland

The content and management of the curriculum are not prescribed by statute, and responsibility rests with education authorities and headteachers, although guidance is provided by the Secretary of State and the Scottish Consultative Council on the Curriculum. The Council has recommended that secondary level pupils follow a broad and balanced curriculum consisting of English, mathematics, science, a modern European language, social studies, technological activities, art, music or drama, religious and moral education, and physical education.

A major programme of curricular review and development has been carried out for the five to 14 age-range. The Government has issued guidance on English language, mathematics, expressive arts, Latin, Gaelic, modern languages, environmental studies and religious and moral education. Under new arrangements, standardised tests in English and mathematics are given to pupils in the five to 14 age group whenever they complete one of five levels. A major programme to extend modern language teaching to primary schools is in progress.

Provision is made for teaching in Gaelic in Gaelic-speaking areas and in some other areas where education authorities have identified this as a priority.

Pupils take the Scottish Certificate of Education (SCE) at Standard Grade at the end of their fourth year of secondary education, normally around the age of 16. The proportion of pupils leaving school with no SCE qualification has fallen significantly from one pupil in four in 1983–84 to fewer than one in ten in 1994–95. SCE Standard and Higher Grade examinations are conducted by the Scottish Examinations Board.

The Higher Grade can be taken in the fifth and/or sixth year of secondary education. Some pupils also sit examinations for the Certificate of Sixth Year Studies or take vocational National Certificate units (see p. 457) awarded by the Scottish Vocational Education Council. A new system of courses for fifth and sixth year pupils is being developed (see p. 458).

Northern Ireland

The Northern Ireland Curriculum, compulsory in all publicly financed schools, is made up of religious education and six broad areas of study: English, mathematics, science and technology, the environment and society, creative and expressive studies, and, in secondary schools, language studies.

The Curriculum also includes four compulsory cross-curricular themes: cultural heritage, education for mutual understanding, health education and information technology. Secondary schools have two additional themes —economic awareness and careers education.

Following reviews of the Curriculum, new arrangements taking effect in September 1996 have reduced its overall content in primary schools and have allowed secondary schools and pupils more flexibility in subject choice. Teaching of the Curriculum takes up about 85 per cent of teaching time in primary schools and 60 to 65 per cent in secondary schools.

Pupil assessment became statutory in September 1996. Pupils are being assessed in English and maths at the ages of 8 and 11; if a pupil is taught in the Irish language, he or she is assessed in Irish and mathematics at the age of 8 and in English, Irish and mathematics at the age of 11. Fourteen-year-olds will additionally be assessed in science. As in England and Wales, the GCSE examination is used to assess 16-year-old pupils.

Religious Education and Collective Worship

In England and Wales state schools must provide religious education and a daily act of collective worship for all registered pupils. Every LEA has to produce a religious education syllabus, which is agreed locally and must be reviewed every five years. Syllabuses must reflect Christianity while taking account of the other main religions practised in Britain.

The School Curriculum and Assessment Authority has published model syllabuses for religious education in England to help promote quality; LEAs may adopt one of the models in full or draw on them when preparing the local syllabus. Parents have the right to withdraw their children from religious education classes and from collective worship. Voluntary-aided schools provide the opportunity for denominational religious education.

Scottish education authorities are required to see that schools practise religious observance and give pupils religious instruction; parents may withdraw their children if they wish. Certain schools provide for Roman Catholic children, but in all schools there are safeguards for individual conscience.

In Northern Ireland, schools must provide religious education and collective worship, although parents have the right to withdraw their children from both. A core syllabus has been approved by the four main churches in Northern Ireland and this must be taught in all grant-aided schools.

Sex Education

All state secondary schools in England and Wales are required to provide sex education for all pupils registered at the school. This must include education about HIV and AIDS and sexually transmitted diseases. In state primary schools the governors must consider whether sex education should be offered beyond the requirements of the National Curriculum Science Order.

Sex education in state schools must encourage young people to have regard to moral considerations and the value of family life. Parents are entitled to withdraw their children from sex education classes other than those required by the National Curriculum. All state schools must publish in their prospectus a summary of the content and organisation of any sex education provided.

In Scotland, government guidance on sex education is provided to education authorities and headteachers, who are responsible for the content of the curriculum.

In Northern Ireland sex education is taught through the compulsory science programme of study and the health education cross-curricular theme.

Curriculum Development and Assessment

The School Curriculum and Assessment Authority in England and the Curriculum and Assessment Authority for Wales are responsible for:

- keeping all aspects of the school curriculum and of school examinations under review;
- advising the Government on the curriculum, and assessment and examination arrangements; and
- publishing information about the curriculum.

All GCSE and other qualifications offered to pupils of compulsory school age in state schools in England and Wales must be approved by the Government. Associated syllabuses and assessment procedures must comply with national guidelines and be approved by the relevant curriculum and assessment authority.

In Scotland curriculum development is undertaken by the Scottish Consultative Council on the Curriculum in consultation with The Scottish Office Education and Industry Department. The Scottish Examination Board liaises with the Council on links between the curriculum and assessment.

The Northern Ireland Council for the Curriculum, Examinations and Assessment is responsible for advising the Department of Education on the Curriculum and its assessment, and for the conduct of examinations.

Information Technology

The National Curriculum places a strong emphasis on the use of information technology (IT) to ensure that all children are appropriately versed in the new technologies. In England the average number of pupils per microcomputer in primary schools in 1993–94 was 18 compared with 25 in 1991–92 and 107 in 1984–85. In secondary schools the average number of pupils per microcomputer was ten in 1993–94 compared with 13 in 1991–92 and 60 in 1984–85. Under a current scheme, managed by the National Council for Educational Technology (see below), two teachers in each of up to 600 schools have been given a multimedia portable computer to develop their expertise. One third of primary schools in England have multimedia computers. The Department for Education and Employment

funds the use of CD-ROM technology in schools in England.

In 1995 the Government announced a £10 million initiative designed to help schools and colleges to pilot the use of intermediate and broadband technologies. The initiative draws together the efforts of educational institutions, private companies, education authorities and Training and Enterprise Councils (TECs).

In Wales the Welsh Office also has a grant programme to support microcomputers in schools and has financed the installation of satellite television equipment in all secondary schools. This is used to teach modern foreign languages and other subjects. A scheme to supply all primary and special schools in Wales with either multimedia equipment and software, or portable computers, has just been implemented.

In Scotland computing studies are included in the five to 14 age group national guidelines on environmental studies. In most secondary schools, first and second year pupils take a short course in computing; third and fourth year pupils choose between a Standard Grade course or a National Certificate module. Similarly, fifth and sixth year pupils are able to choose between Higher Grade and a number of National Certificate modules.

In Northern Ireland, IT is one of the four compulsory educational cross-curricular themes forming part of the curriculum for primary and secondary pupils in publicly financed schools.

The four Government education departments jointly fund the National Council for Educational Technology, which promotes and evaluates the use of new technologies in education and training. The Scottish Council for Educational Technology also develops software and other applications geared to the curriculum and school organisation in Scotland.

Other Educational Aids

The BBC (British Broadcasting Corporation) and the independent Channel 4 transmit radio and television programmes designed for schools (see p. 505). Teachers' notes, pupils' pamphlets and computer software accompany many broadcast series.

School Inspections

Various inspectorates report to the Government on the quality of education provided by schools.

England

In England the independent Office for Standards in Education (OFSTED) advises the Secretary of State on quality, standards and efficiency, and regulates a system of school inspections. The inspection cycle began in September 1993 for secondary schools and in September 1994 for primary and other schools.

Every school has to be inspected every four years by a team of independent inspectors—headed by a registered inspector—containing educationists and lay people. Inspections take place according to agreed national standards monitored by OFSTED. Parents are sent a summary of the inspection report, which is published in full. School governing bodies must prepare action plans to follow it up and report back to parents on their progress. OFSTED is headed by Her Majesty's Chief Inspector of Schools.

A review of the school inspection system is in progress. This proposes that all schools must be inspected at least once within a six-year period, while some may be inspected more often, and that inspection resources should be targeted upon schools which are failing or have serious weaknesses.

Wales

Her Majesty's Chief Inspector of Schools for Wales has similar functions to those of OFSTED. All schools are inspected every five years in the first instance.

Scotland

In Scotland HM Inspectors of Schools (HMI) are responsible for independent evaluation of education standards and for advising the Secretary of State. Reports are published on inspections and given to parents. Inspectors return to the school between one and two years after the publication of the report to assess progress in meeting their recommendations.

Their conclusions about progress are published, together with an indication of any further action which may be required. The school remains a focus for attention by HMI until the recommendations have been satisfactorily addressed.

The Inspectorate's Audit Unit collects, analyses and publishes evidence about the performance of schools and education authorities. Evidence is published on a comparative basis, and recommendations are made for action and improvement.

Northern Ireland

The Education and Training Inspectorate evaluates, reports and advises on quality and standards in schools. Inspection reports are published and a summary is provided for parents. Where follow-up action is judged by an inspection team to be necessary, school governors are required to indicate any action planned and to submit details to the Department of Education. Schools have to be inspected every five years and there is provision for lay involvement in inspections. The Inspectorate is headed by the Chief Inspector, who is the main adviser on professional issues to the Department of Education.

Schools, Careers and Business

One of the Government's key objectives is to help young people develop the skills the economy needs. Some 98 per cent of pupils in their final year of compulsory education in England are offered at least one week of work experience.

Education Business Partnerships, consisting of representatives from industry, education and the wider community, aim to bring about closer links between education and industry in Great Britain and ensure that young people develop the skills to help them succeed in the labour market.

One of the main schemes managed by the Partnerships is the Teacher Placement Service (TPS), funded by the Government. The TPS organises placements in business for teachers and lecturers to extend their professional and personal development, improve learning opportunities for young people, and provide better careers education services. Since 1989 190,000 teachers have been on placements.

Compacts bring together employers, young people, schools, colleges and other bodies involved in training in order to help young people achieve more at school, and to continue their education and training after the age of 16. Under Compact schemes, young people work towards agreed goals, while employers provide a number of incentives for achieving them.

The Government's Project Business scheme offers young people the opportunity to learn how business works and acquire the work skills needed by employers. Business volunteers work with teachers and business/ works visits are arranged for young people.

Careers

All young people in full-time education are entitled to impartial careers guidance. Most schools have a written policy statement on careers education and guidance, a careers co-ordinator and an agreement with their local careers guidance service about the co-ordinated contribution they will make to student development. LEAs are active participants in the majority of careers service organisations.

In Northern Ireland careers education is one of the six compulsory education themes forming part of the secondary school curriculum (see p. 453). The Careers Service is part of the Training and Employment Agency.

All state secondary schools in England and Wales have to provide leavers with a National Record of Achievement setting out their school attainments, including public examination and National Curriculum assessment results. In Scotland the Record is not compulsory.

In Northern Ireland all pupils in secondary education are issued with a Record of Achievement on leaving school, and from 1997–98 this will apply to primary schools too.

EDUCATION AND TRAINING AFTER 16

About 71 per cent of 16-year-old pupils choose to continue in full-time education after 16: in school sixth forms, sixth-form colleges, further education colleges, universities and other higher education institutions. The percentage for 17- and 18-year-olds is 59 per cent and 40 per cent respectively.

Broadly speaking, education after 16 outside schools is divided into further and higher education. Further education (including education for adults) is largely vocational and in England covers courses up to and including GCE A level and AS qualifications, and GNVQ Advanced level or their equivalents (see p. 457). Higher education covers advanced courses at levels higher than GCE A level or equivalent. About 3.8 million people were enrolled on further education courses in 1994–95. Youth credits are on offer from Training and Enterprise Councils in England and Wales and from Local Enterprise Companies in Scotland (see p. 189). They enable 16- and 17-year-olds leaving full-time education to obtain vocational education and training through their employer or a specialist training provider.

In 1994–95 there were 1.7 million home and overseas students in higher education, of whom 49 per cent were women.

Credit accumulation and transfer schemes are in use in many English and Welsh post-school establishments. In Scotland a credit accumulation scheme covers courses in all further and higher education. Similar schemes in higher education in Northern Ireland are compatible with those of institutions in the rest of Britain.

The national computer-based Educational Counselling and Credit Transfer Information Service (ECCTIS) provides prospective students and their advisers with quick and easy access without charge to information on course opportunities at universities and colleges of higher and further education throughout Britain. ECCTIS, which is available to subscribing institutions on CD-ROM, can be found in over two-thirds of secondary schools with sixth forms, as well as the majority of further education colleges, higher education institutions, careers offices and Training and Enterprise Councils; ECCTIS is also available at British Council offices throughout the world.

Schools and Sixth-form Colleges

Having taken the GCSE examination (see p. 452), students in England, Wales and Northern Ireland can stay on at school or be educated in a further education college. Students in England and Wales can also study at sixth-form colleges. They study for examinations which are the main standard for entry to higher education or professional training. These include the academic General Certificate of Education (GCE) Advanced (A) level, the Advanced Supplementary (AS) examination, Advanced General National Vocational Qualifications (GNVQs) and National Vocational Qualifications (NVQs). The GCE A level is usually taken at the age of 18 or 19 after two years' study; part of the qualification is based on course work and the rest on written test papers. AS levels enable sixth-form pupils to study a wider range of subjects. Arts students, for example, can still study science subjects at AS level.

Equality of status for academic and vocational qualifications is being promoted in England, Wales and Northern Ireland. The new GNVQs for young people in full-time education between the ages of 16 and 18 provide a broad-based preparation for a range of occupations and higher education, and are designed to have parity of esteem with GCE A levels. There are three GNVQ levels—Advanced, Intermediate and Foundation. An Advanced GNVQ—called the vocational A level—requires a level of achievement broadly equal to two GCE A levels. GNVQs may also be taken in combination with other qualifications, such as GCE A levels or GCSEs.

GNVQs are accredited by the National Council for Vocational Qualifications. They are awarded by the City and Guilds of London Institute, the RSA Examinations Board and the Business and Technology Education Council (BTEC).

In 1996 an official report was published setting out an agenda for changes designed to raise standards in qualifications for 16- to 19-year-olds and increase participation and achievement in education and training for young people. Consequently, the Government plans to introduce a new qualifications framework in 1998 which will provide for revised and strengthened general and vocational qualifications, offering young people more choice.

Skills valued by employers will be given a higher priority in the new framework. More young people will be offered the opportunity to gain a qualification in the three key skills of communication, numeracy and information technology which are already compulsory in GNVQs and some publicly-funded youth training schemes.

The Government has accepted the report's recommendation that a single organisation should oversee both academic and vocational qualifications in England by taking over the roles of the School Curriculum and Assessment Authority and the National Council for Vocational Qualifications. This will be created in 1997, subject to parliamentary approval. Similar arrangements are being considered for Wales.

Scotland

Pupils staying on at school after the end of compulsory education study for the Higher Grade Scottish Certificate of Education examination between the ages of 16 and 18; passes at this grade are the basis for entry to higher education or professional training. The Certificate of Sixth Year Studies (CSYS) is for pupils who have completed their Higher Grade main studies and who wish to continue studies in particular subjects.

A flexible system of vocational courses for 16- to 18-year-olds has been introduced in schools and colleges in disciplines such as business and administration, engineering and industrial production. These courses are also intended to meet the needs of many adults entering training or returning to education. The courses lead to the award of the non-advanced National Certificate, intended for students over 16 who have successfully completed a programme of vocational courses based on short study units. Similar unit-based courses are also available at advanced levels, leading to the award of a Higher National Certificate or Diploma.

General Scottish Vocational Qualifications (General SVQs) are designed to meet the needs of 16- to 19-year-olds at school or in further education colleges. Broadly compatible with the GNVQs in the rest of Britain, General SVQs are a stepping-stone to higher education or further training. They are accredited and awarded by the Scottish Vocational Education Council (SCOTVEC).

A new five-level system of courses and awards for fifth- and sixth-year pupils will take effect in the late 1990s. Under this, Highers will remain as one of the levels but courses will be based on units of study of 40 or 80 hours. The recommended study time for each Higher will be extended from 120 hours to 160 hours. Existing courses of the Scottish Examinations Board and SCOTVEC will be drawn into a unified system of curriculum and assessment. Advanced Higher courses will be developed, incorporating the current Certificate of Sixth Year Studies and building on Highers to provide a two-year 320-hour course. Group awards will be available at all five levels. The Scottish Examinations Board and SCOTVEC will be replaced in 1997 by a single body called the Scottish Qualifications Authority.

Further Education Colleges

People over the age of 16 can also take courses in further education colleges. Much further education is work-related and vocational. Further education institutions supply much of the education element in government-sponsored training programmes. The number of students in further education is forecast to rise by 20 per cent between 1994 and 1999.

Table 27.2: Students Enrolled in Further Education in Britain

	1984–85	1994–95
Further education enrolments:[a]		
Full-time	400,000	758,000
Part-time	3,126,000	3,061,000
All further education	3,526,000	3,819,000

Source: Department for Education and Employment
[a]Includes enrolments on Youth Training in public sector colleges and adult education centres.

Many students on further education courses attend part-time, either by day release or block release from employment or during the evenings. The system has strong ties with commerce and industry, and co-operation with business is encouraged by the Government and its agencies. Employers are normally involved in designing courses.

Courses are run by some 550 institutions of further education, many of which also offer higher education courses (see p. 459). In England and Wales each is controlled by an autonomous further education corporation and governing body with substantial representation from business. Scottish colleges are controlled by autonomous boards of management.

Funds are allocated to institutions by further education funding councils in England and Wales; part of the funding is not cash limited and is directly related to student numbers. The Scottish Office Education and Industry Department distributes funds to colleges in Scotland. In Northern Ireland further education colleges are financed via the education and library boards by the Department of Education. Institutions in England, Wales and Scotland are obliged to publish information about how they use their financial and other resources.

Funding councils in England and Wales send out independent inspectors to assess the quality of the education provided by colleges. They publish reports containing quality assessments, and colleges are obliged to explain how they will put things right if there are major criticisms. Each college has to publish information about its examination results annually. Colleges in Scotland are inspected by HM Inspectors of Schools (see p. 455) and in Northern Ireland by the Education and Training Inspectorate.

Vocational Qualifications

The National Council for Vocational Qualifications has established a framework of National Vocational Qualifications (NVQs) in England, Wales and Northern Ireland which offers equal access and opportunity for all. NVQs are applicable to nearly 90 per cent of jobs. National standards of competence, knowledge and understanding, which have to be demonstrated by successful candidates, are set by industry lead bodies (consisting of representatives of employers, trade unions and professional groups) supported by the Department for Education and Employment. Lead bodies are often formed by Industry Training Organisations (see p. 189). NVQs are established at five levels:

- Level 1—foundation
- Level 2—basic craft
- Level 3—technician, advanced craft, supervisor
- Level 4—higher technician, middle management
- Level 5—middle to higher management, professional.

NVQs consist of units which set out the standards which the individual must reach in a range of tasks. The individual is assessed on the performance of these tasks, this process consisting of observation in the workplace. Assessment may also include practical simulation, oral questioning, assignments and course work.

In Scotland there is an analogous system of Scottish Vocational Qualifications (SVQs). NVQs and SVQs have mutual recognition throughout Britain.

Modern Apprenticeships, which started in 1995 (see p. 191), are employer-based and designed to train young people at work and qualify them to NVQ level 3 or above.

Awarding Bodies

The National Council for Vocational Qualifications does not award NVQs. The three largest NVQ-awarding bodies are the City and Guilds of London Institute, the RSA Examinations Board and the London Chamber of Commerce and Industry Examinations Board. NVQs are also awarded by a large number of smaller organisations, many of which are industry-specific or professional bodies. The awarding bodies examine and validate vocational education and training and their awards must meet the NVQ criteria and be submitted to the National Council for Vocational Qualifications for accreditation. Accreditation is given for a maximum of five years. Re-accreditation must then be sought.

In Scotland the Scottish Vocational Education Council is the national accreditation body and the main awarding organisation.

National Targets for Education and Training

The Government has endorsed new national targets for education and training announced in 1995 by the National Advisory Council for Education and Training Targets. The main targets, which have been set for the year 2000, are that:

- by age 19, 85 per cent of young people should achieve five GCSEs at Grade C or above, an Intermediate GNVQ or an NVQ Level 2; and
- by age 21, 60 per cent of young people should achieve two GCE A levels, an Advanced GNVQ or an NVQ Level 3.

There is a separate system of targets in Scotland for the year 2000. These are that:

- by the age of 19, 85 per cent of young people should attain SVQ Level II or five standard SCE grades (1-3) or equivalent; and
- by the age of 21, 70 per cent of young people should achieve SVQ level III or three Highers (A-C).

Higher Education

Higher education, which consists of degree and equivalent courses, has experienced a dramatic expansion since the 1980s. The total number of full-time and part-time higher education students in Britain almost doubled between 1979 and 1995 to some 1.7 million. The proportion of young people entering full-time higher education is roughly one in three.

In order to maintain British expertise in science, engineering and technology, the Government has taken steps to promote these subjects at all levels.

Higher education institutions are responsible for providing high-quality education. The Higher Education Quality Council, financed by subscriptions from institutions, ensures that satisfactory quality control arrangements are in place. The higher education funding councils for England, Scotland and Wales (see below) carry out subject assessments of the quality of teaching and learning provision, publish regular reports on their findings and aim to ensure that any serious problems are put right by the university or college concerned. Acting on behalf of the Department of Education for Northern Ireland, the Higher Education Funding Council for England publishes reports on the quality of teaching and learning provision in the two Northern Ireland universities.

The Government has set up a National Committee of Inquiry into Higher Education to make recommendations on how the future shape, structure, size and funding of higher education should develop to meet needs over the next 20 years.

Finance

Higher education is largely financed by public funds, tuition fees for students paid through the student awards system and income received by institutions from research contracts and other sources.

Government finance for higher education institutions in England, Scotland and Wales is distributed by higher education funding councils responsible to their respective Secretary of State. In Northern Ireland grant is paid direct to the two universities by the Department of Education, following advice from the Northern Ireland Higher Education Council. The private University of Buckingham receives no public grants.

Table 27.3: Students Enrolled in Higher Education in Britain

	1984–85	1994–95
Higher education enrolments:[a]		
Full-time	573,000	1,150,000
Part-time[b]	308,000	594,000
All higher education	881,000	1,744,000

Source: Department for Education and Employment
[a]Excludes nursing and paramedic enrolments.
[b]Includes the Open University.

The funding councils and the Department of Education for Northern Ireland help meet the costs of teaching, research and related activities in all publicly funded universities and higher education colleges. In addition to teaching students, institutions undertake paid training, research or consultancy for commercial firms. Many establishments have endowments or receive grants from foundations and benefactors. Some 30 per cent of higher education income originates from private sources.

Student Grants and Loans

Over 95 per cent of full-time students resident in England and Wales on first degree and other comparable higher education courses receive mandatory awards covering tuition fees and a maintenance grant. The level of the grant depends on the income of the student and of the student's parents or spouse. Awards are made by LEAs in England and Wales. The Government reimburses in full the amount spent by education authorities on mandatory awards. Similar schemes are administered by the Student Awards Agency for Scotland and the Northern Ireland education and library boards. LEA grants for other courses can be given at their discretion.

Most students on courses of full-time, non–postgraduate higher education can also take out a loan to help pay their maintenance costs. Loans are not means tested and repayments are indexed to inflation. The scheme is designed to share the cost of student maintenance more equitably between students, parents and the taxpayer. In the academic year 1995–96 loans worth £701 million were made to 559,902 students in Britain, representing 59 per cent of those eligible. Loans are administered by the Student Loans Company in Glasgow. In addition, legislation passed in 1996 allows banks and building societies to operate loan schemes at favourable rates.

Limited access funds administered by universities and colleges are available to people in cases where access to higher and further education might be inhibited by financial considerations or where students face real financial difficulties. In 1996–97, there is provision of £27.7 million in England, £4.3

million in Scotland, £1.7 million in Wales and £868,000 in Northern Ireland for this purpose.

Grants for postgraduate study are offered by the government education departments and by the research councils. Increasing numbers of scholarships are available from research charities, endowments and particular industries or companies.

Access Courses

Access and foundation courses provide a preparation and an appropriate test before enrolment on a course of higher education for prospective students who do not possess the standard entry qualifications (GCE A levels and equivalent qualifications). Many are from the ethnic minority communities.

The Scottish Wider Access Programme (SWAP) is designed to promote greater participation in higher education by mature students and those without the normal entry requirements. Successful completion of a SWAP course guarantees a higher education place.

Universities

There are some 90 universities in Britain, including the Open University. They are governed by royal charters or by Act of Parliament and enjoy academic freedom. They appoint their own staff, decide which students to admit, provide their own courses and award their own degrees. The universities of Oxford and Cambridge date from the 12th and 13th centuries, and the Scottish universities of St Andrews, Glasgow, Aberdeen and Edinburgh from the 14th and 15th centuries. All the other universities in Britain were founded in the 19th and 20th centuries. The 1960s saw considerable expansion in the number of new universities. The number of universities also jumped considerably in 1992, when polytechnics were given their own degree-awarding powers and were allowed to take the university title. At the same time, similar provision was made for higher education colleges which met certain criteria.

Applications for first degree courses are usually made through the Universities and Colleges Admission Service (UCAS), in Cheltenham.

First degree courses are mainly full-time and usually last three years in England, Wales and Northern Ireland. However, there are some four-year courses, and medical and veterinary courses normally require five years. All traditional first degree courses in Scotland require a minimum of three years' study (or four years to honours level). The ratio of staff to full-time students in England is about 1 to 16.5.

Universities offer courses in a wide range of subjects, including traditional arts subjects and science and technology. Some courses lead to the examinations of the chief professional bodies.

Many universities have close links with commerce and industry; some students have a job and attend on a part-time basis.

Degree titles vary according to the practice of each university. In England, Wales and Northern Ireland the most common titles for a first degree are Bachelor of Arts (BA) or Bachelor of Science (BSc) and for a second degree Master of Arts (MA), Master of Science (MSc), and Doctor of Philosophy (PhD). In the older Scottish universities Master is used for a first degree in arts subjects. Uniformity of standards between universities is promoted by employing external examiners for all university examinations.

Some universities are responsible for validating degrees at higher education institutions without degree-awarding powers.

Many staff combine research with teaching duties. The number of postgraduates has increased by over 53 per cent in the last decade; 74 per cent are on taught courses. The Government is encouraging universities to co-operate closely with industry on research. Around 50 science parks have been set up by higher education institutions in conjunction with industrial scientists and technologists to promote the development and commercial application of advanced technology.

The Open University

The Open University is a non-residential university offering degree and other courses for adult students of all ages in Britain, the European Union, Gibraltar, Slovenia and Switzerland.

The University uses a combination of specially produced printed texts, correspondence tuition, television and radio broadcasts, audio/video cassettes and computing. For some courses there are residential schools. There is a network of study centres for contact with part-time tutors and counsellors, and with fellow students. Formal academic qualifications are not required to register for most courses. Its first degrees are the BA (Open) or the BSc (Open), which are general degrees awarded on a system of credits for each course completed. There is also an MMath degree for students who have taken an approved combination of courses specialising in mathematics, and an MEng degree for those who have taken an approved combination of courses to achieve the highest professional status of Chartered Engineer. In 1996 there were 104,373 registered undergraduates, and in all 143,828 first degrees have been awarded since the University started its courses in 1970.

The University also has a programme of higher degrees. About 9,900 students were registered on higher degree courses in 1996. There are also programmes for professionals in a variety of fields.

The University has advised many other countries on setting up similar institutions, and has contributed to projects such as the European Distance Education Network. It is financed by the Higher Education Funding Council for England.

Further Education for Adults

Further education for adults is provided by further education institutions, adult centres and colleges run by LEAs, and voluntary bodies such as the Workers' Educational Association. The duty to secure it is shared by the further education funding councils, The Scottish Office Education and Industry Department and LEAs.

The councils and The Scottish Office Education and Industry Department fund formal academic and vocational courses, courses providing access to higher education and courses in basic literacy and numeracy, including English for speakers of other languages. LEAs are responsible for the less formal leisure and recreational courses. The councils, The Scottish Office Education and Industry Department and the LEAs must take account of adult students with special educational needs.

University departments of continuing education also provide courses for adults.

Basic Skills Agency

The Basic Skills Agency (BSA) is concerned with adult literacy, numeracy and related basic skills in England and Wales. It provides consultancy and advisory services; funds local development projects, including research; publishes materials for teachers and students; and organises and sponsors staff training. Government funding of the BSA was worth about £4 million in 1995–96.

Following a recent review, the BSA has become a more general basic skills unit which covers basic skills training in the workplace for the unemployed and for young people as well as its traditional work with adults.

National Institute of Adult Continuing Education

The National Institute of Adult Continuing Education (England and Wales)—known as NIACE—is the national organisation for adult learning, representing all interests in the education and training of adults. It is a membership body and a registered charity. It convenes conferences, seminars and meetings, collects and disseminates information, conducts inquiries and research, undertakes special projects and works with other organisations.

Open and Distance Learning

The terms 'open' and 'distance' learning broadly mean learning undertaken through use of various media, such as television, without the direct supervision of a tutor. More further education colleges are incorporating many distance learning materials and methods in their mainstream courses.

Scottish Community Education Council

The Scottish Community Education Council advises the Government and promotes all community education matters, including adult literacy and basic education, and youth work.

Educational Research

Educational research is supported financially by government departments, the Economic and Social Research Council, philanthropic organisations, higher education institutions, teachers' associations and other agencies.

The major research institutions outside the universities are the autonomous National Foundation for Educational Research in England and Wales, and the Scottish Council for Research in Education.

LINKS WITH OTHER COUNTRIES

Large numbers of people come to Britain from other countries to study, and British people work and train overseas. The British aid programme encourages links between educational institutions in Britain and developing countries.

There has been an expansion of interest in European studies and languages in recent years, with exchanges of teachers, schoolchildren and students taking place.

European Union Schemes

Exchange of students is promoted by the EU SOCRATES programme, through which grants are provided to enable EU students and those from other countries belonging to the European Economic Area (see p. 127) to study in other states. The programme covers all academic subjects, and the period of study normally lasts between three and 12 months.

Another SOCRATES scheme promotes competence in foreign languages. It offers funding which contributes towards in-service training for teachers, student exchanges based on project work, and the development of new teaching methods. In 1994–95 nearly 12,000 British students were studying in other EU member states.

Youth for Europe III aims to bring together young people from different cultural and social backgrounds in the European Union through a wide range of exchanges. The five-year programme started in 1995 and has an EU budget of £102 million.

A new EU vocational training programme —LEONARDO DA VINCI—came into force in January 1995 and replaces a number of previous programmes, including COMETT (university/industry co-operation) and PETRA (training of young people).

EU member states have created nine European schools, including one at Culham, Oxfordshire, for pupils aged between four and 19, to provide a multilingual education for the children of staff employed in EU institutions.

Overseas Students in Britain

British universities and other higher and further education establishments have built up a strong reputation overseas by offering tuition of the highest standards and maintaining low student-to-staff ratios.

In 1994–95 there were some 158,000 overseas students at publicly funded higher and further education institutions in Britain. Their numbers have more than trebled since 1982–83 when there were about 50,700.

Most overseas students following courses of higher or further education pay fees covering the full cost of their courses.

Nationals of other member countries of the European Union generally pay the lower level of fees applicable to British students; if their courses are designated for mandatory awards, they may be eligible for fees-only awards from LEAs. Students attending Scottish institutions apply either to the Student Awards Agency for Scotland, the appropriate local council or one of the 43 Scottish incorporated further education colleges depending on the place and level of the course.

Government Scholarship Schemes

The Government makes considerable provision for foreign students and trainees through its overseas aid programme and other award and scholarship schemes. In 1994–95 some 15,500 overseas students were supported, at a cost of £115 million.

The Foreign & Commonwealth Office

(FCO) finances the British Chevening Scholarships, a worldwide programme offering outstanding graduate students and young professionals the opportunity to spend time studying at British universities and other academic institutions. In 1995–96 the FCO spent some £32 million on over 4,000 scholarships for students from 150 countries. These included jointly funded scholarships for overseas students co-sponsored by the FCO, business and industry, grant-giving foundations, the Churches and universities; some 760 scholarships were provided under these arrangements in 1995–96.

Outside the aid programme, the Overseas Research Students Awards Scheme, funded by the Higher Education Funding Councils, provides assistance for overseas full-time postgraduate students with outstanding research potential.

Other Schemes

Many public and private scholarships and fellowships are available to students from overseas and to British students who want to study overseas. Among the best known are the British Council Fellowships, the Commonwealth Scholarship and Fellowship Plan, the Fulbright Scholarship Scheme, the British Marshall Scholarships, the Rhodes Scholarships, the Churchill Scholarships and the Confederation of British Industry Scholarships. Most British universities and colleges offer bursaries and scholarships for which graduates of any nationality are eligible.

THE YOUTH SERVICE

The youth service—a partnership between local government and voluntary organisations—is concerned with the informal personal and social education of young people aged 11 to 25 (five to 25 in Northern Ireland).

Many of the voluntary organisations were established at the end of the 19th century and in the first decade of the 20th. In 1944 the Education Act provided for the development of a youth service in England and Wales by LEAs in partnership with the voluntary organisations.

Local authorities maintain their own youth centres and clubs and provide most of the public support for local and regional voluntary organisations. The service is said to reach around 5 million young people, the voluntary organisations contributing a significant proportion of overall provision.

The Department for Education and Employment's Youth Service Unit gives grants to the national voluntary youth organisations to meet 50 per cent of the cost of programmes designed to promote access to the youth service, support training for voluntary youth workers and help improve the efficiency and effectiveness of the organisations.

Funded primarily by local government, England's National Youth Agency provides:

- support for those working with young people;
- information and publishing services; and
- support for curriculum development.

It is also responsible for the accreditation of training and staff development for youth workers.

The Welsh Office provides grant aid to national youth service bodies with headquarters in Wales and has established a Wales Youth Agency.

In Scotland the youth service forms part of the community education provision made by local authorities. It is also promoted by the Scottish Community Education Council. The Scottish Office gives grants to voluntary youth organisations to assist them with their headquarters expenditure and staff training.

In Northern Ireland the education and library boards provide and fund youth clubs and outdoor activity centres, help pay the running costs of registered voluntary youth units, advise and support youth groups and assist young people visiting the rest of Britain, Ireland and overseas in connection with annual camps and award schemes. The Youth Council for Northern Ireland advises the education system on the development of the youth service, promotes the provision of facilities and encourages cross-community activity.

Voluntary Youth Organisations

National voluntary youth organisations undertake a significant share of youth activities through local groups, which raise most of their day-to-day expenses by their own efforts. Many receive financial and other help from LEAs, which also make available facilities in many areas. The voluntary organisations vary greatly in character and include the uniformed organisations, such as the Scouts and Girl Guides. Some organisations are church-based. Some also represent Jews and Muslims. Sport and the arts are catered for by various bodies. In Wales, Urdd Gobaith Cymru (the Welsh League of Youth) provides cultural, sporting and language-based activities for young Welsh speakers and learners.

Thousands of youth clubs encourage their members to participate in sport, cultural and other creative activities. Some youth clubs provide information, counselling and advice.

Many local authorities and voluntary youth organisations make provision for the young unemployed, young people from the ethnic minorities, young people in inner cities or rural areas and those in trouble or especially vulnerable. Other areas of concern are homelessness and provision for handicapped young people.

Many authorities have youth committees on which official and voluntary bodies are represented. They employ youth officers to co-ordinate youth work and to arrange in-service training.

Youth Workers

In England and Wales a two-year training course at certain universities and higher education colleges produces qualified youth and community workers; several undergraduate part-time and postgraduate courses are also available. In Scotland one-, two- and three-year courses are provided at colleges of education. Students from Northern Ireland attend courses run in universities and colleges in Britain and the Irish Republic.

Other Organisations Concerned with Young People

Finance is provided by many grant-giving foundations and trusts for activities involving young people. The Prince's Trust and the Royal Jubilee Trust provide grants and practical help to individuals and organisations; areas of concern include urban deprivation, unemployment, homelessness, and young offenders. Efforts are also made to assist ethnic minorities.

The Duke of Edinburgh's Award Scheme challenges young people from Britain and other Commonwealth countries to meet certain standards in activities such as community service, expeditions, social and practical skills and physical recreation.

Voluntary Service by Young People

Thousands of young people voluntarily undertake community service designed to help those in need, including elderly and disabled people. Many schools also organise community service work as part of the curriculum.

Further Reading

Education, 2nd edn. Aspects of Britain series, HMSO, 1996.

Education after 16. Aspects of Britain series, HMSO, 1994.

Education Reforms in Schools. Aspects of Britain series, HMSO, 1994.

The Government's Expenditure Plans 1996–97 to 1998–99. Department for Education and Employment and Office for Standards in Education. Cm 3210. HMSO, 1996.

28 Religion

Introduction	466	Other Religions	472
The Christian Community	468	Co-operation between Faiths	474

Everyone in Britain has the right to religious freedom without interference from the community or the State. Religious organisations and groups may own property, conduct their rites and ceremonies, run schools, and promote their beliefs in speech and writing, within the limits of the law. There is no religious bar to the holding of public office.

INTRODUCTION

Most of the world's religions are represented in Britain. While there are large Hindu, Jewish, Muslim and Sikh communities, and also smaller communities of Baha'is, Buddhists, Jains and Zoroastrians, as well as numbers of pagans and followers of new religious movements, Britain is predominantly Christian. Non-religious alternatives for humanists and atheists are offered by organisations such as the British Humanist Association and the National Secular Society, although most humanists and atheists do not belong to organised groups. Many Britons would class themselves as agnostic.

There has been a fall in recent years in the number of full-time ministers and the number of adults recorded as members of most of the larger Christian churches. At the same time there has been significant growth in a range of independent churches, and in new religious movements. Surveys have also revealed that many people who do not belong to religious groups claim to be religious and say they believe in God.

Religious Freedom

Freedom of conscience in religious matters was achieved gradually from the 17th century onwards. The older laws discriminating against minority religious groups were gradually enforced less harshly and then finally repealed. Heresy ceased to be a legal offence with the passage of the Ecclesiastical Jurisdiction Act 1677, and the Toleration Act 1688 granted freedom of worship to Protestant minority groups.

In 1828 the repeal of the Test and Corporation Acts gave nonconformist Protestant Christians full political rights, making it possible for them to be appointed to public office. Roman Catholics gained political rights under the Roman Catholic Relief Act 1829, and the Jewish Relief Act 1858 enabled Jews to become Members of Parliament. The religious tests imposed on prospective students and academic staff of the universities of Oxford, Cambridge and Durham were successively abolished by Acts of 1854, 1856 and 1871. Similar restrictions on the staff of Scottish universities were formally removed in 1932.

The past 30 years have seen an increasingly diverse pattern of religious belief and affiliation in Britain. This has been linked both to patterns of immigration and to new religious directions among some of the indigenous population. Social structures have been gradually changing to accommodate this. For example, arrangements are made at many places of work to allow the members of the various faiths to follow their religious observances.

Relations with the State

There are two established churches in Britain, that is, churches legally recognised as official churches of the State: in England the Anglican *Church of England*, and in Scotland the (Presbyterian) *Church of Scotland*. The Monarch is pledged by the coronation oath to defend each Church in its respective territory. There is no longer an established Church in Wales or in Northern Ireland. Ministers of the established churches, as well as clergy belonging to other religious groups, work in services run by the State, such as the armed forces, national hospitals and prisons, and may be paid a state salary for such services. Voluntary schools provided by religious denominations may be wholly or partly maintained from public funds. Religious education in publicly maintained schools is required by law throughout Britain, as is a daily act of collective worship (see p. 453). Religious broadcasting is subject to some legislative controls (see p. 505).

The State does not contribute to the general expenses of church maintenance, although some state aid does help repair historic churches. In 1995–96, for instance, English Heritage grants to churches totalled £10.8 million as compared with the £100 million spent on the buildings by parishes. Assistance is also given to meet some of the costs of repairing cathedrals and comparable buildings; some £4 million is being made available in 1996–97. This funding is not restricted to Church of England buildings.

The Government shares with the Church of England the upkeep of nearly 300 churches of special architectural or historic importance which are no longer required for regular parish use and for which no alternative use can be found. The contribution for the period 1994 to 1997 is about £7.2 million. In 1993 the Historic Chapels Trust was launched, with the aim of preserving the redundant chapels and places of worship of other denominations and faiths, including synagogues and temples, which are of particular architectural or historic interest.

Involvement in Social Issues

Religious involvement in broader social issues was highlighted in the Church of England report *Faith in the City: A Call for Action by Church and Nation*, published in 1985. This led to the establishment of the Church of England's Church Urban Fund, an independent charity which raises money to enable people living in urban priority areas to found projects which alleviate the effects of poverty on their lives. By June 1996 it had made grants totalling £23.5 million to 1,392 projects.

The General Assembly of the Church of Scotland debates annual reports from its Committee on Church and Nation on social, economic, and political matters; and, through its Board of Social Responsibility, is the largest voluntary social work agency in Scotland.

Organisations belonging to other churches and religious groups are also closely involved with a wide range of social issues.

The Inner Cities Religious Council, formed in 1992, is a forum for dialogue between faith communities and the Department of the Environment. The Council promotes policy development and offers advice for religious groups on urban regeneration. Chaired by a government minister, it includes members from the Hindu, Jewish, Muslim, Sikh and Christian faiths, including the majority Black churches.

Statistics on Religious Affiliation

There is no standard information about the number of members of religious groups since questions are not normally asked about religious beliefs in censuses or for other official purposes, except in Northern Ireland. Each group adopts its own way of counting its members, and the membership figures in this chapter—often supplied by the religious groups themselves—are therefore approximate.

THE CHRISTIAN COMMUNITY

Church of England

The Church of England became the established church during the Reformation in the 16th century. Conflicts between Church and State culminated in the Act of Supremacy in 1534 which repudiated papal supremacy and declared Henry VIII to be Supreme Head of the Church of England. The Church of England's form of worship was set out in successive versions of the Book of Common Prayer from 1549 onwards. The Church's relationship with the State is one of mutual obligation, since the Church's privileges are balanced by certain duties it must fulfil.

The Monarch is the 'Supreme Governor' of the Church of England and must always be a member of the Church, and promise to uphold it. Church of England archbishops, bishops and deans of cathedrals are appointed by the Monarch on the advice of the Prime Minister, although the Crown Appointments Commission, which includes lay and clergy representatives, plays a decisive part in the selection of archbishops and diocesan bishops. All clergy swear allegiance to the Crown. The Church can regulate its own worship. The two archbishops (of Canterbury and York), the bishops of London, Durham and Winchester, and 21 other senior bishops sit in the House of Lords. Clergy of the Church, together with those of the Church of Scotland, the Church of Ireland and the Roman Catholic Church, may not sit in the House of Commons.

The Church is divided into two provinces: Canterbury, comprising 30 dioceses, including the Diocese in Europe; and York, with 14 dioceses. The dioceses are divided into archdeaconries and deaneries, which are in turn divided into about 13,000 parishes, although in practice many of these are grouped together. There are, altogether, about 10,265 full-time stipendiary Church of England clergy—men and women—working within the diocesan structure, excluding mainland Europe. In 1994 an estimated 205,990 people were baptised into the Church in the two provinces, excluding the Diocese in Europe; of these, 160,300 were under one year old, representing 25.1 per cent of live births. In the same year there were 45,024 confirmations. Attendances at services on a normal Sunday are around 1,090,400 million. In 1993, 91,214 marriages were solemnised in the Church of England. These accounted for 66.4 per cent of all marriages with religious ceremonies, and 32.2 per cent of all marriages in England. Many people who rarely, if ever, attend services still regard themselves as belonging to the Church of England.

The central governing and legislative body is the General Synod, which comprises separate houses of bishops, clergy and lay members. Lay people are also involved with church government in the parishes. The Synod is the centre of an administrative system dealing with missionary work, inter-church relations, social questions, and recruitment and training for the ministry. It also covers other church work in Britain and overseas, the care of church buildings and their contents, church schools (which are maintained largely from public funds), colleges and institutes of higher education, and voluntary and parish education.

The Church's investment income from historic sources is managed mainly by the Church Commissioners. Most of the remainder of the Church's income is provided by local voluntary donations. The average annual stipend of a Church of England priest is about £14,460; the average value of additional benefits, including free housing and a non-contributory pension, is £7,000.

In 1992 the General Synod voted in favour of legislation allowing the ordination of women to the priesthood. The Measure was subsequently approved by both Houses of Parliament and received the Royal Assent. The first women priests were ordained in 1994 and there are now 783 stipendiary women clergy. The Measure also provided for those, usually from the Anglo-Catholic wing of the Church, unable to accept the ordination of women, including the payment of compensation to clergy who feel they have to leave the ministry of the Church. So far 313 clergy have received compensation payments under the Measure.

> Some 200 former Church of England clergy (many married) have been received into the Roman Catholic Church. Some of these have since been ordained.

Three bishops have been appointed to provide additional pastoral care to those members and parishes of the Church who remain opposed to the ordination of women to the priesthood. Women priests can now be appointed to all offices in the Church, except those of archbishop or bishop.

Other Anglican Churches

The Church of England is part of a worldwide communion of Anglican churches. These are similar in organisation and worship to the Church of England and originated from it. There are four distinct Anglican Churches in the British Isles, each governed separately by its own institutions: the Church of England, the Church in Wales, the Episcopal Church in Scotland, and the Church of Ireland (which operates in both Northern Ireland and the Irish Republic). The Church of Ireland was disestablished in 1869 and the Church in Wales in 1920.

The Anglican Communion comprises 36 autonomous Churches in Britain and abroad, and three regional councils overseas with a total membership of about 70 million. Links between the components of the Anglican Communion are maintained by the Lambeth Conference of Anglican bishops, which is held every ten years, the last Conference being held in Canterbury in 1988. Presided over by the Archbishop of Canterbury, the Conference has no executive authority, but enjoys considerable influence. The Anglican Consultative Council, an assembly of lay people and clergy as well as of bishops, meets every two or three years to allow consultation within the Anglican Communion. The Primates Meeting brings together the senior bishops from each Church at similar intervals.

Church of Scotland

The Church of Scotland has a presbyterian form of government, that is, government by church courts, composed of ministers and elders, all of whom are ordained to office, and also deacons. It became the national church following the Scottish Reformation in the late sixteenth century and legislation enacted by the Scottish Parliament. The Church's status was then consolidated in the Treaty of Union of 1707 and by the Church of Scotland Act 1921, the latter confirming its complete freedom in all spiritual matters. It appoints its own office bearers, and its affairs are not subject to any civil authority.

The adult communicant membership of the Church of Scotland is over 698,500; there are about 1,200 ministers serving in parishes. Both men and women may join the ministry. Twelve hundred and ninety five churches are governed locally by Kirk Sessions, consisting of ministers and elders. Above the Kirk Session is the Presbytery. The General Assembly, consisting of elected ministers and elders, meets annually under the presidency of an elected moderator, who serves for one year. The Monarch is normally represented at the General Assembly by the Lord High Commissioner.

There are also a number of independent Scottish Presbyterian churches, largely descended from groups which broke away from the Church of Scotland. They are particularly active in the Highlands and Islands.

Free Churches

The term 'Free Churches' is often used to describe those Protestant churches in Britain which, unlike the Church of England and the Church of Scotland, are not established churches. Free Churches have existed in various forms since the Reformation, developing their own traditions over the years. Their members have also been known as dissenters or nonconformists. While this historical experience has given these churches a certain sense of shared identity, they otherwise vary greatly in doctrine, worship and church government. All the major Free

Churches—Methodist, Baptist, United Reformed and Salvation Army—allow both men and women to become ministers.

The Methodist Church, the largest of the Free Churches, with over 408,000 adult full members and a community of more than 1.2 million, originated in the 18th century following the Evangelical Revival under John Wesley (1703–91). The present church is based on the 1932 union of most of the separate Methodist Churches. It has 3,600 ministers and 6,950 places of worship.

> MAYC, the youth service of the Methodist Church, has a membership of 50,000. Each year MAYC organises London Weekend, one of the largest youth events in Europe, bringing together dance, drama, rock music and worship produced and performed by youth groups from all over Great Britain.

The Baptists first achieved an organised form in Britain in the 17th century. Today they are mainly organised in groups of churches, most of which belong to the Baptist Union of Great Britain (re-formed in 1812), with about 146,200 members, 2,235 ministers and 2,000 places of worship. There are also separate Baptist Unions for Scotland, Wales and Ireland, and other independent Baptist Churches.

The third largest of the Free Churches is the United Reformed Church, with some 103,000 members, 1,864 ministers and 1,768 places of worship. It was formed in 1972 following the merger of the Congregational Church in England and Wales (the oldest Protestant minority in Britain, whose origins can be traced back to the Puritans of the 16th century) with the Presbyterian Church of England (a church closely related in doctrine and worship to the Church of Scotland). This was the first union of two different churches in Britain since the Reformation in the 16th century. In 1981 there was a further merger with the Re-formed Association of the Churches of Christ.

Alongside these churches are other historic Free Church bodies. The Salvation Army was founded in the East End of London in 1865 by William Booth (1829–1912). Within Britain it is second only to the Government as a provider of social services. It is the largest provider of hostel accommodation, offering almost 3,400 beds every night. Other services include work with alcoholics, prison chaplaincy and a family tracing service which receives 4,900 enquiries each year. The Salvation Army in Britain is served by around 1,800 officers (ordained ministers) and runs some 1,000 worship centres.

The Religious Society of Friends (Quakers), with about 18,000 adult members in Britain and 450 places of worship, was founded in the middle of the 17th century under the leadership of George Fox (1624–91). Silent worship is central to its life as a religious organisation. Emphasis is also placed on social concern and peace-making.

Among the other Free Churches are: the Presbyterian Church in Ireland, the largest Protestant church in Northern Ireland, where it has 291,150 members; the Presbyterian (or Calvinistic Methodist) Church of Wales, with 53,870 members and the largest of the Free Churches in Wales; and the Union of Welsh Independents (45,460 members).

A recent development has been the rise of Pentecostalism and the charismatic movement. A number of Pentecostalist bodies were formed in Britain at the turn of the century. The two main Pentecostalist organisations operating in Britain today are the Assemblies of God (approximately 54,600 members, nearly 900 ministers and over 600 places of worship) and the Elim Pentecostal Church. Since the Second World War immigration from the Caribbean has led to the growth of a significant number of majority Black Pentecostalist churches.

In the early 1960s a Pentecostalist charismatic movement began to influence some followers in both the Church of England and the Roman Catholic Church; it remains a growing influence in both these churches, and in the historic Free Churches. The Christian 'house church' movement (or 'new churches') began in the early 1970s, when some charismatics began to establish their own congregations. Services were originally held in private houses although many congregations have now acquired their own buildings. The movement, whose growth has been most marked in England, is characterised by lay leadership and is organised into a number of loose fellowships, usually on a regional basis, such as the Ichthus Fellowship in south-east London.

Roman Catholic Church

The formal structure of the Roman Catholic Church in England and Wales, which ceased to exist after the Reformation, was restored in 1850. The Scottish Church's formal structure went out of existence in the early 17th century and was restored in 1878. However, throughout this period Catholicism never disappeared entirely. There are now seven Roman Catholic provinces in Great Britain, each under an archbishop, and 30 dioceses, each under a bishop (22 in England and Wales and eight in Scotland, independently responsible to the Pope). There are almost 3,300 parishes and about 7,200 priests (only men may become priests). Northern Ireland has six dioceses, some with territory partly in the Irish Republic. About one British citizen in ten claims to be a Roman Catholic.

The Roman Catholic Church attaches great importance to the education of its children and requires its members to try to bring up their children in the Catholic faith. Two per cent of the teachers in Britain's 2,900 Catholic schools are members of religious orders. These orders also undertake other social work. About 250 Roman Catholic religious orders, congregations and societies are represented in Britain, as are congregations representing about 25 different nationalities who live in Britain. Most Catholic schools are maintained out of public funds.

Other Christian Churches

Other Protestant Churches include the Unitarians and Free Christians, whose origins are traceable to the Reformation.

The Christian Brethren are a Protestant body organised in their present form by J. N. Darby (1800–82). There are two branches: the Open Brethren and the Closed or Exclusive Brethren.

Many Christian communities founded by migrant communities, including the Orthodox, Lutheran and Reformed Churches of various European countries, the Coptic Orthodox Church and the Armenian Church, have established their own centres of worship, particularly in London. All these churches operate in a variety of languages. The largest is probably the Greek Orthodox Church, many of whose members are of Cypriot origin. It is represented in many cities throughout Britain.

There are also several other religious groups in Britain which were founded in the United States in the last century. These include the Jehovah's Witnesses, the Church of Jesus Christ of the Latter-Day Saints (the Mormon Church), the Christadelphians, the Seventh-Day Adventists, the Christian Scientists and the Spiritualists.

Co-operation among the Churches

The Council of Churches for Britain and Ireland (formerly the British Council of Churches) is the main overall body for the Christian churches in Britain. The Council co-ordinates the work of its 31 member churches, in the areas of social responsibility, international affairs, church life, youth matters, world mission, racial justice and inter-faith relations. The Council's member churches are also grouped in separate ecumenical bodies, according to country: Churches Together in England, Action of Churches Together in Scotland, Churches Together in Wales, and the Irish Council of Churches.

The Free Church Federal Council, with 19 member churches, includes most of the Free Churches of England and Wales. It promotes co-operation among the Free Churches (especially in hospital chaplaincy and in education matters).

The Evangelical Alliance, with a membership of individuals, churches or societies drawn from within 20 denominations, represents over 1 million evangelical Christians.

The churches of the Council of Churches for Britain and Ireland and the Free Church Federal Council liaise with the Government through the Churches' Main Committee.

Inter-church discussions about the search for Christian unity take place internationally, as well as within Britain, and the main participants are the Roman Catholic, Orthodox, Anglican, Lutheran, Methodist, Reformed and Baptist Churches. In 1995–96 the Church of England and the Methodist Church had informal meetings to consider moves towards unity.

The Anglican Churches and the Church of Scotland are among the 14 British Churches which are members of the World Council of Churches. This organisation links some 340 churches in over 100 countries around the world.

OTHER RELIGIONS

The Buddhist Community

The Buddhist community in Britain consists largely of adherents of British or Western origin. There are well over 500 Buddhist groups and centres, including some 50 monasteries and temples. All the main schools of Buddhism are represented. The Buddhist Society, founded in 1924, promotes the principles of Buddhism; it does not belong to any particular school of Buddhism.

The Hindu Community

The Hindu community in Britain comprises around 320,000 members and originates largely from India. The largest groups of Hindus are to be found in Leicester, different areas of London, Birmingham and Bradford. The first Hindu temple, or mandir, was opened in London in 1962 and there are now over 150 mandirs in Britain, a number of which are affiliated to the National Council of Hindu Temples.

The Swaminarayan Hindu Mission, in north London, has the largest Hindu temple to be built outside India, together with an extensive cultural complex which has provision for conferences, exhibitions, marriages, sports, and health clinics.

The Jewish Community

Jews first settled in England at the time of the Norman Conquest and remained until banished by royal decree in 1290. The present community in Britain dates from 1656, having been founded by Jews of Spanish and Portuguese origin, known as Sephardim. Later more settlers came from Germany and Eastern Europe; they are known as Ashkenazim.

The Jewish community in Britain numbers about 300,000 and is, after that in France, the largest in Western Europe. The main groups are to be found in London (210,000), Manchester and Salford (27,000), Leeds (9,000), and Brighton and Hove (6,000). About 70 per cent are affiliated to synagogues. The community is divided into two main groups. Of these, some 70 per cent are Ashkenazi Jews, most of whom acknowledge the authority of the Chief Rabbi. The small Sephardi Orthodox element follow their own spiritual head. The recently established Masorti movement, the Reform movement, founded in 1840, and the Liberal and Progressive movement, established in 1901, account for most of the remaining 27 per cent.

Jewish congregations in Britain number about 360. The Board of Deputies of British Jews is the officially recognised representative body for all these groups. Founded in 1760, it is mainly elected by synagogues. The Board serves as the voice of the community to both government and the wider non-Jewish community.

A large-scale survey of British Jews, conducted by the Institute of Jewish Policy Research, was published in 1996. This reports that 44 per cent of Jewish men aged under 40 are married, or living with, non-Jewish partners, and that among Jewish women in this age range, 20 to 25 per cent marry outside the Jewish community.

Roughly one in three Jewish children attend Jewish schools, some of which are supported by public funds. Several agencies care for elderly and handicapped people.

The Muslim Community

Figures for the size of the Muslim community in Britain have ranged from three-quarters of a million to 2 million. Recent estimates, based on extrapolations from the 1991 census, suggest the population is between 1 million and 1.5 million, while estimates from within the Muslim community suggest between 1.5 million and 2 million. The largest number originate from Pakistan and Bangladesh, while sizeable groups have come from India, Cyprus, the Arab world, Malaysia and parts of Africa. There is a growing number of British-born Muslims, mainly the children of immigrant parents, but including an increasing number of converts to Islam.

There are over 600 mosques and numerous Muslim prayer centres throughout Britain. Mosques are not only places of worship; they also offer instruction in the Muslim way of life and facilities for educational and welfare activities.

The first mosque in Britain was established at Woking, Surrey, in 1890. Mosques now range from converted houses in many towns to the Central Mosque in Regent's Park, London, and its associated Islamic Cultural Centre, one of the most important Muslim institutions in the Western world. The Central Mosque has the largest congregation in Britain, and during festivals it may number over 30,000. The Islamic Cultural Centre's activities include a weekend school for children, and regular lectures, seminars and conferences. Pastoral care includes free legal advice, counselling, marriage and funeral services, and hospital visiting.

There are also important mosques and cultural centres in Liverpool, Manchester, Leicester, Birmingham, Bradford, Cardiff, Edinburgh and Glasgow.

Many of the mosques are administered by various local Muslim organisations, and both the Sunni and the Shi'a traditions within Islam are represented among the Muslim community in Britain. Members of some of the major Sufi traditions have also developed branches in British cities. The Ismaili Centre in London provides wide ranging pastoral care and a place of worship for Shi'a Imami Ismaili Muslims, whose current Imam is Prince Karim Aga Khan. There are also several thousand members of the heterodox Ahmadiyya movement in Britain.

The Sikh Community

A large British Sikh community (estimates range from 400,000 to 500,000) originates mainly from India, and particularly from the Punjab. The largest groups of Sikhs are in Greater London, Manchester, Birmingham, Nottingham and Wolverhampton. Sikh temples, or gurdwaras, cater for the religious, educational, social welfare and cultural needs of their community. A *granthi* is normally employed to take care of the building and to conduct prayers. The oldest gurdwara in London was established in 1908 and the largest is in Hounslow, Middlesex (to the west of London). There are over 200 gurdwaras in Britain.

Other Faiths

Small communities of other faiths include that of the Jains, mainly living in London, Leicester and Coventry. Jainism is an ancient religion brought to Britain by immigrants from India. A Jain temple (or derasar) opened in Leicester in 1988. The Zoroastrian religion, or Mazdaism, which originated in ancient Iran, is mainly represented in Britain by the Parsi community, whose ancestors left Iran in the tenth century and settled in north-west India. The Baha'i movement originated in 19th-century Iran; there are an estimated 6,000 Baha'is in Britain, organised in 500 local assemblies and administered by the National Spiritual Assembly in London.

A more recent development is Rastafarianism. This emerged out of the Back to Africa movement in the West Indies early this century, and arrived in Britain through Jamaican immigration in the 1950s. It has no single creed, but draws heavily on the Old Testament.

New Religious Movements

A large number of new religious movements, sometimes popularly referred to as cults, mainly established since the Second World War and often with overseas origins, are active in Britain. Examples include the Church of Scientology, the Transcendental Meditation movement, the Unification Church (popularly known as the 'Moonies') and various New Age groups. In response to public concern about the activities of some of these cults, the Government provided funding from 1987 to 1993 to set up the Information Network Focus on Religious Movements (INFORM). Supported by the main churches, INFORM carries out research and seeks to provide objective information about new religious movements.

CO-OPERATION BETWEEN FAITHS

A number of national organisations seek to develop relations between different religions in Britain. They include the Inter Faith Network for the United Kingdom, which links a wide range of organisations with an interest in inter-faith relations, including representative bodies from the Baha'i, Buddhist, Christian, Hindu, Jain, Jewish, Muslim, Sikh and Zoroastrian faith groups.

Other national organisations include the Council of Christians and Jews, which works for better understanding among members of the two religions and deals with issues in the educational and social fields.

Within each faith tradition are organisations and individuals working to further good relations with other faiths. For example, the Council of Churches for Britain and Ireland (see p. 471) has a Commission on Inter Faith Relations.

Further Reading

Religion. Aspects of Britain series, HMSO, 1992.

Religions in the UK: A Multi-Faith Directory. ed. Paul Weller, University of Derby and The Inter Faith Network for the United Kingdom, 1997 (forthcoming).

UK Christian Handbook, 1996–97 ed. Christian Research Association.

29 The Arts

Introduction	475	Dance	484
Drama	480	Films	486
Music	482	Visual Arts	488
Opera	484	Literature and Libraries	492

A great diversity of artistic and cultural activity is enjoyed in Britain, at both professional and amateur level; a 1994–95 survey showed that 47.6 per cent of adults attended arts activities in that year. Arts funding has received a major boost from the National Lottery in 1995–96, benefiting both national and community-based projects in all areas of Britain.

INTRODUCTION

Britain's artistic and cultural heritage is one of the richest in the world. The origins of English literature, one of the world's most influential bodies of writing, can be traced back to medieval times, while over the centuries Britain has amassed some of the finest collections of works of art. The performing arts also have a long and distinguished history.

London is one of the leading world centres for the arts. Other large cities, including Birmingham, Leeds, Manchester, Edinburgh, Glasgow and Cardiff, have also sustained and developed their reputations as centres of artistic excellence in recent years. Arts festivals attract wide interest. Many British playwrights, craftspeople, composers, film-makers, painters, writers, actors, singers, musicians and dancers enjoy international reputations. They include, for example, Harold Pinter, Sir Colin Davis, Sir Andrew Lloyd Webber, David Hockney, Sir V.S. Naipaul, Vanessa Redgrave, Sir Ian McKellen and Sir Anthony Hopkins. Television and radio bring a range of arts events to a large audience. At an amateur level, numerous groups and societies for the arts make use of local talent and resources.

Department of National Heritage

The Secretary of State for National Heritage, who is a member of the Cabinet, is responsible for government policy in support of the arts for England. The Department of National Heritage (see p. 544) determines government policy and administers expenditure on national museums and art galleries in England, the Arts Council of England (see p. 476), the British Library and other national arts and heritage bodies. Other responsibilities include the regulation of the film industry, broadcasting and the press, the National Lottery and the export licensing of antiques.

The Secretaries of State for Wales, Scotland and Northern Ireland are responsible for the arts in their countries, including the national museums, galleries and libraries and their respective Arts Councils.

The Government's arts policies aim to:

- develop a high standard of artistic and cultural activity throughout Britain;
- encourage innovation; and
- promote public access to, and appreciation of, the arts, crafts and the cultural heritage.

The Government's Arts and Young People initiative, announced in 1996, aims to bring the arts alive for this age group by developing better links between young people and arts organisations, galleries and museums, both within and outside schools.

The Department of National Heritage and the home departments provide funds and advice, and encourage partnership with the private sector, including business sponsorship. National museums and galleries are given an incentive to increase their resources—for example, through trading and other activities. An important concept in funding policy is the 'arm's length' principle, by which government funds are distributed to arts organisations indirectly, through bodies such as the Arts Councils, the British Film Institute and the Scottish Film Council. This principle helps to avoid political influence over funding decisions by ensuring that funds are allocated by those best qualified to do so.

Local Authorities

Local authorities maintain around 1,000 local museums and art galleries and a network of over 4,000 public libraries. They also support many other arts buildings, arts organisations and artistic events in their areas, providing grant aid for professional and voluntary bodies, including orchestras, theatres, and opera and dance companies. They undertake direct promotions of the arts and contribute to the cost of new or converted buildings for the arts. In England revenue support from local authorities is estimated to be about £190 million a year. In Scotland revenue support from local authorities is £35-£40 million a year, and in Wales about £12 million a year.

Finance

Planned central government expenditure through the Department of National Heritage amounts to £937 million in 1996–97, of which about £186 million is channelled through the Arts Council of England mainly to support the performing and visual arts. Grants are also made to the British Film Institute, the Crafts Council, certain other museums and arts bodies, and to the National Heritage Memorial Fund. The Fund helps organisations wishing to acquire, for the public benefit, land, buildings, works of art and other objects associated with the national heritage.

The Scottish Office is providing £39.6 million for Scotland's National Galleries and Museums and National Library, while the Welsh Office is providing £18.3 million for Wales's National Museum and National Library. Planned spending by the Department of Education for Northern Ireland on the three major museums there amounts to about £9.2 million in 1996–97.

Arts Councils

The main channels for government aid to the arts are the independent Arts Councils of England, Scotland, Wales and Northern Ireland.

The aims of the Arts Councils are to:

- develop and improve the knowledge, understanding and practice of the arts;
- make the arts more accessible to the public; and
- advise and co-operate with central government departments, local authorities and other organisations.

The Arts Councils give financial help and advice to organisations ranging from the major arts centres and opera, dance and drama companies to small touring theatre companies and experimental performance groups. They also provide funds for the training of arts administrators and help arts organisations to develop other sources of income, including sponsorship and local authority support. They encourage a variety of art forms, including ballet and contemporary dance, drama, mime, literature, music, opera, visual arts and photography, and help professional creative writers, dramatists, choreographers, dancers, actors, musicians, composers, artists and photographers. The Councils also support art exhibitions and tours of arts events and performances, make funds available for some specialist training courses in the arts and encourage the work of artists in education. Emphasis is being placed on obtaining funds through partnership arrangements with local authorities and other agencies, and from commercial sources.

Planned 1996–97 expenditure by the Arts Councils for Scotland, Wales and Northern Ireland is £24.5 million, £14.2 million and £7.1 million respectively.

Regional Arts Boards

In England the Arts Council and ten Regional Arts Boards comprise the integrated arts funding system. Together, they aim to ensure that a wide range of high-quality arts is accessible to people across the country. The Regional Arts Boards offer financial assistance to artists and arts organisations and advise on, and sometimes help to promote, arts activities. They also advise on the use of National Lottery funding. They are financed mainly by the Arts Council of England, with smaller sums from the British Film Institute and Crafts Council, as well as from local authorities. The Boards also concentrate on business development and sponsorship and many have established 'Business in the Arts' schemes in their areas. Through a system of forward planning and budgeting, the Boards are accountable to their national funders. One-third of the members of each Board are nominated by local authorities. Boards also include representatives of the regional business community as well as others with expertise and interest in the arts.

The Boards are responsible for most of the funding of organisations within their region. The Arts Council of England continues to be responsible for the funding of the national companies—Royal Opera, Royal Ballet and the Birmingham Royal Ballet, the English National Opera, the Royal Shakespeare Company, the Royal National Theatre and the South Bank Centre. It is also responsible for touring companies without a regional base and for other arts organisations which have a national strategic role.

Business Sponsorship

Industrial and commercial companies offer vital sponsorship to a wide range of arts. The Pairing Scheme, managed by the Association for Business Sponsorship of the Arts (ABSA), aims to encourage businesses in Britain to sponsor the arts. Under the scheme, government funding of between £1,000 and £45,000 is awarded to arts organisations to complement the sponsorship from businesses. Launched in 1985, the sponsorship scheme has brought over £95 million into the arts (including a government contribution of £60 million). In 1996–97 the Government is making available £4.9 million to match new sponsorships.

Notable business sponsorships during 1996 include:

- The Tate Gallery's Cézanne exhibition (sponsored by Ernst & Young);
- Ballet Central, an annual programme of public performances across Britain for sixth form graduates of the Central School of Ballet (sponsored by British Gas);
- The Royal Shakespeare Company, which has received the largest single arts sponsorship, amounting to £3.3 million over three years from Allied Domecq, for its seasons of plays by Shakespeare and his contemporaries; and
- Theatre Clwyd's Christmas shows— among them *Great Expectations*, *A Christmas Carol*, *Gulliver's Travels* and *The Snow Queen* (sponsored by Warwick International).

Under ABSA's Business in the Arts scheme, the private sector gives part-time management expertise to arts organisations.

Foundation for Sport and the Arts

The Foundation for Sport and the Arts was set up in 1991 by the Pool Promoters Association to channel funds into sport and the arts. Almost £20 million of the Foundation's annual revenue is used to benefit the arts and is distributed in the form of awards to a variety of organisations.

National Lottery

The National Lottery (see p. 43) generates substantial funds for the arts and Britain's national heritage.

By 1 July 1996, grants of over £728 million had been distributed by the Arts Councils and the Heritage Lottery Fund (see p. 489) to a wide range of arts projects, including:

- £3.8 million to The Tate Gallery in Merseyside;
- £3.7 million to East London's Geffrye Museum, which specialises in domestic interiors;
- £3 million to Armagh City and District Council, Northern Ireland, for a new theatre/arts centre;
- £2.5 million to the Royal Scottish Academy of Music and Drama in Glasgow to create a national opera school; and
- £1.2 million to the Welsh College of Music and Drama, Cardiff.

Substantial funding is also to be channelled into the British film industry (see p. 486).

Cultural Diversity and Disability

The arts activities undertaken by Britain's diverse communities embrace both traditional and new forms of artistic expression. The Arts Council of England has specialist programmes to make the arts more accessible and to develop the knowledge, understanding and practice of diversity in the arts.

Black and Asian Arts

The Arts Council of England and the Regional Arts Boards jointly support the National Black Arts Network, a group of individuals and agencies which is helping to develop black, Asian and Chinese arts across England. The Arts Council also supports other umbrella organisations, including Asian Arts Access, the British Chinese Artists' Association and ADiTi, and has helped in setting up the Institute of International Visual Arts. It also supports Afro-Caribbean and Asian music circuits, the Notting Hill carnival bands, a funding programme for black video and film-makers and the development of black theatre companies.

Arts and Disability

The Arts Council of England has access to experts in arts and disability through its Arts and Disability Advisory and Monitoring Committee, and all its art-form advisory panels include disabled people. The Council's paper on quality of service for disabled people provides practical information and advice for Council and Regional Arts Boards staff. Funding agreements with arts organisations state that they must have an equal opportunities policy; they are also encouraged to adopt the code of practice on employment issued by the Equal Opportunities Commission (see p. 40).

The National Disability Arts Forum and other national agencies are funded by the Arts Council of England, as are creative organisations, such as CandoCo, a company of disabled and non-disabled dancers. The Council also supports an apprenticeship scheme for disabled people in major arts organisations, such as the Royal Shakespeare Company, which is part of an initiative aimed at increasing employment opportunities in the arts for disabled people.

Other schemes supported by the Arts Council of England include an audit of deaf arts conducted by Deafworks and projects involving disabled artists in schools. The Scottish Arts Council supports Art Link and Project Ability, which provide opportunities for people with disabilities to develop creativity in a range of art forms.

The provision of access for disabled people to arts buildings is a basic criterion for all grants made from the National Lottery (see p. 43).

Arts Centres

Over 200 arts centres in Britain give people the chance of enjoying and taking part in a range of activities, with educational projects becoming increasingly important. Nearly all arts centres are professionally managed and most are supported by volunteer groups. They are assisted mainly by Regional Arts Boards and local authorities, while the Arts Council of England funds two national centres—the South Bank Centre and the Institute of Contemporary Arts. Many theatres and art galleries also provide a focal point for the community by making available facilities for other arts.

The British Council

The British Council (see p. 140) is Britain's international network for culture, development and education, and maintains libraries (including film libraries) in many of the 109 countries in which it is represented. The Visiting Arts Office, an autonomous body administered by the British Council, fosters an appreciation and understanding of the arts of other countries. It acts as a broker between Britain and overseas arts organisations, advises on touring matters and makes awards for projects.

Broadcasting

BBC radio and television and the independent companies (see Chapter 30) broadcast a variety of drama, opera, ballet and music, as well as general arts magazine programmes and documentaries. These have won many international awards at festivals such as the Prix Italia and Montreux International Television Festivals. Independent television companies also make grants for arts promotion in their regions.

Broadcasting is a major medium for making the arts available to the public and is a crucial source of work for actors, musicians, writers, composers, technicians and others in the arts world. It has created its own forms—nothing like arts documentaries or drama series, for instance, exists in any other medium. Broadcasters commission and produce a vast quantity of new work. Television and radio provide critical debate, information and education about the arts.

The BBC has five orchestras, which employ many of Britain's full-time professional musicians. Each week it broadcasts about 150 hours of classical and other music (both live and recorded) on its Radio 3 (FM) channel. BBC Radio 1 (FM) broadcasts rock and pop music, along with a range of other programming, 24 hours a day, and a large part of the output of BBC Radio 2 (FM) is popular and light music. There are at present two national commercial radio stations which broadcast music:

- Classic FM, which broadcasts mainly classical music; and
- Virgin 1215, which plays broad-based rock music.

Much of the output of Britain's local radio stations consists of popular and light music.

The BBC regularly commissions new music, particularly by British composers, and sponsors concerts, competitions and festivals. Each summer it presents and broadcasts the BBC Promenade Concerts (the 'Proms'), the world's largest music festival, at the Royal Albert Hall.

The Press

Many national and local newspapers devote considerable space to coverage of the arts, and developments in the arts are also covered in periodicals such as the *Spectator* and *New Statesman and Society* (see Chapter 30). Weekly 'listings' magazines, including *Time Out*, provide details of cultural and other events in London and other large cities.

There are also a large number of specialist publications which cover specific aspects of the arts, including *Classical Music*, *Art Monthly*, *Dance Theatre Journal* and *Opera*. A number of publications publish original literature, including the *London Magazine* and *Granta*, which publishes fiction as well as cultural journalism. *New Musical Express (NME)* and *Melody Maker* cover rock and pop music. The newspaper *Stage and Television Today* is directed at professional actors and others in the industry.

Festivals

Some 650 professional arts festivals take place in Britain each year. The annual Edinburgh

International Festival, featuring a wide range of arts, is held in August and September and is the largest of its kind in the world. Other festivals held in Edinburgh include the annual International Jazz Festival, the International Film and Television Festivals and the biennial Book Festival. The international arts Mayfest takes place in Glasgow. Some well-known festivals concentrating on music are the Three Choirs Festival, which has taken place annually for more than 260 years in Gloucester, Worcester or Hereford; the Cheltenham International Festival of Music, largely devoted to contemporary British music; and the Aldeburgh festival.

Among other festivals catering for a number of art forms are the Royal National Eisteddfod of Wales, the Royal National Gaelic Mod in Scotland, the Belfast Festival at Queen's University, and the festivals in Brighton, Buxton, Chester, St Davids, Harrogate, Llangollen, Malvern, Perth and York. Many smaller towns also hold arts festivals. A major event in London is the Notting Hill Carnival, which is organised largely by the Afro-Caribbean community.

Arts 2000

Arts 2000 is an Arts Council initiative which celebrates the approach of the millennium. During each year between 1992 and 2000, one city, town or region in Britain has been nominated to celebrate a particular art form. Swansea was the City of Literature in 1995; the Northern Region was the Region of Visual Arts for 1996; and the Eastern Region is the Region of Opera and Musical Theatre for 1997. Future years have been designated as follows:

- Yorkshire and Humberside as the Region of Photography and the Electronic Image for 1998; and

- Glasgow as the City of Architecture and Design for 1999.

Arts 2000 is a competitive process judged by expert Arts Council selection committees. Winners are offered between £400,000 and £500,000 from Arts Council funds, and are expected to match this to create a wide-ranging and imaginative programme including a strong international content.

DRAMA

Britain is one of the world's major centres for theatre, and has a long and rich dramatic tradition. There are companies based in London and in many other cities and towns; in addition, numerous touring companies visit theatres, festivals and other venues, including arts and sports centres and social clubs. There are more than 250 companies in receipt of Arts Council or Regional Arts Boards subsidies in 1996–97.

Contemporary British playwrights who have received international recognition, with examples of their works, include:

- David Hare—*Skylight, Racing Demon*;

- Alan Ayckbourn—*The Revengers' Comedies, A Chorus of Disapproval*;

- John Godber—*Up and Under, On the Piste*;

- Caryl Churchill—*Serious Money, The Skriker*; and

- Tom Stoppard—*Arcadia, Indian Ink*.

Among the best-known directors are Sir Peter Hall, Richard Eyre, Nicholas Hytner, Trevor Nunn, Adrian Noble, Jonathan Miller, Deborah Warner and Terry Hands, while the many British performers who enjoy international reputations include Kenneth Branagh, Dame Judi Dench, Ralph Fiennes, Sir John Gielgud, Sir Alec Guinness, Paul Schofield, Sir Ian McKellen, Helen Mirren, Vanessa Redgrave, Dame Diana Rigg, Dame Maggie Smith and Juliet Stephenson. British stage designers such as John Bury, Ralph Koltai and Carl Toms are internationally acclaimed.

Britain has about 300 theatres intended for professional use which can seat between 200 and 2,300 people. Some are privately owned, but most are owned either municipally or by non-profit-making organisations. Over 40 of these have resident theatre companies receiving subsidies from the Arts Councils and Regional Arts Boards. In summer there are also open air theatres, including one in London's Regent's Park and the Minack Theatre, which is on a clifftop near Land's End in Cornwall.

Most theatres are commercially run and self-financing, relying on popular shows and

BROADCASTING

The BBC (British Broadcasting Corporation) is a public body which provides two complementary national television networks—BBC 1 and BBC 2—five national radio networks, and the BBC World Service.

The Middle East Broadcasting Centre (MBC) is an international Arabic television service which has its headquarters in south west London.

ONE HUNDRED YEARS OF CINEMA

Throughout 1996 there were celebrations
of 100 years of cinema, including exhibitions,
special screenings and
National Cinema Day, on 2 June,
when entry to many cinemas cost only £1.00.

The Saturday morning children's picture show—now being revived in many cinemas.

The queue for *Guys and Dolls*
at the Empire, Leicester Square,
1955.

A scene from *Restoration*, premiered in March 1996 to launch the centenary celebrations, and winner of an Oscar for best costume design.

A set of stamps issued to commemorate 100 years of cinema.

Laurel and Hardy lookalikes with Huntley Jefferson Wood, Stan Laurel's only surviving British relative, at the unveiling of a commemorative plaque in Laurel's home town of Bishop Auckland, Durham.

GALLERIES AND EXHIBITIONS

The Evolution House at the Royal Botanic Gardens, Kew, Surrey, tells the story of the development of plant life through the use of realistic landscapes, which include many examples of primitive plants.

An exhibition at the Natural History Museum's Earth Galleries, which opened in 1996.

musicals to be profitable. By contrast, companies funded by the Arts Councils tend to offer a variety of traditional and experimental productions. Experimental or innovative work is often staged in 'fringe' theatres in London and other cities; these are smaller theatres which use a variety of buildings, such as rooms in pubs.

London

London has about 100 theatres, 15 of them permanently occupied by subsidised companies. These include:

- the Royal National Theatre, which stages a range of modern and classical plays in its three auditoriums on the South Bank;

- the Royal Shakespeare Company, which presents plays mainly by Shakespeare and his contemporaries as well as some modern work, in Stratford-upon-Avon and in its two auditoriums in the City's Barbican Centre. Since 1996 the Company has also toured other parts of Britain for six months of the year; and

- the English Stage Company at the Royal Court Theatre in Sloane Square, which stages the work of many new playwrights.

The largest concentration of London's commercial theatres is around Shaftesbury Avenue. West End theatre attendance was over

Table 29.1: Attendances at West End Theatres, 1994 and 1995

| | Percentage | |
Type of Performance	1994	1995
Modern musicals	43	45
Modern drama	10	11
Traditional musicals	14	17
Classical plays	11	8
Comedy	6	4
Opera/operetta	6	6
Ballet/dance	3	4
Thrillers/other	2	2
Revue/variety	2	1
Children's shows/pantomimes	1	1

Source: *The Society of London Theatre Box Office Data Report 1995*

11 million in 1995; over half of these went to musicals.

In 1989 the partial remains of the Globe Theatre, where Shakespeare acted, and the Rose Theatre, where his plays were performed during his lifetime, were excavated on the south bank of the Thames; both have since been listed as ancient monuments. A modern reconstruction of the Globe Theatre, near its original site, was completed in 1996.

Regional Theatres

Outside London most cities and many large towns have at least one theatre. Older theatres which have been restored include the Theatre Royal, Newcastle upon Tyne, which dates from the 18th century; the Alhambra, Bradford; the Lyceum, Sheffield; the Theatre Royal, Bristol; and the Grand Opera House, Belfast, all dating from the 19th century. Others, such as the West Yorkshire Playhouse, Leeds, and the Theatre Royal, Plymouth, have been built to modern designs. Edinburgh's rebuilt and restored Empire Theatre, reopened as the Edinburgh Festival Theatre in 1994, provides an international venue for large-scale productions. A custom-built theatre for new writing recently became the new home of the Traverse Theatre in Edinburgh. Several universities have theatres which house professional companies playing to the public.

Most regional repertory companies mount about eight to ten productions a year; several have studio theatres in addition to the main auditorium, where they present new or experimental drama and plays of specialist interest. Repertory theatres also often function as social centres by offering concerts, poetry readings and exhibitions, and by providing restaurants, bars and shops.

Regional theatre companies with major reputations include the Citizens' Theatre, Glasgow; the Royal Exchange, Manchester; Bristol Old Vic; West Yorkshire Playhouse; the Festival Theatre, Chichester; and the Nottingham Playhouse, one of the first modern regional theatres. Successful productions from regional theatre companies often transfer to London's West End. In addition, the largest regional theatres receive visits from the Royal National Theatre or the Royal Shakespeare

Company, which has three theatres at its base in Stratford-upon-Avon. The Cambridge Theatre Company, Oxford Stage Company and English Touring Theatre Company tour the English regions and worldwide.

Theatre for Young People

Unicorn Theatre for Children and Polka Children's Theatre, both in London, present plays specially written for children; and the Whirligig Theatre tours throughout Britain. The Young Vic Company in London and Contact Theatre Company in Manchester stage plays for young people. Numerous Theatre-in-Education companies perform in schools. Some of these companies operate independently—Theatre Centre, for example, plays in London and tours further afield. Others are attached to regional repertory theatres such as the Wolsey Theatre, Ipswich, and Greenwich Theatre. Most regional repertory theatres also mount productions for younger audiences, and concessionary ticket prices are generally available for those at school, college or university. The first Festival of Theatre for Children and Young People took place in London in 1995.

There has been a marked growth in youth theatres, which number more than 500 in England alone; both the National Youth Theatre in London and the Scottish Youth Theatre in Glasgow offer early acting opportunities to young people.

Dramatic Training

Training for actors, directors, lighting and sound technicians and stage managers is provided mainly in drama schools, among them the Royal Academy of Dramatic Art (RADA), the Central School of Speech and Drama, the London Academy of Music and Dramatic Art (LAMDA), and the Drama Centre (all in London); the Bristol Old Vic School, the Royal Scottish Academy of Music and Drama (Glasgow) and the Welsh College of Music and Drama (Cardiff). Theatre design courses, often based in art schools, are available for people wanting to train as stage designers. A number of universities and colleges offer degree courses in drama.

Amateur Theatre

There are several thousand amateur dramatic societies throughout Britain. They use a variety of buildings, including schools and public halls. Their work is encouraged by a number of organisations, such as the Central Council for Amateur Theatre, the National Drama Conference, the Scottish Community Drama Association and the Association of Ulster Drama Festivals. A nationwide representative body, the Voluntary Arts Network, was established in 1991. Amateur companies sometimes receive financial support from local government and other bodies.

MUSIC

People in Britain are interested in a wide range of music, from classical to different forms of rock, country and pop music. Jazz, folk and world music, and brass bands also have substantial followings.

The 1996 National Music Festival took place in June, with a programme of cultural activity associated with the football European Cup finals, and with the annual National Music Day, which promotes the enjoyment of music by encouraging as many people as possible to take part as performers or listeners in a day of music-making across Britain.

Orchestral and Choral Music

Seasons of orchestral and choral concerts are promoted every year in many large towns and cities. The principal concert halls in central London are the Royal Festival Hall in the South Bank Centre, next to which are the Queen Elizabeth Hall and the Purcell Room, which accommodate smaller scale performances; the Barbican Hall (part of the Barbican Centre for Arts and Conferences in the City of London); the Royal Albert Hall in Kensington; the Wigmore Hall, a recital centre; and St John's, Smith Square. Birmingham has its own recently built concert hall, the Symphony Hall, and a 2,400-seat international concert hall opened in 1996 for Manchester's Hallé Orchestra.

The leading symphony orchestras in London include the London Symphony, the

Philharmonia, the London Philharmonic, the Royal Philharmonic and the BBC Symphony. Important regional orchestras include the Royal Liverpool Philharmonic, the Hallé, the City of Birmingham Symphony, the Bournemouth Symphony, the Ulster Orchestra, the Royal Scottish National Orchestra and the BBC National Orchestra of Wales. The BBC's five orchestras give broadcast concerts which are often open to the public. There are also chamber orchestras, such as the City of London Sinfonia, the Academy of St Martin-in-the-Fields, the Northern Sinfonia, the Bournemouth Sinfonietta and the Scottish Chamber Orchestra. Specialised ensembles include the Orchestra of the Age of Enlightenment, the English Baroque Soloists and the English Concert. The London Sinfonietta and the Birmingham Contemporary Music Group specialise in contemporary music.

British conductors such as Sir Colin Davis, Vernon Handley, Sir Charles Mackerras, John Eliot Gardiner, Andrew Davis, Sir Simon Rattle, Christopher Hogwood, Jane Glover and Richard Hickox reach a wide audience through their recordings as well as by their performances. The works of living composers such as Sir Michael Tippett, Sir Peter Maxwell Davies and Sir Harrison Birtwistle enjoy international acclaim. Other well-established British composers include Michael Berkeley, John Tavener, Sir Malcolm Arnold, Oliver Knussen, Nicola le Fanu, George Lloyd, David Matthews, Mark Anthony Turnage, John Casken, James MacMillan and Judith Weir. The Master of the Queen's Music, Malcolm Williamson, holds an office within the Royal Household with responsibility for organising and writing music for state occasions. Percussionist Evelyn Glennie and clarinettist Emma Johnson are among solo performers currently enjoying great acclaim.

The principal choral societies include the Bach Choir, the Royal Choral Society, the Huddersfield Choral Society, the Cardiff Polyphonic Choir, the Edinburgh International Festival Chorus and the Belfast Philharmonic Society. Almost all the leading orchestras maintain their own choral societies. The English tradition of church singing is represented by choirs such as those of King's College Chapel, Cambridge, and Christ Church Cathedral, Oxford, while other choirs such as the Roman Catholic Westminster Cathedral choir are also well known. There are many male-voice choirs in Wales and in certain parts of England.

The Leeds International Pianoforte Competition for young pianists is one the most prestigious events in the musical calendar; and the biennial Cardiff Singer of the World Competition attracts outstanding young singers from all over the world.

Pop and Rock Music

Hundreds of hours of pop and rock music are broadcast through BBC and independent radio stations every week. Television programmes of both live and recorded music also feature pop and rock, which is by far the most popular form of music in Britain. It covers a diversity of styles, ranging from dance to heavy metal.

In the 1960s and 1970s groups such as the Beatles, the Rolling Stones, Led Zeppelin and Pink Floyd achieved international success. British groups continue to be popular throughout the world and are often at the forefront of new developments in music.

The British record industry recognises the most talented British performers at the annual Brit Awards. In 1996 Oasis won three categories, including best British group. Other winners were Paul Weller (best male singer), Annie Lennox (best female singer) and David Bowie (for an outstanding contribution to the British record industry). Other successful British performers include Blur, Supergrass, Massive Attack, Pulp, Gabrielle, Seal, and East 17.

The pop and rock music industry contributes significantly to Britain's overseas earnings through the sale of recordings, concert tours, and promotional material, including clothing and books.

Jazz

Jazz has a large following in Britain and is played in numerous clubs and pubs. There is also a jazz radio station, Jazz FM, which broadcasts in London and in the north west.

The London Jazz Festival attracts international stars, such as the bandleader Django Bates, saxophonists Pharoah Saunders and Joshua Redman, and the singer Jean Carn. British musicians such as Barbara Thompson, Stan Tracey, Julian Joseph, David Jean Baptiste, Tommy Smith and Courtney Pine have established international reputations. Festivals of jazz music are held throughout Britain, including Cardiff Bay, Brecon, Edinburgh, Glasgow and Birmingham.

Training

Professional training in music is given mainly at colleges of music. The leading London colleges are the Royal Academy of Music, the Royal College of Music, the Guildhall School of Music and Drama, and Trinity College of Music. The City University's music industry course provides training in business practice aimed specifically at musicians and music administrators. Outside London the main centres are the Royal Scottish Academy of Music and Drama in Glasgow, the Royal Northern College of Music in Manchester, the Welsh College of Music and Drama, Cardiff, and the Birmingham Conservatoire. Many universities also offer courses in music.

Other Educational Schemes

Many children learn to play musical instruments at school, and some take the examinations of the Associated Board of the Royal Schools of Music. Music is one of the foundation subjects in the National Curriculum (see p. 451). In Scottish schools music and the expressive arts are also well developed. The National Youth Orchestras of Great Britain, Scotland, Ulster and Wales, and other youth orchestras have established high standards. Nearly a third of the players in the European Community Youth Orchestra come from Britain. There is also a National Youth Jazz Orchestra.

Youth and Music, an organisation affiliated to the international *Jeunesses Musicales*, encourages attendance by young people at opera, dance and concert performances.

OPERA

Interest in opera has been growing markedly in Britain, with an estimated 2.6 million of the adult population attending opera performances in 1995–96. A number of British singers—Thomas Allen, Anne Evans, Philip Langridge, Felicity Lott, Ann Murray and Bryn Terfel, for example—have now established themselves in the international opera houses.

An opera season for which international casts are specially assembled is held every summer at Glyndebourne in East Sussex. This is followed by an autumn tour by Glyndebourne Touring Opera, using casts drawn from the chorus of the festival season. Since 1994 the summer season at Glyndebourne has taken place in a new 1,200-seat opera house, built at a cost of £33 million. All the funding came from private sources.

Regular seasons of opera are held at the Royal Opera House, Covent Garden, London. The English National Opera stages opera in English at the London Coliseum. Scottish Opera has regular seasons at the Theatre Royal in Glasgow, and tours mainly in Scotland and northern England. Welsh National Opera presents seasons in Cardiff and other cities; Music Theatre Wales has become well known for its contemporary work. Leeds-based Opera North tours primarily in the north of England and has gained an international reputation. Opera Factory in London presents experimental work in opera and music theatre. English Touring Opera takes opera to towns throughout England. Opera Northern Ireland presents seasons at the Grand Opera House, Belfast, and tours the province.

The National Opera Studio provides advanced training for young singers.

DANCE

An estimated 6 million people take part in dance, making it one of Britain's leading participatory activities, and audiences are attracted to a widening range of professional dance.

Subsidised Dance Companies

Subsidised dance companies include the Royal Ballet and the Birmingham Royal Ballet, English National Ballet, Northern Ballet Theatre and Rambert Dance Company, which rank among the world's leading companies and are supported by professional orchestras. The Birmingham Royal Ballet tours widely in Britain and overseas; English National Ballet divides its performances between London and the regions; Northern Ballet Theatre is based in Leeds and also tours; and Scottish Ballet is based in Glasgow. Other subsidised companies include the Cardiff-based Diversions Dance Company and the Dundee Repertory Dance Company.

The Arts Councils also subsidise a wide range of other companies and dance organisations, including Rambert Dance Company (which celebrated its 70th anniversary in 1996 with performances at the Coliseum, London), Adzido Pan African Dance Ensemble, Shobana Jeyasingh Dance Company and Richard Alston Dance Company. Also subsidised is Dance Umbrella, which promotes an annual festival of contemporary dance in London. The Arts Councils and the Regional Arts Boards support companies such as Phoenix Dance Company, Adventures in Motion Pictures and CandoCo Dance Company.

Matthew Bourne, Christopher Bruce, Richard Alston, Lloyd Newson, Ashley Page, Shobana Jeyasingh, Siobhan Davies and Jonathan Burrows are among the foremost British choreographers. Leading dancers include Darcey Bussell, Gill Clarke, Adam Cooper and Deborah Bull.

National Dance Agencies

A network of agencies for professional and community dancers has been established in Birmingham, Leeds, Nottingham, London, Newcastle upon Tyne, Swindon (Wiltshire) and Suffolk. The agencies, which receive Arts Council, Regional Arts Board and local authority support, offer classes, provide information and advice, help to co-ordinate activities, and commission dance artists to create work. A new agency based in the north west joined the national network in 1996.

Training

Professional training for dancers and choreographers is provided mainly by specialist schools, which include the Royal Ballet School, the Central School of Ballet, the Northern School of Contemporary Dance (Leeds) and the London Contemporary Dance School; these, with many private schools, have helped to raise British dance to its present standard. Dance is a subject for degree studies at a number of institutions, including the Laban Centre (University of London), the University of Surrey, Dartington College of Arts in Devon and Middlesex University.

Courses for students intending to work with community groups are available at several institutions. The Royal Ballet is running a scheme that aims to widen access to ballet training for children from a different range of cultural backgrounds.

Other Educational Schemes

The Arts Council of England runs Taped, a scheme to finance dance videos for use in education, while the Video Place provides a library of videotape documentation of dance performances for viewing by promoters, choreographers, dancers, teachers and students. The Scottish Arts Council supports Dance Base, which offers a range of classes.

All government-funded dance companies provide dance workshops and education activities. Many have won awards for major projects, such as Phoenix Dance Company's 'Urban Exchange' and English National Ballet's 'Striking a Balance'. Ludus Dance Company, based in Lancaster, works mainly with young people; and Scottish Ballet has a programme of work in schools in Scotland.

The Performing Arts and Technology School in Croydon, Surrey, offers studies in drama, music and dance to pupils aged from 14 to 18, with the emphasis on the application of technology to the performing arts.

The National Youth Dance Company provides opportunities for young dancers to work with professionals and to create and perform dance. Similar opportunities exist for young people to join youth dance companies throughout the country.

FILMS

British films, actors, and producers as well as the creative and technical services supporting them are widely acclaimed. British performers who enjoy international reputations include Kenneth Branagh, Michael Caine, Sean Connery, Ralph Fiennes, Hugh Grant, Sir Anthony Hopkins, Jeremy Irons, Liam Neeson, Miranda Richardson, Alan Rickman, Greta Scacchi and Emma Thompson. Successful British directors include Alan Parker, Mike Newell, Sally Potter, Michael Radford, Ken Loach and Mike Leigh, whose film *Secrets and Lies* won the Palme d'Or at the 1996 Cannes Film Festival.

Throughout 1996 there were celebrations to mark 100 years of cinema in Britain, including special screenings, exhibitions, and National Cinema Day, when there was a greatly reduced entry fee at many cinemas.

British actors and film-makers have won 30 per cent of all Oscars over the last 20 years. In 1996 there were four winners:

- **Emma Thompson (best screenplay)** —*Sense and Sensibility*;
- **Nick Park (best animated short film)**— *A Close Shave*;
- **Jon Blair (documentary feature)** — *Anne Frank Remembered*; and
- **James Acheson (costume)** —*Restoration*.

There are about 2,000 cinema screens in Britain, and estimated attendances are currently running at about 2.5 million a week; cinema admissions have more than doubled (to 124 million a year) since 1984. In London and other large cities a number of art or repertory cinemas show films which have not been more widely distributed. These include films from Britain and abroad; other foreign films, often with English subtitles; and older films which are being shown again, sometimes in a newly edited form.

Animation

The resurgence of interest in animation in Britain is due in part to the pioneering work of British animators, who have created 3D animation and computer animation. British animations have won five Oscars for Best Animated Short Film in recent years, including David Fine and Alison Snowdon's *Bob's Birthday* in 1995 for Channel 4, and in 1996 Nick Park's *A Close Shave* (his third Oscar). Television has proved an important source of production finance.

Government Support

An annual government grant of about £16.5 million is made to the British Film Institute and one of over £1 million to the Scottish Film Council and the Scottish Film Production Fund.

In addition, more than £80 million from the National Lottery (see p. 43) will be provided by the Arts Council of England to support film-making over the next five years.

British Film Commission

The British Film Commission (BFC) was launched in 1991 with government funding to market the British film and television production service industry to overseas production executives with the aim of increasing inward investment. Productions assisted by the BFC since its establishment have contributed in excess of £300 million to the British production industry and the British economy. All services offered by the Commission to overseas producers are free of charge.

The BFC also works alongside the UK Film Commission Network, which currently comprises 20 area or city offices. The growth of this network over the past three years illustrates both the growth of production in Britain and the recognition of local and central government of the effectiveness of such organisations in stimulating increased production activity.

British Screen Finance

British Screen Finance, a private sector company, provides finance for new film-makers with commercially viable productions who have difficulty in attracting funding. The company, investing its own money together with contributions from the Government, makes loans for the production of low- and medium-budget films involving largely British talent. It encourages the early stages of film project development and the production of short films. The Government funds the company with £2 million a year. During 1994 British Screen Finance supported 15 films and recouped £2.2 million from its feature film investments in previous years.

European Co-Production Fund

Funded by the Government with £2 million a year, the European Co-Production Fund (ECPF) offers loans of up to 30 per cent of a film's budget, enabling British producers to collaborate in the making of films in Europe. It has invested more than £6.5 million in 19 feature films, with a total value of more than £46 million.

British Film Institute

The development of film, video and television as art forms is promoted by the British Film Institute (BFI) and in Scotland by the Scottish Film Council. The BFI offers some direct financial and technical help through its Production Board.

The BFI runs the National Film Theatre in London and the National Film and Television Archive, and has the world's largest library of information on film and television. It holds extensive international collections of books, periodicals, scripts, stills and posters. BFI Research and Education Department aims to enable as many people as possible to discover new ways of appreciating film, video and television.

The National Film and Television Archive contains over 300,000 films and television programmes, including newsreels, dating from 1895. BFI on the South Bank comprises the Museum of the Moving Image, which traces the history of film and television, and the National Film Theatre. The latter has three cinemas showing films of historical, artistic or technical interest, and is unique in offering regular programmes unrestricted by commercial considerations. In 1995–96 about 2,000 films, television and video programmes were shown, attracting attendances of over 180,000. In November each year the National Film Theatre hosts the London Film Festival, at which some 250 new films from all over the world are screened. In 1995 over 100,000 people attended Festival screenings.

The BFI promotes, and helps to fund, a network of 35 regional film theatres, and is involved in setting up film and television centres with a range of activities and facilities. It also co-operates with the Regional Arts Boards and grant-aids their film and video work.

The Wales Film Council acts as the BFI's agent in Wales, and in Northern Ireland the BFI works with the Northern Ireland Film Council (NIFC). Both of these Film Councils receive Arts Council funding.

Scottish Film Council

The Scottish Film Council supports regional film theatres, promotes and provides material for media education and administers the Scottish Film Archive. Financial assistance to develop film scripts is available through the Scottish Film Production Fund. Scottish Screen Locations provides advice to film-makers on suitable locations for film productions in Scotland. In 1996 the Secretary of State for Scotland announced plans to merge these three organisations with Scottish Broadcast and Film Training, a privately owned organisation, to form one body—Scottish Screen.

Children's Film

The Children's Film and Television Foundation produces and distributes entertainment films for children, shown largely through video and television.

The Children's Film Unit makes feature films for children (mainly for Channel 4) and runs weekly workshops for children on all aspects of film-making. The Unit caters for about 80 children at any time and has produced 15 feature films.

The Northern Ireland Film Council runs Cinemagic, an award-winning international film festival for young people.

Training in Film Production

The National Film and Television School is financed jointly by the Government and by the film, video and television industries. It offers postgraduate and short course training for directors, editors, camera operators, animators and other specialists. The School enrols about 30 full-time students a year and about 500 on short course programmes. In 1995–96 it received a government grant of £1.8 million. The School is planning to move from its present location in Buckinghamshire to the former BBC film studios in west London.

The London International Film School, the Royal College of Art, and some universities and other institutions of higher education also offer courses in film production.

Cinema Licensing and Film Classification

Cinemas showing films to the public must be licensed by local authorities, which have a legal duty to prohibit the admission of children to unsuitable films, and may prevent the showing of any film. In assessing films the authorities normally rely on the judgment of an independent non-statutory body, the British Board of Film Classification (BBFC), to which films must be submitted. The Board was set up on the initiative of the cinema industry to ensure a proper standard in films shown to the public. It does not use any written code of censorship, but can require cuts to be made before granting a certificate; on rare occasions, it refuses a certificate.

Films passed by the Board are put into one of the following categories:

- U (universal)—suitable for all;
- PG (parental guidance), in which some scenes may be unsuitable for young children;
- 12, 15 and 18, for people of not less than those ages; and

- Restricted 18, for restricted showing only at segregated premises to which no one under 18 is admitted—for example, licensed cinema clubs.

Videos

The BBFC is also legally responsible for classifying videos under a system similar to that for films. It is an offence to supply commercially a video which has not been classified or to supply it in contravention of its classification—for example, to sell or hire a video classified 18 to a person under 18.

VISUAL ARTS

State support for the visual arts includes funding for the national museums and galleries, and funding through local authorities and the Museums and Galleries Commission. It also includes funding for the production, exhibition and distribution of work by contemporary artists and photographers and for the promotion of art to the public, channelled through the Arts Councils, the Crafts Council and the Regional Arts Boards, and grants towards the cost of art education. The Government encourages high standards of industrial design and craftsmanship through grants to the Design Council (see p. 213).

Museums and galleries maintained by local authorities, universities, independent museums and private funds may receive help in building up their collections through grants administered by the Museums and Galleries Commission and the museum councils in Scotland, Wales and Northern Ireland. Support to national and regional public and independent museums and galleries is also given by the Arts Councils and by trusts and voluntary bodies, including the Henry Moore Foundation, the Calouste Gulbenkian Foundation and the National Art Collections Fund. National Lottery proceeds are being distributed in the form of capital grants by the Heritage Lottery Fund, the Arts Councils and the Millennium Commission. The effect of these grants on the infrastructure of galleries, and visual arts provision, will be significant; in the first year of operation the Arts Council of

England allocated £13 million to public arts projects alone.

The Heritage Lottery Fund also distributes grants for the purchase of works of art and items of national significance. In recent years, for example, the Fund has helped towards the acquisition of masterpieces by Hans Holbein and Jacques-Louis David (bought by the National Gallery) and by El Greco (the National Gallery of Scotland).

The Museums and Galleries Commission administers a system whereby pre-eminent works of art may be accepted by the Government in place of inheritance tax and allocated to public galleries; items thus acquired in 1995–96 include paintings by George Stubbs, Yves Tanguy and the 15th century Italian artist Paris Bordone.

In collaboration with the Regional Arts Boards, the Arts Council of England provides some strategic funding for galleries; educational institutions, from art schools and universities to schools; commercial galleries and publishers; artists' agencies; and media centres. It also supports touring exhibitions and the presentation of works of art in a variety of public spaces. The Arts Council of England's unique collection of 20th century British art, with the National Touring Exhibition Service, is managed on its behalf by the South Bank Board, which also runs the Hayward Gallery.

The Arts Council of England also supports the Institute of Contemporary Art in London and five other independent galleries: the Whitechapel and the Serpentine in London, the Museum of Modern Art in Oxford, Ikon in Birmingham and Arnolfini in Bristol, as well as the Institute of International Visual Arts, based in London. The ten Regional Arts Boards also fund galleries and arts centres and provide direct support for artists.

Support for galleries is also given by the Arts Councils in Scotland, Wales and Northern Ireland.

British artists, photographers, architects and sculptors with international reputations include David Hockney, Lucian Freud, David Bailey, Jane Bown, Sir Richard Rogers and Sir Anthony Caro. Younger artists with a similar standing include Damien Hirst, Rachel Whiteread and Anish Kapoor.

Museums and Galleries

About 110 million people a year, across all social groups, visit more than 2,000 museums and galleries open to the public, which include the major national collections, around 1,100 independent museums, and museums receiving support from local authorities.

Museums and galleries in Britain receive about £440 million a year in public expenditure, and by June 1996 they had been awarded over £225 million from the National Lottery. All national museums and galleries are financed chiefly from government funds; they may charge for entry to their permanent collections and special exhibitions. Most of the national collections are managed by independent trustees.

The Museums and Galleries Commission advises the Government on museum issues. The Commission also promotes co-operation between national and regional institutions. Ten area museum councils supply a variety of services and advice to individual museums.

The Government encourages the loan of objects from national and regional collections so that works of art can be seen by as wide a public as possible. The Arts Council of England, through a National Collections Touring Scheme and the National Touring Exhibition Service, is also broadening access to the national collections.

The Museum Training Institute is

Table 29.2: Visitors to National Museums and Galleries 1995–96 in England

	(million)
British Museum	6.15
Imperial War Museum	1.31
National Gallery	4.47
National Maritime Museum	0.58
National Museums and Galleries on Merseyside	1.22
National Portrait Gallery	0.82
Natural History Museum	1.46
Science Museum	2.74
Tate Gallery	2.74
Victoria and Albert Museum	1.49
Wallace Collection	0.16

Source: *Department of National Heritage Annual Report 1995*

responsible for developing training standards and programmes within museums. The Arts Council of England supports an MA course at the Royal College of Art for curating and commissioning contemporary art, and promotes professional practice among artists and curators.

Museums Association

The independent Museums Association, to which many museums and art galleries and their staffs belong, facilitates exchange of information and discussion of matters relating to museums and galleries. The Association, which has many overseas members, provides training, seminars and research; its publications include the monthly *Museums Journal* and a new technical periodical, *Museum Practice*.

National Collections

The national museums and art galleries, many of them located in London, contain some of the world's most comprehensive collections of objects of artistic, archaeological, scientific, historical and general interest. The English national museums are:

- the British Museum (including the ethnographic collections of the Museum of Mankind);
- the Natural History Museum;
- the Victoria and Albert Museum (the V&A, which displays fine and decorative arts);
- the National Museum of Science and Industry, including the Science Museum and its two regional institutes—the National Railway Museum (York) and the National Museum of Photography, Film and Television (Bradford);
- the National Gallery (which houses western painting from around 1260 to 1920);
- the Tate Gallery, with collections in London (British painting and modern art); Liverpool; and St Ives (St Ives School and contemporary art);
- the National Portrait Gallery;
- the Imperial War Museum;
- the Royal Armouries;

- the National Army Museum;
- the Royal Air Force Museum;
- the National Maritime Museum;
- the Wallace Collection (which includes paintings, furniture, arms and armour, and objets d'art); and
- the National Museums and Galleries on Merseyside.

The Royal Armouries, Britain's oldest museum, has collections in the Tower of London (items relating to the Tower's history), Leeds (arms and armoury), and Fort Nelson, near Portsmouth (artillery). The Tate Gallery is to create Britain's first national museum of modern art, situated on the south bank of the Thames. Awarded £50 million by the Millennium Commission, the new museum will house a collection of 20th century art of international importance.

In Scotland the national collections are held by the National Museums of Scotland and the National Galleries of Scotland. The former include the Royal Museum of Scotland, the National Museum of Antiquities of Scotland, the Scottish United Services Museum and the Scottish Agricultural Museum, in Edinburgh; the Museum of Flight, near North Berwick; and the Museum of Costume at Shambellie House near Dumfries. A new Museum of Scotland is being built next to the Royal Museum to house the National Museums' Scottish collection.

The National Galleries of Scotland comprise the National Gallery of Scotland, the Scottish National Portrait Gallery and the Scottish National Gallery of Modern Art. The National Galleries of Scotland also have collections at Paxton House near Berwick and Duff House in Banff. In 1995–96 the National Museums of Scotland attracted 1.5 million visitors and the National Galleries of Scotland some 870,000.

The National Museum of Wales, which has opened new galleries at its main building in Cardiff, has a number of branches, including the Welsh Folk Museum at St Fagans and the Industrial and Maritime Museum in Cardiff's dockland.

Northern Ireland has two national museums: the Ulster Museum in Belfast and the Ulster Folk and Transport Museum in County Down. There are plans to merge these two museums with the Ulster-American Folk Park in County Tyrone to form a single National Museum for Northern Ireland.

Other Collections

Other important collections in London include the Museum of London; Sir John Soane's Museum; the Courtauld Institute Galleries; and the London Transport Museum. The Queen's Gallery in Buckingham Palace has exhibitions of pictures from the extensive royal collection.

Most cities and towns have museums devoted to art, archaeology and natural history, often administered by the local authorities but sometimes by local learned societies or by individuals or trustees. Many are associated with their universities, such as the Ashmolean Museum in Oxford and the Fitzwilliam Museum in Cambridge.

Many collections of art and antiques in historic family houses, including those owned by the two National Trusts (see p. 373) and English Heritage (see p. 372), are open to the public.

There are also a number of national art exhibiting societies, the most famous being the Royal Academy of Arts at Burlington House in London. The Academy holds an annual Summer Exhibition and other important exhibitions during the rest of the year. The Summer Exhibition is the world's largest open contemporary art exhibition and brings together a wide range of work by established artists and by others exhibiting for the first time. The Royal Scottish Academy holds annual exhibitions in Edinburgh. There are also children's exhibitions, including the National Exhibition of Children's Art.

An increasing number of open air museums depict the regional life of an area or preserve early industrial remains. These include the Weald and Downland Museum in West Sussex, and the Ironbridge Gorge Museum in Shropshire. Skills of the past are revived in a number of 'living' museums, such as the Gladstone Pottery Museum near Stoke-on-

Trent and the Quarry Bank Mill at Styal in Cheshire.

Among recently established museums are:

- the Mary Rose Museum in Portsmouth, housing the restored wreck of the flagship of Henry VIII;
- the St Mungo Museum of Religious Life and Art in Glasgow, containing artefacts representing the world's major religions; and
- Eureka!, the first museum designed specifically for children, in Halifax, West Yorkshire.

The Burrell Collection in Glasgow houses world-famous tapestries, paintings and objets d'art. The Design Museum in London's Docklands contains a collection of 20th-century mass-produced consumer objects.

Crafts

The crafts in Britain have an annual turnover estimated at £400 million. Government aid for the crafts, amounting to £3.2 million in 1996–97, is administered in England and Wales by the Crafts Council. The Council supports craftspeople by promoting public interest in their work, and encouraging the creation of works of contemporary craftsmanship. Grants are available to help with setting up workshops and acquiring equipment. The Crafts Council runs the national centre for crafts in London, which houses a gallery, reference and picture libraries, and a gallery shop. It organises the annual Chelsea Crafts Fair, and co-ordinates British groups at international trade fairs. Crafts Council exhibitions tour nationally and internationally, and grants are made to encourage exhibitions, projects and organisations.

Funding is given to the Regional Arts Boards and the Arts Council of Wales for the support of crafts, and to Contemporary Applied Arts, a membership organisation that holds exhibitions and sells work through its London gallery.

Craftworks, an independent company, is the crafts development agency for Northern Ireland, providing training, marketing and business counselling for the crafts sector. The

Arts Council of Northern Ireland also funds crafts promotion, as does the Scottish Office through the Scottish Arts Council.

Training in Art and Design

Most practical education in art and design is provided in the art colleges and fine and applied art departments of universities (these include the Slade School of Art and Goldsmith's College of Art, London); and in further education colleges and private art schools. Many of these institutions award degrees at postgraduate level. Art is also taught at an advanced level at the four Scottish Central (Art) Institutions.

Courses at universities concentrate largely on academic disciplines, such as the history of art. The leading institutions include the Courtauld and Warburg Institutes of the University of London and the Department of Classical Art and Archaeology at University College, London. The Open University also offers courses in art history and theory of art. Art is one of the foundation subjects in the National Curriculum. The Society for Education through Art encourages, among other activities, the purchase by schools of original works of art by organising an annual Pictures for Schools exhibition.

The Open College of the Arts offers correspondence courses in art and design, painting, sculpture, textiles, photography and creative writing to people wishing to study at home.

Export Control of Works of Art

London is a major centre for the international art market, and sales of works of art take place in the main auction houses (two of the longest established being Sotheby's and Christie's), and through private dealers. Certain items are covered by export control; guidance is provided by the Export Licensing Unit of the Department of National Heritage.

A licence from the Department of National Heritage is required before such items can be exported. If the Department's advisers object to the granting of a licence, the matter is referred to the Reviewing Committee on the Export of Works of Art. If the Committee considers a work to be of national importance, it can advise the Government to defer a decision on the licence application for a specified time to provide an opportunity for an offer to be made to buy at or above the recommended fair market price.

LITERATURE AND LIBRARIES

A number of literary activities receive public subsidy through the Arts Councils. In 1995, for example, there was continued support for a programme of tours by writers from other countries; and a partnership between the four Arts Councils and the Republic of Northern Ireland to promote tours of prominent writers from and in each country. There were also innovative broadcasting projects promoting reading and writing.

There are free public libraries throughout Britain (see p. 494), private libraries and several private literary societies. Book reviews are featured in the press and on television and radio, and numerous periodicals concerned with literature are published.

Recognition of outstanding literary merit is provided by a number of awards, some of the most valuable being the Booker and Whitbread prizes. The 1996 Booker Prize was won by Graham Swift for *Last Orders*. In 1995 Harold Pinter was awarded the second David Cohen British Literature Prize for a lifetime's achievement by a living British writer. A part of the £40,000 prize, which is awarded every two years, enables winners to commission new works from younger writers. Other awards to encourage young authors include those of the Somerset Maugham Trust Fund and the E.C. Gregory Trust Fund.

Ulster-born poet Seamus Heaney was awarded the Nobel Prize for Literature in 1995. Other distinguished British poets include Ted Hughes (the Poet Laureate), James Berry, Gillian Clarke, Carol Ann Duffy, U.A. Fanthorpe, Tony Harrison, Geoffrey Hill, Elizabeth Jennings, R.S. Thomas and Carol Rumens. As the Poet Laureate, Ted Hughes is a member of the Royal Household and receives an annual stipend from the Civil List (see p. 51).

Many British writers are internationally recognised. Well-known living novelists, with examples of their works, include:

- Martin Amis—*London Fields, Money, The Information*;
- A.S. Byatt—*Still Life, Possession: A Romance, Babel Tower*;
- Julian Barnes—*Flaubert's Parrot, Letters from London, Cross Channel*; and
- Ruth Rendell—*Crocodile Bird, Demon in my View, Simisola*.

Many writers from overseas, often from Commonwealth countries, live and work in Britain, writing books in English which have a wide circulation in Britain and overseas. English literature is taught extensively at schools, colleges and universities throughout Britain. Creative writing is also taught at a variety of institutions; one of the best known is the University of East Anglia, in Norwich, where writers such as Ian McEwan and Kazuo Ishiguro have studied. The University also houses the British Centre for Literary Translation.

Authors' Copyright and Performers' Protection

Original literary, dramatic, musical or artistic works, films, sound recordings and broadcasts are automatically protected by copyright in Britain. This protection is also given to works from countries party to international copyright conventions. The copyright owner has rights against unauthorised reproduction, public performance, broadcasting and issue to the public of his or her work; and against dealing in unauthorised copies. In most cases the author is the first owner of the copyright, and the term of copyright in literary, dramatic, musical and artistic works is the life of the author and a period of 70 years after death. For films the term is 70 years from the last death among the following: principal director, authors of the screenplay and dialogue, or composer of music for the film. Sound

recordings are protected for 50 years from the year of making or release, and broadcasts for 50 years from the year of broadcast.

Performers are also given automatic protection against broadcasting and recording of live performances, and reproduction of recordings. This lasts for 50 years from the year of performance or release of a recording of it. The Copyright, Designs and Patents Act 1988 revised the law on copyright and performers' rights, and has since been amended to comply with the EC Directives on copyright.

Literary and Philological Societies

Societies to promote literature include the English Association and the Royal Society of Literature. The leading society for studies in the humanities is the British Academy for the Promotion of Historical, Philosophical and Philological Studies (the British Academy).

Other specialist societies are the Early English Text Society, the Bibliographical Society and several societies devoted to particular authors, the largest of which is the Dickens Fellowship. Various societies, such as the Poetry Society, sponsor poetry readings and recitals. London's South Bank Centre runs a programme of literary events.

Libraries

The British Library

The British Library, the national library of Britain, is one of the world's greatest libraries, with a collection of more than 150 million separate items. These include books, journals, manuscripts, newspapers, stamps, maps and recorded sound. Publishers must deposit in the Library a copy of everything published.

A new building for the British Library is being constructed at St Pancras, London, at a cost of £511.1 million. The St Pancras building will offer, for the first time, a purpose-built home for the national library with environmentally controlled storage, increased reader space and seating and greatly improved public facilities, including three exhibition galleries, an auditorium and a bookshop.

The Library's collection grows by about five shelf miles a year and consists of bequests, donations and purchases collected over a period of more than 200 years. It is also the guardian of treasures such as the Magna Carta and Shakespeare's First Folio. Some 450,000 reader visits are made to the Library each year; admission to all reading rooms is free of charge.

The Library's Document Supply Centre at Boston Spa (West Yorkshire) is the national centre for inter-library lending within Britain and between Britain and countries overseas. It dispatches over 4 million documents a year.

The Research and Information Commission is a major source of funding for research and development in library and information services.

Other Libraries

The National Libraries of Scotland and Wales, the Bodleian Library of Oxford University and the Cambridge University Library can also claim copies of all new British publications under legal deposit. At the National Library of Scotland the second phase of a new building, accommodating a map library, lending services and the Scottish Science Library, was opened in May 1995. A major extension of the National Library of Wales was completed in 1995.

Some national museums and government departments have important libraries.

- The Public Record Office in London and in Kew, Surrey, houses the records of the superior courts of law of England and Wales and of most government departments, as well as famous historical documents. The Office has many millions of documents, dating from the time of the Norman Conquest to the present day. Public records, with a few exceptions, are available for inspection by members of the public 30 years after the end of the year in which they were created.

- The Scottish Record Office in Edinburgh and the Public Record Office of Northern Ireland, Belfast, serve the same purpose.

Besides a number of great private collections, such as that of the London Library, there are the libraries of the learned societies and institutions, such as the Royal Institute of International Affairs, the Royal Geographical Society and the Royal Academy of Music. The Poetry Library in the South Bank Centre, owned by the Arts Council of England, is a collection of 20th-century poetry written in or translated into English; the library houses about 60,000 volumes.

University Libraries

The university libraries of Oxford and Cambridge are unmatched by those of the more recent foundations. However, the combined library resources of the colleges and institutions of the University of London total 9 million volumes, the John Rylands University Library of Manchester contains 3.5 million volumes, Edinburgh 2.5 million, Leeds 2.3 million, and Birmingham, Glasgow, Liverpool and Aberdeen each have over 1 million volumes. Many universities have important research collections in special subjects—the Barnes Medical Library at Birmingham and the British Library of Political and Economic Science at the London School of Economics, for example.

Special Libraries

Numerous associations and commercial and industrial organisations run library and information services. Although most are intended primarily for use within the organisation, many can be used, by arrangement, by people interested in the area covered, and the specialist publications held are often available for inter-library lending.

Public Libraries

Local authorities in Great Britain and education and library boards in Northern Ireland have a duty to provide a free lending and reference library service, and Britain's network of about 4,100 public libraries has a total stock of over 130 million books. Public libraries issue an average of ten books a year for every person in Britain. Of these, 58 per cent are works of fiction. Over half of the total population are members of public libraries. Some areas are served by mobile libraries, and domiciliary services cater for people unable to visit a library.

Many libraries have collections of compact discs, records, audio- and video-cassettes, and musical scores for loan to the public, while a number also lend from collections of works of art, which may be originals or reproductions. Most libraries hold documents on local history, and nearly all provide children's departments, while reference and information sections and art, music, commercial and technical departments meet a growing demand. The information role is one of increasing importance for many libraries, and greater use is being made of information technology, including microcomputers, CD-ROMs and reference databases.

The Government remains committed to providing a free basic library service—the borrowing and consultation of printed materials—but believes there is scope for greater private sector involvement. Public libraries charge for some services, such as research services and the lending of non-printed materials.

The Government is advised by the Library and Information Commission, which is a forum for policy on library and information provision in general, and the Advisory Council on Libraries, which advises Government on public libraries in England. In Northern Ireland, the Library and Information Services Council also advises Government on all library matters, including school libraries. The Commission also advises the Government on Britain's representation abroad and research strategy.

The Library Association

The Library Association is the principal professional organisation for those engaged in library and information services. Founded in 1877, the Association has 25,000 members. It maintains a Register of Chartered Librarians and publishes books, pamphlets and an official journal.

The Library Association is the designated authority for the recognition of qualifications gained in other EU member states.

Further Reading

The Arts, Aspects of Britain series, HMSO, 1993.

Department of National Heritage Annual Report 1996. The Government's Expenditure Plans 1996–97 to 1998–99. Cm 3211. HMSO, 1996.

Public Lending Right Scheme

The Public Lending Right Scheme gives registered authors the right to receive payment from a central fund (totalling £4.9 million in 1995–96) for the loans made of their books from public libraries in Britain. Payment is made in proportion to the number of times the authors' books are lent out. The maximum payment an author can receive is £6,000.

Books

In 1995 British publishers issued about 100,000 separate titles. The British publishing industry devotes much effort to developing overseas markets, and in 1995 the estimated value of exports of British books amounted to around £1,089 million.

Among the leading organisations representing publishing and distribution interests are the Publishers Association, which has 200 members; and the Booksellers' Association, with 3,300 members. The Publishers Association, through its International Division, promotes the export of British books. The Welsh Book Council supports the production of books in the Welsh language. Book Trust encourages reading and the promotion of books through an information service and a children's library.

Historical Manuscripts

The Royal Commission on Historical Manuscripts locates, reports on, and gives information and advice about historical papers outside the public records. It also advises private owners, grant-awarding bodies, record offices, local authorities and the Government on the acquisition and maintenance of manuscripts. The Commission maintains the National Register of Archives (the central collecting point for information about British historical manuscripts) and the Manorial Documents Register, which are available to researchers.

30 The Media

Television and Radio	**496**	Technical Developments	510
Recent Changes in		**The Press**	**510**
Regulation	497	National and Regional Titles	511
The BBC	499	The Periodical Press	513
Independent Broadcasting	501	News Agencies	514
Teletext, Cable and Satellite	504	Press Institutions	515
Other Aspects	505	Training and Education	515
International Services	507	Press Conduct and Law	516

Legislation to provide a regulatory framework for digital terrestrial broadcasting in Britain was introduced in 1996. The Government hopes that digital broadcasting will create new opportunities for the broadcasting and programme production industries and extend their contribution to national prosperity and prestige. The Broadcasting Act 1996 will also liberalise the restrictions governing the ownership of broadcasting licences, allowing British media businesses to take advantage of new developments, while at the same time preserving essential safeguards on diversity of viewpoint and plurality of ownership.

Television and Radio

Broadcasting in Britain has traditionally been based on the principle that it is a public service accountable to the people. While retaining the essential public service element, it now additionally embraces the principles of competition and choice.

Three public bodies have the main responsibility for television and radio services. These authorities work to broad requirements and objectives defined or endorsed by Parliament, but are otherwise independent in their day-to-day conduct of business. They are:

- the BBC (British Broadcasting Corporation), which broadcasts television and radio programmes;

- the ITC (Independent Television Commission), which licenses and regulates commercial television services, including cable and satellite services; and

- the Radio Authority, which licenses and regulates commercial radio services, including cable and satellite.

Under the Broadcasting Act 1996, BBC commercial broadcasting services—as opposed to those funded by the licence fee (see p. 500)—will be regulated by the ITC and Radio Authority, just as other commercial broadcasting services.

The Department of National Heritage is responsible for overseeing the broadcasting system; the Secretary of State for National

Heritage is answerable to Parliament on broad policy questions.

Television

Television viewing is Britain's most popular leisure pastime: 97 per cent of households have a colour television set and 77 per cent a video recorder. People spend an average of over three and a half hours a day watching television, including video playbacks.

There are currently four terrestrial television channels offering a mixture of drama, light entertainment, films, sport, educational, children's and religious programmes, news and current affairs, and documentaries. A fifth channel is due to be launched in early 1997 (see p. 503).

The BBC provides two complementary national networks—BBC 1 and BBC 2—which are financed predominantly by a licence fee. The ITC licenses and regulates two commercial television services—ITV (Channel 3) and Channel 4—which complement each other and are largely funded by advertising. In Wales S4C (Sianel Pedwar Cymru) broadcasts programmes on the fourth channel. All four channels broadcast on 625 lines UHF (ultra-high frequency), and over 99 per cent of the population live within range of transmission.

Radio

Almost every home has a radio, and the widespread ownership of portable sets (including personal stereos) and car radios means that people can listen to radio throughout the day.

The BBC has five national networks, which together transmit all types of music, news, current affairs, drama, education, sport and a range of features programmes. There are three national commercial radio stations—Classic FM, Virgin 1215 and Talk Radio UK (see p. 503). The Irish radio station, Atlantic 252, also transmits over much of Britain.

There are 38 BBC local radio stations serving England and the Channel Islands, and national regional radio services in Scotland, Wales and Northern Ireland, including Welsh and Gaelic language stations. About 180

independent local radio (ILR) services are also in operation. Stations supply a comprehensive service of local news and information, sport, music and other entertainment, education and consumer advice.

RECENT CHANGES IN REGULATION

In recent years broadcasting in Britain has seen radical changes. The availability of more radio frequencies, together with satellite, cable and microwave transmissions, has made a greater number of local, national and international services possible. The transition from analogue to digital transmission technology[1] has the potential to expand this capacity greatly (see also p. 498). Digital technology promises improved sound and picture quality, greater potential for wide-screen broadcasts and interactivity, more subscription services, and many more channels.

In response to the rapidly developing technology and the prospect of a much wider choice of programmes and services, the Government has made legislative provision for a more flexible regulatory framework for broadcasting. Its aim is to give viewers and listeners access to a greater range of services, while at the same time promoting competition and plurality of media ownership, and maintaining high standards of taste and decency.

Broadcasting Acts 1990 and 1996

Under the Broadcasting Act 1990, which overhauled the regulation of independent television and radio and opened the way for many more services, the IBA (Independent Broadcasting Authority) was replaced in 1991 by the ITC (Independent Television Commission), the Radio Authority and a transmission and engineering company, National Transcommunications Limited

---

[1]Digital television promises to have a greater impact than the introduction of colour broadcasting. Using a process called digital compression, the transmitter sends not the whole image, but only the information needed to effect changes between frames. This uses much less spectrum than the existing analogue process, thereby releasing transmission capacity for a far greater number of television channels.

(NTL). At the same time the Cable Authority was made part of the ITC and the Radio Authority. The ITC and the Radio Authority issue licences to commercial broadcasters and enforce rules to ensure diversity of ownership. NTL (which took over the IBA's networks and other facilities) transmits television services for the independent television companies, Channel 4 and S4C, and radio services for many independent local radio stations. The Act also provided for the establishment of a new national independent television station—Channel 5—and three national commercial radio stations, with opportunities for launching hundreds of independent local radio and television channels.

> The Government wishes to encourage the eventual transition of all broadcasting and telecommunications services to digital means of transmission. The Broadcasting Act 1996 introduces a new regulatory framework to forward the development of digital terrestrial broadcasting.

The legislation:

- provides for the licensing of at least 18 national digital terrestrial television channels (transmitted on six 'multiplexes',[2] and serving, in the medium term, from 60 to over 90 per cent of the population);

- secures places on the new digital frequencies for the existing public service broadcasters, to ensure that British broadcasting maintains its current standards of programming; and

- encourages the development of digital broadcasting by requiring the ITC and Radio Authority to award licences to those

organisations which pledge to install the new transmission network as quickly as possible, to make consumer receiver equipment as affordable as possible, and to broaden consumer choice of programming.

The Government will review setting a date for switching off analogue frequencies five years after the introduction of digital terrestrial television or once 50 per cent of the population has digital receivers, whichever is the sooner.

Media Ownership

The Broadcasting Act 1990 established rules designed to enable the ITC and Radio Authority to keep ownership of the broadcasting media widely spread and to prevent undue concentrations of single and cross-media ownership. Under that legislation, ownership of broadcasters by companies based outside the European Union is largely prohibited; newspapers are allowed relatively small stakes in Channel 3 (and 5), and national and local radio, but are not restricted in non-domestic satellite broadcasters; public telecommunications operators are not allowed to have controlling interests in any Channel 3, Channel 5, national radio or domestic satellite licence; and political bodies and local authorities are barred from holding licences.

A government review of media ownership regulation issued in 1995 concluded that there was a continuing case for specific regulations beyond those which are applied by the general competition law; but that there was a need to liberalise the existing ownership regulations both within and across different media sectors. Following on from those recommendations, the Broadcasting Act 1996:

- allows greater cross-ownership between newspaper groups, television companies and radio stations, at both national and regional levels; and

- introduces 'public interest' criteria by which the regulatory authorities can assess and approve (or disallow) mergers or acquisitions between newspapers and television and radio companies.

The legislation removes the two-licence limit on the control of ITV licences, replacing

---

[2]Through the process known as multiplexing, the signals of several broadcasters are combined into a single stream on a single frequency channel. There is therefore no longer a direct one-to-one relationship between a television service and a frequency. The signals are finally received and decoded by digital receivers or set-top boxes attached to existing sets.

it by a television ownership limit of 15 per cent share of the total television audience. It also:

- gives the ITC new powers to protect regional programming and production in the event of a merger or acquisition of an ITV licence; and
- allows local newspapers with more than a 50 per cent share of their market to own a local radio station, providing there is at least one other independent local radio station operating in that area.

Programming Obligations

Licence-holders of the independent television Channel 3 (and the forthcoming Channel 5) need to pass demanding quality tests (see p. 502). ITC regulations place a limit on the proportion of non-European material broadcast. Both the BBC and commercial television licensees are required to ensure that at least 25 per cent of their original programming comes from independent producers.

Programme Standards

Recognising that broadcasting is an extremely powerful medium with the potential to offend, exploit and cause harm, the Broadcasting Act 1990 contained guarantees on programme standards which are extended to all British-based broadcasters. These guarantees cover taste, decency, accuracy and balance. The Government can proscribe unacceptable foreign satellite services receivable in Britain, and anyone in Britain supporting such a service can be prosecuted.

THE BBC

The constitution, finances and obligations of the BBC are governed by a Royal Charter and Agreement. The Corporation's Board of Governors, including the Chairman, Vice-Chairman and a National Governor each for Scotland, Wales and Northern Ireland, is appointed by the Queen on the advice of the Government. The Board of Governors is ultimately responsible for all aspects of broadcasting by the BBC. The Governors appoint the Director-General, the Corporation's chief executive officer who heads the executive committee and board of management—the bodies in charge of the daily running of the Corporation.

The BBC has a regional structure throughout Britain. The three English regions—BBC North, BBC Midlands & East and BBC South—and BBC Scotland, BBC Wales and BBC Northern Ireland make programmes for their local audiences as well as contributing to the national network.

The National Broadcasting Councils for Scotland, Wales and Northern Ireland advise on the policy and content of television and radio programmes intended mainly for reception in their areas. Ten Regional Councils in England advise the Board of Governors on the needs and concerns of audiences.

New BBC Charter and Agreement

In May 1996 a new Royal Charter came into effect, providing for the continuation of the BBC as Britain's main public service broadcaster until 2006. The new Agreement between the BBC and the Secretary of State for National Heritage, which runs concurrently with the Charter, formally establishes the Corporation's editorial independence in all matters of programme content, scheduling and management. It also provides for the licence fee (see below) to remain the chief source of finance for the BBC's public service activities until at least 2002.

The new Charter and Agreement give effect to policies set out in a government White Paper (*The Future of the BBC: Serving the Nation, Competing Worldwide*) published in 1994. They maintain the BBC's essential characteristics as a public corporation; preserve its primary objectives of providing broadcasting services of information, education and entertainment; and reinforce the duties laid on the Board of Governors to maintain programme standards and ensure that the BBC is even more accountable to its audiences. They also allow for the development of the BBC's commercial activities, in partnership with the private sector, in Britain and abroad (although these must be separate and distinct from its licence fee-funded services).

Finance

The domestic services of the BBC are financed predominantly from the sale of television licences. Properties with a television must buy an annual licence costing £89.50 for colour and £30.00 for black and white. Nearly 21.2 million licences were current on 30 June 1996; of these, almost 20.6 million were for colour.

Licence income is supplemented by profits from trading activities, such as television programme exports, sale of recordings, publications and other merchandise connected with BBC programmes, hire and sale of educational films, film library sales, and exhibitions based on programmes. The BBC World Service's radio broadcasting operations are financed by a grant-in-aid from the Foreign & Commonwealth Office, while BBC Worldwide Television (see p. 508) is self-financing.

TV Licensing, a subsidiary company of the Post Office, undertakes the licence administration on behalf of the BBC. Since 1988 annual rises in the licence fee have been at, or below, the general rate of inflation, and continues to be until the end of 1996; this is intended to improve the BBC's efficiency even further and encourage it to continue to develop alternative sources of revenue.

In November 1995 the Government announced that the BBC's transmission facilities were to be privatised; this will provide the Corporation with new funds to invest in digital television. In August 1996 an information memorandum describing the transmission businesses and the proposed terms of the sale was issued, on behalf of the BBC, to interested parties.

Structural Reorganisation

In June 1996 the BBC announced a radical reorganisation of its management structure in order to strengthen its existing channels and services and to develop additional digital services for the licence-fee payer. The changes centre on the separation of broadcasting (scheduling and commissioning) from production (television, radio and multimedia) and the creation of a single national and international news operation. From April 1997 the new organisation will comprise six major components:

- BBC Broadcast—to schedule channels and commission services for audiences in Britain and abroad;

- BBC Production—to develop the BBC's in-house radio and television production capability across all genres and media;

- BBC News—to be responsible for an integrated national and international news operation across the full range of BBC news and current affairs services;

- BBC Worldwide (see p. 507)—to be responsible for generating income in Britain and abroad, and for the World Service;

- BBC Resources—to provide support facilities and expertise to BBC programme-makers and broadcasters; and

- the Corporate Centre—to provide strategic services to the BBC as a whole.

BBC Television

BBC Television is based at Television Centre in West London, which houses eight major television studios as well as production and support departments. Its two domestic channels are BBC 1 and BBC 2:

- BBC 1 is the channel of broad appeal. In 1995–96 it broadcast over 1,100 hours of features, documentaries and current affairs programmes, together with over 950 hours of drama and entertainment, 500 hours of sport and over 400 hours of children's programmes.

- BBC 2 is more innovatory. Special audience interests are catered for, with a variety of programmes including documentaries, late-night comedy and leisure and lifestyle shows.

Programmes are made at, or acquired through, Television Centre and six major bases throughout Britain (Scotland, Wales, Northern Ireland and, in England, at Birmingham, Bristol and Manchester), or they are commissioned from independent producers. In addition to a wide range of programmes for the general audience, BBC

Television provides programmes for Open University and further education students and for others learning for leisure or work.

BBC Television celebrated its diamond jubilee in 1996 having started the world's first regular high-definition service 50 years earlier.

BBC Focus

BBC Focus is one of the Corporation's specialist night-time television services. It is a unit within the BBC's Education Directorate and broadcasts education, training, and professional information and updating programmes as part of BBC 2's night-time service, *The Learning Zone* (see p. 505).

BBC Focus does not make any of the programmes that it broadcasts, but works with a variety of public bodies and charities to enable them to communicate with specific audiences as part of the BBC's educational service. All programmes are 'open access' and free. They are designed for recording on video and viewing at a later date.

BBC Network Radio

BBC Network Radio (broadcasting to the whole of Britain) serves an audience of 29 million each week, transmitting 41,000 hours of programmes each year on its five networks:

- BBC Radio 1 is a leading contemporary music station, concentrating on pop music for a target audience of 15 to 24-year-olds (24 hours a day);
- BBC Radio 2 provides a service of popular music and speech for the mature listener (24 hours a day);
- BBC Radio 3 is the largest patron of classical music in Britain, but also offers jazz, drama, documentaries and feature programmes (24 hours a day from 1996);
- BBC Radio 4 (broadcast with some differences on FM and LW) provides authoritative news and current affairs coverage, complemented by drama, science, the arts, religion, natural history, medicine, finance and gardening; it also carries parliamentary coverage, and cricket in season on LW; and

- Radio 5 Live has news and sports coverage (24 hours a day).

INDEPENDENT BROADCASTING

Independent Television Commission

Like the Radio Authority and S4C, the ITC's constitution and finances are governed by the Broadcasting Act 1990. The ITC is responsible for licensing and regulating commercial television services operating in or from Britain. These include:

- ITV (Channel 3);
- Channel 4;
- the forthcoming Channel 5;
- cable and other local delivery services;
- independent teletext services; and
- satellite services transmitted from Britain.

Under the provisions of the Broadcasting Act 1996 the ITC will also have powers to license and regulate commercial digital terrestrial television (see p. 498) and BBC commercial television services.

The ITC monitors the licences and licence conditions but is not involved in detailed scheduling of programmes. It is advised by committees on educational broadcasting, religious broadcasting, charitable appeals and advertising. Ten viewer consultative councils also comment on the commercial services' programmes.

ITV Programmes

The first regular ITV programmes began in London in 1955 (19 years after the BBC launched the world's first regular television service in 1936). ITV programmes are broadcast 24 hours a day throughout the country. About one-third of the output comprises informative programmes—news, documentaries, and coverage of current affairs, education and religion. The remainder covers sport, comedy, drama, game shows, films, and a range of other programmes with popular appeal. Over half the programmes are produced by the programme companies and ITN (Independent Television News—see below).

ITV (Channel 3) Programme Companies

ITV is made up of 15 regionally-based television companies which are licensed to supply programmes in the 14 independent television geographical regions. There are two licences for London, one for weekdays and the other for the weekend. An additional ITC licensee provides a national breakfast-time service, transmitted on the ITV network.

The licensees operate on a commercial basis, deriving most of their revenue from selling advertising time. The financial resources, advertising revenue and programme production of the companies vary considerably, depending largely on the population of the areas in which they operate. Although newspapers may acquire an interest in programme companies, safeguards exist to ensure against concentration of media ownership (see p. 498).

Each programme company plans the content of the programmes to be broadcast in its area. These are produced by the company itself, or by other programme companies, or are bought from elsewhere.

A common news service is provided by ITN. ITN has been appointed to supply a service of national and international news to the ITV network until 31 December 1997.

ITV Network Centre

The ITV Network Centre, which is wholly owned by the ITV companies, independently commissions and schedules those television programmes which are shown across the ITV network. Programmes are commissioned from the ITV companies as well as from independent producers. The Centre also promotes the ITV network and co-ordinates developments in technology and training.

Licences

The ITV licences for Channel 3 (which came up for renewal at the end of 1992) are awarded by the ITC for a ten-year period by competitive tender to the highest bidder who has passed a quality threshold. In exceptional cases a lower bid can be selected, for instance where an applicant is able to offer a significantly better quality of service than that offered by the highest bidder.

There are safeguards for quality programming, with licensees being required to provide a diverse programme service calculated to appeal to a wide variety of tastes and interests. They also have to show high quality news and current affairs programmes and a reasonable proportion of other programmes of high quality. There is a statutory duty to present programmes made in and about the region. There is also a requirement for district and regional programming to be aimed at different areas within regions. Channel 3 licensees are obliged to operate a national programme network. Networking arrangements are subject to the approval of the ITC and the Director General of Fair Trading so that anti-competitive practices are avoided.

Channel 4 and S4C

Channel 4, which began broadcasting in 1982, provides a national television service throughout Britain, except in Wales, which has a corresponding service—S4C (Sianel Pedwar Cymru). In January 1993 Channel 4 became a public corporation, licensed and regulated by the ITC, and funded by selling its own advertising time. It was previously a public limited company owned by the ITC.

Channel 4's remit is to provide programmes with a distinctive character and to appeal to tastes and interests not generally catered for by Channel 3. It must present a suitable proportion of educational programmes and encourage innovation and experiment. Channel 4 commissions programmes from the ITV companies and independent producers and buys programmes from overseas. It broadcasts for around 148 hours a week.

In Wales programmes on the fourth channel are run and controlled by S4C. Members of its authority are appointed by the Government. S4C is required to see that a significant proportion of programming, in practice about 32 hours a week, is in the Welsh language and that programmes broadcast between 18.30 and 22.00 hours are mainly in Welsh. At other times S4C transmits national Channel 4 programmes.

Like Channel 4, S4C has sold its own advertising since 1993. However, it is recognised that S4C will not be self-financing; in practice roughly 10 per cent of its income comes from advertising, with the remainder financed by the Government.

Gaelic TV Fund

The Gaelic Television Committee, appointed by the ITC, administers government finance for making television programmes in Gaelic. The Gaelic Television Fund was created and programmes thus financed came on screen from 1993. In 1995 the Government paid £8.9 million to the ITC, which was credited to the Fund. The Broadcasting Act 1996 extends the scope of the Fund to cover training and other support costs for Gaelic radio.

Channel 5

A new national terrestrial television channel—Channel 5—was originally intended to come into operation in late 1994, financed through advertising, subscription or sponsorship. The ten-year licence was to be awarded by competitive tender. However, in 1992 the ITC rejected the single bid it had received, and in September 1994 announced that it was again inviting applications for the licence. The successful applicant, Channel 5 Broadcasting Limited, was awarded the licence in October 1995. The service, which will serve approximately 70 per cent of the population, is intended to start early in 1997. Channel 5 will be subject to as many of the quality programming requirements as Channel 3.

Local Television

Under the Broadcasting Act 1990 licences for the delivery of local television services are awarded by competitive tender. ITC licence-holders can supply national and local television channels using both cable and microwave transmission systems.

Under the 1996 legislation, a new category of licence—the restricted service licence—has been created to enable television broadcasts to be established in local areas and at special events, subject to the availability of suitable frequencies.

The Radio Authority

Independent national (INR) and local (ILR) radio services are based on principles similar to those of ITV. The programme companies operate under licence to the Radio Authority and are financed mainly by advertising revenue. The Radio Authority is required to ensure that licensed services, taken as a whole, are of a high quality and offer a range of programmes calculated to appeal to a variety of tastes and interests.

The Authority awards national radio licences by competitive tender to the highest bidder. There are three independent national services:

- Classic FM, which broadcasts mainly classical music, together with news and information, came on air in 1992;
- Virgin 1215, which plays broad-based rock music, came on air in 1993 (and is supplemented by a separate Virgin station which operates under a local London licence); and
- Talk Radio UK, which is a speech-based service, came on air in 1995.

Since the early 1990s more local radio stations have continued to come on the air. The Authority has awarded about 60 new local radio licences since it came into operation in 1991. Local radio licences are not allocated by competitive tender; the success of licence applications is in part determined by the extent to which applicants meet the needs and interests of the people living in the area and in part by whether they have the necessary financial resources to sustain programme plans for the eight-year licence period.

Some of the locations for stations have been selected with small-scale 'community radio' in mind. As part of its brief to develop a wide range of radio services, the Authority is licensing a number of more specialist stations.

The Radio Authority also issues restricted service licences. These are issued at the discretion of the Authority (subject to certain conditions and frequency availability), usually for a maximum of 28 days. They enable local events—such as sports events, arts festivals and conferences—to be covered by a temporary radio service in a limited area, for example, part of a city or town or an arena.

TELETEXT, CABLE AND SATELLITE SERVICES

Teletext

The BBC and independent television each operate a teletext service, offering constantly updated information on a variety of subjects, including news, sport, travel, weather conditions and entertainment. The teletext system allows the television signal to carry additional information which can be selected and displayed as 'pages' of text and graphics on receivers equipped with the necessary decoders. Both the BBC and Channels 3 and 4 provide subtitling as part of the text service for certain programmes for people with hearing difficulties. Channel 3 and Channel 4 are required to offer subtitling services for at least 50 per cent of their programmes by 1998, and the BBC is set to match this.

Licences

The Broadcasting Act 1990 introduced a regulatory system for licensing spare capacity within the lines of the television signal. This allows more varied use of the capacity—data transfer, for instance—but the position of the public teletext service and subtitling on commercial television is safeguarded.

In 1991 the ITC advertised three teletext licences. These ten-year licences are awarded by competitive tender, with applicants having to satisfy certain statutory requirements before their cash bid can be considered. The ITC awarded the public teletext licence to Teletext Ltd, which replaced Oracle in 1993, and awarded one of the additional commercial service licences on Channel 3 to the only bidder, Data Broadcasting International. The other additional commercial service licence on Channel 4/S4C was awarded to SimpleActive Ltd in 1994. The ITC will advertise the Channel 5 teletext licence in due course.

Cable Services

Cable services are delivered to consumers through underground cables and are paid for by subscription. The franchising of cable systems and the licensing of cable television services are carried out by the Cable and Satellite Division of the ITC, while the Radio Authority issues cable radio licences.

'Broadband cable', the cable system currently being designed and built, can carry between 30 and 65 television channels (including terrestrial and satellite channels, channels delivered to cable operators by video, and a purely local service) as well as a full range of telecommunications services.

Interactive services such as video-on-demand, home shopping, home banking, security and alarm services, electronic mail and remote meter readings are also possible and are being tested in some locations.

Cable franchises have already been granted covering areas which include three-quarters of all homes and nearly all urban areas in Britain. By July 1996 there were 115 broadband cable franchises in operation in Britain, 23 of which had been set up within the previous year. Regulation is as light as possible to encourage the development of a wide range of services, and flexible enough to adapt to new technology. The ITC awards only one broadband cable franchise in each area so that the new franchisee is protected from direct competition in the early stages. At present there are 7 million homes able to receive broadband cable services and there are over 1.5 million subscribers.

ITC licences are required for systems capable of serving more than 1,000 homes. They are awarded for each area on the basis of competitive tendering. Systems extending beyond a single building and up to 1,000 homes require only an individual licence from OFTEL (see p. 320). Cable investment must be privately financed.

There are no specific quality controls on cable services. However, if cable operators also provide their own programme content as opposed to just conveying services, they need a programme services licence from the ITC, which includes consumer protection requirements.

Direct Broadcasting by Satellite

Direct broadcasting by satellite (DBS), by which television is transmitted directly by satellite into people's homes, has been available throughout Britain since 1989. The signals from satellite broadcasting are received through specially designed aerials or 'dishes'.

Several British-based satellite television channels have been set up to supply programmes to cable operators and viewers with dishes in Britain and, in some cases, throughout Europe. Some offer general entertainment, while others concentrate on specific areas of interest, such as sport, music and children's programmes.

The largest satellite programmer is BSkyB (British Sky Broadcasting), which provides nine channels devoted to light entertainment, news, feature films, sport and home shopping transmitted from the Astra satellite.

Over 30 English language channels were available to viewers with normal satellite dishes at the end of 1995. The ITC also licenses a number of foreign language services, some of them designed for ethnic minorities within Britain and others aimed primarily at audiences in other countries. Viewers in Britain may also receive a variety of television services from other European countries.

OTHER ASPECTS

Educational Broadcasting

Both the BBC and Channel 4 broadcast educational programmes for schools and Continuing Education programmes for adults. Broadcasts to schools deal with all subjects of the National Curriculum (see p. 451), while programmes for adults cover many areas of learning and vocational training. Books, pamphlets, computer software, and audio and video cassettes are produced to supplement the programmes. Ninety four per cent of primary schools and 91 per cent of secondary schools in Britain use BBC schools television; 80 per cent of primary schools use BBC schools radio. Channel 4 and the BBC collaborate to avoid unnecessary duplication or scheduling clashes in schools television. The ITC has a duty to ensure that schools programmes are presented on independent television.

In 1995 the BBC launched *The Learning Zone*, a new night-time education and training service. Broadcast five nights a week on BBC 2, it includes programmes for further

education colleges, schools, the Open University (see p. 461) and BBC Focus.

During 1995–96 the BBC broadcast 797 hours of television and 149 hours of radio on behalf of the Open University.

Advertising and Sponsorship

The BBC may not obtain revenue from the broadcasting of advertisements or from commercial sponsorship of programmes on its public service channels. Its policy is to avoid giving publicity to any firm or organised interest except when this is necessary in providing effective and informative programmes. It does, however, cover sponsored sporting and artistic events.

Advertising and sponsorship are allowed on commercial television and radio services subject to controls. The ITC and the Radio Authority operate codes of advertising standards and programme sponsorship.

Advertisements on independent television and radio are broadcast between programmes as well as in breaks during programmes. Advertisers are not allowed to influence programme content. Advertisements must be distinct and separate from programmes. The time given to them must not be so great as to detract from the value of the programmes as a medium of information, education or entertainment. Advertising on radio has increased markedly in the last few years. Television advertising is limited to an average of seven minutes an hour during the day and seven and a half minutes in the peak evening viewing period. Advertising is prohibited in broadcasts of religious services and in broadcasts to schools.

The ITC and the Radio Authority's codes governing standards and practice in advertising give regulations on the forms of advertisement which are prohibited, alongside rules and guidance on scheduling and creative matters.

Political advertising and advertisements for betting (other than the National Lottery and the football pools) are prohibited. All tobacco advertising is banned on television and cigarette advertisements are banned on radio. Religious advertisements may be broadcast on commercial radio and television, provided they comply with the guidelines issued by the ITC and the Radio Authority.

The ITC and the Radio Authority can impose severe penalties on any television or radio company failing to comply with their codes.

Sponsorship in Independent Broadcasting

In Britain sponsorship is a relatively new way of helping to finance commercial broadcasting, although the practice has long been established in other countries. In return for their financial contribution, sponsors receive a credit associating them with a particular programme.

The ITC's Code of Programme Sponsorship and the Radio Authority's Advertising and Sponsorship Code aim to ensure that sponsors do not exert influence on the editorial content of programmes and that sponsorships are made clear to viewers and listeners. News and current affairs programmes may not be sponsored. Potential sponsors for other categories of programme may be debarred if their involvement could constrain the editorial independence of the programme maker in any way. References to sponsors or their products must be confined to the beginning and end of a programme and around commercial breaks; they must not appear in the programme itself. All commercial radio programmes other than news bulletins may be sponsored.

Government Publicity

Government publicity material to support non-political campaigns may be broadcast on independent television and radio. This is paid for on a normal commercial basis. Short public service items, concerning health, safety and welfare, are transmitted free by the BBC and independent television and radio. All government advertisements and public service information films are subtitled via electronic text to support people with hearing difficulties.

Broadcasting Standards

The independence enjoyed by the broadcasting authorities carries with it certain obligations over programme content.

Programmes must display, as far as possible, a proper balance and wide range of subject matter, impartiality in matters of controversy and accuracy in news coverage, and must not offend against good taste. Broadcasters must also comply with legislation relating to obscenity and incitement to racial hatred.

The BBC, the ITC and the Radio Authority apply codes providing guidance on impartiality and on violence and standards of taste and decency in television programmes, particularly during hours when children are likely to be viewing. By convention, programmes broadcast before 21.00 hours are expected to be suitable for a general audience, including children.

Complaints can be made to the regulators, including the BBC, which opened its own Programme Complaints Unit in early 1994 to investigate serious complaints about BBC television or radio programmes.

The Broadcasting Act 1996 provides for the replacement of the Broadcasting Standards Council (which monitors programmes, examines complaints from the public and undertakes research) and the Broadcasting Complaints Commission (which deals with complaints of unfair treatment or unwarranted infringement of privacy in programmes or in their preparation) by a new Broadcasting Standards Commission. From April 1997 the BSC is required to:

- draw up and review guidance for the avoidance of unjust or unfair treatment and unwarranted infringement of privacy in television and radio;
- draw up and review a code on the portrayal of violence and sexual conduct and on standards of taste and decency (which television and radio broadcasters would have to take into account when drawing up their own guidelines);
- monitor and report on the portrayal of violence, sexual conduct and standards of taste and decency in programmes generally;
- consider and adjudicate on complaints about fairness and standards; and
- represent the Government at international bodies concerned with setting standards for broadcasting.

Parliamentary and Political Broadcasting

The proceedings of both Houses of Parliament may be broadcast on television and radio, either live or, more usually, in recorded and edited form on news and current affairs programmes. The BBC has a specific obligation to transmit an impartial account day by day of the proceedings in both Houses of Parliament.

The BBC and the commercial services provide time on radio and television for an annual series of party political broadcasts. Party election broadcasts are arranged following the announcement of a general election. In addition, the Government may make ministerial broadcasts on radio and television, with opposition parties also being allotted broadcast time.

Audience Research

Both the BBC and the commercial sector are required to keep themselves informed on the state of public opinion about the programmes and advertising that they broadcast. This is done through the continuous measurement of the size and composition of audiences and their opinions of programmes. For television, this work is undertaken through BARB (the Broadcasters' Audience Research Board), owned jointly by the BBC and the ITV Network Centre. For radio, joint research is undertaken for BBC and commercial radio by RAJAR (Radio Joint Audience Research).

Both the BBC and the commercial sector conduct regular surveys of audience opinion on television and radio services. Public opinion is further assessed by the BBC and ITC through the work of their advisory committees, councils and panels. Regular public meetings are also held to debate services, and consideration is given to letters and telephone calls from listeners and viewers.

Training

All ITV (Channel 3) licensees are obliged to provide staff training. Channel 4 also provides a range of training for its staff and for the independent production sector.

The BBC Centre for Broadcast Skills Training (part of BBC Resources) operates on a commercial basis and provides courses on all technical aspects of broadcasting, including craft skills. Courses can be mounted specially to meet particular requirements.

In addition BBC World Service Training runs courses for radio and television broadcasters and their managers from all over the world. Courses and training programmes are tailor-made and carried out both in Britain and in the countries concerned.

The Government finances overseas students on broadcasting training courses at the BBC, the British Council and the Thomson Foundation; the Foundation also conducts courses overseas in broadcast journalism, media management, radio and television production, and technology.

INTERNATIONAL SERVICES

BBC Worldwide

In 1994 the international and commercial interests of the BBC were brought together in BBC Worldwide, to enable the BBC to develop its role in the fast-expanding broadcast and media world. BBC Worldwide comprises BBC World Service, funded by a government grant, and BBC Worldwide Limited, which has three commercial divisions—BBC Worldwide Television, BBC Worldwide Publishing and BBC Worldwide Learning.

BBC World Service

BBC World Service broadcasts by radio in English and 43 other languages worldwide. It has a global weekly audience of at least 140 million listeners. This excludes any estimate for listeners in countries where it is still difficult to survey audiences. The core programming of news, current affairs, business and sports reports is complemented by a wide range of cultural programmes, including drama, literature and music.

BBC World Service programmes in English and many other languages are made available by satellite for rebroadcasting by agreement with local or national radio stations, networks and cable operators. BBC World Service Radio International sells recorded programmes to other broadcasters in over 100 countries.

BBC MPM—Marshall Plan of the Mind—provides a range of business, economic and associated political programmes to the countries of the former Soviet Union. It is mainly funded by the British Government's Know How Fund (see p. 130).

BBC Monitoring, the international media monitoring arm of BBC World Service, provides transcripts of radio and television broadcasts from over 140 countries. As well as providing a vital source of information to the BBC, this service is also used by other media organisations, government departments, the commercial sector and academic institutions.

BBC Worldwide Television

With responsibility for the BBC's commercial television activity, BBC Worldwide Television is a major international broadcaster and a leading distributor and co-producer of BBC programmes.

> In 1995–96 BBC Worldwide Television licensed more than 15,000 hours of programming to 164 broadcasters in 80 countries, making the BBC the largest European exporter of television programmes. Notable successes were *Pride and Prejudice*, *People's Century*, *Alien Empire* and *Dancing in the Streets*.

BBC Worldwide Television works closely with BBC production departments, independent producers and its network of international offices to determine commercial strategies for key programmes with international licensing potential. It is also developing premium channels to compete in the international marketplace. BBC World—the BBC's 24-hour international news and information channel—is available to over 45 million homes worldwide. BBC Prime, an entertainment channel for Europe, has more than 4 million subscribers.

BBC Worldwide Television has a 20 per cent shareholding in UK Gold, an entertainment satellite channel, and UKTV, a new subscription channel in Australia.

BBC Worldwide Publishing

BBC Worldwide Publishing is the BBC's large-scale publishing and licensing operation. Its divisions incorporate:

- BBC Magazines, which publishes popular titles including the *Radio Times* and the best-selling *BBC Music*;

- a consumer publishing division, which publishes a wide range of books, videos and spoken word audio tapes;

- BBC Multimedia, which produces CD-ROMs[3];

- BBC Licensing, which handles the licensing of BBC properties, characters and brands of all forms of merchandising;

- BBC English, which develops English language learning and teaching materials in a variety of formats for international markets;

- BBC Language Publishing, which is a major publisher of multiple media language teaching courses and products; and

- on-line services.

BBC World Publishing is active in over 70 countries, marketing its products and properties alongside BBC Worldwide Television's business operation.

BBC Worldwide Learning

BBC Worldwide Learning was established in September 1995 as a division of BBC Worldwide to develop commercial markets for educational and learning products around the world. Its goal is to establish the BBC as a major player in this field, gaining a significant presence in markets in Britain and internationally, and across all media. It is working to exploit existing assets and has started evaluating the scope for new interactive learning services and products for the digital age. These include CD-ROMs, on-line services and the BBC Learning channel.

---

[3]An abbreviation for compact disc read-only memory, a computer storage device developed from the technology of the audio compact disc.

COI Overseas Radio and Television Services

The Central Office of Information (COI), which procures and provides publicity material and other information services on behalf of government departments and other public agencies, produces radio programmes for overseas. Recorded material is sent to radio stations all over the world. COI television services also distribute material such as documentary and magazine programmes commissioned by the Foreign & Commonwealth Office or acquired from television broadcasters.

News Agencies

WTN (Worldwide Television News), owned by ITN, ABC (the American Broadcasting Corporation) and Channel 9 in Australia, supplies news and a wide range of television services to about 1,000 broadcasters in over 90 countries, as well as to governments and international corporations. It also produces British Satellite News, an international satellite news service, for the Foreign & Commonwealth Office. The service, under FCO editorial control, transmits programmes five days a week. These are distributed, either by satellite or on hard copy compilations, free to television stations throughout Eastern Europe, the Middle East and Asia for use in news bulletins. WTN provides services through the Eurovision network (see below) and by satellite.

For details of Reuters Television, see p. 514.

International Relations

European Agreements

Britain has implemented two important European agreements on cross-border broadcasting: the European Community Directive on Broadcasting and the Council of Europe Convention on Transfrontier Television. Under these, countries have to remove restrictions on the retransmission of programmes originating from other participating countries. They must also ensure that their own broadcasters observe certain minimum standards on advertising, sponsorship, taste and decency and the portrayal of sex and violence on television.

Audiovisual Eureka (AVE), which has a membership of 33 European countries, including Britain, aims to help improve aspects of the European audiovisual industry through practical measures to enhance training, development and distribution. It concentrates its work on the countries of central and eastern Europe. An important task of AVE has also been to establish an Audiovisual Observatory based in Strasbourg which collects, disseminates and standardises European audiovisual data for the industry.

In 1995 Britain played an active part in the negotiations establishing the European Community MEDIA II programme. The programme (succeeding MEDIA I on 1 January 1996) will stimulate a number of initiatives to improve training (especially business and new technology skills) and the development and distribution of films and television programmes.

European Broadcasting Union

The BBC and the Radio Authority are members of the European Broadcasting Union, which manages Eurovision, the international network of television news and programme exchange. The Union is responsible for co-ordinating the exchange of programmes and news over the Eurovision network and intercontinental satellite links. The Union provides a forum linking the major public services and national broadcasters of Western Europe and elsewhere, and co-ordinates joint operations in radio and television.

International Telecommunication Union

The BBC takes part in the work of the International Telecommunication Union, the United Nations agency responsible for regulating and controlling all international telecommunications services, including radio and television. The Union also allocates and registers all radio frequencies, and promotes and co-ordinates the international study of technical problems in broadcasting.

TECHNICAL DEVELOPMENTS

The introduction of computer-based digital production equipment for both television and radio is one of the most significant technical advances affecting the broadcasting industry in Britain in recent years. It allows programmes to be made more quickly and more effectively, with the sound and vision information being held and manipulated on computer disc storage units. A significant proportion of programmes produced by the BBC and independent companies is edited on this type of equipment.

Other recent advances include:

- the introduction of 'all-digital' studios (including digital video recorders and control desks) at both the BBC and independent companies;

- the introduction of digital transmission links, mainly based on optical fibre technology, between studios and from studios to the transmitters; and

- the use of miniature cameras and transmitters.

The BBC and the ITC also undertake long-term research into broadcast technology. Key development areas include:

- digital television transmission (see p. 497);

- the transmission of digital radio broadcasting (DAB) from terrestrial transmitters and by satellite; and

- digital widescreen and high definition television (HDTV), and its associated surround sound.

The Press

More daily newspapers, national and regional, are sold for every person in Britain than in most other developed countries. On an average day nearly 60 per cent of people over the age of 15 read a national morning newspaper; over 65 per cent read a Sunday newspaper. Around 90 per cent read a regional or local newspaper.

National papers have an average total circulation of over 13 million on weekdays and nearly 17 million on Sundays, although the total readership is considerably greater. Men are more likely to read newspapers than women, and more people in the 25–44 age group read a daily newspaper than in any other age group.

There are about 1,400 regional and local newspaper titles and over 6,500 periodical publications.

Several newspapers have had very long and distinguished histories. The *Observer*, for example, first published in 1791, is the oldest national Sunday newspaper in the world, and *The Times*, Britain's oldest daily national newspaper, began publication in 1785.

The press caters for a range of political views, interests and levels of education. Newspapers are almost always financially independent of any political party. Where they express pronounced views and show obvious political leanings in their editorial comments, these may derive from proprietorial and other non-party influences. Nevertheless, during general election campaigns many newspapers recommend their readers to vote for a particular political party. Even newspapers which adopt strong political views in their editorial columns sometimes include feature and other types of articles by authors of different political persuasions.

In order to preserve their character and traditions, some newspapers and periodicals are governed by trustee-type arrangements. Others have management arrangements that endeavour to ensure their editors' authority and independence.

In recent years working practices throughout the newspaper industry have undergone major changes in response to the challenges posed by computer-based technology and the need to contain costs. Newsprint, more than half of which is imported, forms about a quarter of average national newspaper costs; labour represents over half. In addition to sales revenue, newspapers and periodicals earn considerable amounts from their advertising. Total spending on press advertising (including newspapers, magazines and directories) in 1995 was £5,465 million, making the press by far the largest advertising medium in Britain. Unlike most of its European counterparts the British press receives no subsidies and relatively few tax and postal concessions.

NATIONAL AND REGIONAL TITLES

Ownership of the national, London and many regional daily newspapers lies in the hands of a number of large press publishing groups. Although most enterprises are organised as limited liability companies, individual and partner proprietorship survives. The large national newspaper and periodical publishers are major corporations; many are involved in the whole field of publishing and communications.

The National Press

The national press consists of 10 morning daily papers and 9 Sunday papers (see Table 30.1). Formerly they were produced in or near Fleet Street in central London with, in some cases, northern editions being printed in Manchester. All the national papers have now moved their editorial and printing facilities to other parts of London or away from the capital altogether. The *Daily Mirror* and the *Independent*, for example, are printed in Watford and Oldham; the *Financial Times* is printed in London and Leeds. Scottish editions of the *Sun*, the *News of the World* and the *Sunday Times* (Scottish Section) are printed in Glasgow.

In order to improve distribution and sales overseas, editions of the *Financial Times* are printed in Frankfurt, Roubaix (northern France), Hong Kong, New Jersey, Los Angeles, Tokyo and Madrid, while the *Guardian* prints international editions in Frankfurt and Roubaix. *The Times* prints in Charteroix (Belgium), Cork and Dublin, while the *Sun* prints in Barcelona and Tenerife.

National newspapers are often described as either 'quality', 'mid-market' or 'popular' papers on the basis of differences in style and content. Five dailies and four Sundays are usually described as 'quality' newspapers, which are directed at readers who want full information on a wide range of public matters. Popular newspapers appeal to people wanting news of a more entertaining character, presented more concisely. 'Mid-market' publications cover the intermediate market. Quality papers are normally broadsheet (large-sheet) in format and mid-market and popular papers tabloid (small-sheet). *Today*, a mid-market daily which started in the mid-1980s, closed in November 1995.

Many newspapers are printed in colour and most produce colour supplements as part of the Saturday or Sunday paper, with articles on travel, food and wine, and other leisure topics.

The leading Scottish papers, *The Scotsman* and the *Herald*, have considerable circulations outside Scotland.

Regional Newspapers

There are about 100 daily (Monday to Saturday) and Sunday newspapers, and about 1,300 weekly paid-for and free newspapers (not including business, sporting and religious newspapers).

England

Of the morning papers the *Yorkshire Post* (Leeds), the *Northern Echo* (Darlington) and the *Eastern Daily Press* (Norwich) each has a circulation of approximately 75,000, and two provincial Sunday papers—the *Sunday Mercury* (Birmingham) and the *Sunday Sun* (Newcastle upon Tyne)—sell 145,000 and 125,000 copies respectively. Circulation figures of evening papers start at about 10,000 and most are in the 20,000 to 100,000 range. Those with much larger sales include the *Manchester Evening News* (180,600), Wolverhampton's *Express and Star* (208,700) and the *Birmingham Evening Mail* (197,500). Paid-for weekly papers have a mainly local appeal and most have circulations in the 2,000 to 30,000 range.

London has one paid-for evening paper, the *Evening Standard*, with a circulation of 441,300. It covers national and international news as well as local affairs. Local weeklies include papers for every district in Greater London, which are often different local editions of one centrally published paper.

Wales

Wales has one daily morning newspaper, the *Western Mail*, with a circulation of 64,200, and *Wales on Sunday*, with a circulation of 59,300. Both are published in Cardiff. Evening papers published in Wales are the *South Wales Echo*, Cardiff; the *South Wales Argus*, Newport; the *South Wales Evening Post*, Swansea; and the *Evening Leader*, Wrexham. Circulations range

Table 30.1: National Newspapers

Title and foundation date	Controlled by	Circulation[a] average January–June 1996
National dailies		
'Populars'		
Daily Mirror (1903)	Mirror Group plc	2,474,536
Daily Star (1978)	United News & Media plc	669,108
The Sun (1964)	News International plc	4,048,815
'Mid market'		
Daily Mail (1896)	Associated Newspapers Ltd	2,057,593
Daily Express (1900)	United News & Media plc	1,244,749
'Qualities'		
Financial Times (1888)	Pearson	301,961
The Daily Telegraph (1855)	Telegraph Group Ltd	1,043,677
The Guardian (1821)	Guardian Media Group plc	398,057
The Independent (1986)	Mirror Group consortium[b]	279,473
The Times (1785)	News International plc	684,605
National Sundays		
'Populars'		
News of the World (1843)	News International plc	4,607,799
Sunday Mirror (1963)	Mirror Group plc	2,426,431
The People (1881)	Mirror Group plc	2,049,306
'Mid market'		
The Mail on Sunday (1982)	Associated Newspapers Ltd	2,108,298
Sunday Express (1918)	United News & Media plc	1,259,046
'Qualities'		
Sunday Telegraph (1961)	Telegraph Group Ltd	666,938
The Independent on Sunday (1990)	Mirror Group consortium[b]	303,801
The Observer (1791)	Guardian Media Group plc	453,415
The Sunday Times (1822)	News International plc	1,298,998

[a]Circulation figures are those of the Audit Bureau of Circulations (consisting of publishers, advertisers and advertising agencies) and are certified daily or weekly net sales for the period.
[b]The consortium comprises Mirror Group plc, Promotora de Informaciones and Espresso International Holding.

from 30,000 to 77,600. North Wales is also served by the *Daily Post*, published in Liverpool, and the *Liverpool Echo*.

The weekly press (some 70 publications) includes English-language papers, some of which carry articles in Welsh; bilingual papers; and Welsh-language papers. Welsh community newspapers receive an annual grant as part of the Government's wider financial support for the Welsh language.

Scotland

The daily morning papers, with circulations of between 8,300 and 749,000 are *The Scotsman* (published in Edinburgh); the *Herald*, (published in Glasgow); the *Daily Record* (sister paper of the Daily Mirror); the Scottish *Daily Express*; the Scottish edition of the *Sun*; the *Dundee Courier and Advertiser*; the *Aberdeen Press and Journal*; and the *Paisley Daily Express*. The daily evening papers have circulations in the range of 20,600 to 136,000 and include the Edinburgh *Evening News*, Glasgow's *Evening Times*, Dundee's *Evening Telegraph*, Aberdeen's *Evening Express* and the *Greenock Telegraph*. Local weekly newspapers number about 135.

The Sunday papers are the *Sunday Mail*, the *Sunday Post* and a quality broadsheet paper, *Scotland on Sunday*. The national *Sunday Express* has a Scottish edition and the *Sunday Times* carries a Scottish supplement.

Northern Ireland

Northern Ireland has two morning newspapers, one evening and two Sunday papers, all published in Belfast, with circulations ranging from 33,000 to 133,100. They are the *News Letter* (unionist), the *Irish News* (nationalist), the evening *Belfast Telegraph*, *Sunday Life* and *Sunday World* (Northern Ireland edition).

There are about 55 weeklies. Newspapers from the Irish Republic, as well as the British national press, are widely read in Northern Ireland.

Free Distribution Newspapers

About 800 free distribution newspapers, mostly weekly and financed by advertising, are published in Britain; over half are produced by established newspaper publishers. They have enjoyed rapid growth in recent years.

Ethnic Minority Publications

Many newspapers and magazines in Britain are produced by members of ethnic minorities. Most are published weekly, fortnightly or monthly. A Chinese newspaper, *Sing Tao*, the Urdu *Daily Jang* (see below) and the Arabic *Al-Arab*, however, are dailies.

Afro-Caribbean newspapers include the *Gleaner* and *West Indian Digest*. The *Voice* and *Caribbean Times*, both weeklies, are aimed at the black population in general. The *Weekly Journal*, launched in 1992, is the first 'quality' broadsheet aimed at Britain's black community.

The *Asian Times* is an English language weekly for people of Asian descent; the *Sikh Courier* is produced quarterly. Examples of ethnic language newspapers include the Urdu *Daily Jang*, an offshoot of the largest circulation paper in Pakistan, and the weeklies *Garavi Gujarat* and *Gujarat Samachar*. Publications also appear in Bengali, Hindi and Punjabi. The fortnightly *Asian Trader* and *Asian Business* are both successful ethnic business publications, while *Cineblitz International* targets those interested in the Asian film industry.

Many provincial papers print special editions for their local populations. The *Leicester Mercury*, for example, publishes a daily Asian edition, incorporating news from the South Asian sub-continent.

THE PERIODICAL PRESS

The 6,500 periodical publications are classified as 'general consumer', 'consumer specialist' and 'business and professional' titles. There are also many in-house and customer magazines produced by businesses or public services for their employees and/or clients. Directories and similar publications number more than 2,000. The 'alternative' press comprises a large number of titles, many of them devoted to radical politics, community matters, religion, the occult, science or ecology.

General consumer interest and specialist titles comprise magazines for a wide range of interests. These include women's and men's magazines; publications for children; religious periodicals; fiction magazines; magazines dealing with sport, motoring, gardening, youth interests and music; humour; retirement; and computer magazines. Learned societies, trade unions, regiments, universities and other organisations also produce publications.

Weekly periodicals with the highest sales are those which carry full details of the forthcoming week's television and radio programmes, including the satellite schedules. *What's on TV* has a circulation figure of over 1.6 million, followed by the *Radio Times* with 1.4 million and *TV Times* with 1 million.

The top-selling women's magazine is *Take a Break* with a circulation of 1,447,950. *Woman's Weekly*, *Woman's Own*, *Woman*, *Weekly News* (which sells mainly in Scotland), *Woman's Realm* and *My Weekly* have circulations in the 280,000 to 820,000 range. In recent years several women's magazines owned by overseas publishing houses have achieved large circulations; *Prima* and *Best*, for instance, each sell over 550,000 copies, while *Bella* and *Hello!* are also widely read. There is a growing market for men's general interest magazines —for example, *Loaded*, *GQ* and *Esquire*, with circulations ranging from about 107,000 to 239,000.

Smash Hits, with a circulation of 202,000 is a fortnightly magazine dealing with pop music and teenage lifestyles. *Just Seventeen* has a circulation of 162,000. *Viz*, a cartoon comic aimed at young adults, sells 429,000 copies. Of monthly magazines, *Reader's Digest* has the highest circulation (1.65 million).

The leading journals of opinion include *The Economist*, an independent conservative publication covering a wide range of topics. *New Statesman and Society* reviews social issues, politics, literature and the arts from an independent socialist point of view, and the *Spectator* covers similar subjects from an independent conservative standpoint.

New Scientist reports on science and technology in terms that the non-specialist reader can understand. *Private Eye*, a satirical fortnightly, also covers public affairs. Weekly 'listings' magazines, such as *Time Out*, provide details of cultural and other events in London and other large cities.

There are nearly 4,400 business and professional titles, with the highest concentrations in medicine, business management, sciences, architecture and building, social sciences, and computers. Controlled (free) circulation titles represent about two-thirds of the business and professional magazine market. Ninety five per cent of business and professional people regularly read the publications relevant to their sector.

NEWS AGENCIES

Reuters

Reuters is a publicly owned company, employing over 14,600 staff in 91 countries. It has more than 1,930 staff journalists, photographers and cameramen in 153 news bureaux. The company serves subscribers in 158 countries, including financial institutions; commodities houses; traders in currencies, equities and bonds; major corporations; government agencies; news agencies; newspapers; and radio and television stations.

Reuters has developed the world's largest privately leased communications network to transmit its services. It provides the media with a wide range of news, news video, news pictures and graphics. Services for business clients comprise constantly updated financial news, historical information, facilities for computerised trading, and the supply of communications and other equipment for financial dealing rooms. Information is distributed electronically. Reuters wholly owns Reuters Television (RTV), the largest international television news agency in the world. RTV supplies news video to over 170 broadcasters, their networks and affiliates in 89 countries.

The Press Association

The Press Association operates through four companies—PA News, PA Sport, PA Listings and PA Data Design.

PA News, as the national news agency for Britain and the Irish Republic, provides comprehensive coverage of British and Irish news to the national and regional print, broadcast and electronic media. Around 1,500 stories and 100 pictures and graphics are transmitted each day by satellite and telecommunications links. PA also supplies up-to-the-minute news, including live coverage of Parliament, the courts and major international events with a British or Irish interest, to Teletext, on-line information providers and Internet sites. It also offers an on-line news and sports information service—NewsFile—as well as extensive news cuttings and picture libraries.

PA Sport provides a comprehensive sports information and results service. Specialist writers cover all major sports including cricket, soccer, rugby, tennis, boxing, athletics, golf, motor sports and horse racing.

PA Listings creates camera-ready pages of television listings, sports results, share prices, weather reports, and arts and entertainment listings for the national and regional press.

PA Data Design is a development centre for electronic media, tailoring news, sport and listings information for delivery to Internet publishers.

PA is a leading supplier of information and communications services for public relations and investor relations industries in Britain and Canada.

AFX News Ltd

AFX News Ltd, a joint venture news agency owned by the Financial Times Group and Agence France-Presse, is an up-to-the-minute news service of interest to those who monitor corporate economic and market activity in and around Europe. AFX News also reports worldwide general and economic news to which European markets are sensitive. In September 1995 the agency acquired the Examiner financial news service, a leading source of company and stock exchange news for financial market participants. AFX News bureaux are located in 12 European countries, the United States and Japan, with headquarters based in London.

Other Agencies

News services are also provided by Associated Press and United Press International, which are British subsidiaries of United States news agencies, and by UK News. A number of other agencies and news services have offices in London, and there are minor agencies in other cities. Syndication of features is not as common in Britain as in some countries, but a few agencies specialise in this type of work.

PRESS INSTITUTIONS

Trade associations include the Newspaper Publishers Association, whose members publish national newspapers, and the Newspaper Society, which represents British regional and local newspapers. The Scottish Daily Newspaper Society represents the interests of daily and Sunday newspapers in Scotland; the Scottish Newspaper Publishers' Association acts on behalf of the owners of weekly newspapers in Scotland; and Associated Northern Ireland Newspapers is made up of proprietors of weekly newspapers in Northern Ireland. The membership of the Periodical Publishers Association includes most independent publishers of business, professional and consumer journals.

Organisations representing journalists are the National Union of Journalists and the Chartered Institute of Journalists. The main printing union is the Graphical, Paper and Media Union, with some 225,000 members.

The Foreign Press Association was formed in 1888 to help the correspondents of overseas newspapers in their work by arranging press conferences, tours, briefings, and other services and facilities.

The Guild of Editors is the officially recognised professional body for newspaper editors and their equivalents in radio and television. It has approximately 500 members and exists to defend press freedom and to promote high editorial standards. The British Association of Industrial Editors is the professional organisation for editors of house journals. The Association of British Editors represents the whole range of media, including radio, television, newspapers and magazines.

TRAINING AND EDUCATION

The National Council for the Training of Journalists (NCTJ), which represents many regional newspaper publishers, sets and conducts examinations, and organises short training courses for journalists.

The two main methods of entry into newspaper journalism are selection for NCTJ pre-entry courses at a college of further or higher education or direct recruitment by a regional or local newspaper. Both types of entrant take part in 'on-the-job' training. Similar courses exist for press photographers.

Universities and colleges which offer undergraduate and/or postgraduate courses in journalism include City University, London; the University of Central Lancashire; Bournemouth University; Sheffield University; the University of Wales, Cardiff; Strathclyde University; Glasgow Caledonian University; and the London College of Printing, which also provides GCE (General Certificate of Education) Advanced (A) level courses in journalism.

Courses for regional newspapers in such subjects as newspaper sales, advertising, and management are provided by the Newspaper Society's training service. Some newspaper publishers carry out journalist training independently of the NCTJ, awarding their own certificates or diplomas. National Vocational Qualifications (see p. 458) are now available in newspaper journalism.

Specialist training courses for journalists and broadcasters from developing countries and from Eastern Europe are offered by the Thomson Foundation in Cardiff. The Foundation runs training courses overseas and provides consultants to assist newspapers and news agencies in editorial, advertising and broadcast management.

Newspapers in Education, a worldwide scheme using newspapers to improve standards of literacy among young people, is run in Britain by the Newspaper Society. The scheme involves using newspapers in schools for teaching a wide range of subjects at all levels of education. The scheme has over 700 projects operated by regional newspapers in partnership with local schools.

Through its charitable trust—the Reuter Foundation—Reuters offers assistance to overseas journalists to study and train in Britain and other parts of the world. The Foundation awards fellowships to overseas journalists to spend up to one year at Oxford University. It also runs shorter practical training programmes in London for journalists from the former communist countries of Eastern Europe and Central Asia.

The Periodicals Training Council is the official training organisation in periodical publishing. It offers a range of short courses covering management, editorial work, advertisement sales and circulation sales. It has special responsibility for editorial training and administers an editorial training scheme for those already in employment.

PRESS CONDUCT AND LAW

The Press Complaints Commission

The Press Complaints Commission, a non-statutory body, was established in 1991 following recommendations in a report on privacy and related matters by a government-appointed independent committee. The Commission was set up by the newspaper and periodical industry in a final attempt to make self-regulation of the press work properly. It is funded by PRESSBOF (the Press Standards Board of Finance), which co-ordinates and promotes self-regulation within the industry. These measures were prompted by growing criticism of press standards, with allegations of unjustified invasion of privacy and inaccurate and biased reporting, among other abuses, resulting in calls for government regulation of the press.

In its White Paper *Privacy and Media Intrusion: The Government's Response*, published in 1995, the Government rejected proposals for statutory regulation of the press, and for legislation to give protection to privacy. Instead, it endorsed self-regulation under the Commission, and recommended further measures to make it more effective.

The Commission's membership is drawn from newspaper and magazine editors and from people outside the industry. It deals with complaints by members of the public about the content and conduct of newspapers and magazines, and advises editors and journalists. It operates a code of practice agreed by editors governing respect for privacy, opportunity to reply, corrections, journalists' behaviour, references to race and religion, payments to criminals for articles, protection of confidential sources and other matters. The Commission publishes regular reports of its findings.

The industry and the Press Complaints Commission have reinforced voluntary regulation through, for example:

- measures to increase the number of independent members of the Commission to ensure a lay majority;
- a strengthening of the code of practice, and the incorporation of the code into the contracts of employment of most editors and journalists;
- the setting up of a helpline service for members of the public who fear the code of practice has been, or is about to be, breached; and
- the appointment of a Privacy Commissioner with special powers to investigate complaints about privacy.

The Press and the Law

There is no state control or censorship of the newspaper and periodical press, and newspaper proprietors, editors and journalists are subject to the law in the same way as any other citizen. However, certain statutes include sections which apply to the press.

There are laws governing:

- the extent of newspaper ownership in television and radio companies (see p. 498);
- the transfer of newspaper assets; and
- the right of press representatives to be supplied with agenda and reports for meetings of local authorities, and reasonable facilities for taking notes and telephoning reports.

There is a legal requirement to reproduce 'the printer's imprint' (the printer's name and address) on all publications, including newspapers. Publishers are legally obliged to deposit copies of newspapers and other publications at the British Library (see p. 493). Publication of advertisements is governed by wide-ranging legislation, including public health, copyright, financial services and fraud legislation. Legal restrictions are imposed on certain types of prize competition.

Laws on contempt of court, official secrets and defamation are also relevant to the press. A newspaper may not publish comments on the conduct of judicial proceedings which are likely to prejudice the reputation of the courts for fairness before or during the actual proceedings, nor may it publish before or during a trial anything which might influence the result. The unauthorised acquisition and publication of official information in such areas as defence and international relations, where such unauthorised disclosure would be harmful, are offences under the Official Secrets Acts 1911 to 1989. However, these are restrictions on publication—that is, on dissemination to the public by any means—not just through the printed press.

Most legal proceedings against the press are libel actions brought by private individuals.

Defence Advisory Notices

Government officials and representatives of the media form the Defence, Press and Broadcasting Advisory Committee, which has agreed that in some circumstances the publication of certain categories of information might endanger national security. Details of these categories are contained in Defence Advisory Notices (DA Notices) circulated to the media, whose members are asked to seek advice from the Secretary of the Committee, a retired senior military officer, before publishing information in these areas. Compliance with any advice offered by the Secretary is expected but there is no legal force behind it and the final decision on whether to publish rests with the editor, producer or publisher concerned.

The Notices were published for the first time in July 1993 to promote a better understanding of the system and to contribute to greater openness in government.

Advertising Practice

Advertising in all non-broadcast media, such as newspapers, magazines, posters, sales promotions, cinema and direct mail, is regulated by the Advertising Standards

Authority, an independent body funded by a levy on display advertising expenditure. The Authority aims to promote and enforce the highest standards of advertising in the interests of the public through its supervision of the British Codes of Advertising and Sales Promotion.

The Codes' basic principles are to ensure that advertisements:

- are legal, decent, honest and truthful;
- are prepared with a sense of responsibility to the consumer and society; and
- respect the principles of fair competition generally accepted in business.

The Authority monitors advertisements to ensure their compliance with the Codes and investigates any complaints received.

The advertising industry has agreed to abide by the Codes and to support them with effective sanctions. Free and confidential pre-publication advice is offered to assist publishers, agencies and advertisers. The Authority's main sanction is to recommend that advertisements considered to be in breach of the Code should not be published. This is normally sufficient to ensure that an advertisement is withdrawn or amended. The Authority also publishes monthly reports on the results of its investigations.

The Authority is recognised by the Office of Fair Trading as the established means of controlling non-broadcast advertising. It can refer misleading advertisements to the Director General of Fair Trading, who has the power to seek an injunction to prevent their publication.

Further Reading

The Future of the BBC: Serving the Nation, Competing Worldwide. Cm 2621. HMSO, 1994.

Broadcasting. Aspects of Britain series. HMSO, 1993.

Department of National Heritage Annual Report 1996. The Government's Expenditure Plans 1996–97 to 1998–99. Cm 3211. HMSO, 1996.

Media Ownership: The Government's Proposals. Cm 2872. HMSO, 1995.

Privacy and Media Intrusion: The Government's Response. Cm 2918. HMSO, 1995.

Digital Terrestrial Broadcasting: The Government's Proposals. Cm 2946. HMSO, 1995.

31 Sport and Active Recreation

Government Policy	519	Spectator Safety	527
Organisation and Administration	521	Sponsorship and Other Funding	528
Major Sports Facilities	524	Televised Sport	529
Sports Medicine and Science	526	A to Z of Popular Sports	530

Over 100 British sportsmen and women currently hold world championship titles in sports ranging from athletics to windsurfing. Britain won a total of 15 medals at the 1996 Olympics in Atlanta and 122 at the subsequent Paralympics. The finals of the European football championship—Euro 96—were held in England in June 1996, the largest sporting event to be held in Britain for 30 years. A new national stadium is planned in England.

It is estimated that 29 million people in Britain over the age of 16 regularly take part in sport or exercise. The 1993 *General Household Survey* found that almost two-thirds of those interviewed had taken part in at least one sporting activity during the previous four weeks. The most popular participation sports or activities are walking (including rambling and hiking), swimming, snooker/pool, keep fit/yoga and cycling.

Men were more likely than women to have participated in a sporting activity, with 72 per cent of men claiming to have taken part in at least one sport during the previous four weeks compared with 57 per cent of women.

GOVERNMENT POLICY

In July 1995 the Government issued a policy statement—*Sport: Raising the Game*—with a set of proposals designed to develop, encourage and promote sport in Britain. In July 1996 a report was published setting out the action taken to promote sport during the previous 12 months, and a series of policy announcements was made. The Government's aim is to improve sporting opportunity at all levels, from school sport, through clubs and further and higher education institutions, to the highest level.

Separate policy statements were issued in 1995 in Scotland, Wales and Northern Ireland.

British Academy of Sport

The Government wishes to see the establishment of a British Academy of Sport as the pinnacle of a regional network of centres of sporting excellence and academies for individual sports. It will focus on the needs of top-level performers and provide world-class training facilities. Support will be provided to selected sports and their national governing bodies with the intention of developing future British world and Olympic champions. Support services will be provided direct to performers throughout Britain and will include sports science support, sports medicine, coaching, 'lifestyle management services', and financial assistance with training programmes.

A prospectus inviting bids for the Academy was issued in July 1996 and it is hoped that a final decision will be made by the end of January 1997. The cost of the Academy and its network of regional sites is expected to be financed principally from the National Lottery Sports Fund.

Sport in Schools and for Young People

The Government believes that all young children should have the opportunity to learn basic sports skills. Physical education (PE), which includes sport, is a compulsory subject in the National Curriculum (see p. 451) for all pupils aged 5 to 16 in state-maintained schools in England and Wales and in the common curriculum in Northern Ireland. When the National Curriculum was revised in 1995, it placed a greater emphasis on traditional team games and competitive sports.

In Scotland the Secretary of State has issued National Guidelines which contain programmes of study and attainment targets for physical activity for pupils aged 5 to 14.

Assessment of Sporting Facilities

Two new schemes are being set up to assess the sporting merits of schools:

- a Sportsmark scheme to recognise schools that have effective policies for promoting sport; and
- 'Sportsmark Gold' awards for the most innovative schools.

Schools will be expected to aim for four hours of structured sporting activity a week outside formal lessons. The first awards for secondary schools will be made in April 1997. An equivalent scheme for primary schools will be set up in the 1997–98 academic year. In Northern Ireland the scheme will start in primary schools.

Accountability and Inspection

From September 1996 onwards schools have had to include in their annual prospectuses details of their sporting aims and the provision for sport, and to record in their annual governors' reports how they have met these aims. OFSTED (see p. 455) has sent to schools a summary of its survey of good practice in physical education and sport in schools, and OFSTED's framework of school inspections is being extended to look at extra-curricular sporting provision made by the school in addition to timetabled PE.

Partnerships with the Local Community

The Government is encouraging stronger links between schools and the wider community to ensure that children have access to the sports amenities which clubs and associations can make available outside school hours. Efforts to strengthen these links have been promoted by schemes such as 'Team Sport Scotland', which aims to promote the development of school-aged team sport, with support from The Scottish Office. In October 1996 a £2 million challenge fund was established in England to promote links between schools and sports clubs.

National Junior Sport Programme

In 1996 the National Junior Sport Programme (NJSP) was launched in England with the aim of encouraging sporting participation and of developing the range of children's sports skills. It is run by the English Sports Council (ESC, see p. 522). Key partners include the Youth Sport Trust, the physical education profession, local authorities, youth clubs, the National Coaching Foundation (see p. 522) and national governing bodies of sport. One of the programmes in the NJSP is the TOP programme designed to provide 4 million children with sports equipment, qualified coaches and places to play. A total of £14 million is being provided over a three-year period by the National Lottery Sports Fund (£7.7 million), the ESC and private sector funding including business sponsorship.

The scheme contains four main elements:

- Top Play, introduced in schools in April 1996, which is for those aged four to nine and aims to develop core skills, such as co-ordination, ball skills and teamwork;

- BT Top Sport, for those aged seven to 11, which introduces children to games leading up to mini versions of seven sports including cricket, football, hockey, rugby and tennis;
- Champion Coaching (see p. 522), run by the National Coaching Foundation; and
- Top Club, a programme which assists governing bodies of sport and their clubs to develop junior coaching and competitive opportunities for young people—it is being piloted in gymnastics, swimming, athletics, table tennis, basketball and rugby union, and will be fully launched in autumn 1997.

Sport for young people is also given a high priority by the Sports Councils in Scotland, Wales and Northern Ireland.

Other Aspects

Other measures include increasing investment in coaching schemes for teachers with the opportunity for them to acquire coaching qualifications. A further £1 million is to be provided by the ESC for coaching opportunities via the National Coaching Foundation and the governing bodies of sport. About £1 million of funds under the Sportsmatch scheme (see p. 528) are to be set aside for schemes for young people.

ORGANISATION AND ADMINISTRATION

The Secretary of State for National Heritage has responsibility for the Government's policies on sport and recreation in England. The Secretaries of State for Wales, Scotland and Northern Ireland have similar responsibilities in their countries. Responsibility for those aspects of government sports policy of benefit to Britain as a whole rests with the Secretary of State for National Heritage, in association with the respective home country Secretaries of State. Government responsibilities in sport and recreation are largely decentralised and are channelled through the Sports Councils.

Sports Councils

The Sports Councils, appointed and directly funded by the Government, are the principal advisers on sporting matters. The Government works closely with them in implementing its sports policies.

The Sports Councils make grants for sports development, coaching and administration to the governing bodies of sports and other national organisations, administer the National Sports Centres (see p. 524), and manage and allocate the National Lottery Sports Fund. Grants and loans are also made to voluntary organisations, local authorities and commercial organisations to help them provide sports facilities. Facilities receiving support from the Sports Councils include sports halls, indoor swimming pools, intensive-use pitches, indoor tennis halls and school facilities.

During 1996 the structure of the Sports Councils has been reorganised, with the replacement of the former Sports Council— which used to have responsibility for general matters affecting Great Britain and matters specifically concerning England—by two new bodies: the United Kingdom Sports Council (UKSC) and the English Sports Council (ESC). There are three other Councils: the Sports Council for Wales; the Scottish Sports Council; and the Sports Council for Northern Ireland.

The UKSC will lead in all aspects of sport requiring strategic planning, co-ordination and representation for the benefit of Britain as a whole. Key functions include representing British sporting interests overseas and increasing influence at international level, co-ordinating policy for bringing major sporting events to Britain, and identifying areas of unnecessary duplication and waste in the administration of sport. It is giving particular support to the pursuit of high standards of sporting achievement. It will also have an important role in advising and guiding the home country Sports Councils on Lottery projects of significance to Britain. The UKSC has ten members: an independent chairman; the chairmen of the four other Sports Councils; and key individuals from amateur and professional sport, one of whom chairs the British Olympic Association (see p. 523).

The ESC has similar responsibilities to those of the Sports Councils in Scotland, Wales and Northern Ireland. Key ESC functions include young people and sport, the encouragement and development of performance and excellence, and the provision of sporting facilities in England.

Local Authorities

Local authorities are the main providers of basic sport and recreation facilities for the local community. In England local authorities manage over 1,500 indoor centres, largely built in the last 20 years, as well as numerous outdoor amenities. Facilities include parks, lakes, playing fields, sports centres, tennis courts, artificial pitches, golf courses and swimming/leisure pools. Many local authorities employ full-time sports development officers.

National Sports Associations

The Central Council of Physical Recreation (CCPR) is the largest sport and recreation federation in the world. It comprises 209 British bodies and 68 English associations, most of which are governing bodies of sport. The Scottish Sports Association, the Welsh Sports Association and the Northern Ireland Council of Physical Recreation (NICPR) are similar associations. Their primary aim is to represent the interests of their members to the appropriate national and local authorities, including the Sports Councils, from which they receive funding. Award schemes run by the associations include the CCPR's Community Sports Leaders Award scheme and the NICPR's Service to Sport Awards.

Sports Governing Bodies

Individual sports are run by over 400 independent governing bodies, whose functions include drawing up rules, holding events, regulating membership, and selecting and training national teams. Governing bodies receiving funding from the Sports Councils are required to produce four-year development plans, from the grass roots to the highest competitive levels and including their proposals for young people. There are also organisations representing people who take part in more informal physical recreation, such as walking and cycling. The majority of the sports clubs in Britain belong to the appropriate governing body.

National Coaching Foundation

The National Coaching Foundation (NCF) works closely with national governing bodies of sport, local authorities, and higher and further education. Supported by the Sports Councils, it provides a comprehensive range of education and development services for coaches in all sports. The NCF network has ten regional offices in England, and one each in Scotland, Wales and Northern Ireland.

The NCF also runs Champion Coaching, one of the four elements of the National Junior Sport Programme (see p. 520). Champion Coaching provides after-school coaching in a wide variety of sports in England, Wales and Northern Ireland. In 1996–97 there will be 90 schemes, with about 30,000 children and 3,000 coaches participating.

Women and Sport

Efforts to narrow the gap between men's and women's participation in sporting activities have resulted in more women taking part in sport. Women are now being encouraged to adopt leadership roles, such as coaches, officials and administrators. Projects to promote coaching opportunities have been established by the Sports Councils in partnership with the NCF and the Women's Sports Foundation (WSF). The Sports Councils have also supported the provision of management training for women, while a women and sports science and sports medicine network has been established to help increase the number of women in this area and to encourage them to reach senior positions.

The WSF is a voluntary organisation promoting the interests of women and girls in sport and active recreation. It encourages the establishment of women's sports groups throughout Britain and organises a wide range of events and activities. It runs both the Sportswomen of the Year Awards and an annual nationwide awards scheme for girls and young women between the ages of 11 and 19.

Sport for Disabled People

The governing bodies of sport are increasingly taking responsibility for disabled people. Close liaison takes place with the Sports Councils, which provide advice to governing bodies on encouraging the integration of people with disabilities.

The key organisations for people with disabilities are the British Sports Association for the Disabled (BSAD), the United Kingdom Sports Association for People with Learning Disability (UKSAPLD), the British Paralympic Association (BPA—see below) and a range of bodies concerned with individual disabilities and single sports. These include the Riding for the Disabled Association, which caters for some 25,000 riders.

The BSAD is a national body working across all the disabilities. It organises regional and national championships in a wide range of sports and also runs training courses, coaching courses and development days. The Scottish and the Welsh Sports Associations for the Disabled and the Northern Ireland Committee on Sport for People with Disabilities have similar co-ordinating roles.

The UKSAPLD is a co-ordinating body with a membership of over 20 national organisations. It promotes and develops opportunities in sport and recreation for people with learning disability.

There are five national disability sports organisations concerned with individual disabilities: the British Amputee and Les Autres Sports Association; British Blind Sport; the British Deaf Sports Council; the British Wheelchair Sports Foundation; and Cerebral Palsy Sport. They provide coaching and help to organise national competitions in conjunction with the national governing bodies of sport and the BSAD.

British Olympic Association

The British Olympic Association (BOA) is the National Olympic Committee for Britain and comprises representatives of the 33 governing bodies of Olympic sports. Its primary function is to organise the participation of British teams in the Olympic Games.

The BOA determines the size of British Olympic teams and sets standards for selection, raises funds and makes all necessary arrangements for Britain's participation in the Olympics. The British team contained over 300 competitors in the 1996 Olympics and won 15 medals: one gold, eight silver and six bronze.

The BOA also makes important contributions to the preparation of competitors in the period between Games. For example, multi-sport training camps were set up in Tallahassee in the United States to allow athletes to experience training in a climate similar to that in Atlanta. The Association's British Olympic Medical Centre at Northwick Park Hospital in north London supplies a medical back-up service for competitors before and during the Olympics. The BOA is supported by sponsorship and by donations from the private sector and the public.

The BOA is investigating whether a British city could submit a viable bid for the 2008 Olympic Games, in the light of the selection of Manchester or Wembley (London) as the site of the new national stadium (see p. 524).

British Paralympic Association

Britain's participation in the Paralympics is organised by the BPA, which liaises closely with the BOA. The UKSPALD is responsible, in partnership with the BPA, for the preparation and training of the Paralympic team. In 1996, 244 competitors represented Britain in the Paralympics and won a total of 122 medals: 39 gold, 42 silver and 41 bronze.

Sports Clubs

Local sports clubs provide a wide variety of recreational facilities. Some cater for indoor recreation, but more common are those providing sports grounds, particularly for cricket, football, rugby, hockey, tennis and golf. It is estimated that there are over 150,000 voluntary sports clubs affiliated to the national governing bodies of sport. Many clubs linked to business firms cater for sporting activities. Commercial facilities include fitness centres, tenpin bowling centres, ice and roller-skating rinks, squash courts, golf courses and driving ranges, riding stables and marinas.

Countryside Bodies

The Countryside Commission (for England), the Countryside Council for Wales and

Scottish Natural Heritage are responsible for conserving and improving the natural beauty of the countryside, and for encouraging the provision of facilities for open-air recreation. They are also responsible for designating National Parks, Areas of Outstanding Natural Beauty, heritage coasts and National Scenic Areas (see pp. 368–9).

In Northern Ireland the Environment and Heritage Service, an agency within the Department of the Environment, is responsible for protecting and conserving the natural environment and promoting its appreciation. The Council for Nature Conservation and the Countryside provides independent advice on environmental issues to the Service.

British Waterways

British Waterways is a publicly owned body responsible for managing and developing much of Great Britain's inland waterways. Many leisure and recreational pursuits, such as angling and various types of sailing and boating, are enjoyed on waterways and reservoirs. British Waterways, which is responsible for approximately 2,000 miles (3,220 km) of canals and river navigations, actively promotes water safety and community activities.

Playing Fields

The National Playing Fields Association is a charity which aims to ensure that there are adequate playing fields and playspace available for use by the community. There are affiliated associations in the English and Welsh counties and independent organisations in Scotland and Northern Ireland.

Under government action to improve the protection of playing fields, the appropriate Sports Council will have to be consulted on planning applications affecting playing fields, while a government-supported research project will investigate the effectiveness of existing planning guidance.

MAJOR SPORTS FACILITIES

Britain has a range of world-class sporting facilities for training and competition at the highest level including 13 National Sports Centres, operated by the Sports Councils. Facilities are being expanded, notably through the planned new national stadium and developments in Manchester, which will host the Commonwealth Games in 2002. Preparations for the Games include the construction of a £55 million indoor arena with seating for 18,000 people, and a 3,500-capacity velodrome opened in 1994 (see p. 525). These two facilities were assisted by a government grant of £43 million.

National Stadium

A new national sports stadium for England is planned to provide facilities of the highest standard and with a large seating capacity to attract major world sports events. Popular spectator sports likely to use the new stadium include football, rugby league and athletics. A capacity of 80,000 is envisaged. Five venues were nominated—Birmingham, Bradford, Manchester, Sheffield and Wembley (London). This was reduced to a short list of Manchester and Wembley in 1995. A decision is expected to be taken by the ESC by the end of 1996. A major part of the funding is likely to come from the National Lottery Sports Fund.

National Sports Centres

First priority at the National Sports Centres is given to the governing bodies of sport for national squad training and for the training of coaches. However, the Centres also make their facilities available to top sportsmen and women for individual training and to the local community. Most of the Centres provide residential facilities.

England

The ESC operates six major National Sports Centres. Crystal Palace in London is a leading competition venue for a wide range of sports and a major training centre for national squads, clubs and schools, and serious enthusiasts. The Centre is a regional centre of excellence for athletics, netball, weightlifting and swimming.

Crystal Palace stadium is Britain's major international athletics venue, with capacity for 17,000 spectators. Other facilities include Olympic-size swimming and diving pools and a sports injury centre. The Centre also houses the National Boxing Academy.

Bisham Abbey in Berkshire caters for a number of sports, including tennis, football, hockey, weightlifting, squash, rugby union and golf. The England football, rugby union and hockey squads train at the Centre. Bisham Abbey has long-standing partnerships with the British Amateur Weightlifting Association and the Lawn Tennis Association (LTA), which has helped to develop the Abbey as the National Tennis Training Centre and the home of the LTA Rover Tennis School.

Lilleshall National Sports Centre in Shropshire offers extensive sports facilities, which are used by a variety of national teams. Facilities include the Olympic Gymnastics Centre, regularly used by the British gymnastic squads, and extensive playing fields for football and hockey. The Football Association (FA) uses Lilleshall as its base for major coaching activities. The FA school has 32 places for boys aged 15 and 16, who each take up a two-year residency funded by an FA scholarship. Lilleshall also houses the Olympic Archery Centre.

The National Water Sports Centre at Holme Pierrepont in Nottinghamshire is one of the most comprehensive water sports centres in the world. There are facilities for rowing, canoeing, water-skiing, powerboating, ski-racing, angling and sailing. Its main features are a 2,000-metre regatta course and the only purpose-built floodlit canoe slalom course in the world.

The National Cycling Centre, opened in Manchester in 1994, is Britain's first indoor velodrome. The Centre was the venue for the World Cycling Championships in August and September 1996 (see p. 532).

Wales

The Sports Council for Wales runs two National Sports Centres: the Welsh Institute of Sport and the National Watersports Centre.

The Welsh Institute of Sport in Cardiff is the country's premier venue for top-level training and for competition in a large number of sports. Facilities include a world-standard gymnastics hall, a sports science laboratory and a sports injury clinic.

The National Watersports Centre at Plas Menai in north Wales is primarily a centre of excellence for sailing and canoeing, with an extensive range of activities including dinghy and catamaran sailing, offshore cruising and powerboat training.

Plas y Brenin National Mountain Centre, a third centre, is run by the ESC. Situated in Snowdonia National Park in north Wales, it offers courses in rock climbing, mountaineering, sea and river canoeing, orienteering, skiing and most other mountain-based activities. It is renowned as Britain's leading training institution for the development of mountain instructors.

Scotland

Scotland has three National Sports Centres, which are operated by the Scottish Sports Council.

The National Outdoor Training Centre at Glenmore Lodge near Aviemore caters for a wide range of activities, including hill walking, rock climbing, mountaineering, skiing, kayaking and canoeing. Its main purpose is to provide top-quality training for those who intend to lead or instruct others in outdoor activities. A new biathlon and cross-country skiing facility was opened in 1994.

The Inverclyde National Sports Training Centre at Largs has a large number of facilities, including a gymnastics hall, a golf training facility and a laboratory for fitness assessment. The Centre also acts as an important venue for major championships. Inverclyde was used by 28 governing bodies of sport in 1995–96, many of them using it as their national training base.

The Cumbrae National Water Sports Training Centre on the island of Great Cumbrae in the Firth of Clyde offers an extensive range of courses catering for all levels of ability. The Centre has a comprehensive range of modern craft for a wide variety of sailing activities, as well as sub-aqua diving equipment. Cumbrae regularly hosts major sailing championships.

Northern Ireland

The Northern Ireland Centre for Outdoor Activities at Tollymore in County Down, run by the Sports Council for Northern Ireland, offers courses in mountaineering, rock climbing, canoeing and outdoor adventure. Leadership and instructor courses leading to nationally recognised qualifications are also available.

A Northern Ireland Outdoor Team Sports Training Centre is under development in Belfast, with the assistance of a £1 million grant from the Foundation for Sport and the Arts (see p. 528) and £550,000 from the Government. The first phase, involving two new synthetic pitches, was opened in 1995 at Queen's University of Belfast Playing Fields.

SPORTS MEDICINE AND SCIENCE

Sports Medicine

The National Sports Medicine Institute, funded by the UKSC and ESC, is responsible for the co-ordination of sports medicine services. Based at the medical college of St Bartholomew's Hospital, London, its facilities include a physiology laboratory, library and information centre.

Work is in progress to develop a network of regional centres to provide both clinical and educational services, which will be linked with new support services at the National Sports Centres. In Scotland a network of 33 sports medicine centres provides specialist help with sports injuries.

The Scottish Sports Council has developed a partnership with the Universities of Strathclyde and Aberdeen which led to the opening in 1995 of the Scottish Institute of Sports Medicine and Sports Science. The Institute aims to form partnerships with national governing bodies to provide athletes and coaches with high-quality medical and scientific support. A Northern Ireland Sports Medicine Centre was established in June 1996 as a partnership between the Sports Council for Northern Ireland and a local healthcare trust.

Sports Science

The development of sports science support services for the national governing bodies of sport is being promoted by the Sports Councils, in collaboration with the BOA and the NCF, in an effort to raise the standards of performance of national squads. The nature of the support provided may cover biomechanical (human movement), physiological (physical response to exercise and training), or psychological factors (the mental processes that influence performance). There are 15 governing bodies involved in the UKSC's Sports Science Support Programme, and the ESC is supporting 17 projects involving 13 governing bodies. The Sports Council for Wales has established a sports science service at the Welsh Institute of Sport with support from the Welsh Office.

Drug Abuse in Sport

The UKSC's independent drugs-testing regime provides for random testing in and out of competition by independent sampling officers, and the publication of adverse findings and actions taken by governing bodies. Samples are analysed by a laboratory, accredited by the International Olympic Committee, at King's College, University of London, which also carries out research into methods of detection for new drugs which unfairly aid performance.

The Sports Councils have intensified their drugs-testing programmes, with greater emphasis on out-of-competition tests. In 1995–96 the Sports Councils carried out 4,327 tests in 52 sports, with 2 per cent proving positive under the British programme.

In September 1996 anabolic steroids and other anabolic substances (such as growth hormones) became controlled drugs under the misuse of drugs legislation. As a result, greater penalties for their unauthorised supply will take effect. The new controls, which are aimed at those selling such substances, should help to eliminate their abuse in sport and other leisure activities such as bodybuilding.

Britain has fully implemented the provisions of the Council of Europe's Anti-doping Convention, which aims to provide an international framework within which national anti-doping campaigns can work effectively. Britain is also a partner in an international Memorandum of Understanding on doping in sport, with Australia, Canada, France, New Zealand and Norway.

SPECTATOR SAFETY

Safety at sports grounds in Great Britain is governed by legislation. The main instrument of control is a safety certificate which is issued by the relevant local authority. When determining the conditions of a safety certificate, the local authority is expected to comply with the *Guide to Safety at Sports Grounds* produced by the Department of National Heritage and The Scottish Office. The implementation of similar legislation in Northern Ireland is under discussion.

The Taylor Report

Following the Hillsborough stadium disaster in Sheffield in 1989, when 96 spectators died, the Taylor Report was published in 1990. Its major recommendation was that standing accommodation should be eliminated at all grounds designated under the Safety of Sports Grounds Act 1975. The Government accepted the report but limited the all-seating requirement to football in view of the particular problems of safety and crowd control in that sport.

In England and Wales the all-seater policy is being enforced through licences issued by the Football Licensing Authority. Conditions in these licences require all clubs in the Premier League and those in the First Division of the Football League to have all-seater grounds; these conditions have now largely been satisfied. Clubs in the Second and Third Divisions of the Football League are permitted to keep some standing accommodation, providing that the terracing is safe. In Scotland the all-seating policy is being implemented through a voluntary agreement under the direction of the Scottish football authorities.

The Football Trust

The Football Trust provides grant aid to help football clubs at all levels. Annual income is

about £25 million. It is funded partly by the pools companies from their spot-the-ball competition and partly from a 2.5 per cent reduction in pool betting duty which will continue until 2000. This concession has provided £437 million to assist football clubs in financing projects to improve the comfort and safety of spectators in line with the Taylor Report recommendations. A further 0.5 per cent reduction in pool betting duty took effect in May 1996 and is expected to generate up to £3 million a year for the Football Trust.

The Government has given the Football Trust a new wider role to enable it to fund up to £8 million a year of safety work at rugby league, rugby union, cricket and non-league football grounds. The work is being financed through a Sports Ground Initiative by the Foundation for Sport and the Arts (see p. 528).

Crowd Control

The Government has worked closely with the police, football authorities and the governments of other European countries to implement crowd control measures.

Extensive measures were taken to ensure that Euro 96—the final of the European Championship (see p. 533) —held in England was not disrupted by violence or disorder. About 10,000 police officers from ten police forces were involved in security arrangements. The National Criminal Intelligence Service Football Unit, which co-ordinates police intelligence about football hooligans, liaised closely with the forces of all the 15 other participating countries to exchange intelligence about potential troublemakers. A national centre in London ensured effective liaison between eight regional police intelligence centres. Strict crowd control and surveillance measures were taken at the eight grounds where matches were held.

Legislation has made it an offence in England and Wales to throw objects at football matches, run onto the playing area or chant indecent or racist abuse. There are also controls on the sale and possession of alcohol at football grounds and on transport to and from grounds. Courts in England and Wales have the power to prohibit convicted football hooligans from attending football matches, and to impose restriction orders to prevent them travelling abroad to attend specified matches. In Northern Ireland similar legislation is under consideration.

SPONSORSHIP AND OTHER FUNDING

Sport is a major industry in Britain. In addition to professional sportsmen and women, over 450,000 people are employed in the provision of sports clothing, publicity, ground and club maintenance and other activities connected with sport. In total an estimated £9,750 million is spent on sport annually in Britain. The private sector makes a substantial investment in sports sponsorship, contributing an estimated £285 million in 1995. More than 2,000 British companies are involved in sports sponsorship.

Sponsorship may take the form of financing specific events or championships, such as horse races or football/cricket leagues, or of grants to sports organisations or individual performers. Motor sport and football receive the largest amounts of private sponsorship.

Sponsorship of sport is encouraged by a number of bodies, including:

- the Institute of Sports Sponsorship, set up by the CCPR and which comprises some 80 British companies involved in the sponsorship of sport;
- the Sports Sponsorship Advisory Service, administered by the CCPR and funded by ESC, which has helped sporting bodies to raise over £1 million in England over the last three years;
- the Scottish Sports Council's Sponsorship Advisory Service, which raised £200,000 for Scottish sport in 1994–95; and
- the Sports Council for Wales's Sponsorship Advisory Service, which generated £106,200 for Welsh sport in 1994–95.

Successive governments have negotiated voluntary agreements with the tobacco industry to regulate tobacco companies' sponsorship of sport.

Sportsmatch

Launched by the Government in 1992, Sportsmatch is a business sponsorship incentive scheme which aims to increase the amount of business sponsorship going into 'grass roots' sport and physical recreation. The scheme offers matching funding for new sponsorships and extension of existing sponsorships. Priority is given to projects involving groups such as the young, disabled people and ethnic minorities and to projects in deprived areas.

In England the Institute of Sports Sponsorship runs the scheme on behalf of the Department of National Heritage. Since its inception, Sportsmatch has approved over 1,400 awards in England, totalling £12.2 million and covering more than 60 different sports. Rugby union, football, cricket and tennis have each received over 100 awards. Minority sports, such as archery, korfball, orienteering and trampolining, have also received awards. About half the companies involved are sponsoring sport for the first time.

In Scotland and Wales the scheme is managed by the appropriate Sports Council's Sponsorship Advisory Service. In 1994–95 the Scottish Awards Panel approved 149 awards totalling £506,000. In Wales awards of nearly £232,000 were allocated to 78 sporting bodies.

Sports Aid Foundation

The Sports Aid Foundation raises and distributes funds from industry, commerce and private sponsors as well as distributing public funds in order to assist the training of talented individuals. Grants are awarded on the recommendation of the appropriate governing bodies to British competitors who need help preparing for Olympic, World, European and Commonwealth championships. The Scottish and Welsh Sports Aid Foundations and the Ulster Sports and Recreation Trust have similar functions.

Foundation for Sport and the Arts

The Foundation for Sport and the Arts was set up by the football pools promoters in 1991 to channel funds into sport and the arts. The pools promoters are providing the Foundation with some £32 million a year. A further £16 million a year is received as a result of the 2.5 per cent reduction in pool betting duty announced in the 1990 Budget. About £50 million was given to sports schemes in 1995–96. The Foundation has made nearly 12,800 awards to schemes benefiting over 100 sports and totalling over £180 million.

Betting and Gaming

Most betting in Britain takes place on horse racing and greyhound racing. Bets may be made at racecourses and greyhound tracks, or through 9,000 licensed off-course betting offices, which take about 90 per cent of the money staked. A form of pool betting—totalisator betting—is organised on racecourses by the Horserace Totalisator Board (the Tote). Racecourse bets may also be placed with on-course bookmakers.

Bookmakers and the Tote contribute an annual levy—a fixed proportion of their turnover—to the Horserace Betting Levy Board. The amount of levy payable is decided by the racing and bookmaking industries or, in cases where agreement cannot be achieved, by the Home Secretary. The Levy Board promotes the improvement of horse breeds, advancement of veterinary science and the improvement of horse racing.

In 1995–96 the total money staked in all forms of gambling, excluding gaming machines, was estimated at over £15,000 million. The Home Office is proposing measures to deregulate the gambling industry, in order to provide new opportunities for the industry and the consumer. These include relaxation on membership conditions of casinos (of which there are around 120 in Great Britain), 13 new locations for casinos, and the removal of advertising restrictions on bingo and on betting offices.

National Lottery

Sport is one of five good causes to receive awards from funds raised by the National Lottery (see also p. 43). By July 1996 over 1,300 awards totalling £248 million had been made to sports in England alone. Projects have ranged from the provision of small items of equipment and floodlight facilities at grass roots level to the building of major sports venues. Around 50 sports have benefited from Lottery funding. For example, 297 small football clubs have received funds totalling £17.5 million for schemes ranging from floodlighting and drainage of pitches to new purpose-built clubhouses.

> The largest single award from the National Lottery Sports Fund has been for nearly £8 million for a high-quality outdoor multi-sport complex at the University of Central Lancashire. The award has covered 55 per cent of the cost of the sports facilities, including an all-weather, eight-lane running track and field events area, an artificial turf floodlit sports area, a rugby league pitch, a club and community centre, a cricket square with artificial wicket and pavilion, and a cycling road circuit.

Some of the funds from the Millennium Commission are also for sporting and recreational developments. Major schemes include:

- £46 million for the Millennium Stadium in Cardiff, which will be ready for the 1999 Rugby World Cup (see p. 537);
- £42.5 million for a new national cycle network; and
- £23 million for the development of the Hampden Park (Glasgow) football ground.

TELEVISED SPORT

Major sporting events receive extensive television coverage and are watched by millions of viewers. The largest ever audience for a sporting event shown on one channel was achieved by Jayne Torvill and Christopher Dean, who attracted 23 million viewers for their performance in the ice dance competition at the 1994 Winter Olympics. Euro 96 attracted a peak viewing figure of 26 million, spread over two channels. On terrestrial television the sports which receive the most coverage are football, horse racing, snooker and cricket.

Since 1988 the amount of sport on television has more than quadrupled, to over 12,000 hours a year, primarily as a result of the development of satellite and cable broadcasting. Some major events, such as live Premier League football, are now shown exclusively on these channels. As a result, there has been considerable public debate about broadcast sports rights.

Certain important sporting events are not permitted to be shown on television solely on pay-per-view or subscription terms unless these have first been offered to terrestrial channels. These 'listed' events comprise:

- the FIFA World Cup football finals;
- the FA Cup Final;
- the Scottish FA Cup Final;
- the finals weekend of the Wimbledon Tennis Championships;
- the Olympic Games;
- the Grand National;
- the Derby; and
- Test cricket matches involving England.

> The first pay-per-view individual sporting event to be shown in Britain was the world heavyweight title fight in March 1996 between Frank Bruno and Mike Tyson. Over 15 per cent of BSkyB subscribers paid an extra charge to watch the contest.

Following consultation with broadcasters, sports governing bodies, viewers, listeners and other interested parties, the Government has decided on additional protection for listed events. Under the Broadcasting Act 1996, the availability of live coverage of listed events for terrestrial television is guaranteed.
Subscription and pay-per-view services will also be guaranteed live coverage, in order to increase the choice available to viewers.

A TO Z OF POPULAR SPORTS

Some of the major sports in Britain, many of which were invented by the British, are described below.

Angling

Angling, one of the most popular countryside sports, has over seven times as many male as female participants among Britain's 3 million anglers. Many fish for salmon and trout, particularly in the rivers and lochs of Scotland and in Wales. In England and Wales the most widely practised form of angling is for coarse fish (freshwater fish other than salmon or trout). Separate organisations represent game, coarse and sea fishing clubs in England, Wales, Scotland and Northern Ireland, and there are separate national and international competitions in each of the three angling disciplines.

Athletics

Athletics is governed in Britain by the British Athletic Federation (BAF). It is responsible for the selection of British teams for international events, and also administers coaching schemes. For the Olympic Games and the World and European championships one team represents the whole of Britain.

Athletics is attracting increasing numbers of participants. In recent years there has been a significant growth in mass participation events, such as marathons and half marathons. The largest is the London Marathon, which takes place every spring. Nearly 26,800 runners completed the course in the 1996 event.

Jonathan Edwards twice broke the world record in the triple jump, in July and August 1995. In winning the gold medal at the World Athletics Championship in Gothenburg, he became the first man to jump beyond 18 metres. He achieved one of six medals won by British athletes in the 1996 Olympics in Atlanta, winning a silver medal. Silver medals were also won by Roger Black (400 metres), Steve Backley (javelin) and the men's 4 x 400 metres relay team (Jamie Baulch, Roger Black, Mark Richardson and Iwan Thomas), and bronze medals by Denise Lewis (heptathlon) and Steve Smith (high jump).

Badminton

Badminton takes its name from the Duke of Beaufort's country home, Badminton House, where the sport was first played in the 19th century. The game is organised by the Badminton Association of England and the Scottish, Welsh and Irish (Ulster branch) Badminton Unions. Around 5 million people play badminton in Britain and there are over 5,000 clubs. The All England Badminton Championships, held at the National Indoor Arena in Birmingham, is a leading tournament in the world grand prix circuit. The Badminton Association of England has a modern coach education system to develop coaches for players of all levels.

A mini version of the game—Short Badminton—and badminton for the disabled have been introduced in recent years.

Basketball

In Britain over 3 million people participate in basketball. The English Basketball Association is the governing body in England, with similar associations in Wales, Scotland and Ireland (Ulster Branch). All the associations are represented on the British and Irish Basketball Federation, which acts as the co-ordinating body for Britain and the Irish Republic.

The leading clubs play in the National Basketball Leagues, which cover three divisions for men and two for women, while there are also leagues for younger players. Mini-basketball has been developed for players under the age of 13. Wheelchair basketball is played under the same rules, with a few basic adaptations, and on the same court as the running game.

In 1995 the English Basketball Association started a new coaching scheme for schoolchildren which aims to increase participation and improve the quality of basketball throughout England.

Bowls

The two main forms of bowls are lawn (flat green and crown green) and indoor bowls. In recent years the most notable increases have been in the number of women taking part. Bowls is also popular among people with disabilities.

About 4,000 lawn bowling clubs are affiliated to the English, Scottish, Welsh and Irish Bowling Associations, which, together with Women's Bowling Associations for the four countries, play to the rules of the World Bowls Board. Crown green bowls and indoor bowls have their own separate associations.

British bowlers achieved considerable success at the 1996 world outdoor championships in Adelaide. The event is held every four years. Among the winners were Tony Allcock, who became the first man to defend the singles title successfully, while Scotland won the overall team title.

Boxing

Boxing in its modern form is based on the rules established by the Marquess of Queensberry in 1865. In Britain boxing is both amateur and professional, and in both strict medical regulations are observed.

All amateur boxing in England is controlled by the Amateur Boxing Association of England. There are separate associations in Scotland and Wales, and boxing in Northern Ireland is controlled by the Irish Amateur Boxing Association. The associations organise amateur boxing championships as well as training courses for referees, coaches and others. Headguards must be used in all British amateur competitions.

Professional boxing is controlled by the British Boxing Board of Control. The Board appoints inspectors, medical officers and representatives to ensure that regulations are observed and to guard against overmatching and exploitation.

In 1995 the British Boxing Board of Control announced measures designed to give boxers greater medical protection, including: bringing forward the weigh-in time for championship bouts; compulsory annual brain scans; tighter medical checks after fights; longer suspension periods for boxers who have been knocked out or stopped; and more random drug testing.

Britain currently has five world champions. Naseem Hamed (World Boxing Organisation featherweight champion) recorded one of the fastest wins in the history of world title fights when he knocked out his opponent in 35 seconds when retaining his title in March 1996.

Cricket

The earliest extant set of laws for cricket are dated 1744. The rules of the game became the responsibility, in the 18th century, of the Marylebone Cricket Club (MCC), which still frames the laws today. The MCC and the Test and County Cricket Board (TCCB), which represents first-class cricket in England, are both based at Lord's cricket ground in north London, the administrative centre of the English game. Men's cricket in Great Britain is governed by the Cricket Council, consisting of representatives of the TCCB, the National Cricket Association (NCA—representing club and junior cricket), the Minor Counties Cricket Association and the MCC. The Cricket Council, the NCA and the TCCB will be replaced at the beginning of 1997 by an England and Wales Cricket Board, which will govern all domestic cricket.

Cricket is played in schools, colleges and universities, and amateur teams play weekly games in cities, towns and villages. Throughout Britain there is a network of cricket consisting of first class, minor counties and club games with a variety of leagues.

The main competition in professional cricket is the Britannic Assurance County Championship, played by 18 first-class county teams in four-day matches. There are three one-day competitions: the Benson & Hedges Cup, the National Westminster Trophy and the AXA Equity & Law Sunday League.

Every year there is a series of five-day Cornhill Insurance Test matches played between England and one or more touring teams from Australia, India, New Zealand, Pakistan, South Africa, Sri Lanka, the West Indies or Zimbabwe. A team representing England usually tours one or more of these countries in the British winter.

The governing body of cricket for women and girls is the Women's Cricket Association. Women's cricket is played at local, county and international level. In 1993 England won the Women's World Cup for the second time.

Schools cricket in England is organised by the English Schools Cricket Association, to which over 40 counties are affiliated. In 1996 England staged the first international competition for the under 15 age group: the Lombard World Challenge. Ten countries took part and the winners were India.

Cycling

Cycling, one of Britain's fastest growing outdoor activities, includes road and track racing, time-trialling, cyclo-cross (cross country racing), touring and bicycle moto-cross (BMX). All-terrain or mountain bikes have grown significantly in popularity.

The British Cycling Federation has 16,000 members and is the governing body for cycling as a sport. The Cyclists' Touring Club (CTC), with 60,000 members and affiliates, is the representative body for recreational and urban cycling, and holds the CTC rally each year in York. Scotland and Wales have their own Cyclists' Unions. Northern Ireland has two federations for competitive cycling.

The World Cycling Championships were held at the Manchester Velodrome in August and September 1996. Chris Boardman won the 4,000 metres pursuit title and in doing so broke the world record. His time of 4 minutes 11 seconds was around 8 seconds less than the record before the championships. Later in September he regained the world record for the distance covered in 1 hour, when at the Velodrome he rode for over 56.3 km, more than 1 km further than the previous record. At the Atlanta Olympics he had won a bronze in the time trial, while Max Sciandri also won a bronze, in the road race.

Equestrianism

The arts of riding and driving are promoted by the British Horse Society, which is concerned with the welfare of horses, road safety, riding rights of way and training. It runs the British Equestrian Centre at Stoneleigh in Warwickshire. With some 65,200 members, the Society is the parent body of the Pony Club and the Riding Club movements, which hold rallies, meetings and competitions culminating in annual national championships.

Leading horse trials, comprising dressage, cross-country and show jumping, are held every year at a number of locations, including Badminton (Avon) and Gatcombe Park (Gloucestershire). In 1994 the British team won the three-day event team title at the World Equestrian Games in The Hague.

Show jumping is regulated and promoted by the British Show Jumping Association. The major show jumping events each year include the Royal International Horse Show at Hickstead (West Sussex) and the Horse of the Year Show at Wembley in London. Nick Skelton rode Dollar Girl to win the Volvo World Cup in 1995 and finished third in the event in 1996.

The authority responsible for equestrian competitions (other than racing) at international and Olympic level is the British Equestrian Federation, which co-ordinates the activities of the British Horse Society and the British Show Jumping Association.

Football

Association football is controlled by separate football associations in England, Wales, Scotland and Northern Ireland. In England 340 clubs are affiliated to the Football Association (FA) and more than 42,000 clubs to regional or district associations. The FA, founded in 1863, and the Football League, founded in 1888, were both the first of their kind in the world. In Scotland there are 78 clubs under the jurisdiction of the Scottish Football Association, and nearly 6,000 registered clubs.

A new FA Premier League was started in England in 1992 and now comprises 20 clubs. A further 72 full-time professional clubs play in three main divisions run by the Football League. During the season, which lasts from August until May, over 2,000 English League matches are played. A world record transfer fee was established in July 1996 with the transfer of Alan Shearer from Blackburn Rovers to Newcastle United for £15 million.

Three Welsh clubs play in the Football League, while the National League of Wales contains 20 semi-professional clubs. In Scotland the Scottish Football League has 40 clubs, equally divided into four divisions. In Northern Ireland, 16 semi-professional clubs play in the Irish Football League.

> Euro 96, the final stage of the European Championship, was held in June 1996. This was the biggest football tournament to have been held in Britain since the 1966 World Cup. Sixteen teams—including England (as hosts) and Scotland—took part, and the final at Wembley was won by Germany, who beat the Czech Republic. England reached the semi-finals, losing to Germany. About 1.2 million spectators watched Euro 96 and the event was televised in 195 countries. It is estimated that over 250,000 people from overseas attended the tournament, generating over £100 million in extra revenue from tourism. Following the success of the event, the FA announced its intention of putting in a bid to host the World Cup in 2006.

The major annual knock-out competitions are the FA Cup sponsored by Littlewoods and the Coca-Cola Cup (the League Cup) in England, the Tennents Scottish Cup, the Coca-Cola Cup (the Scottish League Cup), the Irish Cup and the Welsh FA Cup.

Gaelic Games

Gaelic Games, increasingly popular in Northern Ireland, cover the sports of Gaelic football, handball, hurling, camogie (women's hurling) and rounders. There are over 700 clubs in Northern Ireland affiliated to the Gaelic Athletic Association and the Camogie Council, the official governing bodies responsible for Gaelic Games.

Golf

Golf originated in Scotland and is ruled by the Royal and Ancient Golf Club (R & A), which is situated at St Andrews on the east coast of Scotland. The Golfing Union of Ireland and parallel unions in Wales, Scotland and

England are the national governing bodies for men's amateur golf. These bodies are affiliated to the R & A and are represented on the Council of National Golf Unions, which is the British co-ordinating body responsible for handicapping and organising home international matches. Women's amateur golf in Great Britain is governed by the Ladies' Golf Union. Club professional golf is governed by the Professional Golfers' Association (PGA) and tournament golf by the European PGA Tour and the Women's PGA Tour. Women's golf in Northern Ireland is governed by the Irish Ladies Golf Union.

The main event of the British golfing year is the Open Championship, one of the world's leading tournaments. Other important events include the Walker Cup and Curtis Cup matches for amateurs, played between Great Britain and Ireland and the United States, and the Ryder Cup and Solheim Cup matches for men and women professionals respectively, played every two years between Europe and the United States. In 1995 Europe regained the Ryder Cup at Oak Hill in the United States.

There are about 1,900 golf courses in Britain. Some of the most famous include St Andrews, Royal Lytham and St Anne's (which hosted the 1996 British Open Championship), Muirfield and Royal Birkdale. Nick Faldo won the US Masters tournament at Augusta in April 1996, his third win in the event and his sixth 'major' title.[1] In the women's game Laura Davies is ranked number one in the world.

Greyhound Racing

Greyhound racing is one of Britain's most popular spectator sports, with about 4.6 million spectators a year. There are 37 major tracks. Meetings are usually held three times a week at each track, with at least ten races a meeting. The main event of the year is the Greyhound Derby, run in June at Wimbledon Stadium, London. There are also about 50 mainly small tracks which operate independently. Like the major tracks, they are licensed by local authorities.

---

[1] The golfing 'major' events are the US Masters, Open and PGA events, and the British Open.

The rules for the sport are drawn up by the National Greyhound Racing Club, the sport's judicial and administrative body. The representative body is the British Greyhound Racing Board.

Gymnastics

Gymnastics is divided into five main disciplines: artistic (or Olympic) gymnastics, rhythmic gymnastics, sports acrobatics, general gymnastics and sports aerobics.

The governing body for the sport is British Gymnastics. Over the past decade the number of affiliated clubs has nearly doubled. The sport is particularly popular with schoolchildren and young adults, and it is estimated that between 3 and 4 million schoolchildren take part in some form of gymnastics every day.

Highland Games

Scottish Highland Games cover a wide range of athletic competitions, including activities such as dancing and piping competitions. The main events include running, cycling, throwing the hammer, tossing the caber and putting the shot.

Over 70 gatherings of various kinds take place throughout Scotland, the most famous of which is the annual Braemar Gathering.

The Scottish Games Association is the official governing body responsible for athletic sports and games at Highland and Border events in Scotland.

Hockey

The modern game of hockey was started by the Hockey Association (of England), which was founded in 1886 and acts as the governing body for men's hockey there. The Irish Ladies Hockey Union was the first women's governing body and assisted in the formation of the controlling body of women's hockey in England, the All England Women's Hockey Association. Separate associations regulate the sport in Scotland and Wales. Cup competitions and leagues exist at national, divisional or district, club and school levels, both indoors (six-a-side) and outdoors, and there are regular international matches and tournaments. A National Hockey Centre in Milton Keynes was opened in March 1996 and is now the venue for all major hockey matches in England.

Horse Racing

Horse racing takes two forms—flat racing and National Hunt (steeplechasing and hurdle) racing. The main flat race season runs from late March to early November, but all-weather flat racing and National Hunt racing take place throughout the year. Britain has 59 racecourses and about 13,000 horses currently in training.

The Derby, run at Epsom, is the outstanding event in the flat racing calendar. Other classic races are: the 2,000 Guineas and the 1,000 Guineas, both run at Newmarket; the Oaks (Epsom); and the St Leger (Doncaster).

The most important National Hunt meeting is the National Hunt Festival held at Cheltenham in March, which features the Gold Cup and the Champion Hurdle. The Grand National, run at Aintree, near Liverpool, is the world's best-known steeplechase and dates from 1839.

The British Horseracing Board is the governing authority for racing in Britain. Its responsibilities include the fixture list, race programmes, relations with the Government and the betting industry, and central marketing. The Jockey Club, as the regulatory authority, remains responsible for licensing, discipline and security.

Ice Skating

Ice skating has four main disciplines: ice figure (single and pairs), ice dance, speed skating and precision skating. The governing body is the National Ice Skating Association of UK Ltd. There are 68 rinks in Britain, with plans in hand for a number of new rinks.

British couples have won the world ice dance championship 17 times, the most recent being Jayne Torvill and Christopher Dean, who won four consecutive world championships between 1981 and 1984. The couple returned to amateur competition briefly in 1994 and won a gold medal at the 1994

European Championships and a bronze medal at the 1994 Winter Olympics in Lillehammer. A second bronze at the Winter Olympics was won by Nicky Gooch in indoor speed skating.

Judo

Judo is popular not only as a competitive sport and self-defence technique, but also as a means of general fitness training. An internationally recognised grading system is in operation through the sport's governing body, the British Judo Association.

Keep Fit

Keep fit encompasses various forms of movement and exercise activities. The Keep Fit Association (KFA), one of the largest governing bodies in England, promotes physical fitness and a positive attitude to health. Its national certificated training scheme for KFA teachers is recognised by local education authorities throughout Britain. Autonomous associations serve Scotland, Wales and Northern Ireland.

In 1994 the Exercise Association of England was established as an impartial advisory authority for the organisations involved in these activities.

Martial Arts

A broad range of martial arts, mainly derived from the Far East, has been introduced into Britain during the 20th century. There are recognised governing bodies responsible for their own activities in karate, ju-jitsu, aikido, Chinese martial arts, kendo, taekwondo and tang soo do. The most popular martial art is karate, with over 100,000 participants.

Motor-car Sports

The main four-wheeled motor sports include motor racing, autocross, rallycross, rallying and karting. In motor racing the Grand Prix Formula 1 World Championship is the major form of the sport.

The governing body for four-wheeled motor sport in Britain is the RAC (Royal

Automobile Club) Motor Sports Association. The Association issues licences for a variety of motoring competitions. It also organises the Network Q RAC Rally, an event in the World Rally Championship, and the British Grand Prix, which is held at Silverstone as part of the Formula 1 World Championship.

Britain has had more Formula 1 world champions than any other country. Nigel Mansell was champion in 1992, and in 1993 became the first person to win the IndyCar World Series Championship in his debut year. Damon Hill (son of Graham Hill, a previous world champion) won the 1996 Formula 1 World Championship, during which he won eight Grand Prix, bringing his total of Grand Prix victories to 21.

British car constructors, including Williams and McLaren, have enjoyed outstanding success in Grand Prix racing and many other forms of racing. British cars won 137 of the 159 Grand Prix held in the ten years to the end of the 1995 Formula 1 season. The motor sport industry in Britain is estimated to generate an annual turnover of over £1,300 million and to employ more than 50,000 people.

> In 1995 Colin McRae became the first British driver to win the World Rally Championship. He is the youngest driver to achieve this feat, winning at the age of 27.

Motor-cycle Sports

Motor-cycle sports include road racing, moto-cross, grass track, speedway, trials, drag racing and sprint. It is estimated that there are between 40,000 and 50,000 competitive motor cyclists in Britain.

The governing bodies of the sport are the Auto-Cycle Union in England and Wales, the Scottish Auto-Cycle Union and the Motor Cycle Union of Ireland (in Northern Ireland). The major events of the year include the Isle of Man TT races and the British Road Race Grand Prix. The Auto-Cycle Union also provides off-road training by approved instructors for riders of all ages.

Mountaineering

A recent survey estimated that there were 700,000 climbers in Britain. The representative body is the British Mountaineering Council, which works closely with the Mountaineering Councils of Scotland and Ireland. The main areas of work include access and conservation. There are over 300 mountaineering and climbing clubs in Britain, and three National Centres for mountaineering activities run by the Sports Councils (see pp. 525–6). Organisations such as the Scottish Mountain Safety Group help to promote the safe enjoyment of the hills.

British mountaineers have played a leading role in the exploration of the world's great mountain ranges. The best-known is Chris Bonington, who has climbed Everest and led many other successful expeditions. Some of the world's hardest rock climbs are found on cliffs in Britain.

Netball

More than 60,000 adults play netball regularly in England and a further 1 million participants play in schools. The sport is played almost exclusively by women and girls.

The All England Netball Association is the governing body in England, with Scotland, Wales and Northern Ireland having their own governing bodies. The number of clubs affiliated to the All England Association has grown steadily in recent years and currently stands at 3,700. The biggest growth has been in the youth development programme. National competitions are staged annually for all age groups. The world championships are held every four years; in 1995 they were staged at the National Indoor Arena in Birmingham, with teams representing 27 countries.

Rowing

Rowing is taught in many schools, universities and rowing clubs throughout Britain. The main types of boats are single, pairs and double sculls, fours and eights. The governing body in England is the Amateur Rowing Association; similar bodies regulate the sport in Scotland, Wales and Ireland (Ulster Branch).

The University Boat Race, between eight-oared crews from Oxford and Cambridge, has been rowed on the Thames almost every spring since 1836. The Head of the River Race, also on the Thames, is the largest assembly of racing craft in the world, with more than 420 eights racing in procession. At the Henley Regatta in Oxfordshire crews from all over the world compete each July in various kinds of race over a straight course of 1 mile 550 yards (about 2.1 km). The 1996 World Rowing Championships were held at Strathclyde Country Park in Scotland.

At the 1996 Olympics Steven Redgrave and Matthew Pinsent won the gold medal in the coxless pairs for the second consecutive Olympics. This was the fourth successive Olympics at which Steven Redgrave had won a gold medal, a feat achieved by only a very few people in Olympic history. The coxless four—Greg Searle, Jonny Searle, Tim Foster and Rupert Obholzer—won a bronze medal.

Rugby League

Rugby league (a 13-a-side game) originated in 1895 following the breakaway from rugby union (see below) of 22 clubs in the north of England, where the sport is still concentrated.

The governing body of the professional game is the Rugby Football League while the amateur game is governed by the British Amateur Rugby League Association. The major club match of the season is the Challenge Cup Final, which is played at Wembley Stadium in London. Rugby league's centenary world cup took place in England and Wales in 1995, and England were runners-up to Australia. A Great Britain team is touring Papua New Guinea, Fiji and New Zealand in autumn 1996.

Rugby league was revolutionised in 1996 with the creation of a summer Super League. This consists of 12 clubs: ten from the north of England, one from London and one representing Paris. Under the new format, there are also a First Division and a Second Division, with 11 and 12 clubs respectively.

Rugby Union

Rugby union football (a 15-a-side game) is thought to have originated at Rugby School in the first half of the 19th century. The sport is played under the auspices of the Rugby Football Union (RFU) in England and parallel bodies in Wales, Scotland and Ireland (Ulster Branch). Each of the four countries has separate national league and knock-out competitions for its domestic clubs.

An annual Five Nations Championship is contested by England, Scotland, Wales, Ireland and France. Overseas tours are undertaken by the national sides and by the British Lions, a team representing Great Britain and Ireland. Tours are also made to Britain by teams representing the major rugby-playing nations.

The Rugby World Cup is held every four years. Wales has been selected by the International Rugby Board to host the finals of the 1999 World Cup. A major new stadium will be built in Cardiff, with a significant financial contribution from the Millennium Commission (see p. 28). Other matches in the competition will be shared among England, Scotland, Ireland and France.

Major changes are occurring in rugby union following the decision in 1995 to end its amateur status. Players may now be paid, and several top players have switched clubs to take advantage of their new professional status.

Skiing

Skiing takes place in Scotland from December to May and also at several English locations when there is sufficient snow. The five established winter sports areas in Scotland are Cairngorm, Glencoe, Glenshee, the Lecht and Nevis Range. All have a full range of ski-lifts, prepared ski runs and professional instructors.

There are over 115 artificial or dry ski-slopes located throughout Britain, and 1.5 million people in Britain take part in the sport. The governing body at the British level is the British Ski Federation, with the home country ski councils being responsible for the development of the sport in their appropriate country, mainly as a holiday activity.

Snooker and Billiards

Snooker was invented by the British in India in 1875 and is currently played by approximately

7 million people in Britain. British players have an outstanding record in the game and have dominated the major professional championships. The main tournament is the annual Embassy World Professional Championship, held in Sheffield. In the 1980s Steve Davis won the world title six times. Stephen Hendry equalled this performance in 1996 when he won the world title for the fifth year in a row.

The controlling body for the non-professional game in England is the English Association for Snooker and Billiards. Scotland, Wales and Northern Ireland have separate associations. The World Professional Billiards and Snooker Association is responsible for professional players, organises all world-ranking professional events and holds the copyright for the rules. The representative body for women is the World Ladies' Billiards and Snooker Association.

Squash

Squash derives from the game of rackets, which was invented at Harrow School in the 1850s. The governing body for squash in England is the Squash Rackets Association; there are separate governing bodies in Wales, Scotland and Northern Ireland. The British Open Championships is one of the major world events in the sport.

The number of players in Britain is estimated at over 2 million, of whom more than 500,000 compete regularly in inter-club league competitions. There are nearly 9,000 squash courts in England, provided mainly by squash clubs, commercial organisations and local authorities.

In 1995 England beat Pakistan in the final of the world team championships in Cairo, to record its first victory in the event. The England team consisted of Mark Chaloner, Del Harris, Simon Parke and Chris Walker. Del Harris was runner-up in the individual event. In July 1996 England won the world junior team championships.

Swimming

Swimming is enjoyed by millions of people with a wide range of abilities from all age groups. All forms of competitive swimming are governed by the Amateur Swimming Association (ASA) in England and by similar associations in Scotland and Wales. These three associations combine to form the Amateur Swimming Federation of Great Britain, which acts as the co-ordinating body for the selection of Great Britain teams and the organisation of international competitions. Northern Ireland forms part of the Irish Amateur Swimming Association. Instruction and coaching are provided by qualified teachers and coaches who hold certificates awarded mainly by the ASA.

In the 1996 Olympics Paul Palmer won a silver medal in the 400 metres freestyle and Graeme Smith took the bronze medal in the 1,500 metres freestyle. Sarah Hardcastle won the 800 metres freestyle at the 1995 world short course championships in Rio de Janeiro and took the bronze medal in the 400 metres freestyle.

Table Tennis

Table tennis developed in Britain in the second half of the 19th century. It is popular with all sections of the community and widely played in a variety of venues. The sport is also a major recreational and competitive activity for people with disabilities. The governing body in England is the English Table Tennis Association. There are separate governing bodies in Scotland, Wales and Northern Ireland.

England is to host the 1997 World Table Tennis Championships in Manchester.

Tennis

The modern game of tennis originated in England in 1872 and the first championships were played at Wimbledon in 1877. The governing body for tennis in Great Britain is the Lawn Tennis Association (LTA), to which the Welsh and Scottish LTAs are affiliated. Tennis in Northern Ireland is governed by Tennis Ireland (Ulster Branch).

The Wimbledon Championships, held within the grounds of the All England Club, are one of the four tennis 'Grand Slam' tournaments. Prize money totalled £6.5

million in 1996. An extensive redevelopment of the All England Club is taking place. The first phase, a new No 1 Court, will be inaugurated in the 1997 Championships. Since 1981 the Championships have generated £153 million for British tennis.

In the 1996 Olympics Neil Broad and Tim Henman won Britain's first medal in tennis since the event was reintroduced to the Olympics. They were runners-up in the men's doubles. Martin Lee became the top-ranked junior in the world in 1996.

> The LTA has a five-year plan for developing tennis in Great Britain in the period to 2001. It will work in partnership with county tennis associations, clubs, schools, further and higher education institutions, and local authorities. The aim is to expand participation, encourage regular competition and produce more world-class tennis players.

Players can take part in national and county championships. National competitions are organised for schools, and short tennis has been introduced for children aged five and over. The game is played in over 3,000 schools and in leisure centres. In all, about 3 million people play tennis in Britain.

Tenpin Bowling

It is estimated that about 4.8 million people take part in tenpin bowling every year in Britain. There are over 200 national tournaments and an annual National Championship. The 1996 World Championships will be held at the Dundonald Ice Bowl in Northern Ireland, involving representatives from around 50 countries.

Britain has over 200 indoor bowling centres, the first having opened in 1960. More than 30,000 people belong to the sport's governing body, the British Tenpin Bowling Association.

Volleyball

The English Volleyball Association and parallel associations in Scotland, Wales and Northern Ireland act as the sport's governing bodies. To encourage more children to play volleyball, the Association organises national, regional and area championships for a variety of ages, from under 13s to under 19s. Mini-Volley is a three-a-side version of the game adapted for children under 13. Grass and beach volleyball tournaments are proving very popular with children and are leading to an increase in the number of schools playing volleyball.

Yachting

Yachting comprises sailing, powerboating and windsurfing on both inland and offshore waters. Racing in sailing boats takes place between one-design classes or under handicap, which provides level racing for boats of different size and shape. Among well-known ocean races are the Whitbread Round The World Yacht Race and the Fastnet Race.

The Royal Yachting Association is the governing body for all yachting in Britain. It is estimated that about 3 million people participate in the sport.

Silver medals were won in two events in the 1996 Olympics, by Ben Ainslie in the Laser class and by John Merricks and Ian Walker in the 470 (double-handed dinghy) class.

Further Reading

The History of Cricket: From the Weald to the World, by Peter Wynne-Thomas. The Stationery Office, June 1997.

Sport: Raising the Game. Department of National Heritage, 1995.

Sport: Raising the Game—The First Year Report. Department of National Heritage, 1996.

Sport and Leisure. Aspects of Britain series. HMSO, 1994.

Appendix 1:
Government Departments and Agencies

An outline of the principal functions of the main government departments and executive agencies is given below.

Cabinet ministries are indicated by an asterisk. Executive agencies are normally listed under the relevant department, although in some cases they are included within the description of the departments' responsibilities.

The work of many of the departments and agencies listed below covers Britain as a whole. Where this is not the case, the following abbreviations are used:

- (GB) for functions covering England, Wales and Scotland;
- (E,W & NI) for those covering England, Wales and Northern Ireland;
- (E & W) for those covering England and Wales; and
- (E) for those concerned with England only.

The principal address and telephone number of each department are given. For details of the addresses of executive agencies see the *Civil Service Year Book*.

Cabinet Office (Office of Public Service)
70 Whitehall, London SW1A 2AS
Tel: 0171 270 1234

The Cabinet Office and the responsibilities of the Office of Public Service—OPS—are described on p. 66.

Executive Agencies

The Buying Agency
Central Computer and Telecommunications Agency
Chessington Computer Centre
Civil Service College
Occupational Health and Safety Agency
Property Advisers to the Civil Estate
Security Facilities Executive

One further agency—the Central Office of Information—reports to the Chancellor of the Duchy of Lancaster but is a department in its own right and not part of OPS (see p. 545).

ECONOMIC AFFAIRS

*Ministry of Agriculture, Fisheries and Food
3–8 Whitehall Place, London SW1A 2HH
Tel: 0171 270 3000

Policies for agriculture, horticulture, fisheries and food; responsibilities for related environmental and rural issues (E); food policies.

Executive Agencies

ADAS (Food, Farming, Land and Leisure)
Central Science Laboratory
Intervention Board
Meat Hygiene Service
Pesticides Safety Directorate
Laboratories Agency
Veterinary Medicines Directorate

*Department of Trade and Industry
1–19 Victoria Street, London SW1H 0ET
Tel: 0171 215 5000

Industrial and commercial affairs; science and technology; promotion of new enterprise and competition; information about new business methods and opportunities; investor protection and consumer affairs. Specific responsibilities include innovation policy; regional industrial policy and inward investment promotion; small businesses; management best practice and business/education links; industrial relations and employment legislation; deregulation; international trade policy; commercial relations and export promotion; competition policy; company law; insolvency; radio regulation; patents and copyright protection (GB); the development of new sources of energy and the Government's relations with the energy industries.

Executive Agencies

Companies House
Insolvency Service
National Weights and Measures Laboratory
Patent Office
Radiocommunications Agency

*Department of Transport
Great Minster House, 76 Marsham Street, London
SW1P 4DR Tel: 0171 271 5000

Land, sea and air transport; domestic and
international civil aviation; international transport
agreements; shipping and the ports industry; marine
pollution; regulation of drivers and vehicles
(including road safety); regulation of the road
haulage industry; transport and the environment.
Motorways and trunk roads; oversight of local
authority transport (E). Sponsorship of London
Transport (E); British Rail; Railtrack (GB) and the
Civil Aviation Authority.

Executive Agencies

Coastguard Agency
Driver and Vehicle Licensing Agency
Driving Standards Agency
Highways Agency
Marine Safety Agency
Transport Research Laboratory
Vehicle Certification Agency
Vehicle Inspectorate

*HM Treasury
Parliament Street, London SW1P 3AG
Tel: 0171 270 3000

Oversight of tax and monetary policy; planning and
control of public spending; international financial
relations; supervision of the financial system; and
responsibility for a range of Civil Service
management issues.

HM Customs and Excise
New King's Beam House, 22 Upper Ground,
London SE1 9PJ Tel: 0171 620 1313

Collecting and accounting for Customs and Excise
revenues, including value added tax; agency
functions, including controlling certain imports and
exports, policing prohibited goods, and compiling
trade statistics.

ECGD (Export Credits Guarantee Department)
P.O. Box 2200, 2 Exchange Tower, Harbour
Exchange Square, London E14 9GS
Tel: 0171 512 7000

Access to bank finance and provision of insurance
for British project and capital goods exporters
against the risk of not being paid for goods and
services; insurance cover for new British investment
overseas; reinsurance to British-based private sector
insurance companies offering insurance for
consumer type exports.

Inland Revenue
Somerset House, London WC2R 1LB
Tel: 0171 438 6622

Administration and collection of direct taxes;
valuation of property (GB).

Executive Agency

Valuation Office

Office for National Statistics
Great George Street, London SW1P 3AQ Tel: 0171
270 3000

An executive agency created in April 1996 by the
merger of the Central Statistical Office and the
Office of Population, Censuses and Surveys. It is
responsible for the full range of functions previously
carried out by both former offices. This includes:

- preparing and interpreting key economic
  statistics for government policy; collecting and
  publishing business statistics; publishing
  annual and monthly statistical digests;

- providing researchers, analysts and those in
  education and other customers with a statistical
  service which assists their work and promotes
  the functioning of industry and commerce;

- administration of the marriage laws and local
  registration of births, marriages and deaths (E
  & W); provision of population estimates and
  projections and statistics on health and other
  demographic matters (E & W); Census of
  Population (E & W). Surveys for other
  government departments and public bodies
  (GB); and

- promoting these functions within Britain, the
  European Union and internationally to provide
  a statistical service to meet European Union
  and international requirements.

PAYMASTER: The Office of HM Paymaster General
Sutherland House, Russell Way, Crawley, West
Sussex RH10 1UH Tel: 01293 560999

An executive agency providing banking services for
government departments and the administration
and payment of public service pensions.

Royal Mint

Llantrisant, Pontyclun, Mid Glamorgan CF72 8YT
Tel: 01443 222111.

An executive agency responsible for producing
and issuing coinage for Britain. It also produces,
among other things, ordinary circulation coins and
coinage blanks for around 100 countries as well as
special proof and uncirculated quality collectors'
coins, commemorative medals, and royal and
official seals.

REGULATORY BODIES

Office of Electricity Regulation (OFFER)

Hagley House, Hagley Road, Birmingham B16 8QG
Tel: 0121 456 2100

Regulating and monitoring the electricity supply
industry; promoting competition in the generation
and supply of electricity; ensuring that companies
comply with the licences under which they operate;
protecting customers' interests (GB).

Office of Gas Supply (OFGAS)

Stockley House, 130 Wilton Road, London SW1V
1LQ Tel: 0171 828 0898

Regulating and monitoring British Gas to ensure
value for money for customers, and granting
licences to other gas suppliers, shippers and
public gas transporters; enabling development of
competition in the industrial and domestic
markets.

Office of the National Lottery (OFLOT)

2 Monck Street, London SW1P 2BQ
Tel: 0171 227 2000

Responsible for the grant, variation and
enforcement of licences to run the National Lottery
and promote lotteries as part of it.

Office for Standards in Education (OFSTED)

29–33 Kingsway, London WC2B 6SE
Tel: 0171 925 6800

Monitoring standards in English schools; regulating
the work of independent registered schools'
inspectors (E).

Office of Telecommunications (OFTEL)

50 Ludgate Hill, London EC4M 7JJ
Tel: 0171 634 8700

Monitoring telecommunications operators' licences;
enforcing competition legislation; representing
users' interests.

Office of Water Services (OFWAT)

Centre City Tower, 7 Hill Street, Birmingham B5
4UA Tel: 0121 625 1300

Monitoring the activities of companies appointed as
water and sewerage undertakers (E & W); regulating
prices, promoting economy and efficiency, protecting
customers' interests and facilitating competition. Ten
regional customer service committees represent
customer interests and investigate complaints. The
OFWAT National Customer Council speaks for
customers at a national level.

LEGAL AFFAIRS

*The Lord Chancellor's Department

Selborne House, 54–60 Victoria Street, London
SW1E 6QW
Tel: 0171 210 8500

Responsibility, through the Court Service, for the
administration of the Supreme Court, county and
crown courts and a number of tribunals. Also
oversees the locally administered magistrates'
courts and the Official Solicitor's Department. All
work relating to judicial and quasi-judicial
appointments. Overall responsibility for civil and
criminal legal aid, for the Law Commission and
for the promotion of general reforms in the civil
law. Lead responsibility for private international
law. Responsibility for national archives and the
Public Trust Office (E & W). The Lord
Chancellor also has responsibility for the
Northern Ireland Court Service.

The Legal Services Ombudsman and the
Advisory Committee on Legal Education and
Conduct are independent of the Department but
report to the Lord Chancellor.

Executive Agencies

The Court Service
HM Land Registry
Public Record Office
Public Trust Office

Crown Prosecution Service

50 Ludgate Hill, London EC4M 7EX
Tel: 0171 273 8000

An independent organisation responsible for the
prosecution of criminal cases resulting from police
investigations, headed by the Director of Public
Prosecutions and accountable to Parliament through
the Attorney General, superintending Minister for
the service (E & W).

Legal Secretariat to the Law Officers

Attorney General's Chambers, 9 Buckingham Gate, London SW1E 6JP Tel: 0171 828 7155

Supporting the Law Officers of the Crown (Attorney General and Solicitor General) in their functions as the Government's principal legal advisers (E, W & NI). The Attorney General, who is also Attorney General for Northern Ireland, is the Minister responsible for the Treasury Solicitor's Department (see below), and has a statutory duty to superintend the Director of Public Prosecutions and the Director of the Serious Fraud Office (see below), and the Director of Public Prosecutions for Northern Ireland.

Parliamentary Counsel

36 Whitehall, London SW1A 2AY
Tel: 0171 210 6633

Drafting of government Bills (except those relating exclusively to Scotland); advising departments on parliamentary procedure (E, W & NI).

HM Procurator General and Treasury Solicitor

Queen Anne's Chambers, 28 Broadway, London SW1H 9JS Tel: 0171 210 3000

Provision of legal services to a large number of government departments, agencies, and public and quasi-public bodies. Services include litigation; giving general advice on interpreting and applying the law; instructing Parliamentary Counsel on Bills and drafting subordinate legislation; and, through an executive agency, providing conveyancing services and property-related legal work (E & W).

Executive Agencies

Government Property Lawyers
The Treasury Solicitor's Department

Lord Advocate's Department and Crown Office (see p. 547)

Serious Fraud Office

Elm House, 10–16 Elm Street, London WC1X 0BJ
Tel: 0171 239 7272

Investigating and prosecuting serious and complex fraud under the superintendence of the Attorney General (E, W & NI).

EXTERNAL AFFAIRS AND DEFENCE

*Ministry of Defence

Main Building, Whitehall, London SW1A 2HB
Tel: 0171 218 9000

Defence policy and control and administration of the armed services.

Defence Agencies

Army Base Repair Organisation
Army Base Storage and Distribution Agency
Army Individual Training Organisation
Army Technical Support Agency
Defence Analytical Services Agency
Defence Animal Centre
Defence Bills Agency
Defence Clothing and Textiles Agency
Defence Dental Agency
Defence Evaluation and Research Agency
Defence Postal and Courier Services Agency
Defence Transport and Movements Executive
Disposal Sales Agency
Duke of York's Royal Military School
Hydrographic Office
Joint Air Reconnaissance Intelligence Centre Agency
Logistic Information Systems Agency
Medical Supplies Agency
Meteorological Office
Military Survey
Ministry of Defence Police
Naval Aircraft Repair Organisation
Naval Recruiting and Training Agency
Pay and Personnel Agency
Queen Victoria School
RAF Maintenance Group
RAF Signals Engineering Establishment
RAF Training Group
Service Children's Education

*Foreign & Commonwealth Office

Downing Street, London SW1A 2AL
Tel: 0171 270 1500

Conduct of Britain's overseas relations, including advising on policy, negotiating with overseas governments and conducting business in international organisations, promoting British exports and trade generally; administering aid (see below). Presenting British ideas, policies and objectives to the people of overseas countries; administering the remaining Dependent Territories; and protecting British interests and influence abroad, including the welfare of British citizens.

Executive Agency

Wilton Park Conference Centre

Overseas Development Administration

94 Victoria Street, London SW1E 5JL
Tel: 0171 917 7000

Responsibility for Britain's overseas aid to developing countries, for global environmental assistance, and also for the joint administration, with the Foreign & Commonwealth Office, of assistance to Central and Eastern Europe and the countries of the former Soviet Union. Responsibility for overseas superannuation.

Executive Agency

Natural Resources Institute

SOCIAL AFFAIRS, THE ENVIRONMENT AND CULTURE

*Department for Education and Employment
Sanctuary Buildings, Great Smith Street, London SW1P 3BT Tel: 0171 925 5000

Overall responsibility for school, college and university education (E). The Careers Service (E); Employment Service; youth and adult training policy and programmes; sponsorship of training and enterprise councils; European social policies and programmes; co-ordination of government policy on women's issues and equal opportunities issues in employment (GB).

Executive Agencies

Employment Service
Teachers' Pensions Agency

*Department of the Environment
2 Marsham Street, London SW1P 3EB Tel: 0171 276 0900

Policies for local government finance and structure; local development; land use planning; housing; construction industry; energy efficiency; environmental protection; water industry and the British Waterways Board; urban and rural regeneration; countryside and wildlife protection; legal and corporate services; Office of the Chief Scientist (E).

Executive Agencies

Building Research Establishment
Planning Inspectorate
Queen Elizabeth II Conference Centre

*Department of Health
Richmond House, 79 Whitehall, London SW1A 2NS Tel: 0171 210 3000

National Health Service; personal social services provided by local authorities; and certain aspects of public health, including hygiene (E).

Executive Agencies

Medical Devices Agency
Medicines Control Agency
NHS Estates
NHS Pensions Agency

*Home Office
50 Queen Anne's Gate, London SW1H 9AT Tel: 0171 273 3000

Administration of justice; criminal law; treatment of offenders, including probation and the prison service; the police; crime prevention; fire service and emergency planning; licensing laws; regulation of firearms and dangerous drugs; electoral matters and local legislation (E & W). Gaming (GB). Passports, immigration and nationality; race relations; royal matters. Responsibilities relating to the Channel Islands and the Isle of Man.

Executive Agencies

Fire Service College
Forensic Science Service
HM Prison Service
United Kingdom Passport Agency

*Department of National Heritage
2-4 Cockspur Street, London SW1Y 5DH Tel: 0171 211 6000.

The arts; public libraries; national museums and galleries; tourism; sport; the built heritage (E); broadcasting; press regulation; film industry; export licensing of antiques; the National Lottery.

Executive Agencies

Historic Royal Palaces Agency
Royal Parks Agency

*Department of Social Security
Richmond House, 79 Whitehall, London SW1A 2NS Tel: 0171 210 3000

The social security system (GB).

Executive Agencies

Benefits Agency
Child Support Agency
Contributions Agency
Information Technology Services Agency
War Pensions Agency

OTHER OFFICES AND AGENCIES

Central Office of Information
Hercules Road, London SE1 7DU
Tel: 0171 928 2345

An executive agency procuring publicity material and other information services on behalf of government departments and publicly funded organisations.

Her Majesty's Stationery Office
St Clements House, 2-16 Colegate, Norwich NR3 1BQ Tel: 01603 621000

A body, within the Office of Public Service, responsible for printing legislation and for control and adminstration of Crown copyright and administration of parlimentary copyright.

Ordnance Survey
Romsey Road, Southampton SO16 4GU
Tel: 01703 792000

An executive agency, which reports to the Secretary of State for the Environment, providing official surveying, mapping and associated scientific work covering Great Britain and some overseas countries.

Office of the Data Protection Registrar
Wycliffe House, Water Lane, Wilmslow, Cheshire SK9 5AF. Tel: 01625 545745

The Data Protection Registrar is an independent officer who reports directly to Parliament. The Officer maintains a public register of data users and computer bureaux; enforces the data protection principles; encourages the development of codes of practice to help data users comply with the principles; and considers complaints about breaches of the principles and other provisions of the Act. Data users must be registered with the Data Protection Registrar.

NORTHERN IRELAND

*Northern Ireland Office
Stormont Castle, Belfast BT4 3ST
Tel: 01232 520700
Whitehall, London SW1A 2AZ Tel: 0171 210 3000

Responsibilities

The Secretary of State for Northern Ireland is the Cabinet minister responsible for Northern Ireland. Through the Northern Ireland Office the Secretary of State has direct responsibility for constitutional developments, law and order, security, and electoral matters.

Executive Agencies

The Compensation Agency
Forensic Science Agency of Northern Ireland
Northern Ireland Prison Service

The work of the Northern Ireland departments, whose functions are listed below, is also subject to the direction and control of the Secretary of State.

Department of Agriculture for Northern Ireland
Development of agri-food, forestry and fisheries industries; veterinary, scientific and development services; food and farming policy; agri-environment policy and rural development.

Department of Economic Development for Northern Ireland
Promotion of inward investment and development of larger home industry (Industrial Development Board); promotion of enterprise and small business (through the Local Enterprise Development Unit); training and employment services; promotion of industrially relevant research and development and technology transfer (through the Industrial Research and Technology Unit); promotion and development of tourism (through the Northern Ireland Tourist Board); energy; mineral development; company regulation; consumer protection; health and safety at work; industrial relations; equal opportunity in employment; and Northern Ireland-wide co-ordination of deregulation.

Executive Agencies

Industrial Research and Technology Unit
Training and Employment Agency (Northern Ireland)

Department of Education for Northern Ireland
Control of the five education and library boards and education from nursery to further and higher education; youth services; sport and recreation; the arts and culture (including libraries); and the development of community relations within and between schools.

Department of the Environment for Northern Ireland
Most of the Department's functions are carried out by eleven Next Step agencies. These include: planning, roads, water and construction services; environmental protection and conservation services; land registries, public records, ordnance survey, rate collection, driver and vehicle testing and licensing.

Core departmental functions include: overall responsibility for housing and transport policies; fire services; certain controls over local government; disposal and management of the Department's land and property holdings; and urban regeneration.

Executive Agencies

Construction Service
Driver and Vehicle Licensing (Northern Ireland)
Driver and Vehicle Testing Agency
Environment and Heritage Service
Land Registers of Northern Ireland
Ordnance Survey of Northern Ireland
Planning Service
Public Record Office of Northern Ireland
Rate Collection Agency
Roads Service
Water Service

Department of Finance and Personnel
Control of public expenditure; liaison with HM Treasury and the Northern Ireland Office on financial matters, economic and social research and analysis; EC co-ordination; policies for equal opportunities and personnel management; central management and control of the Northern Ireland Civil Service.

Executive Agencies

Government Purchasing Agency
Northern Ireland Statistics and Research Agency
Valuation and Lands Agency

Department of Health and Social Services for Northern Ireland
Health and personal social services and social legislation. Responsibility for the administration of all social security benefits and the collection of National Insurance contributions.

Executive Agencies

Northern Ireland Child Support Agency
Health Estates
Social Security Agency (Northern Ireland)

SCOTLAND

*The Scottish Office
St Andrew's House, Edinburgh EH1 3TG.
Tel: 0131 556 8400
Dover House, Whitehall, London SW1A 2AU. Tel: 0171 270 3000

Responsibilities

The Scottish Office is responsible for a wide range of policy matters. These include agriculture and fisheries, education, law and order, environmental protection and conservation of the countryside, land-use planning, local government, housing, roads and certain aspects of transport services, social work and health.

The Secretary of State also has a major role in planning and development of the Scottish economy, and important functions relating to industrial development, including responsibility for financial assistance to industry.

The Secretary of State has overall responsibility for legal services in Scotland and is advised by the two Scottish Law Officers—the Lord Advocate and the Solicitor General for Scotland.

The Scottish Office's responsibilities are discharged principally through its five departments (which include seven executive agencies). There are also four smaller departments: the Registers of Scotland and the Scottish Record Office, which are executive agencies, the General Register Office for Scotland and the Scottish Courts Administration, which is also responsible to the Lord Advocate for certain legal functions.

Relations with Other Government Departments
Other government departments with significant Scottish responsibilities have offices in Scotland and work closely with The Scottish Office.

An outline of the functions of the main Scottish departments is given below.

Scottish Office Agriculture, Environment and Fisheries Department
Promotion and regulation of agriculture: safeguarding public, food, plant and animal health and welfare; land use and forestry; livestock subsidies and commodities. Environment, including environmental protection, nature conservation and the countryside; water and sewerage services; sustainable development. Promotion and regulation of fisheries; protection of the marine environment; research on and monitoring of fish stocks; enforcement of fisheries laws and regulations.

Executive Agencies

Historic Scotland
Scottish Agricultural Science Agency
Scottish Fisheries Protection Agency

Scottish Office Development Department
Housing and area regeneration; new towns; local government organisation and finance; transport and local roads, Roads Directorate; co-ordination of

Scottish Office European interests; land-use planning; building control; protection and presentation to the public of historic buildings and ancient monuments.

Scottish Office Education and Industry Department

Industrial and regional economic development matters; exports, technology; Highlands and Islands co-ordination; enterprise and tourism; industrial expansion; energy; training; education; student awards; arts (including the National Institutions), libraries, museums and galleries, Gaelic language; sport and recreation.

Executive Agencies

The Scottish Office Pensions Agency
Student Award Agency for Scotland

Scottish Office Department of Health

National Health Service; Chief Scientist's Office; Public Health Policy Unit.

Scottish Office Home Department and Scottish Courts Administration

Central administration of law and order (includes police service, criminal justice and licensing, legal aid, the Scottish Court Service and the Scottish Prison Service); civil law, fire, home defence and civil emergency services; social work services; Solicitor's Office.

Executive Agencies

Scottish Court Service
Scottish Prison Service

Central Services are provided to the five Scottish departments. These include the office of the Solicitor to the Secretary of State, The Scottish Office Information Directorate, the Directorate of Administrative Services, Finance and Personnel Group.

The following departments are directly responsible to the Law Officers and are not part of The Scottish Office.

Lord Advocate's Department

2 Carlton Gardens, London SW1Y 5AA. Tel: 0171 210 1010

Provision of legal advice to the Government on issues affecting Scotland; responsibility for drafting government primary legislation relating to Scotland and adapting for Scotland other primary legislation. Provision of advice in matters of parliamentary procedures affecting Scotland.

Crown Office

25 Chambers Street, Edinburgh EH1 1LA Tel: 0131 226 2626

Control of all prosecutions in Scotland.

WALES

*Welsh Office

Cathays Park, Cardiff CF1 3NQ Tel: 01222 825111
Gwydyr House, Whitehall, London SW1A 2ER
Tel: 0171 270 3000

Responsibilities

The Welsh Office is responsible for many aspects of Welsh affairs, including health, community care and personal social services; education, except for terms and conditions of service, student awards and the University of Wales; Welsh language and culture; agriculture and fisheries; forestry; local government; housing; water and sewerage; environmental protection; sport; land use, including town and country planning; countryside and nature conservation; new towns; ancient monuments and historic buildings; arts, museums and libraries.

The Department's responsibilities also include roads; tourism; enterprise and training; selective financial assistance to industry; the Urban Programme and urban investment grants in Wales; the operation of the European Regional Development Fund in Wales and other European Union matters; women's issues; non-departmental public bodies; civil emergencies; all financial aspects of these matters, including Welsh revenue support grant; and oversight responsibilities for economic affairs and regional planning in Wales.

Executive Agency

CADW:Welsh Historic Monuments

Appendix 2:
Recent Legislation

The public Acts of Parliament passed since autumn 1995 are listed below. Eighteen Acts were introduced by Private Members; these are indicated by asterisks. All are available from HMSO.

1995

Atomic Energy Authority Act 1995. Ch 37. £6.30.

*Charities (Amendment) Act 1995. Ch 48. 60p.

Consolidated Fund (No 2) Act 1995. Ch 54. £65p.

Civil Evidence Act 1995. Ch 38. £3.80.

Criminal Injuries Compensation Act 1995. Ch 53. £2.85.

Criminal Law (Consolidation) (Scotland) Act 1995. Ch 39. £7.70.

Criminal Procedure (Consequential Provisions) (Scotland) Act 1995. Ch 40. £8.40.

Criminal Procedure (Scotland) Act 1995. Ch 46. £19.65.

Disability Discrimination Act 1995. Ch 50. £9.25.

Gas Act 1995. Ch 45. £11.

Law Reform (Succession) Act 1995. Ch 41. £1.50.

Medical (Professional Performance) Act 1995. Ch 51. £3.30.

Mental Health (Patients in the Community) Act 1995. Ch 52. £3.30.

Northern Ireland (Remission of Sentences) Act 1995. Ch 47. 65p.

Private International Law (Miscellaneous Provisions) Act 1995. Ch 42. £2.85.

*Proceeds of Crime (Scotland) Act 1995. Ch 43. £8.40.

Statute Law (Repeals) Act 1995. Ch 44. £7.

Town and Country Planning (Cost of Inquiries etc) Act 1995. Ch 49. £3.30.

1996

Appropriation Act 1996. Ch 45. £7.

Arbitration Act 1996. Ch 23. £8.40.

Armed Forces Act 1996. Ch 46. £11.95.

Asylum and Immigration Act 1996. Ch 49. £3.80.

Audit (Miscellaneous Provisions) Act 1996. Ch 10. £1.90.

Broadcasting Act 1996. Ch 55. £16.40.

Chemical Weapons Act 1996. Ch 6. £4.85.

*Civil Aviation (Amendment) Act 1996. Ch 39. 65p.

Commonwealth Development Corporation Act 1996. Ch 28. 65p.

Community Care (Direct Payments) Act 1996. Ch 30. £1.50.

Consolidated Fund Act 1996. Ch 4. 65p.

Criminal Procedure and Investigations Act 1996. Ch 25. £11.

Damages Act 1996. Ch 48. £1.90.

Deer (Amendment) (Scotland) Act 1996. Ch 44. £3.80.

Deer (Scotland) Act 1996. Ch 58. £6.30.

Defamation Act 1996. Ch 31. £4.30.

*Dogs (Fouling of Land) Act 1996. Ch 20. £1.50.

Education Act 1996. Ch 56. £36.50

Education (Scotland) Act 1996. Ch 43. £6.30.

Education (Student Loans) Act 1996. Ch 9. £1.10.

Employment Rights Act 1996. Ch 18. £16.40.

*Energy Conservation Act 1996. Ch 38. 65p.

Family Law Act 1996. Ch 27. £11.

Finance Act 1996. Ch 8. £30.

Health Service Commissioners (Amendment) Act 1996. Ch 5. £2.90.

Hong Kong (Overseas Public Servants) Act 1996. Ch 2. £1.10.

*Hong Kong (War Wives and Widows) Act 1996. Ch 41. 65p.

Housing Act 1996. Ch 52. £18.

Housing, Grants, Construction and Registration Act 1996. Ch 53. £11.

Humber Bridge (Debts) Act 1996. Ch 1. 60p.

Industrial Tribunals Act 1996. Ch 17. £7.

*Law Reform (Year and a Day Rule) Act 1996. Ch 19. 65p.

Licensing (Amendment) (Scotland) Act 1996. Ch 36. £1.50.

London Regional Transport Act 1996. Ch 21. £1.50.

*Marriage Ceremony (Prescribed Words) Act 1996. Ch 34. 65p.

National Health Service (Residual Liabilities) Act 1996. Ch 15. 65p.

*Noise Act 1996. Ch 37. £2.85.

*Non-domestic Rating (Information) Act 1996. Ch 13. 65p.

Northern Ireland (Emergency Provisions) Act 1996. Ch 22. £7.70.

Northern Ireland (Entry to Negotiations, etc) Act 1996. Ch 11. £2.85.

Nursery Education and Grant-Maintained Schools Act 1996. Ch 50. £3.30.

*Offensive Weapons Act 1996. Ch 26. £1.90.

*Party Wall etc. Act 1996. Ch 40. £3.80.

Police Act 1996. Ch 16. £10.

Prevention of Terrorism (Additional Powers) Act 1996. Ch 7. £3.30.

*Prisoner's Earnings Act 1996. Ch 33. £1.50.

*Railway Heritage Act 1996. Ch 42. 1.50.

Rating (Caravans and Boats) Act 1996. Ch 12. 65p.

Reserve Forces Act 1996. Ch 14. £11.

School Inspections Act 1996. Ch 57. £7.70.

Security Service Act 1996. Ch 35. 65p.

*Sexual Offences (Conspiracy and Incitement) Act 1996. Ch 29. £1.90.

Social Security (Overpayments) Act 1996. Ch 51. 65p.

Statutory Instruments (Production and Sale) Act 1996. Ch 54. 65p.

*Trading Schemes Act 1996. Ch 32. £1.10.

*Treasure Act 1996. Ch 24. £1.90.

Trusts of Land and Appointment of Trustees Act 1996. Ch 47. £6.30.

*Wild Mammals (Protection) Act 1996. Ch 3. 65p.

Appendix 3:
Principal Abbreviations

ACAS: Advisory, Conciliation and Arbitration Service

BBC: British Broadcasting Corporation

BR: British Rail

BT: British Telecommunications plc

CAA: Civil Aviation Authority

CAP: Common Agricultural Policy

CBI: Confederation of British Industry

CCW: Countryside Council for Wales

CO$_2$: carbon dioxide

CPS: Crown Prosecution Service

DfEE: Department for Education and Employment

DTI: Department of Trade and Industry

EA: Environment Agency

EC: European Community

ECGD: Export Credits Guarantee Department

EEA: European Economic Area

EFTA: European Free Trade Association

ESAs: Environmentally Sensitive Areas

EU: European Union

FCO: Foreign & Commonwealth Office

GATT: General Agreement on Tariffs and Trade

GDP: gross domestic product

GNP: gross national product

GPs: general practitioners

HMSO: Her Majesty's Stationery Office

HSE: Health and Safety Executive

IPC: integrated pollution control

ITC: Independent Television Commission

ITV: independent television

LEAs: local education authorities

LECs: Local Enterprise Companies

LT: London Transport

MAFF: Ministry of Agriculture, Fisheries and Food

MP: Member of Parliament

NATO: North Atlantic Treaty Organisation

NHS: National Health Service

NO$_x$: oxides of nitrogen

ODA: Overseas Development Administration

OECD: Organisation for Economic Co-operation and Development

OPS: Office of Public Service

PFI: Private Finance Initiative

plc: public limited company

PSBR: public sector borrowing requirement

RAF: Royal Air Force

RPI: Retail Prices Index

SIB: Securities and Investments Board

SNH: Scottish Natural Heritage

SO$_2$: sulphur dioxide

TECs: Training and Enterprise Councils

TUC: Trades Union Congress

TWh: terawatt hours

UKCS: United Kingdom Continental Shelf

UN: United Nations

VAT: value added tax

WEU: Western European Union

WTO: World Trade Organisation

Appendix 4:
Calendar of Events 1997

JANUARY

1: New Year Public Holiday in England, Northern Ireland, Scotland and Wales.
2: New Year Public Holiday in Scotland only.
18: start of Five Nations Rugby Championship, Murrayfield, Edinburgh.

FEBRUARY

1: Five Nations Rugby Championship fixtures in England and Wales.
3: Blessing of Throats, St Ethelreda's Church, Holborn, London.
11: Shrove Tuesday/Pancake Day—pancake races at various venues, including Covent Garden.
15–23: Boat, Caravan and Leisure Show, National Exhibition Centre, Birmingham.

MARCH

1: St David's Day. (St David is the patron saint of Wales.)
1: Five Nations Rugby Championship, Twickenham, London.
6–9: Crufts Dog Show, National Exhibition Centre, Birmingham.
*11–13: Cheltenham Gold Cup, Cheltenham Racecourse, Prestbury, Gloucestershire.
13: start of Ideal Home Exhibition, Earl's Court, London.
15: Five Nations Rugby Championship, Cardiff Arms Park, Cardiff.
17: St Patrick's Day. (St Patrick is the patron saint of the island of Ireland.)
17: St Patrick's Day Public Holiday, Northern Ireland only.
21–25: Liberal Democrat Spring Party Conference, Cardiff.
25: distribution of the Tichborne Dole (a measure of flour to all parishioners), Tichborne, Hampshire.
28: Good Friday Public Holiday in England, Northern Ireland, Scotland and Wales.
29: Oxford v. Cambridge University Boat Race, River Thames, London.
31: Easter Monday Public Holiday in England, Northern Ireland, Scotland and Wales.

APRIL

1–6: Ideal Home Exhibition, Earl's Court, London.
5: Grand National steeplechase, Aintree, Liverpool.
6: Coca Cola Cup, Wembley.
13: London Marathon, starts at Blackheath and ends in the Mall, London.
14–16: Royal Ulster Agricultural Show, Belfast.
19: start of World Professional Snooker Championship, Crucible Theatre, Sheffield.
23: St George's Day. (St George is the patron saint of England.)
24–27: Harrogate Spring Flower Festival, Harrogate, Yorkshire.
26: start of Pitlochry Festival Theatre season, Pitlochry, Tayside. (Continues until 5 October.)

MAY

1: May Day celebrations at various venues, including the Padstow 'Obby 'Oss at Padstow, Cornwall.
*1–4: Badminton Horse Trials, Badminton, Avon.
3: Rugby League Cup Final, Wembley
*3–5: Spalding Flower Parade and Springfields Country Fair, Spalding, Lincs.
5: May Day Public Holiday in England, Northern Ireland and Wales; Spring Public Holiday in Scotland.
*15–29: Mayfest 1997 Arts Festival, Glasgow.
17: F.A. Cup Final, Wembley.
20–23: Chelsea Flower Show, Royal Hospital, Chelsea.
24: Scottish Football Cup Final.
*25: start of Glyndebourne season, Lewes, East Sussex.
26: Spring Public Holiday in England, Northern Ireland and Wales; May Day Public Holiday in Scotland.
29: Oak Apple Day, Worcester.

JUNE

*4–11: Appleby Horse Fair, Appleby, Cumbria.
.6–22: Aldeburgh Festival of Music and the Arts, Aldeburgh, Suffolk.

7: Derby (horseracing), Epsom, Surrey.
*8: Trooping the Colour, Horse Guards Parade, Westminster, London.
10: start of Royal Academy Summer Exhibition.
15–21: Cardiff Singer of the World Competition.
17–20: Royal Ascot (horseracing), Ascot, Berkshire.
19–22: Royal Highland Show, Newbridge, Edinburgh.
23: start of All England Tennis Championship, Wimbledon.
30: start of the Royal Agricultural Show, Stoneleigh, Warwickshire.

JULY

1–3: Royal International Agricultural Show, Stoneleigh, Warwickshire.
1–6: All England Tennis Championship, Wimbledon.
2–6: Henley Regatta, Henley-on-Thames, Oxfordshire.
*6–22: Chichester Festival, Chichester Festival Theatre and other venues in Chichester.
8–13: International Music Eisteddfod, Llangollen, Clwyd, Wales.
*11–13: British Grand Prix (motor racing), Silverstone Circuit, Towcester, Northamptonshire.
12: Durham Miners' Gala.
14: **Battle of the Boyne Public Holiday in Northern Ireland.**
15–16: Royal Tournament, Earls Court, London
17–20: Golf Open Championship, Royal Troon, Scotland.
18: start of Henry Wood Promenade Concerts, various venues in London.
18–26: Cycling, National Track Championships, Manchester.
21–24: Royal Welsh Show, Builth Wells, Powys.
25–27: Cambridge Folk Festival, Cherry Hinton Hall, Cambridge.
29: start of Goodwood, horseracing, Chichester.

AUGUST

1–10: last days of Royal Academy Summer Exhibition.
1–23: Edinburgh Tattoo, Edinburgh Castle, Scotland.
2–9: Cowes Regatta, Isle of White.
4: **Summer Public Holiday in Scotland.**
10–30: Edinburgh Festival (arts), various venues in and around the city. Also Fringe Festival same dates.
24–25: Notting Hill Carnival, London.
25: **Summer Bank Holiday in England, Northern Ireland and Wales.**
29: start of Blackpool Illuminations, The Promenade, Blackpool, Lancashire.

SEPTEMBER

1–13: last fortnight of Henry Wood Promenade Concerts, various venues in London.
6: Braemar Highland Gathering, Braemar, Grampian, Scotland.
7–12: British Association for Advancement of Science Annual Festival, Leeds University.
8–12: Trades Union Conference, Brighton, Sussex.
25: start of Soho Jazz Festival, London.
21–25: Liberal Democrat Autumn Party Conference, Eastbourne, Sussex.
25–27: Plaid Cymru Conference, Aberystwyth, Wales.
29: start of Labour Party Conference, Brighton, Sussex.

OCTOBER

1–3: Labour Party Conference, Brighton, Sussex.
1–4: Soho Jazz Festival.
*1–5: Showjumping, Horse of the Year Show, Wembley Arena.
2–4: Nottingham Goose Fair.
7–10: Conservative Party Conference, Blackpool.
9–19: Norfolk and Norwich Festival, various venues around the county.
*11–12: British National Ploughing Championships, Swinefleet, Humberside.
16–26: London Motor Show, Earls Court Exhibition Centre, London.
20–22: Powerboat racing: Windermere Record Attempts, Windermere.

NOVEMBER

2: RAC London to Brighton Veteran Car Run, starts in Hyde Park, London.
5: Guy Fawkes Night, bonfires and fireworks in parks and other open spaces throughout Britain.
7–24: London Film Festival, various venues throughout London.
8: Lord Mayor's Show, London.
9: Remembrance Sunday, memorial services in churches throughout Britain and wreath-laying ceremony at the Cenotaph, Whitehall, London.
14–23: Welsh International Film Festival, various venues, Aberystwyth, Wales.
30: St Andrew's Day (St Andrew is the patron saint of Scotland.)

DECEMBER

*18–22: Olympia International Showjumping Championships, Olympia, London.
25: **Christmas Day Public Holiday.**
26: **Boxing Day Public Holiday.**
26–31: start of sales in department stores and many other shops throughout Britain.
* indicates a provisional date.

Index

A

Abortion 411
Accidents
    industrial 200–1
    road 305–6
Adoption 428
Adult education 462–3
Advertising 240, 505–6, 516–17
Advisory bodies to Government 68–9
Advisory, Conciliation and Arbitration
  Service (ACAS) 200
Africa, sub-Saharan 132
Agriculture 281–301
    alternative crops 288
    arable 286–7, 294
    BSE 285
    Common Agricultural Policy
      289–90
    conservation schemes 292–4
    Countryside Stewardship 293
    crofting 292
    crops 286–7
    diseases and pests, control of 295–6
    diversification 294
    environment 292–4
    exports 288–9
    grants and subsidies 291–2
    habitats 294
    hill farming 292
    horticulture 287–8
    intervention 290
    landholding 282–3
    less-favoured areas 292
    livestock 283–6
    marketing 289
    moorland 294
    NSAs 293
    organic farming 293–4
    policy 281–2, 289–96, 297–8
    premiums 291
    production 283–6; table 285
    professional, scientific and technical
      services 295
    research 299–300
    rural economy 294–5
    set-aside 292
    schemes 292–4
    shows 289
    smallholdings 292
    tenancies 292
    training 295

    veterinary medicine 295
    welfare 286
    woodland 300–301
    see also Countryside; Fisheries;
      Forestry
Agriculture, Fisheries and Food,
  Ministry of 281, 289, 292–5
Aid
    to developing countries 136–40
    to Central and Eastern Europe and
      Central Asia 130–1
    EU regional 127–8
AIDS 415–16
Air pollution 358–62
Aircraft and aviation
    aero-engine manufacture 252–3
    aerospace industry 251–3
    aerospace, research 335–6
    air safety 318
    air traffic 316–17
    aircraft 244–6, 252, 317
    airlines 317
    airports 318–19; table 319
    and the environment 263
    aviation, civil 316–19
    aviation equipment 253
Alcohol misuse 413–4
Alcoholic drinks industry 253–4
Ambulance services 409
Ancient monuments 371–3
Anglican Communion 468–9
Angling 530
Anti-competitive practices 209
Appeals
    civil 109
    criminal 99–100
Apprenticeships 191–2
Architecture 371, 384
Armed forces 145–6, 148–50
Arms control 133–4
Army 148
Arrest and detention 92–3
Arts
    business sponsorship 477
    centres 478–9
    festivals 479–80
    finance 476
    galleries 489–91
    policies 475–6
    training 482, 484, 485, 488, 492
Arts Councils 476–7
Asia, Central 130–1

Asia-Pacific region 132–3
Assisted areas, map 215
Astronomy 332
Athletics 530
Atomic energy *see* Nuclear power
Auction houses 237
Authors' copyright 493
Aviation *see* Aircraft and Aviation
Awards to Industry and Commerce 214

B

Badminton 531
Bail system 93–4
Balance of payments 182–4; table 183
Ballet *see* Dance
Baltic Exchange 233
Bank of England 222–3
Banks 223–5
Basketball 531
Bathing waters 357
BBC (British Broadcasting
  Corporation) 496, 497, 499–501, 504,
  505, 506, 507–8, 509
Benefits, social security 432–41
Billiards 537–8
Biodiversity 370
Biological weapons 133
Biofuels, energy from 275
Biotechnology 247
Biotechnology and Biological Sciences
  Research Council 332–3
Birth rates 29–30
Blood transfusion 408–9
Books 495
Bosnia 129
Botanic gardens 341
Bowls 531
Boxing 531–2
Brent Spar 267
British Aerospace 251–2
British Airways 317
British Coal 269
British Council 140–1, 464
British Film Institute 487
British Gas 268–9
British Library 493–4
British National Space Centre 338
British Nuclear Fuels 273
British Olympic Association 523
British Overseas Trade Board 181–2

British Paralympic Association 523
British Petroleum 262
British Rail 309–10
British Technology Group *see* BTG
British Telecommunications *see* BT
British Tourist Authority 239
British Waterways 313, 524
Broadcasting 496–510
  and the arts 479
  audience research 507
  complaints 506
  educational 505
  international relations 509–10
  legislation 506
  Parliamentary and political 507
  standards 506–7
  technical developments 510
  see also Radio; Television
BSE 285
BT (British Telecommunications)
  320–2
BTG 339
Buddhism 472
Budget 163
Building *see* Construction industry
Building regulations 257
Building societies 225–6
Bus services 308
Business *see* Financial services;
  Industry and commerce;
  Manufacturing; Construction
  industry; Trade, overseas
Business-education links 212, 455–6
Business Links 212–3
Business sponsorship 477

C

Cabinet 65–6
Cabinet Office 66
Cable & Wireless 323
Cable services 322, 504
Cadw: Welsh Historic Monuments 371
Canals and waterways 313
Cancer
  care 416–17
  screening 417
Capital gains tax 371
Careers education and guidance 456
Careers service 456
Cargo services by sea 314
Caribbean territories 124
Cars *see* Motor vehicles
Catering trade 237–8
CCGTs 272
Central Council of Physical Recreation
  522
Central Office of Information 545
  overseas radio and television 509
Ceramics 244–5
Ceremonial 50
Channel Islands 6
Channel Tunnel 311–12
Charities 41–2, 339

Chemical weapons 133–4
Chemicals industry 245–7, 326
Children
  abuse 426–7
  adoption 428
  benefits 434–5
  day care for 426, 435
  in care 427–8
  films for 487–8
  health and welfare 410–11, 449
  and sport 520–1
  as witnesses 98
Child Support Agency 435
Christian communities 468–72
Church of England 468–9
Church of Scotland 469
Cinema 486–8
Citizen's Charter 69–71
  Charter Mark awards 70
  principles of public service 70
City Challenge 376
City Technology Colleges 377, 444
Civil aviation *see* Aircraft and Aviation
Civil courts 108–11
Civil law 108–11
Civil Service 71–5
Climate 3, 359–60
Clothing industry 255
Coach services 308–9
Coal Authority 269
Coal industry 269
Coasts 367–8
Commerce *see* Industry and commerce
Commission for Racial Equality 35–6
Commodity composition, overseas
  trade 173–7; table 176
Commodity markets 233
Commonwealth 49, 121–3; map 122
Communications 319–24
Community forests 301
Community relations, and police 91
Community service 102
Compacts 377, 380, 456
Competitiveness White Papers 206–7
Complaints
  broadcasting 506
  local government 80
  maladministration 71
  National Health Service 405
  press 516–17
Computers 249, 454
Computing services 240–1
Confederation of British Industry
  (CBI) 200, 205
Conference centres 239–40
Conservation 364–73
Constitution 47
Construction industry 256–8
Consumer protection 210–11
Copyright 493
Coroners' courts 100–1
Corporation tax 168
Council for the Central Laboratory of
  the Research Councils 334
Council of Europe 121, 135

Council tax 170–1
Countryside 293, 364–71
Countryside Commission 364–5
Countryside Council for Wales 364–5
Couriers, private 324
Courts
  civil 108–11
  criminal 94–101
Crafts 491–2
Credit cards 225
Cricket 532
Crime
  international 136
  prevention 85–6
  statistics 84–5
  victims 86
Criminal law 83–108
Crofts 292
Crops *see* Agriculture
Crown *see* Monarchy
Crown Office (Scotland) 547
Crown Prosecution Service 94, 542
Cultural and social affairs 10, 16–17,
  22–3, 28
Curriculum *see* National curriculum
Custody 102–7
Customs and Excise, HM 166, 541
Cycling 532
Cyprus 129–30

D

Dance 484–5
Data Protection Registrar, Office of the
  545
Defence 142–50
  allies 145–6
  armed forces 145–6, 148–9
  arms control 133–4
  dependencies 144–5
  equipment programme 147–8
  finance and management 149–50
  NATO strategy 143–4
  nuclear forces 147
  policy 142–3
  procurement 149–50
  research 336
Defence, Ministry of 118, 336, 543
Defence notices 517
Dependent Territories 123–5, 144–5
Deregulation 208
Design 213, 492
Development co-operation 136–40
Development plans 382–3
Diet 36–8, 417–18
Diplomatic service 73–4
Disabled people
  and the arts 478
  benefits 436–7
  services for 193–4, 424–5
  and sport 253
Discount houses 227
Distribution 233–7
Divorce 30–1

Drama 480–2
Drink *see* Food and drink
Drug misuse 86–7, 411–12
Duchy of Lancaster 51n
Durable goods, availability 37

E

Earnings 195–6
Eating and drinking habits 36–8,
  417–18
ECGD (Export Credits Guarantee
  Department) 182, 541
Economic and monetary union (EMU)
  126
Economic and social pattern 36–44
Economic and Social Research Council
  334
Economy 153–72
  agricultural 283–5
  background 153–7
  government policies 157–9
  indicators, table 154
  management 158–9
  national income and expenditure
    159–61
  strategy 157–9
  see also Balance of payments;
    Expenditure; Finance; Trade,
    overseas
Education 442–65
  administration 443
  after 16 456–63
  broadcasting 505
  finance 443–4, 460
  overseas links and aid 138, 463–4
  post-compulsory 456–63
  prisoners 105–6
  religious 453
  research 463
  schools 443–56
  youth service 464–5
  see also Training, education and
    enterprise
Education and Employment,
  Department for 443, 544
Education, Office for Standards in 455,
  542
Elderly people, services for 423–4,
  433–4
Elections
  general 54–7; table 56
  local government 77–8
Electrical engineering 248–50
Electricity supply industry 271–3
Electricity Regulation, Office of 271,
  542
Electronics, research and development
  331
Emergency relief 140
Emission of harmful gases 358–62
Employees
  conditions of employment 194–6
  involvement 197

share schemes 196
Employers' organisations 200
Employment 154, 185–202
  and European Union 128
  and productivity 154
  patterns 185–8
  rights 194–5
  services 192–4
  table 186
  terms and conditions 194–6
  training 188–92
  workforce 185–8
Energy 139, 259–75
  CCGTs 272
  CHP 261
  consumption 260–1; table 261
  efficiency 261–2
  Energy Saving Trust 262
  fossil fuel levy 275
  interconnectors 272
  liberalisation 260
  policy 260
  renewable sources 274–5
  see also under the types of energy
Energy Saving Trust 262
Engineering 247–53, 330–1
Engineering and Physical Sciences
  Research Council 330–1
England
  cultural life 10
  description 7–10
  economy 9–10
  government 7, 9
  history 7
  statistics (general) 8
English Heritage 371–2
English language 33–4
English Nature 364–5
English Partnerships 376–7
Enterprise zones 378
Environment
  departments and agencies 354–6,
    364–6, 544, 545, 546, 547
  improvement schemes 371
  overseas aid 139–40
  research 333–4
  see also Conservation; Countryside;
    Planning
Environment Agency 355
Environment, Department of the 354,
  364, 375, 385, 544
Environmental health 418–19
Environmentally sensitive areas (ESA)
  292, 351
Equal opportunities 35, 40, 195
Equestrianism 532–3
Ethnic and national minorities 34–5
  arts 478
  education 448
  and police 91
  press 513
Euromarkets 232
Europe, Central and Eastern 130–1
European Broadcasting Union 509

European Union (EU)
  (Association) Agreements 131, 180
  budget 126
  Common Agricultural Policy 127,
    289–91
  common foreign and security policy
    128–9
  crime, action against 136
  currency units 232
  economic and monetary union 126
  employment and social affairs 128
  environment 127
  fisheries 297–8
  and government 63
  and insurers 228
  intergovernmental conferences 126
  law 83–4
  Maastricht Treaty 125
  map 119
  regional policy and aid 127–8, 217
  research and development 128, 342
  select committees on EU affairs 63
  single European market 126, 177,
    180
  trade agreements 127, 180
  trans-European networks 127
  transport 127
  UK membership 118–20
Eurotunnel 311–12
Examinations and qualifications 452,
  454, 456, 457
Excise *see* Customs and Excise, HM
Executive agencies 73
Exhibition and conference centres
  239–40
Expenditure
  personal 159–60; table 160
  public 163–5; diagram 164
Export controls, works of art 492
Exports *see* Trade, overseas
Express services 324
External assets 183
Eye services 403–4

F

Factoring companies 231
Falkland Islands 124
Families, help for 426
Family credit 439
Family health services 405–7
Family planning 411
Farming *see* Agriculture
Festivals, arts 479–80
Fibres, synthetic 247
Films 486–8
Finance
  local government 79–80
  public 161–72
Finance companies 223–8
Financial futures and options 233
Financial markets 231–3
Financial services 219–33
  supervision 220–2

Fines 101
Fiscal policy 158
Fishing (angling) 530
Fishing industry 296–300
    Common Fisheries Policy 297–8
    grants 298
    quota hoppers 298
Food
    exports 288–9
    government role 289–91
    marketing 289
    research 299, 336
    safety 288, 418
Food and drink industries 253–4
Food, farms, land and leisure (ADAS) 295
Football 527–8, 533
Footwear industry 255
Foreign & Commonwealth Office 117–8, 543
Foreign exchange markets 232
Foreign policy, administration of 117–8
Forensic Science Service 90–1
Forestry 300–1
    policy 300–1
    research 301
    schemes 301
    tree planting 366–7
Forestry Commission 300
Foundation for Sport and the Arts 477, 528–9
Fraud 95, 98
Free churches 469–71
Freight
    market 233
    railway 311
    sea cargo 314
Friendly societies 226–7
Fuel see Coal; Electricity; Energy; Gas; Nuclear power
Further education 456, 458, 462

G

Gaelic Games 533
Gardens 341
Gas 262–9; map 267
    see also Oil industry
Gas Supply, Office of 269, 542
Genetically modified organisms 364
Georgia 130
Gibraltar 124
Gold-mining 277
Golf 533–4
Government 47–82
    and civil aviation 317
    departments and agencies 67–9, 540–7
    development of 51–2
    and food 288–91
    and industry 205–18
    local 75–82
    national 47–75
    open 71

overseas 137
    publicity and broadcasting 507
GP fundholders (NHS) 406
Green Belts 383
Greyhound racing 534
Gross domestic product, tables 155, 156, 159
Gross national product, table 159
Groundwork trusts 378
Group of seven (G7) 120
Gymnastics 534

H

Handicapped people see Disabled people
Health
    education 417
    environment 418–19
    prisoners 106
    private medical treatment 410
    professions 419–21
    see also National Health Service; Social welfare
Health and safety at work 200–1
Health, Department of 401–2
Helicopters 252
Higher education 339, 459–62
Highland Games 534
Hindu community 472
Historic buildings 371–2
Historic Scotland 371–2
Historical manuscripts 495
History 3–5
HMSO (Her Majesty's Stationery Office) see Stationery Office, The
Hockey 534–5
Holidays 44, 238–9
Home renovation grants 392
Home Office 85, 544
Home ownership 386–7
Homelessness 392–4
Hong Kong 123–4
Honours 50
Horse racing 535
Horserace Betting Levy 529
Horticulture 287–8
Hospices 409–10
Hospitals and specialist services 407–18
Hotel and catering trade 237–8
House of Commons 52, 54, 56–64
House of Lords 52, 53–4, 56–64
Housing 36, 38, 385–94
    administration 385–6
    construction industry 256–8
    improvements 391–2
    privately rented 388
    rural 391
    sheltered 391
    social 388–91
Housing associations 389–90
Housing benefit 438–9
Hovercraft 314
Human fertilisation 411

Human rights 134–5
Hydro power 271

I

Ice skating 535
Immigration 32–3
Imports see Trade, overseas
Income
    national 159–61
    sources 160–1
    support 437
    taxes on 167–8
    and wealth 36
Independent schools 449–50
Independent Television Commission 496, 498–9, 501
Industrial and intellectual property 214
Industrial associations 205
Industrial financing 204
Industrial innovation 213, 335
Industrial relations 196–200
    legal framework 198–200
Industrial research establishments 336
Industry 203–18
    awards 214
    and government 205–18
    regional development 214–17
    structure and organisation 203–5
Infectious diseases 416
Inflation 156
Information, Central Office of see Central Office of Information
Information technology in schools 454
Inheritance tax 168–9
Inland Revenue, Board of 166–7, 541
Inland waterways 313, 524
Inner cities see Urban regeneration
Innovation 335
Institute of Directors 205
Instrument engineering 248–50
Insurance 228–9
Intellectual property 214
International Maritime Organization 357
International organisations 118–23
International Telecommunications Union 509
Intervention Board 290
Investment 229–30
    funds and trusts 229–30
    inward 184, 217–8
    outward 184
Investors in People initiative 190
Invisible trade 177–9
Iraq 130
Ireland, history 11–12
    see also Northern Ireland
Irish Republic 13
Isle of Man 7

J

Jewish community 472
Jobcentres 193
Jobseeker's Allowance 193
Journalism, training for 515–16
Judges 112
Judo 535
Juries 98–9
Justice *see* Law

K

Keep fit 535
Know How Fund 130–1
Kuwait 130

L

Labour *see* Employment
Land
    pollution 355–6
    use of agricultural 282
Land Authority for Wales 379
Landfill tax 166, 355
Latin America 133
Law 83–113
    administration 111–13
    centres 113
    civil law 108–11
    company 204–5
    criminal law 83–108
    personnel 112
    and press 517
    see also Legal
Learned societies 340–1
Learning difficulties, people with
    424–5
Leasing companies 231
Legal affairs, departments and agencies
    542–3
Legal aid 112–13
Legal profession 112
Legal Secretariat to the Law Officers
    542–3
Legislation 58–60
    list of recent 548
Leisure trends 42–4
Libraries 493–5
Library Association 495
Life expectancy 30
Literature 492–5
Litter control 355–6
Livestock 283–6; table 285
Living standards 36
Lloyd's 228–9
Lobby, Parliamentary 69
Local government 75–81
    and the arts 476
    complaints 80
    finance 79–80
    functions and services 78

revenue 170–1
and sport 522
London, railways 312
London Bullion Market 233
London International Financial
    Futures and Options Exchange 233
London Metal Exchange 233
London Stock Exchange 231–2
Lord Advocate's Department 547
Lord Chancellor's Department 542
Lottery, National 42–4, 477, 529
Lottery, National, Office of the 542

M

Maastricht Treaty 125
Management consultancy 241
Management initiatives, government
    205–6, 212
Manpower *see* Employment
Manufacturing 242–56
Marine
    engineering 251
    environment 357–8
    safety 315–16
Market research 241
Markets
    overseas 177; table 175
    regulation 208–10
Marriage and divorce 30–1
Martial arts 535
Measurement standards 214
Mechanical engineering 247–8
Media *see also* Broadcasting; Films;
    Press
    ownership 498, 512
Medical Research Council 331–2
Medicine *see* Health
Medicines, safety of 419
Mentally ill, services for 106, 425–6
Merchant banks 227
Merchant shipping 314
Mercury Communications 322
Mergers 209
Metal products 242–4, 247–8
Middle East 131–2
Migration 31
Milk 37, 284
Mineral and metal products 242–4,
    275–8; map 276
Ministers, government 64–5
Minorities *see* Ethnic and national
    minorities
Mobile communications 322–3
Monarchy 47–51, 59
Monetary policy 157
Money markets 232
Monopolies 208–9
Mortality 30
Mortgage loans 386
Motor-car sports 535–6
Motor-cycle sports 536
Motor vehicles 250
    emissions 361–2

retailing 237
Mountaineering 536
Museums 341–2, 489–91
Museums Association 490
Music 482–4
    training 484
Muslim community 472–3

N

National Coaching Foundation 522
National Council for Vocational
    Qualifications (NCVQ) 457
National Curriculum 451–4
National Grid 271
National Health Service (NHS) 400–21
    recent developments 402
National Heritage, Department of
    475–6
National Heritage Memorial Fund 372
National income and expenditure
    159–61
National Insurance 170–1, 431–2
National Lottery *see* Lottery
National minorities *see* Ethnic and
    national minorities
National Parks 368–9
National Playing Fields Association 524
National Savings 227–8
National Statistics, Office for 541
Nationalised industries 207–8
Nationality 31–2
NATO *see* North Atlantic Treaty
    Organisation
Natural Environment Research Council
    333–4, 353
Natural resources 259–80
Nature conservation 364–71
Navy *see* Royal Navy
Netball 536
News agencies 509, 514–15
Newspapers 511–13
Next Steps programme 73
Noise, pollution 362–3
Non-departmental public bodies 68–9
Non-fossil fuel obligation 275
North Atlantic Treaty Organisation
    (NATO) 142–6
North Sea oil 262–5
Northern Ireland
    administration 69
    agriculture 283, 287, 292, 293
    appeals 100
    armed forces in 145
    civil courts 109
    criminal courts 96
    cultural and social affairs 16–17
    custodial sentences 103
    departments 545–6
    description 11–17
    Downing Street declaration 13
    economy 15–16
    education 443, 444, 445, 447, 449,
        451, 453, 455

electricity 271
equal opportunities 195
fishing 299
forestry 301
framework document 13–14
geography 11
government 12–14, 545–6
health and safety at work 201
history 11–12
human rights 14–15
industrial development 217
law administration 112
local taxes 171
press 513
prisons 104
prosecutions 95
Royal Ulster Constabulary 89, 145
schools 444
security policy 15
teacher training 451
terrorism, fight against 88, 145
trade unions 198
training and employment 192
urban regeneration 381
water supply 280
young offenders 108
Northern Ireland Office 545
Nuclear power 273–4
Nuclear forces 133, 147

O

Offenders, treatment 101–8
Oil industry 269–8
    map 263
Old people see Elderly people
Ombudsman see Parliamentary
    Commissioner
Open University 461–2
Opera 484
Ordnance Survey 545
Organ transplants 408
Organic food 293
Organisations, international 118–23
Organisation for Security and
    Co-operation in Europe 120–1
OSO 267
Output 153–4
    table 154
Overseas Development Administration
    (ODA) 117, 136–40, 337
Overseas educational links 141, 463–4
Ozone layer 360

P

Parents
    and children, benefits 434–5
    and children, services 410–11
    rights 447
Parliament 51–64
    broadcasting 507

committees 60–2
elections 54–5
financial control 63
functions 52
legislation 58–60
meeting 52–3
origins 51–2
party system 55–7
powers 52
privilege 63–4
procedure 57–8
    see also House of Commons; House
        of Lords
Parliamentary Commissioner for
    Administration 71
    and NHS 404–5
Parliamentary Commissioner for
    Standards 71
Parliamentary Counsel 543
Particle Physics and Astronomy
    Research Council 332
Passenger services
    air 316–17
    rail 310–11
    road 308–9
    sea 314
Patents 214
Patients' Charters 398–9
Pay bargaining 197
Paymaster General's Office 541
Payment systems, banks 224
Peacekeeping 129–30
Pension funds 229
Pensions 433–4, 440
Performing arts 480–8
Periodical press 513–14
Personal Investment Authority 222
Personal social services 421–9
Pesticides 296
Petroleum 262–8
    retailing 237
    revenue 168
Pharmaceuticals 246–7
Photovoltaics 275
Physical geography 3
Planning 381–4
    see also Urban regeneration
Plants, disease control 296
Plastic card technology 225
Plastics 246
Police service 88–94
Political party system 55–7
    broadcasts 507
Pollution control 354–364
Population 29–23
    age and sex structure 31
    distribution 31
    Office of Population Censuses and
        Surveys see Office for National
        Statistics
Ports 313–15
    traffic, table 313
Post Office specialist services 324
Post-compulsory education 456–63
Postal services 323–4

Potatoes 287
Power see Energy
PowerGen 271
Press 510–18
Press Association 514–15
Pressure groups 80–1
Prime Minister 64
Prisons 103–7
Private Finance Initiative 162, 404
Privatisation 207
Privy Council 67
Probation 101–2
Procurator General and Treasury
    Solicitor, HM 543
Productivity 154
Professional institutions 340–1
Prosecution 94–5
Public Accounts Committee 165
Public expenditure see Expenditure,
    public
Public Relations 240
Publishing 255–6, 495, 510–15

Q

Quality and standards 213–14
Quarrying 277
Queen see Monarchy

R

Race relations 35, 195
    see also Ethnic and national
        minorities
Radio 497
    BBC 496, 497, 500, 501, 507
    Radio Authority 497–8, 503
Radioactivity and pollution 363–4
Railtrack 309–10
Railway services 309–13
Rainfall 3
Recreation see Sport
Recycling 356
Regional arts boards 477
Regional newspapers 511, 513
Regions
    EC aid 127–8
    industrial development 214–17
Regulation of markets 208–10
    see also Deregulation
Rehabilitation 409
Religion 466–74
Religious education 453
Renewable sources of energy 274–5
Research and development
    academic 339
    agriculture, fisheries and food
        299–300
    astronomy 332
    coal industry 269
    construction industry 258
    defence 336